Extraterritoriality in Comparative Perspective

Ius Comparatum

VOLUME 5

The titles published in this series are listed at *brill.com/iacl*

Extraterritoriality in Comparative Perspective

Edited by

Hannah L. Buxbaum

BRILL | NIJHOFF

LEIDEN | BOSTON

Library of Congress Cataloging-in-Publication Data

Names: Buxbaum, Hannah L., 1966- editor.
Title: Extraterritoriality in comparative perspective / edited by Hannah L. Buxbaum.
Description: Leiden ; Boston : Brill/Nijhoff, 2025. | Series: Ius comparatum, 2214-6881 ; vol 5 | Includes bibliographical references and index. | Summary: "Extraterritoriality is often understood as an exceptional, sometimes even illegitimate, form of state lawmaking-yet it is pervasive in contemporary practice. Countries around the world rely on extraterritorial regulation to protect local markets, in areas including competition law and data privacy. It is also recognized as a useful strategy to promote international human rights, and to address shared challenges as diverse as transnational crime, tax base erosion, and climate change. The normalization of extraterritoriality as a legal technique, however, has by no means resolved longstanding debates about its place in the international legal order. Containing in-depth studies of fifteen legal systems, this volume provides a critical comparative perspective on those debates" – Provided by publisher.
Identifiers: LCCN 2024046853 (print) | LCCN 2024046854 (ebook) | ISBN 9789004720176 (hardback) | ISBN 9789004720183 (v. 5 ; ebook)
Subjects: LCSH: Exterritoriality.
Classification: LCC KZ3678 .E959 2025 (print) | LCC KZ3678 (ebook) | DDC 341.4–dc23/eng/20241008
LC record available at https://lccn.loc.gov/2024046853
LC ebook record available at https://lccn.loc.gov/2024046854

Typeface for the Latin, Greek, and Cyrillic scripts: "Brill". See and download: brill.com/brill-typeface.

ISSN 2214-6881
ISBN 978-90-04-72017-6 (hardback)
ISBN 978-90-04-72018-3 (e-book)
DOI 10.1163/9789004720183

Contents

Preface

In its famous "Lotus" judgment of 1927, the Permanent Court of International Justice rejected the proposition that international law prohibits states from "extend[ing] the application of their laws and the jurisdiction of their courts to persons, property and acts outside their territory." Over the course of the past century, states have engaged in extraterritorial practices in an ever-increasing range of domains. These practices challenge foundational principles of international law – and provide a valuable lens for critical exploration of power and legitimacy in the international order.

Much of the vast scholarly literature on extraterritoriality approaches the topic from the outside in, assessing the extraterritorial projection of state law from the perspective of international law and the constraints it places on state authority. The goal of this project is to approach the topic from the inside out. Considering a range of legal systems, the authors investigate the geographic scope that states claim for their own laws, and the mechanisms by which states translate and locally implement principles of international jurisdictional law. The book consists of contributions presented at the most recent General Congress of the International Academy of Comparative Law, held in Asunción, Paraguay in 2022. It includes national reports from fourteen countries, a special report on EU law, and a general report. Together, these chapters illuminate significant changes in the morphology of extraterritoriality over the past century. They illustrate the extent to which extraterritoriality has become embedded in, and has contributed to shaping, the transnational legal order.

Hannah L. Buxbaum
Bloomington, Indiana
July 2024

Contributors

Matteo Angelini
Counsel, WilmerHale, London, England

Hannah L. Buxbaum
Professor of Law and John E. Schiller Chair, Indiana University, USA

André de Carvalho Ramos
Professor of Law, University of São Paulo, Brazil

Rong-Chwan Chen
University Distinguished Professor of Law, National Taipei University, Taiwan

Franklin A. Gevurtz
Distinguished Professor of Law, University of the Pacific, Sacramento, USA

Hisashi Harata
Professor of Law, University of Tokyo, Japan

Lena Hornkohl
Assistant Professor, University of Vienna, Austria

Danielle Ireland-Piper
Associate Professor, Australian National University, Australia

John C. Kleefeld
Professor of Law, University of New Brunswick, Canada

Gyooho Lee
Professor of Law, Chung-Ang University, Republic of Korea

Shiping Liao
Professor of Law, Beijing Normal University, China

Quoc Chien Ngo
Professor, Foreign Trade University, Hanoi, Vietnam

Duc Vinh Nguyen
Professor, Foreign Trade University, Ho Chi Minh City, Vietnam

Sergiu Popovici
Assistant Professor, West University of Timisoara, Romania

Lucas Roorda
Assistant Professor of Law, Utrecht University, The Netherlands

Cedric Ryngaert
Professor of Public International Law, Utrecht University, The Netherlands

Frédérique Sabourin
Retired advocate, Canada

Mariana Sebalhos Jorge
Attorney, Sebalhos Advocacia, Brazil

Sören Segger-Piening
Professor of Law, University of Osnabrück, Germany

Timo Zandstra
Assistant Professor of Law, Utrecht University, The Netherlands

Alessandra Zanobetti
Professor and Chair of International Law, Università di Bologna, Italy

PART 1

General Report

Extraterritoriality in Comparative Context: Defining the Scope of State Law in a Global Era

*Hannah L. Buxbaum**

State legal orders operate within a complex and challenging global environment. The ever-increasing transnationalization of economic, social, and political activity, along with the vast expansion of the digital domain, have made it harder for states to regulate local conditions through domestic law alone. In addition, the emergence of international regulatory entities and the proliferation of international treaties have created new intersections between state law and other elements of the transnational legal order. These changes have contributed to a significant expansion in what is often described as "extraterritoriality:" the application of state law in a way that affects persons, activity, or interests outside the lawmaker's territory.[1]

As I have written elsewhere, extraterritoriality has a bad reputation.[2] The label itself tends to evoke one particular type of practice: a state's unilateral action to regulate foreign activity, with the goal of advancing its own economic or policy interests. Much of the scholarship on extraterritoriality focuses on the role of international law in restricting such activity – that is, on establishing the limits of state jurisdiction and authority within the international order. Despite serious challenges to the viability of the territorial paradigm in international law, these accounts typically position extraterritoriality as an exceptional (and contested) mode of regulation, in contrast to the presumed norm of territorial (and thus legitimate) governance. They also tend to cast extraterritoriality as the province solely of dominant states.

This study examines current practices and understandings of extraterritoriality from the perspective of national law. Our inquiry relates not to the limits of state jurisdiction under international law, but rather to the geographic scope that states claim for their own laws. We therefore focus on state practice in enacting, interpreting, and applying statutes and regulations,[3] considering

* Professor of Law and John E. Schiller Chair, Indiana University Maurer School of Law

1 See Menno T. Kamminga, *Extraterritoriality*, in Max Planck Encyclopedia of Public International Law (2012) (recognizing that "In the absence of a universally accepted definition, extraterritoriality is an elusive concept that may include a wide variety of practices.").

2 Hannah L. Buxbaum, *The Practice(s) of Extraterritoriality*, in Extraterritoriality/L'Extraterritorialité (Hannah Buxbaum and Thibaut Fleury Graff, eds., 2022) 3.

3 The report is limited to law made by legislative and administrative bodies, excluding judge-made rules in common law systems.

 | DOI:10.1163/9789004720183_002

international jurisdictional law primarily as translated by and implemented within individual legal systems. The goal of this comparative analysis is to illuminate (a) trends over time in the enactment of provisions with extraterritorial reach and (b) practices of the actors within legal systems charged with interpreting and applying local law in situations involving foreign elements. The study uses the results of that analysis to explore the ways in which current practices both support and challenge traditional accounts of extraterritoriality.

This project was conducted in connection with the XXIst General Congress of the International Academy of Comparative Law. It draws on national reports from fourteen countries, along with a report on extraterritoriality in EU law, that were submitted in response to a survey distributed by the Academy.[4] It yields several overall findings.

First, international law is increasingly irrelevant as a direct constraint on the geographic reach of state law. Rather, general principles of international law serve merely to inform the techniques states use to delimit the scope of their laws. Albeit with some variation across legal systems, an overall trend can be discerned in favor of a sector-specific, purpose-driven (and thus unilateral in nature) approach in enacting, interpreting, and applying laws with extraterritorial reach. This trend indicates a promising shift away from abstract debates about the nature and limits of international jurisdiction and toward consideration of the circumstances in which states may legitimately give their laws extraterritorial scope.

Second, the extraterritorial application of domestic law in order to protect or promote local interests – particularly, although not only, in areas of economic regulation – is no longer a practice only of dominant states. Even the enactment of law that applies to wholly foreign conduct, on the basis of that conduct's effects on local markets, has become utterly routine. This is not to say that all states engage with similar frequency in such practices. Certain states give more of their laws extraterritorial reach on the basis of local effects than others; apply their laws more frequently in situations presenting foreign elements; and/or apply their laws to achieve political rather than purely regulatory ends. As a categorical matter, however, the application of state law to encompass conduct occurring entirely outside the lawmaker's territory should no longer be considered jurisdictionally suspect.

4 The survey is reproduced in the Appendix. The legal systems represented are Australia, Brazil, Canada, China, the European Union, Germany, Italy, Japan, the Netherlands, Quebec, Romania, South Korea, Taiwan, the United Kingdom, the United States, and Vietnam. In this chapter, I also draw on secondary literature covering extraterritorial practices in other legal systems.

Third, states increasingly expand the geographic reach of their laws in order to protect or promote *international* interests, particularly in the domain of criminal law. Many multilateral treaties negotiated in recent decades, for instance, require member states to enact and enforce domestic criminal legislation that reaches foreign conduct and/or actors. Some such treaties not only permit but require states to give their laws extraterritorial reach. This trend affects the normative dimension of extraterritoriality. Traditional accounts equate extraterritoriality with an overreach of state authority; claims that another state has acted extraterritorially are generally meant to signal the illegitimacy of such action. Clearly, claims of extraterritorial authority sourced in multilateral treaties are of a different character – indeed, the extension of national law in this context is often not thought of as extraterritoriality at all.

Finally, practices are emerging that deploy local law to secure *global* goods. In some cases, these practices are multilateral in nature – as in the case of the United Nations Guiding Principles on Business and Human Rights, which encourage states to regulate the activities of their own corporations (and those corporations' supply chains) in other countries. In other cases, though, they are purely unilateral, and as a technical matter align more closely with traditional forms of extraterritoriality in the economic sphere. The European Union in particular has claimed expansive geographic reach for its legislation with the stated goal of addressing global challenges including climate change.

This chapter begins with introductory material regarding the status of extraterritoriality under international law (section 1) and the allocation of authority to enact extraterritorial legislation in federal systems (section 2). It then turns to contemporary practice in extraterritorial lawmaking. Section 3 addresses trends in "explicit" extraterritoriality – that is, the enactment of statutes and regulations with explicitly extraterritorial scope. Section 4 analyzes practices in the interpretation and application of statutes and regulations whose geographic scope is unclear. The report then considers ongoing conflicts created by certain forms of extraterritorial regulation (section 5). Section 6 concludes.

1 Extraterritoriality under International Jurisdictional Law

The geographic scope of state legislation is determined against the backdrop of international jurisdictional law. In 1927, the Permanent Court of International Justice famously declared that:

> [f]ar from laying down a general prohibition to the effect that States may not extend the application of their laws and the jurisdiction of their

> courts to persons, property and acts outside their territory, [international law] leaves them in this respect a wide measure of discretion which is only limited in certain cases by prohibitive rules; as regards other cases, every State remains free to adopt the principles which it regards as best and most suitable.[5]

Even at the time, state practice was not as *laissez-faire* as this statement might indicate. A study of criminal jurisdiction released roughly contemporaneously with the *Lotus* decision outlined five general principles on which states based their claims of lawmaking authority, each of which reflected some specific link between the state and the relevant conduct or occurrence. These are territoriality (based on local conduct); nationality (based on conduct of the state's own nationals, wherever occurring); passive personality (based on conduct affecting the state's own nationals); protective (based on conduct threatening the security or other fundamental interests of the state); and universality (based on a narrow category of particularly serious international offenses).[6] Today, too, the consensus view is that international law permits the exercise of legislative jurisdiction only when there is a "genuine connection" between the lawmaking state and the target of regulation.[7]

Once a genuine link is established, states are under no obligation to take the interests of other states into account when applying their laws – in other words, no normative framework has been developed under international law that imposes additional requirements or constraints on extraterritorial regulation or resolves instances of concurrent jurisdiction. Instead, this area has become the province of international comity.[8] Thus, while general principles of international law inform the tools that states use to mitigate potential conflict, they do not serve as a hard constraint on state action once an acceptable basis for prescriptive jurisdiction has been established.

As a descriptive label, "extraterritoriality" might refer to any exercise of jurisdiction on a basis other than the territorial principle – and, indeed, it is sometimes used simply to describe the location of regulated conduct. As many commentators have observed, however, and as the national reports bear out, the term has acquired multiple meanings and usages. For instance, it is

---

5 SS Lotus (France v. Turkey) [1927] PCIJ Series A. No. 10 at 19.

6 *Codification of International Law: Part II – Jurisdiction With Respect to Crime* (Harvard Report on Jurisdiction), 29 Am. J. Int'l L. Supp. 437 (1935) at 445. As the Harvard Report noted, not all of these bases were universally accepted at the time.

7 See Cedric Ryngaert, Jurisdiction in International Law 35 (2d ed. 2015).

8 See Harold G. Maier, *Jurisdictional Rules in Customary International Law*, in Extraterritorial Jurisdiction in Theory and Practice 64, 69 (Karl M. Meessen ed. 1996).

often used to describe jurisdiction on the basis of local (territorial) effects, or any application of law that has significant effects or implications outside the lawmaking state. Moreover, the term is often used not descriptively but rather normatively – to signal jurisdictional overreach by another state, or the illegitimacy of state action.[9] Here, the location of conduct or the claimed jurisdictional basis is less relevant than the purpose of the regulation or the impact that it has on the interests of other states.[10] In this context, "extraterritoriality" is often equated with the regulatory practices of hegemonic states.[11]

2 The Competence to Enact Extraterritorial Legislation in Federal Systems

2.1 *At the Federal Level*

In systems where legislative authority is divided between federal and subnational governments, questions can arise whether the federal entity has the competence to enact and apply legislation with extraterritorial effect. In Australia, the federal government has the capacity to enact extraterritorial legislation within its sphere of competence – including pursuant to international treaties, which fall within the scope of its external affairs power.[12] In the United States, similarly, the federal government's constitutional powers to regulate foreign commerce and to execute treaties authorize federal lawmaking with extraterritorial effect.[13]

While the EU is not a federal system in this sense, a somewhat analogous issue is presented there. Provisions in the EU's constituent treaties limit the territorial scope of EU law to the territory of EU member states.[14] In a 2017 case, the European Court of Justice held that "in the absence of detail as to the territorial scope of an act of secondary legislation, that scope must be

9 Buxbaum, supra note 2.

10 See Report for Japan, Section 1.1 (stating that although "[t]here are several areas in which extraterritorial application has been practiced in Japan for a long time, … these practices were not explicitly qualified and labeled 'extraterritoriality;' that concept first surfaced only as an objection to foreign practices").

11 See, e.g., Report for Vietnam, Section 1 ("Jusqu'à nos jour, il n'y a pas de politique, ni de pratique d'extraterritorialité au Vietnam…. [L]es lois d'application extraterritoriale sont souvent considérées comme une arme impérialiste utilisée par les pays développés à la merci des pays sous-développés ou en voie de développement").

12 Report for Australia, Section 2.

13 U.S. Const. art. 1, Section 8, clauses 3 and 18.

14 Treaty on the European Union Article 52; Treaty on the Functioning of the European Union Article 355.

determined on the basis of those provisions, since the secondary legislation applies in principle to the same area as the Treaties themselves."[15] This ruling led to some questions about the scope of EU lawmaking authority in international matters.[16] However, as the report for the EU indicates, "Th[o]se rules are relevant in establishing the territorial scope of the rights and obligations of the Member States and Union institutions, but not for the admissibility of extraterritoriality orders in primary or secondary law,"[17] which instead depends on the objective of the particular law.

2.2 *At the Sub-national Level*

In some systems, federal constitutions or other laws address the power of sub-national entities to act extraterritorially. In Canada, for instance, the 1867 Constitution Act limits the legislative power of each province territorially, such that provincial law is permitted to have only incidental extraterritorial effect.[18] As a further consequence, because provinces lack the power to legislate extraterritorially, a strong presumption against extraterritoriality is in place, sourced in the understanding that provincial legislators wish to respect the limits that the Constitution places on their powers.[19] In China, central legislation provides that local law, including regulations adopted within individual provinces, applies only within the relevant locality.[20] Australia's Constitution, by contrast, provides that state laws may have extraterritorial effect as long as they do not conflict with federal law.[21] In the United States, the geographic scope of state law is itself determined at the state level.[22] As in Australia, however, the

15 Case C-17/16 *Oussama El Dakkak* [2017] ECLI:EU:C:2017:341, para 23.

16 See Report for the EU, Section 4.3.

17 Id.

18 Report for Canada, Section 3. This does not necessarily mean that provincial law can never reach foreign conduct, however. In one recent case, Quebec's Securities Act was applied to a foreign transaction that impaired the Quebec securities markets – an instance of what was considered appropriate "territorial" regulation on the basis of local harm. See Report for Quebec, Section 1 (discussing *Sharp* c. *Autorité des marchés financiers*, 2023 CSC 29).

19 Report for Quebec, Section 1.

20 Report for China, Section 2.1 (citing the Legislation Law of the People's Republic of China, arts. 73, 82 (2000)).

21 Report for Australia, Section 1 (citing Section 109 of the Australian Constitution).

22 State laws differ on the question of statutory scope – for instance, some states have adopted a presumption against extraterritoriality similar to that used in interpreting federal statutes, while others have not. For a survey of state law, see William S. Dodge, *Presumptions Against Extraterritoriality in State Law*, 53 U.C. Davis L. Rev. 1389 (2020).

extraterritorial reach of state law is precluded when it conflicts with federal powers, as in the case of laws that affect foreign affairs.[23]

3 Expansions in the Practice of Extraterritoriality

The incidence of extraterritorial lawmaking has expanded significantly over the course of the past half century. Many states today routinely apply domestic law in situations involving foreign elements. In some cases the relevant laws do not include provisions regarding their geographic scope, and so the practice relies on judicial or administrative interpretation of their reach.[24] More notably, there has been a dramatic increase in the enactment of legislation with explicitly extraterritorial scope. The following sections outline worldwide trends in the enactment of such legislation. The discussion touches on the different jurisdictional bases that states invoke to justify the extraterritorial scope of their laws. Its primary goal, however, is to identify and analyze two major drivers of this expansion. Section 3.1 addresses the enactment of laws intended to protect local interests, an area of unilateral practice that focuses primarily on economic regulation. Section 3.2 turns to legislation adopted within the framework of multilateral treaties, examining the use of extraterritoriality to promote the enforcement of international criminal law.

3.1 *Protecting Local Interests*

Over the course of the 20th century, the forces of globalization diminished the power of states to shape local economic conditions. As markets expanded beyond the national scale, and as more corporate activity occurred within large and fluid transnational enterprises, conduct occurring outside the territory of a lawmaking state more frequently affected its local markets. No longer able to protect local interests through purely territorial regulation, states turned to the enactment of statutes and regulations with explicitly extraterritorial scope in order to protect their legislative and regulatory interests.

The trend in favor of expansive scope provisions is most pronounced in the largest and most regulatorily complex states and regions. The EU, for example, despite earlier concerns regarding the legitimacy of effects-based regulation,[25] now routinely enacts legislation providing explicitly for broad geographic

23 See, e.g., Zchernig v. Miller, 389 U.S. 429, 440 (1968) (state regulations "must give way if they impair the effective exercise of the Nation's foreign policy").

24 See Section Four infra.

25 See infra at note 92 and accompanying text.

scope. The United States likewise has incorporated extraterritorial reach into many laws, including anti-discrimination law[26] and a host of market regulations.[27] As the national reports reflect, however, this trend is accelerating in all regions of the world. As economies transition from local to international markets, they tend to adopt laws in these areas with extraterritorial reach, understanding that as a crucial component of an effective regulatory scheme.[28] Countries including Brazil, China, and Vietnam have all enacted market regulations with extraterritorial scope.[29]

The trend in enactment of law with extraterritorial scope is in favor of sector-specific provisions, rather than in general legislation regarding extraterritorial reach.[30]

3.1.1 Competition Law

In most legal systems, the first laws to be given explicitly extraterritorial scope are those governing competition. When Germany enacted its Act against Restraints on Competition in 1958, it included a provision extending its scope to restraints that affected competition within the German market.[31] In the EU, provisions giving competition law extraterritorial reach are included in the founding treaties themselves, and thus "extraterritoriality is in principle as old as the EU law itself."[32] Competition law is also the field in which the adoption of statutes with explicitly extraterritorial reach is most widespread. This results in part from the trend in emerging economies to adopt laws in areas including merger regulation, cartel regulation, and prohibitions on the abuse of market dominant positions.[33] In Asia, for example, many countries, including India,

26 42 USC § 2000e(f) (expressly extending U.S. anti-discrimination law to protect U.S. citizens employed outside the United States).

27 These include regulations in the area of securities law, merger regulation, and derivatives regulation.

28 There are a variety of different drivers here, including legal reform guided by intergovernmental organizations.

29 See Reports for Brazil, Section 1; China, Section 3.5; Vietnam, Section 1.

30 See, e.g., Report for the EU, Section 4 ("In general, there is no universal practice of extraterritorial application of EU law. Extraterritoriality in an EU law context varies according to the respective sub-field of EU law and subject matter"); Report for Australia, Section 2 ("Australia asserts extraterritoriality on specific ad hoc bases, rather than in legislation as a whole"); Report for Germany, Section 4.2.1 ("In the opinion of the Federal Constitutional Court, the definition of a reasonable connecting point needs to be established for each specific field of law separately" (citing BVerfG NJW 2001, 1848, 1852 at III. 6)).

31 Report for Germany, Section 2.1.1.1.

32 Report for the EU, Section 4.

33 See generally Marek Martyniszyn, Report on Developing Countries' Experience with Extraterritoriality in Competition Law, United Nations Conference on Trade and Development, UNCTAD/DITC/CPLP/2021/3 (2021).

South Korea, China, Malaysia, Vietnam, and Cambodia, have enacted competition law with extraterritorial reach.[34] These laws generally permit jurisdiction on the basis of local effects alone, and thus illustrate the paradigmatic case for extraterritoriality in the service of local values: the laws are intended to protect the local market from covered harms.

3.1.2 Other Forms of Financial and Market Regulation

Explicitly extraterritorial legislation is also increasingly common in other areas of market regulation – as one commentator has noted, "extraterritoriality is the 'new normal' in financial law," given the interdependence of markets today.[35] In many systems, securities regulations and other forms of capital market regulation have been amended or introduced to permit extraterritorial application where necessary to protect local markets.[36] This type of regulation can invoke different jurisdictional bases. For instance, some capital requirements directives in the EU extend the nationality principle to cover foreign subsidiaries and branches of EU entities, while financial derivatives regulations extend the territorial principle to cover any transactions with a counterparty located in the EU.[37]

Many states also extend their tax regimes to reach income earned abroad by their nationals or residents – in the case of corporate entities, often also capturing income earned by foreign subsidiaries.[38] Some likewise give their bankruptcy proceedings explicitly cross-border reach. China[39] and the United States, among others, have enacted bankruptcy laws that reach all assets of the debtor, including assets located in other countries.[40]

---

34 See Mari Takeuchi, *Asian Experience With Extraterritoriality*, in Research Handbook on Extraterritoriality in International Law (A. Parrish and C. Ryngaert eds., 2023) 164, 170–71.

35 Matthias Lehmann, *New Challenges of Extraterritoriality: Superposing Laws*, in Continuing Relevance of Private International Law 258 (Franco Ferrari and Diego P. Fernández Arroyo eds., 2019).

36 See, e.g., Report for Germany, Section 2.1.3 (discussing the extraterritorial reach of Germany's Banking Act and Securities Trading Act).

37 Report for the EU, Section 5.1 (noting that "several provisions of the Capital Requirements Directives apply to third country and offshore subsidiaries or branches of EU firms"); Section 5.4 (citing Art 4(1)(a)(IV) Market Instrument Regulation).

38 See, e.g., Report for China, Section 3.1 (discussing China's Individual Income Tax Law, art. 1, and Enterprise Income Tax Law, arts. 2–3). The impact of this form of extraterritoriality is frequently mitigated by the adoption of bilateral tax treaties preventing double taxation and other forms of regulatory overlap.

39 Report for China, Section 3.1 (citing the Enterprises Bankruptcy Law, art. 5).

40 The enforcement of bankruptcy orders affecting foreign assets is of course another matter.

3.1.3 Data Protection and the Digital Economy

The digital economy has emerged as another area where the extraterritorial application of national law is seen as essential to protect local interests.[41] One strand of relevant regulation deals with data privacy. The EU General Data Protection Regulation, to take the single most influential law of this kind, explicitly reaches certain types of foreign activity involving data identifiable to European residents.[42] That regulation has in turn served as a model for data protection reform in multiple other countries, which likewise grant their laws broad geographic scope.[43] In Asia, for instance, Singapore, Japan, and China have all enacted data protection laws with extraterritorial application, and India and Thailand are currently considering proposed legislation along similar lines.[44]

Other laws with extraterritorial effect govern other aspects of digital life, including consumer protection instruments[45] and laws regulating the operations of platform providers and other intermediaries.[46] The EU has enacted significant legislation in this domain, which likewise claims broad extraterritorial reach over foreign actors and activity. The 2022 Digital Markets Act, for instance, applies "to core platform services provided or offered by gatekeepers to business users established in the Union or end users established or located in the Union, irrespective of the place of establishment or residence of the gatekeepers and irrespective of the law otherwise applicable to the provision of service."[47]

---

41 See, e.g., Report for Brazil, Section 1.5 (discussing Law No. 13.709 of 2018); Report for Taiwan, Section 3.5 (discussing the Personal Data Protection Act, Article 51).

42 Regulation 2016/679 of 27 April 2016 on the protection of natural persons with regard to the processing of personal data and on the free movement of such data [2016] OJ 2016 L 119/1, art. 3 (applying to the processing of data identifiable to EU residents regardless of where that processing takes place).

43 See Christopher Kuner, *Data and Extraterritoriality*, in Research Handbook on Extraterritoriality in International Law (A. Parrish and C. Ryngaert eds., 2023) 356, 360 ("As of 2020 there were 142 countries with data protection laws, many of them based on the EU model").

44 Takeuchi, supra note 34, at p. 173.

45 See, e.g., Brazil's Marco Civil da Internet, discussed in the Report for Brazil at Section 1.4.

46 See, e.g., Germany's Network Enforcement Act, discussed in the Report for Germany at Section 2.3.2.

47 Regulation (EU) 2022/1925 of the European Parliament and of the Council of 14 September 2022 on contestable and fair markets in the digital sector and amending Directives (EU) 2019/1937 and (EU) 2020/1828 (Digital Markets Act) [2022] OJ L 265/1, Article 1(2). See generally discussion in Report for the EU, Section 5.3.

3.1.4 Other Areas

The sectors in which national regimes adopt explicitly extraterritorial legislation continue to expand, and include domains beyond core economic regulation. That expansion is sometimes motivated by the desire to protect local social interests. Consumer protection, for example, is another area in which the social interests at stake drive interest in extraterritorial laws.[48] Individual states pursue their own particular priorities in this regard. The report for Italy, for example, identifies social security as a field in which "objectives that are considered crucially relevant to the expression of fundamental [local] values" were served by the enactment of explicitly extraterritorial law.[49]

3.1.5 Conclusion

As this survey indicates, the extension of state law to reach conduct or actors beyond state territory is now routine. It cannot fairly be characterized either as an exceptional form of lawmaking or as a practice only of dominant states. Nevertheless, there remain critical differences across legal systems with respect to the practice of extraterritoriality. Most importantly, enforcement patterns vary significantly. It is one thing to claim broad application of one's laws, and another to enforce those laws with investigations and proceedings affecting foreign entities or conduct.[50] The broad acceptance extraterritoriality has gained as a sometimes-necessary mechanism to protect local interests does not invalidate the legitimacy concerns relating to actual practice.

3.2 *Prosecuting International Crime*

Criminal law is historically more strictly territorial in scope than many other fields of law. In general, local law applies only to offenses committed either wholly or partly in the lawmaking state (which may be deemed to include vessels or aircraft under state registration).[51] Many states do, however, extend their

48 See Report for Brazil, Section 7.1 (citing Claudia Lima Marques on the social interests at stake).

49 Report for Italy, Section 4.

50 See Nico Krisch, *International Law in Times of Hegemony*, 16 E.J.I.L. 369, 400 (2005) ("[D]ominant states tend to use [their domestic law] to a greater extent, and their domestic law 'governs' because other states *de facto* have no choice but to follow it; because of political or economic dependence, or because of the authority the dominant state can command. It is its breadth and actual effectiveness that distinguish it and turn a hegemon's domestic law from a policy tool among equals into an instrument of international government.").

51 Conduct that occurs in part in the state but causes harm in another is treated under the heading of "subjective territoriality," while conduct that occurs in part outside the state but includes an element within it is treated under the heading of "objective territoriality."

laws to encompass crimes committed elsewhere by their own nationals[52] – although those laws are generally enforced only in the case of particularly serious crimes, such as sex offenses involving minors. Many states also enact provisions that extend local criminal law to a more exceptional set of offenses committed entirely outside state territory, regardless of the nationality of the offender. These provisions are often based on the protective principle and involve significant state interests (for example, laws criminalizing the counterfeiting of local currency).

The greatest expansion of extraterritorial provisions in criminal law, however, relates to developments in international criminal law. First, the principle of universal jurisdiction has gained greater purchase, and some states have enacted domestic laws permitting the prosecution of foreign crimes on this basis. Second, treaties addressing the most serious international crimes – including crimes against humanity – turned to domestic criminal law as a tool to enhance enforcement. Third, a number of specialized treaties were adopted to address inherently cross-border criminal activity, likewise relying upon the extraterritorial application of domestic law.

3.2.1 State Laws based on Universal Criminal Jurisdiction

The purpose of this form of jurisdiction is to enhance the enforcement of core international norms by expanding the number of tribunals in which an offender can be prosecuted.[53] It permits a state to apply domestic criminal law regardless of the location of the crime, the nationality of the perpetrator, and the nationality of the victim.[54] The consensus of commentators today is that customary international law permits this form of extraterritoriality[55] – although only in connection with a strictly limited category of crimes, including piracy, slavery, genocide, crimes against humanity, and torture.[56]

52 See, e.g., Criminal Law of the People's Republic of China art. 7.

53 See Princeton Project on Universal Jurisdiction, The Princeton Principles on Universal Jurisdiction 24 (2001) ("[e]nhancing the proper exercise of universal jurisdiction by national courts will help close the gap in law enforcement that has favored perpetrators of serious crimes under international law.").

54 The Belgian law at issue in the *Arrest Warrant* case, for example, stated simply that "The Belgian courts shall have jurisdiction in respect of the offences provided for in the present Law, wheresoever they may have been committed." In that the case, the defendant was not in Belgian territory when the arrest warrant was issued. Arrest Warrant of 11 April 2000 (Democratic Republic of the Congo v. Belgium), Judgment, I.C.J. Reports 2002, pp. 10–11.

55 See U.N. Secretary-General, The Scope and Application of the Principle of Universal Jurisdiction, U.N. Doc. A/66/93 (June 20, 2011).

56 James Crawford, Brownlie's Principles of Public International Law 468 (8th ed. 2012).

Some states have enacted local legislation providing for extraterritorial jurisdiction on this basis – for instance, several African states have laws criminalizing piracy on the high seas.[57] In some cases, national criminal laws claim legislative authority on the basis of universal jurisdiction over a broader set of crimes. Australian criminal law, for instance, includes a category of offenses based on universal jurisdiction that is "quite extensive and far-reaching."[58]

3.2.2 Treaties Enforcing Jus Cogens Norms

A growing number of international treaties include provisions that require member states to enact laws providing for the prosecution of certain foreign crimes.[59] These treaties require member states to criminalize certain offenses in their national regimes and to prosecute offenders. The earliest of these treaties permitted only territorial jurisdiction, such that a member state could prosecute covered crimes only if they occurred within its territory.[60] Over time this was relaxed to incorporate jurisdiction on the basis of nationality, thus permitting states to apply domestic criminal law to extraterritorial offenses. The 1984 Torture Convention, for example, provides that member states shall establish jurisdiction not only if the offense is committed within their territory, but also if it is committed elsewhere by one of their nationals.[61] Other treaties adopting this approach include the Inter-American Convention on

57 See discussion in Magnus Killander, *Extraterritoriality and Africa: in search of justice*, in Research Handbook on Extraterritoriality in International Law (A. Parrish and C. Ryngaert eds., 2023) 195, 200 (citing such provisions in countries including Mauritius and Kenya).

58 Report for Australia, Section 7.1.4. See also Killander, supra note 57, at 196, noting that Eritrea's Penal Code provides that "anyone committing an offence abroad that is a 'serious offence' in Eritrea can be tried in Eritrea where the alleged offender is present in Eritrea after the commission of the offence" (citing Penal Code (2015) art. 44).

59 See generally Matthew Garrod, *The expansion of treaty-based extraterritorial criminal jurisdiction*, in Research Handbook on Extraterritoriality in International Law (A. Parrish and C. Ryngaert eds., 2023) 236 (providing a survey of this trend).

60 The Genocide Convention, for instance, provided only for territorial jurisdiction, assigning authority to prosecute covered crimes to the state in which they occurred. Convention on the Prevention and Punishment of the Crime of Genocide, Article VI (providing that defendants shall be tried either in the territorial state or by an international tribunal with jurisdiction over the matter).

61 Convention against Torture and Other Cruel, Inhuman, or Degrading Treatment or Punishment, 10 December 1984, Article 5 (b). Article 5(c) provides further that in circumstances the state deems appropriate, it may also prosecute foreign offenses when the victim is a national.

Torture,[62] the Inter-American Convention on Forced Disappearances,[63] the International Convention on the Protection of All Persons from Enforced Disappearance,[64] the International Convention for the Suppression of Terrorist Bombings,[65] and the African Union Convention on the Prevention and Combating of Terrorism.[66] Finally, some of the treaties permit states to establish jurisdiction even without the link of nationality. Following the 1998 enactment of the Rome Statute, the founding treaty of the International Criminal Court, many states enacted implementing legislation providing for universal jurisdiction over certain crimes.[67]

It is important to recognize significant regional differences in this area of law. Asian countries have "taken a cautious approach to international criminal law in general"[68] – a sentiment that is reflected in the relatively low rate of accession among those countries to the Rome Statute.[69] Perhaps due to skepticism about the status of universal jurisdiction under customary international law, few countries in the region have enacted domestic law criminalizing international crimes other than genocide and war crimes – and even there have focused on atrocities occurring within the territory of the lawmaking state.[70]

There is also significant variation in the limits states place on the extraterritorial reach of their own criminal law. In Latin America, for example, many states have added significant qualifications to the exercise of extraterritorial criminal jurisdiction. They may require that the accused be located within their territory, that the conduct be criminalized in the state in which the offense was committed, that the statute of limitations in the state in which the offense was committed has not yet run, or some combination of such factors.[71] Perhaps in light of such limitations, along with resource constraints and political factors

62 Article 12.

63 Article IV.

64 Article 9.

65 Article 6.

66 Article 6.

67 As of July 2024, 124 states were parties to the Rome Statute. https://treaties.un.org.

68 Takeuchi, supra note 34, at 166.

69 The International Criminal Court describes Asia-Pacific states as "under-represented in the Court's membership," with only "35% of States in the Asia-Pacific Group [as] parties … as opposed to 75% of States from all other regions of the world." https://www.icc-cpi.int/sites/default/files/2022-09/universality-asia-eng-v.11-web.pdf

70 See Takeuchi, supra note 34, at 166–67.

71 See Alejandro Chehtman, *Strategic Approaches to extraterritorial jurisdiction in Latin America*, in Research Handbook on Extraterritoriality in International Law (A. Parrish and C. Ryngaert eds., 2023) 180, 185–86.

militating in favor of a focus on local crime, the exercise of universal jurisdiction in practice remains extraordinary, although there are exceptions,[72] and some recent studies trace growth in its use.[73]

3.2.3 Treaties Addressing Transnational Crime

There has also been a noticeable increase in international treaties addressing forms of crime that by their nature involve conduct in more than one state. These treaties do not replace national law, but rather enhance enforcement at the global scale by permitting, or in some cases requiring, states to apply their laws extraterritorially to covered conduct. The most common mechanism is nationality jurisdiction, in which the scope of local law is extended to reach the conduct of nationals outside the territory of the lawmaking state.

One of the earliest treaties of this kind is the OECD's anti-bribery convention, adopted in 1997.[74] The Convention obligates member states to adopt legislation criminalizing the bribery of foreign officials, and permits them to prosecute acts of their own nationals overseas.[75] In 2003, the United Nations followed with a global anti-bribery convention, which now has 189 state parties.[76] Like the OECD instrument, this convention requires member states to enact legislation criminalizing acts of corruption and permits the prosecution of offences committed by their nationals.[77] Other regional instruments did the same, including the 2003 African Union Convention on Preventing and Combating Corruption.[78] These are widely signed, with the result that many countries have amended their penal codes to expand the scope of anti-bribery laws in accordance with these international conventions.

Beyond the context of corruption, many other treaties have been developed to address other inherently transnational crimes, such as money laundering

72 Argentina has initiated nearly 100 investigations on the basis of universal jurisdiction, although none has reached trial. Chehtman, supra note 71, at 186–87.

73 See Máximo Langer & Mackenzie Eason, *The Quiet Expansion of Universal Jurisdiction*, 30 Eur. J. Int'l L. 779 (2019). See also Gurgen Petrossian, *Germany's Pursuit of International Criminal Justice Through Universal Jurisdiction*, 27 ASIL Insights 8 (2023) (stating that German courts have recently become more active in prosecuting international crimes under Germany's domestic universal jurisdiction statute).

74 Convention on Combating Bribery of Foreign Public Officials in International Business Transactions, adopted 21 November 1997. See also Inter-American Convention Against Corruption (1996).

75 Id. at Article 4(2).

76 United Nations Convention against Corruption, General Assembly resolution 58/4 of 31 October 2003.

77 Article 42(2)(b).

78 Article 13.

and terrorist financing, that are difficult for individual states to prosecute and deter effectively. These include the International Convention for the Suppression of the Financing of Terrorism;[79] the United Nations Convention on Transnational Organised Crime;[80] and the latter's supplementary protocols focused on human trafficking.[81] Within these treaty frameworks, states have begun more frequently to extend domestic criminal law to foreign activity.[82]

3.3 *Securing Global Goods*

In some areas, extraterritoriality is evolving as a tool to serve not local but rather global interests, or to secure global goods. In the human rights arena, several major soft law initiatives seek to deploy extraterritoriality. The United Nations Guiding Principles, for instance, encourage states to regulate the activities of their own corporations (and those corporations' subsidiaries and affiliates) in other countries.[83] The Principles adopt an explicitly extraterritorial dimension, encouraging states to implement local laws that will operationalize greater control over foreign activities.[84] Likewise, the Maastricht Principles on Extraterritorial Obligations of States in the Area of Economic, Social and Cultural Rights underscore the "general obligation to exercise influence on the conduct of non-state actors where such conduct might lead to human rights being violated outside the state's national territory."[85]

Although such human rights initiatives are multilateral in nature, the EU in particular has engaged in significant unilateral lawmaking intended to advance global welfare. In the case of its extraterritorial emissions regime, for example, the EU chose to address the global problem of climate change unilaterally,

79 International Convention for the Suppression of the Financing of Terrorism.

80 *United Nations Convention on Transnational Organised Crime*, opened for signature 15 November 2000, 2225 UNTS 209 (entered into force 29 September 2003).

81 *Protocol to Prevent, Suppress and Punish Trafficking in Persons, Especially Women and Children*, opened for signature 15 November 2000, 2237 UNTS 319 (entered into force 25 December 2003); *Protocol against the Smuggling of Migrants by Land, Sea and Air*, opened for signature 15 December 2003, 2241 UNTS 507 (entered into force 28 January 2004).

82 For a list and discussion of such treaties, see Danielle Ireland-Piper, Accountability in Extraterritoriality: A Comparative and International Perspective 11–12 (2017).

83 Guiding Principles on Business and Human Rights, HR/PUB/11/04, Principle 1 (Commentary).

84 See https://globalnaps.org/issue/extraterritorial-jurisdiction/ for an overview of these plans in jurisdictions around the world.

85 Commentary 3 to Principle 24. See also General Comment No. 24 on State Obligations Under the International Covenant on Economic, Social and Cultural Rights in the Context of Business Activities of 23 June 2017 (UN Doc. E/C.12/GC/24).

in the absence of progress on a treaty.[86] The Corporate Sustainability Due Diligence Directive similarly claims extraterritorial reach in order to promote fair working conditions worldwide, by indirectly regulating the activities of subsidiaries and subcontractors of EU corporations outside the EU.[87] Here, extraterritoriality of local legislation is promoted either as a substitute for or to spur multilateral action.[88]

3.4 *Assessment*

As noted above, under modern jurisdictional law, the exercise of prescriptive jurisdiction must rest on an acceptable connection or link between the target of regulation and the lawmaking state. Historically, two particular links were widely viewed as acceptable: states were entitled to regulate conduct occurring within their own territory, and the foreign conduct of their own nationals. Since states generally have little interest in regulating the conduct of their nationals outside their own borders, the combined operation of these principles confined the extraterritorial application of state law quite significantly. The trends described above, however, indicate a marked expansion in the circumstances under which states may enact extraterritorial legislation within the limits of international jurisdictional law.

First, at least in certain substantive areas, the "effects basis" for jurisdiction is now widely accepted. Under this principle, a state may legitimately regulate even wholly foreign conduct if it causes effects within its territory – greatly expanding the geographic scope of state law.[89] This is a relatively recent development. Early instances of extraterritorial regulation based solely on the local effects of foreign conduct were challenged as violations of international law. The 1945 *Alcoa* decision,[90] approving the application of U.S. antitrust law to wholly foreign conduct solely on the basis of its local effects, drew widespread condemnation as a breach of international law.[91] As late as 1988, the

86 See Natalie L. Dobson & Cedric Ryngaert, *Provocative Climate Protection:* EU *'Extraterritorial' Regulation of Marine Emissions*, 66 Int'l & Comp. L.Q. 295, 309 (2017).

87 Directive (EU) 2024/1760 of the European Parliament and of the Council of 13 June 2024 on corporate sustainability due diligence and amending Directive (EU) 2019/1937 and Regulation (EU) 2023/2859.

88 See generally Cedric Ryngaert, Selfless Intervention: Exercising Jurisdiction in the Common Interest (2020).

89 In this sense the effects basis represents a significant expansion of the "objective territoriality" principle developed in criminal law, under which a state was permitted to regulate foreign conduct if a constituent element of the relevant offense occurred within its borders.

90 U.S. v. Aluminum Co. of America, 148 F.2d 416 (2d Cir. 1945).

91 See David J. Gerber, Global Competition: Law, Markets, and Globalization (2012).

European Court of Justice – perhaps wary of this critique – offered an alternative rationalization for extending EU competition law to foreign conduct in its first decision on that issue.[92] Over time, however, the local effects of wholly foreign conduct have become generally accepted as a "genuine connection" legitimizing the exercise of prescriptive jurisdiction. The Court of Justice of the European Union, for example, has held that local effects satisfy international jurisdictional requirements as long as it is "foreseeable that the conduct in question will have an immediate and substantial effect in the European Union."[93] Countries including China, Germany, and Japan likewise accept local effects as a basis for jurisdiction; and even in the United Kingdom, long a resister, recent cases apply the effects principle.[94] In sum, international law now permits the extension of state law to wholly foreign conduct in a wide array of fields. Where international law limits are invoked, it is typically only to require local effects to reach some threshold of quantum or significance. Thus, for instance, states may require local effects to be foreseeable, intentional, significant, direct, or some combination of such factors.

Second, in several areas of law, it is becoming more common for states to regulate not only the foreign activity of their own corporations, but that of subsidiaries and other entities within affiliate groups. Under the entity theory of corporate law, each company within an enterprise group is a distinct entity with its own nationality; thus, the home state of a parent company would lack general prescriptive authority over its foreign affiliates. In the past, indeed, efforts to regulate foreign affiliates were criticized as violations of international jurisdictional principles.[95] However, current practice in areas including taxation, anti-corruption, and export controls frequently relies on theories of ownership, control, agency, or attribution to justify the regulation of foreign activity within enterprise groups. The extraterritorial regulation of entities whose accounts are consolidated with a domestic entity, in particular, seems

92 See Wood Pulp, Osakeyhtiö v. Commission of the European Communities, (1988) ECR 5193 (focusing on the local "implementation" of a foreign scheme rather than directly on its local effects).

93 Case C-413/14 *Intel Corp v Commission* [2017] EU:C:2017:632, at para. 49. See also Case C-507/17 *Google v* CNIL [2019] EU:C:2019:772.

94 See generally Restatement (Fourth) of Foreign Relations Law of the United States at § 409 Reporters' Note 2 (compiling examples of effects-based jurisdiction from multiple countries).

95 In the mid-1980s, Mann stated that "the control theory of nationality lacks such general recognition as to render it an internationally permissible test."). F.A. Mann, *The Doctrine of International Jurisdiction Revisited After Twenty Years*, 186 Recueil des Cours 9, 60 (1984).

widely accepted.[96] Broader claims of jurisdictional reach over foreign entities on the basis of control are more contentious, particularly in the area of economic sanctions. Legislation imposing human rights-oriented due diligence obligations on companies, though, frequently rely on attenuated concepts of control and oversight to affect entities throughout the supply chain of local companies.[97]

Third, the extraterritorial application of criminal law – both state-specific legislation and national laws enacted pursuant to treaty obligations – has become routine, in part due to a greater acceptance of universal jurisdiction.

In sum, the "genuine connection" requirement of international jurisdictional law has become a far less meaningful constraint on extraterritorial legislation.

4 The Interpretation of Law's Scope

In some cases, statutes do not speak to their own geographic reach. In others, they expressly contemplate extraterritorial application, but do not include specific tests for that application – as in the case of statutes that authorize the regulation of foreign conduct on the basis of local effects without setting out qualifiers regarding the necessary quantity or severity of those effects. In such cases an interpretive step is required.

In most legal systems, courts are called upon to decide the geographic scope of a statute or regulation when that law is challenged as an excess of legal authority – either in general or in application to a particular case. In systems permitting the private enforcement of regulatory law, courts also interpret scope more routinely, to ascertain whether a cause of action lies under a particular law.

4.1 *Interpreting Ambiguous Statutes*

4.1.1 General Presumptions Regarding the Geographic Scope of Legislation

Many legal systems observe general presumptions against the extraterritorial application of laws that lack an explicit statement of extraterritorial scope.

96 The recent OECD framework for taxing multinational enterprises, for example, uses consolidated accounting to define the MNE.

97 See Report for the Netherlands, Section 6 ("While this does not involve the direct application of Dutch law to foreign companies, incorporation of these provisions in company-wide policies set by (Dutch) parent companies, and in contractual arrangements by end-tier companies in a supply chain, does give Dutch law effect abroad.")

Historically, these presumptions were sourced in the traditional understanding that law was strictly territorial.[98] Some states still observe relatively strict limits of this kind. Romania, for example, continues to adhere to a general principle of territoriality.[99] In addition, in the area of criminal law, a presumption that law can be applied extraterritorially only when expressly authorized is consistent with the doctrine *nullum crimen sine lege*.[100]

Over the course of the twentieth century, with the abandonment of strict territorialism, other explanations emerged for general presumptions against the extraterritorial application of law. These include respect for general principles of international law, including the principle that states must avoid infringing the sovereignty of other states.[101] This justification figures prominently in dualist states that give national legislation primacy over earlier-adopted treaties or customary international law. In such systems, an express indication of legislative intent to give a statute extraterritorial reach will be given effect even if the result is a violation of international law. Because international law does not directly constrain the application of those laws,[102] its indirect role in

98 See, e.g., The Apollon, 22 U.S. 362, 370 (1824) ("The laws of no nation can justly extend beyond its own territories, except so far as regards its own citizens. ... And, however general and comprehensive the phrases used in our municipal laws may be, they must always be restricted in construction, to places and persons, upon whom the Legislature have authority and jurisdiction").

99 Report for Romania, Section 1.5.1 (observing that "almost all the major Romanian normative acts expressly consecrate the principle of territoriality," and citing the "universally accepted rule that extraterritoriality is possible only where expressly mentioned" in legislation).

100 See Report for Japan, Section 1.3.1 ("According to Art. 31 of the Constitution of Japan, criminal punishment must be based on the law (*nullum crimen sine lege*). In this regard, the extraterritorial application of criminal law should always be based on [explicit] legislation.").

101 See, e.g., Report for the United Kingdom, Section 3 (discussing R (On the Application of KBR) v. Director of the Serious Fraud Office [2021] UKSC 2 at para. 24 (stating that the presumption "reflects, in part, the requirements of international law that one State should not by the claim or exercise of jurisdiction infringe the sovereignty of another State in breach of rules of international law"); Report for Quebec, Section 3 and Report for Canada, Section 4.3 (discussing R.v. Hape, 2007 SCC 26, and the "longstanding presumption of conformity with international law as an interpretive principle of domestic law"); Report for Australia, Section 8, quoting *B v T* [2008] 1 Qd R 33 at 13–14 (discussing a presumption that state legislation "is presumed not to deal with persons or matters the jurisdiction over which properly belongs to some other sovereign state").

102 Report for Canada, Section 4.3 at fn 51; Report for United States, Section 3.1 ("if a U.S. statute clearly indicates that it applies in the situation, the fact that such an application violates customary international law does not stop U.S. courts from applying the statute"); Report for Australia, Section 4.

supporting presumptions regarding the scope of laws that do not specifically dictate their scope of application is critical.

The principle of international comity also figures into general presumptions against the extraterritorial application of law.[103] In a landmark Canadian criminal case, the court held that where a statute is unclear as to geographic reach, it applies in cases where a significant element of the offense occurred in Canada, creating a "real and substantial link" to the state, and the assertion of judicial jurisdiction would not offend international comity.[104] This test has been extrapolated to other areas of law, including in the regulatory arena.[105] A recent decision in the United Kingdom explicitly links the presumption against extraterritoriality not only to principles of international law but also to comity.[106] Such presumptions may also be used to indicate restrictions on the extent of a statute's extraterritoriality. In a Korean competition case, for example, the Supreme Court concluded that the law permitting regulation on the basis of local effects must be construed to require "direct, considerable, and reasonably predictable" effects in order to prevent unnecessary international conflict.[107]

4.1.2 Purposive Interpretation of Specific Statutes

In many legal systems, including China and the EU, there is no general presumption against the extraterritoriality of legislation.[108] Instead, when a law does not include an explicit statement regarding its geographic scope, it must be assessed "on a case-by-case basis with regard to [its] objective." Thus, for instance, a 2017 decision of the Japanese Supreme Court construed

103 See Report for Australia, Section 8, describing the presumption of territoriality as "founded in notions of comity" as well as sovereignty.

104 Report for Canada, Section 4.1 (discussing Libman v. The Queen, [1985] 2 SCR 178).

105 Id..

106 Report for the United Kingdom, Section 4 (discussing R (On the Application of KBR) v. Director of the Serious Fraud Office [2021] UKSC 2 at para. 25 (stating that the presumption against extraterritoriality reflects not only principles of international law but also "the usages of States acting out of mutual respect and, no doubt, the expectation of reciprocal advantage," and that "Accordingly, it is not necessary, in invoking the presumption, to demonstrate that the extra-territorial application of the legislation in issue would infringe the sovereignty of another State in violation of international law.").

107 Report for Korea, Section 4.1.1 (discussing Korean Supreme Court on May 16, 2014 (Case No. 2012 Du 5466) (*Asiana Airlines, Co. Ltd., v. Korea Fair Trade Commission*)).

108 Report for the EU, Section 4.3; Report for China, Section 5.3 (noting that "there is no 'presumption against extraterritoriality' or any equivalent doctrine in Chinese law").

the Antimonopoly Act "in light of its object and purpose," determining that it applied to a foreign cartel.[109]

Although the United States does observe a presumption against the extraterritorial application of law, in recent years that presumption has been reframed not as a general presumption based on principles of international law and comity, but rather as a method of purposive interpretation.[110] This shift began with the "focus" test the Supreme Court introduced in the 2010 case *Morrison v. National Australia Bank*.[111] Under this test, when a statute does not include a clear indication of its geographic scope, a court must consider its "focus." As the Court explained in a subsequent decision, "The focus of a statute is 'the object of its solicitude,' which can include the conduct it 'seeks to "regulate,"' as well as the parties and interests it 'seeks to "protect"' or vindicate."[112] If the thing that is the focus of the statute occurs within the United States, then application of the law is territorial and thus permitted even if other factors link the case to another country. If it occurs elsewhere, however, "then the case involves an impermissible extraterritorial application" of the law even if other factors link the case to the United States.[113]

While purposive interpretation is frequently used to impose limits on the reach of statutes that are ambiguous as to scope, it can also support the expansion of a law's scope. For instance, it may indicate that if a statute addresses what is clearly an international problem, it must be assumed to have extraterritorial scope. In one illustrative U.K. case interpreting a money laundering statute, the court held that money laundering "is par excellence an offence which is no respecter of national boundaries," and that the act therefore required extraterritorial application in order to be given effect.[114]

---

109 Case Concerning sales prices of Cathode-ray tubes, Supreme Court of Japan, 12 December 2017, discussed in report for Japan at Section 1.2.4.

110 See generally William S. Dodge, *The New Presumption Against Extraterritoriality*, 133 Harv. L. Rev. 1582 (2020).

111 Morrison v. National Australia Bank Ltd., 561 U.S. 247 (2010).

112 WesternGeco LLC v. ION Geophysical Corp., 585 U.S. 407, 413–14 (2018) (quoting Morrison).

113 RJR Nabisco, Inc. v. European Community, 579 U.S. 325, 337 (2016). In its most recent case, the Supreme Court muddied the waters by implying that whatever a statute's "object of solicitude" might be, some *conduct* within the United States was necessary to justify the application of U.S. law. Abitron Austria GmbH v. Hetronic Int'l, Inc., 600 U.S. 412 (2023).

114 Report for the United Kingdom, Section 1.2 (citing R v. Rogers [2014] EWCA Crim 1680).

4.2 *Case-specific Limitations on the Application of Laws with Extraterritorial Scope*

If a particular law has been interpreted to have extraterritorial reach, an additional question is whether its application can or should be restrained in particular situations based on case-specific factors. The source of a potential requirement to refrain from extraterritorial action in deference to the interests of other states is unclear. Several states have explicitly rejected the proposition that such deference is required as a matter of customary international law.[115] However, the operation of such limits is frequently observed in practice as a matter of domestic law and policy. These limits are typically grounded in the principle of international comity or in considerations of "reasonableness" or "proportionality" that aim to prevent the application of domestic law in factual situations that would create unacceptable conflict with other regulatory regimes.

Such limits are widely observed by public agencies and prosecutorial authorities. In some cases, they are embodied in formal mechanisms that encourage prosecutorial deference where significant foreign interests are involved.[116] They can also be reflected in rules that tailor enforcement mechanisms differently where non-nationals rather than nationals are targeted.[117] And as a matter of policy and practice, regulatory agencies around the world routinely consider case-specific factors that might limit the extraterritorial application of law – both unilaterally and in the context of bilateral or multilateral agreements among agencies.[118]

115 See, e.g., Report for Germany, Section 5.1 (stating that in German discourse "the concept of the comity of nations or *courtoisie* tends not to be considered as customary international law"); Restatement (Fourth) of the Foreign Relations Law of the United States § 405.

116 See, e.g., Report for the United Kingdom, Section 5 (describing the guidelines that Crown Prosecutors follow, and concluding that "While there is no explicit reasonableness requirement in these guidelines, these considerations come close to applying a reasonableness standard to determine the most appropriate forum"); Report for Australia, Section 7.1.4 (noting that if universal jurisdiction is the basis and the accused is not Australian, prosecutorial consent is required).

117 See, e.g., Report for Japan, Section 1.5.1 (describing certain administrative laws whose enforcement mechanisms include coercive orders when directed at Japanese persons, but only "requests" when directed at non-Japanese persons).

118 See, e.g., U.S. Department of Justice and Federal Trade Commission, Antitrust Guidelines for International Enforcement and Cooperation ¶ 4.1 (January 13, 2017) (a unilateral measure requiring U.S. agencies to "take into account whether significant interests of any foreign sovereign would be affected" by application of U.S. law); Agreement between the Government of the United States of America and the Commission of the European Communities regarding the application of their competition laws, OJ L 95, 27.4.1995

Some legal systems also permit or encourage courts to consider case-specific factors at least with respect to certain laws. In the EU, for instance, the 2019 Google v. CNIL decision indicated that individual member states, in applying EU data protection rules regarding the right to be forgotten, should take account of the interests of other affected states.[119] Specific legislation may also explicitly reference comity concerns, as the Report for Canada notes.[120] In other systems, though, statutes that have been interpreted to have extraterritorial reach are applied despite potential conflict in the individual case. In Australia, for example, a court held that comity did not provide a basis to decline jurisdiction conferred on it by statute.[121] The United States went through a period of experimentation with case-by-case comity analysis, but the Supreme Court has moved away from that approach in many areas of law.[122] Lower courts in the United States, however, frequently consider case-specific factors before applying law extraterritorially.[123]

5 Sources of Conflict

While there may be consensus regarding the power of states to apply their laws in situations with foreign elements, there is less consensus on the extent to which – and purposes for which – that power is deployed. In a number of areas, problematic practices persist.

5.1 *Reliance on Weak Links*

As noted above, there is no international law limitation on the exercise of jurisdiction once an acceptable basis of jurisdiction has been established.[124] As a result, states sometimes leverage weak links to engage in regulation with significant extraterritorial impact. These practices understandably generate resistance.

(a bilateral agreement requiring each covered agency to take into account the competing interests of other states before initiating an investigation or proceeding).

119 Case C507/17 *Google v.* CNIL [2019] EU:C:2019:772.

120 Report for Canada, Section 4.4 (citing the Canada Transportation Act).

121 Report for Australia, Section 5.1 (citing *Habib v Commonwealth of Australia* (2010) 183 FCR 61 at 37).

122 Report for the United States, Section 3.3 (discussing F. Hoffmann-La Roche Ltd. v. Empagran S.A., 542 U.S. 155, 168 (2004), an antitrust case concluding that such a case-by-case approach would be "too complex to prove workable".).

123 See Hannah L. Buxbaum and Ralf Michaels, *Reasonableness as a Limitation on the Extraterritorial Application of U.S. Law*, in Stephan and Cleveland (eds), The Restatement and Beyond: The Past, Present, and Future of U.S. Foreign Relations Law 283 (2020).

124 See Section One supra.

5.1.1 Territoriality

Although territorial jurisdiction – jurisdiction based on contacts within the territory of the lawmaking state – is clearly acceptable under jurisdictional law, states sometimes rely on tenuous territorial links to justify legislative jurisdiction over matters with significant foreign elements. The United States, for example, has enacted a number of statutes targeting fraud and other forms of financial misconduct that extend to any situation in which U.S. wires or payment systems are used. U.S. authorities have used such laws to prosecute frauds occurring largely overseas, and targeting only foreign victims.[125] In such cases, where the impact of regulation in other countries seems disproportionate to the quantity or quality of the local contacts, it is often perceived (and described) as illegitimately extraterritorial. Similarly, the United States has used weak territorial links to extend the reach of economic sanctions, extending them to cover not only transactions by U.S. persons, but any transaction involving a nexus with the United States. Controversially, that nexus can be simply channeling payments through U.S. banks, or denominating transactions in U.S. currency.[126]

The EU has also engaged in geographically sweeping legislation based on territorial links, in a process that Joanna Scott has described as "territorial extension."[127] An example of such lawmaking was the 2008 Aviation Directive, which regulated all emissions from flights departing from or arriving in an airport within a member state, not only the emissions related to the EU portion of the flight.[128] The European Court of Justice considered this and concluded that the presence of an airplane in EU territory was a sufficient link to support

125 In 2005, the Supreme Court considered whether the prosecution of a scheme to smuggle liquor into Canada, in order to evade Canadian tax, was impermissibly extraterritorial. It held that it was not, on the basis that the statute punishes only "the domestic element" of such conduct, and therefore that the offense in question was complete as soon as the wires had been used. Pasquantino v. United States, 544 U.S. 349, 371 (2005) (over a dissent by Justice Ginsburg that this would give the law extraterritorial effect; see id. at 375, noting that the decision "fail[s] to take account of Canada's primary interest in the matter at stake").

126 One of the most significant extraterritoriality disputes in recent years involved the decision of U.S. authorities to prosecute BNP Paribas for violating U.S. sanctions law, apparently on the basis that BNP had cleared transactions in dollars, thereby "knowingly and willfully mov[ing] more than $8.8 billion through the U.S. financial system." *See* Statement of Facts, United States v. BNP Paribas, S.A., (S.D.N.Y. 2014), http://www.justice.gov/sites/default/files/opa/legacy/2014/06/30/statement-of-facts.pdf.

127 Joanne Scott, *Extraterritoriality and Territorial Extension in EU Law*, 62 Am. J. Comp. L. 87 (2014).

128 Directive 2008/101/EC of the European Parliament and of the Council of 14 November 2008 amending Directive 2003/87/EC so as to include aviation activities in the scheme for

this broad scope provision.[129] In the later *Zuchtvieh* case, the Court adopted a similarly broad interpretation of a regulation regarding animal transport to reach all stages of a journey beginning in the EU, even the stages taking place in the territory of other countries.[130]

5.1.2 Nationality

Likewise, although jurisdiction based on the nationality of the relevant actor is also clearly acceptable under international law, states sometimes use weak forms of nationality to extend the reach of their laws. For instance, U.S. export control regulations have been granted broad reach in the past, extending not only to U.S. corporations, but also to "any partnership, association, corporation, or other organization, wherever organized or doing business, that is owned or controlled" by a U.S. person or corporation.[131] By using this loose test of corporate control rather than the more traditional test of corporate nationality, the United States has justified the application of its export regulations to prevent non-U.S. companies from engaging in exports that did not originate in the United States.[132] In Australia, anti-cartel laws have been extended to reach the foreign conduct of foreign companies on the basis that they have Australian subsidiaries and are therefore "carrying on business" in Australia.[133]

5.2 *Economic Sanctions*

One of the most contentious forms of extraterritoriality is the economic sanction. Unlike the forms of extraterritoriality described in Section 3.A above, sanctions do not protect and promote local interests embodied in state law – rather, they serve purely foreign policy goals. When primary sanctions claim expansive geographic reach, they become particularly problematic. Moreover, states may impose secondary sanctions, which prohibit relationships between foreign actors and the target of the sanctions even in the absence of a nexus with the sanctioning state. U.S. practice in this regard, including

---

greenhouse gas emission allowance trading within the Community (Aviation Directive) [2009] OJ L8/3, art 1(3)(b).

129 Case C-366/10 *Air Transport Association of America v Secretary of State for Energy and Climate Change* [2011] ECR I – 13755.

130 Case C-424/13 *Zuchtvieh-Export GmbH v Stadt Kempten* [2015] EU:C:2015:259.

131 Export Administration Act; see 21 I.L.M. 891.

132 See discussion in Compagnie Européenne des Pétroles S.A. v. Sensor Nederland B.V., Engl. translation reported in 22 I.L.M. 66 (1983).

133 Report for Australia, Section 7.2 (citing *Australian Competition and Consumer Commission v Yazaki Corporation (No 2)* [2015] FCA 1304).

under the Helms-Burton Act and the Trading With the Enemy Act, has been widely criticized for many years. Other states have likewise engaged in similar activity. The Arab states' boycott of foreign companies doing business with Israel was another such example. More recently, both China and the EU have adopted their own sanctions regimes with explicitly extraterritorial scope.[134]

5.3 *Private Enforcement*

Despite widespread adoption of laws with extraterritorial scope, there is less consensus regarding the private enforcement of those laws in the transnational arena. Civil litigation involves the application of local procedural law, which injects additional conflict into cases involving foreign elements on matters including the extent of discovery, the availability of non-compensatory damages, and the use of representative actions, among others. As a result, even in substantive areas where the extraterritorial application of law is widely accepted, including competition law, private enforcement remains contentious.[135] Likewise, in the human rights arena – where the substantive norms in question are shared – the principle of universal civil jurisdiction has not gained the same acceptance as universal criminal jurisdiction.

5.4 *Countermeasures*

Perceived aggression can lead to significant resistance and diplomatic protest by other countries. Such protest has been common in response to economic sanctions. The notorious dispute over the Trans-Siberian Pipeline project in the early 1980s, for instance, involved widespread protest. It can arise beyond the domain of sanctions, however. In 2008, the EU's directive on aviation emissions, which applied to airlines registered in non-EU countries, led to a joint declaration signed by representatives of 23 countries from all regions of the world. Aggressive extraterritoriality can also be met with counter-extraterritoriality. In Africa, the 2012 African Union Model National Law on

134 See Report for China, Section 3.8 (discussing the Anti-foreign Sanctions Law (AFSL) adopted by the Standing Committee of the Thirteenth National People's Congress on June 10, 2021); Report for the EU, Section 5.3 (discussing the EU's 2017 Venezuela Sanctions Regulation, 2014 Russia Sanctions Regulation, and 2011 Iran Sanctions Regulation).

135 See Hannah L. Buxbaum, *Public Regulation and Private Enforcement in the Global Economy: Strategies for Managing Conflict*, 399 Recueil des Cours 277 (2019) (observing that the use of civil litigation as a regulatory mechanism involves forms of procedural and political conflict that public regulation does not); Paul B. Stephan, *Private Litigation as a Foreign Relations Problem*, 110 AJIL Unbound 40 (2016).

Universal Jurisdiction over International Crimes was adopted as a response to the exercise of universal jurisdiction by some European states over crimes committed in Africa.[136] In 2019, China adopted a policy calling for accelerated extraterritoriality in response to perceived threats from the United States.[137]

At the most extreme, these conflicts can lead to the enactment of blocking statutes – themselves, of course, a form of extraterritoriality. In the 1980s, for example, a number of states implemented blocking statutes in response to perceived U.S. overreach in the area of competition law.[138] In 1996, the EU adopted a regulation in response to "the unlawful effects of extra-territorial legislation of third countries," referring to the U.S. sanctions against Cuba, Iran, and Libya.[139] More recently, shifts in the geopolitical relationship between China and the United States led to the enactment of a blocking statute in China.[140]

6 Conclusion

The extraterritorial application of state law is pervasive in contemporary practice. It is a necessary element of effective regulatory schemes in an era of global markets, and is increasingly recognized as a useful technique to address shared challenges as diverse as transnational crime, tax base erosion, and climate change. To some extent, then, extraterritoriality has been normalized, and integrated into the range of legal instruments – multilateral as well as unilateral, soft law as well as hard law – that constitute the domain of global governance.

---

136 See Killander, supra note 57, at 197.

137 Report for China, Section 2.2, Section 3.8.

138 Report for Italy, Section 7, citing Law no. 488 of 23 July 1980, "Divieto ai cittadini italiani di fornire ad autorità straniere documenti ed informazioni concernenti l'attività marittima," a blocking statute in the particular context of maritime antitrust disputes; Report for the United Kingdom, Section 10, citing the UK Protection of Trading Interests Act 1980; Report for Australia, Section 9, citing the Foreign Proceedings (Excess of Jurisdiction) Act 1984; Report for Quebec, Section 10 (describing the *Loi sur les dossiers d'entreprise*, RLRQ, c. D-12, a provincial law blocking access to business records); Report for Canada, Section 4.9.1, citing the Foreign Extraterritorial Measures Act.

139 Council Regulation (EC) No 2271/96 of 22 November 1996 protecting against the effects of the extra-territorial application of legislation adopted by a third country, and actions based thereon or resulting therefrom, OJ L 309.

140 See Report for China, Section 3.8 (discussing Ministry of Commerce of the People's Republic of China, Rules on Counteracting Unjustified Extraterritorial Application of Foreign Legislation and Other Measures (http://english.mofcom.gov.cn/article/policyrelease/announcement/202101/20210103029708.shtml).

By no means, though, does this normalization of extraterritoriality as a legal technique resolve the longstanding debates about its place in the international legal order. The frequency and intensity of extraterritorial practices (even within multilateral frameworks) map onto the geopolitical power of states, entrenching concerns about the legitimacy of extraterritorial lawmaking and its instrumentalization by dominant states.[141] If anything, we can expect these concerns to intensify in an era of increasing multipolarity, as more states expand their own extraterritorial practices.

---

141 See Krisch, supra note 52; Austen L. Parrish, *Reclaiming International Law From Extraterritoriality*, 93 Minn. L. Rev. 536 (2009).

PART 2

National Reports

The Extraterritorial Application of Statutes and Regulations

Australia

Danielle Ireland-Piper[*]

1 Introduction

Australia was colonised by Britain in 1788, achieving full constitutional independence in 1986. In 1900, the British Parliament passed the *Commonwealth of Australia Constitution Act 1900* (Imp), which came into force as Australia's Constitution on 1 January 1901. That Constitution remains in place, with only minor amendments. In 1942, the *Statute of Westminster Adoption Act* provided that no act of the Australian Parliament could be found invalid for the reason of repugnancy to the laws of the United Kingdom. This act also made it clear that the Parliament of the "Commonwealth of Australia" (Australia) had power to act extraterritorially in its own right.

Australia remains a constitutional monarchy. Unlike the United Kingdom, however, which is a (mostly) unitary system of governance with an "unwritten" constitution, Australia is a federal system with a written constitution.[1] Public power in Australia is divided between the state governments and a central federal government, known as the Commonwealth of Australia ('the Commonwealth'). The federal government has specific "enumerated" powers set out in the *Australian Constitution*,[2] whereas the state governments have general plenary law-making powers and are governed both by individual state constitutions and the *Australian Constitution*. Technically speaking, both state and federal governments in Australia have constitutional capacity to legislate extraterritorially, depending on the subject matter, although in most

* Associate Professor, Australian National University and Honorary Adjunct Associate Professor, Faculty of Law, Bond University.

1 For a discussion on the similarities and differences between the Australia, New Zealand and United Kingdom approaches to extraterritoriality, see: Danielle Ireland-Piper, 'Extraterritoriality in the Commonwealth: Case Studies from Australia, New Zealand, and the United Kingdom' in Austen Parrish and Cedric Ryngaert (Eds.) *Extraterritoriality in International Law* (Edward Elgar, 2023).

2 See, for example, s 51 of the *Constitution of Australia 1901* ('*Australian Constitution*').

 | DOI:10.1163/9789004720183_003

cases, the federal parliament would be the level of government doing so. In instances of direct inconsistencies between federal and state laws (or overlaps where the federal government intended to be the only lawmaker),[3] the *Australian Constitution* expressly provides that federal legislation will prevail. However, this is only the case where the Commonwealth law fits within the scope of an enumerated (or implied) power. In cases that fall outside Commonwealth legislative jurisdiction (such as many aspects of health, criminal law, policing, and education) the laws of states (provinces) have primacy. State laws, as a matter of Australian constitutional law, can extend extraterritorially (provided they do not clash with valid Commonwealth laws). Questions of extraterritorial competence would generally be considered by the High Court of Australia, which is Australia's superior court and exercises both original and appellate jurisdiction.

2 General Trends and Overview

Judicial decision making in Australia favours a permissive approach to jurisdiction. For example, the decision of the High Court of Australia in XYZ *v The Commonwealth*[4] was a key decision on Australian extraterritoriality because it confirmed – as a matter of Australian law – that the federal parliament has legislative competence over matters geographically external to Australia. In that case, an Australian citizen (XYZ) was committed to stand trial on three charges, each alleged to have been committed in Thailand. The charges included engaging and attempting to engage in sexual intercourse with a child under 16 years of age, contrary to provisions in the then Part IIIA of the *Crimes Act 1914 (Cth)*. XYZ challenged the validity of the provisions on the basis that the Commonwealth did not have the authority to assert jurisdiction over offences that occurred in Thailand. On appeal before the High Court, one of the legal questions was whether section 51(XXIX) of the Constitution of Australia, the external affairs power, permitted the Commonwealth to assert extraterritorial jurisdiction over the conduct of its citizens or residents overseas. The Court concluded that, given the conduct proscribed by the extraterritorial components of the relevant child sex offences occurred outside Australia, it was

3 Section 109 of the *Australian Constitution* provides that 'Where a law of a state is inconsistent with a law of the Commonwealth, the latter shall prevail, and the former shall to the extent of the inconsistency be invalid'. This also extends to instances of "indirect inconsistency" where the Commonwealth is taken to have intended to "cover the field".

4 *XYZ v Commonwealth* (2006) 227 CLR 532.

conduct within the scope of the external affairs power.[5] Notably, an earlier decision, *Polyukhovich v the Commonwealth*,[6] had already held that the 'externality of the conduct which the law prescribes as the foundation of the criminal offence is enough without more to constitute it as a law with respect to external affairs'.[7]

Another decision with implications for the Australian approach to extraterritoriality was a 1983 decision, *Commonwealth v Tasmania* (the Tasmanian Dams Case).[8] That case held that the federal parliament may rely on the external affairs power to implement international treaties, provided that the treaty is bona fide, and that the implementing legislation is a faithful pursuit of the spirit and purpose of the treaty. This remains the basis on which international treaties, including those that oblige or permit extraterritorial jurisdiction, are implemented into Australian law today. However, disrupting a trend of permissiveness was the decision in *Moti v The Queen*,[9] where the High Court of Australia considered whether proceedings relating to an offence based on extraterritorial conduct can be maintained against a person who has not properly been brought within the jurisdiction by regular means, or whether to do so would be an abuse of process. The court held the latter. This case is discussed further below.

Australia asserts extraterritorial jurisdiction in a number of statutes, including in the context of criminal law and competition law. Like many other common-law countries, Australia asserts extraterritoriality on specific ad hoc bases, rather than as a whole. Only particular offences specifically identified as having extraterritorial application do so. In short, there is a presumption against extraterritorial application of laws, unless otherwise provided for by express (and in some cases, implied) intent of the legislature. Therefore, assertions of extraterritorial jurisdiction by Australia tend to be motivated by a specific reason or rationale, such as a treaty obligation, a particular cross-border challenge to overcome, or a foreign policy objective (unilateral or otherwise). In that sense, Australian practice is consistent with global trends of increased use of unilateral extraterritorial prescriptiveness.

5 *XYZ v Commonwealth* (2006) 227 CLR 532.

6 (1991) 172 CLR 501.

7 Ibid 531.

8 *Commonwealth v Tasmania* (1983) 158 CLR 1.

9 *Moti v The Queen* (2012) 283 ALR 393.

3 Extraterritoriality under Multilateral Treaties

Australia has enacted legislation in response to multilateral instruments, including instruments that either obligate or permit extraterritorial legislative action. For example, on signing the *Optional Protocol to the Convention on the Rights of the Child on the sale of children, child prostitution and child pornography* on 18 December 2001, amendments were made to relevant legislation at Commonwealth and State and Territory level to ensure that Australia complies with the legislative requirements of the Optional Protocol.[10] The *Criminal Code Act 1995* (Cth) also contains numerous offences that would constitute Australia's implementation of its obligations under the *United Nations Convention on Transnational Organised Crime*[11] and associated instruments. Constitutionally speaking, the federal tier of government does not have a specific legislative power over criminal law, but instead tends to legislate criminal offences relating to federal subject matter, such as defence, taxation, immigration, and – relevantly for this question – external affairs, including treaty obligations. Therefore, obligations in multilateral or regional instruments have the effect of granting the federal government legislative competence, as a matter of Australian law.

By way of further and general background, Australia has signed, ratified or acceded to a number of significant international treaties, including the ICCPR,[12] and other treaties that either permit or oblige assertions of extraterritoriality, such as the *United Nations Convention on Transnational Organised Crime*[13] and supplementary protocols,[14] the *Convention on the Rights of the*

10 See, for example, Parliament of Australia, 'Chapter 3 Optional Protocol to the Convention on the Rights of the Child on the sale of children, child prostitution and child pornography', Parliamentary Business, <https://www.aph.gov.au/Parliamentary_Business/Committees/Joint/Completed_Inquiries/jsct/11october2005/chapter3#fn24 >.

11 *United Nations Convention on Transnational Organised Crime*, opened for signature 15 November 2000, 2225 UNTS 209 (entered into force 29 September 2003).

12 *International Covenant for Civil and Political Rights*, opened for signature 19 December 1966, 999 UNTS 171 (entered into force 28 March 1979).

13 *United Nations Convention on Transnational Organised Crime*, opened for signature 15 November 2000, 2225 UNTS 209 (entered into force 29 September 2003).

14 *Protocol to Prevent, Suppress and Punish Trafficking in Persons, Especially Women and Children*, opened for signature 15 November 2000, 2237 UNTS 319 (entered into force 25 December 2003); *Protocol against the Smuggling of Migrants by Land, Sea and Air*, opened for signature 15 December 2003, 2241 UNTS 507 (entered into force 28 January 2004).

Child,[15] the *Convention against Torture and other Cruel, Inhuman or Degrading Treatment or Punishment*,[16] the *International Convention for the Suppression of Terrorist Bombing*,[17] the *International Convention for the Suppression of the Financing of Terrorism*,[18] the *Convention relating to the Status of Refugees*[19] and the *Rome Statute of the International Criminal Court*.[20]

4 The Role of International Law

Australian courts adopt a dualist approach to international law. That is, in the Australian legal system, international law is considered a separate body of law from domestic legal systems and international law is of little effect unless implemented into domestic legislation. In short, this means that international law is not determinative of the geographic scope of statutes and regulations. However, courts will often refer to international law by way of interpretative and contextual tools, and have done so in adjudicating on extraterritorial assertions by parliament, including by recognising the bases of jurisdiction at international law. For example, in XYZ *v The Commonwealth*,[21] Gleeson CJ specifically noted that the territorial principle of legislative jurisdiction is not the only source of jurisdiction recognised by international law.[22] He found that the principle of national sovereignty, according to the law of nations, grants Australia a right to 'regulate, by legislation, the conduct outside Australia of Australian citizens or residents'.[23]

---

15 *Convention on the Rights of the Child*, opened for signature 20 November 1989, 1577 UNTS 3 (entered into force 2 September 1990).

16 *Convention against Torture and Other Cruel, Inhuman or Degrading Treatment or Punishment*, opened for signature 10 December 1984, 1465 UNTS 85 (entered into force 26 June 1987).

17 *International Convention for the Suppression of Terrorist Bombings*, opened for signature 15 December 1997, 2149 UNTS 256 (entered into force 23 May 2001).

18 *International Convention for the Suppression of the Financing of Terrorism*, opened for signature 9 December 1999, 2178 UNTS 197 (entered into force 10 April 2002).

19 *Convention Relating to the Status of Refugees*, opened for signature 28 July 1951, 189 UNTS 150 (entered into force 22 April 1954).

20 *Rome Statute of the International Criminal Court*, opened for signature 17 July 1998, 2187 UNTS 3 (entered into force 1 July 2002).

21 *XYZ v Commonwealth* (2006) 227 CLR 532.

22 Ibid 536 (Gleeson CJ).

23 Ibid 540 (Gleeson CJ).

Further, the other way in which aspects of international law can influence statutes and regulation in Australia generally is that, constitutionally speaking, federal parliament can only rely on the external affairs power to implement a treaty if the implementing legislation "conforms" with the spirit and purpose of the treaty. In an indirect sense, then, the content of a treaty on extraterritoriality guides what the Australian statute will look like. In *Victoria v Commonwealth*,[24] the High Court held that although 'it is for the legislature to choose the means by which it carries into or gives effect to the treaty',[25] the law must nonetheless 'be reasonably capable of being considered appropriate and adapted to implementing the treaty'.[26] However, although implementing legislation must broadly conform with a treaty obligation to be constitutionally valid under Australian law, it need not follow the treaty precisely. Further, in *Horta v Commonwealth*,[27] it was held that the external affairs power in section 51(XXIX) of the *Australian Constitution* did not require that the treaty be implemented consistent with international law. This means Australia could implement a treaty that did conform with international law into domestic legislation and it would, in theory, be constitutionally sound.

By way of further background on Australia's relationship with international law, the *Australian Constitution* does not expressly refer to international law as having a role in municipal law. It does contain section 51(XXIX), under which, as set out above, the Australia Parliament can enact laws which implement international treaty obligations and which also permits the Commonwealth to act extraterritoriality, and section 75(II), which refers to treaties. As noted above, provisions of an international treaty do not form part of Australian law unless validly incorporated into municipal law by statute. In the 1940s, the view of the High Court was that the idea of the *Australian Constitution* being subject to international law 'ought not to be countenanced'[28] and that 'to limit the constitutional power of sovereign States or their subordinate authorities denies the supremacy of those States within their own territory, which is contrary to the principles of the law of nations itself.'[29] Even as late as the 1990s, the High Court was of the view that the Constitution was 'not to be construed as subject to an implication said to be derived from international law.'

24 (1996) 187 CLR 416.
25 Ibid.
26 Ibid 486–488.
27 (1994) 181 CLR 183.
28 (1945) 70 CLR 60, 78.
29 (1945) 70 CLR 60, 75–76.

However, widely accepted norms of customary international law will be more readily regarded as part of Australian law by Australian courts than a treaty will.[30] Further, while the *Australian Constitution* is not read subject to international law, unless a contrary intention appears, words occurring in a statute are generally to be read as subject to the established rules of international law.[31] Further, the High Court has also been open to international law informing principles of common law, including where human rights are in issue. For example, in *Mabo* (No. 2), it was suggested that:

> The common law does not necessarily conform with international law, but international law is a legitimate and important influence on the development of the common law especially when international law declares the existence of universal human rights.[32]

There are other "soft law" influences of international law on Australian law, and it is possible that as the High Court membership starts to include Justices with greater international law literacy and as time goes on, Australia may develop a closer relationship with international law. However, for now, extraterritorial competence is predominantly a question of domestic rather than international law for Australian purposes.

5 The Role of International Comity

5.1 *Comity*

In essence, comity is concerned with preserving sound relations between nation states. It aims to:

> strike a balance between the sovereign interests of an individual State on the one hand, and the reality that it is also a member of a broader community of States, on the other. In a jurisdictional context, the doctrine of comity may be used by a court to limit the reach of a State's laws in deference to another State that may have a stronger jurisdictional interest.[33]

30 *Polyukovich v The Commonwealth of Australia* (1991) 172 CLR 501 ('War Crimes Act Case').

31 (1945) 70 CLR 60, 77; AMS *v* AIF (1999) 199 CLR 160, 180.

32 (1992) 175 CLR 1, 42.

33 Danielle Ireland-Piper, *Accountability in Extraterritoriality: A Comparative and International Law Perspective* (Edward Elgar, 2017).

By way of background, the doctrine of comity is said to have developed during the seventeenth century in order to resolve jurisdictional uncertainties in the regulation of trade and commerce.[34] The doctrine is still used today, often in a private-law context, to 'mediate between the pretensions of territorial sovereignty and the needs of international commerce'.[35] It is a discretionary concept based on the idea that 'relations among sovereigns are relations among equals.'[36] Harold Maier has described comity as involving 'considerations of high international politics concerned with maintaining amicable and workable relationships between nations.'[37] In the context of extraterritorial jurisdiction, comity has also been described as a 'pragmatic principle of reciprocal expectation' which counsels judicial or governmental restraint when enforcing extraterritorial legislation.[38] The doctrine has been the subject of academic criticism.

However, in the Australian context, a 2016 study revealed that in the period between 2005 and 2006, over 850 Australian court decisions made reference to comity (many of which related to the field of private international law, however).[39] The authors of that study argued that despite its academic unpopularity, 'comity is a relevant, serviceable legal tool',[40] although they argued so in the specific context of private, rather than public, international law.

The key point for the use of comity in Australia is that considerations of comity are relevant and used by courts, but are not ultimately determinative of justiciability of extraterritorial assertions. As observed by Perram J in the Federal Court of Australia in *Habib v Commonwealth of Australia*, 'comity between nations is a fine and proper thing, but it provides no basis whatsoever for this court to decline to exercise the jurisdiction conferred on it by parliament'.[41]

---

34 See, e.g., Hessel Yntema, 'The Comity Doctrine' (1966) 65 *Michigan Law Review* 9; Brian Pearce, 'The Comity Doctrine as a Barrier to Judicial Jurisdiction: A U.S.-E.U. Comparison' (1994) *Stanford Journal of International Law* 30.

35 Hessel Yntema, 'The Comity Doctrine' (1966) 65 *Michigan Law Review* 9.

36 'Predictability and Comity: Toward Common Principles of Extraterritorial Jurisdiction' (1985) 98 *Harvard Law Review* 1310, 1322.

37 Harold Maier, 'Interest Balancing and Extraterritorial Jurisdiction' (1983) 31 *American Journal of International Law* 579, 589.

38 Deborah Senz and Hilary Charlesworth 'Building blocks: Australia's response to foreign extraterritorial legislation', (2001) 2(1) *Melbourne Journal of International Law* 69–121 citing Maier, above, n 36, 589–90.

39 Thomas Schulz and Jason Mitchenson 'Navigating sovereignty and transnational commercial law: the use of comity by Australian courts', 12(2) 2016 *Journal of Private International Law*, 344–378, 344.

40 Ibid 344.

41 *Habib v Commonwealth of Australia* (2010) 183 FCR 61 at 37.

5.2 *The Act of State Doctrine and Extraterritorial Competence*

In addition to comity potentially restraining adjudication by courts of assertions of extraterritorial jurisdiction, there exists in common law countries a related "act of state" doctrine. The "act of state doctrine" has, in some circumstances, impacted the way in which some common law courts adjudicate on extraterritorial conduct. This arises where adjudicating on extraterritorial conduct, including by its own government, would require a court to make a finding of unlawfulness of an act of a foreign state. In particular, the doctrine has been used by courts in Australia, the United States, and the United Kingdom. It is not a principle of international law,[42] but it is theoretically linked with the principle of national sovereignty and with the principle of comity. That Australian courts will generally not enquire into the validity of foreign sovereign acts (whether legislative or executive) done in relation to property that is within the foreign sovereign's territory, for example, if a rule rests partly on international comity.[43]

The act of state doctrine has attracted much criticism due to the inconsistent nature of its application across jurisdictions. It seems that '[b]eyond the certainty that the doctrine exists, there is little clarity as to what constitutes it.'[44] The doctrine was described by Fritz Mann as "one of the most difficult and perplexing topics which, in the field of foreign affairs, may face the municipal judge in England."[45]

In Australia, the High Court in *Moti v The Queen*[46] did not accept it was bound by the doctrine, nor did the Federal Court of Australia in *Habib v The Commonwealth*.[47] In *Moti*, the Australian High Court concluded that the act of state doctrine does not preclude findings as to the legality of the conduct of a foreign government, where such a finding is determinative of an abuse of process.[48] The majority in *Moti v The Queen* rejected an inflexible approach to the act of state doctrine and instead held 'that the decision of a foreign official

42 Richard Garnett 'Foreign States in Australian Courts' (2005) 29(3) *Melbourne University Law Review* 704, 705.

43 *Attorney-General* (UK) *v Heinemann Publishers Australia Pty* Ltd (1988) 165 CLR 30, 41 as cited in James Edelman and Madeleine Salinger, 'Comity in Private International Law and Fundamental Principles of Justice' in: Andrew Dickinson, Edwin Peel and Thomas Pausey, *A Conflict of Laws Companion* (Oxford University Press, 2021) 336.

44 *Habib* (2010) 183 FCR 62, 77 (Perram J).

45 Frederick Mann, *Foreign Affairs in English Courts* (Claredon Press, Oxford, 1986) 164.

46 *Moti v The Queen* (2012) 283 ALR 393 ('*Moti*').

47 *Habib* (2010) 183 FCR 62.

48 For a more detailed discussion of this decision, see: Danielle Ireland-Piper, 'Abuse of Process in Cross-Border Cases: Moti v The Queen'. QUT *Law Review*, (2013) 12(2) 120, 120–121.

is called into question does not of itself prevent the courts from considering the issue.'[49] The Court cited, and agreed with, the following assertion by Mann:

> ... the Courts are free to consider and pronounce an opinion upon the exercises of sovereign power by a foreign government, if the consideration of those acts of a foreign government only constitutes a preliminary to decision of a question, which in itself is subject to the competency of the Court of law.[50]

In *Habib*, the act of state doctrine was similarly held not to apply. That case concerned an Australian citizen, detained by Pakistani authorities and transferred to Egypt in 2001, moved to Bagram airbase in Afghanistan in April or May 2002, and then finally held at Guantanamo Bay where he was detained until his release (without charge) in January 2005. Mr Habib alleged a range of mistreatments amounting to torture and inhumane treatment took place during these times: all, if true, would be contrary to Australian law, even though taking place extraterritorially. Mr Habib's allegations included that Australian officials had visited him during his detention overseas (which was not disputed), been present during questioning, and may even have provided information used in the interrogation. The case against Australian officials for their extraterritorial acquiescence required a determination of the unlawfulness of acts of agents of foreign states outside Australian territory. In turn, this required the Court to consider whether Mr Habib's claim was non-justiciable by virtue of the act of state doctrine. Ultimately, for a number of reasons, it was held that the act of state doctrine did not bar the claim, not least because of the status of the prohibition against torture as a peremptory norm of international law from which no derogation is permitted.

6 Reasonableness in the Extraterritorial Application of Law

There is not a strict or explicit requirement that an assertion of extraterritoriality be "reasonable", particularly given the influences of parliamentary sovereignty on the Australian legal system and judicial thinking in Australia. However, in *Moti v The Queen*,[51] as discussed above, the High Court of Australia considered whether proceedings can be maintained against a person who has not properly been brought within the jurisdiction by regular means, or

49 *Moti v The Queen* (2011) 245 CLR 456, [52].
50 Ibid, 407 [52].
51 *Moti v The Queen* (2012) 283 ALR 393.

whether such proceedings are an abuse of process. In so doing, a majority of six to one concluded that the act of state doctrine does not preclude findings as to the legality of the conduct of a foreign government, where those conclusions are a necessary step to determining a question within the competency of the court. The decision suggests that, in operating extraterritorially, Australian officials will still be accountable in Australian courts, not necessarily because an assertion is unreasonable, but because it is an abuse of process.

7 Jurisdictional Bases for the Extraterritorial Application of Law

Australia asserts extraterritorial jurisdiction in a number of statutes, including, for example, in criminal law and in trade practices/competition law.

7.1 *Criminal Law*

While the *Criminal Code Act 1995* (Cth) ('the *Criminal Code*') provides for a presumption of territoriality,[52] a number of offences have express extraterritorial reach. This is done on a specific and ad-hoc basis and the *Criminal Code* as a whole does not extend extraterritorially. In Division 15, entitled 'Extended geographical jurisdiction', the *Criminal Code* identifies four types of 'extended' jurisdictional assertions, Categories A, B, C and D. Notably, in some instances, this includes, criminal liability for corporate actors, based on the nationality of the corporate body (nationality of registration or nationality of the responsible corporate individual) or if the conduct was wholly or partially based in Australia.

7.1.1 Category A Offences: Objective Territoriality

Category A offences are described in section 15(1) of the *Criminal Code* as those that extend to conduct that occurs wholly or partially in Australia,[53] which is still a type of territorial jurisdiction. It also includes offences that occur wholly outside Australia, if a result of the conduct occurs wholly or partly in Australia.[54] This could be either objective territoriality jurisdiction or, in some circumstances, an assertion of extraterritorial jurisdiction based on the effects principle. Category A offences also include conduct where an ancillary offence occurs wholly outside Australia, but the primary offence to which it relates occurs, or is intended to occur, wholly or partly in Australia.[55] Ancillary

52 *Criminal Code Act 1995* (Cth) s 14.1.

53 '[O]r on an Australian aircraft or ship'. See *Criminal Code Act 1995* (Cth) s 15(1)(a).

54 Ibid.

55 Ibid.

offences are those that are an extension of or relate to another 'primary' offence. For example, offences such as attempts, conspiracies, or incitement are ancillary offences. This means that a conspiracy outside the territory of Australia to commit an offence in Australia can be prosecuted under Australian law. Depending on the nature of the offence, this could be an assertion of extraterritorial jurisdiction based on the protective or effect principles of jurisdiction. Where the accused person is not a citizen of, or a body corporate incorporated in, Australia, this will only apply if the primary offence to which the ancillary offence relates is also an offence in the jurisdiction in which it occurred.[56] In extradition law, this is often referred to as a 'dual criminality' or 'double criminality' requirement. Notably, liability for Category A offences applies to Australian citizens and body corporates incorporated in Australia ('Australian BCs') even where the conduct occurs wholly outside Australia. Examples of Category A offences include fraud offences such as dealing in or possessing fraudulent identification documents.[57] For example, the misuse of Australian passports outside Australia may be caught by this offence, which would be an example of protective principle jurisdiction, or if the accused was an Australian national, nationality principle jurisdiction. Other Category A offences in the *Criminal Code* include computer offences, such as unauthorised access, modification or impairment to data or electronic communication.[58]

7.1.2 Category B Offences: Citizens and Residents

The extraterritorial scope of Category B offences replicates Category A offences, other than that these offences extend to the conduct of Australian residents as well as Australian citizens, and Australian BCs.[59] This is significant because it effectively permits Australia to regulate the overseas conduct of persons who cannot vote in Australia. While this could be considered an assertion of active nationality jurisdiction, it is not necessarily the case that residents are 'nationals' and they are certainly not considered so for the purposes of other parts of Australian law. Examples of Category B offences include conduct such as the importation, exportation, manufacture and possession of plastic explosives,[60] document offences related to migrant smuggling and unlawful entry into

56 *Criminal Code Act 1995* (Cth) s 15.1(2).
57 *Criminal Code Act 1995* (Cth) div 372.
58 Ibid pt 10.7.
59 Ibid s 15.2(1)(c).
60 Ibid div 72.

foreign countries,[61] urging violence against groups or members of groups,[62] slavery offences,[63] trafficking in persons offences,[64] and serious drug offences.[65]

7.1.3 Category C Offences: No Territorial Nexus Required

Category C offences extend outside Australia and do not require any territorial nexus to Australia. These provisions also apply to persons who are not Australian citizens, residents, or Australian BCs. These offences could be considered an example of universal jurisdiction, except that a person who is not a citizen or an Australian BC will not be liable for either ancillary or primary Category C offences if the offence is not also an offence in the jurisdiction in which it occurred.[66] Examples of Category C offences in the Code include 'unwarranted demands',[67] made of or by a Commonwealth public official with 'menaces',[68] causing harm to Commonwealth officials,[69] impersonation of a public official,[70] and crimes against the administration of the justice of the International Criminal Court.[71] Therefore, although the extended geographical reach of Category C offences do provide for a considerable degree of extraterritoriality, none of these offences are particularly controversial, and all would fit into widely accepted assertions of the protective principle.

7.1.4 Category D Offences: Universal Jurisdiction

Category D offences, on the other hand, are truly an example of universal jurisdiction. Unlike the complex array of qualifications for categories A, B, and C, the description of Category D offences simply reads as follows:

> If a law of the Commonwealth provides that this section applies to a particular offence, the offence applies:
> (a) whether or not the conduct constituting the alleged offence occurs in Australia; and

61 Ibid div 73.
62 Ibid div 80.
63 Ibid div 270.
64 Ibid div 271.
65 Ibid div 300.
66 Ibid ss 15.3(2), 15.3(4).
67 Ibid div 139.
68 Ibid.
69 Ibid div 147.
70 Ibid div 148.
71 Ibid div 268.

(b) whether or not a result of the conduct constituting the alleged offence occurs in Australia.

There are a number of offences in the Code that are classified as Category D offences. Most relate to offences against the Commonwealth or to internationally recognised crimes, such as treason and terrorism,[72] and so are not particularly controversial. Nonetheless, the number of offences over which Australia asserts universal jurisdiction is quite extensive and far-reaching, particularly given the offences include attempts and incitement.[73] Further, Category D Jurisdiction also applies to an offence against section 35P of the *Australian Security Intelligence Organisation Act 1979* (Cth). That section makes it an offence to disclose information "relating to" a "special intelligence operation".[74] The offence provisions do not appear to include a public interest exception or exceptions for journalists or whistleblowers.[75]

Notably, any assertion of any of these categories of 'extended geographical jurisdiction' require the consent of the Attorney-General if the conduct in question takes place wholly outside Australia and the accused is not an Australian citizen or an Australian BC. Therefore, assertions of extraterritorial criminal jurisdiction by Australia over non-nationals become a question of political discretion. Offences such as 'associating with terrorist organisations' has the

---

72 Examples of Category D offences in the code include, treason and urging violence against the Constitution, espionage, acts of terrorism,' associating with terrorist organisations, financing terrorist organisations, theft of Commonwealth property, a range of property offences including robbery, burglary and the receipt of property stolen from the Commonwealth, obtaining property or financial advantage from the Commonwealth by deception, dishonestly obtaining a gain from a Commonwealth entity, false or misleading statements to the Commonwealth, bribery of or by Commonwealth officials, forgery of Commonwealth documents, genocide, crimes against humanity and war crimes, and torture.

73 The word 'offence' is expressed in the Code as having a meaning extended by sections 11.2(1), 11.2A(1), 11.3 and 11.6(1), which, in essence, means they apply to ancillary offences too. The first three of these provisions create offences for: aiding, abetting, counselling or procuring the commission of an offence; joint commission of offences; and commission by proxy. Section 11.6(1) provides that a 'reference in a law of the Commonwealth to an offence against a law of the Commonwealth (including this Code) includes a reference to an offence against sections 11.1 (attempt), 11.4 (incitement) or 11.5 (conspiracy) of this Code that relates to such an offence.' This quite considerably extends the range of extraterritorial conduct that could be subject to Australian law.

74 For an extended discussion of the provision, see Danielle Ireland-Piper and Jonathan Crowe, 'Whistleblowing, National Security and the Constitutional Freedom of Political Communication' (2018) 46 *Federal Law Review* 341.

75 Ibid.

potential to include a wide range of conduct and that conduct that may be far removed from any malicious intent against Australia or Australians.

7.2 *Trade Practices*

At the federal level, parts of the *Trade Practices Act 1974* (Cth) extend extra-territorially. Specifically, Parts IV and V have "extended application" to conduct outside Australia where that conduct is by bodies corporate carrying on business in Australia, Australian citizens or residents. For some provisions, this includes any conduct relating to the supply of goods and services.[76] To give context, Part IV relates to restrictive trade practices (such as the regulation of conduct relating to, for example, cartels, secondary boycotts and misuse of market power), and Part V relates to consumer protection (such as the regulation of misleading information, product safety, unsolicited credit, and pyramid schemes).

Judicial consideration of these provisions indicates a foreign parent company will be considered to be "carrying on business" in Australia where an Australian subsidiary acts on its behalf as agent. In short, foreign corporate entities with Australian subsidiaries can be primarily liable for any cartel conduct taking place outside Australia. For example, by supplying corporate services to an Australian subsidiary or directing it when dealing with a global customer, a parent company may be subject to Australia's competition laws. In 2018, the Full Federal Court of Australia upheld a ruling by the Federal Court of Australia that an Italian-based company and electric cable manufacturer engaged in cartel conduct in the supply of high voltage land cables.[77] The Federal Court had found in 2016 that the company entered into and gave effect to agreements involving price guidance to competitors and project allocation. The Court ordered a penalty of $3.5 million.

76 Section 5 of the *Trade Practices Act 1974* (Cth) reads:
Extended application of Parts IV and V.
5. (1) Parts IV and V extend to the engaging in conduct outside Australia by bodies corporate incorporated or carrying on business within Australia or by Australian citizens or persons ordinarily resident within Australia.
(2) In addition to the extended operation that sections 47 and 48 have by virtue of sub-section (1), those sections extend to the engaging in conduct outside Australia by any persons in relation to the supply by those persons of goods or services to persons within Australia.

77 *ACCC v Prysmian Australian Competition and Consumer Commission v Prysmian Cavi E Sistemi S.R.L. (No 12)* [2016] FCA 822.

In a similar case, ACCC *v Yazaki*,[78] the court considered whether a Japanese company "Yazaki" was carrying on business in Australia. In that case, Yazaki's Australian subsidiary was not a party to the proceedings. The court found that the Australian subsidiary was not conducting business in Australia as agent for the Japanese parent company. Nevertheless, the court concluded that the Japanese parent corporation was 'carrying on business' in Australia in dealing with the Toyota Motor Corporation, and was therefore subject to Australian competition law.

7.3 *Human Rights*

Notably, Australia is the only western democracy to have no national bill of rights, either as a statute or entrenched as part of the national constitution.[79] This means human rights, whether territorially or extraterritorially owed, are often protected only by legislation (which is liable to amendment or repeal) or by common law principles,[80] and then, only in part; as well as by principles relating to the separation of powers.[81] The principle of separation of powers has given rise to limits on power that have human rights consequences, such as limits on extra-judicial detention.[82] However, these limits do not appear to operate extraterritorially where another nation state is overseeing arrangements. This can be seen in *Plaintiff M68/2015 v Minister for Immigration and Border Protection*.[83] That decision concerned a Bangladeshi national (M68) who claimed protection from Australia pursuant to Article 1 of the *Convention relating to the Status of Refugees (1954) as amended by the Protocol relating to the Status of Refugees 1967* ('the Refugee Convention').[84] The woman, known as M68, had been detained in Nauru pursuant to an agreement between Nauru

---

78 Australian Competition and Consumer Commission v Yazaki Corporation (No 2) [2015] FCA 1304.

79 Emily Howe et al, 'A Human Rights Act for All Australians', Human Rights Law Resource Centre, Submission to the *National Human Rights Consultation*, May 2009, 74.

80 See, for example, Robert French, 'Protecting Human Rights Without a Bill of Rights' (Speech, John Marchall Law School, Chicago, 26 January 2010).

81 Such, as for example, some limits on some types of extrajudicial detention and punishment. See, for example, *Kable v Director of Public Prosecutions* (NSW) (1996) 189 CLR 51 on preventive detention regimes; and *Chu Kheng Lim v Minister for Immigration, Local Government and Ethnic Affairs* (1992) 176 CLR 1 on extrajudicial detention regimes.

82 See, the Lim Principle: *Kheng Lim v Minister for Immigration, Local Government and Ethnic Affairs* (1992) 176 CLR 1. See, also, a 2023 decision of the High Court of Australia in NZYQ *v Minister for Immigration, Citizenship and Multicultural Affairs & Anor.*

83 (2016) 257 CLR 42 ('*M68*').

84 *Convention Relating to the Status of Refugees*, opened for signature 28 July 1951, 189 UNTS 137 (entered into force 22 April 1954) art 1, as amended by *Protocol Relating to the Status of Refugees*, opened for signature 31 January 1967, 606 UNTS 267 (entered into force 4 October 1967).

and the Australian Government under a scheme to detain a person where that person's status under the Convention had yet to be determined. She was temporarily brought to Australia for medical treatment and the Australian Government subsequently sought to return her to Nauru. The core legal question in this decision was whether the Australian Government had power to detain the woman offshore (or if that were a breach of limits on extra-judicial detention arising loosely from separation of power principles), or alternatively, whether it had power to assist Nauru in doing so. The core factual question, then, became whether it was the Australian Government or the Government of Nauru that was detaining the plaintiff. A majority of the court in this case concluded that it was Nauru and not Australia doing the detaining, putting the question of the legality of the detention beyond the reach of an Australian court in that instance. This is despite both Australian and Nauruan law permitting the use of force in order to prevent a 'protected person', such as the plaintiff, from leaving; despite the Commonwealth Department of Immigration and Border Protection having provided fencing, lighting towers and other security infrastructure, as well as occupying an office where Australian officials carried out functions including managing service provider contracts. Arguably, this decision, while paying homage to the principle of Nauru's sovereign status at international law, overlooks the capacity for collective and ancillary responsibility at international law, particularly as relates to principles of state responsibility for internationally wrongful acts that occur extraterritorially beyond the normal reach of domestic courts.[85] It also arguably represents an accountability gap in terms of extraterritorial accountability for the exercise of extraterritorial authority, particularly in the context of human rights, and in the conduct of international relations and agreements.

8 Interpreting the Geographic Scope of Statutes

Generally speaking, the Australian legal system operates on a presumption of territoriality, which in turn is founded in notions of comity and sovereignty. For example, a decision in a Queensland court in Australia in 2008 observed:

> In the interpretation of general words in a Statute there is always a presumption that the legislature does not intend to exceed its jurisdiction. Most Statutes, if their general words were taken literally in their widest

85 For an extended discussion of this point, see Danielle Ireland-Piper, 'Outdated and Unhelpful: The Problem with the Comity Principle and Act of State Doctrine' (2018) 24 *Australian International Law Journal* 15.

> sense, would apply to the whole world, but they are always read as being prima facie restricted in their operation within territorial limits… [T]his principle was based on the idea of comity of nations and that the legislature of one state is presumed not to deal with persons or matters the jurisdiction over which properly belongs to some other sovereign state.[86]

However, in Australia, comity is a legal presumption, rather than a rule. Therefore, it can be displaced or rebutted by wording to the contrary[87] (as can the presumption of territoriality). It has been observed:

> Usually, it will only be rebutted by explicit statutory language expressing the legislature's intention to legislate extraterritorially. If it is the clear intention of parliament, courts cannot refuse to apply and enforce legislation, even if it might constitute an unacceptable challenge to the doctrine of sovereignty.[88]

In short, both the presumption of territoriality and principles of comity are applicable by rebuttable presumptions in the Australian context.

9 Blocking Statutes

The *Foreign Proceedings (Excess of Jurisdiction) Act 1984* (Cth) gives power to the Australian Attorney-General to limit the effects of extraterritorial practices, including judgments and legislation, of other states. Specifically, where a foreign court gives judgment against a person, the Australian Attorney-General may prohibit compliance with that order if they are satisfied that making such an order is desirable for the protection of the national interest. It also allows

86 *B v T* [2008] 1 Qd R 33 at 13–14 per Lyons J quoting with acceptance the position stated by Dennis Pearce and Robert Geddes in *Statutory Interpretation in Australia*, 5th ed, (Butterworths, 5th ed, 2001) at 133 and as cited by Thomas Schulz and Jason Mitchenson 'Navigating sovereignty and transnational commercial law: the use of comity by Australian courts', 12(2) 2016 *Journal of Private International Law* 344, 352.

87 *Habib v Commonwealth of Australia* (2010) 183 FCR 61 at 37 per Perram J; *Worldplay Services Pty Ltd v Australian Competition and Consumer Commission* (2005) 143 FCR 345; *Trade Practices Commission v Australian Iron & Steel Pty Ltd* (1989) 22 FCR 305.

88 See: Thomas Schulz and Jason Mitchenson 'Navigating sovereignty and transnational commercial law: the use of comity by Australian courts', 12(2) 2016 *Journal of Private International Law* 344, 352 citing *Habib v Commonwealth of Australia* (2010) 183 FCR 61 at 37 per Perram J; *Kartinyeri v The Commonwealth* (1998) 195 CLR 337; *Koowarta v Bjelke-Petersen* (1982) 153 CLR 168 at 204.

for the blocking of extraterritorial application of laws relating to trade and commerce, federal banking, federal insurance, and Australian corporations, as well as granting the power to modify orders relating to anti-trust proceedings (where this is considered to be against the Australian national interest or contrary to international law or comity).

10 Concluding Remarks

In sum, despite Australia only asserting extraterritorial jurisdiction on an ad hoc basis, it does so in a permissive constitutional context and some assertions are quite broad, particularly those identified as "Category D" assertions in the federal criminal code. Australia has a complex relationship with international law. On the surface, a "dualist" approach is adopted. However, obligations to conform with treaty obligations in order to secure constitutional authority - as well as the relationship between the development of customary international law and the development of the common law - mean that international law does influence the development of Australian law on extraterritoriality.

The Extraterritorial Application of Statutes and Regulations

Brazil

André de Carvalho Ramos and Mariana Sebalhos Jorge***

1 Statutes and Regulations with Expressly Extraterritorial Scope

There is a broad provision of extraterritoriality in Brazilian law. The extraterritorial reach of Brazilian law can be seen in criminal law, competition law, labor law, internet law, and in the protection of personal data.

1.1 *Criminal Law: Decree-Law No. 2.848 of December 7, 1940* (*Penal Code*)

In general, the Brazilian Penal Code applies only to criminal offenses occurring within Brazil. Article 7, however, provides for exceptional cases in which the extraterritoriality of the law is in force. Cases in which Brazilian law applies to crimes committed abroad include those committed against the life or freedom of the President of the Republic; committed against the public administration by those in its service; and crimes of genocide, when the perpetrator is Brazilian or domiciled in Brazil.[1]

* Professor at the University of São Paulo Law School (Largo São Francisco). e-mail: carvalhoramos@usp.br.

** PhD in International Law. e-mail: msebalhos@gmail.com.

1 Decree-Law No. 2.848 of December 7, 1940 (Penal Code). Article 7 – They are subject to Brazilian law, although committed abroad: I – The crimes: (a) against the life or liberty of the President of the Republic; (b) against the assets or public faith of the Union, of the Federal District, of the State, of a Territory, of the Municipality, of a public company, mixed capital company, autarchy or foundation instituted by the Public Power; c) against the public administration, by whoever is at its service; d) of genocide, when the agent is Brazilian or domiciled in Brazil; II – The crimes: a) that, by treaty or convention, Brazil was obliged to repress; b) practiced by Brazilians; c) practiced on Brazilian aircraft or vessels, merchants or private property, when in foreign territory and are not judged there. § 1 – In the cases of item I, the agent is punished according to Brazilian law, even if acquitted or convicted abroad. § 2 – In the cases of item II, the application of Brazilian law depends on the concurrence of the following conditions: a) the agent enters the national territory; b) the fact is also punishable in the country where it was committed; c) the crime is included among those for which Brazilian law authorizes extradition; d) the agent has not been acquitted abroad or has not served the sentence there; e) the agent has not been pardoned abroad or, for another reason, the punishment is not extinguished, according to the most favorable law. § 3 – Brazilian law

 | DOI:10.1163/9789004720183_004

1.2 *Competition Law: Law No. 12.529 of November 30, 2011*

In 1994, Law No. 8.884/94 expressly incorporated the effects doctrine into Brazilian law, in a way that validates the extraterritorial application of competition law. This approach has been maintained in Article 2 of Law No. 12.529/11. Thus, it is enough that effects may arise in the national territory for the Brazilian law to apply.

Laws based on the effects doctrine intend to curb activities that produce or may produce effects in the country, even if those effects result from mergers or acquisitions of companies that have taken place entirely abroad, or from anti-competitive activity occurring abroad. It is important, therefore, that the impact of the relevant behavior is felt in the Brazilian market.[2]

In article 2 it is possible to observe the effects doctrine: "This Law is applied, without prejudice to conventions and treaties to which Brazil is a signatory, to practices committed in whole or in part in the national territory or which produce or may produce effects therein".[3]

Brazil embraced the effects doctrine through the provision of article 2 under strong influence of North American doctrine.[4]

---

also applies to the crime committed by a foreigner against a Brazilian outside Brazil, if the conditions set out in the previous paragraph are met: a) extradition was not requested or denied; b) there was a request from the Minister of Justice. Sentence served abroad.

2 Law No. 12.529 of November 30, 2011. Art. 88. They will be submitted to the Administrative Council for Economic Defense by the parties involved in the operation, the acts of economic concentration in which, cumulatively: I – at least one of the groups involved in the operation has registered, in the last balance sheet, annual gross sales or total business volume in the country, in the year prior to the operation, equivalent to or greater than BRL 400,000,000.00 (four hundred million); and II – at least one other group involved in the operation has registered, in the last balance sheet, annual gross sales or total business volume in the country, in the year prior to the operation, equivalent to or greater than BRL 30,000,000.00 (thirty million).

3 Law No. 12.529 of November 30, 2011. Art. 2 This Law is applied, without prejudice to conventions and treaties to which Brazil is a signatory, to practices committed in whole or in part in the national territory or which produce or may produce effects therein. § 1 The foreign company that operates or has a branch, agency, branch, office, establishment, agent or representative in Brazil is considered to be domiciled in the national territory. § 2 The foreign company will be notified of all procedural acts provided in this Law, regardless of power of attorney or contractual or statutory provision, in the person of the agent or representative or person responsible for its branch, agency, establishment or office installed in the Brazil.

4 FORGIONI, Paula. *Os fundamentos do antitruste.* 10 ed. São Paulo: Thomson Reuters Brasil, 2018. p. 523. See WEBBER, Marianne Mendes. *Direito da concorrência e cooperação jurídica internacional.* Belo Horizonte: Arraes Editores, 2015. p. 59.

1.3 *International Employment Contracts: Law No. 7.064 of December 6, 1982*

Historically, Brazil observed the principle of territoriality in international employment contracts. This principle was reflected in Precedent No. 207, of 1865, which stated that "The legal labor relationship is governed by the laws in force in the country where the service is provided and not by those of the place of contracting".[5]

In 1982, however, Brazil enacted Law No. 7.064, which states that the company responsible for the employment contract of the transferred employee shall ensure, regardless of compliance with the legislation of the place where the services are carried out: the rights provided for in this Law; and the application of Brazilian labor protection legislation when more favorable than territorial legislation, in the set of rules and in relation to each subject.[6]

In 2012 the precedent relating to territoriality was officially canceled. As a result, employment law is now given extraterritorial effect, at least in situations involving workers hired in Brazil.

1.4 *Brazilian Civil Rights Framework for the Internet ("Marco Civil da Internet" – Federal Law No 12.965/2014)*

The Brazilian law that regulates activities on the Internet provides for the application of Brazilian law even to activities carried out outside Brazil. In order for Brazilian law to apply, there must be some contact with the national territory, either because 1) at least one terminal is located in Brazil; 2) services are offered in Brazil; or 3) at least one member of the economic group engaged in the relevant activity is established in Brazil.[7]

5 Precedent No. 207 of the Superior Labor Court (TST). CONFLICTS OF LABOR LAWS IN SPACE. PRINCIPLE OF "LEX LOCI EXECUTIONIS". The legal labor relationship is governed by the laws in force in the country where the service is provid-ed and not by those of the place of contracting. Original text: "Súmula nº 207 do TST. CONFLITOS DE LEIS TRABALHISTAS NO ESPAÇO. PRINCÍPIO DA 'LEX LOCI EXECUTIONIS'. A relação jurídica trabalhista é regida pelas leis vigentes no país da prestação de serviço e não por aquelas do local da contratação".

6 Law No. 7.064 of December 6, 1982. Art. 3 – The company responsible for the employment contract of the transferred employee shall ensure, regardless of compliance with the legislation of the place where the services are carried out: I – the rights provided for in this Law; II – the application of Brazilian labor protection legislation, in what is not incompatible with the provisions of this Law, when more favorable than territorial legislation, in the set of rules and in relation to each subject. In compliance with the special provisions of this Law, Brazilian legislation on Social Security, Severance Indemnity Fund – FGTS and Social Integration Program – PIS/PASEP will apply.

7 The application of Brazilian law is conditioned to two situations, clarified in two paragraphs of the same art. 11: a) The established in Art. 11 applies to the data collected in the national

The criterion for extraterritorial application of Brazilian Internet law is the existence of a genuine link to the national territory, expressed in several activities listed in the law itself.

This law establishes principles, guarantees, rights and duties for the use of the internet in Brazil and consumer protection. While the "Marco Civil da Internet" has privacy as one of its main points, the Law No. 13.709 (General Personal Data Protection Law LGPD) creates regulations for the use, protection and transfer of personal data.

1.5 *Protection of Personal Data: Law No. 13.709 of August 14, 2018*

Law No. 13.709 of 2018 was responsible for introducing extraterritoriality in matters of personal data protection in Brazil, through the provision contained in article 3.

> Law No. 13.709 of August 14, 2018
> Art. 3 This Law applies to any processing operation carried out by a natural person or by a legal entity governed by public or private law, regardless of the environment, the country of its headquarters or the country where the data is located, provided that:
> I – the treatment operation is carried out in the national territory;
> II – the processing activity has as its objective the offer or supply of goods or services or the processing of data of individuals located in the national territory; or
> III – the personal data object of the processing has been collected in the national territory.
> § 1º Personal data whose owner is found at the time of collection are collected in the national territory.
> § 2 The processing of data provided for in item IV of the caput of art. 4 of this Law.[8]

territory and to the content of the communications in which at least one of the terminals is placed in Brazil. b) The established in Art. 11 applies even if the activities are carried out by a legal entity placed abroad, provided that it offers services to the Brazilian public or at least one member of the same economic group is established in Brazil. "Art. 11. In any operation of collection, storage, retention and treating of personal data or communications data by connection providers and internet applications providers where at least one of these acts takes place in the national territory, the Brazilian law must be mandatorily respected, including in regard the rights to privacy, to protection of personal data, and to secrecy of private communications and of logs".

8 Original text: "Art. 3º Esta Lei aplica-se a qualquer operação de tratamento realizada por pessoa natural ou por pessoa jurídica de direito público ou privado, independentemente

The criterion for extraterritorial application of Brazilian Personal Data Protection law is the existence of a genuine link to the national territory, expressed in several activities listed in the law itself.

2 The Current Practice of Extraterritoriality in Brazil

The practice of extraterritorial application can be widely observed in judicial decisions under Brazilian criminal law. Regarding competition law, the extensive administrative jurisprudence issued by the Administrative Council for Economic Defense (CADE) likewise supports the extraterritorial application of Brazilian law – decisions that have already been ratified by the Superior Court of Justice (STJ).

In international employment contracts, it is also possible to observe the use of Brazilian law in services rendered entirely abroad. So far, there is no jurisprudence on extraterritorial application in matters of personal data protection in Brazilian law.

2.1 *Criminal Law*

As noted above, the Brazilian Penal Code includes several provisions authorizing the prosecution of crimes committed in foreign territory – in some cases subject to no further qualification (item I, art. 7, Brazilian Penal Code), and in some cases if additional conditions are met (item II and § 3, art. 7, Brazilian Penal Code).

It is possible to affirm that the extraterritoriality of Brazilian criminal law has a wide practical application. Its practical incidence seems to meet less resistance than extraterritoriality in other areas of Brazilian law.

The crimes of false identity or presentation of a false passport provide an example. Habeas Corpus nº 1006581-19.2018.4.01.0000,[9] judged by the Federal Regional Court of the 1st region, addressed the crime of false identity

do meio, do país de sua sede ou do país onde estejam localizados os dados, desde que: I – a operação de tratamento seja realizada no território nacional; II – a atividade de tratamento tenha por objetivo a oferta ou o fornecimento de bens ou serviços ou o tratamento de dados de indivíduos localizados no território nacional; ou III – os dados pessoais objeto do tratamento tenham sido coletados no território nacional. § 1º Consideram-se coletados no território nacional os dados pessoais cujo titular nele se encontre no momento da coleta. § 2º Excetua-se do disposto no inciso I deste artigo o tratamento de dados previsto no inciso IV do caput do art. 4º desta Lei".

9 BRAZIL. Federal Regional Court of the 1st Region. Habeas Corpus No. 1006581-19.2018.4.01.0000. Federal Judge Neviton de Oliveira Batista Guedes. Judged on 06/04/2018.

committed before the Brazilian consulate in French Guiana. The decision stated that the Consulate General of Brazil abroad is a public agency of the Brazilian Government, linked to the Ministry of Foreign Affairs, an agency of the Federal Public Administration. It expressly ratified that art. 7 of the Penal Code applied to the case, providing for the application of Brazilian criminal law to crimes committed abroad (extraterritoriality). The case involved a crime committed against the national public faith, one of the situations in which no additional conditions were necessary: "in the case, despite being committed abroad, the crime committed against the property or public faith of the Union, is subject to national legislation, therefore, Brazilian law applies immediately, without any condition".

In a case of a false passport presented by a Brazilian to the authorities of the United States of America, the decision handed down in Criminal Appeal No. 0002228-21.2008.4.03.6119[10] stated: "For the crime of art. 297 of the Penal Code, the unconditional Brazilian criminal law applies, pursuant to art. 7, I, b, of the Penal Code. The offense of falsifying a public document aims to safeguard the public faith of the Union".

Another example is Criminal Appeal No. 11267 DF 2006.34.00.0011267-5[11] which dealt with the use of an authentic Brazilian passport with a false US consular visa. The decision confirmed that "to the crime committed by a Brazilian abroad – use of a false US consular visa in an authentic Brazilian passport – Brazilian law applies, subject to the rules of conditioned extraterritoriality (art. 7, II, § 2, Brazilian Penal Code)".

It is possible to observe the extraterritoriality of Brazilian law in other areas, such as competition law, protection of personal data and labor law. In those areas, however, the practice is subject to certain limitations, and has met some resistance.

2.2 *Competition Law*

There is a wide practice of extraterritorial application in Brazilian competition law in mergers and acts of economic concentration, as seen in administrative decisions issued by the Administrative Council for Economic Defense (CADE). It can also be seen in court decisions that ratify and support such administrative action. Among the decisions issued by CADE, it is possible to find those targeting operations that took place entirely abroad. What is necessary, however,

10 BRAZIL. Federal Regional Court of the 3rd Region. Criminal Appeal No. 0002228-21.2008.4.03.6119. Federal Judge Nino Toldo. Judged on 07/25/2019.

11 BRAZIL. Federal Regional Court of the 1st Region. Criminal Appeal No. 11267 DF 2006.34.00.0011267-5. Federal Judge Olindo Menezes. Judged on 03/12/2013.

is to recognize that the analysis of these operations in the light of the Brazilian antitrust law rests on the effects doctrine.

An act of economic concentration that takes place entirely abroad and is submitted to CADE for consideration is a direct reflection of the application of Brazilian law extraterritorially. For merger approvals, CADE uses as an objective criterion the amount that the group has invoiced in Brazil during the year prior to the event. If this amount exceeds the legal provision contained in article 88, of Law No. 12,529/11, this act must be submitted for CADE's approval, with justification in article 2 of that law.

CADE's first decision that foreshadowed the adoption of the effects doctrine took place on June 19, 1996, by the former Councilor Rodrigues Chaves, in the concentration act 28/95,[12] which involved the companies *Nalco Chemical Company* and *Exxon Energy Chemicals*. In his vote, he highlights the principle of ubiquity present in Brazilian criminal legislation, which provides for the application of local law in cases that have an effect on the national territory, even if the relevant offense takes place abroad.[13] Drawing an analogy to criminal law, the former Councilor makes it clear that when anti-competitive acts carried out abroad have direct consequences at the domestic level, they are treated as if they had taken place in Brazil.[14]

The vote was extremely important for the enshrinement of article 2 of Brazilian law, and was later widely used in other CADE decisions as a model to

---

12 BRAZIL. Concentration Act No. 28/95 (*Nalco Chemical Company*, and *Exxon Energy Chemicals*). Counselor Rodrigues Chaves. 1996.

13 Excerpt given by former Councilor Rodrigues Chaves: "Brazilian antitrust law – Law 8884, of June 11, 1994 – establishes, for its application, the principle of territoriality, subject only to the exceptions arising from conventions and treaties to which Brazil is a signatory, insofar as it represses the acts contrary to the economic order, practiced in the whole or in part of the national territory. It also applies the principle of ubiquity, insofar as it considers itself competent to punish offenses committed abroad, which produce or may produce effects in the national territory". BRAZIL. Concentration Act No. 28/95 (*Nalco Chemical Company*, and *Exxon Energy Chemicals*). Counselor Rodrigues Chaves. 1996.

14 The vote thus states: "There are certain acts, in Competition Law, which, although practiced abroad, affect the domestic market in such a way that it is as if they were practiced in the national territory: these are the so-called distance practices. For these, Brazilian law concurrently adopts the ubiquity theory, in which the activity theory and the effects doctrine are combined. Consequently, Brazilian law applies not only to acts performed in the whole or in part of the national territory, but to those that produce or may produce effects therein. If these acts constitute infractions against the Brazilian economic order, those responsible must be punished in accordance with Brazilian law, regardless of the fact that they have already been punished or, eventually, acquitted abroad". BRAZIL. Concentration Act No. 28/95 (*Nalco Chemical Company*, and *Exxon Energy Chemicals*). Counselor Rodrigues Chaves. 1996.

be followed. When analyzing existing decisions, it is possible to observe that Article 2 is used in order to determine the need to notify CADE of mergers occurring abroad that meet the requirements.

Another important decision was the concentration act No. 08012.005447/00-56,[15] involving *Davide Campari – Milano S.p.A.* (*Campari*), *Selviac Nederland* BV (*Selviac*) and *Grupo Diageo*, judged by board member Celso Fernandes Campilongo. In that case, Campilongo's report noted the justification offered by the three applicants (companies based in Italy, The Netherlands, and England, respectively) for seeking CADE's approval: "The applicants clarify that this submission is made based on article 2 of Law 8884/94, since it had effects in Brazil even though the operation has been fully formalized abroad".[16] This indicates the international recognition of CADE as an autonomous entity responsible for regulating foreign activity affecting competition in Brazil.

Among the court decisions that ratify CADE's action and recognize the extraterritoriality of Brazilian law, the decision issued in Special Appeal No. 615.628[17] stands out. That decision upheld the fine imposed on the General Electric Company for late presentation of documents relating to a proposed acquisition of the Large Industrial Gas Turbines Division – Heavy Duty from the company Alstom France/SA.

According to the vote by Judge Mauro Campbell Marques, "the defendant company strongly argues, in the initial and in the memorials offered, that the transfer of assets in foreign territory, as well as the inexistence of branches in Brazil, would rule out possible effects on the domestic market". For the Judge, however, it did not matter whether the companies involved had a branch in Brazil, or whether the preliminary contract was agreed in Brazil: "it is enough, that, in theory, the concentration agreement can, under any perspective, impact the national market" so that "the concentration act or the cooperation act can damage the competitive health".

With these arguments, the Superior Court of Justice decided to maintain the fine imposed on General Electric Company by CADE, arguing: "even though they do not have any subsidiary headquartered in the national territory, they actively participated in the Brazilian market, having a significant share, between 8% and 9% each, which makes the operation within the scope of art. 2 of the Antitrust Law".

15 BRAZIL. Concentration Act No. 08012.005447/00-56 (*Davide Campari – Milano S.p.A.*; *Selviac Nederland* BV e *Grupo Diageo*). Board Member Celso Fernandes Campilongo. 2000.

16 Excerpt from the report given by Board Member Celso Fernandes Campilongo, present in the Concentration Act nº 08012.005447/00-56. 2000.

17 BRAZIL. Superior Justice Tribunal. Special Resource No. 615,628. Judge Herman Benjamin. Judged on 06/08/2010.

The extraterritoriality of Brazilian competition law permeates the strong performance of CADE. It is possible to find many administrative decisions that recognize the law's extraterritorial reach. Although the judicial decisions on this issue are scarcer than decisions on the extraterritoriality of criminal law, it is possible to observe the support given to the actions of CADE (recognizing, therefore, the extraterritoriality of Brazilian competition law).

2.3 *International Employment Contracts*

Even before the cancellation of Precedent No. 207 of the Superior Labor Court (TST), it was already possible to find a decision that rejected the principle of territoriality and applied Brazilian law to an employment contract performed entirely abroad. This is the case of Ordinary Labor Appeal No. 0001874-83.2010.5.03.0091.[18]

According to this decision, the hiring of workers in Brazil to provide services abroad was regulated by Law No. 7,064/82, with the application of the Brazilian labor protection legislation "whenever this is more favorable than what is regulated in the workplace law, rejecting the principle of *lex loci executionis contracti*, dealt with in Precedent No. 207/TST, in a generic manner".

With the formal cancellation of Precedent No. 207 in 2012, the principle of territoriality was discarded. For example, Ordinary Labor Appeal No. 0002095-41.2013.5.03.0033[19] approved the application of Brazilian law to the hiring of workers in Brazil to provide services abroad, "whenever more beneficial in the set of rules and in relation to each matter, regardless of compliance with the legislation of the place where the services are performed".

2.4 *Internet Law*

Article 11 of the Brazilian Civil Rights Framework for the Internet ("Marco Civil da Internet" – Federal Law No 12.965/2014) requires Internet conglomerates (if they wish to continue their activities in Brazil) to comply with Brazilian law, stating specifically: "Art. 11. In any operation of collection, storage, safekeeping and processing of records, personal data or communications by Internet connection and application providers in which at least one of these acts occurs in national territory, it shall be mandatory to respect the Brazilian law and the rights to privacy, protection of personal data and confidentiality of private communications and records".[20]

---

18 BRAZIL. Regional Labor Court of the 3rd Region. Ordinary Labor Appeal No. 0001874-83.2010.5.03.0091. Judge Marcio Jose Zebende. Judged on 19/04/2012.

19 BRAZIL. Regional Labor Court of the 3rd Region. Ordinary Labor Appeal No. 0002095-41.2013.5.03.0033. Judge Oswaldo Tadeu B. Guedes. Judged on 7/13/2015.

20 Original text: "Em qualquer operação de coleta, armazenamento, guarda e tratamento de registros, de dados pessoais ou de comunicações por provedores de conexão e de

The fact that certain companies, by business decision, seek to protect the privacy of their users (thereby attracting more consumers) by transferring stored data to places with more protective legislation ("safe haven") does not affect Brazilian jurisdiction or the applicability of Brazilian law, even extraterritorially. Privacy, according to the precedents of the Supreme Federal Court and the Inter-American Court of Human Rights, is not an absolute right, and may yield in the face of others, based on the criterion of proportionality.

In late 2020, the Superior Court of Justice ruled that "it is a *mistake* to imagine that any application hosted outside Brazil cannot be reached by the national jurisdiction or that the Brazilian laws are not applicable to its activities" (Superior Tribunal de Justiça, Recurso Especial n. 1.745.657-SP, Relatoria Min. Nancy Andrighi, 03-11-2020).

3 The Impact of International Treaties on Extraterritoriality in Brazil

There are two types of treaties ratified by Brazil that provide for the extraterritorial application of domestic law: (i) punitive treaties and (ii) human rights treaties. Punitive treaties suggest that Brazil establishes extraterritorial jurisdiction in cases of crimes committed abroad by a Brazilian citizen or by a person residing in Brazil. In addition, they determine that Brazil follows the rule of "aut dedere, aut judicare", whereby individuals located in Brazil who have committed crimes abroad and who, for some reason, cannot be extradited, must be punished according to Brazilian law, which will then have extraterritorial effect, being applied to criminal acts committed outside the national territory.

Four treaties that establish such provisions should be mentioned due to their importance and use: a) the United Nations Convention against Corruption (Merida Convention; art. 42), the Inter-American Convention against Corruption (Caracas Convention, 1996, article V); the United Nations Convention against Illicit Traffic in Narcotic Drugs and Psychotropic Substances (Vienna Convention, 1988, article 4), and the United Nations Convention against Transnational Organized Crime (article 15).

As for human rights, the Brazilian state has ratified the main treaties of the United Nations and the Organization of American States. The extraterritorial application of these treaties prevents the Brazilian State from acting, in cases with foreign elements, in such a way as to violate the human rights of

aplicações de internet em que pelo menos um desses atos ocorra em território nacional, deverão ser obrigatoriamente respeitados a legislação brasileira e os direitos à privacidade, à proteção dos dados pessoais e ao sigilo das comunicações privadas e dos registros."

the individuals involved. In addition, some human rights treaties establish the duty of the Brazilian State to punish perpetrators of human rights violations in cases that occurred abroad, in the event that extradition is not possible. Among the best known are the UN Convention against Torture (art. 5), the Inter-American Convention against Torture (art. 12), and the International Convention for the Protection of All Persons from Enforced Disappearance (art. 9).

4 The Role of International Law in Defining or Limiting the Geographic Scope of Statutes and Regulations

Brazil has a strong tradition of respect for national sovereignty, which translates into the acceptance of the superiority of the Brazilian Constitution over treaties. In addition, the Brazilian Supreme Court recognizes the equivalent status of domestic legislation and treaty law. The superiority of a treaty over domestic laws is only recognized in the case of human rights treaties.

Thus, a new Brazilian law with extraterritorial reach could – in theory – be enforced, even if inconsistent with a previous treaty (other than a human rights treaty).

As seen above, several Brazilian criminal laws with extraterritorial effect implement international conventions signed by Brazil, such as the Merida Convention against corruption (art. 42.3) and the Palermo Convention against Transnational Organized Crime (art. 15.3), among others.

According to the Brazilian Constitution (art. 5, LV), the extradition of native or naturalized Brazilians is forbidden, unless, in the latter case, the crime was committed before naturalization or the naturalized Brazilian committed abroad the crime of drug trafficking. In these two cases, the naturalized Brazilian (never the native Brazilian citizen) can be extradited. To avoid impunity and the transformation of Brazil into a safe haven for Brazilians who have committed crimes abroad, Brazil assumed, through treaties, the duty to apply its criminal law extraterritorially. Even in the absence of treaties, Brazilian criminal law allows such extraterritorial application.

In view of the rule against extraditing nationals, the nations like Brazil that apply this rule are obliged, by a general principle of public international law, to assume jurisdiction over the crime that occurred abroad. This guideline was incorporated into several extradition treaties, as can be seen in the Latin expression "aut dedere aut judicare", which attests to an obligation of States under public international law or a rule of customary international law. Brazil complies with this rule by provision of its Penal Code.

Thus, crimes committed by Brazilians are subject to Brazilian criminal law, even if committed abroad (article 7, II, Penal Code). However, this extension of national jurisdiction depends on the fulfillment of certain conditions (§2°): a) entering the national territory (necessary premise for the usefulness of the criminal action in Brazil); b) the fact is punishable also in the country where it was committed (dual criminality); c) the crime is included among those for which Brazilian law authorizes extradition (extraditable crimes are those with a maximum prison sentence of more than one year, as per art. 77, item IV of Law 6.815/1980); d) the agent has not been acquitted abroad or served his sentence there (to avoid *bis in idem*); e) the agent has not been pardoned abroad or, for another reason, punishability is not extinguished, according to the most favorable law (principle of the most favorable criminal law). Brazilian jurisdiction becomes extraterritorial, to reach facts that occurred in a foreign country.

5 The Role of International Comity

International comity has inspired Brazilian legislation regarding extraterritoriality in a number of ways. First, the extraterritoriality of Brazilian law is limited to cases permitted by law. Second, the establishment of Brazilian civil or criminal jurisdiction is generally based on clear links of the case to the national territory. There has to be a genuine link to Brazil satisfying one of the bases of jurisdiction acceptable under international jurisdictional law, like nationality, territoriality, or protective principle. National jurisdiction that could be considered abusive or extravagant is avoided by the legislator.

6 Reasonableness in the Extraterritorial Application of Statutes and Regulations

The existence of reasonableness in the extraterritorial application of the law is a requirement that does not appear in Brazilian legislation. However, the discussion about the effectiveness of a judicial decision to apply Brazilian law extraterritorially is common. To avoid the situation of adopting a decision that would not be enforced (useless decision), the extraterritorial use of the law, which, hypothetically, would be allowed, is rejected. This situation was seen with regard to the application of Brazilian law on succession to assets located abroad.

Article 10 of Law 12.376 establishes that succession due to death or absence shall obey the law of the country where the deceased or missing person is domiciled, whatever the nature and the situation of the assets. This provision covers all the assets (movable or immovable; tangible or intangible), as well as any type of succession. The only critical factor is the domicile of the deceased or absent person: if domiciled in Brazil, Brazilian law will be applied; if domiciled abroad, foreign law will be applied.

Thus, Brazilian succession law would have, in principle, extraterritorial force. However, since there is no certainty of compliance with the Brazilian judgment by the foreign State in which the assets are located, the dominant jurisprudence of the Superior Court of Justice restricts the application of Brazilian law to the succession of assets located in Brazil. Another argument is that of respect for foreign sovereignty, since Brazil itself would not accept a foreign decision regarding real estate located in Brazil. In this second hypothesis, the Superior Court of Justice decided that if the Brazilian law prevents the foreign succession court from dealing with assets located in Brazil, whether movable or immovable, in a mortis causa succession, then likewise the Brazilian succession court should not deal with assets located abroad, even though the Brazilian decision may be fully effective there" (Superior Court of Justice, Special Appeal no. 397.769-SP, 2002).

7 The Application of Brazilian Law to Wholly Foreign Conduct

7.1 *Consumer Law*

In Brazil, the Consumer Defense Code (CDC) is considered a norm of public order and social interest. As Claudia Lima Marques states, "part of the doctrine argues that the Consumer Defense Code should apply to all consumer contracts with sufficient contacts to Brazil, as an international imperative rule or loi d'application immediate".[21] It is understood that the CDC must provide minimum and imperative standards for consumer protection in all distance contracts, contracts negotiated in Brazil by nationals or foreigners or when marketing or offering is done in Brazil, including in electronic contracts with suppliers with headquarters abroad.

For Claudia Lima Marques, this law of immediate application "has pretensions of generic and extraterritorial application always, regardless of whether they are laws of private or public law, since they have strong interests in the

21 MARQUES, Claudia Lima. A proteção do consumidor de produtos e serviços estrangeiros no Brasil: primeiras observações sobre os contratos à distância no comércio eletrônico. *Revista da Faculdade de Direito da* UFRGS. v. 21. Março/2002. p. 93.

organization of national society".[22] This law is seen in private international law as a technique for materializing the new conflict-of-law rules.

In Brazilian jurisprudence, the famous Panasonic case is observed, in Special Appeal nº 63.981. The product was purchased abroad on a trip by a Brazilian, having already presented a defect in Brazilian territory. The consumer filed the lawsuit in Brazil, claiming that the Brazilian company Panasonic should be responsible for the product, even if it had been obtained abroad.

The São Paulo State Court, at first, understood that the Brazilian company was not obliged to provide a guarantee for the product produced and sold abroad, by the parent company or even branches. The consumer appealed, and the decision of the Superior Court of Justice became historic for Brazilian justice. Judge Aldir Passarinho Júnior followed the understanding of the São Paulo Court of Justice, arguing that the responsibility for the product could not be the company located in Brazil, even if it belongs to the same economic group as the foreign company. His vote was followed by Judge Barros Monteiro.

The divergence came from the vote of Judge Sálvio de Figueiredo Teixeira, who considered the impact of globalization and the advances of the social model: "Because we are living in a new reality, imposed by the globalized economy, we also have a new legal framework, and it is essential that there is an interpretation in tune with this reality. Therefore, protection based on internal limits and traditional legal diplomas is not enough, when it is known that the Brazilian Consumer Protection Code is one of the most advanced legal texts in existence".

This case reflects the application of Brazilian law to a purchase of goods that took place entirely abroad (the only relationship that connects the case to Brazil is the nationality of the consumer). And, even more importantly, it holds a Brazilian company (Panasonic Brasil) liable for a defect in a Panasonic product purchased abroad from another company.

This understanding could be observed later in other cases. The Innominated Resource nº 00199133820158190001 was based on an online purchase made by a Brazilian woman through the American Amazon website. She gave up on the purchase before the product arrived at her residence, which was accepted by the site. However, it was informed that she should receive the product to later return to the origin. The consumer filed a lawsuit against Amazon located in Brazil, since in addition to not being able to return the product, she was charged import tax, which ended up being a surprise for her. In this case, the decision of the Panasonic case was used as a model.

22 MARQUES, Claudia Lima. A proteção do consumidor de produtos e serviços estrangeiros no Brasil: primeiras observações sobre os contratos à distância no comércio eletrônico. *Revista da Faculdade de Direito da* UFRGS. v. 21. Março/2002. p. 92.

The main basis for these decisions is the analysis of consumer vulnerability, which is aggravated when they participate in international trade. In terms of jurisdiction, the Brazilian Civil Procedure Code (Law nº 13.105/2015) provides in article 22, II, that the Brazilian judicial authority is responsible for prosecuting and judging actions arising from consumer relations, when the consumer is domiciled or resident in Brazil (even when the relevant relations unfold entirely outside Brazil).

7.2 *Criminal Law*

In terms of criminal law, it is possible to observe the legislative provision of universal jurisdiction in article 7, II, a, of the Penal Code (Decree-Law No. 2,848 of December 7, 1940). According to this provision, crimes that, by treaty or convention, Brazil is obliged to repress, will be subject to Brazilian law, even if committed abroad. Despite such legal provision, there are yet no judicial decisions that have applied this provision of universal jurisdiction.

Paragraph 3 of article 7 also determines the application of Brazilian law to crimes committed by a foreigner against a Brazilian outside Brazil, provided that the conditions listed above are present and extradition has not been requested or denied; or when there is a request from the Minister of Justice. It should be noted, however, that article 5, LI, of the Brazilian Federal Constitution vetoes the extradition of a Brazilian: "LI – no Brazilian will be extradited, except for a naturalized person, in the case of a common crime, committed before naturalization, or proven involvement in illicit trafficking in narcotics and related drugs, in accordance with the law".

Thus, if a Brazilian has committed a crime abroad and has returned to Brazil before the start of the process, he will be tried in Brazil for the crime committed abroad. This is the understanding already emanated by the Superior Court of Justice (STJ) in Conflict of Competence No. 115.375.[23]

In this precedent, the Supreme Court, Justice Celso de Mello held that: "The *extraterritoriality* of criminal law does not constitute a phenomenon alien to the various legal systems existing in national states, since comparative law – with support in principles such as that of nationality (active and passive), of protection, of universality and of representation (or of the flag) – recognizes the legitimate possibility of the incidence, in foreign territories, of the criminal order of other states. Furthermore, the international community itself has encouraged the adoption of mechanisms that make it possible for the state to repress certain crimes whose seriousness reaches and affects, on a universal scale, the vital interests of the states that make up the society of nations" (Extradição 1151, Justice Min. Celso de Mello, 2011).

---

23 BRAZIL. Superior Court of Justice. Conflict of Competence No. 115.375 SP 2010/0228291-3. Judge Laurita Vaz. Judged on 10/26/2011.

These are examples of the extraterritoriality of Brazilian law that are based on the nationality of the parties involved, regardless of the place where the crime was committed.

8 The Continued Importance of Territorial Links

8.1 *Competition Law*

For a law to be based on the effects doctrine, it means to curb activities that produce or may produce effects in the country, even coming from mergers or acquisitions of companies that have taken place entirely abroad. It is important, therefore, that the impact of the behavior has occurred in the Brazilian market.

Under Article 2 of Law No. 12,529/11, Brazilian competition law applies to practices committed in whole or in part in the national territory, or to foreign practices that produce or may produce effects therein. In the latter case, however, the law uses a territorially-based economic criterion to determine the scope of this extraterritorial application. Article 88 defines that acts of economic concentration must be submitted to the Administrative Council for Economic Defense (CADE) in which, cumulatively: a) at least one of the groups involved in the transaction has registered, in the last balance sheet, annual gross sales or volume of total business in the country, in the year prior to the operation, equivalent to or greater than four hundred million reais (R$400,000,000.00); and b) at least one other group involved in the transaction has registered, in the last balance sheet, annual gross sales or total business volume in the country, in the year prior to the transaction, equivalent to or greater than R$ 30,000,000.00 (thirty million reais). This provision in article 88 of Law No. 12,529/11 corresponded to the provisions of Article 54 of the previous law, Law No. 8,884/94.

In this sense, in the context of Brazilian competition law, it is possible to observe a prevalence of the principle of territoriality. Precedent No. 1 of the CADE states that: "In applying the criteria established in art. 54, §3 of Law No. 8.884/94, the annual gross revenue registered exclusively in the Brazilian territory by the companies or group of companies participating in the concentration act is relevant".

This precedent was the result of the new understanding adopted in CADE's decisions, which began with the vote of Councilor Roberto Augusto Castellanos Pfeiffer in the concentration act No. 08012.002992/2004-14[24] in 2004. In the

24 BRAZIL. Concentration Act No. 08012.002992/2004-14 (ADC *Telecommunications, Inc.* e *Krone International Holding, Inc.*). Vote by Board Member Roberto Augusto Castellanos Pfeiffer.

vote, the reporting Councilor stated that the revenue in the amount provided for in article 54, paragraph 3, of Law No. 8.884/94 (currently provided for in article 88 of Law No. 12,529/11), should be verified by the annual gross revenue of the parties or their economic groups occurring within Brazilian territory.[25]

With this change in understanding, the simple incidence of effects in the national territory is not enough for the concentration act involving large international companies to be considered by the Brazilian entity. For the act to be submitted to Brazilian law, the objective requirements must be met, with the normative predominance of the principle of territoriality.

For some researchers, the new posture adopted by the Administrative Council for Economic Defense is the result of self-restraint. It would respect other jurisdictions when the transaction in question does not produce relevant effects in the Brazilian market, while providing savings in public resources, as it prevents such transactions from reaching CADE's appraisal.[26]

8.2 *International Employment Contracts*

In international employment contracts it is also possible to observe this scenario. Although the provision of services takes place entirely abroad, Brazilian law applies only when the employee is hired in Brazil, through Law No. 7,064 which, since 2009, "regulates the situation of workers hired in Brazil or transferred by their employers to provide services abroad". Article 3 determines the application of Brazilian law to employees hired in Brazil and transferred abroad, regardless of compliance with the legislation of the place where the services are performed.

8.3 *Brazilian Civil Rights Framework for the Internet*

Law No. 12,965/2014 established principles, guarantees, rights and duties for the use of the Internet in Brazil. In its article 11, it is possible to observe the extraterritoriality of Brazilian law on this subject: "In any operation of collection,

---

25 In the vote: "The acts dealt with in the caput include those aimed at any form of economic concentration, whether through merger or incorporation of companies, incorporation of a company to exercise control of companies or any form of corporate grouping, involving the participation of a company or groups of companies resulting in twenty percent of a relevant market, or in which any of the participants has registered annual gross sales in the last balance sheet equivalent to R$400,000,000.00 (four hundred million)". BRAZIL. Concentration Act No. 08012.002992/2004-14 (ADC *Telecommunications, Inc.* e *Krone International Holding, Inc.*). Vote by Board Member Roberto Augusto Castellanos Pfeiffer.

26 VALENTE DOS REIS, Gabriel. Direito concorrencial internacionalizado – Entre a teoria dos efeitos e os efeitos da teoria. *Revista de Direito Constitucional e Internacional.* Ano 18, nº 73. São Paulo, 2010. p. 314.

storage, retention and treating of personal data or communications data by connection providers and internet applications providers where, at least, one of these acts takes place in the national territory, the Brazilian law must be mandatorily respected, including in regard the rights to privacy, to protection of personal data, and to secrecy of private communications and of logs".[27]

This provision applies to data collected in the national territory and to the content of communications in which at least one of the terminals is in Brazil. It also applies to activities carried out by a legal entity located abroad, provided that it offers services to the Brazilian public or at least one member of the same economic group is established in Brazil.

8.4 *Protection of Personal Data*

The General Law for the Protection of Personal Data, Law No. 13,709/2018, provided for the processing of personal data, including in digital media, by a natural person or by a legal entity governed by public or private law, with the objective of protecting the fundamental rights of freedom and privacy and the free development of the personality of the natural person.

Article 3 was responsible for the extraterritorial scope of Brazilian protection. It determined that the law applies to any processing operation carried out by a natural person or by a legal entity governed by public or private law, regardless of the medium, the country of its headquarters or the country where the data are located, provided that: a) the treatment operation is carried out in the national territory; b) the processing activity has the purpose of offering or supplying goods or services or processing data of individuals located in the national territory; or c) the personal data being processed have been collected in the national territory.

Paragraph 1 complemented this provision, determining that personal data whose holder is there at the time of collection are considered collected in the national territory.

9 Extraterritoriality and the Globalization of Corporate Activity

The extraterritorial scope of Brazilian law often raises issues regarding the application of that law to foreign companies, and possible limitations in that regard.

---

27 Translated to English. https://www.cgi.br/pagina/marco-civil-law-of-the-internet-in-brazil/180

The Panasonic case mentioned above, Special Appeal No. 63,981,[28] involved the liability of a Brazilian company due to a consumer contract entered abroad with another company, and it is possible to observe this relationship between a foreign company and the liability on the part of the national company that enjoys the benefits of the brand. This issue involves an unequal relationship with a vulnerable party, which justifies accountability on the part of the national company.

Judge Sálvio de Figueiredo Teixeira (from Superior Court of Justice) sustained: "if the globalized economy does not have rigid borders and encourages and favors free competition, it is necessary that consumer protection laws gain greater expression in their exegesis, in the search for the balance that should govern relations legal issues, including the risk factor inherent to the competitiveness of commerce and commercial business, especially on an international scale, in which powerful, multinational companies with branches in several countries are present, not to mention the sales carried out today by the technological process of information technology and in the consumer market that represents our country".[29]

For him, Panasonic Brazil benefits from the worldwide fame of the Panasonic brand, so that the consumer should not be harmed by any deficiencies in the products. The vote was accompanied by Judges Cesar Asfor Rocha and Ruy Rosado de Aguiar. For Judge Ruy Rosado de Aguiar: "The company that sells its products in different countries of the world, and thus benefits from the commercial globalization regime, must answer for its obligations to the same extent. The breaking of borders for the sale must bring with it the corresponding breaking of borders to maintain the guarantee of the quality of the product. On the contrary, the multinational company receives the bonus that means the possibility of expanding the market for the placement of the goods it produces, elevating it to a universal level, but exempts itself from the burden of assuming the responsibility of manufacturer or supplier, invoking in its favor the existence of the border. This limit, which does not prevent its expansion, cannot serve to reduce its obligation".[30]

When addressing the decision in this case, Paulo de Borba Casella states that "the concrete effect on a given market is a relevant criterion and can be

28 BRAZIL. Superior Court of Justice. Special Appeal No. 63981 SP 1995/0018349-8, Judge Aldir Passarinho Junior, Judgment Date: 04/11/2000.

29 BRAZIL. Superior Court of Justice. Special Appeal No. 63981 SP 1995/0018349-8, Judge Aldir Passarinho Junior, Judgment Date: 04/11/2000.

30 BRAZIL. Superior Court of Justice. Special Appeal No. 63981 SP 1995/0018349-8, Judge Aldir Passarinho Junior, Judgment Date: 04/11/2000.

validly invoked by the State, either judicially or administratively, to enforce the exercise of national Jurisdiction, in relation to a concrete case".[31]

In cases involving competition law, it is possible to observe the submission of totally foreign mergers (involving only foreign companies) to the Administrative Council for Economic Defense (CADE), in situations where the effects of the transaction can be felt in the Brazilian domestic market. As discussed above, as economic globalization has increased the likelihood that foreign mergers affect the Brazilian market, the application of Brazilian law to foreign companies has become more frequent.

10 The Interpretation of Ambiguous Laws

The extraterritoriality of a given law must be expressly contained in its text or be the result of an express provision of a treaty ratified and incorporated into the Brazilian legal system. If the law is silent or there is no treaty, it is understood that the effect of the law is merely territorial and the sovereignty of other countries must be respected. This understanding was seen, for example, in a decision by the Brazilian Supreme Court (Habeas Corpus 102.041, trial on December 18, 2009), which did not accept a request that would generate a decision to be served at a diplomatic mission or even in a foreign country without legal grounds or a treaty.

11 Responses to Extraterritorial Practices by Other States

Brazil has not enacted blocking laws like other countries. It is possible to find, however, norms that act as a block to the extraterritorial application of laws from other States. In this sense, the provision contained in art. 181 of the Federal Constitution of 1988 is viewed to operate as a first-degree blocking norm.[32] It provides that "The fulfillment of a request for a document or information of a commercial nature, made by a foreign administrative or judicial authority, to

31 CASELLA, Paulo Borba. Extraterritorialidade e proteção da livre-concorrência. *Revista da Faculdade de Direito da Universidade de São Paulo*. São Paulo. v. 96. 2001. p. 513.

32 JAEGER JUNIOR, Augusto. Direito Internacional da Concorrência: entre perspectivas unilaterais, multilaterais, bilaterais e regionais. Curitiba: Juruá, 2008, p. 139. FORGIONI, Paula. Os fundamentos do antitruste. 10 ed. São Paulo: Thomson Reuters Brasil, 2018, p. 452.

an individual or legal entity residing or domiciled in the country will depend on authorization from the competent Power".

This article of the Brazilian Constitution establishes a defense mechanism for individuals and companies based in Brazil against orders from a foreign judicial branch. This mechanism seeks to provide legal support for possible disobedience to such foreign judicial orders that have been transmitted informally or privately.

If the judicial order is transmitted through the channels of international legal cooperation between states, whether by letter rogatory or mutual legal assistance, Brazil can refuse to comply with it, alleging a violation of Brazilian public order or even of the human rights violations contained in the foreign judicial decision.

Such blocking rules are foreseen in art. 17 of Introduction to the Rules of Brazilian Law (Law n. 12.376), as follows: "The laws, acts, and sentences from another country, as well as any declarations of will, will not be effective in Brazil when they offend national sovereignty, public order, and good customs."

There is also this type of blocking rule in the Internal Regulations of the Superior Court of Justice, in connection with the recognition of foreign judgments. Article 216-F states that "A foreign decision that offends national sovereignty, human dignity and/or national sovereignty, the dignity of the human person and/or public order;" article 216-P states that "Exequatur will not be granted for letters rogatory that offend national sovereignty national sovereignty, human dignity and/or public order".

12 Extraterritoriality and Private International Law in Brazil: Trends in Applicable Law in Contractual and Non-contractual Obligations

There is a proposal to update the Introduction to the Rules of Brazilian Law (LINDB): Bill No. 3514.[33] Initially, it aimed only to update the Consumer Defense Code (CDC). Now, however, this project includes an update of article 9 of the LINDB, aimed at improving the law on international commercial and consumer contracts and extending to non-contractual obligations, observing the promotion of party autonomy in Brazilian private international law.

33 This Bill: "Amends Law No. 8078, of September 11, 1990 (Consumer Defense Code), to improve the general provisions of Chapter I of Title I and provide for electronic commerce, and art. 9 of Decree-Law No. 4.657, of September 4, 1942 (Law of Introduction to the Rules of Brazilian Law), to improve the discipline of international commercial and consumer contracts and provide for non-contractual obligations".

Article 9, caput, would maintain its wording: "the obligations, except in the specific cases provided for by law, shall be governed by the law of the country in which they are constituted". Innovations would be inserted through the inclusion of Article 9-A, 9-B and 9-C. Article 9-A would be specific for contractual obligations entered between professionals, Article 9-B for international consumer relations and Article 9-C for non-contractual obligations.

This update inserts a specific provision for consumer contracts, providing in Article 9-B that the international consumer[34] contract will be governed by the law of the place of execution or, if executed in Brazil, by Brazilian law, if more favorable to the consumer. It represents an important update, as it breaks with the traditional view of the conflict of laws by requiring the interpreter to carry out an analysis of the material result to determine whether Brazilian law should be applied or the law of the place of conclusion of the contract.

Regarding non-contractual obligations, Article 9-C determines that the law of the place where the effects are felt will be applicable, if none of the parties involved has its domicile or headquarters in the country where the accident occurs. The sole paragraph inserts two special provisions to be applied when dealing with civil liability for traffic accidents. It states that "when the accident involves or affects only people domiciled in another country, the judge may, exceptionally, consider applicable the law of that country, respecting the traffic and safety rules in force at the place and at the time of the accident". It also provides that "when the accident results in damage to things unrelated to the accident vehicles, the law of the country in which the event occurred will apply".

Thus, it is observed that this Bill of Law updates the Brazilian Law regarding contractual and non-contractual obligations, inserting more modern provisions. It allows the choice of law by the parties, the application of Brazilian law to consumer contracts when more favorable to the vulnerable party, and a specific provision for non-contractual obligations – which considers the effects of damage to determine the applicable law.

References

CARVALHO RAMOS, André de. *Curso de direito internacional privado.* 2a ed., São Paulo: Saraiva, 2021.

34 Article 9-B also determines that the international consumer contract will be that "understood as that entered into between a natural person consumer and a supplier of products and services whose establishment is located in a country other than that of the consumer's domicile".

CARVALHO RAMOS, André de. *A construção do direito internacional privado.* Heterogeneidade e Coerência. Salvador: JusPodivm, 2021.

CASELLA, Paulo Borba. Extraterritorialidade e proteção da livre-concorrência. *Revista da Faculdade de Direito da Universidade de São Paulo.* São Paulo. v. 96. 2001. p. 501–519.

FORGIONI, Paula. *Os fundamentos do antitruste.* 10 ed. São Paulo: Thomson Reuters Brasil, 2018.

JAEGER JUNIOR, Augusto. *Direito Internacional da Concorrência: entre perspectivas unilaterais, multilaterais, bilaterais e regionais.* Curitiba: Juruá, 2008.

JAEGER JUNIOR, Augusto; CRAVO, Daniela Copetti. The Extraterritoriality of the Right to Data Portability: Cross-Border Flow Between the European Union and Brazil. *In:* CUNHA RODRIGUES, Nuno (eds). *Extraterritoriality of* EU *Economic Law. European Union and its Neighbours in a Globalized World.* v. 4. Springer, Cham. 2021.

MARQUES, Claudia Lima. A proteção do consumidor de produtos e serviços estrangeiros no Brasil: primeiras observações sobre os contratos à distância no comércio eletrônico. *Revista da Faculdade de Direito da* UFRGS. v. 21. Março/2002. p. 65–99.

MEINERO, Fernando Pedro. O desenvolvimento do princípio da proximidade no direito internacional privado e sua presença no Brasil. *Revista Jurídica Unicuritiba.* v. 02, n. 51, Curitiba, 2018. p. 314–340.

VALENTE DOS REIS, Gabriel. Direito concorrencial internacionalizado – Entre a teoria dos efeitos e os efeitos da teoria. *Revista de Direito Constitucional e Internacional.* Ano 18, nº 73. São Paulo, 2010. p. 303–329.

VALLADÃO, Haroldo. O princípio da lei mais favorável no DIP. *Revista da Faculdade de Direito da Universidade de São Paulo.* vol. 76, 1981. p. 53–61.

WEBBER, Marianne Mendes. *Direito da concorrência e cooperação jurídica internacional.* Belo Horizonte: Arraes Editores, 2015.

The Extraterritorial Application of Statutes and Regulations

A Canadian Perspective

*John C. Kleefeld**

1 Overview

This report was prepared for the 2022 General Congress of the International Academy of Comparative Law held in Asunción, Paraguay. It aims to describe the law and practice in the federal and common-law jurisdictions of Canada and should be read with the companion report by Frédérique Sabourin addressing the civil-law jurisdiction of Québec. The report aims to state the law as of December 2023.

2 Scope of Report

In keeping with the general rapporteur's mandate, the report focuses on prescriptive jurisdiction; any discussion of executive, enforcement or judicial jurisdiction is tangential to that focus. *Prescriptive jurisdiction* is a state's authority to prescribe or make laws that govern the conduct of persons or affect their rights or property. *Executive jurisdiction* is the exercise of prerogative power, such as the sovereign's power to pardon a crime or an immigration minister's power to make decisions about migrants on humanitarian grounds. *Enforcement jurisdiction* is the state's ability to give effect to those laws through measures such as seizure of evidence, mutual legal assistance or extradition requests. *Judicial jurisdiction* is concerned with when a domestic court will oversee civil proceedings, a question that often arises when a case has a foreign element. As the report is about the extraterritorial reach of statutes and regulations, it deals only peripherally with the extraterritorial reach of constitutional law or Canada's extraterritorial obligations under international human rights law – again, in keeping with the report's general mandate.

The report is generally structured in accordance with the questions posed by the general rapporteur. Before responding to them, though, it may help to

* Professor and former Dean of Law, University of New Brunswick Faculty of Law. Dedicated to John P McEvoy, KC, retired law professor and a dedicated comparativist.

 | DOI:10.1163/9789004720183_005

first outline Canada's constitutional framework, particularly the division of legislative authority between the federal and provincial governments.

3 Canada's Constitutional Framework and Legal Systems

Canada is a federal state having ten provinces[1] and three federal territories.[2] Federal legislative authority is vested in the Canadian Parliament, comprising the sovereign (represented by the Governor General) and two legislative chambers: a 338-member elected House of Commons and a 105-member appointed Senate. Mirroring this structure in part, each province has a Lieutenant Governor who serves as the sovereign's representative and a single-chamber elected legislative assembly, typically called a Legislature.

Legislative authority is divided between Parliament and the legislatures in accordance with Canada's Constitution – notably, though not solely, ss 91–92 of the *Constitution Act, 1867*.[3] Under that Act, Parliament has exclusive legislative authority over some 30 enumerated matters of national interest,[4] including trade and commerce[5] and criminal law,[6] both relevant to extraterritoriality, and a residual power to legislate for the "peace, order and good government of Canada" in any subject not under provincial legislative authority. Legislatures have exclusive power to make laws on local matters, some 16 of which are enumerated[7] or, if not, can be characterized as being of "a merely local or private nature in the province."[8] Some subjects are carefully parsed. For

1 British Columbia, Alberta, Saskatchewan, Manitoba, Ontario, Quebec, New Brunswick, Prince Edward Island, Nova Scotia, and Newfoundland and Labrador.

2 Yukon, Northwest Territories and Nunavut.

3 *Constitution Act*, 1867, 30–31 Victoria, c 3 (UK), formerly the *British North America Act, 1867*. Canada's Constitution was patriated in 1982 through the *Canada Act 1982*, c 11 (UK), which enacted the *Constitution Act, 1982*. Among other things, the *Constitution Act, 1982* amended the *British North America Act, 1867*, including renaming it the *Constitution Act, 1867*; enacted the *Canadian Charter of Rights and Freedoms*; guaranteed rights of Aboriginal peoples; set out procedures for amending the Constitution; declared that the Constitution is the supreme law of Canada; and provided a schedule of the acts and orders that are in the Constitution. See *Constitution Acts, 1867–1982*, Government of Canada, https://bit.ly/3nFznEV.

4 *Constitution Act, 1867*, ss 91 and 92(10)(a)–(c).

5 *Ibid*, s 91(2).

6 *Ibid*, s 91(27).

7 *Ibid*, ss 92, 92A and 93.

8 *Ibid*, s 92(16).

example, Parliament has legislative authority over "marriage and divorce,"[9] but a Legislature has authority over laws on "the solemnization of marriage in the province."[10] Certain subjects – notably old age pensions, agriculture and immigration – fall under concurrent legislative authority.[11]

Under the Constitution, only Parliament can legislate extraterritorially.[12] A provincial statute must, in pith and substance, deal only with matters within provincial legislative competence, a limitation reinforced by repetition of the words "in the province" when listing the powers in s 92 of the *Constitution Act, 1867*. Extraterritorial effects must be only incidental or ancillary, failing which courts may hold the legislation constitutionally invalid generally or inapplicable in a specific case.[13] When the pith and substance of a province's legislation relate to a tangible matter, the question of whether it respects territorial limits is relatively easy to answer – one need only look to the physical location of the matter. But when it relates to an intangible matter, one must look to the relationships among the enacting territory, the subject matter of the legislation and those to whom it applies. This is to ensure that the legislation has a meaningful connection to the enacting province and respects other territories' legislative sovereignty.[14]

Canada is also bilingual (English and French) with a bijural legal system. Major areas of law, such as criminal law, fall under federal legislative authority and are thus uniform across the country. Provinces, though, have exclusive authority to make laws on matters of "property and civil rights in the

9 *Ibid*, s 91(26).
10 *Ibid*, s 92(12).
11 *Ibid*, ss 94A and s 95.
12 The power derives from *The Statute of Westminster 1931*, 22 Geo V, c 4 (UK), rep'd in RSC 1985, App II, No 27. This act established the legislative independence of the British Empire's self-governing dominions, including Canada, removing most of the British Parliament's authority to legislate for the dominions and making them largely sovereign nations. By s 3 of the Act, it was "declared and enacted that the Parliament of a Dominion has full power to make laws having extra-territorial operation." The Act is part of Canada's Constitution through s 52(2)(b) of the *Constitution Act, 1982* (*supra*, note 3) which says that the Constitution includes the Acts and orders in the Schedule. *The Statute of Westminster 1931*, as amended, is Item 17 in the Schedule. The federal *Interpretation Act*, RSC 1985, c I-21, which presumptively applies to all enactments made by Parliament, also references the *Statute of Westminster*: s 8(3) says that "[e]very act now in force enacted prior to December 11, 1931 that expressly or by necessary or reasonable implication was intended ... to have extra-territorial operation shall be construed as if, at the date of its enactment, the Parliament of Canada had full power to make laws having extraterritorial operation as provided by the *Statute of Westminster, 1931*."
13 *Reference re Upper Churchill Water Rights Reversion Act*, [1984] 1 SCR 297.
14 *British Columbia v Imperial Tobacco Ltd*, 2005 SCC 49, [2005] 2 SCR 473 at paras 30, 36.

province,"[15] a large domain. Thus, for historical reasons, the private law of Québec, including its rules of private international law, is found in the Civil Code of Québec,[16] while private law in the rest of Canada is based on the English common law.

This is a high-level explanation, all of which could be qualified or elaborated. For example, describing Canada as having two levels of government – federal and provincial – glosses over decades of developments that have set the country on a path to enabling forms of indigenous self-government.[17] And as to the division of legislative power, the demands of a modern state could hardly be met under a strict interpretation of the *Constitution Act, 1867*; rather, Canada has developed through creative judicial interpretation, constitutional convention and executive coordination at the federal and provincial levels of government.

In one example of this pattern, the Supreme Court considered a national egg marketing scheme that required provincial and federal laws to work together.[18] An issue was whether a province could regulate production of eggs that would leave the province, potentially infringing the federal legislative power over international and interprovincial trade and commerce. Despite the effect of the provincial laws on extraprovincial trade, the Court concluded that the provincial law complemented the federal law, and that holding it invalid would make it impossible to create a viable cooperative regulatory scheme.

Cooperative federalism is also evident in Canadian privacy law, where a federal statute, the *Personal Information Protection and Electronic Documents Act* (PIPEDA),[19] casts a wide net over the handling of personal information in commerce while simultaneously recognizing a province's power to regulate the collection, use and disclosure of personal information within its borders. Thus if a province adopts a law substantially similar to PIPEDA, businesses conducting commercial activity within that province are PIPEDA-exempt and need only comply with the provincial law.[20]

---

15 *Constitution Act, 1867*, s 92(13).

16 *Civil Code of Québec*, CQLR c CCQ-1991.

17 See, e.g., *The Canadian Encyclopedia*, *sv* "Indigenous Self-Government in Canada," https://bit.ly/3KN7Sk6 and Government of Canada, "Self-government," https://bit.ly/30oEFZi.

18 *Reference re Agricultural Products Marketing*, [1978] 2 SCR 1198.

19 *Personal Information Protection and Electronic Documents Act*, SC 2000, c 5.

20 For a list of provincial laws declared substantially similar to PIPEDA, see Office of the Privacy Commissioner of Canada, "Provincial laws that may apply instead of PIPEDA," https://bit.ly/3zpRPUS. In 2020, the federal government introduced Bill C-11, the *Digital Charter Implementation Act, 2020*, with a view to updating and reforming PIPEDA and other aspects of federal privacy law. The bill died on the order paper but was reintroduced in 2022 as Bill C-27, the *Digital Charter Implementation Act, 2022*, with debate and committee work on the bill taking place at the time of revising this report for publication.

Another example of federal-provincial coordination can be found in ss 9, 21 and 26 of the *Oceans Act*,[21] by which provincial laws can apply in Canada's coastal waters and other offshore areas under federal jurisdiction. The method allows a province to ask the federal government to pass regulations to extend the application of the provincial laws in question to an offshore area next to the province. Provincial legislation is thereby asserted extraterritorially by federal executive fiat. This power has been used to apply laws of Prince Edward Island to the area of the Confederation Bridge between Prince Edward Island and New Brunswick.[22]

As to the assertion that Canada's legal system is bijural, that at once says too much and too little. For one thing, there is now almost no area of law unaffected by statutes, whether to override the common law, to provide a comprehensive regulatory scheme, or to enact a law of specific application that falls outside the general rules of the Civil Code. Thus to characterize the Canadian legal system as "common law" except for the "civil law" of Quebec is to ignore the profound effect of statutes and regulations in both systems. And while there is diversity in provincial laws, there are also unifying influences, including a court hierarchy with the Supreme Court of Canada at its apex and uniform model legislation available for adoption by provinces, through the work of the Uniform Law Conference of Canada.[23]

Having surveyed Canada's constitutional framework and legal systems, it is now appropriate to turn to the questions posed. The focus is chiefly on federal legislation, since only Parliament may legislate extraterritorially. The discussion is supplemented by an appended table that lists multilateral instruments to which Canada is a party, along with the associated domestic implementing legislation.

4 Questions Posed

4.1 *Trends in Attitude to the Extraterritorial Application of Legislation*

It has long been held that if Parliament wants to legislate extraterritorially, the intent to do so must be clearly expressed or implied as a matter of necessity from the legislation.[24] That presumption is codified in, e.g., s 6(2) (formerly

---

21 *Oceans Act*, SC 1996, c 31.

22 *Confederation Bridge Area Provincial (P.E.I.) Laws Application Regulations*, SOR/97-375 (applying all PEI laws, except the *Highway Traffic Act*, in the Confederation Bridge Area).

23 Uniform Law Conference of Canada, https://ulcc-chlc.ca/.

24 The "intention of Parliament" can be presumed, express or implied. See Elmer Driedger, *The Construction of Statutes*, 1st ed (Toronto: Butterworths, 1974) at 82 and 2d ed (Toronto:

s 5(2)) of Canada's *Criminal Code*,[25] which says that "[s]ubject to this Act or any other Act of Parliament, no person shall be convicted ... of an offence committed outside Canada." Indeed, this provision applies to most Canadian criminal offences. When extraterritoriality is intended, prescriptive language is usually carefully crafted.

Again, using criminal law as an example, the *Criminal Code* creates offences that both extend and limit their extraterritorial reach. For example, under s 7(1), with respect to a Canadian-registered aircraft in flight, or any aircraft in a flight terminating in Canada, everyone who "commits an act or omission in or outside Canada that if committed in Canada would be an [indictable offence] shall be deemed to have committed that act or omission in Canada."[26] That provision applied when a Boston-to-Paris flight was diverted to Newfoundland because of a passenger's behaviour on an American aircraft.[27] The jurisdiction is broad but well accepted, and it is suggested that Canada would generally not object to a foreign state exercising a similar jurisdiction if the passenger had been a Canadian and the flight had been diverted to that other state's territory. This jurisdiction can be contrasted with that in s 7(2) over offences relating to aircraft, international navigation facilities, and international airports, in which a person is deemed to have committed an offence in Canada only "if the person is, after the commission thereof, present in Canada."[28] That is also a well accepted jurisdiction, yet narrower in effect than s 7(1) by its requirement that the alleged offender is present in Canada after commission of the offence.[29]

Butterworths, 1984) at 106, cited in Ruth Sullivan, "Statutory Interpretation in a New Nutshell" (2003) 82 Can Bar Rev 51 at 54, note 8.

25 *Criminal Code*, RSC 1985, c C-46.

26 *Ibid*, s 7(1).

27 *R v Minot*, 2011 NLCA 7. The passenger, a French citizen, was apprehended at the airport and charged with mischief by interfering with the property of American Airlines and engaging in behaviour involving electronic equipment that endangered an aircraft's safety or security. Though the flight was US-bound, the Court was satisfied that it "terminated" at Gander, Newfoundland for the purposes of s 7(1): see paras 63–65 of the decision. The case is notable for the fact that apart from a fine, a sentence of time served awaiting trial, and a probation order, the Court also imposed a stand-alone $22,000 restitution order in favour of American Airlines for refuelling and other costs associated with the flight diversion and landing.

28 *Criminal Code*, *supra* note 25, s 7(1).

29 For more information on the jurisdiction discussed in this paragraph, see the appended table, under the heading entitled "Offences Relating to Aviation, Aircraft and International Airports."

Another example of intentional drafting is the offence of bigamy in s 290 of the *Criminal Code*:

> 290 (1) Every one commits bigamy who
> (a) in Canada,
> (i) being married, goes through a form of marriage with another person,
> (ii) knowing that another person is married, goes through a form of marriage with that person, or
> (iii) on the same day or simultaneously, goes through a form of marriage with more than one person; or
> (b) being a Canadian citizen resident in Canada leaves Canada with intent to do anything mentioned in subparagraphs (a)(I) to (III) and, pursuant thereto, does outside Canada anything mentioned in those subparagraphs in circumstances mentioned therein.

This offence structure can be traced back to the 1800s,[30] showing that bigamy was then viewed, and has long been viewed, as a transnational problem, with the need to extend territorial jurisdiction accordingly. The offence is jurisdictionally bifurcated, the first part defining activities that constitute bigamy if committed in Canada; the second saying that they do so if committed outside Canada in certain circumstances. The second part is a jurisdiction based on nationality (also called "active personality"), but tightly drawn in the elements comprising both *actus reus* and *mens rea*. That is, it operates: (i) only on Canadian citizens (i.e., not on permanent residents or other Canadian nationals), (ii) who are resident in Canada, then (iii) leave Canada, (iv) with the intent to commit bigamy, and (v) succeed in doing so.[31]

Even with such attempts at careful legislative language, courts still often must interpret whether legislation is intended to have extraterritorial reach

30 *An Act respecting Offences relating to the Law of Marriage*, RSC 1886, c 161, s 4. Although the offence is now in the *Criminal Code* rather than its own statute, its bifurcated structure has stayed the same: para (b), previously referring to British subjects resident in Canada, was later amended to refer to Canadian citizens resident in Canada.

31 Because the offence in s 290(1)(b) starts in Canada with the intent requirement and is completed elsewhere with the prohibited marriage, it may be best described as "subjective territoriality": see note 38 and accompanying text, *infra*. Some say the bigamy offence is not relevant to a discussion of extraterritoriality at all: see Steve Coughlan *et al*, *Global Reach, Local Grasp: Constructing Extraterritorial Jurisdiction in the Age of Globalization* (Ottawa: Law Commission of Canada, 2006) at 33 and Currie & Rikhof, *infra* note 38, pp. 507–08.

and, if so, how much. Canadian courts, and particularly the Supreme Court of Canada, have played an important role in this exercise.

The landmark case is the Supreme Court's 1985 decision in *Libman v The Queen*.[32] Libman was charged with fraud and conspiracy to commit fraud. The charges stemmed from a "boiler room" operation in which sales personnel in Toronto phoned U.S. residents to sell them shares in companies based in Costa Rica. The shares were worthless. The purchasers were told to send money to offices in Panama and Costa Rica, with evidence suggesting that Libman met associates there and had the proceeds sent to the Toronto office. Libman sought to have his committal for trial quashed on the basis that the offences occurred outside Canada. The relevant offence provisions at the time contained no extraterritorial language, and if the offences had occurred outside of Canada, Canadian courts would have lacked jurisdiction.

Justice Gérard La Forest gave the Court's judgment. After reviewing the case law, La Forest J explained that Canada had previously dealt with transnational crimes "in a confusing fashion."[33] In response, he adopted a two-part test. First, a significant portion of the facts constituting the offence must have taken place in Canada, such as to create a "real and substantial link" to Canada; second, the assumption of judicial jurisdiction based on those facts should not offend international comity.[34] Though La Forest J did not elaborate on the comity point, an example of judicial self-restraint might arise where another state has a better claim to assert jurisdiction on a basis recognized in international law. In *Libman*, everything that made the operation function – "the directing minds, the boiler room"[35] – took place in Toronto, thus creating the necessary links, and the fact that this approach "would catch cases where the victims of the scheme were harmed outside the country [made] no difference."[36] Justice La Forest also concluded that no aspect of international comity would preclude Canada from prosecuting the offences; indeed, he suggested that comity *required* it to prosecute.[37]

Libman reoriented Canada's complicated history of handling cases with extraterritorial elements, and the tests's open-ended nature has allowed judges to interpret each case based on the links or connections unique to that case. It bears emphasizing that the *Libman* Court characterized the matter as one of domestic jurisdiction, albeit with foreign elements. Academics have since coined the term "qualified" or "extended" territoriality. Qualified territoriality,

32 *Libman v The Queen* [1985] 2 SCR 178.
33 *Ibid*, para 10.
34 *Ibid*, particularly at paras 71–74.
35 *Ibid*, para 72.
36 *Ibid*.
37 *Ibid* at para 77.

the term adopted here, refers to jurisdiction over acts that take place only partly in a state's territory or take place elsewhere but have significant connections to, or effects in, the state's territory – rather than full extraterritorial jurisdiction.[38]

It is hard to overstate *Libman*'s influence, though this has occurred chiefly in the test's first step. Beyond its original criminal law context, the *Libman* test has become an accepted rationale for deciding when to assert various forms of jurisdiction. Thus in Canadian private international law, for example, a court, even if it lacks one of the traditional grounds of jurisdiction such as agreement or attornment, may assume jurisdiction over a foreign defendant or a domestic proceeding with foreign elements if there is a "real and substantial connection" between the forum and the facts on which the proceeding is based.[39] A 2017 study[40] concluded that although the *Libman* test was developed for transnational criminal offences, it was more often applied in other contexts, including breaches of Canadian probation orders outside Canada;[41]

38 On the use of the term "qualified territoriality," see Robert J Currie and Joseph Rikhof, *International & Transnational Criminal Law*, 3d ed (Toronto: Irwin Law, 2020), pp. 65–67 (further subdividing qualified territoriality into *subjective territoriality*, whereby a state asserts jurisdiction over an offence that begins in its jurisdiction but is completed outside it and *objective territoriality*, whereby a state asserts jurisdiction over an offence completed within its territory, even if commenced outside it). *Libman* illustrates subjective territoriality. On this definition, the bigamy offence in s 290(1) of the *Criminal Code*, discussed above, may be understood as a form of subjective territoriality rather than full extraterritoriality. On the use of "extended territoriality" to mean the same as qualified territoriality, see Steve Coughlan *et al*, *Law Beyond Borders: Extraterritorial Jurisdiction in an Age of Globalization* (Toronto: Irwin Law, 2014), c 4: "Extended Territoriality versus Extraterritoriality: A Key Jurisdictional Distinction" (pp. 80–116).

39 The leading case is *Morguard Investments Ltd v De Savoye*, [1990] 3 SCR 1077, also a decision of La Forest J. In response to *Morguard* and later case law, the Uniform Law Conference of Canada (ULCC) aimed to codify that law through the *Court Jurisdiction and Proceedings Transfer Act* (CJPTA). Apart from traditional bases for judicial jurisdiction (called "territorial competence" in the statute), the CJPTA allows for jurisdiction over a person based on "a real and substantial connection between the enacting province … and the facts on which the proceeding against that person is based." This is followed by a list of presumed real and substantial connections, such as a tort committed in the province or contractual obligations to be substantially performed in the province. The CJPTA is in force in British Columbia, Saskatchewan, Nova Scotia and Yukon. In 2021, the ULCC adopted an updated version: See *Uniform Court Jurisdiction and Proceedings Transfer Act (2021)*: https://bit.ly/32tbAhB. As of the date of this report, no Canadian province had yet modified its own legislation in accordance with the updated Uniform CJPTA.

40 Lee-Ann Conrod, "A Closer Look at Libman's Impact on Transnational Crime Cases" 2017 CanLIIDocs 3952: https://www.canlii.org/en/commentary/doc/2017CanLIIDocs3952.

41 *Ibid*, s 8.1, citing *R v Greco* (2001), 159 CCC (3d) 146 (Ont CA), leave to appeal to SCC ref'd (2001), 162 CCC (3d) vi; *R v Stanny*, 2008 ABQB 746; and *R v Rattray*, 2008 ONCA 74.

securities cases;[42] regulatory offences;[43] civil cases;[44] and interprovincial cases.[45]

---

42 Conrod, *ibid*, s 8.1.1, citing *Ontario (Securities Commission) v DaSilva*, 2017 ONSC 4576; *R v Lowman*, 2017 ONCJ 433; *McCabe v British Columbia (Securities Commission)*, 2016 BCCA 7, [2016] 394 DLR (4th) 197; *Doulis (Re) (Ontario Securities Commission)*, [2014] 37 OSCB 8911, 2014 LNONOSC 2043; *Torudag v British Columbia (Securities Commission)*, 2011 BCCA 458, [2011] 343 DLR (4th) 743; *Goldpoint Resources Corp (Re)*, 2011 ONSEC 12 (CanLII), 34 OSCB 5478, 2011 LNONOSC 364; *Lehman Cohort Global Group Inc (Re)*, 2010 LNONOSC 544, 33 OSCB 7041; *Al-tar Energy Corp (Re)*, 2010 ONSEC 11 (CanLII), 2010 LNONOSC 406, 33 OSCB 5535; *Ontario (Securities Commission) v 1367682 Ontario Ltd (cob as De Freitas & Associates)*, 167 ACWS (3d) 825 (ONCJ). These cases typically deal with issuance of, or trading in, securities outside the province. For example, in *Ontario Securities Commission v DaSilva*, the appellants argued that a no-trade order was made outside the Commission's jurisdiction because it concerned trading securities outside Ontario. The Court found a real and substantial connection between Ontario and the trading activities based on the defendants' residence, place for conducting trades, and place where profits were realized (all pointing to Ontario).

43 Conrod, *ibid*, note 216, citing *R v The Stolt Castle*, [1994] 25 WCB (2d) 20 (ONCA) (Liberian ship charged with failing to report to the Canadian Coast Guard Traffic Centre at call-in points on the St. Claire River contrary to s 6 of the *St Clair and Detroit River Navigation Safety Regulations*, SOR/84-335; phrase "every ship" in s 6 held to apply to all ships in the river system covered by the regulations, including a foreign ship when in American waters); and *Pigeon v Ontario (Ministry of Natural Resources)*, 2014 ONSC 236, [2014] 111 WCB (2d) 889 (holding, under Ontario regulation prohibiting the possession of wildlife killed or captured contrary to the laws of another jurisdiction, that Ontario courts had jurisdiction to decide whether two musk oxen and a wood bison were killed in Nunavut or the Northwest Territories – thus applying *Libman* in a federal-provincial context). Also notable, though not cited by Conrod, is *R v Stucky*, 2009 ONCA 151, leave to appeal to SCC granted but appeal abandoned, 2009 CanLII 33009 (SCC), dealing with a regulatory offence under the *Competition Act*, *infra* note 66. Stucky had carried out a direct mail business that sold lottery tickets and merchandise to people outside Canada. He was charged under s 52 of the *Competition Act* with making misleading representations to "the public." Though initially acquitted based on the trial judge's conclusion that the phrase meant "the Canadian public," the Ontario Court of Appeal reversed. The Court found that at the time of the offence, Stucky was in Canada, initiated the alleged misrepresentations in Canada, and received his profits there, thus establishing a"real and substantial connection" to Canada, even if "the public" to whom the representations were made was outside Canada.

44 Conrod, *ibid*, note 217, citing *Overland Custom Coach Inc v Thor Industries Inc* (1999), 46 OR (3d) 788 (SCJ) (referencing adoption of the *Libman* reasoning in *Morguard*, *supra* note 39 and upholding service *ex juris* of a statement of claim); *Vitapharm Canada Ltd v F Hoffmann-La Roche Ltd*, [2002] 20 CPC (5th) 351 (Ont SCJ) (upholding service *ex juris* of a statement of claim in a price-fixing case); *Christensen v Proprietary Industries Inc*, 2002 ABQB 97, [2002] 309 AR 201 (noting, at para 64, that "the source law for finding that events are juridically connected to more than one place is considerably older than even the century[-]old cases mentioned in *Libman*, what with legal fictions being deployed for centuries to establish territorial jurisdiction"); and *Mannix Resources Inc (Trustee of) v Mondial Corp*, 2006 BCSC 175 (dismissing jurisdictional challenge in a price-fixing case).

45 Conrod, *ibid*, note 218, citing *Morguard*, *supra* note 39 (the most frequently cited decision that cites *Libman*); *R v Doer* (1999) 133 Man R (2d) 161 (QB) (accused charged with selling Ontario-marked cigarettes to Manitoba consumers contrary to s 97.1 of the *Excise*

4.2 *Influence of Multilateral or Regional Instruments*

Canada is signatory to treaties, conventions and other instruments that permit, or even require, contracting states to implement legislation with extraterritorial reach, especially in criminal law. Indeed, most of the growth in Canada's assertion of extraterritoriality has arisen from its ratification of international conventions, particularly those aimed at suppressing transnational crime. This "suppression legislation" is summarized in the table appended to this report. It sets out the major multilateral instruments, associated implementing statutes,[46] and types of jurisdiction exercised, together with commentary. The treaties illustrate the full range of possible jurisdictions: territorial; active/nationality (including, in some cases, an expansive definition of nationality, such as any persons employed by Canada in a military capacity); passive personality; protective; and universal custodial.[47] The examples in the appended table are not exhaustive, but show that Canada has a long history of involvement in international agreements.

4.3 *Role of International Law in Defining the Geographic Scope of Legislation*

In *R v Hape*,[48] the Supreme Court of Canada addressed the effect of international law on actions that a state may legitimately take outside its territory. The

Tax Act, RSC 1985, c E-15; in relation to a direct mail business in which there were advertisements in Winnipeg, cigarettes ordered from Winnipeg, money sent from Winnipeg, and cigarettes delivered there, a substantial link to Manitoba was established and the "sale" could be said to have occurred in Manitoba); and *R v Roberge*, 2003 SKPC 74, (2003), 233 Sask R 65 (consideration of s 478(1) of the *Criminal Code*, stipulating that a province shall not try an offence committed entirely in another province, except where the offence takes place within 500 meters of a territorial boundary; on applying *Libman*, Court finding a sufficient factual connection between two related impaired driving charges, one in Alberta and the other across the border in Saskatchewan, that they should have been tried together on the facts of the case).

46 For an international treaty to have direct effect in Canada, it must be incorporated into law through a statute, though the treaty's *values* may bear on statutory interpretation or judicial review. See *Baker v Canada (Minister of Citizenship and Immigration)*, [1999] 2 SCR 817 at paras 69–71. This requirement also applies to instruments relevant to provincial legislative jurisdiction, pursuant to the division of powers. Parliament has no special jurisdiction to implement an international instrument if the field covered is under provincial legislative jurisdiction. See AG *Canada v* AG *Ontario (Labour Conventions)* [1937] AC 326 (PC).

47 For a summary and examples of these types of jurisdiction in international law, see Am. Soc'y Int'l L., "Jurisdictional, Preliminary, and Procedural Concerns," in *Benchbook on International Law* § II.A (Diane Marie Amann ed., 2014) www.asil.org/benchbook/jurisdiction.pdf, pp. A-2–A.4.

48 *R v Hape*, 2007 SCC 26.

case arose from an investigation of the accused, a Canadian businessman, for suspected money laundering in the Turks and Caicos Islands. Working under the supervision and with the consent of the Superintendent of the Turks and Caicos Police Force, Canadian police officers had searched Hape's office and obtained evidence in what Hape maintained was a violation of his right to be free from unreasonable search and seizure under s 8 of the *Canadian Charter of Rights and Freedoms*. The case thus deals with *investigative* jurisdiction (a type of enforcement jurisdiction) rather than prescriptive jurisdiction, but the Court's comments on the role of international law apply beyond that context. On a challenge to admissibility of the evidence, the evidence was admitted and Hape was convicted of money laundering, a result upheld at the Ontario Court of Appeal and the Supreme Court of Canada. Justice LeBel, writing the main judgment of the Supreme Court, held that the *Charter* does not generally apply to searches and seizures in other countries, but rather, the applicable law is that of the state in which the activities occur, subject to the *Charter*'s fair trial safeguards and any limits on comity that may prevent Canadian officers from participating in activities that, though legal in another state, would cause Canada to violate its international human rights obligations.[49]

Justice LeBel explained and confirmed a longstanding presumption of conformity with international law as an interpretive principle of domestic law.[50] The presumption, which is rebuttable, has two aspects. First, Canada is presumed to act in compliance with its obligations as a signatory of international treaties and as a member of the international community. In deciding between possible interpretations, courts will aim to avoid one that would place Canada in breach of those obligations. Second, enactments are presumed to comply with the values and principles of customary and conventional international law. They form part of the context in which statutes are enacted, and courts will therefore prefer a construction that reflects them. Under the principle of Parliamentary sovereignty, though, the presumption is rebuttable: courts *must* give effect to a statute that demonstrates an unequivocal intent to depart from or default on an international obligation.[51]

---

49 *Ibid* at para 90.

50 *Ibid* at para 53 (including the rest of this paragraph).

51 In the 1970s, Canada enacted the *Arctic Waters Pollution Prevention Act*, RSC 1985, c A-12, which asserted regulatory powers over much of the Arctic seas in relation to pollution of those areas. Many states regarded this as breaching the international law of the sea at the time. Canada responded by asserting that the area's environmental fragility required special laws and jurisdiction. This argument succeeded at the UN Conference on the Law of the Sea, with article 234 of the *United Nations Convention on the Law of the Sea* ("Ice-covered areas") upholding Canada's position. See Coughlan *et al*, *supra* note 31, p. 16.

In *Hape*, the Canadian officers were government actors to whom, *prima facie*, the *Charter* would apply, but on the facts it was unreasonable to conclude that Turks and Caicos consented to Canadian extraterritorial enforcement jurisdiction. The trial court found that Turks and Caicos officers always controlled the investigation, making it known to Canadian officers that, at each step, the activities were being carried out pursuant to their authority alone. And because the Canadian officers had a genuine and reasonable belief that they were complying with Turks and Caicos law, there was no basis for claiming that admitting the evidence would cause trial unfairness.[52]

4.4 *Role of International Comity in Defining the Geographic Scope of Legislation*

Comity serves as an interpretive principle, a point reinforced by *Hape*.[53] For offences, the two-step *Libman* test applies. After a court satisfies itself that there is a real and substantial connection between Canada and the facts, the court must also be satisfied that the assumption of judicial jurisdiction based on those facts should not offend international comity.

Given the expansive view of comity advanced in *Libman* (recall that the Court thought that comity considerations *supported*, rather than inhibited, prosecution in Canada), this step is not hard to satisfy. In practice, it is rare, if not unheard of, for prescriptive jurisdiction to pass muster under the first step but fail at the second. Part of the reason is prosecutorial cross-border cooperation: for transnational offences, Canadian authorities may decide not to pursue charges if they are satisfied that another jurisdiction has a stronger connection to the offence and the prosecution will proceed there.[54] A situation could conceivably arise in which another state wished to prosecute but Canada did not – evidenced, perhaps, by a formal diplomatic note or an outstanding extradition request. But in such a situation, Canadian authorities would more likely address it through diplomatic negotiation rather than a contested court case.[55] Thus comity acts as a backdrop to the drafting, administration and interpretation of legislation, but rarely as a show-stopper. That said, comity is not a basis for condoning another state's breach of international law; "[i]ndeed, the need to uphold international law may trump the principle of comity."[56]

---

52 *Ibid* at paras 103–121.

53 *Ibid* at paras 47–52.

54 See the discussion in Currie & Rikhof, *supra* note 38, pp. 490–93.

55 See Coughlan *et al*, *supra* note 38, p. 91.

56 *R v Hape*, *supra* note 48 at 51 (citing *Abbasi v Secretary of State for Foreign and Commonwealth Affairs* [2002] EWCA Civ 1598, regarding a British national captured by U.S. forces in Afghanistan and detained in Guantanamo Bay without access to a lawyer or a court).

Comity is also sometimes explicitly referenced in legislation. An example can be found in s 76(1) of the *Canada Transportation Act*,[57] pursuant to which the Minister of Transport may exercise discretion over the Canadian Transportation Agency's handling of international service (defined in s 55(1) as "an air service between Canada and a point in the territory of another country") if necessary or advisable in the interest of "international comity or reciprocity," the safety or security of international civil aviation, relevant international agreements, or any other matters of public interest concerning civil aviation.

Comity considerations are also implicit in offences that require consent of the Attorney General of Canada to prosecute. These include all the offences in s 7 of the *Criminal Code* where the accused is not a Canadian citizen.[58] In Canada, the Attorney General is also the Minister of Justice and thus a Cabinet member, so the consent provisions give the federal executive a way to consider international implications of prosecuting a person who is not a Canadian citizen for an offence committed outside Canada.[59]

4.5 *Reasonableness in the Extraterritorial Application of Statutes and Regulations*

The approach generally followed by Canadian courts, as reflected in *Libman* and later case law, is tantamount to a reasonableness test. This approach can be seen in the *Hape* Court's conclusion that it would be unreasonable to hold, on the facts of the case, that Turks and Caicos had consented to Canadian extraterritorial *enforcement* jurisdiction. This approach is also reflected in how courts approach prescriptive jurisdiction.

However, when the *Libman* test is answered affirmatively, it means that Canada has *territorial* jurisdiction in the extended or qualified sense, "with all of

57 *Canada Transportation Act*, SC 1996, c 10.

58 *Criminal Code*, s 7(7); see also, e.g., s 7(4.3) (proceedings with respect to an act or omission deemed to have been committed in Canada under s 7(4.1) (sexual offences against children by Canadian citizens or permanent residents) may only be instituted with the Attorney General's consent.

59 See *R v Patel*, 2016 ONCJ 172 at para 19 (court lacking jurisdiction to proceed with a charge under s 7(7(1)(b) of the *Criminal Code* (offence taking place on a flight) because the accused, though a permanent resident, was not a Canadian citizen, and because the consent of the Attorney General had not been sought within the 8-day period provided for in s 7(7)).

the international law solidity that attaches to territorial claims."[60] In contrast, *Libman* should *not* apply when full extraterritorial jurisdiction is asserted. Courts sometimes fail to appreciate this, but the point was noted in *R v Klassen*.[61] The accused was charged with sexual offences against children that occurred over 15 years in Colombia, Cambodia, and the Philippines. Under s 7(4.1) of the *Criminal Code*, the offences were deemed to have been committed in Canada because Klassen was a Canadian citizen – in other words, this was a case of full extraterritorial prescriptive jurisdiction based on the nationality principle. The accused contended that the lack of a real and substantial link between Canada and the facts of his case, along with a correlative absence of support in international law for extraterritorial prescriptive jurisdiction, meant that s 7(4.1) was outside Parliament's authority. The Court disagreed, finding *Libman* distinguishable from cases not relying on the territorial principle to ground jurisdiction,[62] and noted that international law "recognizes nationality or permanent residence as a foundation for prescriptive or adjudicative jurisdiction."[63] The Court articulated a policy rationale for its conclusions; namely, that "[t]he reduced opportunity that states with territorial jurisdiction have to identify, investigate or apprehend those who are only transient within their borders inhibits the likelihood of successful investigation or prosecution" and without extraterritorial laws, "Canada would become a safer harbour for those who engage in the economic or sexual exploitation of children."[64]

4.6 *Statutes or Regulations Applying to Wholly Foreign Conduct on the Basis of Active Nationality, Passive Personality, or Universal Jurisdiction*

Whereas the appended table can be characterized as dealing with "suppression legislation" (legislation pursuant to multilateral instruments aimed at suppressing transnational crime), there is also "sanctions legislation." This is legislation pursuant to resolutions that sanction other states or their nationals. Under these laws, individuals and businesses in Canada as well as Canadian citizens and Canadian-incorporated businesses operating outside Canada are prohibited in their dealings with designated persons, groups or entities in

60 Currie & Rikhof, *supra* note 38, p. 493.

61 *R v Klassen*, 2008 BCSC 1762.

62 *Ibid* at paras 71–73.

63 *Ibid* at para 86.

64 *Ibid* at para 95.

targeted sectors of specified foreign jurisdictions. The legislation also imposes screening, reporting, and asset-freeze obligations on Canadian financial institutions. The laws are based on UN resolutions and other measures that Canada, alone or in cooperation with its international partners, has imposed on foreign jurisdictions or groups.[65]

4.7 *Statutes or Regulations Applying to Activity Occurring Partly in Another Country on the Basis of Local Conduct* (*Territorial Links*)

Several examples have been provided above, but for the purposes of this question, examples are categorized in terms of jurisdiction over subject matter, over persons of any nationality where there is some link to Canada, and over Canadian officials abroad.

Competition law provides examples of actual or potential extraterritorial jurisdiction over subject matter. Part VI of the *Competition Act*[66] deals with competition offences, the main provision being s 45, which makes it an offence for any person to conspire to fix prices, allocate sales, or limit the supply of a product, subject to any defences or exceptions. Like U.S. competition law, the *Competition Act* also provides the basis for a civil action for damages arising from price-fixing.[67] Section 46(1) creates a separate offence for corporations who follow foreign directives to implement a price-fixing agreement entered into outside Canada:

> 46 (1) Any corporation, wherever incorporated, that carries on business in Canada and that implements, in whole or in part in Canada, a directive, instruction, intimation of policy or other communication to the corporation or any person from a person in a country other than Canada who is

---

65 See *Criminal Code*, RSC 1985, c C-46, Part II.1 (Terrorism) and *Regulations Establishing a List of Entities*, SOR/2002-284 (protective principle; nationality-based, but targeted at terrorist groups, wherever located); *United Nations Act*, RSC 1985, c U-2 and extensive associated regulations (protective principle; nationality-based); *Special Economic Measures Act*, SC 1992, c 17 and extensive associated regulations (protective principle; nationality-based, but targeted at foreign states or their nationals); *Freezing Assets of Corrupt Foreign Officials Act*, SC 2011, c 10 (comity-based; nationality-based); and *Justice for Victims of Corrupt Foreign Officials Act* (*Sergei Magnitsky Law*), SC 2017, c 2 (comity-based; nationality-based). The Canadian government maintains a list of current sanctions that can be found on the website of Global Affairs Canada: https://www.international.gc.ca/.

66 *Competition Act*, RSC 1985, c C-34.

67 *Ibid*, s 36.

> in a position to direct or influence the policies of the corporation, which communication is for the purpose of giving effect to a conspiracy, combination, agreement or arrangement entered into outside Canada that, if entered into in Canada, would have been in contravention of section 45, is, whether or not any director or officer of the corporation in Canada has knowledge of the conspiracy, combination, agreement or arrangement, guilty of an indictable offence and liable on conviction to a fine in the discretion of the court.

Section 46 has some built-in jurisdictional limitations. One is that it applies only to corporations (albeit "wherever incorporated"), unlike s 45, which applies to "every person." Another is that it applies only to those corporations that carry on business in Canada, though that requirement has a relatively low evidentiary threshold.[68]

Other parts of the *Competition Act* may also apply extraterritorially, but have links to Canada that, in theory or practice, limit their application to a form of qualified territoriality. For example, under Part IX, dealing with notifiable transactions, participants to a proposed merger must notify the Commissioner of Competition if the merger meets certain criteria. The criteria link the notification requirement to Canada in what amounts to the test for a "real and substantial connection." Under s 109(1), the requirement applies only if the parties to a transaction, together with their affiliates, have assets in Canada over $400 million, calculated as prescribed, or have gross revenues from sales "in, from or into Canada" over $400 million, calculated for such an annual period and in such a manner as prescribed. Section 110 deals with notification requirements for share acquisitions, with a triggering amount of $70 million for assets or sales in the case of an operating business (defined in s 108(1) as a "business undertaking in Canada to which employees employed in connection with the undertaking ordinarily report for work"), with a formula for adjusting the trigger each year after the relevant subsection came into force.[69] Thus, for example, if a U.S. company proposes to buy another U.S. company that owns a Canadian

68 See *Shah v LG Chem, Ltd*, 2015 ONSC 2628 (in multi-defendant class action based on a conspiracy to fix prices of lithium-ion batteries, court granting a jurisdictional challenge to dismiss the action against two Japanese defendants because the plaintiffs tendered no evidence, or insufficient evidence, to counter the evidence of the moving defendants that they did not carry on business in Canada).

69 *Competition Act*, *supra* note 66, ss 7–8.

operating business, both buyer and seller may have to notify the Commissioner even if the transaction takes place entirely in the United States – that is, if both parties meet the size criteria in s 109(1) and if the Canadian affiliate of the target company has assets or sales exceeding the $70 million threshold, as adjusted annually.[70] The justification for the extraterritorial application is that the Canadian affiliate's decisions may be affected by the conduct of the U.S. companies after the transaction.

An example of jurisdiction over extraterritorial persons of any nationality can be found in s 477.1 of the *Criminal Code*, which sets out special maritime jurisdictions for offences outside Canada. These include offences that occur in the exclusive economic zone or the continental shelf of Canada, as well as offences on board Canadian ships at sea, whether committed by a Canadian or a foreign national. Also found in this section is the jurisdiction based on the doctrine that allows a coastal state to pursue onto the high seas any vessel that has apparently violated its laws while within its waters.[71]

Jurisdiction also exists over Canadian officials abroad. For example, Canadian Forces personnel may be charged with most Canadian offences and tried under the *Code of Service Discipline*, whether the alleged offence was committed inside or outside Canada.[72] This jurisdiction extends to dependents and persons accompanying such personnel.[73] In effect, the Canadian military carry Canadian criminal law with them wherever they go. The extraterritorial jurisdiction is broad but linked to Canada since the persons subject to it are employed by, or associated with, the Canadian Forces.

4.8 *To the Extent That Legislation Applies to Foreign Conduct on the Basis of the Actor's Nationality, How Is the Question of Corporate Nationality Addressed?*

Canadian law generally respects the principle of separate corporate personality; it also aligns with the view in public international law that a corporation's nationality can generally be based simply on the state of incorporation or the

70 The example comes from Thanh Phan, "The Legality of Extraterritorial Application of Competition Law and the Need to Adopt a Unified Approach" (2016) 77 Louisiana L Rev 425, 446, though corrected for the threshold figure of $700 million stated there.

71 See *R v Kirchhoff*, 1995 CanLII 16936 (NB QB) (upholding jurisdiction based on "hot pursuit," a concept recognized in international law and codified in the *Criminal Code*, s 477.1(d)).

72 *National Defence Act*, RSC 1985, c N-5 s 67.

73 *Ibid*, s 61(2).

state of the corporation's head office.[74] There are exceptions to the separate corporate personality principle. As noted above, the notification requirement for a merger transaction applies only if the parties, "together with their affiliates," have Canadian assets exceeding $400 million. In other words, there are instances when competition law essentially treats a corporation and its affiliates as a single enterprise. Also, under the *Investment Canada Act*[75] (replacing the *Foreign Investment Review Act*[76]), there are acquisition-of-control rules aimed at non-Canadians seeking to acquire control of a Canadian business. They go beyond simply acquiring voting shares of a Canadian corporation and include, for example, acquiring voting interests in an entity that is carrying on the Canadian business or "controls, directly or indirectly another entity carrying on the Canadian business."[77] Such legislation has been used to thwart foreign mergers that would affect control over Canadian companies; however, despite valiant attempts by counsel at characterizing the legislation as an impermissible regulation of extraterritorial conduct, the courts have construed it as a valid exercise of territorial jurisdiction – later writers would call it "extended" or "qualified" territoriality – whose reach is limited by the fact that it applies only to the acquisition of control of a business carried on in Canada.[78]

4.9 *Has Your Country Enacted Any "Blocking Statutes" Intended to Limit the Effects of Extraterritorial Practices by Other States?*

Yes, both federally and provincially, as discussed below.

74 See *Case Concerning the Barcelona Traction, Light and Power Company, Limited* (*Belgium v Spain*), [1970] ICJ Rep 3 (holding that the national state of the company, in that case Canada, was the only state authorized to make a claim for diplomatic protection of the company). For the earlier Canadian proceedings relating to this case, see *National Trust Company Limited v Ebro Irrigation and Power Company Limited*, [1954] OR 463 (SC).

75 *Investment Canada Act*, RSC 1985, c 28 (1st Supp).

76 *Foreign Investment Review Act*, SC 1973–74, c 46.

77 *Investment Canada Act*, *supra* note 75, s 28(1)(b).

78 See *Dow Jones & Company Inc v Canada* (*Attorney General*), [1981] 1 FC 428, 113 DLR (3d) 395, aff'd [1982] 1 FC 67 (CA), 122 DLR (3d) 731, leave to appeal to SCC ref'd (5 November 1981), [1981] 1 SCR viii; *Fallbridge Holdings Ltd v Canada* (*Minister of Industry, Trade and Commerce*) (1979), 7 BLR 275 (Fed TD), aff'd (1986), 63 NR 17, 31 BLR 57 (FCA), leave to appeal to SCC ref'd (22 May 1986), [1986] 1 SCR viii, 69 NR 76 n. For a discussion of these cases, see William C Graham, "Dispute Resolution in the Canada-United States Free Trade Agreement: One Element of a Complex Relationship" (1992) 37 McGill LJ 544.

4.9.1 Federal Legislation

The most notable federal legislation is the *Foreign Extraterritorial Measures Act* (FEMA),[79] enacted in 1984[80] in response to the extraterritorial reach – both legislative and judicial – of other states, particularly the United States, and modelled in part on laws enacted or contemplated elsewhere at the time, including the United Kingdom's *Protection of Trading Interests Act 1980*.[81] Like its two provincial counterparts (discussed in the next section), the statute's unabashed purpose is to hinder extraterritorial prosecutions or litigation by refusing to recognize a foreign jurisdiction's laws or orders where the Canadian government concludes that those laws or orders are unjustifiably prejudicial to Canadian international trade interests.[82] Unlike its provincial counterparts, though, the statute is drafted not to create a blanket prohibition on document disclosure of business records outside of a province, but to give the Canadian government a high degree of discretion in tailoring orders to specific sets of circumstances.

The background to FEMA is discussed elsewhere;[83] briefly, though, irritants that led to its passage included antitrust litigation such as that by Westinghouse Electric Corporation against foreign corporations participating in a government-sponsored uranium cartel,[84] regulations relating to insider

---

79 *Foreign Extraterritorial Measures Act*, RSC 1985, c F-29.

80 SC 1984, c 49 (by s 11, in force 14 February 1985). The act was originally introduced as Bill C-41 on 11 July 1980 (32nd Parliament, 1st Session) and titled the *Foreign Proceedings and Judgments Act*.

81 Protection of Trading Interests Act 1980 (UK), c 11.

82 Parliament's authority to regulate this area–that is, international or interprovincial trade and commerce–comes from s 91(2) of the *Constitution Act, 1867* (UK), 30 & 31 Vict, c 3, s 132, rep'd in RSC 1985, Appendix II, No 5.

83 See Jean-Gabriel Castel, "The Extraterritorial Effects of Antitrust Laws" in (1983) 179:1 *Recueil Des Cours–Collected Courses of the Hague Academy of International Law* 9 (The Hague: Martinus Nijhoff, 1984); William C Graham, "The Foreign Extraterritorial Measures Act" (1986) 11:4 Canadian Journal of Business Law 410; and Diane Wood, "Extraterritorial Enforcement of Regulatory Laws" in (2019) 401 *Recueil Des Cours–Collected Courses of the Hague Academy of International Law* 9 (Leiden/Boston: Brill | Nijhoff, 2019), pp. 57–63 (antitrust/competition law), 63–72 (securities law), and 72–78 (export controls).

84 For a discussion, see Graham, *ibid*, pp. 416–17; Anthony J Parisi, "The Great Uranium Flap" (9 July 1978) *The New York Times* F1: https://www.nytimes.com/1978/07/09/archives/the-great-uranium-flap-whats-at-stake.html and *Gulf Oil Corporation v Gulf Canada Ltd*, [1980] 2 SCR 39. This litigation involved the *Uranium Information Security Regulations*, originally enacted as PC 1976–2368, SOR/76-644 and replaced by an amended version, PC 1977–2923, SOR/77-836 and included in the *Consolidated Regulations of Canada*: CRC, v III, c 366, p 2347.

trading,[85] export controls,[86] and judicial processes such as subpoenas for production of documents.[87] Later amendments responded to the *Cuban Liberty and Democratic Solidarity* (LIBERTAD) *Act of 1996*, or *Helms-Burton Act*, which extended existing extraterritorial application of US law in relation to the economic embargo of Cuba.[88]

FEMA has five key elements.

First, it allows the Attorney General of Canada (AGC)[89] to respond to a foreign tribunal's exercise of jurisdiction or powers that have adversely affected or are likely to adversely affect "significant Canadian interests in relation to

---

85 See Graham, *ibid* at 415–416.

86 See Graham, *ibid* at 413.

87 See Graham, *ibid* at 414–415 and *United States of America v The Bank of Nova Scotia*, 691 F (2d) 1384 (11th Cir 1982), *cert denied* 469 U.S. 1106 (Canadian bank held in civil contempt and liable to pay $1,825,000 fine to force compliance with grand jury subpoena *duces tecum* for disclosure of narcotics investigation suspects' bank records held by Grand Cayman Islands and Bahamian branches of the bank).

88 *Cuban Liberty and Democratic Solidarity (Libertad) Act of 1996 (Helms–Burton Act)*, Pub L 104–114, 110 Stat 785, 22 USC c 69A (§§ 6021–6091). The *Helms-Burton Act* has four titles. The first codifies the US embargo on transactions with Cuba imposed in the 1960s. The second addresses measures to support a free and independent Cuba. The third and fourth are the most relevant to FEMA. Title III recognizes what the US deems the "wrongful confiscation or taking of property belonging to United States nationals by the Cuban Government, and the subsequent exploitation of this property at the expense of the rightful owner, undermines the comity of nations, the free flow of commerce, and economic development": § 6081. It grants US citizens whose properties were confiscated on or after 1 January 1959 the ability to sue for damages any individual or entity who "traffics" or has "trafficked" in that property if a claim has been certified by the Foreign Claims Settlement Commission: § 6082. Title IV grants authority to deny entry to any alien whom the Secretary of State determines has confiscated or trafficked in in Title III property. The Act has been strongly criticized outside the US, leading to claims that it is inconsistent with US obligations under the rules of the World Trade Organization. These claims led to application of Title III being suspended under the Clinton, Bush and Obama administrations. Under the first Trump administration, though, Secretary of State Mike Pompeo announced on 17 April 2019 that the government would allow suits under Title III: see Brian Hermon and BJ Siekierski, "The Impact of the Helms-Burton Act on Canadian Companies Operating in Cuba" (2 November 2020) *HillNotes*: https://bit.ly/3u61Zso. The U.S.-Cuba Trade and Economic Council, Inc., which casts itself as a provider of "nonpartisan commercial information … relating to the Republic of Cuba" maintains a blog on developments relating to the legislation, including Title III lawsuits and the the Biden administration's treatment of the *Helms-Burton Act*: see https://www.cubatrade.org/.

89 The Attorney General is the chief law officer of Canada and also generally serves as the Minister of Justice. See *Department of Justice Act*, RSC 1985, c. J-2, ss 2(2) and 5.

international trade or commerce…"[90] In particular, the AGC may prohibit or restrict: production, disclosure or identification of records in Canada or "in the possession or under the control of a Canadian citizen or a person resident in Canada;"[91] the doing of any act in Canada in relation to such records that "will, or is likely to, result in [their contents or information being] produced for a foreign tribunal;[92] and the giving, by a Canadian national, of such information to a foreign tribunal. The restrictions extend to receipt of such information by a Canadian tribunal.[93] Orders can be directed to a particular person or class of persons and can relate to a particular tribunal or class of tribunals, or to a particular record or class of records.[94] The orders are complemented by giving the AGC the power to seek warrants that allow for seizure of records for safekeeping.[95]

Second, it allows the AGC, with concurrence of the Minister of Foreign Affairs, to respond to a measure of a foreign state or tribunal "of a kind or in a manner that has adversely affected or is likely to adversely affect significant Canadian interests in relation to international trade or commerce …"[96] The ACG may require a person in Canada to give notice of such a measure and to prohibit any person in Canada from complying with it.[97]

Violation of orders made under either of these aspects of FEMA is an offence punishable by fines of up to $1.5 million and up to five years of imprisonment.[98]

Third, FEMA allows the AGC to respond to a foreign judgment under an antitrust law if it "has adversely affected or is likely to adversely affect significant Canadian interests in relation to international trade or commerce…"[99] The AGC may declare that such a judgment may not be recognized or enforced

90 *FEMA*, *supra* note 79, s 3(1) (disclosure of records to foreign tribunals) and s 2 (defining "foreign tribunal" as "a tribunal of a foreign state or of an organization of states").

91 *FEMA*, *ibid*, s 3(1)(a).

92 *Ibid*, s 3(1)(b).

93 *Ibid*, s 3(2).

94 *Ibid*, s 3(3).

95 *Ibid*, s 4.

96 *Ibid*, s 5(1) (measures of a foreign state or foreign tribunal).

97 *Ibid*, s 5(1).

98 *Ibid*, s 7(1)(a) (on indictment, a fine of up to $1,500,000 for a corporation and, for an individual, a fine of up to $150,000 or up to five years' imprisonment or both) and s 7(1)(b) (on summary conviction, up to $150,000 for a corporation and, or an individual, a fine of up to $15,000 or up to two years' imprisonment or both).

99 *Ibid*, s 8(1) (recognition and enforcement of foreign judgments) and s 2 (defining "antitrust law").

in Canada,[100] or may reduce the amount of a foreign money judgment under such a law to that specified in the AGC's order.[101]

Fourth, FEMA declares that a judgment given under the *Helms-Burton Act* cannot be recognized or enforced in Canada,[102] and for good measure, allows the AGC to declare unenforceable any judgment given under any "foreign trade law" included in a schedule to FEMA, with the only entry in that schedule so far being the *Helms-Burton Act*.[103]

Fifth, FEMA has "clawback" provisions that let a party sue in Canada for recovery from a person who has obtained a foreign judgment that is the object of a non-enforcement order or where the recoverable amount has been capped; these provisions apply both to foreign antitrust judgments and foreign trade law judgments.[104]

Two regulations have been made under FEMA. The *Foreign Extraterritorial Measures (United States) Order, 1992*,[105] prohibits compliance with the US *Cuban Assets Control Regulations*[106] and requires giving the AGC notice of communications made pursuant to those regulations.[107] The *Certain Foreign Extraterritorial Measures (United States) Order, 2014*[108] prohibits any person in Canada, in respect of improvements to be made to premises leased by Alaska from the Prince Rupert Port Authority in British Columbia, to comply with "Buy America" provisions adopted by the United States for construction involving iron or steel.[109] In both cases, the AGC determined that the U.S. provisions contained measures adverse to Canadian international trade or commerce interests.

There has been scant judicial treatment of FEMA, and where courts have considered it, the statute has arisen in contexts that differ from the purposes for which FEMA was enacted.[110]

---

100 *Ibid*, s 8(1(a).

101 *Ibid*, s 8(1)(b).

102 *Ibid*, s 7.1.

103 *Ibid*, s 2 (defining "foreign trade law"), s 2.1 (granting AGC power to amend schedule), and s 8(1.1) (granting AGC power to declare a judgment unenforceable or to reduce the amount of a foreign money judgment to the amount specified in the AGC's order).

104 *Ibid*, s 9.

105 *Foreign Extraterritorial Measures (United States) Order, 1992*, SOR/92-584.

106 *Ibid*, s 5 (referencing *Cuban Assets Control Regulations*, 31 CFR Part 515).

107 *Ibid*, s 3.

108 *Certain Foreign Extraterritorial Measures (United States) Order, 2014*, SOR/2015-12.

109 *Ibid*, s 1 (referencing, in particular, 23 USC § 313 and 23 CFR § 635.410).

110 The main cases are *Germany (Federal Republic) v Canadian Imperial Bank of Commerce* 31 OR (3d) 684 (Gen Div), aff'd 1998 CarswellOnt 1999 (CA) (in objection to a request for let-

Blocking legislation patterned on FEMA also exists in the *Competition Act*.[111] Under ss 82 and 83, the Commissioner of Competition can apply to the Competition Tribunal for preventative orders. Under s 82, if the Tribunal finds that implementing a judgment, decree, order, or other process from outside Canada will adversely affect competition, trade, or commerce in Canada, it can order that no measures be taken in Canada to implement the judgment, decree, order, or other process, except as the Tribunal may prescribe. Under s 83, if the Tribunal finds that a decision has been, or is about to be, made by "a person in Canada or a [Canadian-incorporated] company," and the decision is the result of a foreign law, directive, instruction, intimation of policy or other communication that would adversely affect competition in Canada, it can order that no measures be taken by the person or company in Canada to implement the law, directive, instruction, intimation of policy or other communication.

Finally, Parliament may enact laws that, while not counting as blocking statutes or regulations, have the effect of privileging Canadian laws over foreign laws, even where private parties may have specified those laws in a transaction. An example is s 46 of the *Marine Liability Act*,[112] which allows Canadian shippers and importers of goods by sea to choose a Canadian court or arbitration tribunal regardless of any choice-of-court clause to the contrary.[113]

---

ters rogatory in a German criminal investigation, FEMA held to have no application to the facts); *Desjean v Intermix Media, Inc*, 2006 FC 1395, aff'd 2007 FCA 365 (trial court holding that it lacked jurisdiction over American corporate defendant for alleged violations of the *Competition Act* relating to false advertising since "[i]f Canada reserves the right to refuse enforcement of American antitrust judgments, this Court should not be placed in the position of applying Canadian competition law to American corporations doing business in the U.S. and having no assets in Canada, thereby compelling a plaintiff to seek enforcement in the U.S. of a Canadian antitrust judgment" (para 37); appeal court affirming without reference to FEMA); and *Old North State Brewing Co Inc v Newlands Services Inc*, (1998) 58 BCLR (3d) 144 (CA), [1999] 4 WWR 573 (in contesting enforcement of a U.S. judgment, judgment debtor asserted that treble damages awards were against Canadian public policy, citing FEMA; Court finding that FEMA evinced no generalized Canadian policy against treble damages and that judgment should be enforced).

111 *Supra*, note 66.

112 *Marine Liability Act*, SC 2001, c 6.

113 In practice, the courts have weakened this provision on the basis that it does not *invalidate* such clauses and still leaves the door open to argue that a case should proceed elsewhere on *forum non conveniens* grounds: see *OT Africa Line Ltd v Magic Sportswear*

4.9.2 Provincial Legislation

Provincially, the key statutes are Ontario's *Business Records Protection Act*,[114] enacted in 1947,[115] and Quebec's *Business Concerns Records Act*,[116] enacted in 1958.[117] Some provincial statutes also limit the enforcement of foreign judgments, either in relation to the subject matter[118] or the type or amount of damages.[119]

The Quebec statute was central to *Hunt v T&N plc*,[120] a case that built on *Morguard*[121] to recognize a judicially created "full faith and credit" clause in Canadian constitutional law. The issue in *Hunt* arose out of an action by British Columbia residents against certain companies, some multinational and some Quebec-based, all involved in the manufacturing or distribution of asbestos products. The lead plaintiff, George Hunt, had developed cancer, allegedly from inhaling asbestos fibres at his workplace, and had received compensation from the British Columbia Workers' Compensation Board. To recoup some of its costs of compensating the workers, the Board brought a subrogated claim in British Columbia against the manufacturers and distributors, alleging that they had negligently manufactured the products, failed in their duty to warn about their dangers, and conspired to hide the dangers of asbestos.

The Quebec companies refused to respond to a demand for discovery of documents on the basis that they were precluded from doing so by Quebec's blocking statute. Among other things, that Act stipulated that "no person shall,

---

Corp, 2006 FCA 284 and Nils Daugulis and Shane Nossal, "Eclipse of Section 46 of the Marine Liability Act" (25 October 2006) *Lexology* https://bit.ly/3rZjOGC.

114 *Business Records Protection Act*, RSO 1990, c B.19 [*BRPA*].

115 SO 1947, c 10.

116 *Business Concerns Records Act*, CQLR c D-12 (*Loi sur les dossiers d'entreprises*, RLRQ c D-12) [*BCRA*].

117 SQ 1957–58, 6–7 Eliz II, c 42.

118 See *Court Order Enforcement Act*, RSBC 1996, c 78, s 40 (prohibiting enforcement of judgments from outside British Columbia for loss or injury arising out of exposure to or the use of asbestos mined in British Columbia, though allowing actions to be commenced in British Columbia for loss or injury outside Canada on that basis).

119 See *The Enforcement of Foreign Judgments Act*, SS 2005, c E-9.121, s 6(1) (limiting enforcement of foreign judgments for punitive or multiple damages or other non-compensatory purposes to the comparable damages that could have been awarded in Saskatchewan) and s 6(2) (limiting the enforcement of foreign judgments for compensatory damages to amounts that the enforcing court could have awarded in the circumstances).

120 *Hunt v T&N plc*, [1993] 4 SCR 289.

121 *Morguard*, *supra* note 39.

pursuant to or under any requirement issued by any legislative, judicial or administrative authority outside Québec, remove or cause to be removed, or send or cause to be sent, from any place in Québec to a place outside Québec, any document or résumé or digest of any document relating to any [business] concern."

The case went to the Supreme Court of Canada, where the sole issue was whether the statute was *ultra vires* the National Assembly of Quebec (Quebec's legislature) or constitutionally inapplicable on the facts, due to its pith and substance derogating from extraprovincial rights. Justice La Forest, giving judgment for the Court and casting back to *Morguard*, elevated the "constitutional considerations" that governed interprovincial recognition and enforcement of judgments in *Morguard* to "constitutional imperatives" that applied equally to provincial legislatures and courts. Relying on *Morguard* and other case law, La Forest J held that Quebec's blocking statute was constitutionally inapplicable to other provinces because it did not respect the minimum standards of comity and the demands of territoriality within Canada – in particular, by inhibiting the use of discovery as a tool in Canadian civil litigation. The result is that the legislation was, and still is, within the legislative competence of the provincial legislature, but its extraterritorial effect does not apply between Canadian provinces or territories. In *Hunt*, that meant that the Quebec defendants had to comply with the demand for discovery of documents that emanated from British Columbia.

5 Conclusion

This examination of Canada's extraterritorial application of statutes and regulations reveals a nuanced and evolving approach over time. The foundational principle, enshrined in provisions such as s 6(2) of Canada's *Criminal Code*, emphasizes that clear legislative intent is required for extraterritorial jurisdiction. Legislation reflects a deliberate effort to balance the extension and the limitation of extraterritorial reach. But despite meticulous legislative language, courts often grapple with interpreting the intended reach of statutes. The landmark case of *Libman v The Queen* set a key precedent, introducing a two-part test focused on a "real and substantial link" to Canada and compliance with international comity. This test, known as "qualified" or "extended" territoriality, has significantly influenced Canada's approach to cases with extraterritorial elements, including cases well beyond the criminal law context.

The extraterritorial application of statutes and regulations is also significantly shaped by Canada's commitment to multilateral and regional instruments. The influence of international treaties, conventions, and other agreements is evident in the expansion of extraterritorial jurisdiction, particularly in criminal law. These instruments, many of which are aimed at suppressing transnational crime, serve as catalysts for legislative measures that transcend national borders.

Canadian courts have also emphasized a longstanding presumption of conformity with international law as an interpretive principle. Enactments are presumed to comply with the principles of customary and conventional international law unless there is an unequivocal intent in the statute to depart from international obligations. This was seen, for example, in *R v Hape*, where the Supreme Court found that Canadian investigators, while *prima facie* subject to the *Charter*, were acting under the authority of foreign police forces, and their activities thus did not violate international law.

Courts have adopted a *de facto* reasonableness test for extraterritorial application of statutes and regulations, exemplified by cases like *Libman* and *Hape*. The approach considers the reasonableness of asserting jurisdiction based on the circumstances, avoiding full extraterritoriality while acknowledging extended territorial claims. Yet in cases of full extraterritorial prescriptive jurisdiction, as in *R v Klassen*, courts recognize the importance of international law to address pressing issues like child exploitation.

Like other countries, Canada employs both "suppression" and "sanctions" legislation to assert extraterritorial jurisdiction, influenced by international agreements and UN resolutions. Application of statutes to wholly foreign conduct is evident in the competition law framework, with jurisdiction over corporations implementing foreign directives. The *Competition Act*, particularly s 46, exemplifies extraterritoriality with limitations, linking its application to corporations doing business in Canada. And like other countries, Canada has also adopted "blocking statutes" such as FEMA, although their reach has been circumscribed by executive restraint or judicial interpretation.

In summary, the commitment to multilateral instruments, the influence of international law, a *de facto* reasonableness test, and the employment of "suppression," "sanctions," and "blocking" legislation, underscore the complexity and adaptability of Canada's extraterritorial legal framework.

TABLE 4.1 Sample multilateral instruments to which Canada is a party and associated implementing legislation

Instrument(s)	Associated Legislation	Jurisdiction	Notes/Comments/Cases
Offences Relating to Cultural Property			
Hague Convention of 1954 for the Protection of Cultural Property in the Event of Armed Conflict[a] *First Protocol to the Hague Cultural Property Convention*[b] *Second Protocol to the Hague Cultural Property Convention*[c]	Key legislation: – *Cultural Property Export and Import Act*,[d] s 36.1(3) – *Canadian Cultural Property Export Control List*, CRC, c 448 – *Cultural Property Export Regulations*, CRC, c 449 – *Criminal Code*,[e] s 7(2.01)	nationality (expansive in the case of citizens or stateless persons resident in Canada; limited in the case of permanent residents)	The Convention "aims to protect cultural property, such as monuments of architecture, art or history, archaeological sites, works of art, manuscripts, books and other objects of artistic, historical or archaeological interest, as well as scientific collections of any kind regardless of their origin or ownership."[f] State parties are required to take certain preventative measures and refrain from using such property in any manner that might expose it to destruction or deterioration in the event of armed conflict.

a *Hague Convention of 1954 for the Protection of Cultural Property in the Event of Armed Conflict* (The Hague, 14 May 1954), Can TS 1999 No 52 (*Hague Cultural Property Convention*).

b *First Protocol to the Hague Convention of 1954 for the Protection of Cultural Property in the Event of Armed Conflict* (The Hague, 14 May 1954), Can TS 2006 No 26 (*First Protocol*).

c *Second Protocol to the Hague Convention of 1954 for the Protection of Cultural Property in the Event of Armed Conflict* (The Hague, 26 March 1999), Can TS 2006 No 27 (*Second Protocol*).

d *Cultural Property Export and Import Act*, RSC 1985, c C-51 (enacts the *Hague Cultural Property Convention*, attached as a Schedule).

e *Criminal Code*, RSC 1985, c C-46.

f UNESCO, *1954 Convention for the Protection of Cultural Property in the Event of Armed Conflict with Regulations for the Execution of the Convention*, online: https://bit.ly/3s8zvgH.

Convention on the Means of Prohibiting and Preventing the Illicit Import, Export and Transfer of Ownership of Cultural Property[g]	The combined effect is that a person committing an act or omission relating to cultural property outside Canada that would be an offence if committed in Canada is deemed to have committed it in Canada if the person is: (a) a Canadian citizen; (b) not a citizen of any state but resides in Canada; or (c) a permanent resident and is present in Canada after the act or omission.	The Convention and its First Protocol were signed at The Hague, Netherlands, on 14 May 1954; both entered into force on 7 August 1956. The Convention came into force in Canada on 11 March 1999; the First Protocol, on 28 February 2006. A Second Protocol was signed on 26 March 1999 providing for enhanced protection. It entered into force on 9 March 2004 and came into force in Canada on 28 February 2006. The *1970 UNESCO Convention* entered into force in 1972 and came into force in Canada in 1978. The *Cultural Property Export and Import Act* is the main legislation implementing that Convention. The Act and its regulations aim to protect Canada's national heritage through export controls for objects of historical, scientific, and cultural significance as well as to meet Canada's obligations to recover and return illegally imported cultural property.

g *Convention on the Means of Prohibiting and Preventing the Illicit Import, Export and Transfer of Ownership of Cultural Property* (Geneva, 14 November 1970), 1978 Can TS No 33 (*1970 UNESCO Convention*).

TABLE 4.1 Sample multilateral instruments to which Canada is a party and associated implementing legislation (*Cont.*)

Instrument(s)	Associated Legislation	Jurisdiction	Notes/Comments/Cases
Offences Relating to Aviation, Aircraft and International Airports			
Convention on International Civil Aviation (*Chicago Convention*)[h] *Convention of Offences and Certain Other Acts committed on Board Aircraft* (*Tokyo Convention*)[i] *Convention for the Suppression of Unlawful Seizure of Aircraft* (*Hague Hijacking Convention*)[j] *Convention for the Suppression of Unlawful Acts against the Safety of Civil Aviation* (*Montreal Convention*)[k]	Key legislation: – *Criminal Code*, ss 76–78 – *Criminal Code*, s 7(1) – *Criminal Code*, s 7(2) Sections 76–78 create offences that endanger aircraft and airports. Under s 7(1), with respect to flights of Canadian aircraft or any aircraft in a flight ending in Canada, everyone who "commits an act or omission in or outside Canada that if committed in Canada would be an [indictable offence] shall be deemed to have committed that act or omission in Canada."	qualified territorial; custodial universal	The *Chicago* Convention, now ratified by 193 parties, establishes rules of airspace, aircraft registration, safety and security, and provides that an aircraft has the nationality of the state of its registration. For offences on aircraft in flight, the *Tokyo Convention* allocates jurisdiction between the state of the aircraft's nationality and other states that might be affected. The *Tokyo Convention* has been ratified by 187 states, the most recent being Saint Kitts and Nevis in December 2020.[l] Section 7(1) was applied in *R v Minot*, 2011 NLCA 7. A French citizen, flying from Paris to Boston on American Airlines, was apprehended in Canada after the pilot rerouted the flight to Gander, Newfoundland because of the passenger's behaviour.

h *Convention on International Civil Aviation* (7 December 1944), Can TS 1944 No 36 (*Chicago Convention*).
i *Convention of Offences and Certain Other Acts committed on Board Aircraft* (14 September 1963), Can TS 1970 No 5 (*Tokyo Convention*).
j *Convention for the Suppression of Unlawful Seizure of Aircraft* (16 December 1970), Can TS 1972 No 23 (*Hague Hijacking Convention*).
k *Convention for the Suppression of Unlawful Acts against the Safety of Civil Aviation* (23 September 1971), Can TS 1973 No 6 (*Montreal Convention*).
l See International Civil Aviation Organization (ICAO): https://www.icao.int/secretariat/legal/Pages/TreatyCollection.aspx.

Protocol for the Suppression of Unlawful Acts of Violence at Airports Serving International Civil Aviation (Montreal Protocol)[m]	Under s 7(2), relating to aircraft, international navigation facilities, and international airports, a person is deemed to have committed an offence in Canada only "if the person is, after the commission thereof, present in Canada."	The passenger was arrested and charged with mischief by interfering with the airline's property and engaging in behaviour involving electronic equipment that endangered an aircraft's safety or security. Though the flight was US-bound, the Court was satisfied that it "terminated" at Gander for the purposes of s 7(1). The *Hague Hijacking Convention* "displays a prototypical version of the elements which are now common among modern instruments: a custodial universal jurisdiction provision, an obligation to apprehend and investigate, an extradite[-]or[-]prosecute obligation, and obligations regarding extradition and mutual legal assistance."[n] The *Montreal Convention* supplements the hijacking crime with offences involving acts that could damage or endanger an aircraft's safety in flight, damage or destroy air navigation facilities, or communicate false information. The *Montreal Protocol* extended these provisions to include airports and aircraft not in service.

m *Protocol for the Suppression of Unlawful Acts of Violence at Airports Serving International Civil Aviation* (24 February 1988), 1589 UNTS 474, Can TS 1993 No 8 (*Montreal Protocol*).

n Robert J Currie and Joseph Rikhof, *International & Transnational Criminal Law*, 3d ed (Toronto: Irwin Law, 2020), p. 410 (internal citations omitted).

TABLE 4.1 Sample multilateral instruments to which Canada is a party and associated implementing legislation (*Cont.*)

Instrument(s)	Associated Legislation	Jurisdiction	Notes/Comments/Cases
Offences Relating to Maritime Navigation and Fixed Platforms on the Continental Shelf			
Convention for the Suppression of Unlawful Acts against the Safety of Maritime Navigation (*SUA Convention*)[o] *Optional Protocol for the Suppression of Unlawful Acts against the Safety of Fixed Platforms Located on the Continental Shelf* (*SUA Protocol*)[p]	*Criminal Code*, s 78.1 (maritime safety offences); s 7(2.1) (jurisdiction over offences outside Canada "against or on board a fixed platform attached to the continental shelf of any state or against or on board a ship navigating … beyond [a state's] territorial sea of any state"); and s 7(2.2) (jurisdiction over offences committed outside Canada "against or on board a fixed platform *not* attached to the continental shelf of any state or against or on board a ship *not* navigating … beyond [a state's] territorial sea").	purely territorial (s 7(2.1)(e)); nationality (ss 7(2.1) (c)); passive personality (s 7(2.1)(f)); conditional universal (s 7(2.2(b)).	The SUA *Convention* was sponsored by the International Maritime Organization at the UN's request, following the October 1985 hijacking of the Italian ship *Achille Lauro* and the killing of an American passenger. Offences combine the kinds of crimes in the *Hague Hijacking Convention* and *Montreal Convention* (see above), but transposed to ships. Notable in the implementing provisions for the SUA *Convention* and *Protocol* is *Criminal Code* s 7(2.2)(b), deeming the offence to have been committed in Canada if the offender is found in a state other than that in which the act or omission was committed if the state is party to the SUA *Convention* or SUA *Protocol*.

o *Convention for the Suppression of Unlawful Acts against the Safety of Maritime Navigation* (Rome, 10 March 1988), 1678 UNTS 221, Can TS 1993 No 10 (*SUA Convention*).

p *Optional Protocol for the Suppression of Unlawful Acts against the Safety of Fixed Platforms Located on the Continental Shelf* (Rome, 10 March 1988), 1678 UNTS 304, Can TS 1993 No 9 (SUA Protocol).

			This allows for "the fullest exercise of the *aut dedere aut judicare* ["extradite or prosecute"] obligation by both Canada and its treaty partners, and goes beyond custodial universal jurisdiction to a full-blown (though treaty-based) exercise of extraterritorial jurisdiction."[q]
Offences Against Children			
UN Convention on the Rights of the Child (*UNCRC*)[r] *Optional Protocol to the Convention on the Rights of the Child on the Sale of Children, Child Prostitution and Child Pornography* (*UNCRC Protocol*)[s]	*Criminal Code*, s 7(4.1): everyone who, "outside Canada, commits an act or omission that if committed in Canada would be [one of several specified sexual offences against children] shall be deemed to commit that act or omission in Canada if the person who commits the act or omission is a Canadian citizen or a permanent resident."	nationality	*UNCRC* art 11 requires states to combat the illicit transfer of children abroad and promote the conclusion of agreements for that purpose. The *UNCRC Protocol* is one of two agreements intended to fulfill those requirements, the other being the *Optional Protocol to the Convention on the Rights of the Child on the involvement of Children in Armed Conflict.* In *R v Klassen*, 2008 BCSC 1762, the accused challenged the validity and constitutionality of s 7(4.1). The Court concluded that the section was valid under international law and did not violate the *Canadian Charter of Rights and Freedoms.*

q Currie & Rikhof, *supra* note 14, p. 416.

r *UN Convention on the Rights of the Child* (New York, 20 November 1989), 1577 UNTS 3, Can TS 1992 No 3 (*UNCRC*).

s *Optional Protocol to the Convention on the Rights of the Child on the Sale of Children, Child Prostitution and Child Pornography* (New York, 25 May 2000), 2171 UNTS 227 (not yet in Can TS) (*UNCRC Protocol*).

TABLE 4.1 Sample multilateral instruments to which Canada is a party and associated implementing legislation (*Cont.*)

Instrument(s)	Associated Legislation	Jurisdiction	Notes/Comments/Cases
Crimes Against Humanity and War Crimes			
Rome Statute of the International Criminal Court[t]	*Crimes Against Humanity and War Crimes Act*,[u] with two regimes: offences within Canada (ss 4–5) and offences outside Canada (ss 6–8).	nationality (expansive) (s 8(a) (i)–(ii)); passive personality (s 8(a) (iii)–iv); custodial universal (s 8(b))	The Rome Statute and the *Crimes Against Humanity and War Crimes Act* both came into force in July 2002. The Canadian statute has its own definitions for the core crimes that are separate from the Rome Statute but uses phrasing that allows for incorporation of customary or conventional international law. The extraterritorial offences are in s 6 (genocide, crimes against humanity, and war crimes) and s 7 (breaches of command/superior responsibility leading to these offences) of the Canadian statute. Under s 8(a), a person alleged to have committed an offence under s 6 or s 7 may be prosecuted if, at the time of the offence, (i) the person was a Canadian citizen or employed by Canada in a civilian or military capacity; (ii) the person was a citizen or employee of a state engaged in armed conflict against Canada;

t *Rome Statute of the International Criminal Court* (Rome, 17 July 1998), 2187 UNTS 3, Can TS 2002 No 13 (*Rome Statute*).

u *Crimes Against Humanity and War Crimes Act*, SC 2000, c 24.

(iii) the victim was a Canadian citizen; or (iv) a citizen of a state allied with Canada in an armed conflict. Also included are the inchoate offences of conspiracy, attempts to commit, and accessory after the fact.

Those who commit such offences outside Canada can be tried in Canada, regardless of where or when the events occurred, subject to other jurisdictional requirements. Under s 8(b), a person may be prosecuted if present in Canada after the time the offence is alleged to have been committed. Section 4 links the core crimes to the Rome Statute by stipulating that the crimes in articles 6 and 7 and paragraph 2 of article 8 of the Rome Statute (genocide, crimes against humanity, and war crimes) are crimes according to customary international law (see above).[v]

v For detailed analysis, see Currie & Rikhof, *supra* note 14, p. 283–317. The most significant case is *R v Munyaneza*, 2009 QCCS 2201, aff'd 2014 QCCA 906, leave to appeal to SCC refused 2014 CanLII 76857 (SCC), in which the accused was arrested in Canada under s 8(b) and convicted of genocide and crimes against humanity for acts committed in Rwanda, with the conviction upheld on appeal. One of the unique aspects of the case from an extraterritorial perspective is the "rogatory commissions" conducted in France, Rwanda and Tanzania to take evidence from witnesses in those countries.

TABLE 4.1 Sample multilateral instruments to which Canada is a party and associated implementing legislation (*Cont.*)

Instrument(s)	Associated Legislation	Jurisdiction	Notes/Comments/Cases
Offences Relating to Terrorism[w]			
International Convention against the taking of Hostages[x]	*Criminal Code*, s 279.1 (offence) and 7(3.1) (jurisdiction)	territorial (ss 7(3.1) (a)-(b); nationality (expansive) (s 7(3.1) (a)-(c)); protective (s 7(3.1)d); passive personality (s 7(3.1) (e)); custodial universal (s 7(3.1) (f))	The *Hostages Convention* has its roots in the 1970s, especially the abduction and murder of Israeli athletes at the 1972 Munich Olympics. It has wide adherence and applies when there is any transnational aspect to a hostage-taking. It requires states to take appropriate measures to secure the hostage's release and requires them to assert other forms of jurisdiction that are common in the suppression conventions. The associated legislation is in the *Criminal Code*. Section 279.1 defines hostage-taking (distinct from domestic kidnapping), the salient feature being that the victim's confinement is intended to induce "any group of persons or any state or international or intergovernmental organization to commit ... any act or omission as a condition ... of the release of the hostage."

w See also *Offences Relating to Aviation, Aircraft and International Airports* and *Offences to Maritime Navigation and Fixed Platforms on the Continental Shelf*.

x *International Convention against the taking of Hostages* (New York, 17 December 1979), 1316 UNTS 205, 1986 Can TS No 45 (*Hostages Convention*).

			Under s 7(3.1), jurisdiction applies to a person who takes hostages on a Canadian-registered ship or aircraft; to a hostage-taker who is a Canadian citizen or stateless resident of Canada; when the intent is to induce Canada or a province to commit an act or omission; when the victim is a Canadian citizen; or when the hostage-taker is, after the commission of the offence, present in Canada.
Convention on the Prevention and Punishment of Crimes against Internationally Protected Persons, including Diplomatic Agents[y]	*Criminal Code*, s 2 (definition of "internationally protected person"); s 7(3) (offences and jurisdiction); s 424 (threats to commit an offence); s 431 (attacks on official premises, private accommodation or means of transport)	territorial (ss 7(3)(a)-(b); nationality, custodial universal (s 7(3)(c)); passive personality (expansive) (s 7(3.)(d))	The *Protected Persons Convention* dates to the 1970s and aims to protect: (i) heads of state, heads of government, or foreign affairs ministers, as well as their families, when abroad; and (ii) officials and representatives of states or international or intergovernmental organizations, as well as their families and property, where entitled to protection under international law. It requires states to assert various forms of jurisdiction that are common in the suppression conventions.

y *Convention on the Prevention and Punishment of Crimes against Internationally Protected Persons, including Diplomatic Agents* (New York, 14 December 1973), 1033 UNTS 167, 1977 Can TS No 43 (*Protected Persons Convention*).

TABLE 4.1 Sample multilateral instruments to which Canada is a party and associated implementing legislation (*Cont.*)

Instrument(s)	Associated Legislation	Jurisdiction	Notes/Comments/Cases
			Under s 7(3) of the *Criminal Code*, jurisdiction applies to a person who commits an act against an internationally protected person on a Canadian-registered ship or aircraft; if the person who commits the act is a Canadian citizen or present in Canada after the offence; and if the victim "enjoys the status of an internationally protected person by virtue of the functions that person performs on behalf of Canada." Section 424 criminalizes threats to commit the offences; s 431 criminalizes attacks on premises, residences or means of transport; both fall under the jurisdiction in s 7(3).
Convention on the Safety of United Nations and Associated Personnel[26]	*Criminal Code*, s 2 (definitions of "United Nations operation," "United Nations personnel," "associated personnel"); s 7(3.71) (offences and jurisdiction);	territorial (ss 7(3.71) (a)-(b); nationality (expansive) (s 7(3.71)(c));	The *UN Personnel Convention* works like the *Protected Persons Convention*; it was ultimately drafted separately "in part because of the important symbolic value of such an instrument,

z *Convention on the Safety of United Nations and Associated Personnel* (New York, 9 December 1994), 2051 UNTS 391, 2002 Can TS No 7 (*UN Personnel Convention*).

	s 424.1 (threats to commit an offence); s 431.1 (attacks on official premises, private accommodation or means of transport)	custodial universal (s 7(3.71(d)); passive personality (s 7(3.71)(e)); protective (s 7.371(f))	and also out of a wish not to exclude states which were not parties to the *Protected Persons Convention*."[aa] It applies to UN-controlled operations for restoring or maintaining international peace and security, and not when personnel are engaged as combatants against organized armed forces. Under s 7(3.71) of the *Criminal Code*, jurisdiction applies much as it does for internationally protected persons under s 7(3). Section 424.1 criminalizes threats to commit the offences "with intent to compel any person, group of persons, state or any international or intergovernmental organization to do or refrain from doing any act"; s 431.1 criminalizes attacks on premises, residences or means of transport; both fall under the jurisdiction in s 7(3).
International Convention for the Suppression of Terrorist Bombings[bb]	*Criminal Code*, s 431.2 (definitions, including an expansive one of "explosive or other lethal device" and offence);	territorial (ss 7(3.72) (a)-(b); nationality (expansive) (s 7(3.72)(c));	The *Terrorist Bombings Convention* is one of several instruments that require states to criminalize certain terrorist acts where there is a transnational element and to extradite or prosecute offenders.

aa Currie & Rikhof, *supra* note 14, p. 421.

bb *International Convention for the Suppression of Terrorist Bombings* (New York, 15 December 1997), 2149 UNTS 256, 2002 Can TS No 8 (*Terrorist Bombings Convention*).

TABLE 4.1 Sample multilateral instruments to which Canada is a party and associated implementing legislation (*Cont.*)

Instrument(s)	Associated Legislation	Jurisdiction	Notes/Comments/Cases
	s 7(3.72) (jurisdiction); see also s 7(3.74) (nationality-based jurisdiction for "terrorism offence" committed outside Canada) and s 7(3.75) (passive-personality and protective jurisdiction for "terrorism activity" committed outside Canada)	custodial universal (s 7(3.72(d)) passive personality s 7(3.72(e)), protective (ss 7(3.72(f)-(g))	Tracking the Convention's requirements, the *Criminal Code* defines the necessary elements of the offence (e.g., "explosive or other lethal device," "infrastructure facility," as well as the offence itself, which includes liability for organizing or directing others to commit the offence. Activities of armed forces during armed conflict are exempted.
International Convention for the Suppression of the Financing of Terrorism[cc]	*Criminal Code*, s 2 (definition of "property"); s 83.01 (further definitions, including an expansive one of "terrorist activity" that references the individual suppression conventions; s 83.02 (offences); s 7(3.73) (jurisdiction)	same as above, substituting s 7(3.73) for s 7(3.72)	The *Terrorism Financing Convention* obliges states to criminalize acts of terrorist financing; to identify, detect and freeze or seize funds used for such financing; and to establish regulatory regimes aimed at preventing it. Section 83.02 criminalizes the provision or collection of "property" (more expansive than the term "funds" in the Convention) for terrorism. Section 7(3.73) establishes jurisdiction over those committing the offences in s 83.02, all in accordance with the Convention.

cc *International Convention for the Suppression of the Financing of Terrorism* (New York, 9 December 1999), 2178 UNTS 197, Can TS 2002 No 9 (*Terrorist Financing Convention*).

Sections 83.03 and 83.04 create offences aimed the collection or use of any property, directly or indirectly, to support terrorism, with wording that is broader than the Convention requires. Further sections establish, *inter alia*, lists of entities that the government believes carry out or facilitate terrorist activity (s 83.05); a procedure for admitting foreign information about a listed entity in confidence (s 83.06); and procedures for freezing (ss 83.08–83.12), seizing (s 83.13), and forfeiting (s 83.17) property. Some of these provisions were enacted in earlier legislation and are broader than what the Convention requires. Other legislation, not shown here, sets out regulations that establish lists of terrorist-related entities and impose reporting obligations on banks and other financial institutions).

L'application Extraterritoriale des Lois et Règlements

Québec

*Frédérique Sabourin**

Nous avons été invitée à décrire la portée extraterritoriale donnée par le Québec à ses lois et règlements dans l'exercice de sa compétence législative[1]. Une large part des développements qui suivent est consacrée à la compétence juridictionnelle, la question de savoir si elle fait partie ou non de la compétence législative normative d'un État pouvant être débattue[2].

Comme indiqué par le professeur Kleefeld dans son rapport[3], la *Loi constitutionnelle de 1867*[4] impose au pouvoir législatif des provinces une limite territoriale. Le caractère véritable d'une loi provinciale doit être dans la province; les lois provinciales qui prennent en compte des faits survenus hors de la province sont constitutionnellement valides seulement si elles le font de façon incidente. Compte tenu de ce cadre constitutionnel, les lois et règlements québécois sont généralement silencieux sur leur portée géographique[5]. Dans une situation où un élément d'extranéité[6] est présent, les règles de droit international privé

* Frédérique Sabourin, LL.D., Ad. E., avocate retraitée du ministère de la Justice du Québec. Les opinions exprimées n'engagent que l'auteure et ne lient d'aucune façon le gouvernement du Québec.

1 Le pouvoir d'exécution est exclu du champ de la recherche. H. Kindred et al., *International Law, Chiefly as Interpreted and Applied in Canada*, Emond Montgomery Publications, Toronto, 2014, 869 p., p. 251; J.-M. Arbour et G. Parent, *Droit international public*, Cowansville, éd. Yvon Blais, 7e éd., 2017, p. 353.

2 S. Coughan, R. J. Curie, H. M. Kindersley et T. Scassa, *Portée mondiale et emprise locale : l'interprétation de la compétence extraterritoriale à l'ère de la mondialisation*, préparé pour la Commission du droit du Canada, le 23 juin 2006, p. 11.

3 Voir le rapport canadien.

4 *Loi constitutionnelle de 1867*, 30 & 31 Victoria, ch. 3 (R.-U.).

5 Les lois et de règlements qui réfèrent à des faits s'étant produits à l'extérieur du Québec sans toutefois préciser leur champ d'application territorial fourmillent d'exemples en matière de droits professionnel, sociaux et politiques, de permis, subventions, taxation, parmi d'autres.

6 Dans *Dell Computer Corp. v. Union des consommateurs*, [2007] 2 R.C.S. 801, 2007 CSC 34, par. 26, la majorité a défini l'expression « élément d'extranéité » comme : « un point de contact juridiquement pertinent avec un État étranger », c'est-à-dire un contact suffisant pour jouer un rôle dans la détermination de la juridiction compétente ». Dans cette affaire, la présence au contrat de clauses désignant une organisation américaine d'arbitrage, une loi fédérale américaine et l'anglais pour les procédures d'arbitrage n'ont pas été retenus comme facteurs pertinents aux fins de déterminer si les règles de droit international privé du Québec

 | DOI:10.1163/9789004720183_006

déterminent si la loi ou le règlement s'applique. Tant le fédéral que les provinces et les territoires ont développé chacun dans leur champ de compétence de telles règles. De plus, les provinces et les territoires ont des règles différentes les uns des autres. Or, au Québec, celles-ci sont codifiées au Livre X du *Code civil du Québec* (C.c.Q.), lequel est divisé en quatre titres: I – Dispositions générales (a. 3076–3082); II – Conflits de lois (a. 3083–3133)[7]; III – Compétence internationale des autorités du Québec (a. 3134–3154) et IV- Reconnaissance et exécution des décisions étrangères (a. 3155–3168). Ainsi, les règles de droit international privé sont une expression de la compétence législative normative du Québec même lorsque ces règles concernent les conflits de juridiction.

Par ailleurs, puisque les autorités du Québec doivent avoir compétence pour appliquer le droit québécois, les règles de conflits de juridiction servent aussi à définir le champ d'application du droit québécois[8]. En effet, si la situation a un lien si éloigné avec le Québec que ses tribunaux ne sont même pas compétents, ce ne sont pas les règles de conflits de lois du Québec qui détermineront la portée territoriale des lois québécoises.

Enfin, et bien que les règles de conflits de lois du droit québécois soient neutres et ne favorisent pas systématiquement l'application de la loi québécoise[9], lorsque la question soumise en est une d'un intérêt particulier pour le Québec, le rattachement juridictionnel coïncide avec le rattachement normatif.

Il sera donc principalement question ici, bien que les situations qui font appel au droit international privé québécois soient interprovinciales aussi

---

s'appliquaient. Ainsi, de façon plutôt insatisfaisante, un consommateur québécois qui avait acheté un ordinateur d'une compagnie canadienne ayant son siège en Ontario ne pouvait bénéficier de l'accès aux tribunaux de son domicile. L'article 3149 C.c.Q., protégeait déjà les consommateurs contre leur choix d'un tribunal étranger. La *Loi sur la protection du consommateur*, RLRQ, c. P40.1, a depuis été modifiée afin d'étendre cette protection contre l'arbitrage.

7 Très peu de décisions judiciaires concernant les conflits de lois ont été rendues depuis l'entrée en vigueur du C.c.Q. en 1994, la jurisprudence portant principalement sur les conflits de juridiction et, dans une moindre mesure, sur la reconnaissance et l'exécution des décisions étrangères.

8 F. Rigaux, « Espace et temps en droit international privé », *Revue interdisciplinaire d'études juridiques*, 1989/1 (Volume 22), pp. 107–123. DOI : 10.3917/riej.022.0107. URL : https://www.cairn.info/revue-interdisciplinaire-d-etudes-juridiques-1989-1-page-107.htm

9 L'application par un tribunal étranger d'une loi autre que celle que le tribunal québécois aurait appliquée n'est d'ailleurs pas un motif de refus de reconnaissance et d'exécution des décisions étrangères au Québec.

bien qu'internationales[10], des situations où les autorités du Québec sont compétentes dans une situation internationale et appliquent la *lex fori* (une loi ou un règlement québécois) en privilégiant cette dernière au détriment d'une loi étrangère.

1 Les tendances et la pratique

Il n'existe pas de pratique d'application extraterritoriale des lois et règlements au Québec compte tenu du cadre constitutionnel canadien et, ce cadre étant demeuré le même depuis son adoption en 1867, il n'y a pas eu de changements importants dans l'approche québécoise à cet égard. Cependant, l'interconnectivité de plus en plus grande entre les différents États dans le monde a créé des problématiques qui ont nécessité de trouver des solutions à l'intérieur de ce cadre.

Lorsque le Québec souhaite régir par une de ses lois ou règlements une situation comportant un élément étranger, il ne le fait généralement que si ses propres tribunaux pourront appliquer cette loi ou ce règlement, comme c'est aussi le cas au Canada[11]. Ainsi, il convient de mentionner la particularité du pouvoir d'ordonner des injonctions à portée extraterritoriale qui a longtemps divisé les tribunaux. Dans *Impulsora Turistica de Occidente, S.A. de C.V.* v. *Transat Tours Canada Inc.*[12], la Cour suprême a tranché en indiquant que les tribunaux québécois demeuraient compétents bien que l'injonction recherchée ait eu un effet extraterritorial et qu'elle ait visé des compagnies sans aucun lien avec le Québec. Cette décision a été suivie par la suite[13]. Également, les tribunaux

10 P.-C. Lafond, and G. Goldstein, *JurisClasseur Québec. Droit international privé.* Montréal, LexisNexis, feuilles mobiles; S. Guillemard et L.Van Anh, *Éléments de droit international privé québécois*, Cowansville, Éditions Yvon Blais, 2020, 180 p.

11 S. Coughan, R. J. Curie, H. M. Kindersley et T. Scassa, *Portée mondiale et emprise locale : l'interprétation de la compétence extraterritoriale à l'ère de la mondialisation,* préparé pour la Commission du droit du Canada, le 23 juin 2006, p. 11.

12 *Impulsora Turistica de Occidente, S.A. de C.V.* c. *Transat Tours Canada Inc.*, 2007 CSC 20, [2007] 1 RCS 867. Transat demandait une injonction contre des compagnies mexicaines pour les empêcher de continuer à violer une entente en vertu de laquelle Transat s'était vu octroyer le droit exclusif de louer des chambres d'hôtel pendant trois ans. Le contrat comportait une clause d'élection de for en faveur des tribunaux québécois.

13 *National Bank of Canada* c. *Weir*, 2010 QCCS 402.

québécois peuvent émettre des injonctions pour empêcher des poursuites à l'étranger[14].

Par ailleurs, l'interprète doit recourir au C.c.Q., en tant que droit commun[15], pour compléter les lois et règlements de droit public, bien que ce dernier tire son origine du droit anglais au contraire du droit privé qui tire la sienne du droit français[16].

Cependant, la *common law* conserve un rôle important à jouer. Si bien que le partage entre le C.c.Q. et la *common law*[17] en droit public québécois s'avère une tâche complexe. La question de la compétence des tribunaux administratifs sur les affaires qui présentent un élément d'extranéité pose une difficulté particulière devant le silence des lois qui les créent ou qui énoncent leurs différentes compétences matérielles[18].

Deux approches différentes ont cours relativement à cette question.

---

14 Malgré l'article 513 du *Code de procédure civile* (C.p.c.) selon lequel « une injonction ne peut en aucun cas être prononcée pour empêcher des procédures judiciaires » : *Johns-Manville Corp.* c. *Dominion of Canada General Insurance Co.*, 1991 CanLII 3076.

15 La disposition préliminaire du C.c.Q. prévoit en effet que :
Le Code civil du Québec régit, en harmonie avec la Charte de la langue française (chapitre C-11), la Charte des droits et libertés de la personne (chapitre C-12) et les principes généraux du droit, les personnes, les rapports entre les personnes, ainsi que les biens. Le code est constitué d'un ensemble de règles qui, en toutes matières auxquelles se rapportent la lettre, l'esprit ou l'objet de ses dispositions, établit, en termes exprès ou de façon implicite, le droit commun. En ces matières, *il constitue le fondement des autres lois* qui peuvent elles-mêmes ajouter au code ou y déroger (emphase ajoutée).

16 P. Issalys et D. Lemieux, *L'action gouvernementale, Précis de droit des institutions administratives*, 4e éd., Cowansville, éd. Yvon Blais, 2020, pp. 22–4, pp. 54–6.

17 Certains auteurs différencient les règles qui s'appliquent aux autorités publiques parce qu'elles sont des entités publiques (« *common law* publique »), des règles qui s'appliquent à elles comme à n'importe quel individu (« *common law* privée »). Cette distinction est unique au droit québécois. Daniel Jutras, « Cartographie de la mixité : la *common law* et la complétude du droit civil au Québec », (2010) 88 *R. du B.C.* 247, p. 255. Voir aussi M. Cumyn, « Les lois particulières et le Code civil » dans Y. Emerich et L. Saint-Pierre Harvey, dir, *Le public en droit privé*, Montréal, Centre Crépeau de droit privé et comparé/Yvon Blais, 2019, 89; D. Lemieux, « Le rôle du Code civil du Québec en droit administratif », dans Conférence des juristes de l'État, *Actes de la* XVIIe *Conférence de l'État*, Cowansville, Yvon Blais, 2006, 359; M.-F. Bureau et M. Devinat, dir, *Les livres du Code civil du Québec*, Sherbrooke, Éditions Revue de Droit de l'Université de Sherbrooke, 2014.

18 Ce domaine du droit est sous-développé au Québec. Si l'idée que le droit constitutionnel puisse avoir quelque chose à voir avec le droit international privé s'est imposé relativement récemment en droit canadien (P. Hogg et W. K. Wright, *Constitutional Law of Canada*, 5e éd., 2021, Thomson Reuters Canada Limited, p. §13 et J. Blom. « Constitutionalizing Canadian private international law – 25 years since Morguard », (2017) 13 *J. Priv. Int'l L.* 259), les relations entre le droit administratif et le droit international privé sont encore au stade embryonnaire.

La première est le recours aux règles de compétence internationale établies au C.c.Q. Une décision illustre cette première approche. Dans *Bourgoin* c. *Régie des marchés agricoles et alimentaires du Québec*[19], la Cour supérieure a retenu la compétence de la Régie des marchés agricoles et alimentaires du Québec (« Régie ») sur un résidant de la province du Nouveau-Brunswick qui avait acheté du sirop d'érable de producteurs du Québec. La Régie l'a trouvé coupable de ne pas avoir retenu les contributions dues à La Fédération des producteurs acéricoles du Québec[20], de s'être exempté de la classification et de l'inspection des produits et de ne pas avoir agi à l'intérieur du système de vente mis en place par la *Loi sur la mise en marché des produits agricoles alimentaires et de la pêche*[21] et ses règlements. En se fondant sur l'article 3148 (par. 3) C.c.Q., la Cour a trouvé que plusieurs fautes d'omission avaient été commises au Québec, qu'un préjudice y avait été souffert, et que les obligations prévues à l'arrangement de mise en marché devaient y être exécutées[22]; par conséquent la Régie était compétente[23].

De plus, dans *Bourgoin*, la Cour supérieure a appliqué la loi québécoise en se basant soit sur l'article 3076[24] soit sur l'article 3126 C.c.Q.[25]. En effet, l'article 3076 introduit la notion de « loi d'application immédiate » ou « loi

19 *Bourgoin* c. *Régie des marchés agricoles et alimentaires du Québec*, 2008 CSQ 5348.

20 La Fédération a changé son nom en 2018 pour celui de Producteurs et productrices acéricoles du Québec.

21 *Loi sur la mise en marché des produits agricoles, alimentaires et de la pêche*, RLRQ, c. M-35.1.

22 Un seul de ces facteurs aurait été suffisant pour que la Régie ait compétence en vertu de l'article 3148 par. 3 C.c.Q. Dans *Langford Sharp* c. *Autorité des marchés financiers*, 2021 QCCA 1364, le juge de la Cour d'appel Mainville, minoritaire, avait tenu un raisonnement similaire et appliqué l'article 3148 C.c.Q. par analogie. Cependant en appel, tous les juges de la Cour suprême ont estimé que l'article 3148 C.c.Q. ne pouvait s'appliquer puisqu'il ne s'agissait pas en l'espèce d'une action personnelle à caractère patrimonial. *Sharp* c. *Autorité des marchés financiers*, 2023 CSC 29.

23 Bien que l'ordonnance de la Régie à l'effet que M. Bourgoin paye plus d'un million de dollars à la Fédération ait été annulée en appel, les conclusions de la Cour relatives à la compétence font autorité. La demande d'autorisation d'appel de l'arrêt de la Cour d'appel du Québec, 2010 QCCA 1593, a été rejetée avec dépens en faveur de l'intimé Bourgoin par la Cour suprême du Canada, no 33903, le 23 décembre 2010.

24 Article 3076 C.c.Q.: « Les règles du présent livre s'appliquent sous réserve des règles de droit en vigueur au Québec dont l'application s'impose en raison de leur but particulier ».

25 Article 3126 C.c.Q.: « L'obligation de réparer le préjudice causé à autrui est régie par la loi de l'État où le fait générateur du préjudice est survenu. Toutefois, si le préjudice est apparu dans un autre État, la loi de cet État s'applique si l'auteur devait prévoir que le préjudice s'y manifesterait. Dans tous les cas, si l'auteur et la victime ont leur domicile ou leur résidence dans le même État, c'est la loi de cet État qui s'applique ».

d'application nécessaire », aussi appelée « loi de police »[26] aux côtés de la méthode traditionnelle des conflits de lois pour solutionner les affaires comportant un élément d'extranéité.

Par conséquent, pour justifier la compétence de la Régie, la Cour aurait pu se fonder également sur la constatation que la loi québécoise était applicable.

Trois décisions illustrent cette seconde approche à la question de la compétence des autorités administratives relativement à des situations de droit international privé. Dans *Commission des droits de la personne et des droits de la jeunesse* (*C.G.*) c. *Gomez*[27], le Tribunal des droits de la personne a conclu à l'application de la *Charte des droits et libertés de la personne*[28] en se fondant sur l'article 3126 C.c.Q. puisque l'auteur et la victime du harcèlement sexuel, qui avait eu lieu en Allemagne, étaient domiciliés au Québec. Le Tribunal a considéré avoir compétence sur l'affaire, ayant déterminé que la Charte était applicable et la Charte instituant le Tribunal. Dans *3141705 Canada Inc. c. Brueckner*

---

26 Cette disposition a été utilisée pour refuser la reconnaissance et l'exécution de jugements étrangers (*Kuwait Airways Corp.* v. *Iraq*, 2010 CSC 40, [2010] 2 RCS 571; *McKinnon* c. *Polisuk*, 2009 QCCS 5778, par. 19; *Adoption-106*, 2010 QCCQ 2040, par. 65). L'article a aussi été utilisé pour appliquer la loi québécoise plutôt qu'une loi étrangère dans des situations se déroulant au Québec. Dans *Al-Salem* c. *Procureure générale du Québec* (*Directeur de l'état civil*), 2019 QCCS 1287, un mariage célébré au consulat égyptien à Montréal a été invalidé, le célébrant n'ayant pas été autorisé par le ministre de la Justice comme le requiert l'article 366 C.c.Q. Cet article a été déclaré d'application immédiate tout comme certaines exigences formelles qui n'avaient pas été respectées. Depuis, la règle de conflit de loi (a. 3088 C.c.Q.), qui prévoyait la possibilité d'appliquer la loi du domicile ou de la nationalité de l'un des époux aux conditions de forme du mariage comme facteurs de rattachement alternatifs a été modifiée pour ne retenir que la loi du lieu de sa célébration, et ce, malheureusement, que le mariage soit célébré à l'étranger ou au Québec et quel que soit le domicile des époux.

Un certain nombre de décisions ont également appliqué la *Loi sur la protection de la jeunesse*, RLRQ, P-34.1 de façon immédiate: *Protection de la jeunesse-44*, 1981 T.J. 2073; *Protection de la jeunesse – 222*, 1986 R.J.Q. 2541; *Protection de la jeunesse – 1378*, 2013 QCCS 1063, par.11. Dans d'autres affaires, les dispositions en cause n'ont pas été qualifiées de cette nature (celles sur le patrimoine familial: *B.*(*G.*) c. *C.*(*C.*), 2001 CanLII 20627 (QC CA); celle qui interdit de déroger au droit du tiers lésé d'exercer son droit d'action contre l'assuré ou l'assureur ou les deux (a. 2414 et 2501 C.c.Q.): *Ferme Avicole Héva Inc.* c. *Boréal assurances agricoles Inc.*, 2003 CanLII 47539 (QC CS); celles de la *Loi sur la protection du consommateur,* RLRQ, c. P40.1: *Bousquet c. Acer America Corporation* (*Canada*), 2012 QCCQ 1261 *contra* C. Emanuelli, *Droit international privé québécois*, Montréal, 3e éd., Wilson & Lafleur, 2011, par. 547).

27 *Commission des droits de la personne et des droits de la jeunesse* (*C.G.*) c. *Gomez*, 2015 QCTDP 14.

28 *Chartre des droits et libertés de la personne*, RLRQ, c. C-12. Contrairement à la *Chartre canadienne des droits et libertés*, Partie I de la *Loi constitutionnelle, 1982,* constituant l'annexe B de la *Loi de 1982 sur le Canada,* (R.-U.), 1982, c. 11), la charte québécoise s'applique aux parties privées.

Group[29], la *Loi sur la compétition*[30] a été trouvée d'application immédiate et par conséquent seuls les tribunaux canadiens étaient compétents bien que les défendeurs aient été domiciliés à l'étranger et que la loi de la Floride ait été applicable au contrat liant les parties.

Dans *Sharp* c. *Autorité des marchés financiers*[31], la Cour suprême devait déterminer si le Tribunal administratif des marchés financiers (TAMF) avait compétence pour imposer des pénalités administratives à des résidents de la Colombie-Britannique qui, par le biais de compagnies incorporées dans plusieurs pays différents et ayant des comptes bancaires en Europe, avaient pris part à une opération de gonflage et de largage en influençant ou en manipulant de façon irrégulière le cours d'une action en contravention de la *Loi sur les valeurs mobilières* (LVM)[32].

Les juges de la majorité ont observé qu'aucune disposition ne prévoit expressément que le TAMF peut se déclarer compétent sur des parties de l'extérieur de la province, ni ne limite autrement la portée territoriale du régime québécois des valeurs mobilières à l'égard d'opérations interprovinciales ou internationales (par. 102). Ils ont déterminé que le C.c.Q. peut, en principe, s'appliquer à un tribunal administratif comme le TAMF (par. 70)[33] mais, qu'en l'espèce, ces dispositions ne conféraient pas compétence au TAMF (par. 92). À leur avis, le test développé dans *Unifund Assurance Co.* c. *Insurance Corp. of British Columbia*[34], relatif à l'applicabilité (et non pas à la validité)

29 *3141705 Canada Inc. c. Brueckner Group*, 1997 CanLII 9270 (C.S.).

30 *Loi sur la compétition*, SRC 1985, c. C-34.

31 *Sharp* c. *Autorité des marchés financiers*, 2023 CSC 29. Voir S. Blake, « The Territorial Jurisdiction of a Provincial Tribunal », Law360 Canada, 11 décembre 2023; J. Maciura, « Real and Substantial Connection », 17 novembre 2023; S. Pitel, https://conflictoflaws.net/2023/is-this-a-conflicts-case.

32 *Loi sur les valeurs mobilières*, RLRQ, c. V-1.1 (LVM). Ils auraient ainsi agi de concert pour acquérir les actions d'une société américaine (Solo) et faire la promotion de ses activités dans le but d'accroître frauduleusement la valeur de ses actions et de les vendre à profit, profit qu'ils se seraient partagé. Les actions de Solo se négociaient à un marché hors bourse à New York. Solo était un émetteur assujetti au Québec dont l'adresse d'affaires se situait à Montréal et aurait été dirigée par un résident québécois. Les communiqués de presse et le matériel de promotion trompeurs, dont une partie provenait de Montréal, étaient accessibles aux résidents du Québec, et environ quinze investisseurs québécois auraient perdu au total 5 000 $. L'AMF demandait d'ordonner que les défendeurs cessent toute activité à l'égard d'une opération en valeurs mobilières; de leur interdire d'agir en tant qu'administrateurs ou dirigeants d'un émetteur, courtier, conseiller ou gestionnaire d'un fonds de placement pendant cinq ans; et de leur imposer des pénalités administratives.

33 Au contraire des juges majoritaires de la Cour d'appel. On ne peut qu'approuver ce raisonnement de la Cour suprême.

34 *Unifund Assurance Co.* c. *Insurance Corp. of British Columbia*, 2003 CSC 40, [2003] 2 R.C.S. 63.

constitutionnelle[35] d'une loi à une personne de l'extérieur de la juridiction[36] devait servir de critère d'interprétation législative (par. 110). Ils ont souligné que ce test concerne la compétence législative normative, plutôt que la compétence juridictionnelle, en ajoutant que cette dernière peut découler de la première[37]. En appliquant ce test, ils ont déterminé que le TAMF était nécessairement compétent puisqu'aux termes de l'article 93 de la *Loi sur l'Autorité des marchés financiers*[38] (LAMF), le TAMF exerce la compétence prévue par la LVM et que la conduite que l'on reprochait aux appelants avait un lien réel et substantiel avec le Québec[39]. Ainsi, la compétence juridictionnelle du TAMF découlait de la compétence législative normative de la province (par. 136)[40].

L'espace et le temps restreint dont nous disposons ne nous permettent pas d'aller très loin dans l'analyse de cette importante décision qui vient tout juste d'être rendue. On peut toutefois lancer quelques pistes de réflexion.

---

35 On peut remarquer que le droit constitutionnel ne conduit pas ici à établir une règle limitée à un contexte interprovincial comme dans *Hunt* c. *T&N plc*, [1993] 4 R.C.S. 289, puisque la limite territoriale au pouvoir législatif d'une province s'applique également et à plus forte raison dans un contexte international.

36 L'examen de l'applicabilité du point de vue constitutionnel s'articule autour des propositions suivantes :

1. La limitation territoriale de la portée du pouvoir de légiférer des provinces empêche les lois d'une province de s'appliquer aux affaires qui ne présentent pas de lien suffisant avec cette dernière.
2. Le caractère « suffisant » du lien dépend du rapport qui existe entre le ressort ayant légiféré, l'objet du texte de loi et l'individu ou l'entité qu'on cherche à assujettir à celui-ci.
3. L'applicabilité d'une loi provinciale par ailleurs valide à un défendeur de l'extérieur de la province concernée est fonction des exigences d'ordre et d'équité qui soustendent les structures fédérales canadiennes.
4. Comme ils visent une finalité, les principes d'ordre et d'équité sont appliqués d'une manière souple, en fonction de l'objet de la loi. *Unifund Assurance Co.* c. *Insurance Corp. of British Columbia*, 2003 CSC 40, [2003] 2 R.C.S. 63, par. 56.

37 Nous appuyons également ce raisonnement de la Cour suprême.

38 *Loi sur l'Autorité des marchés financiers* (LAMF). Le titre de cette loi ayant été remplacé en 2018 par le suivant : « Loi sur l'encadrement du secteur financier », on le retrouve maintenant sous RLRQ, c. E-6.1.

39 Ils ont sur ce point confirmé le point de vue exprimé par les juges majoritaires de la Cour d'appel : *Langford Sharp* c. *Autorité des marchés financiers*, 2021 QCCA 1364, par. 78.

40 La juge Côté, dissidente, estime que la compétence du TAMF ne peut être déterminée par l'utilisation du critère développé dans *Unifund Assurance Co.* c. *Insurance Corp. of British Columbia*, 2003 CSC 40, [2003] 2 R.C.S. 63, s'agissant d'un critère visant à établir l'application d'une loi et non pas la compétence d'un tribunal. À son avis, puisque ni la LVM ni la LAMF ne dérogent, ni expressément ni implicitement, aux règles du C.c.Q. en ce qui a trait à la compétence du TAMF en matière administrative et que ces dernières ne sont pas applicables en l'espèce, le TAMF était sans compétence. *Sharp* c. *Autorité des marchés financiers*, 2023 CSC 29, par. 139 et s.

Premièrement, on peut observer que puisque l'affaire ne consistait pas à déterminer quelle loi, québécoise ou étrangère, avait vocation à s'appliquer, la Cour n'examine pas les dispositions du C.c.Q. relatives aux conflits de lois. Pourtant, les juges majoritaires ont indiqué que le Livre dixième du C.c.Q. s'applique, en tant que droit commun du Québec, dans les contextes de droit public et administratif (par. 61) sans limiter cette affirmation aux règles de compétence. De plus, c'est bien finalement en déterminant que la loi québécoise s'applique que les juges majoritaires concluent que le tribunal est compétent. Si la Cour avait fait une certaine analyse des règles de conflits de lois prévues au Code, quitte à conclure qu'elles ne s'appliquaient pas même par analogie à la situation en cause, comme elle l'a fait pour les règles de compétence, l'utilisation du critère du lien réel et substantiel aurait pu être confinée aux lois auxquelles ne correspond aucune règle de conflits, plutôt que de sembler en consacrer l'application générale[41]. On peut en effet se demander quel rôle pourraient jouer à l'avenir les règles de conflits dans des contextes de droit public et administratif[42].

Deuxièmement, tout en rejetant l'application du critère du lien réel et substantiel de *common law* pour établir la compétence juridictionnelle en droit québécois[43], elle le réintroduit pour déterminer si la loi s'applique[44] tout en soulignant qu'il s'agit d'une famille de critères mettant en jeu différentes considérations dans chacun des divers contextes dans lesquels la même formule – soit « lien réel et substantiel » – est employée (par. 118). De plus, sans recourir expressément à la notion de loi d'application nécessaire, elle détermine que le TAMF était nécessairement compétent. Or, le recours au test du lien réel et suffisant pour déterminer l'applicabilité constitutionnelle d'une loi dans un contexte de droit international privé sans recourir aux règles de conflits de loi

41 E. Edinger et V. Black. « A New Approach to Extraterritoriality: *Unifund Assurance Co.* v. *I.C.B.C.* » (2004), 40 *Rev. can. dr. comm.* 161, p. 185.

42 Un tribunal administratif peut-il appliquer une loi étrangère? Doit-il plutôt se déclarer sans compétence? Faut-il renoncer à faire usage des règles de conflits de lois dans ce contexte puisqu'aucun réel conflit entre la loi québécoise et une loi étrangère n'existera jamais, un tribunal administratif ne pouvant appliquer une loi étrangère de par la limitation de ses pouvoirs?

43 L'arrêt *Club Resorts Ltd. c. Van Breda*, 2012 CSC 17, [2012] 1 R.C.S. 572 « établit le critère du lien réel et substantiel dans le contexte d'actions en responsabilité délictuelle en *common law* et ne s'applique pas au Québec », *Sharp* c. *Autorité des marchés financiers*, 2023 CSC 29, par. 123. Voir aussi *Charbonneau* c. *Apple Canada Inc.*, 2016 QCCS 5770, par. 100.

44 Le C.c.Q. comporte un certain nombre de dispositions qui réfèrent à la notion de lien suffisant (a. 3136 C.c.Q.), étroit (a. 3079 C.c.Q. et 3082 C.c.Q.), ou les plus étroits (a. 3077, 3107, 3112, 3113 C.c.Q.).

n'équivaut-il pas à qualifier la loi d'application immédiate[45]? D'un point de vue méthodologique, le recours aux lois d'application immédiate pour déterminer la compétence juridictionnelle est-il correct[46]?

Finalement, la Cour aurait-elle pu conclure à la compétence du tribunal sans s'appuyer sur l'applicabilité de la loi québécoise? Quel rôle la notion d'un ordre public de rattachement[47] (lequel d'ailleurs appelle pour son application un certain lien de proximité avec le for)[48] aurait-il pu jouer?

45 Dans *Langford Sharp* c. *Autorité des marchés financiers*, 2021 QCCA 1364, par. 71, les juges majoritaires de la Cour d'appel ont indiqué que les sanctions civiles prévues à la LVM étaient d'application immédiate. En appel à la Cour suprême, la juge Côté, minoritaire, indique que « ces règles de droit en vigueur au Québec dont l'application s'impose en raison de leur but particulier » pourraient comprendre la LVM et la LAMF : *Sharp* c. *Autorité des marchés financiers,* 2023 CSC 29, par. 186. Dans *Daphnis* c. *Bello*, 2022 QCCS 4790, note 37, le juge observe que « du point de vue du droit comparé, ce critère du « lien réel et important » pour déterminer l'application dans l'espace de la *Loi sur le droit d'auteur*, L.R.C. (1985), ch. C-42, – et qui en fait pratiquement l'équivalent d'une « loi d'application immédiate » (cf. a. 3076 C.c.Q.) -, est assez singulier. En matière de droit international privé de droit d'auteur, la plupart des juridictions ou des traités internationaux utilisent plutôt la méthode conflictuelle classique ».

46 Commentant l'affaire *Kuwait Airways Corp.* v. *Iraq*, 2010 CSC 40, [2010] 2 RCS 571, le prof. Goldstein souligne que l'article 3076 C.c.Q., n'est pas conçu pour jouer un rôle en matière de compétence des tribunaux: G. Goldstein, « Méthodes alternatives: lois de police, règles matérielles et méthodes de la reconnaissance », in *JurisClasseur Québec, Droit international privé*, Montréal, LexisNexis, éd. feuilles mobiles, fasc. 6, par. 25. On observera cependant que l'article 3076 C.c.Q. est situé dans le Titre I – Dispositions générales du Livre X et peut donc avoir vocation à s'appliquer aux règles juridictionnelles prévues au Titre III.

47 Voir en droit français, Petra Hammje, « L'ordre public de rattachement», (2009) 18 *Travaux du Comité français de droit international privé*, pp. 153–86, pp. 165 et s. P. Callé, indique que : « la détermination de la compétence générale des autorités [publiques françaises] ne paraît poser qu'une seule difficulté : il s'agit de l'hypothèse où la règle de conflit déclarerait applicable la loi française, tandis qu'aucune règle de compétence classique ne donnerait compétence aux autorités françaises. Il conviendrait alors d'admettre un chef exorbitant de compétence » : *L'acte public en droit international privé*, à https://www.biicl.org/files/1046_l%5C'acte_public_en_droit_international_prive_-_pierre_calle.pdf, p. 130. Bernard Audit, *Droit international privé*, Paris, éd. Economica, 6e éd., 2010, par. 353 et s. regroupe les actions mettant en cause le fonctionnement d'un service, l'urgence, et un déni de justice sous le titre des compétences fondées sur le bon ordre sur le territoire.

48 Appelé en droit allemand « *inlandsbeziehung* » et en droit suisse « binnenbeziehung » ; voir A. Bucher, « L'ordre public et le but social des lois en droit international privé », (1993) II R.C.A.I. 9, tome 239, par. 25 et s.

2 Les instruments multilatéraux ou régionaux

Selon le droit constitutionnel canadien les instruments internationaux sont mis en œuvre par le fédéral ou les provinces suivant leur champ de compétence respectif[49]. Par exemple, les conventions internationales contre la corruption[50] ont été mises en œuvre au Québec par la *Loi concernant la lutte contre la corruption*[51].

La firme québécoise d'ingénierie Lavalin a été au cœur de décisions judiciaires relatives à des paiements dans le but de conclure des contrats importants en Libye[52]. Plus récemment, une autre compagnie basée au Québec et quatre de ses ex-administrateurs ont été poursuivis en lien avec l'obtention de contrats aux Philippines[53].

3 Le rôle du droit international

À notre connaissance, le droit international ne joue aucun rôle pour définir ou limiter le champ d'application géographique des lois et règlements au Québec, sauf dans le champ limité de la protection contre les violations aux droits de

49 En droit canadien, « le traité n'a aucun effet juridique formel en droit interne – même s'il est contraignant sur le plan international – tant qu'il n'a pas été transformé ou mis en œuvre dans le cadre d'un processus législatif interne, habituellement par l'édiction d'une loi (Harrington, pp. 482–485; Currie, p. 235) » : *Nevsun Resources Ltd*, c. *Araya* 2020 CSC 5, par. 159. Voir F. Sabourin, « Les conventions multilatérales de droit international privé conclues par le Canada et leur mise en œuvre en droit québécois », dans N. Vezina, dir, *Le droit uniforme : limites et possibilités, Actes du colloque 2008 de l'Association québécoise de droit comparé et rapports québécois au 1er congrès thématique de l'Académie internationale de droit comparé*, éd. Yvon Blais, Cowansville, 2009, pp. 87–160.

50 Voir le rapport canadien.

51 *Loi concernant la lutte contre la corruption*, RLRQ, c. L-6.1.

52 Des officiers publics lybiens ont reçu de l'argent afin que Lavalin obtienne plusieurs contrats en lien avec le projet de la Grande rivière artificielle. Lavalin a admis sa responsabilité. Voir *R.* c. SNC-*Lavalin international inc.*, C.Q. Montréal, no 500-73-004261-158, 18 décembre 2019, Leblond j.c.q. (non publié). Lavalin a poursuivi notamment deux de ses anciens employés et administrateurs, (« Ben Aïssa »et « Bebawi »), des sociétés ainsi qu'un avocat suisse agissant pour ces dernières (« Kaufmann ») afin de récupérer plus de $127 millions détournés frauduleusement et compenser l'atteinte à sa réputation. Kaufmann et Ben Aïssa ont été trouvés coupables en Suisse et ce dernier a été extradé au Canada où il fait face à d'autres accusations. Bebawi a été trouvé coupable dans *R.* c. *Bebawi*, 2020 QCCS 22.

53 *R.* c. *Ultra Electronics Forensic Technology Inc.* (*UEFTI*), 2022 QCCS 4401.

la personne fondée sur les chartes canadienne et québécoise[54] ou sur le droit international coutumier[55].

Contrairement aux traités qui requièrent une incorporation législative, la coutume fait partie intégrante du droit québécois sans qu'aucune action ne soit requise[56]. Selon un principe d'interprétation législative bien établi, les tribunaux sont légalement tenus d'éviter une interprétation du droit interne qui conduirait l'État à contrevenir à ses obligations internationales, sauf lorsque le libellé de la loi commande clairement un tel résultat[57].

Dans deux affaires qui méritent d'être mentionnées, plutôt que le droit international, c'est le *forum non conveniens* (a. 3135 C.c.Q.) qui a joué un rôle en mettant un terme à la saisine des tribunaux québécois et à toute possibilité que les lois ou règlements du Québec puissent s'appliquer: *Bil'in (Village Council), Late Ahmed Issa Abdallah Yassin, Basem Ahmed Issa Yassin, Maysaa Ahmed Issa Yassin* v. *Green Park International inc., Green Mount International inc. and Annette Laroche*[58] et *Recherches internationales Québec* v. *Cambior inc.*[59].

---

54 *Chartre canadienne des droits et libertés*, Partie I de la *Loi constitutionnelle, 1982*, constituant l'annexe B de la *Loi de 1982 sur le Canada*, (R.-U.), 1982, c. 11); *Chartre des droits et libertés de la personne*, RLRQ, c. C-12.

55 Dans *Nevsun Resources Ltd. v. Araya*, 2020 CSC 5, la Cour suprême du Canada a décidé que la réclamation de trois travailleurs érythréens devait être autorisée à procéder. Ils alléguaient avoir été conscrits indéfiniment, par l'entremise de leur service militaire, dans un régime de travail forcé dans le cadre duquel ils ont dû travailler à une mine en Érythrée appartenant à une société canadienne, Nevsun Resources Ltd. Les travailleurs ont réclamé des dommages-intérêts pour des violations à des interdictions de droit international coutumier relatives au travail forcé, à l'esclavage, aux traitements cruels, inhumains ou dégradants, et aux crimes contre l'humanité. La décision s'appliquerait également au Québec bien qu'elle provienne de la ColombieBritannique.

56 *Nevsun Resources Ltd.* c. *Araya*, 2020 CSC 5, par. 86.

57 *R. c. Hape*, 2007 CSC 26, [2007] 2 R.C.S. 292, par. 53. P.-A. Côté et M. Devinat, *Interprétation des lois*, 5e éd., Montréal, Thémis, 2021, pp. 421–25, par. 1301–07; S. Beaulac et F. Bérard, *Précis d'interprétation législative*, 2e éd., Montréal, LexisNexis, 553 p., pp. 465–85.

58 Dans *Bil'in (Village Council), Late Ahmed Issa Abdallah Yassin, Basem Ahmed Issa Yassin, Maysaa Ahmed Issa Yassin* c. *Green Park International inc., Green Mount International inc. and Annette Laroche*, 2011 CanLII 10843 (CSC), les demandeurs alléguaient que les défendeurs, des compagnies ayant leurs sièges sociaux à Montréal, et qui construisaient des immeubles d'habitation dans des territoires occupés par Israël, le faisaient sur des parcelles de terrain dont ils étaient propriétaires, en contravention de la *Convention* (IV) *relative à la protection des personnes civiles en temps de guerre*. Ils intentèrent une action en responsabilité civile en Cour supérieure du Québec, sollicitant une injonction et un jugement déclaratoire ainsi que des dommages-intérêts punitifs. La Cour supérieure a accueilli une requête en exception déclinatoire au motif de *forum non conveniens* (2010 QCCA 1455). La Cour d'appel a rejeté l'appel (2010 QCCA 1455) et la Cour suprême la demande d'autorisation d'appel.

59 Dans *Recherches internationales Québec* v. *Cambior inc.*, 1998 CanLII 9780 (QC CS), un déversement de cyanure dans un important fleuve en Guyana à la suite du bris d'une

4 Le rôle de la courtoisie internationale

Les règles de droit international privé du Québec sont fondées sur la courtoisie, particulièrement dans le contexte interprovincial[60]. Comme les dispositions du C.c.Q. et du C.p.c. n'y renvoient pas directement, et qu'au mieux la courtoisie y est vaguement définie, elle ne constitue pas une règle contraignante. Elle sert plutôt de guide à l'interprétation des différentes règles de droit international privé[61].

5 L'exigence de caractère raisonnable

Une exigence constitutionnelle du droit canadien veut que les tribunaux ne soient compétents que lorsqu'il existe un lien réel et substantiel[62]. La Cour suprême a souligné qu'au Québec, le C.c.Q. vise à assurer la présence d'un « lien réel et substantiel » entre l'action et la province et à empêcher l'exercice inapproprié de la compétence du for québécois. Par conséquent, il n'était pas nécessaire d'imposer le critère constitutionnel supplémentaire du lien réel et substantiel[63].

Dans le cas de la loi applicable, l'article 3082 C.c.Q.[64], parfois appelée « clause échappatoire », permet d'écarter la loi désignée par les règles de conflits (mais pas celle désignée dans un acte juridique) s'il n'existe pas de lien suffisant entre

digue d'une mine d'or a engendré une action collective au Québec contre une compagnie guyanaise appartement à 65% à une compagnie québécoise. La Cour supérieure a décliné sa compétence en se fondant sur le *forum non conveniens.*

60 *Morguard Investments Ltd.* c. *De Savoye*, 1990 CanLII 29 (CSC), [1990] 3 RCS 1077; *Hocking* c. *Haziza*, 2008 QCCA 800; *Newfoundland and Labrador* (*Attorney General*) c. *Uashaunnuat* (*Innu of Uashat and of ManiUtenam*), 2020 CSC 4, par. 16. Dans cette dernière affaire, des Premières Nations intentent une poursuite contre deux compagnies minières responsables d'un mégaprojet comprenant de nombreuses mines à ciel ouvert exploitées au Québec et à Terre-Neuve-et-Labrador, de même qu'un port, un chemin de fer et des installations industrielles au Québec, et des chemins de fer sillonnant les deux provinces.

61 *Spar Aerospace Ltd.* v. *American Mobile Satellite Corp.*, 2002 CSC 78, [2002] 4 SCR 205, par. 23.

62 *Club Resorts Ltd.* v. *Van Breda*, 2012 CSC 17, [2012] 1 CSC 572, par. 24: « Dans les provinces canadiennes de *common law*, le critère du lien réel et substantiel « à l'instar de Janus, se présente sous deux aspects – l'un de droit international privé et l'autre de nature constitutionnelle – ... ».

63 *Spar Aerospace Ltd.* v. *American Mobile Satellite Corp.*, 2002 CSC 78, par. 55 et 63.

64 Article 3082 C.c.Q. : « À titre exceptionnel, la loi désignée par le présent livre n'est pas applicable si, compte tenu de l'ensemble des circonstances, il est manifeste que la

la situation et cette loi et de lui en substituer une autre qui respecte mieux le lien de proximité. En vertu de cette disposition, dans une affaire de responsabilité civile, après un accident d'avion en Ontario, les parties étant toutes du Québec, à l'exception de certains beaux-parents domiciliés en Colombie-Britannique, la loi québécoise a été trouvée applicable plutôt que la loi ontarienne désignée par l'article 3126 C.c.Q.[65]. Dans deux affaires, la loi québécoise s'est également appliquée à des enfants qui résidaient au Québec afin de déterminer leur admissibilité à l'adoption[66]. Dans d'autres cas, la loi québécoise a été écartée au profit d'une loi étrangère en application de cette disposition[67].

6 Les bases d'application des lois ou des règlements à une conduite entièrement étrangère

6.1 *La nationalité de l'acteur ou d'une personne lésée par le comportement (principe de la « personnalité passive »)*

La nationalité n'est pas un facteur de rattachement généralement retenu au Québec[68]. Comme Emanuelli l'explique[69] il en est ainsi parce que: (1) jusqu'à

---

situation n'a qu'un lien éloigné avec cette loi et qu'elle se trouve en relation beaucoup plus étroite avec la loi d'un autre État. ....».

65 Dans *Giesbrecht* c. *Succession de Nadeau*, 2017 QCCA 386, demande d'autorisation d'appel à la Cour suprême rejetée, 2017 CanLII 75043 (CSC), M. Fournier avait acheté un avion qui se trouvait en Alberta. Il avait engagé M. Nadeau et Nadeau Air Service Inc. pour inspecter l'avion et le ramener au Québec mais l'avion s'est écrasé pendant ce voyage et seul M. Fournier a survécu. L'épouse, les parents, les frères et sœurs ainsi que la belle-famille de l'une des victimes ont intenté des poursuites contre le pilote et son employeur.

66 *Dans la situation de : M. (D.)*, 1999 CanLII 10301 (QC CQ), la mère était domiciliée aux Philippines et dans *Adoption (en matière d')*, 2006 QCCQ 8524, l'enfant avait été placée sous la tutelle des requérants au Maroc alors que ceux-ci y étaient domiciliés.

67 Dans une poursuite contre un assureur, la Cour a écarté la loi québécoise, applicable en vertu de l'article 3119 C.c.Q., au profit de la loi de la Colombie-Britannique: *Univar Canada Ltd.* c. *Aslchem international inc.*, 2014 QCCS 401. En appel, l'action a été rejetée mais cette conclusion quant à la loi applicable ne fut pas remise en question (2016 QCCA 500).

68 La nationalité est retenue comme facteur de rattachement alternatif pour désigner la loi applicable par les articles 3091, al. 1 (établissement de la filiation), 3109, al. 3 (validité formelle d'un testament) et 3123, al. 2 (régime matrimonial ou d'union civile) ainsi qu'en matière de reconnaissance et d'exécution des décisions étrangères par les articles 3166 (filiation) et 3167 (divorce) C.c.Q. La nationalité ne joue aucun rôle pour la compétence des tribunaux québécois.

69 C. Emanuelli, *Droit international privé québécois*, Montréal, 3e éd., Wilson & Lafleur, 2011, par. 26 et 127.

une époque relativement récente, les pays qui composaient l'empire britannique n'avaient pas leur propre nationalité. Leurs citoyens étaient sujets britanniques[70]; (2) au Canada, la nationalité relève des compétences fédérales alors que, pour la plupart, les questions qui intéressent le droit international privé sont du ressort des provinces; (3) un pays qui encourage l'immigration à des fins de peuplement n'adoptera pas une règle de conflit donnant de larges compétences à la loi nationale des étrangers, afin de faciliter leur intégration dans leur pays d'adoption, et y substituera la loi de leur domicile ou de leur résidence.

Jusqu'à récemment, les articles 59 et 71, paragraphe 3, C.c.Q. imposaient une exigence de nationalité pour demander un changement de nom ou de désignation de sexe. La Cour supérieure a biffé les mots "et ayant la citoyenneté canadienne" de ces articles les considérant invalides au regard des chartes qui interdisent la discrimination. L'exigence de nationalité empêchait les personnes transgenres et non-binaires domiciliées au Québec d'avoir leur identité de genre reflétée dans les documents d'identification dont elles ont besoin pour s'engager dans la vie de leur société d'adoption[71].

6.2 *Les effets internes du comportement en question*

Les décisions qui ont été mentionnées jusqu'à présent dans ce rapport et qui concernent un défendeur domicilié et ayant agi à l'étranger ont été portées à l'attention des autorités du Québec en raison précisément des effets de la conduite en question.

On peut ajouter à ces exemples, l'affaire *Ordre des optométristes du Québec* c. *Coastal Contacts Inc. et al.*[72] où la vente par Internet de lentilles cornéennes à des résidents du Québec par une compagnie de la Colombie-Britannique n'a pas été considérée comme un acte de la compétence exclusive des optométristes du Québec. Par conséquent, la question de l'application extraterritoriale de *Loi sur l'optométrie*[73] et du *Code des professions*[74] ne se soulevait pas. À *contrario*, on peut penser qu'une personne hors du Québec qui poserait un acte de la

70 Jusqu'au 1er janvier 1947 au Canada, le statut juridique de citoyen canadien n'existait pas. Voir : https://www.canada.ca/fr/immigration-refugies-citoyennete/organisation/publications-guides/bulletins-guides-operationnels/citoyennete-canadienne/apercu/historique-legislation.html

71 *Centre for Gender Advocacy* c. *Attorney General of Québec*, 2021 QCCS 191, par. 253–54, 332.

72 *Ordre des optométristes du Québec* c. *Coastal Contacts Inc. et al.*, 2017 CanLII 442 (CSC) a rejeté la demande d'autorisation d'appel de 2016 QCCA 837. Le juge de première instance avait donné effet à la loi de la Colombie-Britannique choisie par les parties : 2014 QCCS 5886.

73 *Loi sur l'optométrie*, RLRQ, c. O-7.

74 *Code des professions*, RLRQ, c. C-26.

compétence exclusive d'un professionnel québécois à l'égard d'une personne du Québec pourrait y être poursuivie avec succès.

Dans un tout autre ordre d'idées, il convient de mentionner l'article 3100 C.c.Q. qui prévoit que lorsque l'application de la loi successorale sur des biens situés à l'étranger ne peut se réaliser, des correctifs peuvent être apportés à même les biens situés au Québec notamment au moyen d'un rétablissement des parts, d'une nouvelle participation aux dettes ou d'un prélèvement compensatoire constatés par un partage rectificatif. Cette disposition pourrait mener à l'application tant d'une loi étrangère que d'une loi québécoise. Si le Québec semble indifférent à la loi applicable, il ne semble pas l'être à l'application de sa règle de conflit de loi qu'il vise à imposer à l'étranger[75].

6.3 *Le principe de la compétence universelle*

Le principe de la compétence universelle existe en droit canadien dans des matières de compétence fédérale comme le droit criminel[76] ou le divorce[77], mais le droit constitutionnel limite la possibilité pour les provinces d'en établir une.

Le C.c.Q. comporte néanmoins une disposition, l'article 3136[78], qui retient la compétence des tribunaux ainsi que possiblement l'application de la loi québécoise, et qui relève de la notion de compétence universelle. Cependant,

---

75 La jurisprudence n'a pas encore fait usage de cette disposition mais peut-être la pratique notariale y recourt-elle.

76 Voir le rapport canadien et *Munyaneza* c. *R.*, 2014 QCCA 906, demande d'autorisation d'appel rejetée dans *Désiré Munyaneza* c. *Sa majesté la Reine*, 2014 CanLII 76857 (CSC).

77 La *Loi sur le mariage civil*, L.C. 2005, ch. 33, prévoit que tous les mariages célébrés au Canada entre non-résidents, qu'ils soient de même sexe ou de sexe opposé, et qui seraient valides au Canada si les époux y avaient leur domicile, sont valides pour l'application du droit canadien, même si les non-résidents ou l'un deux n'ont pas, au moment du mariage, la capacité de le contracter en vertu du droit de l'État de leur domicile respectif. Elle permet également aux tribunaux canadiens d'accorder le divorce aux époux qui résident dans un État où le divorce ne peut leur être accordé parce que la validité de leur mariage n'y est pas reconnue.

78 Article 3136 C.c.Q. : « Bien qu'une autorité québécoise ne soit pas compétente pour connaître d'un litige, elle peut, néanmoins, si une action à l'étranger se révèle impossible ou si on ne peut exiger qu'elle y soit introduite, entendre le litige si celui-ci présente un lien suffisant avec le Québec ». Dans *Langford Sharp* c. *Autorité des marchés financiers*, 2021 QCCA 1364, le juge de la Cour d'appel Mainville, minoritaire, avait estimé que l'article 3136 C.c.Q. pouvait également fonder la compétence du TAMF. Cependant en appel, tous les juges de la Cour suprême ont estimé que cet article ne s'appliquait pas notamment parce que la demanderesse-intimée ne l'avait pas invoqué: *Sharp* c. *Autorité des marchés financiers*, 2023 CSC 29.

ses conditions d'application étant difficiles à rencontrer[79], il n'a pas encore été retenu[80] excepté dans quelques affaires relatives à la garde d'enfants ayant leur résidence dans des États n'étant pas parties à la *Convention de La Haye sur les aspects civils de l'enlèvement international d'enfants*[81].

Il semble également y avoir une compétence universelle au Canada pour les procédures en reconnaissance et en exécution des décisions étrangères et, dans ce contexte, pour l'application des lois canadiennes[82].

---

79 J. P. McEvoy, « Forum of necessity in Québec Private International Law: C.C.Q. art. 3136 », (2005) 35 *R.G.D.* 61, 2005 CanLIIDocs 410; S. Guillemard, « Règles générales de compétence des tribunaux québécois » dans P.-C. Lafond, and G. Goldstein, *JurisClasseur Québec – Droit international privé*, Montréal, LexisNexis, feuilles mobiles, fasc. 8, par. 7 et s.; C. Emanuelli, *Droit international privé québécois*, Montréal, Wilson & Lafleur, 2011, par. 168; G. Goldstein, *Droit international privé, vol. 2 – Compétence internationale des autorités québécoises et effets des décisions étrangères (art. 3134 à 3168 C.C.Q.)*, coll. Commentaires sur le Code civil du Québec, Montréal, Éditions Yvon Blais, 2013, par. 3136.560, EYB2013DCQ1276; H.P. Glenn, « Droit international privé », dans Barreau du Québec et Chambre des notaires du Québec, *La réforme du Code civil*, t. 3, Sainte-Foy, Presses de l'Université Laval, 1993, no 74 ; J.A. Talpis et J.-G. Castel, « Le Code civil du Québec : Interprétation des règles du droit international privé », dans Barreau du Québec et Chambre des notaires du Québec, *La réforme du Code civil, ibid.*, par. 423; A.D. Johnston, « (Almost) Any Port in a Storm – Forum of Necessity Jurisdiction in Québec and Canada », (2010–2011) 20 R.J.E.U.L. 130; S. Peari, « Three Objections to Forum of Necessity: Global Access to Justice, International Criminal Law, and Proper Party », 2018 55–1 *Osgoode Hall Law Journal* 225, 2018 CanLIIDocs 10751.

80 *Mamadou Zoungrana* c. *Air Algérie*, 2017 CanLII 6745 (CSC) (écrasement d'avion au Mali tuant 110 nationaux de différents pays, dont seulement 12 pouvaient poursuivre au Canada en vertu de la *Convention pour l'unification de certaines règles relatives au transport aérien international* conclue à Montréal en 1999); *Anvil Mining Ltd. c. Association canadienne contre l'impunité*, 2012 CanLII 66221 (CSC); G. Saumier, « Commentaire sur Anvil Mining », (2013) 9 RDDDM. 145 (plusieurs civils tués lors de la répression d'une insurrection au Congo par des militaires avec la complicité d'une compagnie minière australienne ayant un établissement au Québec); *Lamborghini (Canada) Inc. c. Automobili Lamborghini S.P.A.*, 1996 CanLII 6047 (QC CA), [1997] R.J.Q. 58 (C.A.) (les coûts et les inconvénients relatifs à un procès en Italie en vertu d'une clause d'élection de for); *Souffrant c. Haytian American Sugar Company*, 2006 QCCS 5580 (action pour redevances impayées en vertu d'un bail haïtien pour l'occupation de terres situées en Haïti au profit d'une famille domiciliée et résidant en Haïti).

81 *Droit de la famille-1830*, 2018 QCCA 24 et *Droit de la famille – 082431*, 2008 QCCS 4493 (garde d'enfants domiciliés en Arabie Saoudite et illégalement déplacés au Québec par leur mère); dans *L.F.* c. *N.T.*, 2001 CanLII 27958 (QC CA), la mère a été invitée à présenter un argument basé sur l'article 3136 C.c.Q pour appuyer sa demande de garde pour ses enfants domiciliés en Côte d'Ivoire qu'elle avait illégalement déplacés au Québec. Dans *N. (H.H.)* c. *Ng. (O.X.)*, 2002 CanLII 63084 (QC CS), les enfants avaient été déplacés de la Thaïlande par leur mère qui en demandait la garde au Québec.

82 Dans *Chevron Corp.* c. *Yaiguaje*, 2015 CSC 42, [2015] 3 R.C.S. 69, par. 72, la Cour suprême a indiqué à l'unanimité qu'il n'est pas nécessaire d'établir un lien réel et substantiel entre le défendeur ou le litige et le tribunal saisi de la demande de reconnaissance et d'exécution

7 Les liens territoriaux

Certaines décisions qui ont été mentionnées jusqu'à présent dans ce rapport démontrent que les lois et les règlements du Québec s'appliquent aux activités qui se déroulent à l'étranger sur la base d'agissements au Québec. Le *forum non conveniens* et la clause échappatoire sont des moyens de balancer l'importance relative des liens avec l'étranger et avec le Québec de manière à parvenir à un équilibre. On peut ajouter à ces exemples, l'affaire *Paquette* c. *Comité de discipline de la Corporation professionnelle des médecins du Québec*[83] dans laquelle il a été décidé que la Corporation professionnelle des médecins et son Comité de discipline pouvaient sanctionner un médecin qui avait administré un traitement en Haïti puisque tous les patients étaient des Québécois, qu'ils avaient été examinés au Québec, où le diagnostic avait été posé et la recommandation pour le traitement faite. Le médecin était un membre de la corporation du Québec et les sanctions disciplinaires sont destinées à protéger le public en maintenant la qualité professionnelle des membres de la corporation. Par conséquent, le professionnel n'est pas exonéré de sa responsabilité du fait que la conduite ait lieu à l'étranger[84].

8 La nationalité de l'entreprise

Comme il a été mentionné, la nationalité n'est pas utilisée au Québec comme facteur de rattachement pour les lois et règlements, mais le domicile (siège) d'une personne morale, le lieu de son établissement ou le lieu où ses activités sont conduites sont à considérer. Certaines lois retiennent plutôt si le capital social d'une personne morale fait partie du domaine de l'État. La *Loi sur l'accès aux documents des organismes publics et sur la protection des renseignements personnels* (LA)[85] en est un exemple.

---

du jugement étranger. Bien que ce jugement émane de l'Ontario, les juges ont ajouté en *obiter* qu'ils croyaient que le législateur québécois avait voulu la même chose.

Depuis qu'il a été rendu, *Chevron* n'a jamais été cité au Québec sauf dans une affaire qui ne concernait pas la question qui nous occupe et qui a été renversée par la suite en appel : *International Air Transport Association* v. *Instrubel*, N.V., 2019 CSC 61.

83 *Paquette* c. *Comité de discipline de la Corporation professionnelle des médecins du Québec*, 1995 CanLII 5215 (QC CA).

84 *Ibid.*

85 *Loi sur l'accès aux documents des organismes publics et sur la protection des renseignements personnels*, RLRQ, c. A-2.1. La *Loi sur la protection des renseignements personnels et les documents électroniques* (LPRPDE), L.C. 2000, c. 5, ne s'applique pas au Québec. Depuis le 22 septembre 2023, avant de communiquer à l'extérieur du Québec un renseignement personnel, une organisation publique ou privée (*Loi sur l'accès aux documents des organismes*

Ainsi, lorsque M. Boyer a demandé à Hydro-Québec International (HQI) en se fondant sur la LA des copies de certains documents mais que celui-ci a refusé de les lui communiquer, il a demandé à la Commission d'accès à l'information du Québec (CAI) de réviser cette décision[86]. La CAI a conclu que les documents que HQI détenait étaient ceux d'une filiale (HQIC) d'Hydro-Québec, une société d'État, et donc que HQIC était soumise à la LA. Le lieu d'incorporation de HQIC et son siège social (Bermudes), ou la localisation de ses affaires (Chine) ne devaient pas être pris en considération. En appel de la décision de la CAI, la Cour du Québec[87] a au contraire conclu que les actions de HQIC appartenaient à HQI et non pas à Hydro-Québec. La Cour a distingué le capital social du patrimoine. Alors que le premier est la propriété de l'État, le second l'est de la personne morale. Quoiqu'il en soit, les documents de HQIC pouvaient être accessibles.

9 Les règles d'interprétation

Les lois et règlements sont généralement silencieux en ce qui concerne leur champ géographique. Une règle d'interprétation contre l'extraterritorialité existe qui se confond, étant donné le cadre constitutionnel canadien en matière de lois provinciales, avec celui qui commande de préférer l'interprétation permettant d'affirmer la validité d'un texte à celle qui le rend invalide[88].

---

publics et sur la protection des renseignements personnels dans le secteur privé, RLRQ, c. P-39.1), doit procéder à une évaluation des facteurs relatifs à la vie privée. Le Québec est officiellement la première juridiction au Canada à mettre à jour ses lois en matière de protection des renseignements personnels suivant la tendance initiée par le Règlement général sur la protection des données (« RGPD ») de l'Union européenne selon Bordner, Ladner, Gervais, Réforme des lois québécoises en matière de protection des renseignements personnels : guide de conformité pour les entreprises, novembre 2021. https://www.blg.com/-/media/insights/documents/blg-quebec-loi-64-guide.pdf?spid=4366DC9F7C8F45FB8B279931C3153818

86 La société d'État Hydro-Québec, constituée en vertu de la *Loi sur Hydro-Québec*, RLRQ, c. H-5, détient 100 % des actions d'Hydro-Québec International (HQI) qui détenait la totalité des actions de HQI China Limited (HQIC). HQIC est dissoute et tous les documents de HQIC demandés par M. Boyer sont devenus en la possession de HQI.

87 *Hydro-Québec international inc.* c. *Boyer*, 2015 QCCQ 7681. Dans *Boyer* c. *Hydro-Québec International inc.*, 2018 QCCAI 157, sur le mérite de l'action, la CAI a conclu que les documents demandés étaient protégés par des exceptions prévues à la LA.

88 P.-A. Côté et M. Devinat, *Interprétation des lois*, 5e éd., Montréal, Thémis, 2021, pp. 236–38, par. 782; S. Beaulac et F. Bérard, *Précis d'interprétation législative*, 2e éd., Montréal, LexisNexis, 553 p.

10 Les « lois de blocage »

Quatre exemples méritent d'être mentionnés.

Le premier est la *Loi sur les dossiers d'entreprise*[89] qui interdit le transport hors de la province de documents qui se rapportent à une affaire commerciale à la suite d'une ordonnance judiciaire étrangère. Dans *Hunt* v. *T&N plc*[90], la Cour suprême a indiqué: « la Loi, tout comme son équivalent ontarien dont elle s'inspire, a été adoptée, ..., pour faire obstacle à l'application extraterritoriale des lois américaines antitrusts et peut-être à d'autres formes d'ingérence judiciaire étrangère »[91]. Elle a déclaré l'application de la loi entre les provinces inconstitutionnelle mais celle-ci s'applique toujours à l'international.

Le second exemple a trait aux matières premières. Les articles 3129, 3151 et 3165 C.c.Q. prévoient : (1) l'application obligatoire de la loi québécoise en ce qui concerne la responsabilité civile pour le préjudice souffert au Québec ou à l'étranger et résultant de l'exposition ou de l'utilisation d'une matière première qu'elle ait été transformée ou non, qui origine du Québec; (2) la compétence exclusive des autorités québécoises et (3) la non-reconnaissance de la compétence des autorités étrangères et par conséquent celles des décisions rendues à l'extérieur du Québec lesquelles ne peuvent donc pas être rendues exécutoires par les autorités du Québec. Des dispositions similaires avaient été adoptées dès 1989[92].

Il ne peut être nié que ces dispositions ont été adoptées afin de protéger des intérêts économiques locaux au détriment de droits étrangers, en particulier américains[93]. Il doit être souligné que l'ordre public ne peut être soulevé pour

---

89 *Loi sur les dossiers d'entreprise*, RLRQ, c. D-12.

90 Dans *Hunt* c. *T&N plc*, 1993 CanLII 43 (CSC), [1993] 4 SCR 289, le demandeur alléguait avoir souffert un préjudice causé par son exposition à des fibres d'amiante distribuées dans la province de sa résidence par les défendeurs, des compagnies québécoises. Le demandeur a obtenu une ordonnance de la Colombie-Britannique visant la production de documents du Québec liés à son action mais les défendeurs ont refusé de s'y conformer.

91 Une allocution prononcée par le premier ministre du Québec d'alors au moment du dépôt du projet de loi l'établit clairement. À maintes reprises, les tribunaux du Québec ont affirmé que c'était vraiment là le but de la Loi. En dépit de ce prétendu objectif restreint, les tribunaux québécois ont donné à la Loi une interprétation généreuse conforme à son texte très général. *Hunt* c. *T&N plc*, 1993 CanLII 43 (CSC), [1993] 4 SCR 289.

92 Les articles 8.1 du *Code civil du Bas Canada* et 21.1 et 181.1 C.p.c., ont été abrogés en 1994 avec l'entrée en vigueur du nouveau C.c.Q.

93 *Worthington Corp.* c. *Atlas Turner Inc.*, 2004 CanLII 21370 (QC CA), par. 35. Voir H. P. GLENN, « La guerre de l'amiante », (1991) 80 *R.c.d.i.p.* 41–60.

refuser la reconnaissance et l'exécution d'un jugement étranger pour la seule raison que des dommages comparables n'auraient pu être octroyés au Québec. Les jugements américains en sont un bon exemple.[94]

Le troisième exemple concerne précisément cette exception d'ordre public qui s'applique lorsqu'une loi étrangère est désignée (a. 3081 C.c.Q.) et quand un jugement étranger doit être reconnu et exécuté (a. 3155, par. 5 C.c.Q.). La Cour supérieure du Québec a ainsi refusé de reconnaître et d'exécuter un jugement du Royaume-Uni qui avait sommairement maintenu un contrat de prêt assujetti à la loi du Royaume-Uni laquelle prévoyait un taux d'intérêt annuel de 438% auquel s'ajoutait, en cas de défaut, un taux d'intérêt annuel de 73%[95].

Un dernier mot sur les actions collectives multiterritoriales. Dans *Vivendi Canada Inc.* v. *Dell'Aniello*[96], la Cour suprême du Canada a statué que le fait que les membres du groupe vivent dans différentes provinces au Canada ne devait pas empêcher la Cour d'autoriser l'action collective. Dans *Canada Post Corp.* v. *Lépine*[97], la Cour a souligné que le besoin de former des classes nationales de

---

94 *Beals v. Saldanha*, [2003] 3 R.C.S. 416, 2003 CSC 72. Dans *Cortas Canning & Refrigerating Company* v. *Suidan Bros. Inc./Suidan Frères inc.*, 1999 CanLII 12203 (QCSC), il n'a pas été nécessaire pour la Cour de se prononcer sur la violation de l'ordre public parce qu'elle était parvenue à la conclusion que la cour américaine aurait dû décliner sa compétence. Pour une valeur de $96 de marchandises achetées au Texas, 9 millions de dollars américains avaient été octroyés en dommages au plaignant par le tribunal américain pour compétition intentionnelle et illégale.

95 *Awanda* c. *AMBC Ventures Inc.*, 2022 QCCA 1133.

96 *Vivendi Canada Inc.* v. *Dell'Aniello*, 2014 CSC 1, par. 62–63. Le litige résultait d'une modification unilatérale apportée par l'employeur au régime d'assurance-maladie dont il était le promoteur pour ses retraités et leurs conjoints survivants. Le groupe proposé incluait 250 retraités, qui avaient travaillé dans six provinces, ou leurs conjoints survivants. Puisqu'aucune loi applicable n'avait été désignée dans les contrats de travail, la loi de la province où l'employé effectuait son travail s'appliquait en vertu de l'article 3118 C.c.Q. Un règlement a été approuvé par la suite dans *Dell'Aniello* c. *Vivendi Canada inc.*, 2015 QCCS 6557.

97 *Société canadienne des postes.* v. *Lépine*, 2009 CSC 16, par. 56–57. En 2000, la Société canadienne des postes commercialise un service d'Internet à vie sur le marché canadien, mais met fin à son engagement l'année suivante. Cela provoque des plaintes et des recours divers. La Cour supérieure du Québec autorise le recours collectif au Québec pour un groupe incluant seulement les résidents du Québec. Plus tard, en Ontario, la Cour supérieure de justice certifie un recours collectif puis entérine une transaction aux termes de laquelle les consommateurs canadiens pourront se faire rembourser le prix d'achat du cédérom et recevoir trois mois de service Internet gratuit. La Société tente alors d'obtenir la reconnaissance du jugement ontarien. La Cour supérieure du Québec rejette sa demande au motif que l'avis de la certification du recours ontarien était inadéquat au

demandeurs en provenance de deux provinces ou plus semble se soulever de temps en temps. Cela: « peut poser le problème délicat de la constitution de sous-groupes en leur sein et de la détermination du régime juridique qui leur serait applicable… [ainsi que] des rapports entre tribunaux supérieurs égaux, mais différents, dans un système fédéral où la procédure civile et l'administration de la justice relèvent des provinces ».

Un tribunal qui est saisi d'une action collective multiterritoriale fait face à l'application possible d'une multitude de lois de différentes juridictions. Certaines auront un régime de « *opt-in* »; d'autres comme le Québec, de « *opt-out* ». Cela n'est pas une raison de refuser de les autoriser. Le plus souvent, en substance, les lois sont similaires. S'il est démontré que les lois d'une autre province sont si substantiellement différentes qu'elles rendent difficile le procès relativement aux membres de cette province, la classe peut être redéfinie. De plus, si un groupe de membres est autorisé dans une autre province, ce groupe peut être retranché de l'action collective de la cour saisie à l'origine[98].

La compétence des tribunaux du Québec doit être établie à l'égard de la demande de chaque membre d'une action collective – qu'il soit un résident du Québec ou non – selon les critères prévus au C.c.Q.[99]. Des actions collectives

---

Québec et créait de la confusion avec le recours collectif entamé au Québec, ce qui violait les principes essentiels de la procédure (a. 3155 (3) C.c.Q.). La Cour d'appel du Québec confirme le jugement sur cette question et ajoute que, bien que la cour ontarienne ait compétence à l'égard du recours, elle aurait dû la décliner sur les résidents québécois en application du *forum non conveniens* (a. 3135, 3155(1) et 3164 C.c.Q.). Enfin, il y avait litispendance entre les deux recours collectifs, la procédure québécoise ayant été engagée la première (a. 3155 (4) C.c.Q.). La Cour suprême du Canada a rejeté l'appel.

98 *Union des consommateurs* c. *Bell Canada*, 2012 QCCA 1287.

99 *Zoungrana* c. *Air Algérie*, 2016 QCCS 2311, par. 70–71. Dans ce cas, les tribunaux du Québec sont compétents quel que soit le domicile du plaignant et pourront donc autoriser une action collective pour un groupe qui inclut des membres qui résident à l'extérieur du Québec : *Benamor* c. *Air Canada*, 2020 QCCA 1597; *Union des consommateurs* v. *Bell Canada*, 2012 QCCA 1287; *Patterson* c. *Ticketmaster Canada Holdings*, 2022 QCCS 1998; *Neale* v. *Groupe Aéroplan inc.* (jugement corrigé le 2012-05-11), 2012 QCCS 902; *Picard* v. *Air Canada*, 2011 QCCS 5186; *Brito* v. *Pfizer Canada inc.*, 2008 QCCS 2231; *Recherches internationales Québec* v. *Cambior inc.*, 1998 CanLII 9780 (QC CS).

mondiales peuvent même être autorisées si le défendeur a son domicile au Québec[100] ou s'il se soumet à la compétence du tribunal québécois[101].

Parmi les règles spécifiques aux actions collectives, il y en a deux au C.p.c. qui concernent les actions multiterritoriales: l'article 577 C.p.c. qui permet à la Cour supérieure, si une action collective multiterritoriale est introduite à l'extérieur du Québec, de décliner sa compétence ou de surseoir à statuer et l'article 594 C.p.c. qui concerne certaines vérifications que la Cour supérieure doit faire si une demande d'homologation d'une transaction ou de reconnaissance et d'exécution d'un jugement portant sur une action collective étrangère lui est faite. Ce dernier peut avoir l'effet d'un « blocking statute » lorsqu'il y a contravention aux principes essentiels de la procédure[102].

La jurisprudence illustre qu'un certain nombre d'actions collectives multiterritoriales ont été autorisées au Canada qui concernaient la même cause d'action à l'encontre d'un même défendeur dont on recherchait la même réparation en ce qui concerne divers traitements médicaux (filtre de veine cave inférieure[103], contraceptifs injectables[104] et antipsychotiques[105]), des valeurs

---

100 *Catucci* v. *Valeant Pharmaceuticals International Inc.*, 2017 QCCS 3870, requêtes pour permission d'appeler rejetées, voir : *Goldman, Sachs & Co. v. Catucci*, 2017 QCCA 1890; *PricewaterhouseCoopers v. Catucci*, 2017 QCCA 1891; *Valeant Pharmaceuticals International Inc. v. Catucci*, 2017 QCCA 1892; *Pearson v. Catucci*, 2017 QCCA 1893; *Schiller v. Catucci*, 2017 QCCA 1894; *Halfon* v. *Moose International Inc.*, 2017 QCCS 2651.

101 *Derome* v. *Stars Group Inc.*, 2020 QCCS 1089; *Majestic Asset Management* v. *Toronto-Dominion Bank*, 2019 QCCS 2781.

102 *Société canadienne des postes.* c. *Lépine*, 2009 CSC 16, et *Hocking* v. *Haziza*, 2008 QCCA 800, sont des exemples de refus de reconnaître et d'exécuter des jugements ontariens avant l'adoption de ces dispositions.

103 Les parties ont conclu une entente pour mettre fin à l'action collective en Ontario lequel a été approuvé par la Cour supérieure de justice de l'Ontario. *Kenneth A. Winter and Jacqueline Winter* v. *C.R. Bard inc., Bard Peripheral Vascular, Inc. and Bard Canada Inc.*, no 1068/16CP. La Cour supérieure du Québec a refusé d'autoriser le désistement mais suspendu le déroulement de l'action collective au Québec bien que, ou peut-être parce que, M. Boehmer avait obtenu un règlement confidentiel avec le défendeur: *Boehmer* c. *Bard Canada inc.*, 2021 QCCS 108). Des actions collectives sont pendantes en Saskatchewan (*Douglas Bussey* c. *Cook Group, Inc. and others*, Court of Queen's Bench of Saskatchewan, 2016 no QBG 2729) et en Colombie-Britanique (*Irene Fraser* c. *Cook Group, Inc. and others*, Supreme Court of British Columbia, NO 178129).

104 Un règlement canadien a été approuvé par la Cour supérieure du Québec, *Brito* c. *Pfizer inc.*, 2021 QCCS 4562, après qu'elle eut autorisé l'action collective nationale: *Brito* c. *Pfizer Canada inc.*, 2008 QCCS 2231.

105 Trois actions collectives nationales ont été autorisées: une en Ontario (*Kirsh* v. *Bristol-Myers Squibb*, 2021 ONSC 6190), une en Alberta (le déroulement de cette action a été suspendu pour permettre le déroulement de l'action ontarienne) et une au Québec (*Scheer* c. *Bristol-Myers Squibb Canada Co.*, 2018 QCCS 4725).

mobilières[106], des produits informatiques[107], des dispositifs de contrôle des émissions[108] et l'encéphalopathie spongiforme bovine[109].

Il y aura parfois des raisons parfaitement valables pour qu'il en soit ainsi[110], par exemple, des préoccupations relatives à la possibilité que le défendeur puisse régler l'affaire avec le demandeur le plus faible ou le moins exigeant. Ce défendeur pourrait ensuite tenter d'opposer ce règlement au demandeur qui aura pour sa part investit temps et efforts pour parfaire ses procédures.

Conclusion

Étant donné les contraintes imposées par le cadre constitutionnel canadien, il n'y a pas actuellement au Québec de pratique à l'effet d'appliquer extraterritorialement les lois et les règlements et il n'y en a jamais eu. Cependant, en se fondant sur le Code civil, les tribunaux sont compétents et appliquent la *lex fori* dans un grand nombre de situations où un élément d'extranéité existe lorsque le domicile de l'une des parties, plutôt que leur nationalité, est au

106 Il y a deux actions collectives nationales substantiellement semblables autorisées contre SNC Lavalin au Québec (*Graaf* c. *SNC-Lavalin Group Inc.*, 2020 QCCS 1232) et en Ontario (*DALI 675 Pension Fund* v. *SNC Lavalin*, 2019 ONSC 6512 (Sup. Ct.) L'action collective québécoise a été intentée en premier. Celle de l'Ontario est considérablement plus complète. Par ailleurs, une autre action collective a été autorisée laquelle concerne les pertes encourues par les investisseurs dans des actions de Volkswagen: *Volkswagen Aktiengesellschaft* c. *Chandler*, 2019 QCCA 641. Une action collective similaire s'est vue refuser l'autorisation de procéder sur la base d'une absence de compétence ou de *forum non conveniens* dans *Leon* v. *Volkswagen* AG, 2018 ONSC 4265 soulignant que des procédures parallèles étaient en cours aux États-Unis et en Allemagne.

107 Une conspiration alléguée pour fixer le prix d'une puce informatique a donné lieu à des actions collectives nationales au Québec (*Micron Technology Inc.* v. *Hazan*, 2020 QCCA 1104) et devant la Cour fédérale du Canada (*Jensen* v. *Samsung Electronics Co., Ltd.*, 2019 FC 373). La Cour d'appel du Québec a maintenu le refus de suspendre le déroulement de la procédure soulignant la différence entre les deux recours et les avantages pour les membres.

108 Plusieurs actions collectives ont été intentées en Ontario (*Maginnis and Magnaye* v. FCA *Canada et al*, 2020 ONSC 5462 rejetant la requête des demandeurs en certification pour les EcoDiesel Dodge Ram 1500 et EcoDiesel Jeep Grand Cherokee; *Quenneville* v. *Volkswagen Group Canada, Inc.*, 2018 ONSC 2516) et au Québec (FCA *Canada inc.* c. *Garage Poirier & Poirier inc.*, 2019 QCCA 2213; *Frank-Fort Construction inc. c. Porsche Cars North America Inc.*, 2018 QCCS 1727) Parmi ces dernières, certaines ne visaient que des résidents québécois et d'autres étaient multiterritoriales. Finalement un règlement global est intervenu.

109 *Flying E Ranche Ltd.* v. *Canada* (*Attorney General*), 2020 ONSC 8076; *Bernèche* c. *Canada* (*Procureur général*), 2010 QCCS 6480.

110 *Boehringer Ingelheim* (*Canada*) *Ltd.* v. *Englund*, 2007 SKCA 62, par. 40.

Québec, qu'elles y ont agi ou que leur conduite y a eu des effets. Il convient de mentionner à cet égard, la notion de lois d'application immédiate, le pouvoir d'ordonner une injonction, la clause échappatoire, le forum de nécessité, l'objectif de blocage de la *Loi sur les dossiers d'entreprise* et des dispositions du Code civil sur les matières premières. Si les traités internationaux et la coutume ont joué un rôle limité, la courtoisie et le *forum non conveniens* permettent d'équilibrer l'exercice délicat de l'application extraterritoriale. Ainsi même des actions collectives multiterritoriales peuvent être entreprises et menées à bien. Ces développements mettent en lumière des zones d'ombre où des questions subsistent telles la compétence d'autorités administratives et la loi applicable par ces autorités en présence d'un élément d'extranéité, et la compétence des tribunaux pour reconnaître et exécuter un jugement étranger.

Extraterritoriality in China

*Shiping Liao**

1 Introduction

The traditional view on extraterritoriality is that the exercise of extraterritorial jurisdiction is permissible in exceptional circumstances. However, in the era of globalization, sovereign states tend to exercise extraterritorial jurisdiction more frequently to protect their nationals' interest and sovereign rights. As one of the increasingly major players in the international arena, China has recently put more emphasis on extraterritoriality. This report tries to depict a full picture of extraterritoriality in Chinese law.[1] Part 2 will give a short introduction of the hierarchy in the Chinese legal system and the historic development of extraterritoriality in Chinese law. Part 3 will describe the different categories of extraterritoriality in Chinese law. In the following part, an analysis concerning the implications of international law on extraterritoriality in Chinese law will be offered. Part 5 will conclude with some features of the Chinese legal system of extraterritoriality as a whole.

2 The Chinese Legal System and the Evolution of Extraterritoriality in Chinese Law

2.1 *The Chinese Legal System: a Hierarchal Picture*

China is a centralized state and Chinese law is divided into central and local levels. The hierarchy of Chinese law is established by the Legislation Law adopted in 2000. At the central level, the hierarchy of the law is listed as the Constitution; the laws adopted by the National People's Congress and its Standing Committee (hereafter "central law"); the administrative regulations adopted by the State Council; and the rules adopted by the Ministries and Commissions of the State Council, the People's Bank of China, the State Audit Administration, and other Divisions with administrative functions directly

* Professor of Law, Beijing Normal University

1 In the context of Chinese law, extraterritoriality and extraterritorial application are not the same and are treated differently. Extraterritoriality only refers to prescriptive extraterritorial jurisdiction and excludes extraterritorial adjudicatory and enforcement jurisdiction, both of which fall within the scope of extraterritorial application.

 | DOI:10.1163/9789004720183_007

under the State Council (hereafter "central departmental rules").[2] The hierarchy of local law is as follows: local regulations adopted by the People's Congress and its Standing Committee of province, autonomous region, special economic zone, ethnic autonomous area, or municipality directly under the State Council; local rules adopted by people's government of province, autonomous region, municipality directly under the Central Government, a districted city, or an autonomous prefecture.[3] The local regulations and rules are inferior to the Constitution, central laws, and the administrative regulations.[4] The central departmental rules share an equal hierarchy with the local rules.[5] Where there is an inconsistency between the local regulations and the central departmental rules, it is up to the State Council to decide which shall prevail. If the State Council considers the local regulations shall prevail, it shall decide the local regulations be applied in the locality concerned. If the State Council considers the central departmental rules shall prevail, the case shall be submitted to the Standing Committee of the National People's Congress for the final ruling.[6]

Local Chinese law, including local regulations and local rules, the legal effect of which is inferior to that of the Constitution, the central law and the administrative regulations, applies only within the relevant locality.[7] Thus, the extraterritoriality of Chinese law refers to the extraterritoriality of Chinese law at the central level, which is the main subject of this research.

2.2 *The Evolution of Extraterritoriality of Chinese Law*

China has pursued integration into the international system since 1979, and one of the most important changes during the integration is that the philosophy of domestic governance is moving from a policy orientation to a law-based orientation. During the past decades, China has enacted numerous laws and regulations, covering almost all the topics with regards to economy, politics, society and culture. However, when looking into the content, it can be observed that China rarely puts emphasis on the extraterritoriality of domestic law. Only a few legislative acts include explicit extraterritorial jurisdiction clauses, and can indeed be applied extraterritorially. The substantive areas these acts cover are taxation, anti-monopoly, and criminal offences. Since the justification of

2 See articles 87 and 88 of the Legislation Law.
3 See articles 63, 73 and 80 of the Legislation Law.
4 See articles 78 and 79 of the Legislation Law.
5 See article 82 of the Legislation Law.
6 See article 95.1.2 of the Legislation Law.
7 See articles 72 and 82 of the Legislation Law.

establishing and exercising extraterritorial jurisdiction in these fields is widely accepted by most states in the world, no state expressed objections or negative responses to this development in Chinese law.

Things changed dramatically when Donald Trump first took charge of the White House and launched a "Trade War" and numerous sanctions against China. Recognizing extraterritoriality as a tool for counter-sanctions and an impetus for improving the rule of law in the regulation of international business transactions and the movement of capital, China accelerated the pace of constructing the legal system of extraterritoriality and extraterritorial application of domestic law.

On February 25, 2019, President Xi Jinping pointed out in his open and important speech at the second meeting of the Central Committee for Comprehensive Law-based Governance of the Country that China should accelerate the construction of a legal system for the extraterritorial application of domestic laws.[8] On this basis, "The Decision of the Central Committee of the Communist Party of China on Several Major Issues concerning Adhering to and Improving the Socialist System with Chinese Characteristics and Promoting the Modernization of the National Governance System and Governance Capacity" issued at the Fourth Plenary Session of the 19th Central Committee of the Chinese Communist Party further emphasizes that "legislation in important areas shall be strengthened and the construction of a legal system for the extraterritorial application of Chinese laws shall be accelerated."[9] Therefore, extraterritoriality will be a key element in future Chinese legislation.

In fact, from 2016 till now, China has enacted quite a few laws with extraterritorial reach, covering more areas than before, such as cyber security, export control, data protection, and finance regulation. China even enacted a blocking statute trying to relieve the impact of various sanctions imposed by Western states. In the following part, the report will give a quick glance at these newly and previously adopted laws.

8 See Xi Jinping Presides over the Second Meeting of the Central Committee for Comprehensive Law-based Governance of the Country and Delivers an Important Speech, available at Xinhua, http://www. xinhuanet.com/politics/leaders/2019-02/25/c_1124161654.htm, last accessed on August 5, 2021.

9 https://news.china.com/zw/news/13000776/20191105/37354178.html, last accessed on August 5, 2021.

3 Extraterritoriality of Chinese Law: a Quick Glance

The Permanent Court of International Justice, in its far-reaching Lotus Case, held that whether a State may lawfully exercise extraterritorial jurisdiction is a matter of international law, and the exercise of extraterritorial prescriptive and adjudicative jurisdiction is permitted only if there is a sufficient connection between the state exercising it and the extraterritorial event.[10] The sufficient connection may be established initially with reference to certain general principles of jurisdiction. Thus, in the following sections, this report will introduce the extraterritoriality of Chinese law mainly based on different jurisdictional principles. However, it should be noted that the exercise of extraterritorial jurisdiction in conformity with one of these principles in a particular case is not necessarily lawful under international law, since these principles differ considerably in the extent to which they offer a legitimate basis for exercising jurisdiction.[11]

3.1 *Principle of Active Nationality Jurisdiction*

This Principle refers to the jurisdiction a state exercises with regards to its own nationals, not limited to natural persons, abroad. Under Chinese law, the indicative sufficient connections between the state exercising active nationality jurisdiction and the extraterritorial event varies with respect to natural persons, companies, ships and aircraft. Here are some examples.

Article 7 of Chinese Criminal Law (Central Law)

This law is applicable to PRC citizens who commit the crimes specified in this law outside the territory of the PRC; but those who commit crimes carrying a maximum sentence of less than three-year imprisonment as stipulated in this law may be exempt from prosecution.

Article 5 of Enterprises Bankruptcy Law (Central Law)

The procedures for bankruptcy which have been initiated according to the present Law shall have binding force over the assets of the relevant debtor beyond the territory of the People's Republic of China.

10 See Lotus Case, PCIJ Series A, No.10, at 18–19.

11 Menno T Kamminga,Extraterritoriality,Max Planck Encyclopedia of Public International Law, https://opil.ouplaw.com/view/10.1093/law:epil/9780199231690/law-9780199231690-e1040?print=pdf.

Article 81 of Coast Guard Law (Central Law)

When a coast guard agency performs law enforcement tasks in an area outside the waters under the jurisdiction of China in accordance with laws, regulations, and international treaties concluded or acceded to by China, the relevant procedures may be governed, *mutatis mutandis*, by the relevant provisions of this Law.

With regards to the determination of the nationality of a corporation or entity, state practice has developed several criteria, such as the place of seat, the place of incorporation, and the control test. The criteria Chinese law adopts are the location test as a general principle, with the control test available as an exception.

Generally speaking, an entity which is incorporated under Chinese law acquires the status of a Chinese legal person, except for the branch of a foreign company established in the territory of China,[12] whether the majority of the shares of the entity are owned by nationals of another State or not.[13] In very rare circumstances, Chinese law may apply to an entity incorporated abroad and controlled by an entity located within Chinese territory. A case to that point is regulation in finance.

Article 2 of Banking Supervision Law (Central Law)

... The term "banking financial institutions" as mentioned in the present Law refers to the commercial banks, urban credit cooperatives, rural credit cooperatives and other financial institutions and policy banks established within China and engaged in taking in deposits of the general public....

The banking supervision institution of the State Council shall, in accordance with the relevant provisions of the present Law, conduct supervision over the financial institutions established abroad upon its approval and the overseas operations of the financial institutions as mentioned in the preceding two paragraphs.

According to article 2, China will supervise financial institutions such as commercial banks established in the territories of other states and controlled by a financial institution incorporated under Chinese law. However, the rationale in Chinese law is not the traditional control test based on the majority of

12 Article 195 of Company Law is as follows: The branch of a foreign company established within the territory of China does not have the status of a legal person.

13 Article 2.2 of Foreign Investment Law is as follows: For the purposes of this Law, "foreign-funded enterprise" means an enterprise formed and registered within China under the laws of China in which all or part of investment is made by a foreign investor.

shares, but the functional control test, with various indications including but not limited to the majority of shares, the right to appoint senior management staff, and veto on vital items affecting business operation.

Unlike the legislation described above, the extraterritoriality of Chinese tax law is based not on nationality, but on domicile. According to the Individual Tax Law, individuals are categorized as residents and non-resident individuals, and a resident individual is an individual who is domiciled in China or who is not domiciled in China but has stayed in the aggregate for 183 days or more of a tax year in China. A resident individual shall pay individual income tax on his or her income obtained both inside and outside China.[14] According to the Enterprise Income Tax Law, enterprises are also classified into resident and non-resident enterprises. Resident enterprise refers to an enterprise that is established inside China, or which is established under the law of a foreign country (region) but whose actual office of management is inside China, and non-resident enterprise refers to an enterprise established under the law of a foreign country (region), whose actual institution of management is not inside China but which has offices or establishments inside China; or which does not have any offices or establishments inside China but has income sourced in China. For a non-resident enterprise having offices or establishments inside China, it shall pay enterprise income tax on its income derived from China as well as on income that it earns outside China but that has real connections with the said offices or establishments.[15]

3.2 *Principle of Passive Nationality Jurisdiction*

The passive personality principle refers to the jurisdiction a State may exercise in respect of conduct abroad which injures its own nationals, especially in the area of criminal procedure. This principle, in the past, has been considered controversial, since it may result in tensions between states who want to exercise jurisdiction.[16] Nevertheless, more and more states, including China, tend to incorporate it into domestic law. The most typical example in Chinese law is Article 8 of the Criminal Law.

Article 8 clearly states that the Chinese Criminal Law may be applied to foreigners who, outside PRC territory, commit crimes against its citizens, provided that this law stipulates a minimum sentence of not less than a three-year

14 See article 1 of Individual Income Tax Law.

15 See articles 2 and 3 of Enterprise Income Tax Law.

16 Menno T Kamminga, Extraterritoriality, Max Planck Encyclopedia of Public International Law, https:// opil.ouplaw.com/view/10.1093/law:epil/9780199231690/law-9780199231690-e1040?print=pdf.

fixed term of imprisonment for such crimes; but an exception is to be made if a crime is not punishable according to the law of the place where it was committed. This Article established the extraterritoriality of Chinese Criminal Law based on the passive personality principle together with *non bis in idem*.

3.3 *Principle of Protective Jurisdiction*

This principle, a well-established concept in international law, provides that states may exercise jurisdiction over aliens who have committed an act abroad which is deemed prejudicial to the security of the particular state concerned, although there are uncertainties as to how far it extends in practice and particularly which acts are included within its net.[17] The example in Chinese law is again article 8 of the Criminal Law, which is also applicable to foreigners committing crimes against the PRC outside its territory, if the crime involves a sentence of imprisonment no less than three years, with the exception that the crime has been punished by the law of the place where it was committed.

Based on article 8 of Chinese Criminal Law, the principle of protective jurisdiction has been incorporated into other areas, such as data security.

Article 2.2 of Data Security Law (Central Law)

Those that conduct data processing activities outside the territory of the People's Republic of China to the detriment of the national security, public interest……shall be held legally liable in accordance with the law.

3.4 *Principle of Universal Jurisdiction*

There is no internationally codified definition of universal jurisdiction at present. The Max Planck Encyclopedia defines it as the (criminal) jurisdiction a State may or is required to exercise in respect of certain serious crimes irrespective of the location of the crime and irrespective of the nationality of the perpetrator or the victim.[18] The Institut de droit international (IDI), in its 2005 resolution on universal jurisdiction, tried to define it by the "absence" of the normal jurisdictional links to the national legal system necessary to exercise jurisdiction. In paragraph 1, the resolution states: "Universal jurisdiction in criminal matters, as an additional ground of jurisdiction, means the

17 Malcolm N. Shaw, International Law, Ninth Edition, Cambridge University Press 2021, p. 573.

18 Menno T Kamminga, Extraterritoriality, Max Planck Encyclopedia of Public International Law, https://opil.ouplaw.com/view/10.1093/law:epil/9780199231690/law-9780199231690-e1040?print=pdf.

competence of a State to prosecute alleged offenders and to punish them if convicted, irrespective of the place of commission of the crime and regardless of any link of active or passive nationality, or other grounds of jurisdiction recognized by international law."[19]

Chinese law, interestingly, incorporated universal jurisdiction in a way linked with international law. Article 9 of Chinese Criminal Law states: "This law is applicable to the crimes specified in international treaties to which the PRC is a signatory state or of which it is a member and the PRC exercises criminal jurisdiction over such crimes within its treaty obligations."

Besides universal crimes under treaty law, China may also exercise jurisdiction over limited universal crimes under customary international law. According to the Speech on the Sixth Committee in the 69th UN General Assembly, the Chinese government referenced an extremely limited number of serious crimes under customary international law, such as piracy on the high seas, as the recognized universal crimes.[20]

3.5 *Effects Principle*

The effects principle refers to the (civil) jurisdiction a State may exercise when foreign conduct produces substantial effects in its territory, and first appeared in the case of United States v. Aluminum Co of America.[21] This principle was originally controversial, but is now more and more accepted by several jurisdictions including Mainland China, especially in commercial areas such as antitrust and securities regulation. Here are some examples.

Article 2 of Anti-monopoly Law (Central Law)

... This Law shall apply to monopolistic conduct outside the territory of the People's Republic of China that has the effect of eliminating or restricting competition on the domestic market of China.

Article 2 of Securities Law (Central Law)

... Where any offering of or trading in securities outside the People's Republic of China disrupts the order of the domestic market of the People's Republic of China and causes any damage to the lawful rights and interests of domestic investors, it shall be handled, and the violators shall be held legally liable, according to the applicable provisions of this Law.

---

19 Institut de droit international (IDI), Resolution on universal criminal jurisdiction with regard to the crime of genocide, crimes against humanity and war crimes, adopted in Krakow, 2005 (http://www.idi-iil.org/idiF/ resolutionsF/2005_kra_03_fr.pdf), para. 1.

20 A/C.6/69/SR.11, para.85.

21 148 F 2d 416 [2nd Cir 1945].

Article 3.1 of Provisions of the State Council on the Standard for Declaration of Concentration of Business Operators 2018 (Administrative Regulations Adopted by State Council)

Where the concentration of business operators reaches any of the following standards, the business operators concerned shall declare it to the anti-monopoly law enforcement institution of the State Council beforehand, otherwise, the concentration is not allowed:

> ... the worldwide business volume of all the business operators involved in the concentration exceeds 10 billion yuan in the last accounting year, and the business volume in China of at least two business operators among them exceeds 400 million yuan separately in the last accounting year.

The references to "the effect of eliminating or restricting competition on the domestic market of China" in the Anti-monopoly Law and "the order of the domestic market of the People's Republic of China" in the Securities Law are strong indications of the effects principle. Pursuant to these clauses, the Chinese authorities, such as the State Administration for Market Regulation (SAMR), the National Development and Reform Commission (NDRC), the Chinese Ministry of Commerce (MOFCOM), and the Chinese Securities Regulatory Commission (CSRC) are able to exercise their jurisdiction in enforcing the Anti-Monopoly Law and the Securities Law against conduct outside the territory of China.

Practices concerning the extraterritorial application of the Chinese Anti-monopoly Law thrived in recent years as the amount of transnational business transactions increased. In June 2014, the MOFCOM prohibited three European shipping companies, namely, Maersk, Mediterranean Shipping and CMA CGM, from setting up a close joint venture in Europe. Considering that the relevant service market was the international container liner shipping service market while the relevant geographic market was the Eurasia route, the trans-Pacific route and the trans-Atlantic route, the MOFCOM determined that the coalition had the effect of eliminating and restricting competition in the container liner shipping service market for the Eurasia route in China.[22] The NDRC also imposed administrative penalties respectively on Samsung, LG and Taiwan Qimei, who coordinated product prices;[23] eight Japanese enterprises

22 Announcement of MOFCOM, No.46, 2014. http://fldj.mofcom.gov.cn/article/ztxx/201406/20140600628586.shtml Accessed on July 30 2021.

23 http://jjs.ndrc.gov.cn/gzdt/t20130117_523203.htm Accessed on July 30 2021.

including Hitachi, who negotiated the pricing of auto parts;[24] and four Japanese enterprises including Seiko, who reached an agreement on the sales price of bearings in the Chinese market,[25] all because of negative impact on the relevant Chinese market.

Chinese entities are also entitled to bring lawsuits against foreign entities whose conduct is subject to article 2 of the Anti-Monopoly Law. In the case of Huawei v. IDC, the defendant was domiciled in the United States and all the alleged conduct took place outside China. Guangdong Higher People's Court held that, since Huawei's products would be exported to the United States, IDC's licensing of Huawei's SEPs to Huawei would have a significant, substantial, and reasonably foreseeable impact on Huawei's production and exports in China. Based on that, the Court held that exorbitant pricing and unreasonable tie-in sales damaged the legitimate rights and interests of Huawei, and ordered IDC to cease relevant infringing acts and compensate Huawei for economic losses of RMB 20 million.[26]

3.6 *Compound Jurisdiction Basis*

As the structure and design of transnational business transactions become more and more complicated, it is not feasible to regulate cross-border business behaviors on a single jurisdictional basis. Recently, there is a tendency in Chinese law to establish extraterritoriality on a compound jurisdiction basis through various provisions. The Export Control Law adopted in 2020 is an example.

Article 44 of Export Control Law (Central Law)

Where any organization or individual outside the territory of the People's Republic of China violates the provisions of this Law regarding the administration of export control, which compromises the national security and interest of the People's Republic of China or interferes with the fulfillment of nonproliferation and other international obligations, the organization or individual shall be dealt with in accordance with the law and held legally liable.

---

24 See NDRC Decisions on Administration Penalty, Fa Gai Ban Jia Jian Chu Fa, No.2, No.3, No.5, and No.7, 2014.

25 See NDRC Decisions on Administration Penalty, Fa Gai Ban Jia Jian Chu Fa, No.10, No.11, No.12, and No.13, 2014.

26 Huawei v. IDC, No.306, Yue Gao Fa Min San Zhong Zi (2013), http://www.pkulaw.cn/case / pfnl_a6bdb 333 2e c0adc42de5f7a40d0f73ccab81af49b42cd5a9bdfb.html?match=Exact Accessed on July 30 2021.

The jurisdiction basis of article 44 is obviously the protective jurisdiction for criminal liability if an individual or entity outside China violated the Export Law. However, considering the inherently transnational nature of export trade and export control as the main purpose of the Export Control Law, without the appropriate definition of export control, it is nearly impossible for the executive and judicial branches to enforce the law only on the basis of protective jurisdiction. Thus, the Export Control Law also establishes its extraterritoriality on other jurisdictional bases:

Article 2.3 of Export Control Law
For the purposes of this Law, "export control" means the prohibitive or restrictive measures imposed by the state on the outward movement of controlled items from the territory of the People's Republic of China and the provision of controlled items by a citizen, legal person, or unincorporated organization of the People's Republic of China to a foreign organization or individual.

Article 2 defines the legal meaning of export control. Firstly, the transfer of controlled items is subject to Export Control Law if it occurs within the territory of China, regardless of whether conducted by a Chinese citizen, legal person or non-legal person organization.[27] Secondly, if the transfer of controlled items occurs between a Chinese citizen, legal person or non-legal person organization, it is still subject to Export Control Law even if such transfer occurs outside of the territory of China. Thus, based on nationality jurisdiction, the legal binding force of the law is extended to transfers conducted outside China.

Article 45 of the Export Control Law
The transit, transshipment, through shipment, or re-export of controlled items, or the export of controlled items to overseas parties from areas under special customs supervision such as bonded areas and export processing zones and from bonded places under customs supervision such as export supervision warehouses and bonded logistics centers, shall be governed by the relevant provisions of this Law.

Furthermore, article 45 extends the law's scope of application to reach re-export, which is always conducted overseas by the foreign importer and

27 An non-legal person organization is an organization which does not have the legal person status but may engage in civil activities in its own name in accordance with law. Non-legal person organizations include sole proprietorships, partnerships, professional service institutions that do not have the legal person status, and the like. See article 102, Civil Code of the People's Republic of China.

end-user. Although the legal definition of re-export is absent in the Chinese Export Control Law, the extraterritoriality of the law has been reinforced by the extension of the subject matter.

3.7 *Regulation Based on Partly Territorial Links*

Read literally, the word "extraterritoriality" clearly excludes territorial jurisdiction from its connotation. As practice in various jurisdictions indicates, however, there is in fact debate as to whether extraterritorial prescriptive jurisdiction refers exclusively to the governance of situations that are wholly located abroad, or whether it includes the governance of situations that are partially located abroad. As to the latter, three approaches have been taken to determine how substantial the "abroad portion" has to be to qualify as extraterritorial jurisdiction. One approach defines extraterritoriality as jurisdiction in the absence of a territorial link. Another approach qualifies it as jurisdiction in the absence of a *substantial* territorial link. Yet another approach defines extraterritoriality as jurisdiction in the presence of a non-exclusive territorial link.[28] China, taking its practices into consideration, is a follower of the third approach, and some activities involving partly territorial links will be subjected to Chinese law even if another part of them occurs abroad.

Article 6.3 of Criminal Law

When either the act or consequence of a crime takes place within PRC territory, a crime is deemed to have been committed within PRC territory.

This article mainly applies to transboundary crimes. For instance, crimes related to telecommunication fraud sometimes occur abroad and cause financial loss of persons or entities located within PRC territory. The financial loss within the territory, as the consequence of the crime, is a critical nexus when Chinese courts exercise jurisdiction.

Article 272 of Civil Procedure Law

Where an action is instituted against a defendant which has no domicile within the territory of the People's Republic of China for a contract dispute or any other property right or interest dispute ... if the subject matter of action is located within the territory of the People's Republic of China ... the people's court at the place ... where the subject matter of action is located ... may have jurisdiction over the action.

28 Susan Emmenegger, Extraterritorial Economic Sanctions and Their Foundation in International Law, 33 Ariz. J. Int'l & Comp. L. 639 (2016).

Article 44 Law of the People's Republic of China on Choice of Law for Foreign-related Civil Relationships

> The laws at the place of tort shall apply to liabilities for tort, but if the parties have a mutual habitual residence, the laws at the mutual habitual residence shall apply. If the parties choose the applicable laws by agreement after any tort takes place, the agreement shall prevail.

In transboundary civil litigation, if the location of the tort is within Chinese territory, the Chinese courts are entitled to exercise jurisdiction over the case. Similar to the definition of the location where a crime takes place, the location of tort in civil proceedings also comprises the locations of the conduct and the resulting consequence. On the one hand, the legislation above enables Chinese courts to seize the civil cases based on partly territorial links. However, on the other hand, the legislation will give rise to competing jurisdiction between Chinese and foreign courts.

The escalation of Sino-U.S. confrontation will definitely be catastrophic for the fragile international order. When shaping extraterritoriality, two ideas must be always borne in mind. First and foremost, the primary purpose of constructing the Chinese legal system is to further improve the rule of law in China, especially incorporating some aspects of foreign relations into the domestic legal framework, defending its core interests such as territorial integrity and essentially national security – not to take countermeasures or sanctions against foreign individual or entities, which risks the Chinese business environment becoming eroded and isolated from the contemporary international market. Second, China must be very cautious when exercising extraterritorial jurisdiction, considering the reasonable connections between the subject matter and exercising jurisdiction, not only for shaping the image of a responsible state, but for maintaining the stability of the international order.

3.8 *Blocking Statute and Sanctions*

China did not have any blocking statutes, laws, or regulations concerning sanctions until 2020. It is noted that China rarely openly declares its economic sanctions and prefers to use vague threats, variation in leadership visits, selective purchases (or non-purchases), and other informal measures instead.[29] These informal measures may afford Chinese leaders greater flexibility in the international arena, but on the other hand may also weaken the legitimacy of the sanctions due to the lack of justification in domestic law. After suffering a lot from U.S. economic sanctions since Donald Trump took the White House

29 James Reilly (2012) China's Unilateral Sanctions, The Washington Quarterly, 35:4, 121–133.

in 2016, China determined to design its blocking statute and sanctions law as a response, which indicated that its sanction policy was switching from informal measures to measures with legal basis.

China's legal system of sanctions now comprises one central law and two central departmental rules: the Anti-foreign Sanctions Law (AFSL) adopted by the Standing Committee of the Thirteenth National People's Congress on June 10, 2021, and the Provisions on the Unreliable Entity List (PUEL)[30] and Rules on Counteracting Unjustified Extraterritorial Application of Foreign Legislation and Other Measures (RCUEAFL),[31] both adopted by the Chinese Ministry of Commerce. AFSL, as one of the basic laws for Chinese foreign policy, has been the focus of the international community since immediately after its adoption.

The AFSL tries to impose Chinese sanctions and countermeasures in two circumstances: (1) when a foreign country violates international law and basic norms of international relations, containing or suppressing China, adopting discriminatory restrictive measures against any Chinese citizen or organization, and meddling in China's internal affairs under various pretexts or pursuant to its own laws;[32] and (2) when it acts compromising China's sovereignty, security, and development interests.[33] Sanctions and countermeasures imposed under these two circumstances are implemented through different approaches.

The first approach is to establish a countermeasure list. The departments of the State Council may decide to include in a countermeasure list the individuals and organizations directly or indirectly involved in the development, decision-making, and implementation of the discriminatory restrictive measures as mentioned above,[34] and may also decide to adopt countermeasures against the spouses and immediate family members of individuals included in the countermeasure list, senior executives or actual controllers of organizations included in the countermeasure list, organizations where individuals included in the countermeasure list serve as senior executives and organizations that are actually controlled by individuals and organizations included in the countermeasure list or of which the said individuals and organizations participate in the formation or operation.[35] The countermeasures directed against the indi-

30 Order No. 4 [2020] of the Ministry of Commerce of the People's Republic of China

31 Order No. 1 [2021] of the Ministry of Commerce of the People's Republic of China.

32 See article 3 of Anti-foreign Sanctions Law.

33 See article 13 of Anti-foreign Sanctions Law.

34 See article 4 of Anti-foreign Sanctions Law.

35 See article 5 of Anti-foreign Sanctions Law.

viduals and organizations in the list include: refusing to issue a visa, denying entry, canceling a visa, or deportation; placing under seal, impounding, or freezing movables, immovables, and other types of property in the territory of China; prohibiting or restricting organizations and individuals in the territory of China from carrying out relevant transactions, cooperation, and other activities with them and other necessary measures.[36] The decisions above shall be final, and the determination, suspension, modification, or removal of the countermeasure list and countermeasures shall be announced by an order issued by the Ministry of Foreign Affairs or any other relevant department of the State Council.[37] For the purpose of guaranteeing the implementation of the countermeasures above, AFSL denies the legal effect of all the discriminatory restrictive measures above within China's territory, prohibits organizations and individuals to implement or assist in the implementation of discriminatory restrictive measures adopted by foreign countries against Chinese citizens and organizations, and authorizes the Chinese citizen or organization to file a lawsuit in Chinese courts against the organizations and individuals above for the cease of the infringement and the compensation for possible losses.[38] Furthermore, organizations and individuals in the territory of China shall implement the above countermeasures adopted by the relevant departments of the State Council, otherwise, they may be subject to the prohibition on carrying out relevant activities.[39] Although with a seemingly powerful and profound effect, no countermeasure list has been issued since the adoption of AFSL.

The second approach is to take measures without issuing a countermeasure list. AFSL shall apply *mutatis mutandis* to the circumstance where foreign countries, organizations, or individuals conduct, assist in, or support acts that undermine China's sovereignty, security, or development interests, and the countermeasures China may take are not limited to the content in AFSL, but include the sanctions provided for by central laws, administrative regulations and central departmental rules.[40] Thus, the countermeasures in PUEL and RCUEAFL have been logically incorporated into the Chinese legal system of sanctions and the blocking statute.

---

36 See article 6 of Anti-foreign Sanctions Law.

37 See articles 7, 8 and 9 of Anti-foreign Sanctions Law.

38 See article 12 of Anti-foreign Sanctions Law.

39 See article 11 of Anti-foreign Sanctions Law.

40 See articles 13 and 15 of Anti-foreign Sanctions Law.

4 International Law and Extraterritoriality in China

4.1 *Exercising Extraterritorial Jurisdiction in the Territory*

International law today, in certain areas such as punishing crimes, encourages the sovereign state to exercise jurisdiction in its territory in respect of any case which relates to acts which have taken place abroad. As an increasingly active player in the international arena, China has joined several international conventions authorizing exercising extraterritorial jurisdiction. For instance, China ratified the Convention on the suppression of unlawful acts endangering the safety of civil aviation[41] in 1972, and Article 5.1 of this Convention requires that China establish criminal jurisdiction over the offence jeopardizing the safety of civil aviation even if the crime occurs outside its territory, if other requirements are satisfied.[42] In order to fulfill its obligations under this Convention, China incorporated the crime against the safety on civil aviation into its domestic Criminal Law in 1997.[43] Similarly, China amended its Criminal Law to criminalize the bribery of foreign and international officials[44] committed abroad after ratifying the United Nations Convention against Corruption[45] in 2006, which requires contracting parties to establish giving undue advantage to a foreign public official as a criminal offence.[46]

41 U.N.T.S. 974.

42 Article 5. 1 is listed as follows: Each Contracting State shall take such measures as may be necessary to establish its jurisdiction over the offences in the following cases: (a) when the offence is committed in the territory of that State; (b) when the offence is committed against or on board an aircraft registered in that State; (c) when the aircraft on board which the offence is committed lands in its territory with the alleged offender still on board; (d) when the offence is committed against or on board an aircraft leased without crew to a lessee who has his principal place of business or, if the lessee has no such place of business, his permanent residence, in that State.

43 Article 123 of Criminal Law read: Whoever uses violence against any person on board an aircraft and thereby endanger air safety, if there are no serious consequences, shall be sentenced to fixed-term imprisonment not more than five years or criminal detention; if there are serious consequences, shall be sentenced to fixed-term imprisonment not more than five years or criminal detention.

44 Whoever gives any property to a functionary of a foreign country or an official of an international public organization for any improper commercial benefit shall be sentenced to imprisonment of not more than three years or limited incarceration in addition to a fine if the amount of property is relatively large; or be sentenced to imprisonment of not less than three years but not more than ten years in addition to a fine if the amount of property is huge. See article 164 of Criminal Law.

45 U.N.T.S. 2349.

46 Article 16.1 of United Nation Convention against Bribery provides: Each State Party shall adopt such legislative and other measures as may be necessary to establish as a criminal offence, when committed intentionally, the promise, offering or giving to a foreign public official or an official of a public international organization, directly or indirectly, of an

Implementing United Nations Security Council Resolutions (UNSCR) regarding sanctions in China is another international legal justification for exercising extraterritorial jurisdiction, since China is under the obligation to comply with the UNSCR.[47] There is no central law in China concerning the enforcement of UNSCR. It is under the responsibility of the Ministry of Foreign Affairs to issue the Notice to other competent authorities on a case-by-case basis for the purpose of carrying on UNSCR concerning international sanctions.[48]

4.2 *Exercising Extraterritorial Jurisdiction Outside Territory Permitted by International Law*

It is also a widely accepted idea that a State may exercise its power abroad if authorized by a permissive rule derived from international law.[49] There are several Chinese laws granting the right to the executive branch to enforce its competence abroad, according to permissive rules in multilateral conventions and bilateral agreements or arrangements.

After joining the World Trade Organization (WTO) in 2001, China published two administrative regulations, namely the Anti-dumping Regulations and the Countervailing Regulation, in the same year,[50] both of which incorporated

---

undue advantage, for the official himself or herself or another person or entity, in order that the official act or refrain from acting in the exercise of his or her official duties, in order to obtain or retain business or other undue advantage in relation to the conduct of international business.

47 See article 25 of United Nations Charter.

48 For instance, United Nations Security Council adopted Resolution 2397 on the intercontinental ballistic missile launch conducted by the Democratic People's Republic of Korea ("the DPRK") and further expanded sanctions against the DPRK based on its previous resolutions. In order to enforce the Resolution 2397, Chinese Ministry of Foreign Affairs issued the Notice by the Ministry of Foreign Affairs of Implementation of UN Security Council Resolution 2397 (No. 84 [2017] of the Ministry of Foreign Affairs) to all the Ministries and Commissions of and all the Institutions directly under the State Council, requiring them to implement the Resolution under the competence respectively. See https://www.pkulaw.com/en_law/71258942c57585 48bdfb.html [CLI Code] CLI.4.309735(EN). As a Ministry and an Institution under the State Council, Chinese Ministry of Commerce and General Administration of Customs jointly published Notice of Implementation of UN Security Council Resolution 2397 (No. 4 [2018] of Ministry of Commerce) subsequently, prohibiting the export of iron, steel and other metals to DPRK, restricting the export of crude oil, refined petroleum products and other products to DPRK, restricting the import of certain food, agricultural products, machinery, electrical equipment, earth and stone including magnesite and magnesia, wood, and vessels from DPRK. See http://www.mofcom.gov.cn/article/b/g/201804/ 20180402 7277 1 8.shtml.

49 See Lotus Case, PCIJ Series A, No. 10, at 45.

50 The Anti-Dumping Regulation of the People's Republic of China is promulgated on November 26, 2001 by the Order No. 328 of the State Council of the People's Republic of China, and amended according to the Decision of the State Council about Amending the

foreign on-site inspections as provided in the WTO Anti-dumping Agreement and Countervailing Agreement.[51] Thus, the Chinese Ministry of Commerce (MOFCOM) is authorized to send functionaries to the relevant country (region) to conduct investigations when necessary, except where the relevant country (region) concerned objects to the investigation. From 2001 to the present, a lot of investigations abroad have been conducted and all the information is available in official investigation documents, such as preliminary and final decisions, and are published on the official website.[52]

With regards to the import of medicine and medical apparatus, the Chinese government seeks to conclude bilateral agreements since no relevant multilateral conventions or arrangements are available. Early in 2000, China reached several bilateral memorandums on cooperation on medical supervision and regulation, and the memorandum with the United States on the same topic was concluded in 2007. In 2007, the Chinese National Food and Drug Administration (CFDA)[53] promulgated Provisions for Drug Registration authorizing the CFDA to conduct an on-site inspection of the development and production conditions of import drugs and take samples.[54] In the following years, a series of regulations and documents has been published in regard to the on-site inspections of import drugs, drugs producers, and medical apparatus.[55]

Antidumping Regulation of the People's Republic of China on March 31, 2004. The Countervailing Regulation of the People's Republic of China is promulgated by Order No.329 of the State Council of the People's Republic of China on November 26, 2001, and amended on the Basis of the Decision of the State Council on Amendments to the Countervailing Regulation of the People's Republic of China on March 31, 2004.

51 See article 20.3 respective of The Anti-Dumping Regulation of the PRC and the Countervailing Regulation of the PRC.

52 See China Trade Remedy Information, http://cacs.mofcom.gov.cn/

53 The CFDA was cancelled in 2018 and its function was incorporated into the National Medical Products Administration (NMPA) under the supervision of the State Administration of Market Regulation (SAMR).

54 See article 86.2 of Measures for the Administration of Drug Registration 2007. Measures for the Administration of Drug Registration 2007 was repealed and replaced by Measures for the Administration of Drug Registration 2020, with the provision for on-site inspection retained and specified. See articles 45–49 of Measures for the Administration of Drug Registration 2020.

55 See Oversea Inspection on Import Drug Testing Working Plan, promulgated in 2011 by CFDA, Working Procedure of Oversea On-site Inspection on Import Drug Production (pilot program), promulgated in 2011 by CFDA, Regulatory Measures of Inspection on Oversea Drug Production Enterprise (For Trial), promulgated in 2012 by CFDA, Oversea Inspection on Drug and Medical Apparatus, promulgated in 2018 by NMPA, Implementation Measures for the Supervision and Administration of Drug Production, promulgated

It was reported that, from 2011 to 2019, China has approved a total number of 3,739 import medicines, conducted on-site investigations of 171 thereof, and declared 22 import prohibitions thereof.[56] All the information regarding the procedure, determination, and declaration of the investigation is available on the official website of the Center for Food and Drug Inspection of NMPA.[57]

4.3 *Limitations Imposed by International Law on Extraterritoriality*

It is a widely accepted idea that a State may exercise jurisdiction in its territory unless there exists a prohibitive rule in international law.[58] China seems to be very cautious and puts considerable emphasis on the consistency between extraterritoriality and its obligations under international law. Requiring a violation of international law as a precondition to apply AFSL, as discussed in the previous part, is a case on point.

Another case of the limitation on extraterritoriality is the rules concerning the exercise of extraterritorial judicial jurisdiction. Although there is no comity requirement in Chinese law for the court to meet, for the purpose of avoiding unnecessary parallel procedures and competing jurisdictions, the non-convenient forum has been incorporated into the Chinese legal system. Chinese courts may render a ruling to dismiss the plaintiff's action and inform the plaintiff to institute an action in a more convenient foreign court under the following circumstances: (1) The defendant raises a claim that the case shall be subject to the jurisdiction of a more convenient foreign court, or raises an objection to jurisdiction; (2) The parties do not have an agreement specifying the jurisdiction of a court of the People's Republic of China; (3) The case does not fall under the exclusive jurisdiction of a court of the People's Republic of China; (4) The case does not involve the national interest, or the interest of any citizen, legal person or any other organization of the People's Republic of China; (5) The people's court has great difficulties in the determination of facts and the application of laws since major facts of disputes in a case do not occur within the territory of the People's Republic of China, and the laws of the People's Republic of China do not apply to the case; (6) The foreign court

---

in 2020 by NMPA, Measures for the Administration of Drug Registration, promulgated in 2020 by SAMR.

56 Ni Zhang, 'China Increases the Intensity of Oversea Inspection on Import Drug with 22 prohibitions on Import in the Past Nine Years', https://www.chinanews.com/sh/2020/01-11/9057043.shtml.

57 See https://www.cfdi.org.cn/cfdi.

58 See Lotus Case, PCIJ Series A, No. 10, at 45.

has jurisdiction over the case and it is more convenient for it to try the case.[59] In *Baron Motorcycles, Inc. v. Awell Logistics Group, Inc.*, both parties are foreign entities and the key facts had no connection to China, the court noticed that even after the seizure of the case and the delivery of the judgment, it was still necessary to require a petition in a foreign country for enforcement. Thus, the court finally declined to exercise jurisdiction and advised the plaintiff to open the case in other forum.[60]

5 Extraterritoriality in China: a Concise Appraisal

5.1 *A Comparatively Modest Approach to Extraterritoriality*

Extraterritoriality is closely related to the comprehensive capacity of a sovereign state. This explains why China did not develop its extraterritoriality until recent years. As one of the countries that exercises extraterritorial jurisdiction most frequently in the world, the United States has expanded its extraterritorial jurisdiction, if not in all areas, but at least in most areas, in the past generations, although the expansion is subject to various criticisms.[61] It seems that China intends to take a modest approach to its capacity building of extraterritoriality in contrast with the United States, to exercise its extraterritorial jurisdiction in a way not too excessive. Incorporating the requirement of international law into the AFSL, and setting a high threshold on invoking the countermeasure list in AFSL, are clear examples. Besides, China chooses to claim extraterritorial jurisdiction on several topics which are tolerated by international law, such as export control and financial supervision, and few countries make objection to the underlying rationale.

5.2 *A System with Both Defensive and Offensive Functions*

Extraterritoriality in China, as mentioned in Part I, thrives in the increasing tensions of Sino-U.S. relations. Therefore, the Chinese legal system on

59 See article 530, Interpretation of the Supreme People's Court on the Application of the Civil Procedure Law of the People's Republic of China, Interpretation No. 11 [2022] of the Supreme People's Court.

60 Baron Motorcycles, Inc. v. Awell Logistics Group, Inc. High People's Court of Zhejiang Province, 2009, [CLI Code] CLI.C.1174141(EN), https://www.pkulaw.com/en_case/a25051f3312b07f3fbec47624c3092255270b08 e058e0f77bdfb.html.

61 Lea Brilmayer, The Extraterritorial Application of American Law: A Methodological and Constitutional Appraisal (1987) 50 Law and Contemporary Problems 11. Alexander Layton and Angharad M Parry, Extraterritorial Jurisdiction – European Responses (2004) 26 Hous J Int'l L 309.

extraterritoriality in its initial stage is destined to be a defensive tool with the function of preventing Chinese nationals and entities from harm arising out of the extraterritorial application of U.S. law. A case to this point is the quick enactment of the AFSL by the Standing Committee of the National People's Congress, the main function of which is to nullify the legal effect of foreign sanctions within China's territory. Nevertheless, it does not necessarily mean that China will not exercise its jurisdiction in an active way. After the Export Control Law was enacted in 2020, China successively published several central departmental rules facilitating its enforcement.[62] Besides, although mainly serving as a defensive tool, the AFSL leaves room for actively imposing sanctions in the future when China's core interest is undermined.[63]

5.3 *An Imperfect Legal System with Areas Needing to be Improved*

China is an obvious freshman and a newcomer on the playing field of extraterritoriality. The lack of experience and skill will definitely lead to several flaws and gaps in the design and architecture of legislation. Furthermore, China had put more weight on legislation than on law enforcement, and the reinforcement of the latter is much more critical to bringing the legal doctrines from the book into reality. Unlike in the U.S. legal system, there is no "presumption against extraterritoriality"[64] or any equivalent doctrine in Chinese law. Thus, if there is no explicit permissive language in legislation, whether the Chinese court will exercise extraterritorial jurisdiction remains unclear. This uncertainty will inevitably result in the unpredictability and inconsistency of the judicial system, and creates some uncertainty to the expectation of foreign individuals and entities doing business in the Chinese market.

62 Shortly after the adoption on Export Control Law, the Ministry of Commerce, the State Cryptography Administration and the General Administration of Customs jointly published the Announcement No. 63 [2020], issuing the List of Commercial Cryptography under Import Licensing, the List of Commercial Cryptography under Export Control and the Related Regulation Measures. In June 2021, Ministry of Industry and Information Technology published Provisional Measures on Monitoring the Administration on General License on Chemical Products Export (Exposure Draft). After that, Ministry of Commerce chronologically issued several documents, such as Announcement No. 10 [2021] (Guidance on Establishing Internal Compliance Mechanism of Export Control for Dual-items Exporters), and Announcement No. 48 [2021] (Catalogue of Dual-Use Items and Technologies Subject to Import and Export License Administration).

63 See article 13 of AFSL.

64 Morrison v. National Australia Bank Ltd., 130 S. Ct. 2869 (U.S.2010).

6 Concluding Remarks

China is one of the most influential economies in the world, but its capacity building with respect to extraterritoriality is still at an early stage. Although quite a few laws been enacted in the past five years, legislation as a whole is still far away from a mature system. Thriving in the circumstance of Sino-U.S. confrontation, extraterritoriality in China was initially designed as a defensive tool, not as a tunnel to expand its jurisdiction for facilitating the free flow of Chinese goods and capital in the world. Nevertheless, China's attitude to extraterritoriality is rather contradictory. On the one hand, China is frequently injured by the extraterritoriality of U.S. law and has a strong motive to discipline it under the international legal framework; on the other hand, since international law has left too much room for extraterritoriality, China has to rely more on its domestic law to fight back. As a sovereign state, China has the inherent right to exercise extraterritorial jurisdiction. However, China should make every effort to claim its extraterritoriality in a modest and reasonable way, otherwise the Sino-U.S. confrontation will be inevitably escalated and further bring catastrophic influence to the fragile international order.

Extraterritoriality in Germany

Sören Segger-Piening *

1 Introduction[1]

Extraterritoriality of statutes and regulations is a topic widely discussed in Germany.[2] In this respect, it first appears necessary to define the term in the sense used here. This is followed by some subject matter delimitations of the topic, and finally by an explanation of the concept behind this country report.

1.1 *Definition of the Term Extraterritoriality*

It should be pointed out right at the beginning that the term 'extraterritoriality' itself is not clearly defined.[3] In part, the term is associated in international writing with a valuation in the sense that a certain element of illegality or illegitimacy is inherent to an extraterritorial regulation, especially under consideration of recognised principles of international law.[4] On the other hand, there

* Prof. Dr., LL.M. Eur., University of Osnabrück, Germany.

1 For helpful comments, I would like to thank Professor Dr. Oliver Remien († 24.04.2023) and Prof. Hannah Buxbaum; for editorial help I would like to thank Leon Uebelhör, Marie-Theres Beyer and Fenna Kruse. All web pages were last accessed on 31.05.2023. This country report is based on the Questionnaire of the General Rapporteur Prof. Hannah Buxbaum.

2 A few numbers taken from relevant German legal databases shall demonstrate the sheer number of 'results' when searching for 'extraterritorial': Beck-online: over 4,000 results; juris: 2,906 results; Nomos e-Library: 1,201 results; Duncker & Humboldt eLibrary, 304 results. However, if you take a look at the U.S. journals and conduct a search via Westlaw you find more than 10,000 results. Furthermore, some of the German results refer to identical cases that are published in different journals. Nevertheless, these numbers demonstrate at least two things: 1. Extraterritoriality is a topic widely discussed in Germany. 2. It is impossible to take account of all the developments in all the different fields of law. Thus, this report naturally does not cover all the different fields of law; the subject matter delimitations are further spelled out below at 1.2.

3 Recently in German writing on this subject, C. Kurkin, *Extraterritorialität*, Mohr Siebeck, Tübingen 2021, pp. 44–48; see further i.a. W. Meng, *Extraterritoriale Jurisdiktion im* öffentlichen *Wirtschaftsrecht*, Springer, Berlin 1994, p. 73 with different potential meanings; in international writing with further references C. Ryngaert, *Jurisdiction in International Law*, 2nd ed., Oxford University Press, Oxford 2015, p. 7.

4 C. Ryngaert, *Jurisdiction in International Law*, 2nd ed., Oxford University Press, Oxford 2015, p. 7; however, this does not seem to be the common approach to this notion; C. Kurkin,

 | DOI:10.1163/9789004720183_008

is also an understanding of the term according to which an extraterritorial regulation is precisely one that constitutes a lawful regulation due to certain connecting factors legitimised under international law.[5] This ambiguity in the understanding of the term is also emphasised in international literature.[6] In the following, extraterritoriality is understood in a technical sense, following questions 6 and 7 of the Questionnaire. An extraterritorial regulation is one that is factually linked to a situation that occurs either wholly or in part outside the territory of the law-making state and/or prescribes a legal consequence for such a situation.[7] Thus, the extraterritorial application of the law is important, be it by means of a connection to a circumstance located abroad in the broadest sense or a legal consequence attached to such a circumstance.

Such an understanding of extraterritoriality is on the one hand restrictive, because it excludes a number of areas such as enforcement by focusing on the application of rules and regulations, and on the other hand boundless, especially against the background of private international law. Therefore, the need arises to clarify the areas not covered by this study and also to add a demarcation from private international law in general. Finally, it should be noted that the foregoing definition of extraterritoriality does not so much lead to the formation of a legal term, but rather circumscribes a legal phenomenon.

1.2 *Subject Matter Delimitations*

1.2.1 Exclusion of the Jurisdiction to Enforce and Adjudicate

In accordance with the delimitations of the questionnaire, the issue of jurisdiction to enforce is not addressed.[8] Excluded as well is the limitation of

---

Extraterritorialität, Mohr Siebeck, Tübingen 2021, p. 47 refers in this context to a naturalistic understanding (*naturrechtliches Begriffsverständnis*).

5 M. Herdegen, Völkerrecht, 20th ed., C.H.Beck, München 2021, sect. 26 n. 3; C. Kurkin, *Extraterritorialität*, Mohr Siebeck, Tübingen 2021, pp. 47–48 refers in this context to a positivistic understanding (*positivistisches Begriffsverständnis*).

6 See i.a. H. Buxbaum, *Territory, Territoriality, and the Resolution of Jurisdictional Conflict*, 2009, 57 Am. J. Comp. L 631, 635.

7 C.f. W. Meng, *Extraterritoriale Jurisdiktion im öffentlichen Wirtschaftsrecht*, Springer, Berlin 1994, pp. 73 et seqq.; A. K. Schnyder, *Wirtschaftskollisionsrecht*, Schulthess, Zürich 1990, pp. 58 et seqq.; H.-J. Schlochauer, *Die extraterritoriale Wirkung von Hoheitsakten nach dem öffentlichen Recht der Bundesrepublik Deutschland und nach internationalem Recht*, Klostermann, Frankfurt a. Main 1962, p. 10.

8 Comp. in this regard however i.a. K. P. Mössle, *Extraterritoriale Beweisbeschaffung*, Nomos, Baden-Baden 1990, passim; O. Remien, *Rechtsverwirklichung durch Zwangsgeld*, Mohr, Tübingen 1992, passim.

jurisdiction to adjudicate in matters involving certain foreign persons, such as diplomats.[9]

1.2.2 Exclusion of Non-special Interest based Private International Law

While the two preceding limitations of this report result at least indirectly from the choice of subject matter, the demarcation from private international law in general is much more difficult to accomplish. According to the common continental European understanding of modern conflict-of-law rules developed by *Savigny*, these rules aim to reveal the closest connection of a legal relationship to a legal system.[10] Thus, German law may still apply although the facts of the case occur at least partly abroad – and vice versa foreign law in Germany.[11] For example, Art. 4 para. 1 Rome II Regulation[12] is based on the place of the damage, so that German law applies to a person acting abroad if the place where the damage occurs is situated in Germany. If one considers the numerous other conflict-of-law rules, it quickly becomes clear that there can be virtually innumerable cases in which conduct takes place exclusively or partly abroad and is nevertheless subject to a German rule, since the conflict-of-law rule leads to the application of German law. The background to this is the search for a connecting factor that best realises the interests from a private international law point of view; in other words, the search for the legal order that appears to be the most suitable from a territorial point of view. In principle, the consideration of state interests is not in the foreground.

However, in today's modern conflict of laws, there are a number of rules whose connecting factors also take state interests into account.[13] Particularly in the field of international economic regulation, there are many examples

---

9 Comp. sects. 18–20 of the Courts Constitution Act (*Gerichtsverfassungsgesetz*) in this sense.

10 Instead of all G. Kegel, K. Schurig, *Internationales Privatrecht*, 9th ed., C.H.Beck, München 2004, p. 131 and pp. 181–88 on the history of modern conflict of laws.

11 C.f. W. Meng, *Extraterritoriale Jurisdiktion im öffentlichen Wirtschaftsrecht*, Springer, Berlin 1994, pp. 161 et seqq., 468–69; K. Siehr, *Internationales Privatrecht*, C.F. Müller, Heidelberg 2001, pp. 368–69.

12 Regulation (EC) No 864/2007 of the European Parliament and of the Council of 11 July 2007 on the law applicable to non-contractual obligations [2007] OJ L 199 ('Rome II'), pp. 40–49. This regulation unifies private international law for non-contractual obligations within the Union; it also contains rules on applicable (private) antitrust law (see infra, 2.1.1.1.), unfair competition (see infra, 2.1.1.2.) and intellectual property (see infra, 2.1.2.).

13 See esp. A. K. Schnyder, *Wirtschaftskollisionsrecht*, Schulthess, Zürich 1990, pp. 121 et seqq.; J. v. Basedow, *Wirtschaftskollisionsrecht: Theoretischer Versuch über die ordnungspolitischen Normen des Forumstaates*, RabelsZ 52 (1988), 8, 20 ff.

of this, which will be considered infra, 2.[14] In this report, the extraterritorial effect of private international law norms will be examined only to the extent those norms also serve the realisation of state interests. The focus will be on the broad field of economic regulation.

1.2.3 Exclusion of Fundamental Rights and Constitutional Law

This country report also does not address the possible extraterritorial effects of human rights in particular and fundamental rights or constitutional law in general; these areas were excluded by the Rapporteur General. Comparable questions arise, however, in part in criminal law, taking into account the principle of universal jurisdiction, see infra, 7.4.

1.3 *Outline of the Report – Methodology*

Section 2 first provides an overview of current practice and trends in Germany. In addition to a brief introduction into each subject-matter, particular attention is paid to the connecting factors in question and the impact of European law. In the following sections, certain cross-cutting principles related to the issue of extraterritoriality will be examined in relation to several different areas of law. On the one hand, this refers to principles or rules that lead to a limitation of an extraterritorial application of the relevant law, see 4.–6. On the other hand, it is also conceivable to examine the various connecting factors that support extraterritorial applicability, such as the active and passive personal principle, the effects doctrine, and the principle of universality, see 7. and 8. Furthermore, the topics of corporate nationality, presumption against extraterritoriality and blocking statutes are dealt with under 9.–11.

2 Overview of Current Practice and Trends

In Germany, there are a number of very different regulations that are applied extraterritorially. International economic regulation plays a particularly prominent role. The relevant sub-areas are presented below under 1. without claiming to be exhaustive; the term economic regulation is understood broadly here and also includes, for example, intellectual property and data protection law.

14 However, state interests can also play a role in the field of international family law, i.a. Art. 10 Council Regulation (EU) No 1259/2010 of 20 December 2010 implementing enhanced cooperation in the area of the law applicable to divorce and legal separation [2010] OJ L 343/10 ('Rome III'), c.f. L. Rademacher in C. Rupp et al. (eds.), IPR *zwischen Tradition und Innovation*, Mohr Siebeck, Tübingen 2019, pp. 121–140.

Subsequently, the important field of criminal law is to be dealt with under 2. Finally, some current trends will be discussed in subsection 3.

2.1 *Extraterritoriality and Economic Regulation*

The extraterritorial application of law is particularly important in economic regulation. In the course of the ever increasing globalisation during the 20th century, the question also came to the fore in Germany to what extent regulations should be applied extraterritorially.[15]

2.1.1 Competition Law

The term competition law (*Wettbewerbsrecht*) in Germany is used in two senses.[16] First, competition law can be understood in the sense of antitrust law. Thus, protection is provided for the creation and preservation of a relevant market, i.e. competition as an institution. However, it is also conceivable to understand competition law in the sense of fair-trading practices law. This aims at regulating behaviour on a market, for example in the sense of prohibiting misleading advertising.

2.1.1.1 *Competition Law in the Sense of Antitrust*

Antitrust law in Germany is governed by the Act against Restraints of Competition[17] (*Gesetz gegen Wettbewerbsbeschränkungen*, hereafter: GWB). The international applicability of the GWB is governed by sect. 185 para. 2. The effects doctrine is established by stipulating that the [relevant] 'provisions of ... this Act shall be applied to all restraints of competition having an effect within the area of application of this Act, even if they were caused outside the area of application of this Act.' For example, the GWB applies to a cartel agreement or a merger of foreign companies that has an effect in Germany. The wording of the provision has remained unchanged since the entry into force of the GWB.[18] The extent to which sect. 185 para. 2 GWB is to be interpreted restrictively, also against the background of international law considerations, the extent to which principles of comity play a role and, finally, whether there is a need for a balancing requirement in the case of conflicting interests in the

15 See for the historical development i.a. G. Erler, *Grundprobleme des internationalen Wirtschaftsrechts*, Otto Schwartz, Göttingen 1956, pp. 5 and passim.

16 For a demarcation, see i.a. K. Thorn in C. Grüneberg (ed.), Bürgerliches Gesetzbuch, 82th ed., C.H.Beck, München 2023 Art. 6 Rome II n. 5.

17 Translation available at https://www.gesetze-im-internet.de/englisch_gwb/.

18 See i.a. A. Klees, P.-T. Stoll, T. P. Holterhus and A. Schebstadt in J. Busche and A. Röhling (eds.), *Kölner Kommentar zum Kartellrecht*, Carl Heymanns, 2014, sect. 130 GWB, n. 64 et seqq.

sense of reasonableness, are disputed and frequently discussed. All these questions will be returned to infra, 4.–6.

Furthermore, it should be noted that the substantive scope of application of sect. 185 para. 2 GWB is limited.[19] The provision governs the applicability of the GWB only in constellations in which German authorities enforce German antitrust law, i.e. cases of antitrust administrative law. Private antitrust law, which is also becoming increasingly important for private enforcement in Germany as well as the European Union, is not covered by sect. 185 para. 2 GWB. Instead, Art. 6 para. 3 Rome II is applied here in a harmonised manner across Europe. However, Art. 6 para. 3 Rome II is also based on the effects principle or marketplace principle and thus a similar approach is taken.[20] Furthermore, the international applicability of the European prohibitions of cartels (Art. 101 et seq. TFEU) is not determined by sect. 185 para. 2 GWB, but derives from the corresponding norms themselves;[21] the Rome II Regulation is not applicable either.[22] The applicability of European antitrust law depends on 'agreements and practices on the part of undertakings which 'may affect trade between Member States'.[23] This criterion is traditionally interpreted broadly.[24] In particular, in cases of lack of appreciability (*Spürbarkeit*, the translation appreciability is used by the EU Commission), national law remains applicable, for example in the case of market shares of less than 5 per cent and a turnover of no more than 40 million euros.[25]

---

19 On this and the following i.a. G. Mäsch in W. Berg and G. Mäsch (eds.), *Kartellrecht*, 4th ed., Luchterhand, München 2022, sect. 185 n. 28, 36; A. Klees, P.-T. Stoll, T. P. Holterhus and A. Schebstadt in J. Busche and A. Röhling (eds.), *Kölner Kommentar zum Kartellrecht*, Carl Heymanns, 2014, sect. 130 GWB, n. 78 et seqq., 82 et seqq.

20 See i.a. O. Remien in W. Siebert (ed.), *Soergel* BGB Bd. 27/1, 13th ed., Kohlhammer, Stuttgart 2019, Art. 6 n. 51. There are also some differences esp. with regard to multi state scenarios; furthermore sect. 185 para. 2 GWB is a unilateral rule, whereas Art. 6 para. 3 Rome II also leads to the application of foreign law (*allseitige Kollisionsnorm*).

21 See i.a. E. Rehbinder in U. Immenga and E.-J. Mestmäcker (eds.), Wettbewerbsrecht, Bd. 1, 6th. ed., C.H.Beck, München 2019, II. A. esp. n. 6 et seqq.

22 P. Mankowski, *Das neue Internationale Kartellrecht des Art. 6 Abs. 3 der Rom II-Verordnung,* RIW 2008, 177, 179.

23 See Commission Notice, Guidelines on the effect on trade concept contained in Art. 81 and 82 of the Treaty, OJ C 101, 27/04/2004 P. 0081, n. 1, quoting Art. 81, 82 EC treaty, now 101, 102 TFEU.

24 See i.a. CJEU, Case C-56/65, *Société Technique Minière v. Maschinenbau Ulm GmbH*, ECLI:EU:C:1966:38, 249; D. Zimmer in U. Immenga and E.-J. Mestmäcker (eds.), *Wettbewerbsrecht*, Bd. 1, 6th. ed., C.H.Beck, München 2019, Art. 101 Abs. 1 n. 173 et seqq.

25 See Commission Notice, Guidelines on the effect on trade concept contained in Art. 81 and 82 of the Treaty, OJ C 101, 27/04/2004 P. 0081, n. 1, quoting Art. 81, 82 EC treaty, now 101, 102 TFEU, n. 51 et seqq., esp. 53.

2.1.1.2 *Unfair Competition*

Unfair competition law is also part of competition law. Pursuant to a memorandum of the EU Commission regarding the Rome II regulation, unfair competition includes 'acts calculated to influence demand (misleading advertising, forced sales, etc.), acts that impede competing supplies (disruption of deliveries by competitors, enticing away a competitor's staff, boycotts), and acts that exploit a competitor's value (passing off and the like).'[26] Many of those acts are governed by European directives.[27] These are implemented into the Act against Unfair Competition[28] (*Gesetz gegen den unlauteren Wettbewerb*, hereafter: UWG).

With regard to the international dimensions of unfair competition, the Rome II Regulation again plays an important role. Article 6 para. 1 and para. 2 Rome II contain the conflict-of-law rules for claims resulting from a violation of fair competition practices. The connecting point pursuant to para. 1 is the place 'where competitive relations or the collective interests of consumers are, or are likely to be, affected'. Even though the term 'market' is not directly mentioned, the rule is associated with the 'effects' or 'market effects principle'.[29] It has a number of similarities to the effects doctrine pursuant to Art. 6 para. 3 Rome II. However, most authors agree that Art. 6 para. 1 Rome II is to be differentiated from Art. 6 para. 3 Rome II.[30] The former refers to the market where the behaviour affects competitors and consumers, while the latter asks whether free competition is restricted because of the anti-competitive act.[31] In practice however, differences are rather minimal and thus Art. 6 para. 1 Rome II will be dealt with when looking at the effects principle, infra 7.3.

---

26 *Regulation of the European Parliament and the Council on the Law Applicable to Non-Contractual Obligations ('Rome II')*, COM(2003) 427, p. 15; the exact definition of the term varies from member state to member state, however in the sense of Rome II reg. a coherent and autonomous interpretation of the term is called for, with the CJEU as authoritative instance.

27 For an overview see O. Sosnitza in A. Ohly and O. Sosnitza (eds.), *Gesetz gegen den unlauteren Wettbewerb*, 8th ed., C.H.Beck, München 2023, Einf. C.

28 Translation available at https://www.gesetze-im-internet.de/englisch_uwg/.

29 See i.a. M. Illmer in U. Magnus and P. Mankowski (eds.), ECPIL – *Rome* II, Otto Schmidt, Köln 2019, Art. 6 n. 69.

30 Esp. P. Mankowski in P. W. Heermann and J. Schlingloff (eds.), *Münchener Kommentar zum Lauterkeitsrecht*, 3rd ed., C.H. Beck, München 2020, A. II. n. 142 et seqq.; doubting O. Remien in W. Siebert (ed.), *Soergel* BGB Bd. 27/1, 13th ed., Kohlhammer, Stuttgart 2019, Art. 6 n. 16 with whom it must be agreed that many similarities exist.

31 P. Mankowski in P. W. Heermann and J. Schlingloff (eds.), *MünchKomm-Lauterkeitsrecht*, 3rd ed., C.H. Beck, München 2020, A. II. n.144.

By focusing on the place where the interests are affected, it also becomes clear that actions abroad can be covered by German regulations. If, for example, advertising is placed on the German market from abroad, the admissibility of this advertising is determined according to the German regulations on unfair competition.[32]

2.1.2 Intellectual Property

Extraterritoriality is also discussed in the domain of intellectual property.[33] Regarding substantive law, a distinction is traditionally made in Germany between copyright (*Urheberrecht*), including the law of related rights (*verwandte Schutzrechte*), and industrial property (*gewerblicher Rechtsschutz*) – although intellectual property (*Geistiges Eigentum*) is increasingly accepted as a generic term in the specific legal context, especially for questions of applicable law.[34] While copyright arises informally and ipso iure and serves to protect cultural achievements, industrial property protection comprises rights that, generally, must be registered and serve commercial activity, such as patent and trademark rights as well as utility model and design rights.

The international dimensions of intellectual property in Germany are a web of national and European regulations. Traditionally, the law of the state for which protection is sought (*Schutzlandprinzip*), the lex loci protectionis, has prevailed as the conflict rule in Germany, both in the field of copyright and industrial property rights.[35] According to the prevailing opinion, this results from national conflict of laws principles and/or international conventions on the question of whether a protected right exists at all.[36] The question of which

32 See i.a. O. Remien in W. Siebert (ed.), *Soergel* BGB Bd. 27/1, 13th ed., Kohlhammer, Stuttgart 2019, Art. 6 n. 16; from case law i.a BGH GRUR 2004, 1035; OLG Hamm, MMR 2014, 17.

33 See i.a. J. Drexl in F. J. Säcker et al., *Münchener Kommentar zum* BGB, Bd. 13, 8th ed., C.H. Beck, München 2021, Art. 8 Rome II n. 306 et seqq.; *F. Beckstein, Einschränkungen des Schutzlandprinzips*, Mohr Siebeck, Tübingen 2010, p. 152 et seqq.

34 For a closer look at the term intellectual property from the German perspective, see H.-P. Götting, *Der Begriff des Geistigen Eigentums*, GRUR 2006, 353.

35 Essential E. Ulmer, *Die Immaterialgüterrechte im internationalen Privatrecht*, Carl Heymanns, Köln 1975, p. 12; from today's commentary literature, for example J. Drexl in F. J. Säcker et al., *Münchener Kommentar zum* BGB, Bd. 13, 8th ed., C.H. Beck, München 2021, Art. 8 n. 199; from the case law BGH, IIC 1999, 227, 229; see below on the partly divergent conception for the partly universally conceived copyright.

36 I.a. J. Drexl in F. J. Säcker et al., *Münchener Kommentar zum* BGB, Bd. 13, 8th ed., C.H.Beck, München 2021, Art. 8 n. 176 et seqq.; C. v. Bar and P. Mankowski, *Internationales Privatrecht/2*, 2nd ed., C.H.Beck, München 2019, sect. 2 n. 356, 358 et seq.; the opposing opinion, i.a. M. Grünberger, *Das Urheberrechtsstatut nach der Rom II-VO*, ZvglRWiss 108 (2009), 134, 157 ff. wants to apply the Rome II reg. to the question of the existence of the property right as well and in this respect denies the construction via a preliminary question. This

law applies to the legal consequences of the infringement (remedies) as well as the scope of protection, on the other hand, is decided with recourse to Art. 8 Rome II. The latter, however, also refers to the lex loci protectionis in paragraph 1 for intellectual property rights that are not standardised throughout the Union, such as copyright. In this respect, there is, in principle, a parallelism between the question of the applicable law regarding the existence of an IP-right as well as the applicable law for questions regarding infringements.[37]

If, for example, protection of a trademark is sought in Germany, then German substantive law must decide how far the protection of the trademark extends. For both copyright law and industrial property rights, it is generally assumed in Germany that the so-called territoriality principle applies in this respect – at the level of substantive law.[38] Accordingly, intellectual property rights are only valid for the state that grants or recognises the right.[39] Such an understanding conceptualises all intellectual property rights as objects of a national state, which are only protected within its borders, and thus initially stands in the way of an extraterritorial application. However, it is worth noting that in the field of copyright, a universalistic and thus inevitably extraterritorial approach is also advocated,[40] although this approach has not prevailed, either in case law or in the prevailing doctrine.

The consequence of this principle of territoriality is also that an act of infringement must in principle take place within domestic territory, since according to the ideas of the principle of territoriality the protected right does not exist abroad and therefore cannot be infringed.[41] However, the limits of

---

is less convincing; after all, it is not evident why the impairment of intellectual property should be treated differently from the impairment of physical property.

37 Deviations may occur, as under German private international law the *renvoi* is still applicable, Art. 4 para. 1 s. 1 EGBGB, whereas it is excluded by Art. 24 Rome II, see further C. v. Bar and P. Mankowski, *Internationales Privatrecht/2*, 2nd ed., C.H.Beck, München 2019, p. 369.

38 See i.a. M.-R. McGuire in C. Budzikiewicz et al., *BeckOGK. Rom II-VO*, ed. 01.12.2016, C.H Beck, Art. 8 n. 30; *F. Beckstein, Einschränkungen des Schutzlandprinzips*, Mohr Siebeck, Tübingen 2010, pp. 113–120; K.-.JhH.H. Fezer in K.-H. Fezer (ed.), *Markenrecht*, 4th ed., C.H. Beck, München 2009, part H n. 11. However, this is disputed.

39 M.-R. McGuire in C. Budzikiewicz et al., *BeckOGK. Rom II-VO*, ed. 01.12.2016, C.H Beck, Art. 8 n. 28.

40 I.a. U. Drobnig, *Originärer Erwerb und Übertragung von Immaterialgüterrechten im Kollisionsrecht*, RabelsZ 1976, 195–208; H. Schack, *Urheber- und Urhebervertragsrecht*, 10th ed., Mohr Siebeck, Tübingen 2021, n. 1026 et seqq..

41 Very clear already E. Ulmer, *Die Immaterialgüterrechte im internationalen Privatrecht*, Carl Heymanns, Köln 1975 p. 9; from the current writing i.a. K.-H. Fezer and S. Koos in J. Staudinger (fdr.), *Internationales Wirtschaftsrecht*, ed. 2019, Otto Schmidt/De Gruyter, Berlin 2019, n. 897; from case law i.a. BGH GRUR 1994, 798, 799.

this approach became apparent at an early stage. A first step was taken to the effect that even an impairment of an IP right occurring partly in Germany and partly abroad was considered a sufficient act of infringement under certain conditions. The details in this regard are dealt with infra, 8.

Another significant development in the present context was to consider acts abroad as domestic acts of infringement and/or to allow them to fall under the principle of territoriality while defining certain limitations.[42] Initially, these were in particular cases where television broadcasts were deliberately transmitted from abroad to domestic territory in order to take advantage of weaker copyright protection at the place of the act.[43] Based on the so-called *Bogsch*-theory,[44] the courts gradually accepted that the law of the receiving state should also be taken into account.[45] Similar to the effects doctrine, the extent to which an act abroad could affect domestic IP rights was increasingly taken into account. In the context of the internet, it was gradually recognised that the mere accessibility of an internet page would, in principle, be sufficient to meet the criterion of using/offering within the meaning of i.a. sect. 14 para. 2 of the Act on the Protection of Trade Marks and other Signs[46] (*Gesetz* über *den Schutz von Marken und sonstigen Kennzeichen*) or sect. 17 para. 1 of the Act on Copyright and Related Rights[47] (*Gesetz* über *Urheberrecht und verwandte Schutzrechte*). At the same time, however, German courts have always been aware that such a broad understanding requires limitation. The Hotel Maritime case of the Federal Court of Justice (*Bundesgerichtshof*) concerning trademark

42 See i.a. *F. Beckstein, Einschränkungen des Schutzlandprinzips*, Mohr Siebeck, Tübingen 2010, p. 51–59; J. Drexl in F. J. Säcker et al., *Münchener Kommentar zum* BGB, Bd. 13, 8th ed., C.H.Beck, München 2021, Art. 8 n. 287 et seqq.

43 From case law i.a. OLG München ZUM 1995, 328, 332–33; LG Stuttgart GRUR Int 1995, 412, 413; comp. also K.-H. Fezer and S. Koos in J. Staudinger (fdr.), *Internationales Wirtschaftsrecht*, ed. 2019, Otto Schmidt/De Gruyter, Berlin 2019, n. 1102.

44 Originally P. Katzenberger, *Urheberrechtsfragen der elektronischen Textkommunikation*, GRUR Int 1983, 895, 913–17; today i.a. J. Drexl in F. J. Säcker et al., *Münchener Kommentar zum* BGB, Bd. 13, 8th ed., C.H.Beck, München 2021, Art. 8 n. 289 et seq.

45 For trademark law i.a. BGH GRUR Int 2005, 433, 434 (Hotel Maritime); BGH, GRUR 2018, 417 Rn 37; comp. K.-H. Fezer and S. Koos in J. Staudinger (fdr.), *Internationales Wirtschaftsrecht*, ed. 2019, Otto Schmidt/De Gruyter, Berlin 2019, n. 1019. Especially for internet cases and the field of copyright law, for example OLG München ZUM-RD 2012, 88, 91; comp. K.-H. Fezer and S. Koos in J. Staudinger (fdr.), *Internationales Wirtschaftsrecht*, ed. 2019, Otto Schmidt/De Gruyter, Berlin 2019, n. 1113.

46 Translation available at https://www.gesetze-im-internet.de/englisch_markeng/englisch_markeng.html.

47 Translation available at https://www.gesetze-im-internet.de/englisch_urhg/englisch_urhg.html.

law is significant in this respect.[48] First, the Federal Court of Justice stated that offering services in Germany using the trademark was sufficient in principle. However, a restriction was then made to the effect that 'not every offer of foreign services on the internet that can be accessed in Germany may justify claims under trade mark law if there is a risk of confusion with a domestic trade mark'. Rather, it is necessary 'that the offer has a sufficient economically relevant domestic connection (referred to by WIPO as 'commercial effect')'. This is ultimately a criterion similar to the requirement of appreciability[49] or a *de minimis* rule[50] as known in antitrust law.[51] In the case at hand, the Federal Court of Justice denied such a connection even though the website was also directed at Germans, on the basis that it had only a minimal impact on the plaintiff's economic activity. Furthermore, on the legal consequences side, it must be taken into account that possible claims under German law can only relate to infringements in Germany, so claims for damages are limited to the domestic infringement and claims for injunctive relief should be limited to the legal order of the country for which protection was sought.[52]

2.1.3 Financial Regulation and Supervision

Extraterritorial application of the law also takes place in so-called international financial regulation (*internationales Finanzmarktrecht*). The regulation of financial markets from a German perspective is a complex interplay of international standards,[53] European law[54] and national German legislation.[55] Of the

48 BGH, GRUR Int 2005, 433, it concerned advertising of a Danish hotel; all the following quotations are taken from the decision, translation by author.

49 In this sense K.-H. Fezer and S. Koos in J. Staudinger (fdr.), *Internationales Wirtschaftsrecht*, ed. 2019, Otto Schmidt/De Gruyter, Berlin 2019, n. 1116.

50 In this sense A. Metzger in U. Magnus and P. Mankowski (eds.), ECPIL – *Rome* II, Otto Schmidt, Köln 2019, Art. 8 n. 28.

51 See infra, 4.2.2.1.

52 See i.a. J. Drexl in F. J. Säcker et al., *Münchener Kommentar zum* BGB, Bd. 13, 8th ed., C.H.Beck, München 2021, Art. 8 n. 324 et seqq.

53 International standards are often set by soft law instruments, thus non-binding rules, for a current overview see i.a.H. Kronke and J. Haubold in H. Kronke, W. Melis and H. Kuhn (eds.), *Handbuch Internationales Wirtschaftsrecht*, 2nd ed., Otto Schmidt, Köln 2017, part L. n. 8; 1.

54 Since the financial crises of 2008 the amount of European directives and regulations has substantiality grown; many of the German acts referred to hereafter implement European directives. Good overview by H. Kronke and J. Haubold in H. Kronke, W. Melis and H. Kuhn (eds.), *Handbuch Internationales Wirtschaftsrecht*, 2nd ed., Otto Schmidt, Köln 2017, n. 9 et seqq., with n. 26 giving an overview about all the different directive and regulations.

55 Complete overview i.a. I. Freis-Janik in S Kümpel, P. O. Mülbert, A. Früh and T. Seyfried (eds.), *Bankrecht und Kapitalmarktrecht*, 6th ed., Otto Schmidt, Köln 2022, passim.

many different subareas of the regulation of the financial market, two shall be looked at more closely. One subarea is the institutional regulation and supervision of banks and financial service providers in terms of a prudential supervision, i.a. minimum capital, risk management and so forth.[56] In Germany this is governed by the Banking Act[57] (*Gesetz über das Kreditwesen*, hereafter: KWG). Another area is the regulation and supervision of stock exchanges and other (electronic/virtual) trading venues. From a German perspective this is mostly governed by the Securities Trading Act[58] (*Wertpaphierhandelsgesetz*, hereafter: WpHG), which is also referred to as the basic law of capital market law (*Grundgesetz des Kapitalmarktrechts*).[59] According to this, there are, inter alia, organisational and conduct rules for certain trading platforms (sects. 72 et seq. WpHG); a special licensing requirement arises from the KWG.[60]

The challenge in the *international* regulation of the capital market is the increase in globalisation and digitalisation.[61] This makes it much easier for credit institutes or electronic trading platforms to look for a location in an offshore centre or a 'tax haven', for example, and thus circumvent regulatory requirements. Here, lawmaking states adopt counter-strategies by extending the scope of their law extraterritorially. As with antitrust law and fair trading law, the effects doctrine is applied on the basis of the market place principle.[62]

An example is sect. 102 WpHG, according to which 'markets in financial instruments whose registered office is outside the European Union ..., or their operators, require written authorisation from BaFin if they grant trading participants whose registered office is in Germany direct market access by means of an electronic trading system.' This is also referred to as the target market

56 For an overview see i.a. C. Köhler in H.-P. Schwintowski (ed.), *Bankrecht*, 6th ed., Carl Heymanns, Köln 2022, ch. 5 part B. (*Gegenstand der Aufsicht*).

57 Translation available at https://www.bafin.de/SharedDocs/Downloads/EN/Aufsichtsrecht/dl_kwg_en.html.

58 Translation available at https://www.bafin.de/SharedDocs/Veroeffentlichungen/EN/Aufsichtsrecht/Gesetz/WpHG_en.htm.

59 H. Hirte, T. A. Heinrich in H. Hirte, T. M. J. Möllers (eds.), Köllner Kommentar zum WpHG, 2nd ed., Carl Heymanns, Köln 2014, Einl. n. 3

60 See sect. 1 para. 1a no. 1b, d, sect. 2 para. 6 no. 16 para. 12 KWG.

61 These risks have been discussed already before the financial crises of 2008, see i.a. T. Marauhn in R. Grothe and T. Marauhn (eds.), *The Regulation of International Financial Markets*, Cambridge University Press, Cambridge 2006, p. 14–18; more recently esp. T. Dornis in C. Budzikiewicz et al., *BeckOGK. Internationales Gesellschaftsrecht*, ed. 01.11.2022, C.H Beck, München, n. 82 et seq. with further references.

62 See i.a. F. L. Christoph, Zulässigkeit grenzüberschreitender Bankenaufsicht nach dem Marktortprinzip, ZBB 2009, 117, 119; M. Lehmann in F. J. Säcker et al., *Münchener Kommentar zum BGB*, *Finanzmarktrecht*, Bd. 13, 8th ed., C.H.Beck, München 2021, n. 121 et seq.

principle, whereby this is synonymous with the effects doctrine.[63] The foreign provider therefore does not formally have to meet the requirements of sects. 72 et seqq. WpHG and does not regularly require an authorisation pursuant to the KWG,[64] but similar standards are applied when granting the authorisation pursuant to sect. 102 WpHG. In practice, 18 companies have already received an authorisation according to sect. 102 WpHG or the identical predecessor standard of sect. 37i WpHG.[65]

A similar approach is taken by sect. 32 KWG for banks or other financial service providers that serve national consumers from foreign territory. However, here a closer connection is needed since financial services need to be provided in Germany, sect. 32 para. 1 S. 1 KWG. The Federal Administrative Court (*Bundesverwaltungsgericht*) decided in the FIDIUM Case that such a provision of services can also take place virtually, especially by disseminating a credit application formula via the internet.[66] This is very similar to a marketplace principle.[67]

2.1.4 Data Protection and Data Economy

An increasingly important field in terms of the extraterritorial application of the law is the protection of personal data and as an underlying goal the protection of privacy. Of course, this also entails the regulation of companies whose business model lies in the processing of such personal data and thus the regulation of the most valuable companies worldwide.[68] Against this background,

---

63 J. v. Hein in E. Schwark and D. Zimmer (eds.), *Kapitalmarktrechts-Kommentar WpHG*, 5th ed., C.H.Beck, München 2020, sect. 102 n. 4.

64 On the problematic overlap regarding a so-called Organised Trading Facility while pleading for a teleological reduction D. Döhmel in H.-D. Assmann, U. W. Schneider and P. O. Mülbert (eds.), *Wertpapierhandelsrecht*, 7th ed., Otto Schmidt, Köln 2019, before sects. 102–105 WpHG n. 9

65 The authorisation must be published in the Federal Gazette (*Bundesanzeiger*) pursuant to sect. 102 para. 3 WpHG. The Bundesanzeiger is available at www.bundesanzeiger.de and is fully searchable. The authorisations are published as follows: BAnz AT 08.03.2022 B5; for the following citations the addition 'BAnz AT' has been omitted: 31.08.2021 B4; 20.08.2020 B2; 20.09.2019 B5; 06.05.2019 B3; 06.05.2019 B4; 03.05.2019 B4; 03.05.2019 B6; 03.05.2019 B7; 03.05.2019 B5; 10.11.2017 B6; 16.05.2017 B7; 16.05.2017 B8; 03.09.2014 B2; 22.08.2014 B3; 28.03.2014 B3; eBAnz AT 116 2009 B3; eBAnz AT 45 2007 B1.

66 BVerwGE 133, 358; see also CJEU, C-452/04, *Fidium Finanz v. Bundesanstalt für Finanzdienstleistungsaufsicht*, ECJ ECLI:EU:C:2006:631.

67 Profound discussion of the international dimension of sect. 32 KWG and references to the FIDIUM-case with further references i.a. by T. Dornis in C. Budzikiewicz et al., *BeckOGK. Internationales Gesellschaftsrecht*, ed. 01.11.2022, C.H Beck, München, n. 306 et seqq.

68 See i.a. https://www.statista.com/statistics/263264/top-companies-in-the-world-by-market-capitalization/.

the overriding economic importance of data protection law in the age of the information society becomes apparent. At the European level, the General Data Protection Regulation (hereafter: GDPR), which is applicable since May 2018, is particularly relevant. Even though this instrument covers a number of regulatory areas, it only aims for a *general* data protection regulation. Thus, a number of areas are left for the member states to further specify and regulate.[69] In Germany, such national regulations can be found in the Federal Data Protection Act[70] (*Bundesdatenschutzgesetz*, hereafter: BDSG) as well as in the data protection laws of the states (*Bundesländer*).

With regard to the international and extraterritorial applicability of both the GDPR and the BDSG, the active personality principle in the form of the establishment principle and the effects doctrine in the form of the marketplace principle apply. The former will be dealt with infra, 7.1, the latter is scrutinized here. Sect. 1 para. 4 sentence 2 no. 3 BDSG refers in this respect to the rules of the GDPR. Article 3 of the GDPR governs the geographical – and thus international – applicability, whereby para. 2 refers to the marketplace principle.

First of all, Art. 3 para. 2 lit. (a) GDPR establishes a link to the offering of goods or services to persons in the Union; they do not need to be residents or citizens. This is comparable to the principle of targeting/directing, as it is also laid down in the extraterritorial provisions of international consumer protection law in Art. 6 para. 1 Rome I and Art. 17 para. 1 Brussels Ia Regulation.[71] Thus, it is decisive, whether, for example, a website specifically offers goods or services to persons within the Union; according to the 23rd recital, criteria for this can be a special linguistic design (offer of a U.S. company in German) or an offer in the currency of an EU citizen. Against this background, Art. 3 para. 2 lit. (a) GDPR is considered to be less problematic and, with its 23rd recital, is obviously aimed at offers that are directed at persons within the Union and not merely offers that can be accessed via a website from the Union.

The situation is completely different – and much more problematic – with regard to the behavioural monitoring provided for in Art. 3 para. 2 lit. (b) GDPR. According to this provision, it is sufficient for the GDPR to apply that

69 Depending on how one counts up to 70 opening clauses in the GDPR can be found, see S. Simitis, G. Hornung and I. Spiecker genannt Döhmann in S. Simitis, G. Hornung and I. Spiecker gen. Döhmann (eds.), *Datenschutzrecht*, 1st ed., Nomos, Baden-Baden 2019, Einl. n. 226.

70 Translation available at https://www.gesetze-im-internet.de/englisch_bdsg/.

71 See for this and the following i.a. M. Brkan, *Data protection and conflict-of-laws: A challenging relationship*, EDPL 2016, 324, 338; ; EDPB, Guidelines 3/2018 on the territorial scope of the GDPR, p. 17.

the behaviour of individuals in the Union is – for example – monitored by tracking internet activities through the placing and/or reading of cookies.[72] All third-country websites that provide access to their content, for example on the basis of behavioural advertising – and thus monitor the behaviour via cookies –, would therefore be covered by the GDPR according to the prevailing view.[73] Hence, press companies from non-EU countries partly exclude Europeans from their websites since data protection standards would be too expensive to comply with – extraterritorial data protection is paid for by means of a restricted offer of information for Europeans.[74] More recently, attempts have been made to interpret the GDPR in this sense contrary to its wording and contrary to the systematics arising from the recitals,[75] in part also by invoking international law arguments; the latter will be returned to under 4. Although such a restrictive interpretation is quite understandable, even welcome, in terms of its underlying policy, this seems impossible in my opinion; the wording and recitals are clear-cut.

Against the background of the actual economic dimensions of international data protection in an information society, the fundamental rights debate about the status of data protection in Germany and the European Union, and the doubtful connecting factors of the GDPR regarding behavioural monitoring this sub-area appears to me to be the one with the greatest need for future discussion. In this report, the problems under international law are dealt with under 4., a possible conflict-of-law rule in the sense of a balancing requirement under 6. and the connecting factors again under 7. and 8.

72 Comp. further the 24th recital as well as S. Segger-Piening, Extraterritorialitätsauswirkungen und fehlender Privatrechtsbezug im Internationalen Datenprivatrecht in K. Duden et. al. (eds.), IPR *für eine bessere Welt?*, Mohr Siebeck, Tübingen 2022, pp. 114–15 with further references.

73 See i.a. S. Segger-Piening, Extraterritorialitätsauswirkungen und fehlender Privatrechtsbezug im Internationalen Datenprivatrecht in K. Duden et. al. (eds.), IPR *für eine bessere Welt?*, Mohr Siebeck, Tübingen 2022 pp. 114–15 with a critical evaluation; W. Däubler in W. Däubler, P. Wedde, T. Weichert and I. Sommer (eds.), DSGVO/*BDSG*, 2nd ed., Bund-Verlag, Frankfurt a. Main 2020, Art. 3 n. 20; T. Zerdick in E. Ehmann and M. Selmayr (eds.), DSGVO, 2nd ed., C.H.Beck, München 2018, Art. 3 n. 20.

74 On this with a number of examples S. Segger-Piening, Extraterritorialitätsauswirkungen und fehlender Privatrechtsbezug im Internationalen Datenprivatrecht in K. Duden et. al. (eds.), IPR *für eine bessere Welt?*, Mohr Siebeck, Tübingen 2022, pp. 109–11.

75 F. Jotzo, *Der Schutz personenbezogener Daten in der Cloud*, 2nd ed., Nomos, Baden-Baden 2020, p. 167; S. Herrmann, *Völkerrechtliche Jurisdiktionsgrundlagen für den Datenschutz im Netz*, Mohr Siebeck, Tübingen 2021, pp. 336–47.

2.1.5 *Foreign Trade Law and Sanctions*

An important domain for questions of extraterritorial application of the law is, by its very nature, foreign trade law and the sanctions associated with it. Foreign trade law is codified in Germany in the Foreign Trade and Payment Act[76] (*Außenwirtschaftsgesetz*, hereafter: AWG) and the complementary Foreign Trade and Payments Ordinance[77] (*Außenwirtschaftsverordnung*, hereafter: AWV).

The structure of the German system is based on the principle of free trade,[78] although restrictions are expressly permitted.[79] However, these restrictions are mainly linked to domestic actions, such as the prohibition to export or import certain goods.[80] The active personality principle is only implemented in isolated cases, with the consequence of extraterritorial application, which will be discussed later.[81] Consequently, foreign trade law is less extraterritorial than it might initially appear.[82]

With regard to the important field of sanctions, but also otherwise, it should be noted that European Union law is becoming increasingly important.[83] Union law comprehensively regulates trade within the internal market, see only Art. 26 et seqq. TFEU. In relations with third countries, the EU also has an exclusive competence in the field of foreign trade, Art. 206 et seqq. TFEU. Therefore, the imposition of economic sanctions and embargo measures is in principle within the exclusive competence of the European Union, Art. 215 TFEU. Only smaller residual fields, in which limited member state competence exist, remain.[84] It should be noted, however, that foreign trade sanctions are of particular importance within the European Union. In the recent past, the

---

76 Translation available at https://www.gesetze-im-internet.de/englisch_awg/.

77 Translation available at https://www.bmwi.de/Redaktion/DE/Downloads/A/awv-englisch.html.

78 Sect. 1 para. 1 s. 1 AWG; comp. further O. Remien, *Außenwirtschaftsrecht in kollisionsrechtlicher Sicht*, RabelsZ 54 (1990), 431, 442–43.

79 See sect. 4 et seqq. of the AWG.

80 Export control is especially governed by sects. 8 et seqq. AVV; imports are governed by sect. 29 et seqq. AVV.

81 See infra, 7.1.

82 Comp. also O. Remien, *Außenwirtschaftsrecht in kollisionsrechtlicher Sicht*, RabelsZ 54 (1990), 431, 446 et seqq., esp. 454.

83 See in this regard and for the following C. Herrmann and M. Niested in H.G. Krenzler et al., EU-Außenwirtschafts- und Zollrecht, 20th ed., C.H.Beck, München 2022, Einl., n. 10 ff.; A. Thoms in R. Rüsken (ed.), Zollre*cht*, 214th ed, Stollfuß, Bonn 2023, Einf. n. 29 ff.

84 Especially in the case of weapons embargoes, there is also a competence of the member states, cf. Art. 346 para. 2 lit. (b) TFEU; see also M. Niested in H.G. Krenzler et al., EU-*Außenwirtschafts- und Zollrecht*, 20th EL., C.H.Beck, München 2022, part 50. n. 57.

extensive sanctions against Russia in the context of the war against Ukraine stand out in particular.[85] There are also numerous other sources that illustrate the extent of the sanctions currently imposed.[86]

2.2 *Extraterritoriality and Criminal Law*

The extraterritorial application of criminal law norms can be seen as the beginning of the debate on the permissibility of such a practice under international law with the International Court of Justice's Lotus decision,[87] which was rather favourable towards an extraterritorial application in its outcome.[88] In Germany, the principle of territoriality applies pursuant to sect. 3 StGB of the German Criminal Code[89] (*Strafgesetzbuch*, hereafter: StGB), according to which 'German criminal law applies to offences committed on German territory'.[90] However, many criminal law provisions can be applied extraterritorially, some of which will be discussed infra. A discussion from the point of international law can be found infra at 4. The different connecting factors will also be analysed infra, 7. focusing not only on criminal law. Due to the definition of the place of commitment in sect. 9 StGB an extraterritorial application may also take place on the basis of partly foreign conduct as will be demonstrated infra, 8. Questions of corporate nationality will be answered separately infra at 9.

2.2.1 General Part of the German Criminal Code

The provisions of the General Part (*Allgemeiner Teil*) of the StGB apply in principle to all provisions of the Special Part; they are, so to speak, placed in front of the parenthesis. The territorial scope of German criminal law is codified in sects. 3–7 StGB. As already seen, sect. 3 StGB refers to the principle of territoriality (also called the principle of the place of the offence). Extraterritorial

---

85 See https://www.consilium.europa.eu/en/policies/sanctions/restrictive-measures-against-russia-over-ukraine/; from a legal point of view i.a. G. Schwendinger, K. Göcke, *Die Russland-Sanktionen der* EU, EuZW 2022, 499.

86 For an overview see https://www.sanctionsmap.eu/#/main; see also https://www.bundesbank.de/de/service/finanzsanktionen/sanktionsregimes.

87 PCIJ, Ser. A., No. 10 (1927).

88 For a discussion of the decision in German criminal law writing see i.a.G. Werle and F. Jeßberger in G. Cirener et al., *Leipziger Kommentar,* 13th ed., De Gruyter, Berlin 2020, before sects. 3, n. 24 et seq.; for a broader and most recent perspective from the German writing i.a. C. Kurkin, *Extraterritorialität*, Mohr Siebeck, Tübingen 2021, pp. 38–44.

89 Translation available at https://www.gesetze-im-internet.de/englisch_stgb/englisch_stgb.html.

90 The place of the commission of offences is defined in sect. 9 StGB; this provision is discussed infra, 8.

regulations are to be found in sects. 4–7 StGB, the basic structure and special features of which are to be illustrated in the following.

Section 4 StGB establishes the *flag principle* (*Flaggenprinzip*);[91] German criminal law applies 'regardless of which law is applicable at the place where the offence was committed' 'to offences committed on a ship or an aircraft which is entitled to fly the federal flag or to carry the national insignia of the Federal Republic of Germany.'

Section 5 StGB refers to 'Offences committed abroad with specific domestic connection'; German criminal law applies 'regardless of which law is applicable at the place where the offence was committed' for a variety of specifically enumerated crimes, no. 1–17. Each number refers to one or more criminal offences from the special part of the StGB (sects. 80 et seqq. StGB) and stipulates the method of connecting these crimes to behaviour abroad. The individual connecting measures can then be assigned to different well recognized connecting factors and principles.[92] This shall be demonstrated hereafter, however the list will not be complete:[93]

- *principle of state protection* (*Staatsschutzprinzip*): refers to offences abroad that particularly endanger the interests of the German state; aims to protect these state interests;
- examples: crimes such as high treason (sect. 5 no. 2 StGB with reference to sects. 81 to 83 StGB); treason and endangering external security (sect. 5 No. 4 StGB with references to sects. 94 to 100a StGB); offences against national defence (sect. 5 No. 5 lit a) with references to sects. 109 as well as 109e to 109g StGB);
- *passive personality principle*: refers to offences abroad that particularly endanger and/or violate the individual rights (*Individualrechtsgüter*) of German natural and in some instances also juridical/legal persons (*juristische Person* such as corporations); aims to protect these individual interests; connecting factor is the nationality of the victim;

---

91 See i.a. T. Fischer, *StGB*, 70th ed., C.H.Beck, München 2023, sect. 4 n. 2.

92 A good overview of the different principles, also in respect of delimitations derived from international law is provided i.a. by: A. Eser, B. Weißer in A. Schönke, H. Schröder (eds.), *StGB*, 30th ed., C.H.Beck, München 2019, before sect. 3, n. 17 et seqq.; K. Ambos in V. Erb, J. Schäfer (eds.), *MünchKomm-StGB*, 4th ed., C.H.Beck, München 2020,before sect. 3 n. 10 et seqq.; G. Werle and F. Jeßberger in G. Cirener et al., *Leipziger Kommentar*, 13th ed., De Gruyter, Berlin 2020, before sect. 3, n. 235 et seqq. For the following, reference is made to these sources.

93 For a rather complete overview see A. Eser, B. Weißer in A. Schönke, H. Schröder (eds.), *StGB*, 30th ed., C.H.Beck, München 2019,sect. 5 n. 2;, sect. 5, n. 10.

- example: 'violation of the business or trade secrets of a business which is physically located within the territorial scope of this statute or of an enterprise which has its seat therein or of an enterprise which has its seat abroad and which is dependent on an enterprise which has its seat within the territorial scope of this statute and which forms a corporate group with the latter' (sect. 5 No. 7 StGB);[94] however, it would also be possible to understand this as an example of the effects doctrine or the principle of state protection.
- *passive domicile principle*: refers to offences abroad that particularly endanger and/or violate the individual rights of natural persons, whose domicile or habitual residence is in Germany at the time of the offence; connecting factor is the domicile or habitual residence of the victim;
- example: offences against personal liberty (sect. 5 no. 6 lit. c) second alternative StGB with reference to sect. 237 StGB regarding forced marriages);
- *active personality principle*: refers to offences abroad committed by a German national; thus, connecting factor is the nationality of the perpetrator;
- example: sect. 5 No. 8 StGB: 'offences against sexual self-determination in the cases under sect.174 (1), (2) and (4), sects.176 to 178 and sect.182 if the offender is a German national at the time of the offence';
- *combination* of these principles: i.a. combination of active personality principle and active domicile principle in case of an offence endangering the democratic state under the rule of law (sect. 5 no. 3 lit. c StGB regarding 'a German national whose livelihood is based within the territorial scope of this statute' with reference to sects. 89, 90a para. 1 and 90b StGB).

Section 6 StGB refers to 'offences committed abroad against internationally protected legal interests'. In this respect, the *principle of universality* is established. The catalogue of individually covered crimes is exemplified infra, 7.4.

In contrast to sects. 5 and 6 StGB, sect. 7 StGB does not refer to a specific catalogue of offences but covers certain specific victim- or offender-related situations. The common prerequisite for all paragraphs and variants of this section is that 'the act is a criminal offence at the place of its commission or ... that place is not subject to any criminal law jurisdiction.'[95] Furthermore, the following must be cumulatively fulfilled: According to para. 1, the offence must be directed against a German, thus again establishing the passive personality principle.[96] Pursuant to para. 2 no. 1 the offender must be 'a German national

94 For the last alternative regarding a corporate group comp. further infra, 9.

95 Thus, the provision is to be regarded in conformance with international law, see i.a. G. Werle and F. Jeßberger in G. Cirener et al., *Leipziger Kommentar*, 13th ed., De Gruyter, Berlin 2020, sect. 7, n. 3 et seqq.

96 See i.a. T. Fischer, *StGB*, 70th ed., C.H.Beck, München 2023, sect. 7 n. 1.

at the time of the offence or became a German national after its commission', thus the active personality principle is established.[97] Para. 2 no. 2 refers to a special situation where extradition would be permissible, but the offender 'is not extradited because no request for extradition is made within a reasonable period, is rejected or the extradition is not feasible.' This is referred to as *Prinzip der stellvertrenden Strafrechtspflege* (vicarious criminal justice).[98]

2.2.2 Further Criminal Law Provisions (Nebenstrafrecht)

Furthermore, there are numerous acts and provisions outside the Criminal Code that stipulate their own extraterritorial applicability. A few examples illustrate:[99]

- According to sect. 1 s. 1 of the Code of Crimes against International Law[100] (*Völkerstrafgesetzbuch*), German criminal law applies to genocide (sect. 6 of the International Criminal Code), crimes against humanity (sect. 7 of the International Criminal Code) and war crimes (sects. 8 to 12 of the International Criminal Code) 'even when the offence was committed abroad and bears no relation to Germany'. The provision implements (again) the principle of universality.
- Regarding foreign trade law there is also a number of specific criminal provisions, such as sects. 17, 18 AWG. These provisions mostly refer to domestic conduct and a domestic place of action.[101] However, in sects. 17 para. 7, 18 para 10, 79 AWV the active personality principle applies. This will be further analysed infra, 7.1.
- There are also a number of criminal law provisions in the field of international financial market law.[102] However, their applicability is usually determined by the applicability of the corresponding administrative provisions, which is why reference can be made to this.

---

97 See i.a. T. Fischer, *StGB*, 70th ed., C.H.Beck, München 2023, sect. 7 n. 1.

98 see i.a. A. Eser, B. Weißer in A. Schönke, H. Schröder (eds.), *StGB*, 30th ed., C.H.Beck, München 2019, sect. 7 n. 1.

99 For a more detailed overview see i.a. G. Werle and F. Jeßberger in G. Cirener et al., *Leipziger Kommentar*, 13th ed., De Gruyter, Berlin 2020, before sect. 3, n. 476 et seqq.

100 Translation available at http://www.iuscomp.org/wordpress/wp-content/uploads/2014/03/voestgb.pdf.

101 See R. M. Stein, L. von Rummel in R. Rüsken (ed.), *Zollrecht*, 214th EL, Stollfuß, Bonn 2023, before sect. 17 et seqq. AWG, n. 19

102 See for this and the following i.a. M. Lehmann in F. J. Säcker et al., *Münchener Kommentar zum* BGB, *Finanzmarktrecht*, Bd. 13, 8th ed., C.H.Beck, München 2021, n. 487 et seqq.; T. Dornis in C. Budzikiewicz et al., *BeckOGK. Internationales Gesellschaftsrecht*, ed. 01.11.2022, C.H Beck, München, n. 493 et seqq.

2.3 *Trends*

2.3.1 Dominance of European Law

Questions of extraterritorial application of law have been increasingly discussed in Germany since the second half of the 20th century. Parallel to this, there have been a number of significant developments, for example with regard to the increase in economic sanctions,[103] or the recent increase in considerations about an end to concepts of territoriality and extraterritoriality altogether since global challenges to humanity such as climate change or migration can only be solved in a global sense.[104] From a German perspective, however, all these topics are characterised by a very special trend: the dominance of European law regarding questions of extraterritoriality.

As has been seen, the subject area of international economic regulation under consideration here are more or less dominated by European regulations. The unification achieved in this respect strengthens the European internal market and reduces trade barriers. But also externally, the concentrated power of 27 member states allows for a strong presence in a variety of economically relevant fields. The Brussels Effect described by *Anu Bradford* has illustrated this,[105] including negative downsides such as in international data law.[106] On the other hand, or at the same time, the special constitution of the European Union still allows for a multitude of member state competences, so that for many questions a veritable thicket of national and European regulations exists. It is the task of European legal scholars in the 21st century to maintain an overview here, also with regard to the international dimensions and obligations under international law.

2.3.2 Regulation of Cyberspace – The Netzwerkdurchsetzungsgesetz

Another trend concerns the regulation of cyberspace and the respective online intermediaries, i.e. platforms, social networks or instant messaging services. This area is also shaped by European regulations[107] and at the same time the subject of national laws.

---

103 See supra, 2.1.5.

104 See in this regard i.a. the recent presentations of *Ralf Michaels* and *Peer Zumbansen* at the international conference 'Extraterritoriality and International Law', Indiana Law School, 15th to 17th of September 2021 via Zoom.

105 A. Bradford, *The Brussels Effect,* 107 Nw. U. L. Rev., 1 (2012).

106 See supra, 2.1.4.

107 I.a. Regulation (EU) 2019/1150 on promoting fairness and transparency for business users of online intermediation services OJ 2019 L 186, pp. 57 et seqq., comp. for the extraterritorial

Subject of the current discussion – and of particular interest from a German perspective – is the extraterritorial application of the German Network Enforcement Act[108] (*Gesetz zur Verbesserung der Rechtsdurchsetzung in sozialen Netzwerken*, hereafter: NetzDG) of 2017 to the Dubai-based messenger service Telegram.[109] This service is inter alia used by large user groups to incite violence against state authorities as a reaction to the current policy in connection with the containment of the Corona pandemic. The German Federal Office of Justice (*Bundesamt für Justiz*) recently imposed a fine of 5,125 million Euro against Telegram.[110] The complaint filed against this fine is pending before the *Amtsgericht* (district court) Bonn.[111] Recently, proceedings were also initiated against Twitter.[112] In this context, Federal Minister of Justice Bushman stated, "Our laws apply to everyone."[113]

The NetzDG obliges platform providers[114] to delete illegal content according to certain requirements and to provide reporting mechanisms for this purpose. Illegal content is defined by reference to certain provisions of the German Penal Code (StGB); according to sect. 1 para. 3 NetzDG, this includes for example insults, denial of the Holocaust, but also child pornography. The obligations under the NetzDG also apply to foreign providers, as long as these have no 'fewer than two million registered users in the Federal Republic of Germany', sect. 1 para. 2 NetzDG. Furthermore, it is important to note, that it is not necessary to scrutinize whether or not German criminal law is applicable to the offense at hand, since the criminal law provisions referred to by sect. 1

applicability Art. 1 para. 2; Regulation (EU) 2022/2065 on a Single Market For Digital Services, OJ 2022 L 277, p. 1–102, comp. for the extraterritorial applicability Art. 2 para. 1.

108 Translation available at https://www.bmj.de/DE/Themen/FokusThemen/NetzDG/NetzDG_EN_node.html.

109 For the facts of the case see the good report of the Handelsblatt, available at https://www.handelsblatt.com/politik/deutschland/messengerdienst-corona-radikalisierung-innenminister-nehmen-telegram-ins-visier/27888986.html as well as the report of the Spiegel available at https://www.spiegel.de/netzwelt/telegram-was-die-politik-gegen-die-gefaehrliche-chat-app-unternehmen-kann-a-7245e6fd-b057-41b9-9b50-69095458cd54.

110 https://www.bundesjustizamt.de/DE/ServiceGSB/Presse/Pressemitteilungen/2023/20230302.html.

111 https://www.lto.de/recht/nachrichten/n/bussgeldbescheide-in-millionenhoehe-gegen-telegram-verstoesse-netzdg-ag-bonn/.

112 https://www.bundesjustizamt.de/DE/ServiceGSB/Presse/Pressemitteilungen/2023/20230404.html.

113 https://www.bmj.de/SharedDocs/Zitate/DE/2022/1017_Telegram.html. However, a genuine link is needed, when applying German laws extraterritorially, see infra, 4.2; in the case of the NetzDG such a link can be established with regard to sect. 1 para. 2 NetzDG, see infra.

114 For a closer definition, see sect. 1 para. 1 NetzDG.

para. 3 NetzDG are only the substantial criterion for determining whether or not the content is unlawful.[115] If a provider of a social network does not comply with the duties of the NetzDG a regulatory fine can be imposed pursuant to sect. 4 NetzDG, even if the offence is not committed in Germany, sect. 4 para. 3 NetzDG.[116] The outcome of the proceedings before the Amtsgericht Bonn can be eagerly awaited, not least because the constitutionality of the NetzDG is often doubted in the literature.[117] Moreover, even in the event of victory an eventual enforcement of the judgement is likely to be challenging.

The international regulation of cyberspace is a particularly pressing and significant issue for the future development of both European and German law.

3 Multiple Interconnections with the Law of the European Union

As has already been made clear several times, European Union law has a great influence on the extraterritorial application of German law. In part, German rules implement European law, i.e. directives, and thus extraterritorial application orders, such as in the field of capital market law and banking supervision.[118] In part, there is a broad convergence between extraterritorial applicability according to European principles and German practice, such as in the field of antitrust (administrative) law.[119] In part, it is European conflict-of-law rules that lead to German law being applied extraterritorially, as in the field of private enforcement of antitrust law and fair trading law.[120] In part, reference is also made to European regulations, as in the field of data protection law.[121] Overall, there is considerable interaction between German and European law at the regulatory level, particularly in the field of economic regulation.[122] This is far less often the case in the field of criminal law, although

115 See further E. Hoven, H. Gersdorf in H. Gersdorf, B. P. Paal(eds.), *BeckOK Info- u. MedienR*, 39th ed., C.H.Beck, München 2023, NetzDG § 1 n. 45; however, this is also questioned, see i.a. M. Liesching, *Netzwerkdurchsetzungsgesetz*, 1st ed., Nomos, Baden-Baden 2018, sect. 1 n. 11.

116 Thus, pursuant to the prevailing opinion, also foreign companies can be fined, see in this regard infra, 9.

117 See i.a. E. Hoven, H. Gersdorf in H. Gersdorf, B. P. Paal(eds.), *BeckOK Info- u. MedienR*, 39th ed., C.H.Beck, München 2023, NetzDG § 1 n. 5–8 with further references.

118 See supra, 2.1.3.

119 See supra, 2.1.1.1.

120 See supra, 2.1.1.

121 See supra, 2.1.4.

122 See also in terms of intellectual property and foreign trade law supra, 2.1.2., 2.1.5.

some of the extraterritorial provisions there must also be seen against the background of European requirements.[123]

4 Role of International Law in General, as a Limitation and as a Foundation

International law in general has a high significance within the German legal system, as will be briefly clarified infra, 1. This is also evident in connection with the question of an extraterritorial application of domestic law. International law has both a negative, limiting function and a positive, enabling function. The former function refers to the classical understanding of international law as a limit to extraterritorial applicability and will be clarified infra under 2. In addition, international law itself also serves as a basis for extraterritorial applicability, as will be explained infra under 3.

It should be noted at the outset that there is some discussion of the extent to which international law also contains a conflict of laws rule for the case of conflicting extraterritorial laws. This question is dealt with infra, under 6.

4.1 *Preliminary: the Basic Law's Friendliness towards International Law*

The law of the Federal Republic of Germany is governed by the principle of friendliness towards international law.[124] The principle is decisively derived from Art. 25 of the Basic Law[125] (*Grundgesetz für die Bundesrepublik Deutschland*, hereafter: GG). Pursuant to sentence 1 '[t]he general rules of international law shall be an integral part of federal law.' Therefore, customary international law is directly incorporated into the German legal system; an implementing act is not needed.[126] This is an important provision, as international law itself does not demand such a result.[127] However, a restriction must be made insofar as international treaties require implementation in accordance with Art. 59 para. 2 GG for their domestic validity. Pursuant to Art. 25 sentence 2 GG general

123 For example sect. 5 no. 8 StGB, see in this regard G. Werle and F. Jeßberger in G. Cirener et al., *Leipziger Kommentar*, 13th ed., De Gruyter, Berlin 2020, before sect. 5, n. 125.

124 I.a. BverfGE 6, 309, 362 f; BverfGE 111, 307, 317–18; M. Herdegen, Völkerrecht, 20th ed., C.H.Beck, München 2021, sect. 22 n. 8.

125 Translation available at: https://www.gesetze-im-internet.de/englisch_gg/englisch_gg.html.

126 BVerfGE 6, 309, 363.

127 Comp. further in this respect F. Wollenschläger in H. Dreier (ed.), *Grundgesetz*, 3rd ed., Mohr Siebeck, Tübingen 2015, Art. 25 n. 7 with references to the international writing, left out in this country report.

rules of international law 'shall take precedence over the laws and directly create rights and duties for the inhabitants of the federal territory.' Accordingly, general rules of international law rank below the Basic Law but above federal law;[128] this is also significant and by no means self-evident, as practice in many common law countries shows.[129] Thus, Art. 25 GG clearly illustrates the principle of friendliness towards international law. This is also reflected in the decision-making practice of the courts in Germany, as considerations of international law are taken into account in a large number of cases.[130]

4.2 *International Law as a Limit on the Extraterritorial Application of Law*

4.2.1 General Requirement: Genuine Link

Against the backdrop of the Basic Law's friendliness towards international law there is a basic consensus in Germany that limits under international law must be observed when applying law extraterritorially. This is predominantly linked to the principle of non-interference or prohibition of intervention under international law (*völkerrechtliches Einmischungs- bzw. Interventionsverbot*).[131] From this, the Federal Constitutional Court (*Bundesverfassungsgericht*) derives the requirement of a 'reasonable connecting point';[132] this corresponds to a genuine link.

In the opinion of the Federal Constitutional Court, the definition of a reasonable connecting point needs to be established for each specific field of law

128 BVerfGE 6, 309, 363; 37, 271, 279; 141, 1, 17 n. 41; D. Koenig, König in H. v. Mangoldt, F. Klein, C. Starck (eds.), *Grundgesetz*, 7th ed., C.H.Beck, München 2018, Art. 25 n. 4.

129 Comp. for example Sect. 115 para. 1 lit. (a), comment a) and Reporters' Note 2, Restatement (Third) of the Foreign Relations Law of the United States; comp. further the constitution of South Africa, Art. 232; on this point from the German writing F. Wollenschläger in H. Dreier (ed.), *Grundgesetz*, 3rd ed., Mohr Siebeck, Tübingen 2015, Art. 25 n. 11.

130 See infra, 4.2., for matters of extraterritoriality. See in general, with the formation of case groups and further references to case law i.a. F. Wollenschläger in H. Dreier (ed.), *Grundgesetz*, 3rd ed., Mohr Siebeck, Tübingen 2015, Art. 25 n. 40 et seqq.; M. Herdegen in G. Düring, R. Herzog, R. Scholz (eds.), *Grundgesetz*, 99th EL, C.H.Beck, München 2022, Art. 25 n. 50 et seqq.

131 BVerfGE 3, 343, 369; BVerfG NJW 2001, 1848, 1852 at III. 6.; from the literature i.a. M. Herdegen, *Völkerrecht*, 20th ed., C.H.Beck, München 2021, sect. 26 n. 3; comp also. C. Engel, *Die Bedeutung des Völkerrechts für die Anwendung in- und ausländischen Wirtschaftsrechts*, RabelsZ 52 (1988), 271, 281–82; see further infra, with references for different fields as antirust, data protection and criminal law.

132 BVerfGE 63, 343, 369; BVerfG NJW 2001, 1848, 1852 at III. 6.; from the writing i.a. W. Meng, *Extraterritoriale Jurisdiktion im öffentlichen Wirtschaftsrecht*, Springer, Berlin 1994, pp. 541 et seqq.; O. Sandrock, *Völkerrechtliche Grenzen staatlicher Gesetzgebung*, ZVglRWiss 115 (2016), 1, 79.

separately.[133] In this respect, some areas are to be exemplified hereafter, i.e. antitrust law, data protection law and criminal law. In other areas also considered above, however, an incipient discussion of international law limits takes place,[134] even though the case law tends to discuss any limits only against the *implicit* background of international law considerations and does not link them directly to international law.[135] The restrictions on extraterritorial applicability discussed there are therefore discussed infra, 7., in connection with the effects doctrine.

4.2.2 Sector Specific Analysis

4.2.2.1 *Principle of Non-interference and* de minimis *Rule in Antitrust Law*

Of particular interest is (administrative) antitrust law.[136] There, as seen, the so-called effects doctrine has always applied – for German antitrust law pursuant to sect. 185 para. 2 GWB – which by its very nature also covers conduct abroad as long as it has an effect on the domestic market.[137] Thus, the admissibility of the effects doctrine under international law was discussed early on.[138] In principle, there is a general agreement that local effects are also a suitable connecting factor under international law.[139] Both in practice and in

133 BVerfG NJW 2001, 1848, 1852 at III. 6.

134 For the starting discussion in intellectual property law see J. Drexl in F. J. Säcker et al., *Münchener Kommentar zum* BGB, Bd. 13, 8th ed., C.H.Beck, München 2021, Art. 8 n. 308. In matters of financial regulation there is acceptance of the requirement of a genuine link, M. Lehmann in F. J. Säcker et al., *Münchener Kommentar zum* BGB, *Finanzmarktrecht,* Bd. 13, 8th ed., C.H.Beck, München 2021, n. 118; for trademarks and unfair competition see T. *Dornis, Trademark and Unfair Competition Conflicts*, Cambridge University Press, Cambridge 2017, pp. 436–37. For package travel see Weber in W. Hau and R. Poseck (eds.), *BeckOK* BGB, 64th ed., München 2022, sect. 651v n. 32.1 with references to the Lotus case.

135 See for intellectual property i.a. BGH GRUR Int. 2005, 433 Hotel Maritime with a discussion supra, 2.1.2.

136 As seen, Art. 6 para. 2 Rome II applies to so-called private antitrust law, supra 2.1.1.1. There, a requirement of appreciability is controversially discussed, comp. O. Remien in W. Siebert (ed.), *Soergel* BGB Bd. 27/1, 13th ed., Kohlhammer, Stuttgart 2019, Art. 6 n. 53 with further references.

137 Supra, 2.1.1.1.

138 Particularly noteworthy in this regard is K. M. Meessen, *Völkerrechtliche Grundsätze des internationalen Kartellrechts,* Nomos, Baden-Baden 1975; for further references see i.a. C. Stadler in H.-J. Bunte (ed.), *Kartellrecht,* 14th ed., Luchterhand, München 2022, sect. 185 n. 136 et seqq.

139 From case law see i.a, BGH, GRUR 1979, 790, 792; KG, WuW/E OLG 3051, 3052 et seqq.; OLG Düsseldorf, WuW/E DE-R 2477 n. 31 et seq.; from the writing i.a. F. Wagner-von Papp, W. Wurmnest in F. J. Säcker (ed.), *MünchKomm-Wettbewerbsrecht*, Bd. 1, 3rd ed., C.H.Beck, München 2020, Grdl. n. 1339 et seqq.; W. Meng, *Extraterritoriale Jurisdiktion im öffentlichen Wirtschaftsrecht*, Springer, Berlin 1994, pp. 526 et seqq., 541 et seqq.

academic writing, the principle of non-interference under international law is often used as a limit.[140] However, other principles are also mentioned in some cases.[141]

It also remains somewhat unclear which criteria should be used to determine the extent from which on interference appears inadmissible.[142] Insofar as the literature, in particular, refers to a balancing of interests in this respect,[143] this seems to me to be a subordinate second step towards a possible solution of a conflict between different legal systems that are applied in parallel, but not as a criterion for the exclusion of the application of one's own law per se. More promising – and favoured by the courts – seems to be the approach of excluding effects that are not very appreciable, i.e. a *de minimis* rule;[144] in part, foreseeability is also required as well as an immediate, in part also significant effect.[145] However, with all these criteria, ambiguities remain, which can also be explained against the background of a largely lacking practice of a restriction of the impact principle based on international law. With regard to the criterion of appreciability, completely marginal domestic effects are excluded.[146] In the case of restrictions of competition, for example, a low domestic turnover of less than 2 to 3 million euros is sometime referred to, however, others want to differentiate according to

140 OLG Düsseldorf, WuW/E DE-R 2–477 n. 31 et seq.; KG WuW/E OLG 2419, 2420; KG WuW/E OLG 3051, 3052 n. 9, 14; OLG Frankfurt a. M. WuW /E DE-R 801; G. Wiedmann in G. Wiedemann (ed.), *Kartellrecht*, 4th ed., C.H.Beck, München 2020, sect. 5 n. 7.

141 For example, the so-called prohibition of abuse of rights, OLG Düsseldorf, WuW/E DE-R 2–477 n. 31 et seq.; for a broad overview comp. further F. Wagner-von Papp, W. Wurmnest in F. J. Säcker (ed.), *MünchKomm-Wettbewerbsrecht*, Bd. 1, 3rd ed., C.H.Beck, München 2020, n. 1353 et seqq.

142 Discussed i.a. by C. Stadler in H.-J. Bunte (ed.), *Kartellrecht*, 14th ed., Luchterhand, München 2022, sect. 185 n. 139 et seqq., 144 et seqq. with further references; see in this regard also BGH WuW/E DE-R 2133 n. 19.

143 K. M. Meessen, *Völkerrechtliche Grundsätze des internationalen Kartellrechts*, Nomos, Baden-Baden 1975, pp. 198 et seqq.; comp. also C. Stadler in H.-J. Bunte (ed.), *Kartellrecht*, 14th ed., Luchterhand, München 2022, sect. 185 n. 142 et seq. with reference to extreme cases, that could need such an interest balancing; from case law see KG WuW/E OLG 3051, 3053, 3061–62.

144 BGH, GRUR 1979, 790, 791; WuW/E DE-R 2133 n. 19; OLG Düsseldorf WuW /E DE-R 2477 n. 28; E. Rehbinder, J. von Kalben in U. Immenga, E.-J. Mestmäcker (eds.), *Wettbewerbsrecht*, Bd. 2, 6th. ed., C.H.Beck, München 2020, sect. 185 n. 128.

145 See i.a. M. Herdegen, *Internationales Wirtschaftsrecht*, 12th ed., C.H.Beck, München 2020, sect. 3 n. 69; F. Wagner-von Papp, W. Wurmnest in F. J. Säcker (ed.), *MünchKomm-Wettbewerbsrecht*, Bd. 1, 3rd ed., C.H.Beck, München 2020, n. 1348 et seqq.

146 In this sense C. Stadler in H.-J. Bunte (ed.), *Kartellrecht*, 14th ed., Luchterhand, München 2022, sect. 185 n. 132.

the respective legal standard in question.[147] In the case of mergers, it is usually referred to a certain domestic turnover of the companies involved.[148]

From a practical point of view, it is significant that although authorities and courts do refer to the limits of the effects doctrine under international law with recourse to the prohibition of interference, German antitrust law is nevertheless often applied to foreign cases on the basis of the effects doctrine.[149] However, an exception is made in this respect in the field of merger control. In particular, there are some decisions in which the prohibition was limited to the domestic part of a divisible merger.[150]

4.2.2.2 *Discussion in the Field of Data Protection*

For data protection law, it has already been pointed out that Art. 3 para. 2 lit. (b) GDPR, to which German law refers, is very far-reaching.[151] If the provision were not to be interpreted restrictively, a violation of international law would be established in the opinion of some commentators;[152] case law is missing so far. This is linked to a lack of limitation of the effects doctrine by criteria such as a direction of the activity towards a specific country or a 'direct, substantial and reasonably foreseeable' effect. Although this criticism is shared here in the result, it seems to me that it is still completely open which preconditions international law requires in detail with regard to data protection. After all, one must also take into account that behavioural monitoring via cookies enables the creation of far-reaching personality profiles of persons within the Union. At least in the case of a limitation de lege ferenda to EU citizens – and thus the establishment of the passive personality principle in combination with the effects doctrine –, the current legal situation seems to me to be not at

147 See R. Bechtold and W. Bosch in R. Bechtold and W. Bosch (eds.), GWB, 9th ed., C.H.Beck, München 2018, sect. 185 n. 20; C. Stadler in H.-J. Bunte (ed.), *Kartellrecht*, 14th ed., Luchterhand, München 2022, sect. 185 n. 132.

148 See for a detailed discussion i.a. F. Wagner-von Papp, W. Wurmnest in F. J. Säcker (ed.), *MünchKomm-Wettbewerbsrecht*, Bd. 1, 3rd ed., C.H.Beck, München 2020, n. 1438 et seqq.; today specific values can also be found in sect. 35 GWB. However, these values refer to substantive law and not the question of applicable law; the result will be the same, though.

149 Comp. further F. Wagner-von Papp, W. Wurmnest in F. J. Säcker (ed.), *MünchKomm-Wettbewerbsrecht*, Bd. 1, 3rd ed., C.H.Beck, München 2020, n. 1425.

150 See i.a. KG WuW/E OLG 3051, 3052; KG WuW/E OLG 2419, 2420–21 and with further references F. Wagner-von Papp, W. Wurmnest in F. J. Säcker (ed.), *MünchKomm-Wettbewerbsrecht*, Bd. 1, 3rd ed., C.H.Beck, München 2020, n. 1449.

151 See supra, 2.1.4.

152 See esp. S. Herrmann, *Völkerrechtliche Jurisdiktionsgrundlagen für den Datenschutz im Netz*, Mohr Siebeck, Tübingen 2021, pp. 336–47 and passim; comp. also P. Uecker, Extraterritorialer Anwendungsbereich der DS-GVO, ZD 2019, 67.

all certain from a purely international law perspective. However, this does not change the fact that the current connecting factor is clearly too far-reaching and should be corrected de lege ferenda, even though international law might not require this.[153]

4.2.2.3 *Criminal Law*

In the field of criminal law, the principle of non-interference and the resulting requirement of a reasonable connecting factor ('genuine link') are also taken into account. In this context, the Federal Constitutional Court has classified a number of connecting factors as reasonable in matters of criminal law, namely: active and passive personality principle, the protection principle, the principle of vicarious criminal justice (*stellvertretende Strafrechtspflege*), and the universality or world law principle.[154] Thus, the connecting factors discussed above[155] are justified under international law. However, the conformity with international law is doubted by parts of the German writing with regard to the passive personality principle if the requirement of criminal liability at the place of commission is waived.[156] The same holds true for the active personality principle. Against the background of the rather clear decision of the Federal Constitutional Court, however, this view hardly seems to play a role in practice. Furthermore, if the Federal Supreme Court considers the mere stay of the victim in the country to be insufficient,[157] it is questionable whether this also applies to the place of residence/domicile. In recent years, the connection to habitual residence has increased considerably, especially in private international law.[158]

153 For a proposal see S. Segger-Piening, Extraterritorialitätsauswirkungen und fehlender Privatrechtsbezug im Internationalen Datenprivatrecht in K. Duden et. al. (eds.), IPR für eine bessere Welt?, Mohr Siebeck, Tübingen 2022, pp. 121–23.

154 BVerfG, NJW 2001, 1848, 1852.

155 Supra, 2.2.

156 See i.a. K. Ambos in V. Erb, J. Schäfer (eds.), *MünchKomm-StGB*, 4th ed., C.H.Beck, München 2020, before sect. 3, n. 40 et seqq. However there are also strong voices that do not see a conflict with international law see i.a. G. Werle and F. Jeßberger in G. Cirener et al., *Leipziger Kommentar*, 13th ed., De Gruyter, Berlin 2020, before sect. 3 n. 249.

157 BGH NStZ 1999, 236.

158 See i.a. B. Rentsch, *Der gewöhnliche Aufenthalt im System des Europäischen Kollisionsrechts*, Mohr Siebeck, Tübingen 2017.

4.3 *International Law as a Foundation of the Extraterritorial Application of Law*

Partly, international law also serves as a foundation for the extraterritorial application of law. Especially in the field of criminal law several examples can be found. First of all, the active personality principle is now linked to the idea of international solidarity.[159] Crimes committed by Germans abroad should not go unpunished despite the ban on extradition that applies in principle. Sect. 7 para. no. 1 StGB must be seen against this background. Some sections of the StGB also serve to implement obligations under international law, as for example sect. 5 no. 8 regarding certain offences against sexual self-determination[160] or sect. 5 no. 15 regarding certain corruption offences.[161] Furthermore, the whole concept of universal jurisdiction can also be regarded as being based on international law.[162]

5 Limited Role of International Comity

5.1 *Comity in General*

The principle of 'comity' is recognized in German legal discourse. However, this institution does not have the same significance here as it does in U.S. law and is rather studied from a comparative, academic point of view.

In Germany, the concept of comity is associated with the requirement of mutual consideration under international law (*völkerrechtliches Rücksichtnahmegebot*), i.e. some sort of reasonableness also termed as international *courtoisie*.[163] According to this, foreign interests must be taken into account,

---

159 See i.a. G. Werle and F. Jeßberger in G. Cirener et al., *Leipziger Kommentar*, 13th ed., De Gruyter, Berlin 2020, before sect. 3, n. Rn 254.

160 Partly a result of the implementation of the Council of Europe Convention on the Protection of Children Against Sexual Exploitation and Sexual Abuse (CETS No. 201), see i.a. A. Eser, B. Weißer in A. Schönke, H. Schröder (eds.), *StGB*, 30th ed., C.H.Beck, München 2019, sect. 5. n. 20.

161 Partly a result of the implementation of the Criminal Law Convention on Corruption (ETS No. 173), see i.a. A. Eser, B. Weißer in A. Schönke, H. Schröder (eds.), *StGB*, 30th ed., C.H.Beck, München 2019, sect. 5. n. 32.

162 See i.a. G. Werle and F. Jeßberger in G. Cirener et al., *Leipziger Kommentar*, 13th ed., De Gruyter, Berlin 2020, before sect. 3, n. Rn 258 et seqq.; for a discussion of the concept of universal jurisdiction see infra, 7.4.

163 See i.a.M. Herdegen, *Internationales Wirtschaftsrecht*, 12th ed., C.H.Beck, München 2020, sect. 3 n. 72; from case law regarding international *courtoise* i.a. BverfGE 66, 39; BverwGE 37, 116; NJW 1984, 574; NJW 1989, 678. In this regard also W. Meng, *Extraterritoriale Jurisdiktion im öffentlichen Wirtschaftsrecht*, Springer, Berlin 1994, p. 101.

for example, when applying the law extraterritorially. However, the concept of the comity of nations or *courtoisie* tends not to be considered as customary international law.[164]

Regarding subject matter, comity is discussed in particular in the field of antitrust law, which will be discussed in more detail below. However, certain approaches can also be found in the areas of data protection law,[165] intellectual property[166] and financial market law.[167] There, it is being considered to what extent comity can help with conflicts of application of the law or serve as a limitation to the effects doctrine, although predominantly other instruments are used for this purpose.[168]

5.2 *Comity and Antitrust Law*

The principle of comity is repeatedly emphasised in antitrust law, especially in the academic writing. Generally, it is understood as a manifestation of the principle under international law for nations to treat each other in a friendly manner.[169] The common view is that this is not a duty under international law, but rather a requirement of mutual consideration.[170] As far as it can be seen, it is not used in the practice of the German cartel authorities and courts. They rather rely on the principle of non-interference under international law.

164 I.a. M. Herdegen, Völkerrecht, 20th ed., C.H.Beck, München 2021, sect. 14 n. 6; from the U.S. writing i.a. W. Dodge, *International Comity in American Law,* 115 Colum. L. Rev. 2071, 2140–41 (2015).

165 See M. Melcher in S. L. Gössl et al.(eds.), *Politik und Internationales Privatrecht,* Mohr Siebeck, Tübingen 2017, pp. 141–43; discussed also by S. Herrmann, *Völkerrechtliche Jurisdiktionsgrundlagen für den Datenschutz im Netz,* Mohr Siebeck, Tübingen 2021, pp. 377–80.

166 J. Drexl in F. J. Säcker et al., *Münchener Kommentar zum* BGB, Bd. 13, 8th ed., C.H.Beck, München 2021, Art. 8 n. 308.

167 T. Dornis in C. Budzikiewicz et al., *BeckOGK. Internationales Gesellschaftsrecht,* ed. 01.11.2022, C.H Beck, München, n. 98 et seqq.

168 For limits pursuant to international law see supra, 4.2.; methods for solving conflicts are discussed infra, 6.

169 See i.a. T. Käseberg in H.-J. Bunte (eds.), *Kartellrecht,* 14th ed., Luchterhand, München 2022, Einl. zum EU-Kartellrecht, n. 77; specifically on the limits of international law and the principle of comity in the context of European merger control, for example T. Körber in U. Immenga, E.-J. Mestmäcker (eds.), *Wettbewerbsrecht,* Bd. 1, 6th. ed., C.H.Beck, München 2019,Art. 1 FKVO n. 62.

170 See i.a. T. Käseberg in H.-J. Bunte (eds.), *Kartellrecht,* 14th ed., Luchterhand, München 2022, Einl. zum EU-Kartellrecht, n. 77.

Regarding content, the principle of comity or the comity of nations is initially discussed in the academic writing with regard to the effects doctrine.[171] Even if a conduct has an effect on the German or the European market, a balancing of the interests of the law-applying state and the foreign state should take place under the aspect of comity. This form of comity is also referred to as negative comity and has the overall effect of limiting the effects principle.[172] In this respect, comity is attributed a function that is already fulfilled by other instruments.[173]

In addition, so-called positive comity is recognized in German and European antitrust law.[174] This describes a special type of cooperation between two states. According to this, the state concerned about the effects of an antitrust infringement in its territory informs the state from which the behaviour originates about the possible infringing practices. It is then up to the state of origin to prevent the practices, so that the first state does not have to apply its antitrust law extraterritorially. Such an understanding of positive comity can be found in particular in a number of international antitrust treaties, such as the EC-US Agreement[175] or the Agreement between the EU and Switzerland.[176] However, despite such principles at the European level, the Commission has already re-examined a merger approved by the US antitrust authorities according to the standards of European antitrust law and imposed additional

171 L.-P. Rudolf in W. Jaeger, J. Kokott, P. Pohlmann, D. Schroeder (eds.), *Frankfurter Kommentar zum Kartellrecht,* 104th ed., Otto Schmidt, Köln 2023, AT des Europ. Kartellrechts C n. 9.

172 See for the European case law EGC, Case T-102/96, *Gencor,* ECLI:EU:T:1999:65; from the writing i.a. A. Klees, P.-T. Stoll, T. P. Holterhus, A. Schebstadt in J. Busche, A. Röhling (eds.), *Kölner Kommentar zum Kartellrecht,* Carl Heymanns, 2014, sect. 130 n. 117; comp. also P. Späth, *Zum gegenwärtigen Stand der Doctrine of Comity im Recht der Vereinigten Staaten von Amerika,* IPRax 2006, 184,188.

173 See supra, 4.2.2.1., and infra, 6.2.

174 See i.a. L.-P. Rudolf in W. Jaeger, J. Kokott, P. Pohlmann, D. Schroeder (eds.), *Frankfurter Kommentar zum Kartellrecht,* 104th ed., Otto Schmidt, Köln 2023, AT des Europ. Kartellrechts D. n. 45 et seqq.; T. Käseberg in H.-J. Bunte (ed.), *Kartellrecht,* 14th ed., Luchterhand, München 2022, Art. 1 FKVO n. 52.

175 See for the original agreement OJ 1995 L 95/47 and for the addition regarding comity see OJ 1998 L 173/28; see further T. Käseberg in H.-J. Bunte (ed.), *Kartellrecht,* 14th ed., Luchterhand, München 2022, Art. 1 FKVO n. 52; S. Völcker in U. Immenga, E.-J. Mestmäcker (eds.), *Wettbewerbsrecht,* Bd. 1, 6th. ed., C.H.Beck, München 2019, II. Int. Wettbewerbsrecht, n. 55 et seqq.

176 See Art. 5 of the agreement, available at https://ec.europa.eu/competition/international/bilateral/agreement_eu_ch_en.pdf; and regarding comity i.a. S. Völcker in U. Immenga, E.-J. Mestmäcker (eds.), *Wettbewerbsrecht,* Bd. 1, 6th. ed., C.H.Beck, München 2019, II. Int. Wettbewerbsrecht, n. 101 et seq.

conditions[177] or, in one case, even prohibited[178] it. Positive comity does not seem to be relied upon in antitrust practice.

6 Requirement of Reasonableness as a Conflict Rule

6.1 *Reasonableness as a Conflict Rule in General*

In German writing, it is discussed how to deal with the case of a jurisdictional conflict.[179] If one agrees with the predominant national as well as international opinion – and thus in accordance with customary international law – that there are rather few restrictive requirements of international law with regard to an extraterritorial application of the law,[180] an important question arises: To what extent are conflicts of law to be resolved between, for instance, two national states, where state A extends its laws, with regard to antitrust law for the respective individual case, to state B and state B to state A. For it is clear: The more states extend their rules extraterritorially (and unilaterally), the greater the danger that a legal subject will find itself exposed to different and possibly also contradictory legal systems.

In the United States, some past practice suggested the possibility that conflicts might be at least partly avoided by the requirement of reasonableness, which would provide for consideration and, if necessary, balancing of the different interests. However, there is by no means a uniform practice either.[181] In Germany, such reasonableness is most commonly associated with the discussion concerning a balancing of interests. Thus, it is discussed to what extent the interests of foreign states can also be taken into account in the question of

177 *Boeing v. McDonnell Douglas* (Case No IV/M.877), Commission Decision, 30.07.1997, WuW/E EU-V 7, see T. Käseberg in H.-J. Bunte (ed.), *Kartellrecht,* 14th ed., Luchterhand, München 2022, Art. 1 FKVO n. 52

178 *General Electric v. Honeywell* (Case COMP/M.2220), Commission Decision, 03.07.2001, WuW/E EU-V 631, see T. Käseberg in E. Langen, H.-J. Bunte (eds.), *Kartellrecht,* 14th ed., Luchterhand, München 2022, Art. 1 FKVO n. 52.

179 From a broader perspective i.a. W. Meng, *Extraterritoriale Jurisdiktion im öffentlichen Wirtschaftsrecht*, Springer, Berlin 1994, pp. 648 et seqq.; C. Kurkin, *Extraterritorialität*, Mohr Siebeck, Tübingen 2021, pp. 193–236; A. K. Schnyder, *Wirtschaftskollisionsrecht*, Schulthess, Zürich 1990, passim; J. Schwarze, *Die Jurisdiktionsabgrenzung im Völkerrecht*, Nomos, Baden-Baden 1994, passim; for a sector specific discussion see infra.

180 See supra, 4.2.

181 Comp. further Sect. 403, Restatement (Third) of the Foreign Relations Law of the United States vs. sect. 402 Restatement (Fourth); the latter being far more reserved towards a balancing of interests.

whether extraterritorial application of the law should take place. At present, no clear legal status can be discerned for Germany in this regard. Nevertheless, this will be clarified a bit further for some areas of law.

6.2 *Sector Specific Analysis*

For antitrust law, a balancing requirement is demanded in part,[182] but also firmly rejected by others.[183] The details are again not very clear. As already seen, a requirement to weigh up interests is partly derived from the requirement of comity[184] and is thus not regarded as a duty, but partly a duty to balance interests under international law is also assumed.[185] Others want to understand the balancing requirement in terms of conflict of laws or substantive law.[186] It is also postulated that a balancing of interests should be carried out solely in extreme cases of conflict.[187] In particular, in cases where the predominant focus of the competition restriction is abroad, it is assumed that the domestic interest should then recede.[188] In this case, however, it might be more

182 I.a. K. M. Meessen, *Völkerrechtliche Grundsätze des internationalen Kartellrechts*, Nomos, Baden-Baden 1975, pp. 198 et seqq.; C. Stadler in H.-J. Bunte (ed.), *Kartellrecht*, 14th ed., Luchterhand, München 2022, sect. 185 n. 139, 143 et seqq.; G. Wiedmann in G. Wiedemann (ed.), *Kartellrecht*, 4th ed., C.H.Beck, München 2020, sect. 5 n. 7

183 K.-H. Fezer and S. Koos in J. Staudinger (fdr.), *Internationales Wirtschaftsrecht*, ed. 2019, Otto Schmidt/De Gruyter, Berlin 2019, n. 149 et seqq.; F. Wagner-von Papp, W. Wurmnest in F. J. Säcker (ed.), *MünchKomm-Wettbewerbsrecht*, Bd. 1, 3rd ed., C.H.Beck, München 2020, n. 1361 et seqq.

184 See supra, 6.2.

185 See esp. K. M. Meessen, *Völkerrechtliche Grundsätze des internationalen Kartellrechts*, Nomos, Baden-Baden 1975, pp. 198 et seqq.; W. Meng, *Völkerrechtliche Zulässigkeit und Grenzen wirtschaftsverwaltungsrechtlicher Hoheitsakte mit Auslandswirkung*, ZaöRV 1984, 675, 771; comp. also KG WuW/E OLG 2419, 2420–21; BKartA WuW/E BKartA 2521, 2539 et seqq.; however, it is unclear from which principles of customary international law such a balancing of interests can be derived, for an overview P. Hector, *Das völkerrechtliche Abwägungsgebot*, Duncker und Humblot, Berlin 1992, pp. 133 et seqq.; G. Schuster, *Die internationale Anwendung des Börsenrechts*, Springer, Berlin Heidelberg 1996, p. 683 thus speaks of a rule of customary international law in statu nascendi.

186 See i.a. KG WuW/E OLG 3051, 3059; E. Rehbinder, J. von Kalben in U. Immenga, E.-J. Mestmäcker (eds.), *Wettbewerbsrecht*, Bd. 2, 6th. ed., C.H.Beck, München 2020, sect. 185 n. 129; R. *Deville, Die Konkretisierung des Abwägungsgebots im internationalen Kartellrecht, Nomos, Baden-Baden 1990, pp.* 15 et seqq.

187 I.a. J. Basedow, *Entwicklungslinien des internationalen Kartellrechts: Ausbau und Differenzierung des Auswirkungsprinzips*, NJW 1989, 627, 638; C. Stadler in H.-J. Bunte (ed.), *Kartellrecht*, 14th ed., Luchterhand, München 2022, sect. 185 n. 143.

188 E. Rehbinder, J. von Kalben in U. Immenga, E.-J. Mestmäcker (eds.), *Wettbewerbsrecht*, Bd. 2, 6th. ed., C.H.Beck, München 2020, sect. 185 n. 132; comp. also C. Stadler in H.-J. Bunte (ed.), *Kartellrecht*, 14th ed., Luchterhand, München 2022, sect. 185 n. 151; OLG Düsseldorf, WuW/E DE-R 2477, 2484.

appropriate to assume a lack of appreciability.[189] It would also be conceivable to carry out a kind of cost-benefit analysis, taking into account the resulting welfare aspects in each case,[190] although there is probably no sufficient legal basis for this.

In the field of financial market law too, such a balancing of interests is sometimes seen as a solution for conflicts of jurisdiction.[191] In this context, the respective welfare gains and losses are again taken into account, even though these are still rather preliminary considerations.

In data protection law, such an approach oriented towards economic interests usually fails. If a balancing requirement is nevertheless discussed, an attempt is made to solve any conflicts through technical solutions such as geo-blocking[192] or otherwise to focus on the intensity of the link, for example with regard to the focus of a website.[193]

Insofar as a balancing of interests is also discussed in the field of intellectual property, one could also ask whether a website is directed at the domestic market. However, in the case of multi-state infringements it seems to be more reasonable to consider a general limitation of the connecting factor.[194]

6.3 *Comparative Assessment*

On the whole, the principle of a balancing of interests derived from international law in the sense of a requirement of reasonableness is certainly discussed in Germany and is also partly applied by courts and authorities in antitrust law. Nevertheless, there is a high degree of different opinions in this field in particular. The basis of a balancing requirement remains largely unclear: should it derive from international law or from conflict of laws or substantive law? The substantive criteria of the balancing are also unclear or specific to the respective legal area. Nevertheless, there is a general trend across legal areas to weigh interests in considering extraterritorial application of the law.

---

189 In this sense K.-H. Fezer and S. Koos in J. Staudinger (fdr.), *Internationales Wirtschaftsrecht*, ed. 2019, Otto Schmidt/De Gruyter, Berlin 2019, n. 152; see also supra, 4.2.2.1.

190 Comp. R. *Deville, Die Konkretisierung des Abwägungsgebots im internationalen Kartellrecht, Nomos, Baden-Baden 1990*, pp. 101 et seqq.

191 T. Dornis in C. Budzikiewicz et al., *BeckOGK. Internationales Gesellschaftsrecht*, ed. 01.11.2022, C.H Beck, München, n. 93, 104; G. Schuster, *Die internationale Anwendung des Börsenrechts*, Springer, Berlin Heidelberg 1996, pp. 691–92.

192 S. Herrmann, *Völkerrechtliche Jurisdiktionsgrundlagen für den Datenschutz im Netz*, Mohr Siebeck, Tübingen 2021, pp. 402–18.

193 S. Herrmann, *Völkerrechtliche Jurisdiktionsgrundlagen für den Datenschutz im Netz*, Mohr Siebeck, Tübingen 2021, pp. 419–22.

194 See supra, 2.1.2.

7 Wholly Foreign Conduct – Connecting Factors

There are a number of different connecting factors for establishing an extraterritorial application of the law. These shall be summed up hereafter. References will be made to areas discussed supra.

7.1 *Nationality of the Actor – Active Personality Principle*

The active personality principle refers to conduct abroad, committed by a German national.[195] In the field of criminal law in particular, its introduction goes back to an authoritarian view of the state during the National Socialist era, which is why its importance steadily declined after 1945.[196] Today, the active personality principle is mostly used in criminal law for reasons of international solidarity.[197] Some examples are listed above,[198] i.a. sect. 5 no. 8 StGB or sect. 7 para. 2 No. 1 StGB. Sect. 5 no. 15 lit. (a) StGB establishes the active personality principle for crimes as accepting benefits or taking bribes and thus establishes an extraterritorial effect for anti-corruption laws.

The active personality principle can also be found in matters of foreign trade law.[199] Pursuant to sect. 5 para. 5 AWG '[r]estrictions or obligations to act pursuant to Section 4 subsection 1 [this section referrers generally to restrictions that are further specified in the AWV] can also be imposed with regard to legal transactions or actions of Germans abroad which refer to goods within the meaning of subsection 1 including their development and manufacture.' The mentioned goods consist of military goods, weapons and the like. The provision aims to prevent problematic military and commercial activities regarding arms of 'Germans living abroad' from being politically attributed to Germany.[200] The reference to the active personality principle in sects. 17 para. 7, 18

195 For a general description see i.a. M. Herdegen, *Völkerrecht*, 20th ed., C.H.Beck, München 2021, sect. 26 n. 9 et seq.; broad analysis from the international literature esp. by C. Ryngaert, *Jurisdiction in International Law*, 2nd ed., Oxford University Press, Oxford 2015, pp. 104 et seqq.

196 Comprehensive overwiew A. Eser, B. Weißer in A. Schönke, H. Schröder (eds.), *StGB*, 30th ed., C.H.Beck, München 2019, before sect. 3–9, n. 20.

197 See supra, 4.3.

198 See supra, 2.2.

199 See i.a. O. Remien, Außenwirtschaftsrecht in kollisionsrechtlicher Sicht: *Zur internationalen Reichweite von Aus- und Einfuhrverboten,* RabelsZ 54 (1990), 431, 447.

200 See R. M. Stein in R.Rüsken (ed.), *Zollrecht,* 214th EL, Stollfuß, Bonn 2023, sect. 5 AWG n. 43; comp. also BT-Drs. 11/7218, p. 6.

para. 10 AWG regarding criminal offences in connection with foreign trade law must also be seen against this background.[201]

Within the framework of sect. 1 para. 4 s. 2 no. 2 BDSG as well as Art. 3 para. 1 GDPR, there is a link to the active personality principle, as these provisions refer to a domestic establishment.[202] Although the data processing must take place 'in the context of the activities of an establishment', this requirement is interpreted very broadly.[203] It is sufficient that the establishment only economically promotes the business purpose. In this respect, companies with their headquarters in the Union must also observe European data protection regulations, even if they act abroad.

The active personality principle is also codified in other fields of law, such as tax law.[204]

7.2 *Nationality of the Person Harmed – Passive Personality Principle*

The passive personality principle refers to conduct abroad that particularly endangers and/or violates the interests/rights of a German national.[205] It is a more or less common connecting factor in criminal law.[206] This has already been exemplified in terms of trade secrets.[207] It is also worth mentioning in this context that the protection of trade secrets is now regulated in a separate law with its own sanctions, the Act on the Protection of Trade Secrets (*Gesetz zum Schutz von Geschäftsgeheimnissen*, hereafter: GeschGehG). There, sect. 23 GeschGehG also specifically regulates criminal liability; sect. 23 Para. 7 GeschGehG then refers to sect. 5 no. 7 StGB. Thus, the passive personality principle

201 See R. Junck, C. Kirch-Heim in H. Achenbach, A. Ransiek, T. Rönnau (eds.), *Handbuch Wirtschaftsstrafrecht*, 5th ed., C.F. Müller, Heidelberg 2019, II. Räumlicher Anwendungsbereich, n. 11.

202 See S. Herrmann, *Völkerrechtliche Jurisdiktionsgrundlagen für den Datenschutz im Netz*, Mohr Siebeck, Tübingen 2021, pp. 251–54; comp. in general K. Ambos in V. Erb, J. Schäfer (eds.), *MünchKomm-StGB*, 4th ed., C.H.Beck, München 2020, before sect. 3 n. 34.

203 Comp. with further references to the case law of the CJEU S. Segger-Piening, Extraterritorialitätsauswirkungen und fehlender Privatrechtsbezug im Internationalen Datenprivatrecht in K. Duden et. al. (eds.), IPR für eine bessere Welt?, Mohr Siebeck, Tübingen 2022, pp. 114–15.

204 See sect. 1 para. 1 EStG, according to which 'natural persons who have a domicile or habitual residence in Germany are subject to unlimited income tax liability', so actually this is more the active domicile principle; C. Ryngaert, *Jurisdiction in International Law*, 2nd ed., Oxford University Press, Oxford 2015, pp. 106 et seqq.

205 For a general description see i.a. M. Herdegen, *Völkerrecht*, 20th ed., C.H.Beck, München 2021, sect. 26 n. 11.

206 See supra, 2.2.

207 Supra, 2.2.1.

is referred to again.[208] A further example is sect. 5 no. 14 StGB regarding 'acts committed against public officials, persons entrusted with special public service functions or soldiers in the Federal Armed Forces in the discharge of their duties or in connection with their duties'. However, this is also connected with the principle of state protection.[209] Some voices in the academic writing doubt the conformity with international law, unless the act is also punishable abroad.[210] However, this is not the prevailing view.

A certain variation of the passive personality principle is the use of or combination with the domicile principle. Some examples have already been illustrated.[211] Further examples refer to 'offences against physical integrity in the cases under sect. 226a [covering female genital mutilation] if the ... offence is directed against a person whose domicile or habitual residence is in Germany', sect. 5 no. 9a lit. (b) alternative 2 StGB.

Finally, it should be noted that companies are also partly covered by the passive personality principle, for example in the field of the protection of trade secrets, infra, 9.

7.3 *Effects Doctrine and Comparable Approaches*

Domestic effects of the conduct in question are an important connecting factor for the extraterritorial application of statutes and regulations in Germany. Such a practice is called most often *Auswirkungsprinzip*, which is more or less equivalent to the so-called 'effects doctrine'. As in the United States, the effects doctrine has its roots in antitrust law.[212] In Germany, it is now codified in sect. 185 para. 2 GWB. Regarding the private enforcement of antitrust law Art. 6 para. 3 Rome II applies, which also establishes the effects principle. The effects doctrine is believed to be in accordance with international law, however, the details are disputed.[213]

The effects doctrine as a connecting factor can also be found in a number of further fields of law: Regarding unfair commercial practices Art. 6 para. 1 Rome II establishes the so-called 'market effects principle'.[214] Even though it is not identical with the effects doctrine in antitrust law it is very similar. A

208 See also C. Alexander in H. Köhler, J. Bornkamm, J.Feddersen, *Gesetz gegen den unlauteren Wettbewerb*, 41st ed., C.H.Beck, München 2023, GeschGehG sect. 23 n. 94.

209 A. Eser, B. Weißer in A. Schönke, H. Schröder (eds.), *StGB*, 30th ed., C.H.Beck, München 2019, sect. 5 n. 31.

210 See supra, 4.2.2.3.

211 Supra, 2.2.1.

212 See supra, 2.1.1.1.

213 See supra, 4.2.2.1.

214 See supra, 2.1.1.2.

limitation of the connection in the sense of a requirement of appreciability is controversially discussed.[215] The argument in favour of such a requirement is that in the absence of appreciability, neither the market nor the market participants are likely to be adversely affected. However, the question then arises as to which law applies to the effects that are not appreciable. In this respect, a substantive law solution seems more appropriate.

The effects doctrine is also known in the area of data protection,[216] Art. 3 para. 2 lit. (a) GDPR in connection with sect. 1 para. 4 BDSG. Regarding the monitoring of behaviour pursuant to lit. (b) it seems rather questionable to refer to the effects doctrine since a criterion such as a direction of the activity towards a specific country is missing. One could speak of an extended market principle.[217]

In the field of the regulation of the financial market the effects doctrine is also known. This has already been illustrated with a few examples regarding sect. 102 WpHG and sect 32 KWG. Further examples can be found in terms of prospectus liability,[218] insider trading,[219] and short selling.[220] However, these examples all refer to European legislation and are thus not treated in this report.

In the field of intellectual property, as already mentioned, the country of protection principle is applied.[221] However, with the possibility of taking into account certain foreign acts of infringement in the sense of the *Bogsch*-theory, there are certainly similarities to an effects principle.[222] This is evident not least in the restrictions discussed, such as the requirement of appreciability.

---

215 In favour i.a. P. Mankowski in P. W. Heermann, J. Schlingloff (eds.), *MünchKomm-Lauterkeitsrecht,* 3rd ed., C.H. Beck, München 2020, A. II. n. 211 et seqq.; declining i.a, O. Remien in W. Siebert (ed.), *Soergel* BGB, Bd. 27/1, 13th ed., Kohlhammer, Stuttgart 2019, Art. 6 n. 17.

216 See supra, 2.1.4.

217 In this sense S. Segger-Piening, Extraterritorialitätsauswirkungen und fehlender Privatrechtsbezug im Internationalen Datenprivatrecht in K. Duden et. al. (eds.), IPR für eine bessere Welt?, Mohr Siebeck, Tübingen 2022, pp. 114–15.

218 See Art. 3 para. 1 Regulation (EU) 2017/1129, [2017] OJ L 168/12 and M. Lehmann in F. J. Säcker et al., *MünchKomm-BGB, Finanzmarktrecht,* Bd. 13, 8th ed., C.H.Beck, München 2021, n. 306 et seqq.

219 See Art. 2 Regulation (EU) No 596/2014, [2014] OJ L 173/1 and M. Lehmann in F. J. Säcker et al., *MünchKomm-BGB, Finanzmarktrecht,* Bd. 13, 8th ed., C.H.Beck, München 2021, n. 363, 367.

220 See Art. 1 Commission Delegated Regulation (EU) 2021/236 of 21 December 2020, [2021] OJ L 56/1 and M. Lehmann in F. J. Säcker et al., *MünchKomm-BGB, Finanzmarktrecht,* Bd. 13, 8th ed., C.H.Beck, München 2021, n. 467.

221 Supra, 2.1.2.

222 Supra, 2.1.2. as well as J. Drexl in F. J. Säcker et al., *MünchKomm-BGB,* Bd. 13, 8th ed., C.H.Beck, München 2021, Art. 8 n. 318 et seqq.

7.4 *Universal Jurisdiction*

The concept of universal jurisdiction is known in criminal law.[223] On the one hand, it is realised in the Code of Crimes against International Law, which has already been pointed out above. This means that offences such as genocide, crimes against humanity and war crimes are encompassed by the concept of universal jurisdiction.

On the other hand, sect. 6 StGB refers to 'offences committed abroad against internationally protected legal interests'. Such offences include i.a. 'no. 2. serious crimes involving nuclear energy, ...; no. 3. attacks on air and maritime traffic (sect. 316c); no. 4. human trafficking (sect. 232); ... no. 9. offences which, based on an international agreement which is binding on the Federal Republic of Germany, are to be prosecuted even though they are committed abroad.' Regarding these offences German criminal law is applicable, 'regardless of which law is applicable at the place where they are committed', sect. 6 StGB, and thus the concept of universal jurisdiction is realised.

8 Partly Foreign Conduct – Territorial Links

In the German legal system, various situations are conceivable in which conduct takes place partly in Germany and partly abroad and nevertheless falls within the scope of application of a German statute.

In the field of economic regulation, one might refer first to antitrust law. For example, a cartel agreement could be entered into by both a German and a foreign company and could be agreed upon in the course of several meetings both at home and abroad. Both sect. 185 para. 2 GWB and Art. 6 para. 3 Rome II are only concerned with the domestic effects and would therefore cover this conduct as long as domestic effects appear. Sect. 185 para. 2 GWB explicitly states that German antitrust law also applies if restraints of competition are 'caused outside the area of application of this Act'. Conversely, conduct that only partially takes place abroad is of course also covered. With regard to a limitation of the coverage of foreign conduct, the comments above on a general limitation of the effect principle apply.[224]

The situation in antitrust law can in principle also be applied to other fields of economic regulation. In data protection law sect. 1 para. 4 s. 2 no. 2 BDSG as well as Art. 3 para. 1 GDPR only require 'the processing of personal data in the context of the activities of an establishment'. If the data processing takes

223 Supra, 2.2., 4.3.

224 Supra, 4.2.

place both domestically and abroad, this is sufficient in any case. No restrictions apply in this respect. In the field of intellectual property, it is recognised that partial acts abroad may also be sufficient to qualify as domestic infringement.[225] In trademark law, for example, it is sufficient for domestic use within the meaning of sect. 26 MarkenG if goods are exported abroad; in particular, use abroad may have to be taken into account.[226] The same is true for copyright[227] and patent[228] law. The link to acts abroad is limited insofar as merely preparatory acts in Germany cannot be the basis for a link to an additional infringing act abroad.[229] However, this limitation does not apply if the act abroad itself qualifies as a domestic act because of its economic effects.[230]

Finally, situations may arise in criminal law where parts of the offence are committed abroad. According to sect. 3 StGB 'German criminal law applies to offences committed on German territory.' Section 9 StGB specifies the place of commitment as follows: '[a]n offence is deemed to have been committed at every place where the offender acted … or in which the result … occurs'. In the case of offences where the place of the act and the place of the result differ – so-called distance offences (*Distanzdelikte*) – it can therefore happen that part of the offence is committed abroad and another part in Germany and German criminal law is nevertheless applicable.[231] This is particularly problematic in cases involving the internet, since for offences such as insult or incitement of the masses, a result could also be seen in the mere possibility of retrieving content which was uploaded abroad.[232] Due to the potential breadth of the scope of application of German criminal law in the case of the fulfilment of even partial acts of the offence domestically, it is generally agreed upon that there

225 For a overview see i.a. J. Drexl in F. J. Säcker et al., *MünchKomm-BGB*, Bd. 13, 8th ed., C.H. Beck, München 2021, Art. 8 n. 310 et seqq.

226 BGH GRUR 1980, 52; J. Bogatz in A. Kur, V. v. Bomhard, F. Albrecht (eds.), *BeckOK MarkenR*, 32nd ed., C.H.Beck, München 2023, sect. 26 MarkenG n. 93.1.

227 BGH GRUR 1994, 798, 799; K.-H. Fezer and S. Koos in J. Staudinger (fdr.), *Internationales Wirtschaftsrecht*, ed. 2019, Otto Schmidt/De Gruyter, Berlin 2019, n. 1025.

228 J. Drexl in F. J. Säcker et al., *MünchKomm-BGB*, Bd. 13, 8th ed., C.H.Beck, München 2021, Art. 8 n. 286.

229 BGH GRUR 1994, 798, 799; J. Drexl in F. J. Säcker et al., *MünchKomm-BGB*, Bd. 13, 8th ed., C.H.Beck, München 2021, Art. 8 n. 315

230 Supra, 2.1.2.

231 See i.a. K. Ambos in V. Erb, J. Schäfer (eds.), *MünchKomm-StGB*, 4th ed., C.H.Beck, München 2020, StGB sect. 9 n. 26 et seqq.; A. Eser, B. Weißer in A. Schönke, H. Schröder (eds.), *StGB*, 30th ed., C.H.Beck, München 2019, sect. 9 n. 3.

232 See esp. K. Mey, *Die Anwendbarkeit des deutschen Strafrechts bei Straftaten via Internet*, Nomos, Baden-Baden 2020; G. Werle and F. Jeßberger in *LeipzigerKommentar*, 13th ed., De Gruyter, Berlin 2020, sect. 9 n. 73 et seqq.

is a need for a reduction in this scope of application.[233] However, the details are controversial. In a significant case, the Federal Court of Justice has determined the extent to which 'a weighty domestic legal interest which, moreover, objectively has a special reference to the territory of the Federal Republic of Germany' is given.[234] In the case at hand, the Holocaust was denied by means of a website operated from Australia. The negation of this crime naturally has a special connection to Germany, so that German criminal law could be applied.

9 Corporate Nationality

Corporate nationality and extraterritoriality are discussed particularly against the background of sanctions.[235] The United States has enacted laws that exercise jurisdiction over corporations abroad that are controlled by a U.S. (natural) person. This has been criticized by European courts and thus the European Union does not pursue such an approach. Insofar as European sanctions also apply to legal persons, these must be legal persons 'incorporated or constituted under the law of a Member State' or related to transactions carried out in the Union.[236] Control by an EU person is not sufficient, as the persons acting are legally independent.[237]

Otherwise, German law has the special feature that there is no criminal law relating to associations (*Verbandsstrafrecht*). Legal persons are thus not covered by §§ 3–9 StGB beyond the cases expressly provided for.[238] Only sect. 30 of the Act on Regulatory Offences[239] (*Ordnungswidrigkeitengesetz*) provides a possibility to impose a fine on legal persons in case a representative of a legal person or such like 'has committed a criminal offence or a regulatory offence

233 See G. Werle and F. Jeßberger in *LeipzigerKommentar*, 13th ed., De Gruyter, Berlin 2020, sect. 9, n. 91 et seqq.; BGHSt 46, 212, 224.

234 BGHSt 46, 212, 224, translated by the author.

235 See in this regard and for the following i.a. C. Ryngaert, *Jurisdiction in International Law*, 2nd ed., Oxford University Press, Oxford 2015, pp. 108–09; see for a discussion Sect. 414 Restatement (Third) of the Foreign Relations Law of the United States, esp. Reporters' Notes 3 and 4.

236 Quote taken from Art. 49 lit. d) of the Council Regulation (EU) No 267/2012, [2012] OJ L 88/1.

237 M. Niested in H.G. Krenzler et al., EU-*Außenwirtschafts- und Zollrecht*, 20th EL., C.H.Beck, München 2022, part 50. n. 36

238 See i.a. K. Ambos in V. Erb, J. Schäfer (eds.), *MünchKomm-StGB*, 4th ed., C.H.Beck, München 2020, sect. 7 n. 23.

239 Translation available at https://www.gesetze-im-internet.de/englisch_owig/englisch_owig.html.

as a result of which duties incumbent on the legal person or on the association of persons have been violated, or where the legal person or the association of persons has been enriched or was intended to be enriched.' Pursuant to the prevailing opinion this also encompasses foreign corporations (and thus also subsidiaries of German corporations) as long as German criminal law applies to the criminal offence in question.[240]

As seen, the active personality principle is also applied in part in the field of foreign trade law.[241] However, the provisions refer either to 'a German national' (sect. 17 para. 7 and 18 para. 10 AWG) or to 'Germans' (sect. 5 para. 5 GWB). Thus, a reference is made to a German natural person and corporations are excluded.[242] The question of corporate nationality does not arise.

In the field of data protection Art. 3 para. 1 GDPR refers to an establishment in the Union. It is regarded as sufficient if such an establishment is part of a corporate group and only economically promotes the business purpose.[243] From this point of view, the GDPR has been applied to subsidiaries of foreign corporate groups. However, this line of argumentation should also be possible for the reversed situation, i.e. a European corporate group with a subsidiary established e.g. under the law of Delaware and acting in Delaware. As long as the subsidiary promotes the business purpose of the corporate group the GDPR could apply. However, this situation has not been decided yet and thus an amount of uncertainty remains.

Finally, it should be noted that in the case of the passive personality principle, subsidiaries with their seat abroad are protected in terms of trade secrets, provided they are 'dependent on an enterprise which has its seat within the territorial scope of this statute [StGB] and which forms a corporate group with the latter', sect. 5 no. 7 StGB.

10 Presumption against Extraterritoriality

A presumption against extraterritoriality as it is known in U.S. law[244] does not exist in German law. However, restrictions on extraterritorial applicability do

240 See i.a. K. Rogall in W. Mitsch (ed.), *Karlsruher Kommentar zum OWiG*, 5th ed., C.H.Beck, München 2018, sect. 30 n. 88; but comp. A. Schneider, *Der transnationale Geltungsbereich des deutschen Verbandsstrafrechts – de lege lata und de lege ferenda*, ZIS 2013, 488, 492.

241 Supra, 7.1.

242 Comp. R. M. Stein in R. Rüsken (ed.), *Zollrecht*, 214th EL, Stollfuß, Bonn 2023, sect. 5 AWG n. 43.

243 Supra, 7.1.

244 See i.a. Sect. 404, Restatement (Fourth) of the Foreign Relations Law of the United States.

arise, as seen, when taking into account the principles of international law.[245] Otherwise, extraterritorial applicability in Germany is only established by special connecting factors such as the principle of effect, the marketplace principle or the passive personality principle.[246] If such a connecting factor exists, it also implies that a provision can be applied extraterritorially. A presumption against an extraterritorial application would then be contradictory. In the absence of such a rule, the provisions should only apply domestically. However, it must then be examined to what extent there are special conflict-of-law rules for the respective area. In the area of private law, various different conflict-of-law rules can be found, although these often do not serve the extraterritorial enforcement of state interests, but rather try to find the closest connection to a certain legal order.[247] Exceptions in terms of economic regulation have been dealt with above.[248] For criminal law, too, there are generalising provisions with regard to applicability, some of which also explicitly provide for an extraterritorial connection.[249]

A special situation exists in the field of intellectual property.[250] The principle of territoriality and the *lex loci protectionis* do not provide any information on how to deal with foreign acts that might also have domestic effects, for example via the internet. However, there is a restrictive practice, as illustrated by the *Hotel Maritime* case. Even if this cannot be interpreted as a presumption against extraterritoriality, it serves as an example of the fact that, as a rule, limits to extraterritoriality are also taken into account when applying German law extraterritorially.

11 Blocking Statutes

Germany has not enacted any blocking statues. However, on the EU level there is the so-called EU-Blocking Regulation from 1996.[251] Originally, it aimed against the far-reaching U.S. secondary sanctions enacted by the 1996 Helms-Burton-Act as well as other acts. In 2018, however, the EU-Blocking Regulation was amended to include the secondary sanctions of the United States with

245 Supra, 4.2.
246 Supra, 7.
247 Supra, 1., 1.2.2.
248 Supra, 2.1.
249 Supra, 2.2.
250 Supra, 2.1.2.
251 Council Regulation (EC) No 2271/96, [1996] OJ L 309, 1–6.

regard to Iran in the list of measures to be averted.[252] The EU-Blocking Regulation contains a number of different instruments, the central one being the prohibition to comply as stipulated in Art. 5, according to which no person – including legal persons – shall comply with sanctions specified in the Annex of the Regulation and covering i.a. the aforementioned ones.

This prohibition to comply has recently become the subject of a number of German court decisions.[253] In one case, Deutsche Telekom terminated a contract with an Iranian bank because it feared that it would otherwise fall within the scope of U.S. sanctions.[254] The Iranian bank argued that this would violate Art. 5 of the Blocking Regulation. In this context, the Hamburg Higher Regional Court submitted a series of questions to the ECJ on the interpretation of the Blocking Regulation.[255] First, it was questioned, if Art. 5 para. 1 of the EU-Blocking Regulation only applies 'where the acting EU operator ... is issued directly or indirectly with an official or court order on the part of the United States of America' or whether it suffices 'for its application that the action of the EU operator is predicated on compliance with secondary sanctions without any such order'.[256] Secondly, it was questioned whether or not the Telekom could terminate the contract without 'ever having to justify its decision' and thus in accordance with an ordinary termination or whether it had to explain its motives.[257] Thirdly, it was questioned whether 'ordinary termination in breach of the [EU-Blocking Regulation must] necessarily be regarded as ineffective or [if] the purpose of the [statute can] be satisfied through other penalties, such as a fine.' Finally the court asked, if indeed an ordinary termination was in non-conformity with the blocking regulation pursuant to the interpretation of the CJEU, whether such a general prohibition was compatible with the freedom to conduct a business, which is protected by Art. 16 of the Charter

252 Commission Delegated Regulation (EU) 2018/1100, [2018] OJ L 199 I/1; for the background see i.a. M. Niested, K. Göcke in H.G. Krenzler et al., EU-*Außenwirtschafts- und Zollrecht*, 20th EL., C.H.Beck, München 2022, VO (EG) 2271/96 Art. 1 n. 1 et seq. with reference to President Trump's refusal to extend the waiver that has been in place so far.

253 I.a. LG Dortmund, BeckRS 2016, 3046; OLG Köln, BeckRS 2020, 4132; OLG Hamburg EuZW 2020, 390; for an overview see L. Harings, *Die EU-Blocking-Verordnung in der Rechtsprechung,* RdTW 2020, 442 445 et seqq.

254 OLG Hamburg EuZW 2020, 390; English translation of the facts of the case and the preliminary questions can be found in the opinion of the Advocate General *Hogan*, 12.05.2021, Case C124/20, *Bank Melli Iran v. Telekom Deutschland GmbH*, ECLI:EU:C:2021:386.

255 Preliminary references are governed by Art. 267 TFEU.

256 The question can be found at opinion of the Advocate General *Hogan*, 12.05.2021, Case C124/20, *Bank Melli Iran v. Telekom Deutschland GmbH*, ECLI:EU:C:2021:386, n. 49.

257 Opinion AG of the Advocate General *Hogan*, 12.05.2021, Case C124/20, *Bank Melli Iran v. Telekom Deutschland GmbH*, ECLI:EU:C:2021:386, n. 99.

of Fundamental Rights of the EU (CFR), and the principle of proportionality enshrined in Art. 51 CFR, especially against the background that this 'expose the EU operator to considerable economic losses on the US market (in this case: 50% of group turnover)'.[258]

The advocate general answered all questions in favour of the Iranian Bank and thus to the disadvantage of the Telekom, even though he added that it gives him 'no particular pleasure to arrive at this particular result' and asks for the EU legislature to 'ponder and consider' parts of the Blocking Regulation. The CJEU essentially agreed with the Advocate General and also decided the questions to the disadvantage of Telekom in a recent judgement.[259] However, it left some room for a proportionality test, which also had to take into account that Telekom had not applied for a derogation from Art. 5 para. 1 of the Regulation, which would have been possible pursuant to Art. 5 para. 2.[260]

---

258 See also L. Harings, *Die EU-Blocking-Verordnung in der Rechtsprechung,* RdTW 2020, 442, 448–49.

259 CJEU, Case C124/20, *Bank Melli Iran v. Telekom Deutschland GmbH,* ECLI:EU:C:2021:1035.

260 CJEU, Case C124/20, *Bank Melli Iran v. Telekom Deutschland GmbH,* ECLI:EU:C:2021:1035 n. 92 et seq.

The Extraterritorial Application of Statutes and Regulations

Italy

*Alessandra Zanobetti**

1 Extraterritoriality and Italian Legal Thinking

The issue of extraterritoriality has always been widely discussed, and in recent times it meets a rekindling of interest as a response to growing globalization in economic, social and political life.[1] Extraterritorial legislation is an instrument in matters of foreign policy and a tool in the economic regulation of transnational activities; it also serves a function in the promotion of human rights, the protection of the environment, and the fight against corruption, in addition to the pursuit of specific economic or political interests of a State. The multifaceted character of extraterritoriality jurisdiction is reflected by the fact that it is possible to adopt a plural approach to the theme,[2] and its legitimacy may be difficult to apprehend.[3]

In Italy, the legal studies devoted to the matter are, however, few and mainly discuss foreign practice, in connection with particular issues: the US Export Administration Regulations,[4] the extraterritorial effects of anti-trust

* Università di Bologna.

1 The Hague Academy of International Law hosted in recent years several courses dealing with extraterritoriality. Some explicitly refer to the notion in their title: D.P. Wood, 'Extraterritorial Enforcement of Regulatory Laws' (2019) 401 *Collected Courses of the Hague Academy of International Law*, pp. 9–126, and Y. Shany, 'The Extraterritorial Application of International Human Rights Law' (2020) 409 *Collected Courses of the Hague Academy of International Law*, pp. 9–152.

2 As evidence of this character, cf. the title of the 2019 Workshop of the Société française de droit international, which uses the term in a plural form: *Extraterritorialités et droit international.*

3 This difficulty is probably the reason for which the draft resolution of the Institut de droit international, 'The extraterritorial jurisdiction of States', included in the final report of the 1993 session of Milan, has not, so far, been formally adopted.

4 On export controls and US practice, see M. Benedettelli, 'Sull'applicazione extraterritoriale delle misure di embargo degli Stati Uniti relative al « gasdotto siberiano »' (1984) *Rivista di diritto internazionale*, pp. 529–574; A. Bianchi, *L'applicazione extraterritoriale dei controlli all'esportazione: contributo allo studio dei fenomeni di extraterritorialità nel diritto internazionale*, Padova, Cedam 1995; G. Garbone, 'Extraterritorialità della *jurisdiction* statunitense' (1996) *Diritto del commercio internazionale*, pp. 557–564; L. Bellodi, 'L'extraterritorialità rivisitata' (2013) *Diritto del commercio internazionale*, pp. 1023–1033.

 | DOI:10.1163/9789004720183_009

legislation,[5] and the international and European aspects of the subject in connection with specific topics.[6] There is hardly any Italian case-law dealing with the issue. Recently, the EU Regulation on Data Protection and its extensive field of application awakened the interest of Italian legal scholars, but the debate concerns only the supranational framework, with negligible reference to the Italian legal system or Italian practice.[7]

The word 'extraterritorialità' in Italian is itself ambiguous as, even in a legal context, it may be employed with more than one meaning.[8]

---

5 For an extensive analysis on the legitimacy of the extraterritorial application of national rules, specifically from the angle of antitrust regulations, see P. Picone, 'L'applicazione extraterritoriale delle regole sulla concorrenza e il diritto internazionale', in F. Capotorti et al. (eds), *Il fenomeno delle concentrazioni di imprese nel diritto internazionale*, Padova, Cedam 1989, pp. 81–209.

6 The journal *Diritto del commercio internazionale* promoted in 2019 a 'Special Focus on unexplored dimensions of extraterritoriality'. The five contributions on different aspects of extraterritoriality contain very little – if any – reference to Italian practice: G. Gagliani, 'The Extraterritorial and Post-Discrimination Dimension of the SPS Agreement put to the test in Korea-Radio-nuclides (Japan) Case', pp. 647–673; A. Mensi, 'Breaking the Ice: Reconciling Extraterritoriality and Multilateralism in the light of the Carbon Offsetting and Reduction Scheme for International Aviation (CORSIA)', pp. 675–693; M. C. Meneghetti, 'The different shapes of extraterritoriality in EU Data Protection Law and its international justifications', pp. 695–716; M. Soprana, 'Extraterritoriality in US-China relations: the ZTE and Huawei cases', pp. 717–733; L. Scollo, 'The Petrobras settlement: a global governance analysis and potential implications for foreign countries', pp. 735–753. In their 'Introduction' to the 'Special Focus', P. Mariani and M. Winkler underline the relevance of the topic, and yet they make no mention of an Italian perspective.

7 On the EU protection of data, see M. Catanzariti, 'La dimensione extraterritoriale della sorveglianza di massa' (2019) *Rassegna di diritto pubblico europeo*, pp. 335–363; M.C. Meneghetti, 'The different shapes of extraterritoriality' (2019) *Diritto del commercio internazionale*, pp. 695–716.

8 The word 'extraterritorialità' may refer to the special status of the Holy See properties in the Italian territory and specifically in Rome, as in G. Caputo, 'Extraterritorialità (dir. eccles.)', in *Enciclopedia del diritto*, Milano, Giuffré 1967, vol. XVI, pp. 154–161; G. Dalla Torre, *L'"extraterritorialità" nel Trattato del Laterano*, Torino, Giappichelli 2016; it may still be employed to indicate the immunities granted by international law to foreign countries and to international organizations' headquarters, as well as to diplomatic and consular personnel and to international officers, as in the entry 'Extraterritorialità' of the *Enciclopedia Treccani* https://www.treccani.it/vocabolario/extraterritorialita/; it may also refer to the status of foreign ships. This is the same meaning given to the notion in the first courses professed at the Hague Academy of International Law: see L. Strisower, 'L'exterritorialité et ses principales applications' (1923) 1 *Collected Courses of the Hague Academy of International Law*, pp. 229–287. All the mentioned meanings must be considered – and are in fact unanimously considered – as misleading and based on unacceptable conceptions; see the comparatively recent observations of M.R. Ferrarese, *Diritto sconfinato. Inventiva giuridica e spazi nel mondo globale*, Bari, Laterza 2006, 70, who underlines the new usages of an old notion that is still in

2 A Renewed Interest in Extraterritoriality: the Regulation of Economic Activities

The renewed interest in the scope of national statutes and their extraterritorial effects is prompted primarily by the increasing intertwining of economic activities. In Italy – as in all European countries – the Euro-Siberian gas pipeline project, started in 1981–82, raised a debate on the extraterritorial reach of U.S. export controls enacted as a reaction to that operation. In particular, the debate concerned the legality, from the standpoint of international law, of extraterritorial jurisdiction to prescribe and on the existence of boundaries to the normative power of each State.[9] The prevailing opinion expressed at the time matched the decision adopted in 1927 by the Permanent Court of International Justice in its *S.S. Lotus* judgment, according to which 'the first and foremost restriction imposed by international law upon a State is that – failing the existence of a permissive rule to the contrary – it may not exercise its power in any form in the territory of another State'. However, this did not entail 'that international law prohibits a State from exercising jurisdiction in its own territory, in respect of any case which relates to acts which have taken place abroad, and in which it cannot rely on some permissive rule of international law.'[10] The admissibility of the exercise of jurisdiction to prescribe was counterbalanced by the limits of jurisdiction to enforce.

The debate opened by the affair of the Euro-Siberian pipeline and the US practice on extraterritorial export controls regained relevance with the adoption of the first economic sanctions against foreign States by the European Community. These measures required interventions of the Italian authorities, albeit only in the implementation of decisions approved in Brussels.[11] More generally, economic interventions in foreign policy entailed the adoption of

---

use even in a legal context. It is worth mentioning that P. Fedozzi, an Italian legal scholar, in his two courses given at The Hague Academy in 1925 and in 1929 ('La condition juridique des navires de commerce' et 'De l'efficacité extra-territoriale des lois et des actes de droit public'), referred to 'extraterritoriality' in the proper sense in which it is intended in the present Report.

9 M. Benedettelli, 'Sull'applicazione extraterritoriale delle misure di embargo degli Stati Uniti relative al « gasdotto siberiano »' (1984) *Rivista di diritto internazionale*, 529 ff.

10 PCIJ, *The case of the S.S. "Lotus", Publications of the Permanent Court of International Justice*, Series A.-No. 10, 1927. The decision was adopted by the President's casting vote.

11 On the development of the practice of the European Community in this respect, both in case of the implementation of economic sanctions adopted by the United Nations and of unilateral measures, see A. Davì, *Comunità europee e sanzioni economiche internazionali*, Napoli, Jovene 1993.

reactions, also of a normative character, by European countries, including Italy. We will examine these interventions in § 7.

Similarly, the extraterritorial effects of antitrust regulations received much attention in Italy;[12] yet the debate focused on foreign rules – in particular, US rules – or rules of a supranational origin, because Italy did not possess its own legislation on the matter and competition activities with a transnational character were, and still are, governed by European rules. Accordingly the role of Italian authorities was, and still is, restricted to enforcement actions.[13] The Italian law enacted in 1990 concerns solely issues relevant 'all'interno del mercato nazionale o in una sua parte rilevante',[14] and does not apply to activities performed, totally or in part, beyond Italian territory. Italian authorities maintain, however, the duty to fully cooperate with the EU institutions, and specifically with the Commission, in the implementation of antitrust regulations, and participate in the European Competition Network set up by Regulation 1/2003.[15] It is worth mentioning that more than forty years ago Italy adopted specific statutes aimed at counteracting some extraterritorial effects of foreign practice in this respect; an example is mentioned in § 7.

3 Scope of Application of Italian Rules in Civil and Commercial Matters: the Codification of Private International Law

One of the reasons for the scarcity of debate on the boundaries of Italian jurisdiction to prescribe may reside in the early codification of Italian conflict of laws rules. These rules, whose first function is to regulate relationships connected with more than one legal system, also offer some guidance in establishing the scope of application for both domestic and foreign rules, as well as

---

12 See P. Picone, 'Introduzione, Tutela della concorrenza', in P. Picone and G. Sacerdoti, *Diritto internazionale dell'economia*, Milano, F. Angeli 1982, pp. 865–879, 868 ff.; the analysis is conducted on the perspective of the compatibility with international law of national rules with extraterritorial effects, and, once more, it is mostly founded on an analysis of the US practice.

13 The classical work of B. Goldman, 'Les champs d'application territoriale des lois sur la concurrence' (1969) 128 *Collected Courses of the Hague Academy of International Law*, pp. 631–729, mentions Italy only incidentally, with reference to a protestation of the Governments of several countries. Italy is included once, in reference to their protestation against US regulations.

14 Article 1, Law 10 October 1990, no. 287, 'Norme per la tutela della concorrenza e del mercato'.

15 Council Regulation (EC) No 1/2003 of 16 December 2002 on the implementation of the rules on competition laid down in Articles 81 and 82 of the Treaty.

their territorial or extraterritorial application.[16] In 1865, only four years after the proclamation of its unification, Italy adopted its first *codice civile*. Following the ideas of Pasquale Stanislao Mancini,[17] the 1865 code contained a comprehensive, albeit concise, system on private international law based on the well-known theories expressed by Friedrich Carl von Savigny in the eighth volume of his extensive treatise on Roman law. Transcending the necessity of establishing the scope of application of the domestic rules typically linked to the thought of the medieval Statutists, whose ideas informed legal thinking from the 12th to the 18th century,[18] Italy's codified conflict of laws rules, strategically inserted in the introductory part of the *codice*, adopted the methodology of localizing the fact-situations and relationships by way of connecting factors.[19] National rules were consequently put on a footing of equality with foreign norms. The prospect of an extraterritorial reach of Italian statutes – together with the corresponding possibility of the application of foreign rules in the Italian territory – was entrenched in the approach adopted by the codified rules; the opinion of the leading scholars was that a legal system ('ordinamento giuridico') may be considered as universal, and that the normative power of a

16 On the relationship between conflict of laws and the principles of territoriality and extraterritoriality see, in Italian literature, E. Vitta, *Dirito internazionale privato*, Torino, UTET 1972, vol. I, 23; A. Bianchi, *L'applicazione extraterritoriale dei controlli all'esportazione: contributo allo studio dei fenomeni di extraterritorialità nel diritto internazionale*, Padova, Cedam 1995, 8; for a very clear expression of this approach, compare D.T. Trautman, 'The Role of Conflicts Thinking in Defining the International Reach of American Regulatory Legislation' (1961) *Ohio State Legislation Journal*, 586, 616: 'Once it is recognized that the problem may be to decide which of the statutes of two or more countries should be applied to a particular case it is apparent that the court faces a problem much like that dealt with in the conflict of laws. Choice-of-law rules are designed to resolve precisely such problems.'

17 For a recent reassessment of the contribution of Mancini to the development of the Italian private international law codification see S. Tonolo, 'L'Italia e il resto del mondo nel pensiero di Pasquale Stanislao Mancini' (2011) *Cuadernos de Derecho Transnacional*, 2, pp. 178–193.

18 Many legal scholars had made advances in the comprehension of the problems connected with a plurality of statutes enacted by different sovereign powers and had offered useful contributions to the comprehension of the issues at stake, along with the changes in the political structure of the European territories, specifically after the dissolution of the Holy Roman Empire. However the basic methodology – establishing the spatial scope of application of each domestic provision – did not change until the Copernican revolution advocated by Savigny.

19 The bibliography on the history of private international law and on the change of paradigm triggered by Savigny's and Mancini's new perspective is quite extensive. See, ex multis, R. De Nova, 'Historical and comparative introduction to conflict of laws' (1996) 118 *Collected Courses of the Hague Academy of International Law*, pp. 437–621, 441 ff.

State is not restrained by its physical borders. The adoption of the 1942 new Italian system of private international law (included in the introduction of the new *codice civile*) further reinforced these assumptions.[20]

However, the universal character of the Italian legislation, even for those who expressly embraced this view, was purely hypothetical: first, because the operation of conflict of laws provisions itself restrained the application of Italian law to facts and relationships having a significant connection with Italy,[21] and, second, because the theoretical limitlessness of jurisdiction to prescribe was counterbalanced by the stringent limits of Italian jurisdiction to adjudicate and to enforce. It was also seen, moreover, as restricted by the existence of obligations imposed by international law; a traditional example are the rules on the protection of aliens.[22]

With the adoption of a codified system of conflict of laws rules, together with rules on the exercise of jurisdiction to adjudicate, the Italian lawmaker established the regulation of facts and relationships connected with more than one legal system, on the assumption that strict territoriality is unable to offer a just solution. The theory which considered that conflict rules' mission is the distribution of fact situations among the different legal systems and, accordingly, to fix the scope of application of domestic rules still echoed in the

20 For this position see R. Ago, *Diritto internazionale privato*, Milano, Giuffré 1955, 20; G. Morelli, 'Limiti dell'ordinamento statale e limiti della giurisdizione' (1933) *Rivista di diritto internazionale*, 382; Id., 'Sull'universalità dell'ordinamento dello Stato' (1951) *Rivista di diritto processuale*, I, 9. For a critical assessment of this theory, G. Balladore Pallieri, 'I limiti di efficacia dell'ordinamento italiano' (1940) *Jus*, p. 74; Id., 'L'universalità dell'ordinamento dello Stato' (1950) *Jus*, p. 57.

21 This assumption is subject, however, to several exceptions. The operation of the public policy clause imposes the application of Italian rules upon relationships that are possibly deprived of a significant connection with Italy, because the clause functions by replacing foreign rules which are considered contrary to the forum's fundamental values with the domestic norms. Domestic rules also apply when it is impossible to establish the content of the foreign law (Article 14, Italian law on private international law). Moreover, the Italian legal system has always granted the parties to an international contract a broad power of choice-of-law, permitting the choice of any law, even unrelated to the contract, as is still the case under the authority of EU Regulation 593/2008 (Rome I). For an interesting perspective see H.L. Buxbaum, 'Determining the Territorial Scope of State Law in Interstate and International Conflicts: Comments on the Draft Restatement (Third) and on the Role of Party Autonomy' (2017) 27 *Duke Journal of Comparative & International Law*, pp. 381–403, 396 ff.

22 See B. Nascimbene, *Il trattamento dello straniero nel diritto internazionale ed europeo*, Milano, Giuffré 1984, 17 ff.

presentation of the matter offered in treatises on private international law.[23] But these portrayals were incorrect and did not explain the functioning of the system based on bilateral norms. The logical consequence of such position would be that each country could only fix the scope of spatial application of its own norms; this is clearly contradicted by the mode of operation of the Italian rules.

The subsequent Italian codification enacted in 1995 (law 218/1995, reforming the private international law Italian system) has maintained the same approach, consisting of conflicts rules establishing the applicable law to fact situations.

It may be argued that this approach affects mainly matters of private law; rules of a public or regulatory character, such as those concerning tax,[24] administrative, procedural, and criminal issues, were and still are considered to have a mostly territorial reach. This is a general principle of the Italian legal system, which was made explicit by Article 11, 'Preleggi' of the 1865 codice civile and by Article 28, 'Disposizioni sulla legge in generale' of the 1942 codice civile.[25] Even if both provisions are not in force any more, the principle that they express maintains its authority. Even so, the spatial scope of those rules is generally expressed, and not presumed. Besides, the boundaries between private and public norms are often blurred, especially in economic matters; and even in private matters, or in matters having a direct influence over private relationships, there are exceptions to the functioning of conflict rules. Furthermore, although the conflict of laws methodology, in the Italian legal experience, can indicate with sufficient certainty in most situations which rules should be applied, private parties may find themselves in the difficult situation of being

23 See T. Perassi, *Lezioni di diritto internazionale. Parte seconda*, Roma, Il Foro italiano 1938, 55; see also the title of a textbook on private international law by R. Monaco, *L'efficacia della legge nello spazio*, Torino, UTET 1954; compare, for a similar view, R. Quadri, *Lezioni di diritto internazionale privato*, Napoli, Liguori 1969, 27.

24 The territoriality of Italian taxation needs, however, to be assessed with reference to international activities of individuals and legal entities: see R. Cordeiro Guerra, 'I limiti alla potestà impositiva ultraterritoriale' (2012) *Rivista Trimestrale di Diritto Tributario*, pp. 31–64.

25 Both provisions, drafted in very similar terms, established that 'Le leggi penali e di polizia e sicurezza pubblica obbligano tutti coloro che si trovano nel territorio [italiano]'. These rules were modelled on Article 3 of the French *code civil*. The former was replaced by the latter, which, in turn, was abrogated by the new 1995 Italian law on private international law; the lawmaker did not consider useful to maintain the rule.

the recipients of contrasting commands from different legal orders, all purporting to regulate a single matter.[26]

This study will give an overview of the sectors where territoriality, and conversely extraterritoriality, are relevant for the Italian legal system, notwithstanding the theoretical universality – in the absence of provisions stating the opposite – of the statutes enacted by the Italian lawmaker.

4 The Protection of Crucial Values through the Extension of Application of Internal Rules: the Examples of Social Security and Adoption of Children

In a few, very specific, areas, the Italian lawmaker has considered that widening the scope of some specific rules of law was the most efficient way to pursue objectives that are considered crucially relevant to the expression of fundamental values. This may be exhibited by two examples: (a) the regulation of social security and (b) the law on adoption of children.

(a) Italian legislation on social security applies, as a general rule, to all labour relations performed in Italian territory. This is consistent with European Regulation 1408/71, whose Article 13, again as a general rule (accompanied by some specifications and a few exceptions), states that workers 'employed in the territory of one Member State shall be subject to the legislation of that State', notwithstanding their domicile or residence, or the place of business of their employer.

In 1985, with decision no. 365, the Italian Constitutional Court declared contrary to the Italian Constitution, and accordingly abrogated, the Italian rules restricting the application of the social security provisions to activities accomplished in the Italian territory, because, in the absence of agreements with the extra-European foreign country where a labour relationship was carried out, the worker could be left without social coverage, or with a coverage insufficient to meet the prescriptions of Article 38, par. 2, of the Italian Constitution.[27] The Italian legislator, in compliance with the ruling of the Court, has thus issued law no. 398 of 1987, which prescribes the registration in the Italian public

26 On this perspective, M. Lehmann, 'New challenges of extraterritoriality: superposing laws', in F. Ferrari and D.P. Fernández Arroyo (eds), *Private International Law. Contemporary Challenges and Continuing Relevance*, Cheltenham/Northampton, Elgar 2019, pp. 258–291, offers some interesting thoughts on possible answers to the problem.

27 Article 38, par. 2, affirms (in the English translation made available on the Italian Senate's website): 'Workers have the right to be assured adequate means for their needs and necessities in the case of accidents, illness, disability, old age and involuntary unemployment.'

system of social security of all Italian citizens,[28] hired in Italy or abroad, who work in non-EU countries where an international agreement on social security has not been adopted, or where the existing agreement covers only some branches of social security. The obligation applies to employers established in Italy and to companies incorporated abroad under Italian control or having an Italian shareholder participation, but also, quite surprisingly, to the unlimited category of foreign employers ('datori di lavoro stranieri': Article 1, par. 2, *d*). The scope of the rules thus embraces all Italian citizens working in any non-EU country lacking an agreement with Italy, or having only a partial agreement; this may produce conflicting obligations for the employers, when the labour activity is performed in a country where a mandatory social security system is also in effect. The provisions, therefore, appear clearly disproportionate, even if their rationale is to protect an employee's right to social security. This is particularly true with reference to obligations imposed on foreign companies and firms devoid of any connection with Italy. However, so far the Italian authorities do not seem to have yet been asked to enforce these norms towards alien employers not established in Italy, almost certainly because the link with the Italian legal system offered by the mere nationality of the worker is insufficient to grant jurisdiction to the Italian authorities when the respondent is a foreign firm. The effects of the very wide exercise of the jurisdiction to prescribe by the adoption of Law 398/1987 are, therefore, restricted by the limits of the jurisdiction to adjudicate and to enforce.

(b) A law with an extraterritorial reach was enacted in 1983 in matters of adoption. The law establishes in Italy a form of adoption of mandatory application to all children under the age of 18.[29] Title III of the law specifically governs international relationships: it applies to the adoption of foreign children by Italian or foreign couples residing in Italy, and to the adoption of Italian children by Italian or foreign couples residing abroad, even when the child's residence is in a foreign country. Therefore, the law applies to the adoption of a foreign child by a couple having the same nationality, but residing in Italy, as well as to the adoption in a foreign country of an Italian child by a local couple. The rationale of this ultra-inclusive and uncompromising approach is, firstly, the belief of the Italian lawmaker that adoption is always the best solution for children deprived of the care of their parents and relatives – contrary to the

28 In compliance with the principle of non-discrimination, the rules apply also to EU nationals and other workers legally hired in Italy and posted abroad.

29 Law no. 184 of 1983 (revised several times); the form of adoption introduced by this law creates a status between the child and the adoptive parents that is identical to that of children born in wedlock. The Italian *codice civile* maintains a different form of adoption, establishing less stringent bonds, which applies to the adoption of adults.

international standards codified in Articles 20 and 21 of the 1989 Convention on the rights of the child – and, secondly, the distrust towards the possible application of other laws on the assumption that they might be less respectful of the private and public interests involved.[30]

A difficult aspect concerning the application of this law involves internationally displaced children and unaccompanied migrant children, whose situation is often quite critical, as denounced by NGOs.[31] According to Article 8 of Law 183/1984, all children who are found in Italian territory in a non-temporary state of abandonment are eligible for adoption according to the same Italian law. Children are considered in a state of abandonment when they lack the moral and material care of parents or relatives, even when they are in a foster family or in an institution, as long as the lack of care is not due to temporary force majeure.

A strict interpretation and application of Italian law would entail the declaration of the state of abandonment and the consequent adoption of all children, whatever their nationality or their country of residence. The consequences may be particularly severe with reference to internationally displaced children and to unaccompanied migrant children. This was the case with children from Rwanda, who were brought to Italy for humanitarian reasons and to receive medical assistance. Some of these children were orphans; they were adopted in 1994 by Italian families notwithstanding the opposition of the Rwandan authorities and the existence, in some cases, of relatives in the country of origin. A wave of protest arose when the repatriation of these children was denied.[32] The application of Law 1984/183 has progressively changed

30 According to A. Davì, 'Adozione nel diritto internazionale privato', in *Digesto delle discipline* privatistiche, Torino, UTET 1987, pp. 3–52, 27, the scope of application of the provisions of the law concerning the adoption of children by foreign nationals residing in Italy and by Italian couples living abroad exceeds the purpose of submitting to specific controls the adoptions performed abroad by Italian couples living in Italy and may give rise to difficulties. For an account of the consequences of the prescriptions of the Italian law in the relationships between Italy and Germany, see E. Jayme, 'L'adozione internazionale nelle relazioni italo-tedesche' (1985) *Rivista di diritto internazionale privato e processuale*, pp. 453–464.

31 For an overview of the situation of unaccompanied migrant children in Italy and in other European countries, see the reports of Save the Children, https://www.savethechildren.it/.

32 See R. Thomas, *L'adozione*, Milano, Feltrinelli 2006, 297. The Italian and the Rwandan authorities had agreed that the children should be returned to Rwanda after a sojourn in Italy for being medically treated following the deprivations suffered during the civil war. However, the judges of the juvenile Corte d'appello of Brescia in their decision of 16 January 1995 decided that remaining in Italy and being adopted by Italian families corresponded to the best interest of the children involved and was in line with the

and public authorities seem more inclined to accept that severing ties with the family and the country of origin, as a consequence of the procedure of adoption, may be inappropriate, in particular when it is not possible to exclude that the unaccompanied children have relatives in their country of origin or in a different country. Consequently, Italian handling of unaccompanied foreign children now shows that adoption is not considered as an adequate answer, although it is not altogether excluded if the circumstances of a specific case suggest that this is, in fact, the preferable solution. The practice, recently codified in Law 7 April 2017, no. 47, 'Disposizioni in materia di misure di protezione dei minori stranieri non accompagnati', primarily consists in unaccompanied children being placed in foster families or, when this is not possible (in particular when their age, often approaching adulthood, discourages families from hosting them), in public institutions, as provisional measures, without cutting their ties with their family and their country of origin.

5 Territorial Scope of Italian Criminal Law and Its Exceptions

According to Article 6 of the Italian *codice penale*, enacted in 1931 but modified several times, anyone who commits a crime in the territory of the State is punished according to Italian law. The provision specifies that the offence is considered to have been committed in the territory of the State when the action or omission has either fully or partially taken place there, or in the event that the consequence of the action or omission has occurred there.[33] Thus Italian criminal law is indisputably based on the principle of territoriality, although ascertaining the place where the conduct was carried out might at times give rise to difficulties. There are, nevertheless, exceptions: Articles 7–10 of the code list activities performed in a foreign country that fall under the scope of Italian criminal provisions when certain conditions are met. These provisions are similar to those adopted by other legal systems, as they aim to protect vital interests of the Italian Republic, or to give effect to international obligations such as the principle *aut dedere aut iudicare* which justifies Article 10 (which provides for the prosecution – albeit under certain conditions – of a

prescriptions of the Italian law on adoption, and that the Italian engagement towards the Rwandan authorities should be disregarded.

33 Article 6 states: 'Chiunque commette un reato nel territorio dello Stato è punito secondo la legge italiana. Il reato si considera commesso nel territorio dello Stato, quando l'azione o l'omissione, che lo costituisce, è ivi avvenuta in tutto o in parte, ovvero si è ivi verificato l'evento che è la conseguenza dell'azione od omissione.'

foreign citizen who is in Italian territory and has perpetrated a serious criminal offence in a foreign country).[34]

Specific recourse to the extraterritorial application of Italian criminal law was introduced in 1998, with Law no. 269, for strengthening the fight against the exploitation of children, in particular sexual exploitation. A special provision concerns the prosecution of organizers or promoters of trips that are aimed at the fruition of prostitution activities with underage victims. The sexual exploitation of children is punished by Italian law when it is perpetrated by Italian citizens in foreign countries, or when the victim is Italian. The territorial reach of these criminal offences in Italy is in agreement with Article 19 of the UN 1989 Convention on the Rights of the Child;[35] it has moreover anticipated the prescriptions included in 2000 in a specific optional Protocol to that Convention,[36] and those of the 2007 Convention on the Protection of Children against Sexual Exploitation and Sexual Abuse, adopted in Lanzarote under the auspices of the Council of Europe and now in force in all 46 members of the Organization, plus Russia and Tunisia. It seems, accordingly, that the extraterritorial scope of these rules is justified by the erga omnes character of the obligations imposed on Italy as well as on the international community as a whole.[37]

Another example of the application of Italian criminal law to activities which are not performed in Italian territory is the prosecution for the smuggling of migrants, following an interpretation favorable to the spatial extension of the incriminating rules beyond the Italian borders and specifically on the high seas.[38] The expansion of Italian criminal jurisdiction, although difficult to

---

34 For an analysis of the relationship between the principle and the territoriality of criminal law see A. Caligiuri, *L'obbligo* aut dedere aut judicare *nel diritto internazionale*, Milano, Giuffré 2012, 97 ff.

35 Article 19: 'States Parties shall take all appropriate legislative, administrative, social and educational measures to protect the child from all forms of physical or mental violence, injury or abuse, neglect or negligent treatment, maltreatment or exploitation, including sexual abuse, while in the care of parent(s), legal guardian(s) or any other person who has the care of the child'.

36 Optional Protocol to the Convention on the Rights of the Child on the sale of children, child prostitution and child pornography, New York, 25 May 2000.

37 It is worth mentioning that the Convention on the Rights of the Child is the international agreement that has attracted the highest number of ratifications: 196 so far, with the notable absence of the United States.

38 A. Annoni, 'L'esercizio dell'azione penale nei confronti dei trafficanti di migranti: le responsabilità dell'Italia… e quelle degli altri' (6 May 2015) *Sidiblog*, http://www.sidiblog.org, considers this interpretation, endorsed by the Italian Corte di cassazione, as 'fantasiosa'; see also J. Drisch, 'Compétence pénale italienne et interception de passeurs de migrants lors d'opérations internationales en haute mer', in *Extraterritorialités et droit international*, Paris, Pedone 2020, pp. 275–292.

endorse in strict legal terms, appears justified by the universal condemnation of smuggling practices.

It is, however, difficult to formulate criminal rules with an extraterritorial reach for the protection of less internationally accepted values. Italy has a very stringent law on Assisted Reproductive Technologies and in particular forbids surrogacy agreements as criminal offences. However, no prosecution reaches an agreement performed abroad: the Italian Corte di cassazione has made clear that surrogacy motherhood agreements performed in a foreign country are not prosecutable under Italian law, even when part of the forbidden activity takes place in Italy (in the case decided by the Court, the first contacts between the prospective parents and the practicing institution had taken place in Italy, but were considered only preliminary to the agreement itself).[39] On the civil plane, if there is a biological link with a parent, the parenthood will be automatically recognized in Italy.[40]

In order to strengthen the prohibition of surrogacy agreements, two proposals which aim to prosecute the performance of such agreements in foreign countries as a criminal offence, even where the agreements are legal according to the local law, were presented to the Italian Parliament. However, both proposals were rejected. For one thing, as the debate on the ethical admissibility of surrogacy sees very divergent positions in Italy, the political admissibility of extending the territorial application of the Italian criminal rules to activities performed legally in a foreign country is a highly controversial issue. For another, from a more technical point of view, these rules appear difficult to formulate.[41]

---

39 See, Cassazione penale, Sezione 3, 10 February 2021 no. 5198. This decision is the most recent of similar judgments.

40 The outcome of a surrogacy agreement is now clearly established in Italian practice and case-law. If there is a biological link, parenthood is recognized automatically. However, in the absence of such a link, recognition will be refused, and the child will be considered eligible for adoption (see European Court of Human Rights, Grand Chamber, *Paradiso and Campanelli* v. *Italy*, judgment 24 January 2017, Appl. no. 25358/12; the Court considered that the Italian law refusing the recognition of the parenthood in such a case was not contrary to Article 8 of the European Convention on Human Rights). In the case of a surrogacy agreement performed by a couple, the parent without a biological link (intentional parent in the lexicon of the European Court of Human Rights) will be entitled under Italian law to adopt the child, by recourse to the adoption 'in casi particolari' which permits the adoption of the child of the partner. The Italian practice can be considered in line with the case-law of the European Court and specifically with the *Manesson/Labassee* judgments.

41 One of the proposals simply stated that the crime of surrogacy could be prosecuted even if performed in a foreign country; the other specified that surrogacy performed abroad could be prosecuted in Italy when performed by an Italian national. In the first case, this would

6 The Application in Italy of Foreign Extraterritorial Rules to Specific Private Matters: the Example of Mandatory Rules in Contract

From the standpoint of the Italian legal system, the effects on a contractual relationship of extraterritorial foreign rules aiming at regulating the matter, when the relevant conflict of laws provisions of the forum would prescribe the application of domestic law or of the rules of a different foreign country, would call into play the category of foreign overriding mandatory rules ('norme di applicazione necessaria straniere'). As is well known, the possibility of recourse in contractual matters to the application of mandatory rules of a country which has a close connection with the contract, but which were neither the *lex causae* nor the *lex fori*, was introduced by Article 7, par. 1, of the 1980 Rome Convention on the law applicable to contractual obligations. The provision, which was described as leading to the so-called 'third dimension' of conflict of laws reasoning, was highly controversial; indeed, seven contracting States had lodged reservations in its respect. When the Rome Convention was converted into Regulation 593/2008, Article 7 was replaced by Article 9; the new provision is more precise than its predecessor, because it gives a definition of what is to be considered as an overriding mandatory norm,[42] and its application is limited to the possibility of giving effect to foreign rules of this special character insofar as they belong to 'the country where the obligations arising out of the contract have to be or have been performed' (*lex loci executionis*) and only 'in so far as those overriding mandatory provisions render the performance of the contract unlawful.' This restriction was the price to be paid for maintaining the provision itself; otherwise some

amount to an exercise of criminal universal jurisdiction, and in the second case to an exercise of jurisdiction based on nationality, clearly difficult to reconcile with the principle of equality; see M. Pelissero, 'Surrogazione di maternità: la pretesa di un diritto punitivo universale' (29 June 2021) *Sistema penale* https://www.sistemapenale.it/it/articolo/pelissero-surrogazione-maternita-diritto-punitivo-universale.

42 The definition is the following: 'provisions the respect for which is regarded as crucial by a country for safeguarding its public interests, such as its political, social or economic organisation, to such an extent that they are applicable to any situation falling within their scope, irrespective of the law otherwise applicable to the contract under this Regulation.' The provision was modelled on a statement the Court of Justice made in its *Arblade* decision (23 November 1999, joint cases C-369/96 and C-376/96), inspired to the Court by a well-known contribution on the topic by Ph. Francescakis, 'Quelques précisions sur les "lois d'application immédiate" et leurs rapports avec les règles sur les conflits de lois' (1966) *Revue critique de droit international privé*, pp. 1–18, and that the Court itself in all probability did not intend to be a final definition of that category of norms.

member States would not have accepted it.[43] Accordingly, in the regulation of a contractual matter the Italian courts may decide to apply foreign overriding mandatory rules of the country where the obligations set out in the contract must be performed.

The European Court of Justice has confirmed in its judgment of 18 October 2016, *Nikiforidis*,[44] that Article 9 of the Rome I Regulation precludes 'the court of the forum from applying, as legal rules, overriding mandatory provisions other than those of the State of the forum or of the State where the obligations arising out of the contract have to be or have been performed' (para. 50). However, the Court held that Article 9 does not preclude such other overriding mandatory provisions to be taken into account 'as matters of fact in so far as this is provided for by the national law that is applicable to the contract pursuant to the regulation' (para. 56).[45] Italian courts could give effect to a foreign extraterritorial rule 'as a matter of fact', in the implementation of its own conceptions, such as, in particular, the notions of 'impossibilità sopravvenuta' and of 'eccessiva onerosità sopravvenuta'.[46] It is thus possible to evaluate the effects on a contract of extraterritorial measures adopted by a foreign State under this perspective. This should enhance the efficiency of the Rome I Regulation beyond the rigid boundaries of its Article 9, as it permits to take into account cases in which parties to a contract may be faced with conflicting duties produced by overlapping rules.[47]

43 See A. Bonomi, 'Le régime des règles impératives et des lois de police dans le Règlement "Rome I" sur la loi applicable aux contrats', in E. Cashin Ritaine and A. Bonomi (eds), *Le nouveau règlement européen « Rome I »* relatif à la loi applicable aux obligations contractuelles, Genève/Zurich/Bâle, Schultess 2008, pp. 217–237, 233.

44 ECJ (Grand Chamber), 18 October 2016, *Nikiforidis*, case C 135/15.

45 See M. Schmidt-Kessel, 'Article 9 Overriding Mandatory Provisions', in F. Ferrari (ed), *Concise Commentary on the Rome I Regulation*, Cambridge, Cambridge University Press 2020, pp. 236–260, 259, who refers to 'frustration, force majeure, hardship, good morals etc.'

46 Articles 1463 and 1467 Italian *codice civile*, respectively. Both provisions concern cases in which it is possible to ask for the termination or the renegotiation of the contract, the former when the performance has become impossible and the latter when the obligation of one of the parties has become excessively onerous due to extraordinary and unpredictable events.

47 See A. Bonomi, 'Le régime des règles impératives et des lois de police dans le Règlement "Rome I" sur la loi applicable aux contrats', in E. Cashin Ritaine and A. Bonomi (eds), *Le nouveau règlement européen « Rome I »* relatif à la loi applicable aux obligations contractuelles, Genève/Zurich/Bâle, Schultess 2008, pp. 217–237, 235, who refers to a 'conflit de devoirs'.

7 Counteracting Foreign Extraterritorial Measures: Implementation in Italy of So-Called Blocking Statutes

The adoption by a State of extraterritorial rules and practices can provoke the reaction of other countries, to begin with in the form of political complaints, but possibly also through the adoption of countermeasures.

Under this second perspective, Italy had in some situations enacted domestic statutes, because at the time cooperation among European countries was achieved through the adoption of national laws in view of the protection of common interests. An example of the very few Italian pieces of legislation adopted against that background is Law no. 488/1980.[48] This law, a form of 'blocking statute', was a reaction against the extraterritorial reach of US antitrust measures. Some Italian ship-owners and their representatives were the recipients of formal requests from US antitrust officers for information and the production of documents concerning the management and the commercial activity of their vessels. Law no. 488 states that all ship-owners of Italian navigation companies and their representatives receiving requests of information from foreign authorities must inform the Ministry of the Merchant Navy and ask to be authorized to give such information. It is explicitly forbidden, and it is considered a criminal offence, to give any information or document without the prescribed authorization.

More recently, Italy has participated as a member of the European Union in enacting instruments intended to protect European interests from the effects of foreign extraterritorial measures.

A relevant EU Act is Regulation 2271/96, which is known as the Blocking Statute Regulation, and has been revised on several occasions.[49] As indicated in the recitals of its original text, this instrument was adopted because 'a third country has enacted certain laws, regulations, and other legislative instruments which purport to regulate activities of natural and legal persons under the jurisdiction of the Member State', the reference being to the United States. By their 'extra-territorial application' these instruments, listed in an Annex to the Regulation, were seen as violating international law and hampering the

48 Law no. 488 of 23 July 1980, 'Divieto ai cittadini italiani di fornire ad autorità straniere documenti ed informazioni concernenti l'attività marittima'; see L. Fumagalli, 'Problemi di conflitto tra convenzione dell'Aja del 18 marzo 1970 e leggi locali: il caso « Aérospatiale »' (1987) *Rivista di diritto internazionale privato e processuale*, pp. 709–736, 717; Id., *Conflitti tra giurisdizioni nell'assunzione di prove all'estero*, Padova, Cedam 1990, 148 ff.

49 Council Regulation (EC) No 2271/96 of 22 November 1996 protecting against the effects of the extra-territorial application of legislation adopted by a third country, and actions based thereon or resulting therefrom.

attainment of European objectives. Accordingly, these instruments were 'likely to affect the established legal order and have adverse effects on the interests of the Community and the interests of natural and legal persons exercising rights under the Treaty establishing the European Community'; this required the adoption of EU rules providing protection against, and counteracting the effects of, 'the extra-territorial application of the laws specified in the Annex of [the] Regulation' (Article 1 of the Regulation). The reference in the Annex was to several US Acts and Regulations related to the economic and financial embargo concerning Cuba and the 1996 sanctions against Iran and Libya. The Regulation forbids European citizens, persons residing in a member country and companies incorporated in the EU from complying with the laws included in the Annex or acts resulting therefrom (Article 5.1), unless an exemption from that prohibition is obtained. The exemption can be granted by the European Commission where non-compliance with those foreign laws would seriously harm the interests of the persons covered by the Regulation or those of the European Union.

Regulation 2271/96 received, at the time of its enactment, little implementation. The scope of the original text was extended in 2018, by Commission Regulation 2018/1100,[50] to cover other US measures and specifically those affecting Iran. Quite a few judicial proceedings have recently been brought before the courts of EU member States and have also prompted requests of preliminary rulings to the Court of Justice.[51]

There is mention in trustworthy websites of two interesting Italian cases.[52] However the decisions, both quite recent, have not been published and the information is thus incomplete. The first decision concerns an Italian bank that had notified its client, an Italian company, of the termination of services, alleging that the company was controlled by partners in Iran. The Italian court ordered an injunction against the bank because the cessation of banking

50 Commission Delegated Regulation (EU) 2018/1100 of 6 June 2018 amending the Annex to Council Regulation (EC) No 2271/96 protecting against the effects of extra-territorial application of legislation adopted by a third country, and actions based thereon or resulting therefrom.

51 See L. Di Lullo, 'L'attuazione nell'Unione europea dei meccanismi di blocco alle sanzioni extraterritoriali: profili sostanziali e processuali' (2020) *Ordine internazionale e diritti umani*, pp. 134–150, 145 ff.

52 See 'Italian judgments on the EU Blocking Regulation' (2 October 2019) https://www.europeansanctions.com; 'EU Blocking Regulation – where are we now?' (8 October 2019) https://www.eversheds-sutherland.com. The two cases are mentioned also in the Report from the Commission to the European Parliament and the Council relating to Article 7(a) of Council Regulation (EC) No 2271/96 ('Blocking Statute'), Brussels, 3.9.2021, COM(2021) 535 final, p. 14, quoting the first source indicated in this footnote.

services would be a violation of the EU blocking regulation. The second case also relates to bank activities: an Italian bank had frozen the funds of one of its clients, an Italian company, to be allocated to a payment to an Iranian company. The Italian court considered that the US rules, applied by the bank, could not be enforced in the EU member states on account of the Blocking Statute Regulation, and ordered the release of the funds. The interpretation to the Regulation given by the Italian courts, as far as it is possible to infer from these short reports, seems in line with the subsequent decision rendered by the European Court of Justice on 21 December 2021 in the *Bank Melli* case.[53]

In the future, I envisage further applications of extraterritoriality, especially in the context of ongoing digitalisation. The GDPR and other data and digital law, in particular, provides for far-reaching extraterritorial rules that have yet to be fully explored in the CJEU's case law. Furthermore, globalisation will also remain a relevant factor for extraterritoriality. This is demonstrated by developments such as the Foreign Subsidies Regulation or the FDI Screening Regulation. It remains to be seen to what extent the EU Green Deal will impact further extraterritorial EU environmental law. Moreover, the global application of EU universal principles will also remain a topic of conversation. The discussions on supply chain liability show this. On the other hand, *Bank Melli* demonstrated the general value of blocking statutes in the EU, especially in relation to US extraterritorial regulations. Concerning the blocking statute rules of the GDPR, the United States and its CLOUD Act will likely also become the subject of future proceedings at the highest court of the EU.

53 ECJ, 21 December 2021, *Bank Melli Iran*, c. C-124/20. The case concerned a dispute between the German branch of Bank Melli Iran, a bank owned by the Iranian state, and the German company Telekom Deutschland GmbH, a subsidiary of Deutsche Telekom AG. The Court decided, inter alia, that the prohibition laid down in Article 5.1 of the Regulation 'is drafted in clear, precise and unconditional terms with the result that it may be relied on in civil proceedings, such as the present case.'

The Extraterritorial Application of Statutes and Regulations

Japan

Hisashi Harata[*]

This report begins by describing the practice in Japan as of July 2023, as far as the reporter has gathered information (Part 1). It then sheds analytical light on the conceptual framework and rationale behind the practice (Part 2). Finally, it points out some general problems of extraterritorial application in our globalized era (Part 3).

In this report, the concept of extraterritorial application is used to refer to the application of law in situations involving any elements associated with foreign countries, such as nationality, domicile, or residence, as well as the location of subjects, acts or things. This definition follows the current understanding broadly shared in Japan.

This report follows the objectives and settings suggested by the General Reporter. However, it is almost impossible to describe the practice in a comprehensive way, as it involves a great deal of interpretation of statutes, especially by administrators in Japan, which is very difficult to observe from the outside.

1 Practice: Historical Development and Current Status

1.1 *Historical Development*

There are several areas in which extraterritorial application has been practiced in Japan for a long time, such as foreign exchange and foreign trade law,[1] tax

* *The University of Tokyo.*

1 This Act was first enacted in 1949 as the Foreign Exchange and Foreign Trade "Control" Act to prohibit, in principle, foreign trade under the government's control. It was liberalized by the legislative reform of 1980 (Art. 1). The regulations on FDI were amended in 1991. The name of the Act was changed in 1997. Art. 5 of the Act introduced the principle of active personality. For other provisions expressly referring to the extraterritorial scope of application, see Art. 20 item 7, 21 (1) (with criminal sanction according to art. 70 item 11), 25 and 27 (with criminal sanction according to art. 70 (1) item 25), the last of which concerns the regulation of FDI on the national-security grounds. With regard to this regulation, there is a case in which the purchase of J-Power's shares by a foreign institutional investor, TCI Fund, was prevented by

 | DOI:10.1163/9789004720183_010

law,[2] criminal law, and private law.[3] However, these practices were not explicitly qualified and labeled "extraterritoriality;" that concept first surfaced only as an objection to foreign practices.[4] In accordance with the territoriality principle, practice in Japan under the laws identified above was not very aggressive. (See infra 1.2.1.)

The situation has changed since the 1990s. Scholars emphasized the possibility and necessity of extraterritorial application, and legislation and administrative practices gradually changed.[5] In criminal law, there is a tradition of legislation based on several principles, such as protection, personality, territoriality, and universality. In other fields, such as competition law and other

---

a suspension order under Art. 27 (10) for national security reasons. On the other hand, it is noteworthy that there is no regulation of re-export by the Act.

2 See Income Tax Act, art. 7 (1) items 3 and 5. Both non-resident individuals and foreign companies may be subject to income tax based on PE located within Japan. Regarding PE, see infra note 88. On the other hand, taxation under the Consumption Tax Act (cf. Art. 4 (3) item 1 and 5 (1)) is considered as based on the principle of territoriality.

3 Even in civil cases, if Japanese law is chosen as applicable, Japanese private law is applied extraterritorially. In particular, Art. 22 of the Act on General Rules for the Application of Laws, regarding the choice of law for torts, adopts the so-called double actionability principle, which results in the cumulative application of Japanese tort law. Public policy (Art. 42) and overriding mandatory rules of Japanese law are applied.

4 See infra 2.4.2.1. There are some cases in which Japanese government diplomatically or unilaterally expressed objection to U.S. government, such as the cases of Siberian pipeline (in 1982) and of Iran Libya Sanctions Act (in 1996), and JFTC's press release on antitrust enforcement policy of U. S. Department of Justice for the anti-competitive practice to limit export of America (in 1992), and FSA and BOJ's letter on U.S. CFTC's interpretation guidelines on financial transactions accompanied with the letter of Japan and EU (2012). There are also some court cases in which the government expressed its opinion, such as U.S. vs. Itoh & Co. Ltd et al. (1982 83 Trade Cases p.65010) (regarding the import cartel of Japanese companies), in U.S. et al. v. Toyota Motor Corporation (569 F.Supp. 1158 (C.D.Cal. 1983)), in U.S. v. Nippon Paper Industries Co., 109 F. 3d 1 (1st Cir., 1997), in the Vitamin C antitrust litigation, in Inquivosa S.A. v. Ajinomoto Co. (477 F.3d 535(8th Cir. 2007)), in F. Hoffman-La Roche Ltd. v. Empagran S.A., 542 U.S. 155 (2004), and in Motorola Mobility LLC v. AU Optronics Corp. – 775 F.3d 816 (7th Cir. 2014). With respect to China's extraterritorial application, there has been some reaction by the Japanese Center for Information and Security Trade Control with the Federation of Economic Organizations and other organizations, resulting in the comments made at the press conference by the Minister of Economy, Trade and Industry in November 2020.

5 There are two main official mechanisms by which administrative authorities explain the scope of application of regulations, namely, their response to questions through public comments and the non-action letter. The public comment system is based on a Cabinet decision (March 23, 1999) as amended on December 26, 2000. See Administrative Procedure Act, arts. 38 to 45. The no-action letter system is also based on a Cabinet decision (March 27, 2001).

administrative regulations, the effects doctrine has become more and more mainstream.

Recently, there has been a stronger legislative and interpretative tendency to broaden the scope of law's application based on the need to regulate in accordance with domestic policies. The consideration of the conflicting policies of foreign countries is not absent, but it is not so routine as to keep the current in check. The need for regulation combined with the pretext of the effects doctrine or the principle of territoriality promotes extraterritorial application. The limits of the jurisdiction imposed by the international law are not taken into consideration as seriously as the reach of laws' application expected on the basis of domestic policies.

1.2 *Theory and Practice of Extraterritorial Application in the Field of Competition Law*

According to the general understanding, it is the field of competition law that first brought up the issue of extraterritorial application of foreign laws, as well as Japanese law, in Japan.

1.2.1 Traditional Approach Pre-1980s

The Antimonopoly Act (hereinafter referred to as the AMA), the main part of Japanese competition law, includes several provisions that explicitly refer to extraterritorial application (Art. 6 and Art. 9 which was amended in 1949). However, it was widely recognized that the application of the AMA should be limited due to the principle of territoriality, and therefore it should not be applied to foreign companies that did not have a branch office in Japan. The scope of Art. 6 prohibiting international cartels was also understood in this way.[6]

1.2.2 Shift to Extraterritorial Application

This modest attitude began to change around 1990. A report of the Japan Fair Trade Commission (JFTC) published in 1990 recognized extraterritorial

6 For instance, see the Supreme Court's judgment of 28th Nov 1975 regarding a continuous sale contract between a Japanese company and a Danish company including the duty not to compete after determination of contract. JFTC made a decision of recommendation only regarding the Japanese company, and the Supreme Court denied standing for the Danish company to appeal the decision. In JFTC's decision of recommendation on 28th Sep 1971, an international export cartel was treated as a domestic case with consideration of the cartel's effect on domestic supply of production.

application based on the effects doctrine.[7] The Chairman of the JFTC explicitly mentioned the JFTC's stance in support of the effects doctrine in 2009.[8]

The regulations on mergers and business combinations were amended in 1998 to impose notification and reporting requirements on mergers between foreign corporations.[9] Extraterritorial application is also stipulated in the Guidelines on the Regulation of Business Combinations, as amended in 2007.[10] Finally, although the rules on unfair competition and restraint of competition do not explicitly address extraterritoriality, there are cases in which those laws have been interpreted to permit extraterritorial application (see infra 1.2.3.).

1.2.3 Cases of Extraterritorial Application

With the change of attitude of the Japanese government, especially the JFTC, several cases have been decided on the issue of extraterritoriality in competition law. As for the restraint of competition, a cease and desist order was imposed on a foreign company for the first time in 2008,[11] and a fine (surcharge payment) order was imposed in 2017[12] (the so-called CRT case discussed below), in addition to cases closed with administrative recommendation that occurred in 1995, 1998, and 2004.[13] The Supreme Court's ruling in the CRT case

7 See 公取委事務局編 (JFTC Secretariat Office ed.), ダンピング規制と競争政策·独禁法の域外適用 (Dumping Regulation and Competition Policy/Extraterritorial Application of Anti-monopoly Act) (1990) pp. 67, 84, 97. There is also a report of the research commissioned by the Ministry of Foreign Affairs, published in March 2001, which suggests the adoption of the basic criterion of "close connection" for the examination of international jurisdiction.

8 The practice of extraterritorial application of the AMA is heavily influenced by the mechanism and limits of the service of notices to addressees located abroad. In 2002, the Act was amended with new provisions, one of which allowed the service by publication (Art. 70-8). Although it is out of main scope of this report, it is to be noted that, even though there is a difference between legislative jurisdiction and enforcement jurisdiction in public international law, the feasibility of enforcement and the measures for enforcement may affect the determination of the scope of application of domestic laws and regulations.

9 Due to the amendment of the AMA in 1998, sales made not only by the place of business located in Japan, but also by the directly owned subsidiary company are taken into account for the assessment of asset value as a criterion for regulation.

10 See the JFTC's "Guidelines to the Application of the Antimonopoly Act Concerning the Review of Business Combination," as amended in 2011 and 2019.

11 JFTC order on February 20, 2008 (the Marine Horse case). See infra note 94.

12 The Supreme Court's judgment of Dec. 12, 2017 regarding the JFTC's decision of Oct. 7, 2009.

13 As other cases, the JFTC's decision of October 13, 1995 (Asahi Denka Kogyo case), that of the same day (Okishiran Kagaku case), and that of September 3, 1998 (Nordion case), all

is worth a closer look in order to reflect on the difficulties and issues of extraterritorial application in our globalized era.

1.2.4 Case Study of the CRT Case

1.2.4.1 *The Facts of the Case*

The case relates to price fixing for cathode ray tubes (CRTs) used in the production of CRT televisions. In 2009, the JFTC issued a cease and desist order and imposed administrative fines (surcharge payment order) on the cartel members, including Samsung SDI Company and its subsidiary Samsung Malaysia, MT Picture Display Co., Ltd (a Japanese company) and its Malaysian, Thai and Indonesian subsidiaries, Chunghwa Picture Tubes Company Ltd (a Taiwanese company) and its Malaysian subsidiary, LG Philips Displays (a Korean company) and its Indonesian subsidiary, and Thai CRT Company Ltd.

In its orders, the JFTC mainly considered Japanese CRT television manufacturers on the demand side. They were incorporated under Japanese law and were headquartered in Japan. These five Japanese companies had subsidiaries or affiliates established and located in Southeast Asia to produce CRT televisions using purchased CRTs. The sales contracts were entered into between the CRT manufacturers and the subsidiaries/affiliates of the Japanese companies and not by the Japanese companies themselves. However, the sales negotiations were conducted by the Japanese companies and they decided who would be their counterparty sellers as well as the price and quota of purchase. The subsidiaries and affiliates followed their instructions, concluded the relevant contracts, received CRTs, and produced CRT televisions.

1.2.4.2 *International Point Missed by the Supreme Court*

The critical issue in this case is the rationale for the extraterritorial application of Japan's AMA, which involves two separate issues. One regards domestic law: does Japan's AMA intend to cover this case in terms of domestic legal policy? The other regards international law: even if Japan's AMA itself wants to cover it, is it rational in accordance with the limitation of legislative jurisdiction imposed by international law? The cartel companies claimed that this case is beyond the limits of the AMA's scope of application, in terms of

of which are not orders but recommendations. As a case of export-cartel regulation, the JFTC's decision of December 27, 1972 (Chemical Fiber International Cartel Case), that of March 31, 1983 (Soda Ash Case), that of May 30, 1994 (Zenkoku-Mozaiku-Tairu-Kogyo-Kumiai Case), which all involve recommendation. There are also cases of admonition by the JFTC made on March 18, 1989 (Jinzo-Kokuen-Marugata-Denkyoku case) and April 5, 1991 (Vitamin case). For cases of regulations on business combinations, see the JFTC's website.

both domestic law and international law. However, the Supreme Court did not directly address the issue of international law in upholding the JFTC's extraterritorial application.[14]

1.2.4.3 *The Court's Reasoning on the Scope of the AMA*

From the perspective of domestic law, the Supreme Court, after setting forth the general principle regarding the geographical scope of the AMA based on the effects doctrine, applied that principle to the case as follows:

> the trade of the purchasing of the Cathode-ray Tubes can be evaluated as trade conducted by the Business Operators Engaged in the Manufacturing and Selling of Televisions in Japan and the Local Manufacturing Subsidiary Companies, etc. as a unit with regard to economic activities, and therefore it can be held that the Agreement impaired the competitive function of the market pertaining to the trade in which Business Operators Engaged in the Manufacturing and Selling of Televisions in Japan, who were located in Japan, were part of the counterparties.[15]

This assessment of the case has an impact on the scope of application of the AMA. As a first characteristic, the difference in legal personality between Japanese companies and foreign companies was not decisive for the court. Instead of the legal form of the corporation, the court considered the substantial economic unit of the enterprise. Even if there are several legal entities incorporated in the same enterprise, the court considered it as one unit on the demand side of trade. As a second characteristic, the ruling does not take into account whether the CRTs themselves were imported into Japan or instead were incorporated into CRT televisions abroad. Nor does the court consider the final destination of the televisions as an end product in determining the applicability of the AMA.

These two features of the judgment facilitate the regulation of global cartels in the globalized economy. The conventional way of thinking about the

14 In competition law, some scholars hold that there is essentially no limit of international law on legislative jurisdiction. See, 小寺彰A. Kodera, "独禁法の域外適用·域外執行をめぐる最近の動向"(Recent trends of extraterritorial application and enforcement of anti-monopoly law),ジュリスト1254号(2003) p. 64, at 65. 白石忠志T. Shiraishi, 独占禁止法 第3版 (Competition Law of Japan, 3rd ed.)(有斐閣, 2016) p. 180. Such a view may influence the Supreme Court's blindness to the issue.

15 The Supreme Court's judgment of Dec. 12, 2017. English translation is available at the Supreme Court's website (https://www.courts.go.jp/app/hanrei_en/detail?id=1557) (emphasis added).

applicability of competition law, which is narrowly based on the place of consumption and delivery and on the legal form of the entity, may not fit well with such a complicated situation of the globalized economy. The judgment of the Supreme Court seems to try to overcome the difficulties caused by the conventional framework of competition law in terms of scope of application.[16]

But why did the Supreme Court uphold the application of the AMA to the case? What is the policy underlying such an extraterritorial application of the AMA? What is to be protected? Is it to protect Japanese-origin business groups from the global cartel? Is such protectionism justified on the basis of similarity to the passive personality principle? Or on some other basis?

1.3 *Practice in Other Fields: Legislation and Interpretation*

The Competition Law was the first runner of extraterritorial application in Japan. But it was and is recognized in other fields as well. In particular, the Criminal Code includes provisions regarding crimes outside Japan. In addition, the provisions concerning "crimes within Japan" are also applied extraterritorially by way of interpretation based on the ubiquity principle. In other areas of administrative law, the practice used to be moderate, but recently some legislation and interpretative practices have shifted to expand extraterritorial application.

1.3.1 Criminal Law

According to Art. 31 of the Constitution of Japan, criminal punishment must be based on the law (*nullum crimen sine lege*). In this regard, the extraterritorial application of criminal law should always be based on legislation. The Japanese Criminal Code distinguishes between "crimes committed within Japan" (Article 1) and "crimes committed outside Japan". The punishment of crimes outside Japan shall be explicitly stipulated by law (Art. 8). Any criminal punishment for violation of administrative regulations applies in principle only to infringements committed within Japan, unless the laws explicitly provide for crimes outside Japan.[17]

---

16 As a criticism of both the JFTC and the Supreme Court's view, see T. Shiraishi, "Customer Location and the International Reach of National Competition Laws," Japanese Yearbook of International Law, Vol. 59 (2016), pp. 202–215 (arguing for limiting the scope of the AMA based on the location of the customer to be protected in Japan). However, there is no justification for limiting the legislative purpose of the AMA so narrowly to protect demanders located within the country. See also infra note 53.

17 Regarding the scope of application of the regulations with criminal penalties of the Fisheries Act, which has no explicit provision regarding crimes committed outside Japan, the Supreme Court decision of September 30, 1970 applied the Act to the case of fishing conducted in foreign territorial waters without any explanation regarding applicability of the

Crimes outside Japan are classified according to a number of categories. Their respective rationales for extraterritorial application differ, permitting reflection on the basis and limits of extraterritorial application compared to the very vague dictates of the effects doctrine.

Art. 2 of the Criminal Code provides for the punishment of some crimes committed outside Japan regardless of the nationality of the offender, such as rebellion, conspiracy, and forgery. They are related to the protection of important national or social interests, invoking the so-called protective principle. In this regard, Art. 971 of the Companies Act is the provision regarding the punishment of corporate crimes outside Japan. The interests protected by this provision based on the same principle seem to be not completely similar to those of the Criminal Code, since they are not directly related to national or social interests but affect individual and also legal institutional interests of corporate law.[18]

There are several special statutes that apply Art. 2 of the Criminal Code, but they are considered as based not only on the principle of national protectionism, but also on the principle of universality.[19]

Art. 4-2, as amended in 1998, comprehensively allows punishment of crimes outside Japan as required by international conventions.[20]

Art. 3 of the Code deals with the punishment of various crimes committed by Japanese citizens abroad, and Art. 4 concerns crimes committed abroad by Japanese officials. Both are considered to be based on the active personality principle. Personal loyalty to the nation is regarded as a rationale of this principle.

---

regulation on such a case like crimes outside Japan. Supreme Court judgments on April 22, 1971 applied the Act to the similar situation by interpreting the criminal provisions of the Act as including the crimes outside Japan.

18 There are also provisions in the Bankruptcy Law regarding crimes outside Japan. See the Bankruptcy Act (Art. 276), the Civil Rehabilitation Act (Art. 264), the Corporate Reorganization Act (Art. 274), and the Act on Recognition and Assistance for Foreign Insolvency Proceedings (Art. 70). The provision (1) of these articles seems to correspond to art. 2 of the Criminal Code, which is based on the principle of protection, but the interest to be protected by those of the Insolvency Law concerns not national/social but legal institutional of insolvency procedure.

19 For example, the Act on Punishment of Unlawful Seizure of Aircraft (Art. 5), the Act on Punishment of Acts to Endanger Aviation (Art. 7), the Act on Punishment of Coercion and Other Related Acts Committed by Those Who Have Taken Hostages (Art. 5), the Narcotic Drugs and Psychotropic Substances Control Act (Art. 69-6), the Act on Special Provisions for the Narcotics and Psychotropic Drugs Control Act, etc. and Other Matters for the Prevention of Activities Encouraging Illegal Conduct and Other Activities Involving Controlled Substances through International Cooperation (art. 10), etc.

20 For instance, Convention on Cybercrime adopted by Japan in 2001.

Art. 3-2 was added by a 2003 amendment.[21] It concerns extraterritorial application based on the passive personality principle. Historically, a similar principle had been adopted in the 1907 Criminal Code as art. 3 (2). But it was abolished by an amendment in 1947 for the reason of "internationalism", i.e. to show consideration for the country of the *locus delicti commissi*. Recently, there has been a criminal case which advocated for criminal legislation to protect Japanese citizens abroad,[22] which was realized in 2003 with respect to a very limited number of crimes outside Japan against the life and security of individuals, whether committed by Japanese or not.

There are some noteworthy points regarding the provisions of Japanese criminal law concerning crimes outside Japan. First, extraterritorial application based on the protective principle is mainly limited to important national and social interests. Since it is very likely that other countries would tolerate Japan's punishment for these crimes, these provisions seem to take into account possible conflicts with foreign countries.

On the other hand, Art. 3-2 of the Code for the protection of Japanese citizens abroad does not impose conditions such as dual criminality or predictability of the offender. Japanese criminal law has not adopted the principle of *non bis in idem* or the principle of *lex minor*, i.e., lighter punishment, in the international context. In this sense, this article does not show any serious consideration of potential conflicts with other countries, but seems to be based only on the need for protection.

Regarding the extraterritorial application of criminal law, the interpretation of Art. 1 on crimes within Japan is not to be ignored. It is interpreted in accordance with the principle of ubiquity, although there is no explicit provision like the German Criminal Code Art. 9.[23] According to this principle, any case in which a part of the constituent element of a crime is located in Japan is to be punished as a crime realized in Japan.

---

21 Art. 3-2 of the Criminal Code stipulates: "This Code shall apply to any non-Japanese national who commits one of the following crimes against a Japanese national outside the territory of Japan ……".

22 It is said that the TAJIMA case gave a chance to this amendment of Art. 3-2. This case concerned the murder of Japanese on a Panamanian-registered ship committed by a Filipino on the high seas. The Panamanian government was initially reluctant to punish, and there was no provision in Philippine criminal law for crimes committed outside the country. But it might have been possible to apply Japanese criminal law as a case of crime within Japan, somehow considering the inside of the ship as within Japanese territory. At least, the criminalization of any case committed within the territory of a foreign country is not the same with the case.

23 For instance, Tokyo District Court's judgment on 30th March 1981.

As for this theory, it should be noted that the theory could be considered as a justification for international jurisdiction, but there is room for doubt about the rationale of punishment in line with domestic policy. This theory can extend extraterritorial scope to a case which could not be covered by the effects doctrine, i.e. a case where no effect occurs within the country, while just a part of the constituent element, such as an act, happens to be located in the country. In this sense, the punishment based on the ubiquity theory could be excessively broad.

The punishment of complicity also shows some extraterritorial extension of punishment. First, there is a case where the act of an accomplice outside Japan was punished as a crime inside Japan because the principal offense was located within Japan.[24] Second, even if the principal offense is outside Japan but the accomplice is inside Japan, the accomplice will be punished.[25] In this respect, the scope of the ubiquity theory is extended by the accomplice relationship.

1.3.2 Administrative Regulations

In addition to the Antimonopoly Law and the Criminal Law, there are other laws that expressly stipulate their application to cases involving foreign elements, such as the Financial Instruments and Exchange Act (hereinafter referred to as FIEA), the Unfair Competition Prevention Act (UCPA) (regarding bribery of foreign public officials),[26] and the Act on the Protection of Personal Information (APPI).[27] And in several business laws that regulate particular

---

24 The decision of the Supreme Court on December 9, 1994 (regarding the case where the principal offense was committed in Japan and the accomplice was abroad, but the latter was punished as a domestic offense).

25 The judgment of the Sendai District Court (Kesen-numa Branch) of July 25, 1991 (regarding the case where only the conspiracy took place on a ship registered in Japan).

26 The provisions on bribery of foreign public officials were amended by the 1998 amendment to the UCPA as Art. 18 with Art. 21 on criminal punishment. Then, after further amendment in 2001, the provision regarding crimes committed by citizens outside Japan was added in 2004 as Art. 21 (8). For cases, see the METI website.

27 Art. 75 of the APPI, as amended in 2015, stipulated the scope of application of the APPI's provisions covering a certain type of acts outside Japan by the foreign business operator, i.e. the cases "in those cases where a personal information handling business operator who in relation to supplying a good or service to a person in Japan has acquired personal information relating to the person being as a principal handles in a foreign country the personal information or anonymously processed information produced by using the said personal information".

The extraterritorial application of the APPI is considered to be based on "target criteria", according to which those who open a website for Japanese customers can and should anticipate and comply with domestic regulations. In this regard, it can be said that this view considers the legitimacy of subjects' forced obedience to domestic law in terms of predictability.

business and industry sectors, there are provisions that specifically concern foreign entrepreneurs, such as in the FIEA, the Insurance Business Act, and the Banking Act. Moreover, in the Companies Act, there are provisions regarding foreign companies. However, these provisions regarding foreign companies, especially the obligation of registration accompanied by penalties in case of violation, are not regularly enforced.[28]

1.3.3 Extraterritorial Application based on International Conventions

The aforementioned APPI and the anti-bribery provisions of the UCPA were enacted as domestic implementations of international conventions. The former refers to the eight principles of the OECD Recommendation of the Council concerning Guidelines governing the Protection of Privacy and Transborder Flows of Personal Data (1980); the latter, the OECD Anti-Bribery Convention (1997), to which Japan acceded in 1999, and in the same year received such a critical recommendation for monitoring as to demand the adoption of the active personality principle. Subsequently, the principle was adopted by amendment in 2004 (Art. 21 (8)).

In addition, there is some legislation based on international conventions and agreements that explicitly refer to extraterritorial application. This is particularly the case in the field of criminal law,[29] with regard to drug trafficking,

---

In this regard, it is said that the effects doctrine cannot cover and justify the whole scope of application of APPI, especially due to the ambiguity or indirectness of the effect on the country. In addition, like the lack of re-export regulation by the Foreign Exchange and Foreign Trade Act (see supra note 1), the subsequent acquirer abroad is out of the area of coverage of the APPI.

The power of the competent administrative authority of the Personal Information Protection Commission (PIPC) has been so strengthened by the amendment of 2020, that the scope of extraterritorial application now covers the whole APPI and the service of publication and the system of disclosure of offender's name are available.

There is a case of administrative guidance by the PIPC to Facebook Inc. on October 22, 2018. It is also reported that there are other cases regarding foreign major IT companies, etc. For the PIPC's practice, see its website.

28 The regulations of foreign companies are divided into two categories, namely the regulations of foreign companies in general and the regulations of pseudo-foreign companies in particular, both of which are set forth in Part VI of the Companies Act. The main part of the regulations concerns the obligation to appoint a representative in Japan and the obligation to publish balance sheets. Non-compliance with the regulations may result in prohibition to continue business in Japan, liquidation order, etc. The registration requirement as a condition for a foreign company to continuously conduct business in Japan (Art. 818), which is sanctioned by criminal penalty (Art. 933 and 976 (1)), is almost unpracticed.

29 As an example of international conventions leading to domestic implementation with extraterritorial application, see the United Nations Convention on the Law of the Sea

organized crime and terrorism.[30] Article 4-2 of the Criminal Code, as amended in 1998, comprehensively enabled the punishment of crimes outside Japan in line with international conventions. However, this article has been criticized for creating ambiguity in its scope and for violating the constitutional principle of *nullum crimen sine lege*.

1.3.4 Impact of International Concordance as Soft Law on Domestic Practice

Some international concordances, other than international conventions, may have influence on domestic legislation leading to extraterritorial application. This is the case for some concordances within summit meetings and other international conferences.

For example, in the field of money laundering, the government upon recommendation of the Financial Action Task Force enacted the Act on Prevention of Transfer of Criminal Proceeds in 2007. Criticism expressed in the report of the third phase in 2008 also pushed the government to revise the Act in 2013. A recommendation as well as a report of the FATF has no legally binding effect, but it is said that the Japanese government as a summit member takes political responsibility and it led to the enactment as a domestic implementation.

There are also other examples, including domestic financial regulations following the 1988 Basel Accord I, 2004 Basel Accord II, and 2010 Basel Accord III of the BCBS; regulations on foreign securities dealers (1998) following the intergovernmental understanding indicated in the IOSCO report on securities activities on the internet (1998); and the tax reform to adopt the destination principle (2015) following the international VAT/GST Guidelines adopted by the OECD Global Forum on VAT in 2015, among others. These domestic regulations, which include the legislation of rules as well as interpretation practice,

(Art. 100 and 105), and the domestic law implementing it which is the Act on Punishment of and Measures against Acts of Piracy. However, this Act (Art. 3 and 4) does not explicitly stipulate the punishment of crimes outside Japan (cf. Criminal Code, Art. 8). For case law, see the judgments of the Tokyo High Court of December 18, 2013 and January 15, 2014.

30 Another example is the Control of Illicit Export and Import of and other matters of Cultural Property Act, which was enacted in 2002, following Japan's adoption of the 1970 Convention on the Means of Prohibiting and Preventing the Illicit Import, Export and Transfer of Ownership of Cultural Property in 2002. Art. 4 addresses regulations on the import of stolen cultural property. According to the resolution of the United Nations Security Council (No. 2199, on February 12, 2015), regarding the regulations on cultural properties illegally exported from Iraq and Syria, the import control was applied in accordance with the Foreign Exchange and Foreign Trade Law.

are settled by the administrators within their competence through negotiation and cooperation with foreign authorities.

1.3.5 Prohibition or Chilling Effect of International Conventions

In addition to encouraging the extraterritorial application of domestic laws and regulations, international conventions may also prohibit or restrict it. For example, there is a debate in Japan as to whether the requirement for foreign entrepreneurs to establish a branch or appoint a representative or agent in Japan is contrary to the GATS or FTAs.[31]

Another issue is the extraterritorial application of domestic patent law. The decision of the Supreme Court of Japan of September 26, 2002 concerns a claim for damages and for an injunction in a case concerning the infringement of a U.S. patent alleged to have been committed with active inducement in Japan.[32] In this case, the Supreme Court held that the extraterritorial application of U.S. patent law to acts within Japan was contrary to Japan's public order and therefore could not be acceptable. The Court not only declared the territorial limitation of Japanese patent law, but also imposed the same limitation on U.S. patent law. The supplementary opinion of Justice IJIMA considers this kind of bilateral limitation based on the territoriality principle to be part of the international framework of patent law. The law clerk of the Supreme Court also stated in her case note that the U.S. patent law is so idiosyncratic that it breaches "the international order" in this regard.[33]

Regarding this judgment, it is necessary to note that there is no explicit explanation as to why this kind of territorial limitation should be imposed on Japanese substantive law, nor why the same limitation should be imposed on foreign substantive law, nor why this kind of bilateral territoriality principle should be considered as an international framework for patent law. In fact, there are scholars who refer to the Paris Convention in this regard, but the Convention itself does not seem to provide for this kind of territoriality principle.

---

31 For example, with regard to the Telecommunications Business Act, which selectively requires a foreign company to appoint a representative or agent in Japan, the Ministry of Internal Affairs and Communications is of the opinion that this regulation does not violate international trade agreements such as GATS, according to 渡部友一郎 Y. Watanabe, 域外適用の類型とイコールフッティングに関する実務的展望 (Practical Prospect on Types of Extraterritorial Application and Equal-Footing) NBL 1180 (2020) 37, note 20.

32 For this case, the English translation provided by the Supreme Court can be found at https://www.courts.go.jp/app/hanrei_en/detail?id=619.

33 高部眞規子(M. Takabe), 調査官解説, 法曹時報56巻9号(2004) 2246, at 2281.

1.4 *Extraterritorial Application through Interpretation: Overview of Examples*

In addition to competition law and criminal law, there are other examples of laws that have been interpreted to apply extraterritorially, such as several business acts, the Labor Standards Act, the FIEA, and several acts related to e-commerce and digital platform business, including the Act on Specified Commercial Transactions, the Act on Improving Transparency and Fairness of Digital Platforms, and the Act against Unjustifiable Premiums and Misleading Representations, whose extraterritorial application by interpretation has recently attracted much attention. In addition, a case has also applied the Social Security Act extraterritorially.[34]

1.4.1 Labor Law[35]

Labor administration[36] generally uses the criterion of the location of "business" within the country to determine the scope of application of regulations (e.g., Art. 9 of the Labor Standards Act). Notably, extraterritorial application can occur even when the "business" is located within the country, but the actual employment is in a foreign country.[37]

The scope of application of the Labor Union Act is yet to be clarified. As for the administrative remedy for unfair labor practices, there are cases of extraterritorial orders issued by the Labor Relations Commission. Even for a

---

34 As an example of extraterritorial application of social insurance law, see Supreme Court judgment of June 13, 2016 (regarding suspension of payment of healthcare allowance to atomic bomb victim resident in Korea). As another example of extraterritorial grant of rights, the Act on Access to Information Held by Administrative Organs opens access to "any person," including foreign citizens as well as residents abroad (Art. 3).

35 With regard to subcontracting closely related to the labor relationship, the Act Against Delay in Payment of Subcontract Proceeds, Etc. to Subcontractors (enacted in 1956) has unclear points regarding the scope of its application. For example, it is not clear whether the case of a Japanese general contractor with a foreign subcontractor is covered by the provisions of the Act. There may be an inconsistent gap between the Act and the Labor Law in terms of extraterritorial application.

36 For the private law aspect of labor relations, there is room for extraterritorial application of Japanese law. In the decision of the Tokyo District Court of April 26, 1965, regarding the case of dismissal of an American pilot employed by a company incorporated in California and dispatched to work in Japan, the Japanese Labor Union Act was applied as an unfair labor practice. On the other hand, in the judgment of the Tokyo District Court of May 14, 1969, the principle of abuse of right for dismissal, which is peculiar to Japanese law, was not applied to the case of employment of an American employed by a company incorporated in New Jersey.

37 For an example of the extraterritorial application of the Industrial Accident Compensation Insurance Act, see the Tokyo High Court judgment of April 27, 2016. For the regulation on the foreign parent company, see infra 2.3.1.

labor union organized abroad, if it fulfills the conditions prescribed in Art. 2 and 5(2) of the Labor Union Act and the labor-management dispute takes place in Japan, the Labor Relations Commission will order administrative remedies.[38]

1.4.2 Financial Laws and Regulations

The ambiguity of the scope of application of financial regulations was already pointed out.[39] And the Financial Law Commission of the Financial Services Agency (FSA) published an Interim Report on Cross-Border Application of Financial Laws and Regulations in 2002 (hereinafter referred to as the Report).[40]

The Report acknowledges that the traditional idea was to limit the scope of application of financial regulations in accordance with the principle of territoriality. It then implicitly proposes the adoption of the effects doctrine, taking into account the necessity of extraterritorial application based on domestic policy to protect investors and the price-setting function of the market.[41]

The Report then proposes a general formula for determining the scope of application of regulations, based primarily on the territoriality principle but with the effects doctrine as a supplement. This formula, keeping the territoriality principle as the main element, can be more easily accepted by practice. In fact, this formula is currently referred to by administrative officials for legislation and interpretation.[42]

---

38 In the case of application of the Labor Union Act, the orders of the Tokyo Local Labor Relations Commission dated February 20, 1965 and February 15, 1994. As a case of refusal to apply the Act, the decision of the Central Labor Relations Commission of December 6, 2006 and the judgment of the Tokyo High Court of December 26, 2007. Both concern the same case involving the collective dispute between the Japanese automobile company Toyota and the employees of Toyota's Philippine subsidiary. The local Filipino union cooperating with the Japanese union requested Toyota for collective bargaining but was refused. The Central Labor Relations Commission as well as the Tokyo High Court denied the application of the Japanese Labor Union Act because a "foreign labor relationship" is outside the scope of the Act.

39 In Japan, the Securities and Exchange Act was amended and renamed in 2007. The renewal Act, called Financial Instruments and Exchange Act, has a wide range of coverage of regulations from securities and exchange transactions to doing certain types of business to disclosure and unfair trading.

40 The Report is available on http://www.flb.gr.jp/jdoc/publication11-j.pdf.

41 It should be noted that there is no mention here of the limitation based on the subjective purpose of the actor or the "substantial" or "direct" effect of the act. On the other hand, the Report states in paragraph 2 (3) that extraterritorial application may be abstained from in consideration of coordination with foreign regulations.

42 It is said that not only the FIEA, but more generally the administration of financial regulation has adopted this approach. See Nishimura & Asahi Law Firm ed., ファイナンス

The FSA's position on the scope of application of the FIEA is often presented in fragments, both in response to questions posed in public comments and in no-action letters. According to this position, first, a transaction in which one party is a foreigner may be covered by the regulations.[43] Second, the FIEA is in principle designed to protect investors resident in Japan.[44] In this regard, it is not appropriate to exclude all transactions involving foreign accounts from its scope.[45] And if acts of solicitation of offers to purchase are directed only at non-resident investors and are conducted abroad, such acts are in principle outside the scope of the FIEA.[46] On the other hand, if a foreign securities company advertises on its website for "business operations related to securities business", it falls under the concept of "solicitation" for transactions in financial instruments and is therefore covered by the FIEA.[47] Third, even transactions with non-resident customers are covered in the case of solicitation conducted within Japan.[48]

However, there are still some unclear points regarding the scope of application of the FIEA, which require further examination, especially with regard to the consistency of the law's application. For example, with respect to disclosure, certain public offerings conducted abroad are also covered by the Act.[49] And even in the case of foreign sales of shares by non-resident investors, if the shares sold are of domestic companies listed on the stock market in Japan,

法大全〔全訂版〕(Corpus Juris Finance, Completely revised Ed.)(商事法務, 2017) p.1132 (written by 松尾直彦 N. Matsuo).

43 FSA's response to public comments on 31 July 2007.

44 FSA's response to public comments on 31st July 2007. See also FSA's Financial Law Commission's Report's case-study analysis 2 referring to the viewpoint of investor protection.

45 FSA's response to public comments on 31st July 2007.

46 FSA's response to public comments on July 31, 2007, that the obligation to register sales representatives, etc. will not be applied. According to the FSA's "Answer to Questions of Financial Instruments and Exchange Act" dated February 2008, if a foreign branch of a Japanese bank engages in local currency-based transactions with a foreign customer, such a case is outside the scope of application of the FIEA. What about the case of yen-based transactions? 松尾直彦 N. Matsuo, 金融商品取引法〔第6版〕(Financial Instruments and Exchange Act, 6th ed.)(商事法務, 2021) holds that the FIEA shall not be applied to the case. Compare with the scope of a regulation on yen-based transactions by the Foreign Exchange and Foreign Trade Act.

47 FSA's Comprehensive Guidelines for the Supervision of Financial Instruments Business Operators, etc. X-1-2 (as of Nov. 2021). See also Case Study Analysis 2 of the FSA's Financial Law Commission's Report.

48 FSA's response to public comments dated July 31, 2007. According to the FSA's response to public comments dated December 28, 2009, whether an offer to sell is deemed to have been made in Japan depends on whether the securities sold are in circulation in Japan.

49 Art. 24-5 (4) of the FIEA.

they are said to be covered by the provisions of the FIEA regarding reports of possession of large volume, TOB, sales report and insider trading.[50]

On the other hand, there are different views on the FIEA's reach to sales of shares issued by foreign companies listed in Japan. A response from the FSA (as of 2002) held that the regulations on sale reports related to insider trading did not apply to the sale of shares issued by foreign companies listed in Japan by non-resident directors or major shareholders.[51] However, the Report suggests the application of the sale report regulations as well as the redemption of short-term margin[52] in such a case. Remarkably, the Report thus characterizes regulations on insider trading and market rigging as protecting the fairness of market transactions and the price-forming function of the market rather than the individual interests of investors (in the Report, 3 (2)). However, it is unclear how much and what kind of "effect" on the Japanese market will trigger the application of domestic regulations.

With the formula of territoriality plus the effects doctrine as a complement proposed by the Report, it is unclear what kind of effect can necessitate and justify the application of FIEA or other financial regulations. The focus on the protection of individual interests of investors cannot explain the application of regulations in the case of non-resident investors.[53] Other focuses on the protection of market order or fairness of trading in relation to domestic listed companies could be considered to clarify the effect needed to trigger the application of the law.[54]

---

50 FSA's Financial Law Commission's Report's Case Study Analysis 5①. See also 松尾直彦 N. Matsuo, 金融商品取引法〔第6版〕(Financial Instruments and Exchange Act, 6th ed.)(商事法務, 2021) 67.

51 The FSA Planning and Coordination Bureau's response to the Financial Law Commission (referred to in note 24 of the report).

52 FSA's Financial Law Commission's Report's case-study analysis 4.

53 There is a view that the FIEA should be applied to protect such a non-resident investor if the financial instruments business operator solicits and sells the instruments from Japan, based on the subjective territoriality principle. For this view, see infra note 75. On the other hand, there is another view that, in principle, the protection of investors should be left to the country where they are located, and that it is neither necessary nor appropriate to apply Japanese regulations for further protection in such a case. 森下哲朗 Tetsuo Morishita, 金融関係法の国際的適用範囲 (The international scope of application of financial laws and regulations) 金融商事判例 1294(2008)1. For a similar view on competition law, based on the customer's location theory, see supra note 16.

54 See Art. 971 of the Companies Act (see supra note 18). It certainly applies to companies incorporated under Japanese law, but it is not clear whether foreign companies are excluded from the scope of application. It would be possible to apply to them at least some regulations concerning the market and institutions based on Japanese laws. The

1.4.3 Regulations on E-commerce and Digital Platform Business

The regulation of cyberspace activities such as e-commerce requires a higher degree of extraterritoriality. In Japan, this is also done by interpreting the geographic scope of laws and regulations, such as the Specified Commercial Transactions Act,[55] the Digital Platform Transparency and Fairness Improvement Act,[56] the Private Lodging Business Act,[57] the Unjustified Premium and Misleading Representation Act,[58] and the Payment Services Act.[59] The scope of application of these statutes is determined by interpretation based on the location of the consumer/client, the location of the accommodation, domestic sales, etc.[60]

Report refers to the case of rigging committed abroad but having some influence on the market in Japan (Case Study Analysis of the Report, 3).

55 Regarding online sales to consumers resident in Japan from overseas, the Consumer Affairs Agency has published guidelines. See https://www.no-trouble.caa.go.jp/qa/foreign.html.

56 It is said that the regulations of digital platforms based on the Act presuppose the use of administrative guidelines in principle. The scope of the regulations does not depend on the distinction between domestic and foreign entrepreneurs. Whoever provides a digital platform to the Japanese market should be considered a "specified digital platform providers" (Article 4(1)) and should be subject to the regulations. Whether or not the provider is targeting the "Japanese market" is determined on the basis of domestic income. The Act implies the disclosure of the terms and conditions for providing the digital platform, and it would be possible to require the provider to suspend providing the service to pernicious tenants.

57 The scope is limited based on the location of the lodging within Japan. The Act applies not only to entrepreneurs engaged in the business of lodging, but also to lodging managers and agents. The use of unregistered agents is prohibited (Art. 12), and in case of infringement, the business improvement order (Art. 15) and the business suspension order (Art. 16) may be imposed with criminal penalties (Art. 75). For the regulation of entrepreneurs without an office in Japan, " an order" is replaced by " a request" as an administrative measure. See infra 1.5.1.

58 There is a case of a foreign entrepreneur located in China for whom the administrative order based on Art. 7 of the Act (on January 26, 2018) as well as the administrative fine under Art. 8 (1) (on March 29, 2021) for violating Art. 5 item 2 of the Act were issued.

59 Registration is required to engage in the business of payment services (Art. 37). Non-registered foreign entrepreneur is prohibited from conducting "solicitation of a person in Japan" (Art. 63, and 63–22). As a case of admonition to non-registered foreign entrepreneur, the case of Binance (located in HK) on March 23, 2018 and Binance Holdings Ltd. (whose location was unknown) on June 25, 2021.

60 For the insurance business, the Insurance Business Act requires foreign insurance companies to obtain a license and establish a branch office to conduct business in Japan. An unlicensed foreign insurance company that does not have a branch in Japan is not only prohibited from conducting insurance business in Japan, but is also generally prohibited from concluding individual insurance contracts "with persons having an address or residence in Japan, or with property located in Japan, or with vessels or aircraft of Japanese

However, as suggested above in relation to the CRT case and the FIEA, it is doubtful that a narrow focus on protecting domestic investors can alone justify all types of extraterritorial application of these regulations to cyberspace activities.

1.4.4 Business Acts

1.4.4.1 *General Framework of Business Acts*

In business acts, i.e., statutes that specifically regulate certain types of business, such as banking, insurance, etc., the system of licenses, permissions, or registrations is generally applied in order to grasp entrepreneurs as the target of regulations. Failure to comply with such a system will result in criminal penalties and prohibition from conducting a particular business. This framework generally applies to foreign companies, even if they do not have a branch in Japan.[61] However, the scope of application of this framework is not always clear.[62]

1.4.4.2 *Scope Demarcation*

The scope of application of business acts in Japan is generally delimited with some reference to the country. While some provisions explicitly address geographic scope, certain ambiguity in their terms may leave room for interpretation. For example, according to Art. 47 of the Banking Act, if a foreign bank intends to "conduct banking business in Japan", it must establish a licensed branch office in Japan. Strictly speaking, the meaning of "conducting business in Japan" is not clear, as suggested by a case in which a foreign bank received deposits from Japanese customers without having a branch in Japan.[63] Art. 187 of the Insurance Business Act, which defines "insurance business in Japan," is similarly unclear.

---

nationality" (Art. 186 (1), with criminal penalties under Art. 316 (item 4)). For securities transactions, the FIEA not only requires foreign securities firms to register (Art. 58) to conduct business in Japan, but also generally prohibits them from engaging in even a single one-time transaction with a customer in Japan (Art. 58-2, but without criminal penalty).

61 As for the assistance to foreign banks in receiving deposits in Japan, the operator providing such assistance is not required to be registered under the Banking Act, according to the FSA's no-action letter dated March 20, 2012. The system of Foreign Bank Agency Services revised in 2008 (Banking Act, 52-2-2 item 1) does not require the license (Art. 4 (1)) of the foreign bank.

62 For example, the term " intermediary or agency services " as stipulated in Art. 2(2) of the Real Estate Brokerage Act is unclear as to its scope. For some questionable terms used to indicate some connection with Japan, see infra 1.4.4.2.

63 FSA's request to Credit Suisse regarding unlicensed banking business in Japan through an overseas branch, March 16, 2007. See infra note 67.

For the FIEA, the scope is clarified to a greater extent by the FSA's responses as observed above, especially in the case of transactions and relationships with investors resident in Japan.[64] However, in the case of non-resident investors, the demarcation is not so clear. This ambiguity may have an impact on the scope of the registration requirement (Art. 29 of the FIEA).

Like these examples, the commonly used concept of "conducting business in Japan" requires further clarification in order to delineate the scope of application of regulations under these business acts.

1.4.4.3 *Money Lending Business Act: Tokyo High Court's Judgment of Dec. 12, 2016*

The Tokyo High Court's judgment of December 12, 2016 concerns the scope of application of the provisions of the Money Lending Business Act. This Act establishes the registration requirement for entrepreneurs wishing to engage in the money lending business in Japan (Art. 2(1), 3(1)), prohibiting them from doing so without registration and imposing a criminal penalty for failing to comply (Art. 11(1) and 47). According to the FSA's interpretation,[65] the regulations based on the Act apply to "money lending within Japan". The Act seems to cover lending including that between a foreign lender and a borrower resident in Japan, due to the location of the borrower to be protected by these regulations and the connection of the lending with Japan.[66] Then, what about lending from a foreign lender to a foreign borrower? Is this also covered by the Act? The judgment refers to the case in which a loan was made to only one borrower, a foreign company, by means of money transferred from Japan.

The Tokyo High Court held that the registration requirement of the Act applies to the extent that any part of the money lending business is conducted in Japan, even in the case of a single foreign borrower. The Court reasoned that (1) it is not contrary to the principle of territoriality, (2) there is a more obvious need to regulate money lending to foreign borrowers, and (3) "ensuring the proper management of business operations conducted by persons engaged in

64 With respect to the business operations related to securities business, Art. 58-2 of the FIEA deals with transactions with clients in Japan. As for self-directed business, registration of the operator is also required for foreign investment funds in the case of investment by resident investors. The same applies to investment advisory and investment management businesses. FSA's response to public comments dated July 31, 2007.

65 FSA's response to public comments on December 2, 2008.

66 This point is reported by 八木俊則 T. Yaghi, 金融規制法のクロスボーダー適用に関する試論 (Some thoughts on extraterritorial application of financial regulations), 資本市場 303 (2010)16, at 26.

the money lending business" is also the purpose of the Act, as distinguished from protecting "the interests of persons seeking funds".

However, the extension of the scope of the registration requirement is not entirely clear. First, the distinction between a domestic borrower and a foreign borrower, whether based on the place of residence or the place of receipt of funds, etc., is unclear. Further, the relevance of such a distinction, even if possible, is not clear in terms of demarcating the scope of application.

Second, as a more critical point in the case, there is no clear explanation as to why Japanese regulations should be applied to the case of a foreign borrower. The general need for regulations on entrepreneurs who lend money to foreign borrowers cannot necessarily justify the application of Japanese regulations specifically. The rationale and scope of application of the Japanese regulations to "ensure the proper management of business operations conducted by persons engaged in the money lending business" has yet to be clarified.

If the protection of foreign borrowers cannot easily be considered as a rationale for the application of Japanese regulations, there should be other factors related to the country. What is such a connecting factor that necessitates and justifies the application of domestic laws? One view may point to the connection of the relevant transactions with the market order based on the Japanese legal system. In order to establish and maintain this market order, it may be justified to apply Japanese laws to such a transaction. The protection of individual interests of customers will then be of secondary importance in this regard.

For social relations such as financial transactions and especially virtual e-commerce, where a real and physical element is not decisive, the regulations may be legitimate and necessary to ensure some virtual order based on domestic legal systems, although the consideration of conflicts with other countries as well as the consideration regarding the subjects to be regulated need to be addressed further (see infra 2.3 and 2.4).

The observations on the FIEA, the CRT case of competition law, and this case of the Money Lending Business Act raise questions regarding the necessity and justification of extraterritorial regulations based on virtual connections with the domestic legal order without relevant real physical contact in our globalized era.

1.5 *Moderate Application of Administrative Measures or Shift toward Aggressiveness?*

1.5.1 "Request" to Foreigners

As noted above, Japan has moved away from the categorical denial of the extraterritorial application of domestic laws and regulations on the basis of the territoriality principle. Instead, there is a recent tendency among administrative authorities to justify it almost exclusively on the basis of the need for regulation in line with domestic policy or merely on the basis of formal consistency with principles such as the subjective territoriality principle. (See infra 2.2.).

On the other hand, several Acts contain provisions that seem to indicate a moderate attitude toward imposing administrative measures on foreigners. Where these provisions indicate "orders" to Japanese persons, they indicate merely "requests" to foreigners.[67]

Such a "request" to foreigners, unlike an order as an administrative measure, has an ambiguous character. The "request" is not considered to have the coercive force of an "order". However, it also differs from an administrative guidance, on the basis of which disadvantageous treatment is prohibited (Art. 33 of the Administrative Procedure Act), in the sense that the failure to comply with a "request" can be one of the reasons for the rescission of a business registration.[68] At least we can find here some indication of the moderate attitude of Japanese authorities in imposing administrative measures against foreigners.[69]

However, if we look at the whole administration, we can see that such a moderate attitude is not consistently maintained. There are several statutes that do not contain such a substitution of order with request.[70] There are also statutes that explicitly impose mandatory obligations on subjects resident

---

67 For example, the Private Accommodation Business Act (Art. 61 (2)), the Radio Act (Art. 24-13 (2)), the Act on Ensuring the Quality, Efficacy and Safety of Products, including Medicines and Medical Devices (Art. 75-2-2 (2)).
Other than "request", there is a case of mere request for voluntary action without any disadvantageous treatment. Such a case is the FSA's request to Credit Suisse regarding unlicensed banking business in Japan through a foreign base on March 16, 2007. (See supra note 63).

68 For example, see art. 63 (1) item 3 of the Private Lodging Business Act.

69 Regarding the Atomic Bomb Survivors' Assistance Act, the foreign medical institution is said to be outside the scope of legally binding and mandatory provisions of the Act. The judgment of the Osaka High Court of June 20, 2004.
On the other side of the treatment of foreigners, there is some insufficient part as for procedural protection for them to make a claim against administrative measures. The Administrative Complaint Review Act seems to limit its application to Japanese citizens (Art. 1). There is no such limitation in the Administrative Case Litigation Act and the State Redress Act.

70 Art. 75 of the APPI does not contain such a substitution but Art. 42 (1) provides for a "recommendation" which can also be applied to foreign subjects.

abroad, regardless of their nationality.[71] And there are even cases of administrative measures applied to foreign companies.[72]

2 Overview and Examination of Japan's Practices

The practice of extraterritorial application in Japan discussed in Part 1 reveals several characteristics and problems in terms of conceptual framework.

2.1 *Divergence between Different Fields of Law*

Historically, the framework of extraterritorial application in Japan has been formed mainly by the discussion, including legislation and interpretation, in criminal law and competition law. The discussion in both fields shows an obvious divergence.

As for criminal law, extraterritorial application is discussed and at least allegedly justified by some principles of international legislative jurisdiction, namely territoriality (including subjective/objective territoriality and ubiquity theory), active/passive personality, and protectionism, in relation to different categories of crimes. In competition law, the effects doctrine predominates as a basis of justification. And in other areas of administrative law, such as financial regulation, the effects doctrine, including as a complement to the territoriality principle, is becoming increasingly influential.

This divergence is probably due to the difference between criminal sanctions, which are limited by the constitutional principle of *nullum crimen sine lege*, and other administrative measures. As for the administrative regulations and measures, the explicit delimitation of the scope of application in legislation is rare or incomplete and requires further interpretive operation. For interpretive identification, the formula of the effects doctrine or its combination with the territoriality principle is vague enough to be adopted as a comprehensive general framework.

71 Art. 36 of the Payment Services Act prohibits subjects abroad from certain types of conduct (but without sanction). The order of business improvement and suspension by Art. 60-8 (1) of the FIEA is also the case. See also FSA's Comprehensive Guidelines for Supervision of Financial Instruments Business Operators (as of Sept. 2014), X-2-1 (3) and X-2-2 (3).

72 For the competition law, regarding the JFTC's order to foreign companies, see supra notes 12 and 13. For the order of the Labor Relation Commission, see the order of the Tokyo Local Labor Relation Commission of Sept. 5, 1988, and the order of the Tokyo Local Labor Relation Commission of Feb. 15, 1994.

2.2 *International Jurisdiction and the Unilateral Domestic Perspective: Confusion or Ignorance?*

The difference between the limits of international jurisdiction and the self-definition of the scope of application of domestic law is to some extent recognized in theory. In practice, however, the former is often overlooked and the focus is almost exclusively on the latter, as the Supreme Court's judgment in the CRT case shows.[73]

Moreover, the principles of territoriality, personality, and protectionism, which are and can be invoked in relation to international jurisdiction, are confusingly applied to justify the scope of application of domestic laws.[74] Such a way of relying on the principles in relation to domestic-law perspective seems problematic as below.

2.2.1 Territoriality: Especially, Ubiquity Theory and Subjective Territoriality

The ubiquity theory is based on the concept of territoriality, as it rests on real physical contacts with the relevant territory. It could be used to justify international jurisdiction. However, the identification and justification of the scope of application based on the theory from the perspective of domestic law leaves room for doubt, since it would lead to the application in cases where no direct effect reaches the country, and thus cannot be covered by the effects doctrine. Similarly, as for the principle of subjective territoriality, it is not always clear why such an application is necessary and justified from the perspective of domestic law,[75] even if the same principle could be invoked from the perspective of international law.

---

73 The same is true of the Social Security and Assistance Act. In its decision of November 1, 2007, the Supreme Court ruled that the right to health care benefits under the Atomic Bomb Survivors' Assistance Act is not disqualified on the grounds of relocation abroad. It should be noted that this argumentation of the Court is only from the point of view of the domestic law in order to determine the scope of application.

74 The Report of the FSA's Financial Law Commission does not make a clear distinction between international and domestic issues. See note 19 of the Report.

75 The FSA's Financial Law Commission Report refers to the extraterritorial application of the registration requirement in the case where a Japanese entrepreneur conducts transactions for a non-resident customer. See case study analysis 1 in the Report. See also 松尾直彦 N. Matsuo, 金融商品取引法〔第6版〕(Financial Instruments and Exchange Act, 6th ed.)(商事法務, 2021) 96. He considers that the extraterritorial application based on the subjective territoriality principle justifies Art. 2 (3) item 2-ロ-(2) and art. 2 (31) item 4 of the FIEA. The applicability of the provisions of the FIEA in the case of an investment fund without a resident investor but managed directly from Japan is confirmed by art. 2 (8) item 14 with its related rules and regulations (as amended in 2010). See also

2.2.2 Active Personality Principle

A similar problem can be found as for the active personality principle, which is used in Art. 3 of the Criminal Code. Although nationality can be used in terms of international jurisdiction, it is not clear why it is also used to determine the scope of application from the perspective of domestic law.[76]

2.2.3 Objective Territoriality and the Protective Principle: Convergence with the Effects Doctrine

The objective territoriality principle focuses on where harm, as a constituent element of an offense, took place, while the protective principle, which is used only for important national and social interests in Japanese criminal law, presupposes that the effect caused by the constituent act reached these interests of the country. Both principles presuppose some concrete "result" or "violation of national/social interests", unlike the effects doctrine, which, at least by definition, has no limit as to "effect". But these principles can converge into the effects doctrine as a more general and comprehensive framework. In this respect, the effects doctrine has the potential to become a flattened general framework, but with the risk of excessive abstraction. In fact, in competition law and other administrative law, the effects doctrine has already become the general framework for legislation and interpretation. And there is a tendency among scholars to conflate the objective territoriality principle with the effects doctrine without recognizing any essential difference.[77] They do not take the difference between "result" and "effect" seriously.

FSA's response to public comments dated December 21, 2010. Matsuo, op. cit. 96, explains that the applicability of the FIEA in this case is based on the principle of subjective personality. This is also the case when a director of a Japanese listed company engages in insider trading of ADRs on the NYSE (Art. 27-2(1)(1) and related rules and regulations), as well as TOB regulations (Art. 27-2(1)(1) and related rules and regulations). However, such an explanation based on the principle of subjective personality may raise doubts as a rationale for the application of domestic laws and regulations from the point of view of domestic law. Is there any other substantial consideration as a basis for application? In this regard, see 1.4.4.3 on the case of the Money Lending Business Act.

76 In criminal law, the principle of active personality is generally understood to be based on national allegiance to the country. Theoretically, it can also be based on and limited by such an idea as the "Prinzip der stellvertretenden Strafrechtspflege," although Japanese criminal law has not adopted it (See supra 1.3.1.).

77 In the case of the protective principle, as opposed to the objective territoriality principle, the constituent elements themselves cannot always determine the scope of extraterritorial application, as they can cover and be related with only the similar interests of foreign countries. In such a case, it is necessary to additionally examine whether the to-be protected national/social interests belongs to Japan, other than the verification of constituent elements. It is also the case for the effects doctrine.

As noted above, Japanese administrative authorities, especially the JFTC, the FSA and ministries such as METI, show a tendency to adopt the effects doctrine and use it as a complementary tool to the territoriality principle to determine the scope of application from the standpoint of domestic policy.

This tendency to use the combined formula has several characteristics and problems. First, there is no strong caution against the excessive application based simplistically on the territoriality principle.[78] Second, the main concern as a result focuses almost exclusively on the existence of effects within the country, and insufficient attention is paid to the necessary constraints against the excessive exercise of jurisdiction.[79] Third, the idea of identifying and at the same time justifying the scope of application on the basis of the effects doctrine almost always confuses the issue of international law with the issue of domestic law. As a result, the former is very often ignored in practice.[80]

2.2.4 Ambiguity of the Concept of "Effect" in the Effects Doctrine

As mentioned above, the formula with the effects doctrine has the potential of flattening and the risk of excessive abstraction in comparison with the discussion related to criminal law.

In criminal law, as for the protective principle, the divergence of interests to be protected is seriously considered in Japan. Even if we had used the formula of the effects doctrine to explain the punishment of crimes based on the protective principle, the "effect" can be presumed with the fulfilment of the constituent elements prescribed by law.

On the other hand, in competition law and other administrative laws and regulations, the assessment of "effect" as the trigger and justification for application is not always easy,[81] because the prescribed constituent

78 As an exceptional warning, Ministry of Labor, Employment Security Bureau, 国外にわたる労働力需給制度研究会報告書 (Report of Research on Labor Demand and Supply System Reaching Abroad)(Feb. 1983) 3.イ. This report holds that the location of acts as well as results within Japan itself cannot sufficiently justify extraterritorial application, and it is necessary to consider the necessity and rationale of such application.

79 Ministry of Posts and Telecommunications, Broadcasting Bureau, ed., 国境を超えるテレビ(Television exceeding national boundaries)(第一法規, 1983) 24. It supports the extraterritorial application based on the effects doctrine but also refers to the necessity of consideration for international relationship and coordination.

80 See Supreme Court's judgment on CRT case (supra 1.2.4). As for academia, see infra note 103.

81 The FSA's Financial Law Commission Report (supra note 40), 2 (3). The report provides a case-study analysis of the rigging regulation, in particular, whether the FIEA should be applied to the rigging of shares of a foreign company that are primarily listed in the

elements themselves do not always allow the presumption of "effect" within the country.

2.2.5 Ambiguity of the Effects Doctrine and Excessiveness

In Japan, there are scholars and lawyers who consider the objective territoriality principle and the effects doctrine to be gradually related to each other (see supra 2.2.3.).[82] As we have observed above, they have commonalities but show divergences. The difference between the "result" as a constituent element and the "effect", which is implicitly behind the provision, is not taken into consideration.[83]

In Japan, the "effects doctrine" is very often referred to without any limitation or constraint, focusing only on the need for application in terms of domestic policies related to "effects."[84]

2.2.6 Blind Spot of the Effects Doctrine

There is an area that cannot easily be covered by the effects doctrine and its combination with the territoriality principle, namely, a part of the cases to be covered by the passive personality principle. Should we dare to make the latter principle converge with the effects doctrine with a very indirect and minor effect within the country? In what kind of general theoretical framework can we integrate the effects doctrine and the passive personality principle?

2.2.7 Necessity of Reconstructing the Active/Passive Personality Principle

The passive personality principle is applied in criminal law with the criterion of nationality. In other areas, there are extraterritorial provisions that

---

foreign home market but are also traded in the Japanese market. The Report points out the need to consider the degree of direct effect on the Japanese market caused by the rigging committed abroad. For similar considerations, see also the case study analysis given in the Report regarding insider trading (Case Study 4 ②), mass acquisition reporting requirement (5②), TOB (6①, ②).

82 小寺彰 A. Kodera, 独禁法の域外適用·域外執行をめぐる最近の動向(Recent trends of extraterritorial application and enforcement of Anti-monopoly Act), ジュリスト1254号 (2003) p. 64, at 67. 松尾直彦 N. Matsuo, 金融商品取引法〔第6版〕(Financial Instruments and Exchange Act, 6th ed.)(商事法務, 2021) 94.

83 The FSA Financial Law Commission Report (supra note 40) suggested extraterritorial application on the basis of the effects doctrine, with the concept of "effect" as distinct from "result" as a constituent element. See the Report, note 12 and the corresponding main text.

84 This is the case with the FSA Financial Law Commission Report (supra note 40).

protect those who are connected with Japan on the basis of criteria other than nationality.

The appropriateness of nationality as a connecting factor for identifying those to be protected may raise doubts. Moreover, personal ties to the country such as nationality, domicile and residence are not the exclusive criteria for defining the scope of application.

Furthermore, it should be noted that these personal or physical ties to the country are not exclusive. There could be room for extraterritorial application even in a case without any personal and physical connection with the country in our global era, as suggested by the observation of the CRT case.

On the other hand, regarding the subjects to be regulated, the principle of active personality should also be re-examined. The need for regulation has already been pointed out with regard to business groups controlled by a Japanese parent company and doing business abroad, as in the case of the Money Lending Business Act. It is said that the active personality principle adopted in Japanese criminal law is based on national allegiance. However, the rationality of citizenship as a criterion of obedience may be doubtful in some cases, and there may be other criteria to justify it. For example, compulsory obedience for participants in the market order based on domestic legal systems could be based on their active involvement, which is not limited by personal and physical factors.

2.3 *Coverage of Subjects to be Regulated and Consideration of Their Compulsory Compliance*

Although we must still be cautious in drawing generalized conclusions from our limited observation regarding the coverage of "to be protected" and "to be regulated" subjects by domestic regulations, we can point out some tendencies, especially in the case of enterprise groups, which involve several legal entities.

2.3.1 Subjects to be Regulated

In general, foreign enterprises are also subject to domestic laws.[85] Regulations target each legal entity within an enterprise group separately.[86] However, the

85 In the past, it was said, especially by public officials, that Japanese corporate law could not be applied to foreign subsidiaries of Japanese companies. However, this view is not supported at present.

86 For the FIEA, the provisions of the Act are applied on a legal entity basis. See the FSA's response to public comments dated December 21, 2009. If a foreign subsidiary of a Japanese company gives instructions on investment trust abroad, the FIEA is applied to the former as a legal entity. If a Japanese company manages an investment trust through a branch office abroad, the FIEA applies to the Japanese company itself as an investment trust manager. See the FSA's response to public comments dated December 21, 2010.

legal entity to be regulated is determined by considering the substance and actual state of the enterprise.[87] In the case of an enterprise group formed in other ways than a shareholding relationship, the agency relationship can be considered as the substance and scope of an enterprise unit.[88]

Thus, although the regulations are applied to a legal entity as a unit, the target entity is identified by considering the substance as an enterprise unit as well as the purpose and necessity of the regulations.[89] In this last respect, this type of identification is similar to the effects doctrine.[90]

2.3.2 Compulsory Obedience of Subjects to be Regulated and Its Legitimacy

There is a tendency that the scope of domestic laws with regard to the subjects to be regulated is determined on the basis of the purpose and necessity of the regulations. This could lead to the risk of extraterritorial application so excessive that those who are not aware of the need to comply with regulations are forced to do so, violate rules, and face sanctions. As a matter of fact, the

---

The so-called separate entity doctrine applies to the regulation of banks, and banking regulations also apply to the branch of a foreign bank in Japan. See, Banking Act, art. 47 (2).

87 There is a labor law case regarding the validity of layoffs due to the closure of the company in which the Labor Relations Commission's order is applied even to the wholly owned foreign parent company that has no direct connection with Japan but through this Japanese subsidiary. Tokyo Local Labor Commission's Order, Sept. 5, 1988. See supra 1.4.1.
For the regulation of banking business, the scope of the prohibition of other business reaches to the foreign subsidiary and foreign branch. See Banking Act Art. 12 and the FSA's Comprehensive Guideline for Supervision of Major Banks, etc., V-3-3-3 (as of July 2021). In this regard, there is a view that the regulations of registered financial institutions do not apply to transactions with non-resident customers by foreign branches of Japanese banks.

88 Under Japanese tax law, income tax is also imposed on foreign companies if they have a PE (permanent establishment) in Japan (Art. 4(2) and 138 of the Corporation Tax Act). The rationale for taxation in this case is the connection with Japan based on the PE. The practical issue is in which case the PE is verified to be within Japan, which is governed by Art. 141 of the Act. The case decided by the Tokyo High Court on March 14, 1984, concerns the taxation of a Panamanian company operating through the office of a sister company registered in Japan as the domicile of the former company. In this case, the Tokyo High Court did not apply Art. 141 item (1) regarding the company's own office located in Japan, nor item (3) regarding the location of the agency located in Japan, but Art. 141 item (2) regarding the location of equipment of construction as its activities within Japan.

89 There are also some examples in which the regulations are imposed not only on legal entities, but also on natural persons who are involved in the activities of enterprises. For example, see Art. 972 of the Companies Act (with punishment of crimes outside Japan by virtue of Art. 971), and Art. 8-2 of the Act on Certain Commercial Transactions.

90 With respect to the subjects to be protected, the Japanese court takes into account the substance of the enterprise and the relationships. See supra 1.2.4 on the CRT case.

examination of the legitimacy or justification in terms of compelled obedience is not always paid sufficient attention by administrative authorities.

In tax law, double taxation is an issue traditionally dealt with internationally, through bilateral treaties. In criminal law, the *ne bis in idem* principle is not applied in the international context, but only the reduction of the penalty is applied (Art. 5 of the Criminal Code) (cf. supra 1.3.1). In other fields, although the consideration in this regard is often made in terms of foreseeability,[91] the explicit and systematic examination of the legitimacy of compelling the targeted subjects to obey has yet to be incorporated into the framework of the discussion. As mentioned above, this point is easily left out of consideration from the perspective of the effects doctrine, which focuses narrowly on the necessity of applying domestic laws.

2.4 *Conflicts with Foreign Laws and Coordination*

2.4.1 Coordination Mechanisms: International Treaties, Domestic Legislation and Interpretation

Regarding the coordination of conflicts with foreign laws and policies, there are cases where a mechanism of coordination is established through international treaties, such as in the field of criminal law, tax law, competition law and social security law. In addition, positive comity is also recognized in some international agreements.[92]

Other coordination mechanisms adopted outside of treaties, especially those based on intergovernmental agreements, are difficult to view from the outside. As for cases before the courts applying domestic laws,[93] some of

91 The consideration regarding the legitimacy of the forced compliance of the subjects to be regulated seems to be reflected in the concept of "solicitation" to the Japanese market as stipulated in the FIEA and the APPI, which is said to be based on the target criteria.

92 As examples of mechanisms based on positive comity, i.e. the accommodation of foreign requests, see the Agreement between the Government of the United States of America and the Government of Japan concerning Cooperation on Anti-Competitive Activities (1999), Art. 5, and the Agreement between the Government of Japan and the European Community concerning Cooperation on Anti-Competitive Activities (2003), art. 5. For mutual assistance in enforcement, there are several treaties in such areas as punishment of crimes, extradition, investigation of criminal activities, tax collection, etc. However, there is a constitutional problem with this type of mechanism in view of the principles of *nullum crimen sine lege* (Art. 31) and no taxation without law (Art. 30 and 84). In addition, it is still doubtful whether the condition of double criminality is sufficient to meet the requirements of these two constitutional principles.

93 As for criminal law, there are no explicit provisions for self-restraint of domestic regulations based on passive comity, such as the principle of dual criminality, *lex minor*, and *no bis in idem* in the international context.

them can be seen as examples of passive comity for foreign countries.[94] And the need to refrain from applying domestic laws is often argued on the basis of consideration for foreign laws and policies.[95] In addition, there are some cases of so-called "substituted compliance", i.e. recognition of substitution of domestic regulations with foreign ones.[96]

Some commentators still suggest that extraterritorial application of law may violate the requirement of non-interference, and should be prohibited not by comity but by international law.[97] However, the criteria for such a limit are not at all clear.

2.4.2 Considerations Regarding Conflicts with Foreign Countries

What is the position of the Japanese government, including the administration and the courts, regarding conflicts with foreign countries? How does it respond to extraterritorial application by foreign countries? Is there any correlation between such response to foreign countries and Japan's own practices of extraterritoriality?

2.4.2.1 *Japan's Opposition to Foreign Extraterritorial Application*

There is a case of legislation as a countermeasure to foreign laws, namely the Act on Special Measures concerning the Recovery of Damage Resulting from the United States Anti-Dumping Act of 1916. It is noteworthy that this was not

94 For the international cartel in the Marine Horse case (see supra note 11), the JFTC verified the infringement of the AMA only with respect to customers within Japan. In the case of price-fixing for the North American route for the transportation business of automobiles, the JFTC verified the infringement of the AMA only for the part of the route from Japan to the United States.

95 Supreme Court Law Clerk 池原桃子(M. Ikehara)'s note on the case in 法曹時報71巻1号 (2019)198, at 217. See also JFTC Commissioner H. Odagiri's Supplementary Opinion to the decision of the JFTC of May 22, 2015 on the CRT Case (available at http://www.jftc.go.jp/shinketsu/itiran/160225.html).

96 Regarding gambling, which is generally illegal in Japan except for public gambling, the Tokyo District Court, in its judgment of January 29, 1993 regarding the junket tour from Japan to Las Vegas, referred to the casino authorized under the control and regulation of the Nevada State Government as similar in legality to Japanese public gambling.
Regarding the substitution of foreign regulations for domestic regulations on margin deposits for financial transactions, see Cabinet Office Order on Financial Instruments Business, etc., Art. 123 (10) and the FSA's response to public comments dated October 21, 2016.

97 小寺彰A. Kodera, 独禁法の域外適用·域外執行をめぐる最近の動向 (Recent trends of extraterritorial application and enforcement of Anti-monopoly Act), ジュリスト1254号 (2003) p. 64, at 65.

a response by the Japanese government alone, but was adopted after a dispute resolution by the WTO and in parallel with similar measures taken by the EU.[98]

Apart from such a legislative countermeasure, the Japanese government has often expressed its opposition to foreign countries (see supra note 4).

2.4.2.2 *Consideration of Consistency with the Application of Japanese Laws*

It is worth noting that there is a view that the extraterritorial application of Japanese law must be consistent with the government's reaction or opposition to foreign extraterritorial application.[99] This may lead to the view that Japan should (and could) abstain from extraterritorial application, even if it is required in accordance with the purpose and necessity of regulation, if it wishes to avoid or express opposition to foreign regulation.[100]

2.4.2.3 *Phase of Consideration Related to Conflicts: Examination of International Jurisdiction or Avoidance of Conflicts in a Specific Case*

As noted in this view, the consideration related to conflicts, even if made ad hoc, focuses mainly on the conflicts that actually occur in a particular case, i.e. the case of real conflict.[101] But we should keep in mind that there is always a need for international coordination of jurisdiction even in the case of false conflict, i.e. in the case where there is no real opposition. In this respect, the narrow focus on real conflict may lead to our view being excluded from the examination of international jurisdiction.

According to this view, if there were no fear of extraterritorial regulation by foreign countries, there would be no inherent impulse to limit Japan's extraterritorial regulation. On the other hand, Japan's extraterritorial application,

98 The Transfer Pricing Tax System, introduced in 1986, also has such a characteristic as legislation with extraterritorial scope by taking into account foreign tax systems.

99 For the Japanese government's amicus curiae brief in F. Hoffman-La Roche Ltd. v. Empagran S.A., see 白石忠志 T. Shiraishi, 独占禁止法 第3版 (Competition Law of Japan, 3rd ed.) (有斐閣, 2016) p. 182 note 141 (holding that it is necessary for the Japanese government, including the courts, to maintain consistency between the scope of application of Japanese laws and opposition to foreign extraterritorial application).

100 See also the Supreme Court's judgment on the extraterritorial application of U.S. patent law, which rejected it on public policy grounds. See supra 1.3.5.

101 Such a way of thinking is reflected in the opinion of the public official in charge of the APPI 2020 amendment, who says that what criteria are used by foreign laws in terms of scope should be considered by the Japanese government in delimiting the scope of Japanese laws and regulations. 田宮寿人 H. Tamiya, 行政法の域外適用に関する立法政策上の諸論点-個人情報保護法·令和2年改正の視点から-(Some issues of legislative policy on extraterritorial application of administrative law from the viewpoint of APPI 2020 amendment) 情報法制研究8号(2020) 63, 66.

even if required by domestic policy, would be abstained from in order to avoid foreign regulations.[102] This kind of abstention is passively less problematic in terms of international jurisdiction, but domestically it may raise the issue of equal treatment between "intra-territorial" and "extraterritorial" application of the same regulations.

3 Concluding Remarks: General Lessons from Japan's Experience

In Japan, the principle of protection and the principle of passive personality are not advocated unreservedly with regard to international jurisdiction. They are accompanied by considerations of possible conflicts with foreign countries. It is not necessary to recall Japan's own experience of imperialist invasion under the pretext of protecting its own citizens and self-preservation. The effects doctrine, which is becoming more and more dominant in the country, gives a more general and comprehensive formula that covers these two principles, but often lacks considerations of such conflicts with foreign countries.

With such a flattened formula of the effects doctrine, the focus is on the existence of an effect in the territory to justify extraterritorial application. A detailed assessment of the quality of the interests to be protected, whether national and social or individual, and of the scope of such protection, whether to cover only one's own citizens or not, is jeopardized.

Moreover, in focusing only on the necessity and demands of domestic policy, the effects doctrine runs the risk of ignoring the limits imposed by international law and comity, as well as the legitimacy of compelled obedience of the subjects to be regulated.

3.1 *Necessity of Examining the Limits of International Law*

It is necessary to distinguish the examination of international jurisdiction from the unilateral examination of the scope of application of domestic laws and regulations, which is mainly based on domestic policy. The verification of the existing basis of international jurisdiction does not lead directly to the latter. And the necessity of application based on domestic policy does not justify the former. It is always necessary to consider international jurisdiction separately from domestic policy.

102 The public official in charge of the amendment of the APPI of 2020 referred, as a personal opinion, to the need to consider diplomatic pros and cons in the case of extraterritorial application. See Tamiya, supra note 101, at 67–68, 74.

However, the consideration of international jurisdiction has not had much presence in the current practice and background thinking in Japan. Some Japanese scholars believe that a general international law on international jurisdiction has not been sufficiently established, especially for resolving the conflicts of jurisdiction, and continue to say that the exercise of jurisdiction is actually left to domestic ruling.[103]

But there is a leap of logic in their argument. Even if international law has not provided sufficiently clear principles or rules on international jurisdiction, this does not mean that there is no international law on it. The exercise of jurisdiction is not left to the full discretion of each country. The national exercise should be found to comply with international law with accountable justification. This kind of accountability will hopefully lead to the international refinement of a framework for the examination of international jurisdiction.

3.2 *Framework for the Examination of International Jurisdiction*

As a framework for examining international jurisdiction, the effects doctrine is too vague and flat. We need to list different kinds of connecting factors as well as interests and consider which factor is relevant for which kind of regulation and for which interests to be protected. It is also necessary to consider when and how extraterritorial application creates conflicts with other countries. The location of the actor, the act, and the things in foreign countries particularly and potentially cause conflicts. What additional considerations may justify extraterritorial application in such a case? (Point 1).

Even if the international jurisdiction is verified in an abstract way, it is necessary to examine the conflicts that the extraterritorial application of law creates with foreign countries in a concrete case. (Point 2) In addition to the verification of the jurisdiction as well as the tolerance by foreign countries (if any), it is necessary to justify the compelled obedience of the subject who is governed by the extraterritorial application. (Point 3).[104]

The problem is which of these points are to be regarded as limits imposed by international law. Point 1, by definition, refers to international law. What about point 2? Is it not left to international law, but to comity and diplomacy? What about point 3? Is there no limit imposed by the international law for

103 酒井啓亘他 (H. Sakai et al.), 国際法 (International Law) (有斐閣, 2011) pp.97–98. 小寺彰 A. Kodera, 国家管轄権の構造 (Structure of International Jurisdiction), 法学教室 254号 (2001) p. 121, at 117. 白石忠志 T. Shiraishi, 独占禁止法 第3版 (Competition Law of Japan, 3rd ed.) (有斐閣, 2016) p. 180.

104 See supra 2.3.2 and note 91 in particular.

imposing certain domestic regulations on a particular subject? Especially for individuals, it is necessary to take international human rights into account.

3.3 *Problems of Domestic Policy for Extraterritorial Application*

Determining the scope of application of domestic laws and regulations is a different issue from that of international jurisdiction. For the former, the examination of the domestic policy for application is most relevant. It should be clarified what kind of interest is considered to be protected by the regulations. In this regard, there may be a need to apply regulations for the protection of some interests where the cases concerned are not directly connected with the country in terms of nationality, domicile, residence of the subjects and the location of the actor, act and/or thing.

In our globalized era, economic activities may be merely virtually connected with the legal order of the home country, without any real physical connection. This is especially the case with the activities of multinational enterprise groups.[105] It is our urgent task to deal with such cases, both with respect to the unilateral identification of the scope of application of domestic regulations, and to the examination of international jurisdictional limits on such extraterritorial application.

---

105 See supra 1.2.4 and 1.4.4.3.

The Extraterritorial Application of Korean Laws

*Gyooho Lee**

1 Trends and General Practices

In general, the extraterritorial application of statutes and regulations is not preferred in Korea because Korean lawmakers are concerned about the potential violation of the sovereignty of foreign countries that might result. However, in some specific legal fields, prescriptive jurisdiction has been extended to activities carried out outside Korea. These exceptions are as follows: (i) the Monopoly Regulation and Fair Trade Act (hereinafter "Fair Trade Act");[1] (ii) the Financial Investment Services and Capital Markets Act (hereinafter "KCMA");[2] (iii) the Telecommunications Business Act;[3] (iv) the Act on Promotion of Information and Communications Network Utilization and Information Protection, etc.;[4] and (v) the Act on Reporting and Using Specified Financial Transaction

* Professor of Law, Chung-Ang University School of Law; Seoul, Republic of Korea.

1 The current version of this Act is Act No. 17799, comprehensively revised on December 29, 2020 and effective since December 30, 2022. See K. Suk, *Private International Law and International Litigation*, Pakyoungsa Publ. Seoul (2012) Vol. 5, Chapter 3; S. Choi, 'Extraterritorial application of Competition Law' (2009) HUFS *Law Review*, Vol. 33, No. 1, pp. 205–233; D. Suh & D. Lee, 'A Study on the Extraterritorial Application of the Korean Fair Trade Act' (June 2005), *Public Law*, Vol. 33, No. 5, pp. 579–602.

2 Act No. 19211, revised on December 31, 2022 and effective since January 1, 2023 in accordance with the revision of another law. See K. Suk & S. Jung, 'An Introductory Study on the International Capital Market Regulations' (2010) *The Korean Journal of Securities Law*, Vol. 11, No. 2, pp. 27–82; S. Cheong, 'Extraterritoriality of the Capital Markets Act in Connection with Cross – Border Securities Transactions–Focused on the Entry Regulation on Foreign Brokers and Dealers' (2016) *Korean Journal of International Trade and Business Law*, Vol. 25, No. 1, pp. 247–298; J. D. Lee, 'Extraterritorial Application of Financial Investment Services and Capital Markets Act: Focused on the Overseas Securities Issuance' (2016) *Journal of Financial Regulation and Supervision*, Vol. 3, No. 2, pp. 23–58.

3 Act No. 18869, revised on June 10, 2022 and effective since December 11, 2022. See H. Kim, 'A Study on Extraterritorial Applications to Global Platform Operators: Focused on the Introduction of the Status Survey on Vaule-added Telecommunications Business under the Telecommunications Business Act' (June 2020) *Journal of Cybercommunication Academic Society*, Vol. 37 No. 2, pp. 103–136.

4 Act No. 19154, revised on January 3, 2023 and effective since July 4, 2023.

 | DOI:10.1163/9789004720183_011

Information.[5] Each of these laws applies to acts done outside Korea if such acts affect the domestic market.[6]

The development of extraterritoriality in Korea was influenced by an important case initiated under a previous version of the Fair Trade Act. In that case, a group of manufacturers and sellers of graphite electrodes had reached an agreement in a foreign country to determine and maintain the prices of graphite electrodes for the global market. The implementation of that agreement affected the Korean market, since it determined the sales prices of graphite electrodes in Korea.[7]

The Korean Supreme Court held in that case that "Even if a foreign company has reached an agreement in a foreign country to jointly restrict competition with other companies, the Korean Fair Trade Act applies to the agreement to the extent that the agreement has affected the domestic market if the domestic market is included in the subject of the agreement, so that it has the resulting impact on the domestic market."[8] At the time, the Fair Trade Act contained no explicit provision regarding its extraterritorial reach. The Court explained its holding as follows:

> In consideration of the fact that the purpose of the Fair Trade Act is to encourage creative business activities and protect consumers as well as facilitate balanced development of the national economy by promoting fair and free competition through the regulation of unfair collective activities of business operators (Article 1), the fact that the business operator who conducts unfair collective activities is stipulated to be the "operator of manufacturing business, service business and other businesses" and is not limited to be domestic business operators (Article 2), and the fact that there is a need to include foreign business operators in the scope of the application of the Fair Trade Act in the case where an unfair collective activity in a foreign country affects the domestic market, the Fair Trade Act shall be applied within the limit of the effect on the domestic market of a consensus, if a foreign business operator reaches a consensus jointly

5 Act No. 18662, revised on December 28, 2021 and effective since the same date.

6 Article 3 of Monopoly Regulation and Fair Trade Act; Article 6 of the Act on Reporting and Using Specified Financial Transaction Information; Article 2 of Financial Investment Services and Capital Markets Act; Article 2 bis of Telecommunications Business Act; and Article 5 bis of the Act on Promotion of Information and Communications Network Utilization and Information Protection.

7 Korean Supreme Court Decision on March 24, 2006 (Case No. 2004 Du 11275) (*Showa Denko K.K.* (昭和電工) Co. Ltd. v. Korea Fair Trade Commission).

8 Id.

with another business operator to limit competition and that such consensus includes the domestic market and affected the domestic market.

In order to eliminate unnecessary controversy over the extraterritorial application of the Fair Trade Act, an explicit provision regarding the law's scope was inserted, stating that "This Act shall also apply to acts done outside Korea, if such acts affect the domestic market." This provision was introduced by Act No. 7315, revised on December 31, 2004 and effective since April 1, 2005.[9] In other words, the graphite electrode case marked a significant shift in Korea's approach to extraterritoriality in the field of fair trade law.

The resulting concern was that the law's scope of application might be overly extended to all acts affecting competition in domestic markets. Hence, the Korean Supreme Court limited the scope of application of the Korean Fair Trade Act to acts having a direct, substantial, and reasonably predictable effect on the domestic market.[10] In this context, the Korean Supreme Court held that a court should determine specifically on a case-by-case basis whether an act affects the domestic market, while comprehensively taking into account the content of the act at issue and the intention with which the act was pursued, the features of the goods or services that are subject to the act, the transaction structure, and the content and extent of its impact on the domestic market.[11] However, in *Asiana Airlines, Co. Ltd., v. Korea Fair Trade Commission*, the Korean Supreme Court held that if the domestic market is included in the subject of an agreement restricting competition jointly conducted by business

9 Article 2 bis (Application to Overseas Acts) of the Fair Trade Act prior to its revision of 2020 prescribed that "This Act shall also apply to acts done outside Korea, if such acts affect the domestic market." This Article was newly inserted by Act No. 7315 on December. 31, 2004. Article 2 bis of the Fair Trade Act was moved to Article 3 under the Fair Trade Act of 2020 (Act No. 17799, comprehensively revised on December 29, 2020 and effective since December 30, 2021). Hence, it is currently prescribed under Article 3 of the Fair Trade Act.

10 Korean Supreme Court on May 16, 2014 (Case No. 2012 Du 5466) (*Asiana Airlines, Co. Ltd., v. Korea Fair Trade Commission*); S. Cho, 'The Study on the Limits of Extraterritorial Application in Monopoly Regulation Law-Centered on Hoffman-La Roche Cases' (June 30, 2022) *Culture, Media and Entertainment Law*, Vol. 16, No. 1, p. 194.

11 Korean Supreme Court on May 16, 2014 (Case No. 2012 Du 5466)(*Asiana Airlines, Co. Ltd., v. Korea Fair Trade Commission*); Korean Supreme Court on May 16, 2014 (Case No. 2012 Du 13269)(*Nippon Cargo Airline Co. Ltd. v. Korea Fair Trade Commission*); Korean Supreme Court on May 16, 2014 (Case No. 2012 Du 13689) (*All Nippon Airways Co., Ltd.* (全日本空輸株式会社) *v. Korea Fair Trade Commission*); Korean Supreme Court on December 24, 2014(Case No. 2012 Du 6216)(*Air France-KLM v. Korea Fair Trade Commission*). See J. Ju, 'A Comment on Some Problems of Extraterritorial Application of Korean Monopoly Regulation Act – Supreme Court 2014. 5. 16. declared 2012 Du 13689 Decision concerning International Cartel of Air Cargo Carriers –' (April 2017) *International Trade Law*, Vol. 134, pp. 53–83.

operators abroad, the agreement will affect the domestic market unless there are special circumstances and the act conducted abroad constitutes an illegal cartel conduct under Article 19 (1)[12] of the former Fair Trade Act.[13]

The other laws mentioned above likewise include provisions explicitly permitting their application to foreign conduct on the basis of domestic effects. Article 2 of the Financial Investment Services and Capital Markets Act provides that "Any activities conducted in a foreign country the effects of which extend to the territory of the Republic of Korea shall be governed by this Act." It was introduced into the Act by Act No. 8635, enacted on August 3, 2007 and effective since February 4, 2009.[14] Article 2 bis of the Telecommunications Business Act prescribes that "This Act shall apply to any conduct committed overseas if such conduct affects the Korean market or users in the market." It was newly introduced by Act No. 16019, revised on December 24, 2018. Article 5 bis of the Act on Promotion of Information and Communications Network Utilization and Information Protection, etc states that "This Act shall apply to any conduct committed overseas if such conduct affects the Korean market or users in the market." It was newly inserted into the Act on by Act No. 17358, revised on June 9, 2020. Article 6 paragraph 2 of the Act on Reporting and Using Specified Financial Transaction Information, under the title "Notification of Data of Foreign Exchange Transactions, etc., stipulates that "Any activities conducted in a foreign country in terms of financial transactions of virtual asset service providers the effects of which extend to the territory of the Republic of Korea shall be governed by this Act." This provision was introduced into the Act by Act No. 17113 revised on March 24, 2020 and effective since March 25, 2021. These extraterritorial application provisions are based on the effects doctrine established by the precedents of the federal courts of the United States.[15]

---

12 Article 19 (1) of the Fair Trade Act prior to its revision of 2020 was moved to Article 40 (1) of the Fair Trade Act of 2020 (Act No. 17799, comprehensively revised on December 29, 2020 and effective since December 30, 2021).

13 Korean Supreme Court on May 16, 2014 (Case No. 2012 Du 5466) (*Asiana Airlines, Co. Ltd., v. Korea Fair Trade Commission*).

14 There have been no court cases related to the extraterritorial application of this law in virtual asset cases. See E. Lee, 'A Study on the Extraterritorial Application of Virtual Assets-Focused on U.S. Laws and Regulations-' (February 2022) *Law Review (Institute of Law Studies, Pusan National University)*, Vol. 63 No. 1 p. 24.

15 J. Lee, 'Capital Markets Law and Its Implication to Choice-of-law Rules for Prospectus Liability', *The 10th China-Korea Symposium on Private International Law held on October 29, 2021*, p. 151; J. Lee, 'A Function of the Extraterritorial Application Clause in the Korean Capital Markets Law: Focusing on the Applicable Law of Prospectus Liability in Cross-border Securities Offering' (July 2020) *Dong-A Journal of International Business Transactions Law*, Issue No. 30, pp. 179–225.

The table below illustrates the interaction between the Korean Criminal Code (KCC) and the Korean Capital Markets Act (KCMA), and the resulting outcome in different factual constellations. For example, consider a case where a domestic financial investment business entity violates the KCMA abroad. Article 3 of the KCC (applicability to crimes committed by a Korean national

TABLE 10.1 Interrelations between the applicability of the KCC and Article 2 of the KCMA

<table>
<tr><th>No.</th><th>Issuer's nationality</th><th>Market's location</th><th>Investor's location</th><th>Type of the scope of application of the KCC</th><th>Possibility of punishment and function of extraterritorial application provision</th></tr>
<tr><td>1</td><td>Korean</td><td>Korean</td><td>Korean</td><td rowspan="2">Territoriality principle (Article 2)</td><td rowspan="2">Punishable, irrespective of extraterritorial application</td></tr>
<tr><td>2</td><td>Korean</td><td>Korean</td><td>Foreign</td></tr>
<tr><td>3</td><td>Korean</td><td>Korean</td><td>Korean</td><td rowspan="2">Nationality principle (Article 3)</td><td rowspan="2">Punishable, illegality deniable</td></tr>
<tr><td>4</td><td>Korean</td><td>Korean</td><td>Foreign</td></tr>
<tr><td>5</td><td>Foreign</td><td>Korean</td><td>Korean</td><td rowspan="2">Territoriality principle (Article 2)</td><td rowspan="2">Punishable, irrespective of extraterritorial application</td></tr>
<tr><td>6</td><td>Foreign</td><td>Korean</td><td>Foreign</td></tr>
<tr><td>7</td><td>Foreign</td><td>Korean</td><td>Korean</td><td rowspan="2">Foreigner's crime at foreign country (Article 6)</td><td>Punishable, possibly limiting Article 6</td></tr>
<tr><td>8</td><td>Foreign</td><td>Korean</td><td>Foreign</td><td>Unpunishable, confirming no effects on Korea</td></tr>
</table>

SOURCE: J. LEE, 'CAPITAL MARKETS LAW AND ITS IMPLICATION TO CHOICE-OF-LAW RULES FOR PROSPECTUS LIABILITY', *THE 10TH CHINA-KOREA SYMPOSIUM ON PRIVATE INTERNATIONAL LAW HELD ON OCTOBER 29, 2021*, P. 163.

abroad) would indicate that a punishment could be imposed under Korean law. In this context, however, due to the restrictions under Article 8 of the KCC (regarding exceptions if there are special provisions in other statues) and Article 2 of the KCMA (reflecting the principle of territoriality), the crime would not fall within the scope of Korean law.

2 Extraterritorial Laws Related to Multilateral or Regional Treaties

The Republic of Korea signed the OECD Anti-Bribery Convention and the UN Convention against Corruption (hereinafter "UNCAC") in 2003. The Act on Special Cases Concerning Confiscation and Recovery of Stolen Assets was passed by the National Assembly on February 29, 2008, resulting in the official ratification and implementation of the convention.[16] However, it does not include any provisions which encourage the extraterritorial application of the domestic law.

3 The Role of International Law

Article 6(1) of the Korean Constitution prescribes that "Treaties duly concluded and promulgated under the Constitution and the generally recognized rules of international law shall have the same effect as the domestic laws of the Republic of Korea." Hence, treaties ratified, accessed or approved by South Korea have the same effect as the domestic laws of the Republic of Korea. For example, South Korea adheres to the territoriality principle set forth in the Paris Convention for the Protection of Industrial Property[17] and the Berne Convention for the Protection of Literary and Artistic Works[18] as their signatory.[19]

---

16 Act No. 8993, enacted on March 28, 2008 and effective on April 26, 2008.

17 Paris Convention for the Protection of Industrial Property, March 20, 1883, revised at Brussels on Dec. 14, 1900, revised at Washington on June 2, 1911, revised at the Hague on Nov. 6, 1925, revised at London on June 2, 1934, revised at Lisbon on Oct. 31, 1958, revised at Stockholm on July 14, 1967, 21 U.S.T. 1538, 828 U.N.T.S. 305.

18 Berne Convention for the Protection of Literary and Artistic Works of Sept. 9, 1886, completed at Paris on May 4, 1896, revised at Berlin on Nov. 13, 1908, revised at Berne on Mar. 20, 1914, revised at Rome on June 2, 1928, revised at Brussels on June 26, 1948, revised at Stockholm on July 14, 1967, revised at Paris on July 24, 1971, amended on Oct. 2, 1979, S. Treaty Doc. No. 27, 99th Cong., 2d Sess. (1986), 828 U.N.T.S. 221.

19 G. Lee, 'Extraterritorial Application of Intellectual Property Law' (June 2022) *Korea Private International Law Journal*, Vol. 28, No. 1, pp. 243–292.

Korean law also takes the view that the international law principle of non-interference prevents extraterritoriality unless the lawmaking state has established an acceptable jurisdictional basis for regulation.

4 The Role of International Comity

The Korean Supreme Court has taken the principle of international comity into account with respect to Article 2 bis of the Korean Fair Trade Act.[20] In a case involving the airline industry, it held as follows:

> If the conduct of a foreign business in a foreign country affects the domestic market, the requirements of Article 2 bis of the Korean Fair Trade Act are met. Hence, even if it is an act that is allowed under a foreign law or policy of a foreign government with respect to the act, it does not necessarily result in the limitation to the application of the Korean Fair Trade Act. However, if a domestic law conflicts with a foreign law with respect to the same act and, thus, the business cannot end up choosing a legitimate act, the exclusive application of the domestic law cannot be forced. Hence, if the necessity to respect foreign laws and policies is significantly superior to the one for the application of the Korean Fair Trade Act, the application of the Korean Fair Trade Act should be limited. In determining whether the application of the Korean Fair Trade Act should be limited, the court should take into account comprehensively the following factors: (i) The impact of the act on the domestic market, (ii) The degree of the foreign government's involvement in the act; (iii) The degree of conflict between domestic and foreign laws and policies, (iv) The disadvantage to foreign businesses and the extent to which the legitimate interests of the foreign government are hindered in cases where the Korean Fair Trade Act is applied to the act in question due to conflict between domestic and foreign laws and policies.[21]

20 G. J. Choi, 'Standards of Extraterritorial Application of Competition Law: Case Study of Air Cargo Cartel' (2016) *Korean Economic Law Association*, Vol. 15, No. 1, p. 42.

21 The Korean Supreme Court Decision on May 16, 2014 (Case No. 2012 Du 5466) (*Asiana Airlines, Co. Ltd., v. Korea Fair Trade Commission*).

5 Bases for the Application of Statutes or Regulations to Foreign Conduct

5.1 *Nationality of the Actor*

The Korean Criminal Act prescribes that it shall apply to all Korean nationals who commit crimes outside the territory of the Republic of Korea.[22] This provision applies to all crimes committed by Korean nationals outside Korea. For example, a Korean who gambles in Las Vegas will be punished for the gambling crime even though it is not a crime in Nevada. It is a good example which applies to wholly foreign conduct on the basis of the nationality of the actor.

In addition, Article 3 (2) of the Act on Punishment of Crimes Under Jurisdiction of the International Criminal Court applies to any Korean national who commits a crime provided for in this Act outside the territory of the Republic of Korea.

5.2 *Nationality of a Person Harmed by the Conduct ("Passive Personality")*

Article 3 (4) of the Act on Punishment of Crimes under Jurisdiction of the International Criminal Court states that "This Act shall apply to any foreigner who commits a crime provided for in this Act against the Republic of Korea or its people outside the territory of the Republic of Korea."

5.3 *Domestic Effects of the Conduct in Question*

5.3.1 An Overview

As discussed above, there are several statutes that apply to wholly foreign conduct on the basis of the domestic effects of the conduct in question in Korea. They are as follows: (i) the Monopoly Regulation and Fair Trade Act;[23] (ii) the Financial Investment Services and Capital Markets Act;[24] (iii) the Telecommunications Business Act;[25] (iv) the Act on Promotion of Information and Communications Network Utilization and Information Protection, etc.;[26] and (v) the Act on Reporting and Using Specified Financial Transaction

22 Article 3 (Crimes by Koreans outside Korea) of the Korean Criminal Act.

23 The current version of this Act is Act No. 17799, comprehensively revised on December 29, 2020 and effective since December 30, 2022.

24 Act No. 19211, revised on December 31, 2022 and effective since January 1, 2023, followed by the revision of another law.

25 Act No. 19153, revised on January 3, 2023 and effective since July 4, 2023.

26 Act No. 19154, revised on January 3, 2023 and effective since July 4, 2023.

Information.[27] Those laws shall apply to acts done outside Korea if such acts affect the domestic market.[28]

5.3.2 Act on Promotion of Information and Communications Network Utilization and Information Protection, etc.

Pursuant to Article 136 of the Korean Copyright Act, which allows for criminal sanctions in the event of copyright infringement crimes, online information which violates the Korean Copyright Act can fall within the scope of Article 44-7 (1) 9 of the Act on Promotion Of Information And Communications Network Utilization And Information Protection (hereinafter "Information and Communications Network Act"). Article 44-7 (Prohibition on Circulation of Unlawful Information) of that Act states that "(1) No one may circulate any of the following information through an information and communications network: [...]

9. Other information with content that attempts to commit, aids, or abets a crime."

Currently, the Korea Communications Standards Commission is actively responding to overseas copyright infringement by treating information resulting from overseas online piracy as illegal information under Article 44-7 (1) 9 of the Information and Communications Network Act, and by requesting a correction measure which blocks access to overseas online sites from domestic key telecommunication operators. Therefore, the Copyright Act applies to copyright infringement on domestic online sites, but the Information and Communications Network Act and the Korea Communications Standards Act apply to copyright infringement on overseas online sites. In this sense, the regulations on online piracy are bifurcated.[29]

We recognize that regular access blocking measures are not suitable for effectively preventing online copyright infringement. Due to the technical structure of the Internet, access blocking measures can be easily bypassed, and in order to avoid access blocking measures, the infringing server can be moved abroad and the pirated contents can be re-hosted and transmitted again.

---

27 Act No. 18662, revised on December 28, 2021 and effective since December 28, 2021.

28 Article 3 of Monopoly Regulation and Fair Trade Act; Article 6 of the Act on Reporting and Using Specified Financial Transaction Information; Article 2 of Financial Investment Services and Capital Markets Act; Article 2 bis of Telecommunications Business Act; and Article 5 bis of the Act on Promotion of Information and Communications Network Utilization and Information Protection.

29 H. Lee, 'Research on Legislative Measures to Prevent the Spread of Copyright Infringement by Links' (Summer 2020) *Copyright Quarterly*, Vol. 33, No. 2, p. 196.

5.4 *The Principle of Universal Jurisdiction*

5.4.1 Criminal Act

Korea has revised the Korean Criminal Act to implement the United States Convention against Transnational Organized Crime and its supplementary protocols (the Protocol on the Prevention of Trafficking in Persons and the Protocol to Prevent, Suppress and Punish Trafficking in Persons Especially Women and Children). The Korean Criminal Act of 2013 adopted the universality principle[30] to prevent those transnational organized crimes in terms of trafficking in persons.[31] The universality principle applied to crimes of (i) kidnapping or abduction of minors,[32] (ii) kidnapping, abduction, etc. for purpose of indecent acts, etc.,[33] (iii) trafficking in persons,[34] (iv) inflicting or causing another's bodily injury while in kidnapping, abduction, trafficking

---

30 Article 296-2 (Universality) of the Korean Criminal Act prescribes that "Articles 287 through 292 and Article 294 shall also apply to aliens who commit any of the crimes in these Articles outside the territory of the Republic of Korea."

31 Act No. 11731, revised on April 5, 2013 and effective on June 19, 2013. The current version of the Korean Criminal Act is Act No. 17571, revised on December 8, 2020 and effective since December 9, 2021.

32 Article 287 (Kidnapping or Abduction of Minors) of the Korean Criminal Act prescribes that "A person who obtains and maintains a minor under the control of his or hers or a third person by means of the threat, use of force or other forms of coercion, or by means of fraud, deception or enticement shall be punished by imprisonment with labor for not more than ten years."

33 Article 288 (Kidnapping, Abduction, etc. for Purpose of Indecent Acts, etc.) of the Korean Criminal Act prescribes that

(1) A person who obtains and maintains another under the control of his or hers or a third person by means of the threat, use of force or other forms of coercion, or by means of fraud, deception or enticement for the purpose of engaging in an indecent act, sexual intercourse or marriage, or for gain shall be punished by imprisonment with labor for at least one year up to ten years.

(2) A person who obtains and maintains another under the control of his or hers or a third person by means of the threat, use of force or other forms of coercion, or by means of fraud, deception or enticement for the purpose of labor exploitation, sex trafficking, sexual exploitation, or the acquisition of organs, shall be punished by imprisonment with labor for at least two years up to 15 years.

(3) The preceding paragraph shall apply to a person who obtains and maintains another under the control of his or hers or a third person by means of the threat, use of force or other forms of coercion, or by means of fraud, deception or enticement for the purpose of transporting him or her out of the Republic of Korea, or a person who transports such a victim out of the Republic of Korea.

34 Article 289 (Trafficking in Persons) of the Korean Criminal Act prescribes that

(1) A person who buys or sells another shall be punished by imprisonment with labor for not more than seven years.

in persons, transportation, etc.,[35] (v) killing another or causing death of another while in kidnapping, abduction, trafficking in persons, transportation, etc.,[36] (vi) receiving, harboring, etc. of person kidnapped, abducted, trafficked, or transported,[37] and (vii) their attempts.[38] Articles 287 through 292 and Article 294 of the Criminal Act shall apply to aliens who commit any of the crimes in these Articles outside the territory of the Republic of Korea.

---

(2) A person who buys or sells another for the purpose of engaging in an indecent act, sexual intercourse, marriage, or for gain, shall be punished by imprisonment with labor for at least one year up to ten years.

(3) A person who buys or sells another for the purpose of labor exploitation, sex trafficking, sexual exploitation, or the acquisition of organs shall be punished by imprisonment with labor for at least two years up to 15 years.

(4) The preceding paragraph shall apply to a person who buys or sells another for the purpose of transporting him or her out of the Republic of Korea, or a person who transports a purchased person out of the Republic of Korea."

35 Article 290 (Inflicting or Causing Another's Bodily Injury while in Kidnapping, Abduction, Trafficking in Persons, Transportation, etc.) of the Korean Criminal Act prescribes that

(1) A person who commits any of the crimes of Articles 287 through 289, thereby inflicting the injury of a victim of such crime, shall be punished by imprisonment with labor for at least three years up to 25 years.

(2) A person who commits any of the crimes of Articles 287 through 289, thereby causing the injury of a victim of such crime, shall be punished by imprisonment with labor for at least two years up to 20 years.

36 Article 291 (Killing Another or Causing Death of Another while in Kidnapping, Abduction, Trafficking in Persons, Transportation, etc.)

(1) A person who commits any of the crimes of Articles 287 through 289, thereby killing a victim of such crime, shall be punished by death or imprisonment with labor for life or for at least seven years.

(2) A person who commits any of the crimes of Articles 287 through 289, thereby causing the death of a victim of such crime, shall be punished by imprisonment with labor for life or for at least five years.

37 Article 292 (Receiving, Harboring, etc. of Person Kidnapped, Abducted, Trafficked, or Transported) of the Korean Criminal Act prescribes that

(1) A person who receives or harbors a victim of any of the crimes of Articles 287 through 289, shall be punished by imprisonment with labor for not more than seven years.

(2) The preceding paragraph shall apply to a person who recruits, transfers or delivers another with the intent to commit any of the crimes of Articles 287 through 289.

38 Article 294 (Attempts) of the Korean Criminal Act prescribes that "Attempts to commit any of the crimes of Articles 287 through 289 and Articles 290 (1), 291 (1) and 292 (1) shall be punished."

5.4.2 The Act on Counter-Terrorism for the Protection of Citizens and Public Security

The Act on Counter-terrorism for The Protection of Citizens and Public Security applies also to a foreigner who commits a crime organizing a terrorist group outside Korea.[39,40] It applies the principle of universal jurisdiction. The purpose of this Act is to protect the life and property of citizens and to ensure national and public security against terrorism by prescribing matters necessary for the prevention of terrorism, counter-terrorism activities, etc. and compensation for damage, etc. caused by terrorism. It applies the universality principle to a crime(s) organizing a terrorist group(s).

5.4.3 The Act on Punishment of Crimes under Jurisdiction of the International Criminal Court[41]

The Rome Statute of the International Criminal Court is the treaty that established the International Criminal Court (ICC). It was adopted at a diplomatic conference in Rome, Italy on 17 July 1998 and it entered into force on 1 July 2002. The Act on Punishment of Crimes under Jurisdiction of the International Criminal Court was enacted to domestically implement the Rome Statute on the International Criminal Court ratified on November 13, 2002. It intended to provide punishment rules for genocide, crimes against humanity and war crimes under the jurisdiction of the International Criminal Court and special provisions in the criminal law, such as the ones punishing crimes committed by foreigners abroad. It is viewed to adopt the principle of universal jurisdiction.[42]

6 The Application of Statutes and Regulations on the Basis of Local Conduct (Territorial Links)

6.1 *Unfair Competition Prevention and Trade Secret Protection Act*[43]

The Unfair Competition Prevention and Trade Secret Protection Act provides a criminal sanction for any person who uses trade secrets in a foreign country

39 Article 19 (Universality) of The Act on Counter-terrorism for The Protection Of Citizens And Public Security prescribes that "A foreigner who commits a crime provided for in Article 17 outside the territory of the Republic of Korea shall also be subject to the application of domestic Acts."

40 J. Ahn, 'Cyberterror Regulatory Legislations and Extraterritorial Application of Domestic Law : Focused on Standards of Exercising Protective Jurisdiction' (October 2016) *Korean Journal of Military Art and Science*, Vol. 72, No. 3, pp. 25–52.

41 Act No. 10577, revised on April 12, 2011 and effective since the same date.

42 S. Kim, *Criminal Law*, 9th ed., Sojin Publishing Co. 2020, p. 52.

43 Act No. 18548, revised on December 7, 2021 and April 20, 2022. See D. Choi, 'A Possibility of Extraterritorial Application of a Trade Secrets Protection Act in International Litigation –

or commits certain acts while knowing that trade secrets will be used in the foreign country. In other words, in addition to prescribing a criminal sanction for any person who uses trade secrets in another country, it states that it punishes any person who commits covered acts within Korea, while knowing that trade secrets will be used in a foreign country. Covered acts include: (i) Acquiring, using or leaking to any third party trade secrets for the purpose of making an improper profit or causing damage to a person who possesses trade secrets; (ii) Unauthorized release of trade secrets out of a designated place for the purpose of making an improper profit or causing damage to a person who possesses trade secrets; (iii) Continuing to possess trade secrets even after a request to delete or return them by the person who possesses such trade secrets for the purpose of making an improper profit or causing damage to a person who possesses trade secrets; (iv) Any act of acquiring trade secrets by theft, fraud, threat, or other improper means; or (v) Any act of acquiring or using[44] trade secrets with knowledge of the commission of an act enumerated in (i) to (iv).[45]

A Prediction Through the Principle of Formation of Customary International Law -' (2021) *Hanyang Law Review*, Vol. 38, No. 1. pp. 227–276.

44 It excludes an act using trade secrets by a person who has properly acquired them through a transaction within the scope of the rights the person has properly acquired through the transaction. See Article 13 (1) of Unfair Competition Prevention and Trade Secret Protection Act.

45 Article 18 paragraph 1 of Unfair Competition Prevention and Trade Secret Protection Act prescribes that "Any person who uses trade secrets in a foreign country or commits any of the following acts while knowing that trade secrets will be used in a foreign country, shall be punished by imprisonment with labor for not more than 15 years or by a fine not exceeding 1.5 billion won: Provided, That where he/she is punished by a fine and the amount equal to ten times the amount of proprietary benefits acquired by the violation exceeds 1.5 billion won, a fine equal to two to ten times the amount of proprietary benefits shall be imposed.

1. Any of the following acts committed for the purpose of making an improper profit or causing damage to a person who possesses trade secrets:
    (a) Acquiring, using, or leaking to any third party, trade secrets;
    (b) Unauthorized release of trade secrets out of a designated place;
    (c) Continuing to possess trade secrets even after a request to delete or return them by the person who possesses such trade secrets;
2. Any act of acquiring trade secrets by steal, fraud, intimidation, or other improper means;
3. Any act of acquiring or using (except for the uses permitted under Article 13 (1)) trade secrets with knowledge of the commission of an act described in subparagraph 1 or 2."

6.2 *Act on Prevention of Divulgence and Protection of Industrial Technology*[46]

The Act on Prevention of Divulgence and Protection of Industrial Technology (hereinafter 'Industrial Technology Protection Act') identifies a group of technologies that have been designated as particularly important to Korea's technological, economic, and security interests.

The Act provides enhanced protection of "national core technology," whose leak abroad could have a material adverse effect on national security and development of the national economy, since it has high technological and economic value in the Korean and overseas markets or brings high growth potential to its related industries.

The Act provides that no person shall engage in any of the following acts:

(i) Acquiring the industrial technology of any institution possessing industrial technology obtained by means of theft, deception, threat, or other improper means or using or publicizing such industrial technology (including providing information to a specific person in secret; hereinafter the same shall apply);

(ii) In cases of a person who has a duty to maintain confidentiality of industrial technology under Article 34 or in accordance with a contract, etc. with an institution possessing industrial technology, divulging industrial technology for the purpose of obtaining unjust enrichment or causing loss to the institution possessing industrial technology; using or publicizing the divulged industrial technology; or causing a third person to make use thereof;

(iii) Acquiring, using, or publicizing industrial technology, knowing that any act under (i) or (ii) is involved in the industrial technology, or using or publicizing industrial technology, knowing, after acquiring the industrial technology, that any act under (i) or (ii) is involved in the industrial technology;

(iv) Acquiring, using, or publicizing industrial technology without knowing, by gross negligence, that any act under (i) or (ii) is involved in the industrial technology; or using or publicizing industrial technology without knowing, by gross negligence after acquiring the industrial technology, that any act under (i) or (ii) is involved in the industrial technology;

(v) Exporting national core technology without obtaining approval under Article 11 (1) of the Act on Prevention of Divulgence and Protection of

46 Act No. 19166, revised on January 3, 2023 and effective on April 4, 2023.

Industrial Technology or with such approval approved by improper means;

(vi) Conducting cross-border acquisition, merger, etc. without obtaining approval under Article 11-2 (1) of the Act on Prevention of Divulgence and Protection of Industrial Technology or with such approval obtained by fraud or other improper means, with intent to use national core technology in a foreign country or to cause national core technology to be used in a foreign country;

(vii) Conducting cross-border acquisition, merger, etc. without filing a report under Article 11-2 (5) and (6) of the Act on Prevention of Divulgence and Protection of Industrial Technology or with such report filed by fraud or other improper means, with intent to use national core technology in a foreign country or to cause national core technology to be used in a foreign country;

(viii) In cases of a person who has a duty to maintain confidentiality of industrial technology under Article 34 of the Act on Prevention of Divulgence and Protection of Industrial Technology or in accordance with a contract, etc. with an institution possessing industrial technology and is requested by a relevant institution possessing industrial technology to return the special media records, such as documents, drawings, and electronic records concerning industrial technology, or to delete the industrial technology; refusing to comply with, or evading, such request or keeping a copy for the purpose of obtaining unjust enrichment or causing loss to the institution possessing industrial technology;

(ix) Failing to comply with an order issued by the Minister of Trade, Industry and Energy under Article 11 (5) or (7) or Article 11-2 (7) or (9) of the Act on Prevention of Divulgence and Protection of Industrial Technology.[47]

Any person who commits an offense under any of (i) through (iii) mentioned above with intent to use national core technology in a foreign country or to cause national core technology to be used in a foreign country shall be punished by imprisonment with labor for a limited term of not less than three years. In such cases, a fine not exceeding 1.5 billion won shall be concurrently imposed.[48]

---

47 Article 14 of the Act on Prevention of Divulgence and Protection of Industrial Technology.

48 Article 36 (1) of the Act on Prevention of Divulgence and Protection of Industrial Technology.

Any person who commits an offense under any of the subparagraphs (excluding (iv) with intent to use industrial technology in a foreign country or to cause industrial technology to be used in a foreign country (excluding a person who commits an offense under (i)) shall be punished by imprisonment with labor for not more than 15 years or by a fine not exceeding 1.5 billion won.[49]

Violation of a confidentiality order without good cause is punished outside Korea.[50] It shall be prosecuted for a crime of violation of the confidentiality order without a criminal complaint filed by a person who moved for the confidentiality order.[51]

6.3 *Foreign Exchange Transactions Act*[52]

The scope of the Foreign Exchange Transactions Act covers acts occurring a foreign country, for example, (i) acts conducted by an individual having a domicile or residence in the Republic of Korea, or his or her agents, employers or other employees in connection with his or her assets or business in a foreign country; and (ii) acts conducted by a representative, agents, employers or other employees of a legal entity having its main office in the Republic of Korea in connection with assets or business of the legal entity in a foreign country.[53]

6.4 *Customs Act*[54]

The head of a customs office shall not grant permission for customs clearance of any goods with a false label on their quality, details, manufacturing method, use and quantity (hereafter referred to as "quality, etc." in this Article) or with a misleading label or mark on their quality, etc. which violate the statutes governing the labels on quality, etc. including but not limited to the Unfair Competition Prevention and Trade Secret Protection Act, the Act on Labeling and Advertising of Foods, and the Industrial Standardization Act.[55]

---

49 Article 36 (2) of the Act on Prevention of Divulgence and Protection of Industrial Technology.

50 Article 36 bis (1) of Act On Prevention Of Divulgence And Protection Of Industrial Technology (Prescribing that "any person who violates a confidentiality order in or outside Korea, without good cause, shall be punished by imprisonment with labor for not more than five years or by a fine not exceeding 50 million won.").

51 Article 36 bis (2) of Act On Prevention Of Divulgence And Protection Of Industrial Technology.

52 Act No. 18244, revised on June 15, 2021 and effective on September 16, 2021.

53 Article 2 (1) of the Foreign Exchange Transactions Act.

54 Act No. 19186, revised on December 31, 2022 and effective on January 1, 2023.

55 Article 230 bis of the Customs Act.

The following goods may not be exported or imported:

(i) Books, publications, drawings, films, records, videos, sculptures and other similar goods which disrupt constitutional order, disturb the public safety and order or corrupt public morals;

(ii) Goods which reveal confidential information of the Government or are used to carry out intelligence missions;

(iii) Currencies, bonds and securities which are counterfeited, forged or copied.[56]

No goods which infringe on any of the following intellectual property rights may be imported or exported:

(i) Trademark rights, the enactment of which is registered under the Trademark Act;

(ii) Copyrights and neighboring rights pursuant to the Copyright Act (hereafter referred to as "copyright, etc." in this Article);

(iii) Variety protection rights created and registered pursuant to the Act on the Protection of New Varieties of Plants;

(iv) Geographical indications rights or geographical indications (hereinafter referred to as "geographical indications right, etc.") registered under the Agricultural Products Quality Control Act or the Quality Control of Fishery Products Act, or designated for the protection under treaties, agreements, etc.;

(v) Patent rights, the enactment of which is registered under the Patent Act;

(vi) Design rights, the enactment of which is registered under the Design Protection Act.[57]

However, the border measures under the Customs Act lacks the importation of goods misappropriating trade secrets.[58]

6.5 *The Act on the Investigation of Unfair International Trade Practices and Remedy against Injury to Industry*[59]

The purpose of the Act on the Investigation of Unfair International Trade Practices and Remedy Against Injury to Industry is to ensure the establishment

56 Article 234 of the Customs Act.

57 Article 235 (1) of the Customs Act.

58 G. Lee, 'Extraterritorial Application of Trade Secret Protection Law' (July 2022) *Korean Forum on International Trade and Business Law*, Vol. 31 No. 1, p. 521 (July 2022)(hereinafter 'G. Lee, Trade Secret Protection').

59 Act No. 17758, revised on December 29, 2020 and effective on January 1, 2021 in accordance with the revision of another law.

of fair trade orders and the protection of domestic industries through determining the procedures for investigating and remedying the injury to domestic industries caused by unfair trade practices and increase in imports, etc., and to prescribe necessary matters to comply with international treaties on trade, including the Marrakesh Agreement Establishing the World Trade Organization.[60]

No one shall engage in any of the following acts (hereinafter referred to as "unfair international trade practices"):

(i) The following acts related to goods, etc. which violate patent rights, utility model rights, design rights, trademark rights, copyrights, neighboring copyrights, publishing rights, database producer's rights, lay-out design rights of semiconductor integrated circuits, geographical indications, geographical indication rights, or trade secrets protected by the statutes of the Republic of Korea or the treaties signed by the Republic of Korea as a party concerned (hereinafter referred to as "goods, etc. violating intellectual property rights"):
   (a) Supplying goods, etc. violating intellectual property rights into Korea from overseas, or importing goods, etc. violating intellectual property rights or selling such imported goods domestically;
   (b) Exporting goods, etc. violating intellectual property rights, or manufacturing such goods domestically for export;

(ii) Acts of exporting or importing the following goods, etc.:
   (a) Goods, etc. whose marks of origin are false or misleading;
   (b) Goods, etc. whose marks of origin are damaged or modified;
   (c) Goods subject to origin marking, whose origin is not marked;

(iii) Acts of exporting or importing goods, etc. whose quality, contents, manufacturing method, purpose of use, quantity, etc. (hereinafter referred to as "quality, etc.") is falsely or exaggeratedly stated;

(iv) With respect to the implementation of export or import contracts, acts of disrupting import from or export to relevant areas by damaging Korea's international credibility, including export and import of goods, etc. which are profoundly differently from the details of contracts, and disputes arising therefrom.[61]

---

60 Article 1 of the Act on the Investigation of Unfair International Trade Practices and Remedy against Injury to Industry.

61 Article 4 (1) of the Act on the Investigation of Unfair International Trade Practices and Remedy against Injury to Industry.

Where the Korea Trade Commission judges that unfair international trade practices exist, the Trade Commission, upon consultation with the Minister of Trade, Industry and Energy, order the relevant actor to do one or more of the following:

(i) Suspending import, export, sale, or manufacture of the goods, etc. concerned;
(ii) Banning the landing of such goods, etc. or abandoning such goods;
(iii) Making corrective advertising;
(iv) Publishing the fact of receiving a corrective order from the Trade Commission in violation of the Act;
(v) Other necessary measures to correct unfair international trade practices.[62]

Hence, the Act on the Investigation of Unfair International Trade Practices and Remedy against Injury to Industry is extraterritorially applicable to importation of goods misappropriating trade secrets as administrative remedies. However, the scope of the goods misappropriating trade secrets should be extended to goods used only to misappropriate trade secrets. Otherwise, it is difficult to prevent domestic distribution of goods used only to misappropriate trade secrets.[63]

7 The Treatment of Corporate Nationality

The question of corporate nationality is not addressed to the extent that the Criminal Act is applied to foreign conduct on the basis of the actor's nationality. However, it is fair to say that the application of Article 3 of the Criminal Act, which prescribes that "This Act shall apply to all Korean nationals who commit crimes outside the territory of the Republic of Korea," extends to corporations incorporated in Korea.

Another statute whose application is extended to foreign corporations is the Financial Investment Services and Capital Markets Act. Under this Act, the term "foreign corporation, etc." in this Act means any of the following entities:

(i) A foreign government;
(ii) A foreign local government;
(iii) A foreign public institution;

62 Articles 10 (1) 1 and 4 (1) 1 of the Act on the Investigation of Unfair International Trade Practices and Remedy against Injury to Industry.

63 G. Lee, Trade Secret Protection, p. 521.

(iv) A foreign company established pursuant to statutes or regulations of a foreign country;
(v) An international organizations specified by Presidential Decree;
(vi) An entity specified by Presidential Decree among other corporations, etc. in foreign countries.[64]

With respect to trading and other transactions involving securities or exchange-traded derivatives by foreigners (referring to individuals with no address or residence for not less than six months in the Republic of Korea; hereafter the same shall apply in this Article), foreign corporations, etc., restrictions may be placed on the limit of acquisition, etc. in accordance with the guidelines and methods prescribed by Presidential Decree.[65] With respect to the acquisition of stocks of a public purpose corporation by foreigners, foreign corporations, etc., a separate restriction may be set in accordance with the articles of incorporation of the public purpose corporation in addition to the restrictions enumerated above.[66]

8 The Interpretation of Ambiguous Statutes and Regulations

Article 3 of the Korean Constitution prescribes that "The territory of the Republic of Korea shall consist of the Korean peninsula and its adjacent islands." According to the principle of a sovereign state based on Article 3 of the Korean Constitution, the laws of South Korea are geographically applied to the Korean peninsula and its adjacent islands.[67] Hence, unless prescribed otherwise, the scope of the laws of South Korea are geographically limited to the Korean peninsula and its adjacent islands.

64 Article 9 (16) of the Financial Investment Services and Capital Markets Act.

65 Article 168 (1) of the Financial Investment Services and Capital Markets Act.

66 Article 168 (2) of the Financial Investment Services and Capital Markets Act.

67 A Study on Scope of Personal Information Protection Act: Focused on the Scope Based on Persons, Subjects, and Geography, Naver Privacy White Paper, p. 37 https://privacy.naver.com/download/2021_chapter2_ScopeOfPrivacyAct.pdf(accessed on March 1, 2023). Cf. see Korean Supreme Court Decision on November 12, 1996 (Case No. 96 Nu 1221); Koran Supreme Court Decision on September 28, 1990 (Case No. 89 Nu 6396)(holding that the laws of South Korea are applied to North Korea because the geographical scope of the sovereignty of South Korea includes North Korean territory based on Article 3 of South Korean Constitution).

9 Blocking Statutes

Unlike the EU[68] and China,[69] South Korea has not enacted any blocking statutes to limit the effects of extraterritorial practices by other countries.

68 Council Regulation (EC) No 2271/96 of 22 November 1996 protecting against the effects of the extra-territorial application of legislation adopted by a third country, and actions based thereon or resulting therefrom.

69 On January 9, 2021, the Ministry of Commerce of the People's Republic of China (the "MOFCOM") issued the MOFCOM Order No. 1 of 2021 on Rules on Counteracting Unjustified Extraterritorial Application of Foreign Legislation and Other Measures (the "Chinese Blocking Statute"). See Z. Zhang, 'Rules on Counteracting Unjustified Extra-territorial Application of Foreign Legislation and Other Measures' (2021) *Chinese Law Review*, Vol. 45, pp. 421–426.

The Extraterritorial Application of Dutch Statutes and Regulations

*Lucas Roorda, Cedric Ryngaert and Timo Zandstra**

1 Introduction and General Trends

No single overarching rule or framework determines the extraterritorial scope of Dutch law. Rather, the scope of any individual law is determined by that law itself, and hence may differ among individual laws and fields of law. But that does not mean that no general rules, frameworks, principles, and practices can be observed. Upon analysing recent developments, we observe that over time, the active nationality principle has come to play a significant role in applying Dutch law to conduct abroad. Overall, however, we find that, in practice, the Netherlands appears committed to a relatively restrictive attitude to extraterritoriality and the exercise of extraterritorial jurisdiction. In very broad terms, our conclusion is that most instances of the Netherlands asserting extraterritorial jurisdiction are connected to the Netherlands via the Dutch nationality of the person (either natural or legal) who committed the conduct in question. The notable exception is the exercise of universal jurisdiction for prosecuting international crimes. Although Dutch practice is not as far-reaching as was the case in Spain and Belgium, universality is still more widely used than in other states.

This first section will discuss the general rules, frameworks, principles, and practices that govern the extraterritorial scope of Dutch law. It is divided into two sub-sections, each focusing on a different field of Dutch law. The first sub-section will discuss the grounds for extraterritorial jurisdiction in Dutch criminal law. Criminal law is the field in which the grounds for extraterritorial jurisdiction have been most developed and are also most explicit.[1] But – as will become clear – its principles are not necessarily applicable to other fields of law, such as administrative law. The second sub-section will discuss the grounds for extraterritorial jurisdiction of Dutch administrative law. Throughout this report, where necessary we will make a distinction between direct

* Utrecht University.

1 A.H. Klip & A.-S. Massa, *Communicerende grondslagen van extraterritoriale rechtsmacht*, 2010 WODC/Universiteit Maastricht.

 | DOI:10.1163/9789004720183_012

extraterritorial application of Dutch law and indirect extraterritorial effect – the latter referring to the regulation of conduct on a basis that is strictly speaking territorial, but that indirectly affects conduct abroad.

1.1 *Criminal Law*

In the Netherlands, the doctrine of extraterritoriality has mainly been developed in the criminal law. In 1881, the first version of the Dutch Criminal Code (Sr; *Wetboek van Strafrecht*) was adopted,[2] whose initial provisions were (and still are) jurisdictional in nature. Since 1881, the jurisdictional provisions have been amended multiple times. An Act of 1 July 2014 renumbered the provisions (now Articles 2-8d Sr),[3] thereby making them more coherent and accessible.[4]

Dutch criminal law traditionally provided for jurisdiction based on the principles of territoriality, active personality, and universality (the latter at least in relation to some crimes). Dutch criminal law was skeptical towards the passive personality principle, but this skepticism was abandoned in 1983.[5] The Act of 2014 extended the active and passive personality principles to *foreign residents* of the Netherlands (as opposed to just Dutch nationals), thereby introducing domicile-based criminal jurisdiction. The law of 2014 also introduced the new principle of 'derivative jurisdiction' (*afgeleide rechtsmacht*), pursuant to which all foreigners in the Netherlands are amenable to Dutch jurisdiction if they have committed an offense punishable with at least eight years of imprisonment, insofar as extradition has been refused or proves impossible (Article 8c Sr).

Jurisdiction over core crimes under international law used to be governed by the War Crimes Act (*Wet Oorlogsstrafrecht*, 1952), the Act implementing the Torture Convention (1988), and the Act implementing the Genocide Convention (1964). These laws have been replaced by the International Crimes Act (WIM; *Wet Internationale Misdrijven*), at least with respect to crimes committed after 1 October 2003. Under Dutch law, universal jurisdiction can be exercised over core crimes, also under pre-2003 legislation. However, as was confirmed by the Dutch Supreme Court in the *Bouterse* case,[6] the presence of the offender on Dutch territory is required for the exercise of universal jurisdiction.

2 Stb. 1881, 35.
3 Stb. 2013, 484.
4 *Kamerstukken* II 2012/13, 33572, 3, p. 2.
5 *Kamerstukken* II 1983/84, 18439, 3, pp. 11–12.
6 HR 18 september 2001, NJ 2002/559.

That Dutch statutory criminal law provides for extraterritorial jurisdiction does not mean that the Netherlands will in practice exercise such jurisdiction. Prosecutions, let alone trials, in respect of core international crimes remain few and far between, in spite of the broad jurisdictional grants in the International Crimes Act and its predecessors. Also, the Netherlands has long remained a laggard in terms of prosecution of foreign corrupt practices, although it had clear jurisdictional authority, in particular under the nationality principle (Dutch firms bribing persons abroad). Only in 2013 did Dutch law-enforcement agencies start to more actively prosecute foreign corrupt practices involving Dutch firms.[7]

1.2 *Administrative Law*

Dutch law contains a large body of norms that regulate the intra- and extra-territorial actions of national regulatory agencies. Dutch law does not employ the category of 'regulatory law' to denote that body of norms but considers it under the umbrella of administrative law. Dutch administrative law generally provides the rules that public authorities should apply in their decision-making, and it regulates relations between the government and its citizens.[8] The various sub-fields of Dutch administrative law regulate the activities of a wide range of administrative authorities. Our discussion of the extraterritorial scope of Dutch administrative law will focus on regulatory agencies – most importantly, the Netherlands Authority for Financial Markets (AFM);[9] the Netherlands Authority for Consumers and Markets (ACM);[10] the Dutch Central Bank (DNB);[11] and the Dutch Data Protection Authority (AP).[12] Moreover, while some questions concerning the scope of Dutch administrative law concern *intranational* extraterritoriality (for example, in the context of municipal-level rulemaking and enforcement), this report will focus on questions concerning *international* extraterritoriality of the rules that regulate these agencies.

The territorial scope of any rule of Dutch administrative law is determined by the individual statutory provision on which it is based. Dutch administrative law comprises general and specific rules. Since 1994, the Netherlands has

7 See F. Haijer, *Corporate Crime Conundrums and Globalization: Transnational Anti-Corruption Enforcement in the Netherlands and the* USA*, 2001–2017*, PhD Utrecht, 2021.

8 See for a general overview of the scope of Dutch administrative law T. Barkhuysen, W. Ouden & Y.E. Schuurmans, 'The Law on Administrative Procedures in the Netherlands' (2012) NALL 1.

9 https://www.afm.nl/en, accessed 13 December 2023.

10 https://www.acm.nl/en, accessed 13 December 2023.

11 https://www.dnb.nl/en, accessed 13 December 2023.

12 https://www.autoriteitpersoonsgegevens.nl/en, accessed 13 December 2023.

had the General Administrative Law Act (AWB; *Algemene wet bestuursrecht*),[13] which contains general rules for orders issued by administrative authorities and that creates the right of appeal before an administrative court (Article 1:3 AWB).[14] Specific rules exist as a patchwork of individual statutory provisions that grant administrative authorities the power to act for the purpose of performing a public service and that regulate such action in a detailed manner.[15] This includes specific rules in numerous areas of law, such as financial law, immigration law or environmental law. The prescriptive jurisdiction of Dutch administrative law is not explicitly provided in the AWB. And while the AWB explicitly regulates the jurisdiction of Dutch administrative courts (Article 8:7 AWB), it does not contain general rules concerning the enforcement jurisdiction of Dutch administrative bodies. The territorial scope of specific rules of Dutch administrative law is determined on the basis of individual statutory provisions. Nonetheless, some generally accepted rules and practices can be observed.

Dutch administrative law is generally considered to be applicable to all activity that takes place on Dutch territory. The nationality of the offender will often be legally irrelevant. For example, a foreign company may come under the jurisdiction of Dutch financial supervisory law by entering Dutch financial markets.[16] In addition, Dutch administrative law is applicable to all seagoing vessels registered in the Netherlands,[17] all aircraft registered in the Netherlands,[18] Dutch civil servants – including military personnel, for example – and Dutch nationals, even if they reside outside Dutch territories.[19]

13 Stb. 1993, 693.

14 Most rules in the GALA relate to specific acts, namely 'orders' (*besluiten*) issued by adminstrative authorities. Article 1:3 GALA includes a definition of an order made by an administrative authority: a written decision of an administrative authority constituting a public-law juridical act (T. Barkhuysen, W. Ouden & Y.E. Schuurmans, 'The Law on Administrative Procedures in the Netherlands' NALL 2012, p. 9). This provision largely determines the scope of Dutch administrative law.

15 See T. Barkhuysen, W. Ouden & Y.E. Schuurmans, 'The Law on Administrative Procedures in the Netherlands' (2012) NALL 1.

16 See e.g. R. Stijnen, 'Territorialiteit' in R. Stijnen, *Rechtsbescherming tegen bestraffing in het strafrecht en het bestuursrecht: een rechtsvergelijking tussen het Nederlandse strafrecht en bestraffende bestuursrecht, mede in Europees perspectief* (Wolters Kluwer 2011).

17 See e.g. Article. 1 and 20 of the Maritime Traffic Act (*Scheepvaartverkeerswet*; Stb. 1988, 389).

18 See Article 1.1 of the Aviation Act (*Wet Luchtvaart*; Stb. 1992, 368).

19 See e.g. O. Jansen, 'Rechtsmacht in Het Bestuursrecht' in T. Barkhuysen, A.T. Marseille, W. den Ouden, J.A.F. Peters & R.J.N. Schlössels (eds.), *25 jaar Awb in eenheid en verscheidenheid* (Wolters Kluwer 2019).

1.3 *Civil Law*

There is no general determination of jurisdictional scope of Dutch civil law. The Dutch Civil Code (BW; *Burgerlijk Wetboek*) is divided into 9 parts or 'books', each concerning a particular subject: for example, Book 1 concerns persons and family law, Book 2 concerns legal persons, Book 6 concerns contracts generally, et cetera. Each book sets its own jurisdictional scope which can also vary depending on the particular provision and topic regulated by that provision, although a few general tenets can be identified: parallel to the criminal code discussed above, Dutch civil law applies within Dutch territory, and all persons resident in the Netherlands enjoy the rights afforded by Dutch civil law (Art. 1:1(a) BW). Dutch civil law is further applicable to property registered in the Netherlands, to contracts drafted under Dutch law and/or whose primary performance is in the Netherlands, and to non-contractual disputes where the impugned acts took place in the Netherlands. In transboundary matters, choice of law and potential extraterritorial application are determined by applying relevant private international law. This is codified in Book 10 of the Civil Code and several EU instruments, and is not discussed further in this contribution.

While not strictly concerned with extraterritorial prescription, one instrument of civil litigation that merits a short discussion is the Collective Settlements Act (WCAM; *Wet Collectieve Afhandeling Massaschade*).[20] The WCAM creates the possibility to come to collective settlements on behalf of groups of injured parties and declare those settlements binding on all parties involved, somewhat akin to the mass settlement regimes of the United States, United Kingdom, and Canada. The original intent was to create a regime for settling mass (medical) liability claims that could then be declared binding on all by the District Court of Amsterdam. The WCAM itself does not include a procedure for collective litigation or class actions beyond the already existing possibility of non-profit organizations filing representative actions, Art. 3:305A BW.[21] In this incarnation, it has been used extensively for settling securities litigation and commercial actions.[22] Some of these actions had only a marginal connection to the Netherlands, with mostly foreign parties involved in the

20 Stb. 2005, 340.

21 A possibility for collective actions has since been introduced in the Collective Actions Law (*Wet Afhandeling Massaschade in Collectieve Actie*, WAMCA, Stb. 2019, 130) to supplement the WCAM.

22 See e.g. X.E. Kramer, 'Securities Collective Action and Private International Law Issues in Dutch WCAM Settlements: Global Aspirations and Regional Boundaries', 2014 *Pac. McGeorge Global Bus. & Dev. L.J.* 27.

settlement.[23] Such settlements do not constitute a direct extension of Dutch statutory law, but do declare settlements under Dutch law binding on all or some groups of interested parties, including those outside the Netherlands.[24] The WCAM regime has been criticized extensively for encouraging forum shopping and extending Dutch interpretations of reasonableness and appropriateness of settlement agreements.[25]

2 The Influence of International and Regional Instruments on the Extraterritorial Application of Dutch Law

2.1 *Criminal Law*

International and regional instruments have had a major influence on the extraterritorial application of Dutch criminal law.

In principle, the Netherlands can exercise extraterritorial jurisdiction if there is an obligation under international law to this effect. Indeed, pursuant to Article 6(1) Sr, Dutch criminal law applies to everyone who has committed an offence outside the Netherlands, insofar as a treaty or a decision of an international organization requires the Netherlands to exercise jurisdiction. However, this treaty or decision must be expressly named in a Dutch administrative regulation (*algemene maatregel van bestuur*). If the treaty or international decision is not listed in the regulation, there will be no jurisdiction over extraterritorial offenses. Also, if the treaty or decision is listed, but it only provides for optional extraterritorial jurisdiction, there will be no jurisdiction under Dutch law pursuant to Article 6(1) Sr. Obviously, such jurisdiction could be based on other statutory provisions or specific statutes (such as the International Crimes Act).

The 2014 'Regulation international obligations extraterritorial jurisdiction' (*Besluit internationale verplichtingen extraterritoriale rechtsmacht*)[26] contains a long list of relevant treaties and other legal instruments which require the Netherlands to exercise extraterritorial jurisdiction. The Regulation lists obligations in the framework of the UN, the Council of Europe, and the European Union in Articles 2, 3 and 4 specifically. Relevant instruments may require that the Netherlands exercise jurisdiction based on the principle of *aut dedere aut*

23 This was made possible by a purposefully broad reading of personal jurisdiction rules under Article 2(4) and 8(1) of the Brussels-I Regulation.

24 See i.e. Court of Appeal Amsterdam, 12 November 2010, ECLI:NL:GHAMS:2010:BO3908 and 17 January 2012, ECLI:NL:GHAMS:2012:BV1026 (*Converium*) and Court of Appeal Amsterdam, 29 May 2009, ECLI:NL:GHAMS:2009:BI5744 (*Shell*).

25 J. Kortmann, 'Case note *Converium*', 2011 *Jurisprudentie Ondernemingsrecht* 46, p. 46.

26 Stb. 2014, 47; most recently amended Stb. 2021, 315.

judicare (*i.e.*, requiring the establishment of jurisdiction in case the Netherlands does not extradite the suspect), but also on other permissive principles of jurisdiction. The advantage of having an administrative regulation is that the Dutch Criminal Code does not have to be amended each time an international instrument becomes binding on the Netherlands.[27] Administrative regulations, in contrast, can easily be amended, and indeed the Regulation has been amended repeatedly to reflect international developments.

Relevant international instruments listed in the 2014 Regulation include various anti-terrorism conventions, the UN Convention against Transnational Crime, the Budapest Cybercrime Convention, the Istanbul Convention on Preventing and Combating Violence against Women and Domestic Violence, and the EU Directive on the Fight against Fraud to the Union's Financial Interests by Means of Criminal Law. All of these instruments have provisions mandating the exercise of types of extraterritorial jurisdiction.

2.2 *Administrative Law*

Dutch administrative law, for its part, is heavily impacted by, and converging with, EU law. A relevant development concerning the operations of the Dutch Data Protection Authority (AP; *Autoriteit Persoonsgegevens*) is the introduction of the EU General Data Protection Regulation (GDPR). The Implementation Law of 16 May 2018 (*Uitvoeringswet Algemene verordening gegevensbescherming*) implemented the GDPR into Dutch law,[28] and thereby repealed the Dutch Data Protection Law (*Wet bescherming persoonsgegevens*), which served to implement EU Data Protection Directive 95/46/EC.[29] The introduction of the GDPR limited the applicability of Dutch law in the context of data protection investigations. The main objective of Article 4 of the Directive was to define which Member State's national law is applicable, whereas Article 3 of the GDPR defines the territorial scope of the directly applicable text. The European Data Protection Board has provided guidelines for the uniform interpretation of Article 3 of the GDPR, adopted after consultation with national data protection authorities, including the AP.[30] From interviews with legal staff members of the Dutch AP, we gathered that there is little to no extraterritorial extension of Dutch (implementation) laws under the GDPR. Dutch law might become relevant to investigations conducted in cooperation between relevant

---

27 Kamerstukken II 2012/13, 33572, 3, p. 5.

28 Stb 2018, 144.

29 Stb. 2001, 337.

30 <https://edpb.europa.eu/our-work-tools/our-documents/guidelines/guidelines-32018-territorial-scope-gdpr-article-3-version_nl> accessed 19 October 2021.

supervisory authorities under Articles 60-62 of the GDPR: to the extent that the Dutch AP might conduct an investigation or other activity in the territory of another Data Protection Authority, the Dutch rules that regulate that activity are applied extraterritorially. However, due to close intra-EU cooperation within the framework of the GDPR, the effect on foreign state sovereignty is kept to a minimum.

Pursuant to Article 6 of the Dutch Competition Act (Mw; *Mededingingswet*), Dutch competition law applies to prohibited conduct (such as collusion or the formation of cartels) producing economic effects on the Dutch market, regardless of the domicile of the market actors involved or the place where the cartel was formed.[31] This scope is in line with the scope of EU competition law as contained in Articles 101 and 102 TFEU and the provision is essentially the same, with the Competition Act substituting 'Dutch market' for 'internal market'.[32] The Competition Act also empowers the Dutch competition authority (ACM; *Autoriteit Consument en Markt*) to enforce competition rules, both Dutch competition law and European competition law, with the same territorial scope. For demarcating and interpreting the extraterritorial application of the Competition Act and the competences of the ACM, the legislator has aligned itself with European case law.[33] This case law will not be discussed here.[34]

3 The Role of International Law

3.1 *Customary International Law*

In the area of criminal law, as noted under question 2, Dutch law applies to everyone who has committed an offence outside the Netherlands, insofar as a treaty or a decision of an international organization requires that the Netherlands exercise jurisdiction (Article 6 Sr). Customary international law alone cannot provide a basis for the application of Dutch criminal law, as pursuant to articles 93 and 94 of the Constitution Dutch courts can only directly apply treaty law and decisions of international organizations to the extent they are considered self-executing ('*eenieder verbindend*').[35] Courts can apply

31 Stb. 1997, 242.

32 13 December 2007, 2008/C 115/01.

33 E.J. Zippro, 'Privaatrechtelijke handhaving van mededingingsrecht' 174 *Recht & Praktijk* 2009 1.4.2.1.

34 See for this discussion R. Klein & R.E. Tak, 'Over de grens gaan: grensoverschrijdende handhaving van het mededingings- en consumentenrecht' in R. Klein, R.E. Tak, F.C. van der Jagt & M.B. (eds.) Weijers, *Grensoverschrijdend bestuursrecht* (Jonge VAR-reeks 15 2016).

35 HR 18 September 2001, NJ 2002/559 (*Bouterse*).

customary norms if they have been codified in treaty or statute, and interpret the written analogues in the light of customary international law.

While Dutch courts rarely rely on customary international law for interpreting criminal statutes, customary international law has affected the extent to which Dutch statutes can be applied extraterritorially. A number of statutes have transposed customary international law authorizations to exercise jurisdiction into Dutch law. For instance the International Crimes Act or WIM provides for universal jurisdiction over genocide, crimes against humanity and certain violations of the law of non-international armed conflict based on customary international law. Indeed, as outlined below, the Genocide Convention Implementation Act (*Uitvoeringswet Genocideverdrag*) did not establish universal jurisdiction for the crime of genocide, on the basis that this was not required by the Genocide Convention itself. This has however been amended with the adoption of the WIM, based on both the Rome Statute and developments in international custom.[36]

3.2 *The Law of Immunities*

The international law of immunities limits the exercise of jurisdiction by Dutch courts. This is provided in general Dutch law (Article 13a *Wet Algemene Bepalingen*) as well as in the criminal law (Article 8d Sr). Both articles stipulate that jurisdiction is 'limited by the exceptions recognized in international law'. It is widely understood that these exceptions refer to immunities.[37] Such immunities may also be based on customary international law, notably the immunities of foreign states and foreign state officials which are, by and large, not governed by treaty law.

3.3 *International Treaties as a Source of Extraterritoriality*

The extent to which the scope of Dutch competition law is governed by the TFEU has already been outlined above; most other instances of treaties as a source for extraterritoriality concern the application of criminal statutes. The explanatory memorandum of the International Crimes Act,[38] discussed more extensively below, refers directly to several international instruments the Netherlands is a party to.[39] This includes Article 146 (2) of the fourth Geneva

36 Wetsvoorstel 32.475 tot Wijziging van het Wetboek van Strafrecht, het Wetboek van Strafvordering, de Wet internationale misdrijven, de Wet overlevering inzake oorlogsmisdrijven en de Uitleveringswet (verruiming mogelijkheden tot opsporing en vervolging van internationale misdrijven), Stb. 2011, 605.

37 T&C Strafrecht, commentaar op art. 8d Sr.

38 Stb. 2003, 340.

39 *Kamerstukken* II, 2001–2002, 28 337, nr. 3.

Convention and Article 5 of the Convention Against Torture as examples of treaty provisions that oblige the Netherlands to establish universal jurisdiction over certain international crimes. It further references the complementarity principle, pursuant to Article 17(a) of the Rome Statute of the International Criminal Court, to note that the crimes contained in the Rome Statute should also be criminalized under domestic law to ensure that effective domestic prosecution can take place.[40] The memorandum also refers to international law to justify limiting the application of universal jurisdiction to offenders present on Dutch territory. The memorandum recalls that universal jurisdiction *in absentia* is considered controversial, and not mandated by the relevant international instruments.

4 Bases for the Application of Dutch Law to Conduct Occurring Outside the Netherlands

In the **criminal law**, there are detailed regulations on the application of Dutch law to wholly foreign conduct, *i.e.*, extraterritorial jurisdiction. In general Dutch criminal law, these are laid down in Articles 3-8d Sr.

4.1 *General Grounds for Extraterritorial Application: Nationality and Registration*

Dutch criminal law is applicable to any person who commits an offense outside the Netherlands on board a Dutch-registered vessel or aircraft (Art. 3 Sr), *i.e.*, **flag state or registration-based jurisdiction.**

Dutch criminal law applies to extraterritorial conduct which threatens Dutch interests, *i.e.*, an application of the **protective or security principle of jurisdiction** (Art. 4 Sr). Relevant offenses are terrorist offences, such as hijacking aircraft, offenses against the state or monarchy, and counterfeiting currency; in practice however, this type of jurisdiction is usually exercised in conjunction with other types of jurisdiction, in particular passive personality jurisdiction (see examples below).

The Dutch Criminal Code provides for **passive personality-based jurisdiction** over anyone who has committed an offence against a Dutch national or resident, a Dutch official, or a Dutch vehicle, vessel, or aircraft, insofar as this offense is punishable with at least eight years of imprisonment, and is also punishable in the state where the offense occurred (Art. 5 Sr). The latter

40 *Id.*, p. 5.

limitations do not apply insofar as international law obliges the Netherlands to exercise jurisdiction (Art. 6 Sr). During the overhaul of the jurisdictional provisions of the Criminal Code, there was a proposal to lower the eight years requirement to three years, but this was rejected.[41] The Dutch trial regarding the downing of the MH17 aircraft over Ukraine, in which many Dutch nationals perished, was based on the passive personality principle insofar as it concerns Dutch victims. The trial extended to non-Dutch victims on the basis of an agreement on transfer of jurisdiction concluded between Ukraine and the Netherlands (2017).[42]

Dutch criminal law applies to any Dutch national or resident who commits any act classified as a crime under Dutch law (thus excluding misdemeanours) outside the Netherlands, provided that the act is punishable in the state where it is committed, *i.e.*, an application of the **nationality or active personality principle of jurisdiction** (Art. 7 Sr). The dual criminality requirement does not apply to a number of specific offenses, *e.g.*, genital mutilation, sexual abuse of minors, or forced marriage (Art. 7(2) Sr), so as to signal that some conduct cannot be tolerated, regardless of where it is committed or whether it is punishable elsewhere.[43] This requirement also does not apply to certain acts committed by Dutch military personnel outside of the Netherlands and criminalized by the Dutch Military Criminal Law act (Art. 7 *Wetboek van Militair Strafrecht*).[44] The active nationality principle also applies to aliens who have their habitual residence in the Netherlands, and to aliens who became Dutch nationals by means of naturalization after committing the relevant criminal acts (Art. 7(3) Sr); the latter is with exception of certain offences enumerated in Art. 7(2)(a) Sr (concerning for instance polygamy and disclosure of corporate secrets; these represent specific policy choices). Nationality-based jurisdiction may also flow from international legal instruments to which the Netherlands is a party, and which require the Netherlands to exercise such jurisdiction (Art. 6 Sr).

4.2 *Residual Grounds for Jurisdiction*

The Dutch Criminal Code also provides for some residual grounds of extraterritorial jurisdiction (Arts. 8a–8c Sr), in particular transfer-based jurisdiction and jurisdiction based on *aut dedere aut judicare.*

---

41 Kamerstukken II 2012/13, 33572, 3, p. 18.

42 See at length on the MH17 trial: https://www.prosecutionservice.nl/topics/m/mh17-plane-crash.

43 T&C Strafrecht, commentaar op art. 7 Sr.

44 Stb 1911, 5.

In case of **transfer-based jurisdiction**, Dutch criminal law applies extraterritorially to the extent that the Netherlands has concluded a treaty with the relevant foreign state (normally the state where the offense took place) providing for the transfer of jurisdiction (Art. 8b(1) Sr). As noted above, in respect of non-Dutch nationals, the MH17 trial was based on the transfer of jurisdiction from Ukraine to the Netherlands. Dutch criminal law also applies extraterritorially to the extent that an international criminal tribunal has transferred its jurisdiction to the Netherlands on the basis of a treaty or a decision of an international organizations (Art. 8b(4) Sr). This jurisdictional basis was inserted into the Criminal Code after the Dutch Supreme Court held that there was no legal basis for the transfer of cases from the International Criminal Tribunal for Yugoslavia to Dutch courts.[45] A transfer of jurisdiction may notably be needed if an *ad hoc* international criminal tribunal is about to close its doors before all cases have been tried.

Dutch ***aut dedere aut judicare*-based jurisdiction** ('extraditing or prosecuting') may flow from international obligations which the Netherlands has to implement (Art. 6 Sr), but may also apply outside this context. Dutch criminal law applies to terrorist offences committed extraterritorially where extradition has been declined, refused, or declared impermissible (Art. 8b(3) Sr), in situations not covered by international obligations (the latter only relate to *specific* terrorist offences). Also, Dutch criminal law applies to any foreigner who commits a crime outside the Netherlands, which is punishable with at least eight years of imprisonment, provided that extradition has been refused or is impossible, and subject to a dual criminality requirement (Art. 8c Sr). This provision resembles the provision on passive personality-based jurisdiction, discussed above, but applies to offenses with no link to the Netherlands other than the alleged offender's later presence on Dutch territory. The provision was inserted into the Criminal Code during the 2014 revision, and was informed by the desire to prevent impunity, in particular for murder, drug trafficking, and rape.[46] It could prove useful to prosecute a refugee who, pursuant to Art. 1F of the Refugee Convention, is not entitled to protection under the Convention on the ground that there are serious reasons for considering that 'he has committed a serious non-political crime outside the country of refuge prior to his admission to that country as a refugee' (Art. 1F(b) 1951 Refugee Convention). Doubts have been cast over whether international law allows for such expansive jurisdiction.[47]

---

45 HR 21 oktober 2008, NJ 2009/108.

46 *Kamerstukken* II 2012/13, 33572, 3, pp. 6, 60.

47 T&C Strafrecht, commentaar op art. 8c Sr.

4.3 *Universal and Quasi-Universal Jurisdiction*

The Dutch Criminal Code provides for particular types of **(quasi-)universal jurisdiction**, over crimes including piracy (Art. 381 Sr), terrorism, and even counterfeiting currency (Arts. 4 and 6 Sr). Such universal jurisdiction often finds its legal basis in treaties, such as the UN Convention on the Law of the Sea (regarding piracy) and the 1929 Geneva Convention for the Suppression of Counterfeiting Currency. In most cases, the exercise of such jurisdiction is based on the presence of the offender in the Netherlands. In the absence of Dutch interests being affected, Dutch prosecutors will be reluctant to exercise universal jurisdiction, however.[48] In one (rare) case, universal jurisdiction was asserted to prosecute and convict Somali nationals accused of piracy who had been transferred to Dutch authorities from Danish naval vessels, on which they had been held after their arrest in the Gulf of Aden.[49]

Dutch law also recognizes **universal jurisdiction** over international 'core' crimes, primarily pursuant to art. 2(1)(a) of the aforementioned WIM.[50] The crimes over which universal jurisdiction can be exercised are genocide (art. 3), crimes against humanity (Art. 4), war crimes (Arts. 5-7), torture committed by a state official (Art. 8) and the crime of aggression (Art. 8b), generally regarded as the 'core crimes' of international criminal law. The material elements of the crimes are analogous to the relevant provisions of the Rome Statute of the International Criminal Court, with the exception of Art. 8 (torture), which reflects the UN Convention Against Torture (CAT). According to the explanatory memorandum, courts are supposed to interpret both the material provisions and the modes of liability in accordance with the case law of the international criminal tribunals.[51]

Before the adoption of the WIM, universal jurisdiction could not be exercised over the crime of genocide and over crimes against humanity. The Genocide Convention Implementation Act (*Uitvoeringswet Genocideverdrag*) only provided for active and passive nationality jurisdiction in addition to territorial jurisdiction, and crimes against humanity were not explicitly criminalized under Dutch law.[52] Universal jurisdiction could only be exercised over torture (Art. 5 *Uitvoeringswet Folteringverdrag*),[53] and war crimes (Art. 3 lid 1 *Wet*

48 T&C Strafrecht, commentaar op art. 4 Sr, regarding piracy.

49 Gerechtshof 's-Gravenhage, 12 December 2012, ECLI:NL:GHSGR:2012:BY6937, ECLI:NL:GHSGR:2012:BY6938, ECLI:NL:GHSGR:2012:BY6940 and ECLI:NL:GHSGR:2012:BY6943; confirmed by HR 11 February 2014, ECLI:NL:HR:2014:286.

50 Stb. 2003, 270.

51 Kamerstukken II, 2001–2002, 28 337, nr. 3, p. 5.

52 Stb. 1964, 243.

53 Stb. 1988, 478.

Oorlogsstrafrecht).[54] This has now mostly been harmonized by the enactment of the WIM, which also partially repealed the aforementioned acts.

The WIM was further amended in 2011, making it possible to retroactively apply the WIM and establish jurisdiction over international crimes committed before 2003. This in particular affected prosecution of the crime of genocide, which was criminalized under Dutch law but for which universal jurisdiction was not available. However, the amendment did not retroactively establish universal jurisdiction over crimes against humanity committed prior to 2003, as crimes against humanity were not criminalized under Dutch law prior to the WIM.[55]

As noted above, universal jurisdiction can only be asserted over persons present on Dutch territory; prosecution in absentia based on universal jurisdiction is not possible.[56] In practice, that means that universal jurisdiction pursuant to the WIM is mostly asserted over aliens who reside in, or have applied for residence in, the Netherlands, often as asylum-seekers. In some cases, this concerns persons who had already been residents of the Netherlands for some time before investigations were opened into their involvement in the commission of international crimes.[57] In other situations, investigations and prosecutions are initiated after a person is flagged as being suspected of international crimes when applying for asylum in the Netherlands – the so-called '1F'-procedure, pursuant to which asylum seekers can be denied asylum when there is a reasonable suspicion of involvement in serious crimes, including the aforementioned international crimes, terrorism and other serious crimes.[58]

Additionally, universal jurisdiction can be and has been asserted in the Netherlands over suspects of international crimes surrendered to Dutch courts by an international tribunal; this is particularly relevant for the Netherlands as the host state of the ICC, the ICTY and the ICTR. Indeed, the 2011 amendment of the WIM was partially prompted by jurisdictional barriers to the prosecution

54 Stb. 1952, 408, and HR 1 November 1997 (*Knesevic*), NJ 1998, 463, m.nt. 'tH).

55 Wetsvoorstel 32.475 tot Wijziging van het Wetboek van Strafrecht, het Wetboek van Strafvordering, de Wet internationale misdrijven, de Wet overlevering inzake oorlogsmisdrijven en de Uitleveringswet (verruiming mogelijkheden tot opsporing en vervolging van internationale misdrijven), Stb. 2011, 605, and for a critical reflection C. Ryngaert, Opsporing en Vervolging van Internationale Misdrijven in Nederland: Enige reflecties over de verruiming van de mogelijkheden tot opsporing en vervolging van internationale misdrijven in Nederland, 2012 NTM|*NJCM-Bulletin*, no. 37, pp. 24–26.

56 HR 18 September 2001 (*Bouterse*), ECLI:NL:HR:2001:AB1471, para. 8.5.

57 see i.e. Rb 's Gravenhage 15 December 2017, (*Eshetu A.*), ECLI:NL:RBDHA:2017:14782.

58 See for example the prosecution of a Afghan for torture committed during the Soviet-Afghan war, Rechtbank 's-Gravenhage 14 October 2005, ECLI:NL:RBSGR:2005:AU4347.

of Rwandese *genocidaires* referred to the Netherlands by the ICTR, the crimes having taken place before enactment of the WIM.[59]

4.4 *Extraterritorial Jurisdiction beyond Criminal Law*

Outside of the domain of criminal law, certain provisions of Dutch **labour law** apply to labour conducted outside of the Netherlands. Both the Labour Conditions Act (ARBO; *Arbeidsomstandighedenwet*)[60] and the Working Hours Act (*Arbeidstijdenwet*) apply to employment aboard vessels flying the Dutch flag, and airplanes registered in the Netherlands, operating outside of the Netherlands.[61] This mirrors the **registration- or flag-based** jurisdiction also applied in criminal law. The Working Hours Act also applies to work for a Dutch employer performed outside the Netherlands aboard airplanes or in motor vehicles (Art. 2.8) – for example, truck drivers employed by Dutch companies but performing most or all of their work outside of the Netherlands.

As mentioned in section 1, Dutch administrative law is applicable to all seagoing vessels registered in the Netherlands (Art. 1 and 20 *Scheepvaartverkeerswet*)[62] and all aircraft registered in the Netherlands (Art. 1.1 *Wet luchtvaart*),[63] i.e. some form of **flag state or registration-based jurisdiction.** It is also applicable to Dutch civil servants – including military personnel – and Dutch nationals in general, even if they reside outside Dutch territories – i.e. some form of **nationality or active personality principle of jurisdiction.**

5 Territorial Ubiquity and Possible Territorial Links to the Netherlands

Dutch criminal law espouses a relatively broad interpretation of the territorial ubiquity principle when determining the *locus delicti*; i.e., it recognizes multiple potential connections to Dutch territory that support the application of Dutch law. Dutch courts follow three doctrines when interpreting the territoriality principle: (1) the doctrine of the physical act; (2) the doctrine of the

59 HR 21 October 2008, LJN BD656, C. Ryngaert, 'The Failed Referral of Michel Bagaragaza from the ICTR to the Netherlands', *Hague Justice Journal* 2009, pp. 237–243; in some cases, this problem was circumvented by charging torture and war crimes rather than the crime of genocide, see Gerechtshof 's-Gravenhage 7 July 2011 (*Joseph Mpambara*), ECLI:NL:GHSGR:2011:BR0686; confirmed on cassation HR 26 November 2013, ECLI:NL:HR:2013:1420.

60 Stb. 1999, 450.

61 Stb. 1995, 600.

62 Stb. 1988, 389.

63 Stb. 1992, 368.

instrument; and (3) the doctrine of the constitutive effect. These doctrines are jurisprudential creations and do not follow from the text of the Criminal Code, which only provides in Art. 2 Sr that Dutch criminal law applies to anyone who commits an offence in the Netherlands.

According to the doctrine of the physical act, the *locus delicti* is determined by the place where the offender personally acts.[64] According to the doctrine of the instrument, the *locus delicti* is determined not by the place where the offender is found, but where he acts by means of an instrument. In the famous case of the horse of Azewijn, a village on the Dutch-German border, Dutch territorial jurisdiction was established over a person in Germany who pulled a horse with a rope from the Netherlands into Germany.[65] According to the doctrine of the constitutive effect, the *locus delicti* is the place where the offense is completed, provided that a particular consequence is a constitutive element of the offense (*e.g.*, murder).[66] Furthermore, there are specific arrangements regarding territorial ubiquity in case of participation, co-perpetration, complicity, and instigation.[67]

This relatively wide conception means that even in cases where there is a link to Dutch territory, other states may have concurrent territorial claims. Dutch law has no established rule or doctrine for determining which connection is strongest or takes precedence, nor do Dutch courts explicitly apply any form of comity when asserting jurisdiction. This has created some concern over jurisdictional overreach where effects in the Netherlands are merely fortuitous.[68] This concern is somewhat mitigated by the broad discretion enjoyed by Dutch public prosecutors, who are expected not to pursue cases if the connection with the Netherlands is tenuous, especially if this means there is no realistic prospect of an effective investigation and/or enforcement. Similarly, while individuals can ask courts to overrule prosecutorial discretion and order criminal investigations based on Art. 12 of the Code of Criminal Procedure (Sv, *Wetboek van Strafvordering*), courts can reject such requests on expediency grounds. For example, in 2011 the Court of Appeal of The Hague refused to order the prosecution of commodity trader Trafigura for dumping toxic waste in Ivory Coast after exporting it

64 HR 16 October 1899, W 7347; HR 7 May 1996, NJ 1997/7.

65 HR 6 April 1915, NJ 1915/427, *Azewijnse paard.*

66 HR 6 April 1954, NJ 1954/368 (Singapore).

67 T&C Strafrecht, commentaar op art. 2 Sr.

68 T&C Strafrecht, commentaar op art. 2 Sr.

from Amsterdam,[69] in response to an Art. 12 complaint by the Dutch branch of Greenpeace. This decision was primarily based on admissibility criteria, but the Court also reasoned that while a (tenuous) jurisdictional connection might theoretically be established, the relevant acts had occurred exclusively abroad, and all named defendants were domiciled outside of the Netherlands. Combined with the refusal of Ivorian authorities to cooperate, this meant that an effective prosecution was neither expedient, nor likely to result in a conviction.[70]

In the context of the regulatory dimension of **administrative law**, there have been some developments toward the creation of specific obligations on companies with extraterritorial effects, beyond the application of competition law as outlined above. In particular, following the EU tendency to use a territorial link to indirectly affect actors and conduct not necessarily within the EU, Dutch regulators are increasingly applying administrative regulations to nominally territorial acts, but with the intent to produce extraterritorial effects.

The recently adopted Child Labour Law (WZK; *Wet Zorgplicht Kinderarbeid*)[71] is a good illustration of this. It obliges companies to monitor their supply chain, publish a due diligence plan, and take measures to prevent the use of child labour in that supply chain – also with regard to foreign business partners in that supply chain. The law applies based on either of two territorial links: it applies to companies registered in the Netherlands, and to companies that sell products to end-users on the Dutch market. The former could also be described as a nationality link, although it is based on registration and habitual presence in the Netherlands; the latter is more similar to how the effects doctrine is used in competition law as discussed above: the presence of products creates effects on the Dutch market that are targeted by the law; additionally, the sale to Dutch consumers creates a link to Dutch nationals, although this should not be fully read as a passive personality connection. Both however are utilized to induce changes in supply chains outside of the Netherlands, and otherwise outside of the scope of Dutch legislation.

The WZK is not yet in force and is likely to be revoked when the Netherlands adopts implementation legislation for the EU Corporate Sustainability

---

69 Note that both the captain of *Probo Koala*, and the Amsterdam port authority were initially convicted of illegal transfer of hazardous material; the case against the port authority was later dropped on immunity grounds.

70 Hof Den Haag, 12 April 2011, K09/0334.

71 Stb 2019, 401.

Due Diligence Directive (CSDDD).[72] The CSDDD applies to large companies domiciled in EU Member States, and companies supplying goods to end users on the single market.[73]

6 Extraterritorial Regulation and Corporate Nationality

The **nationality of corporations** is determined by corporate law. 'Corporation' is defined here as for-profit legal entities owned by shareholders, and that themselves can also own shares in another company. Dutch law recognizes the Naamloze Vennootschap (NV), a publicly traded entity akin to the US incorporated entity (Inc) and the English Public Limited Company (Plc), and the privately traded Besloten Vennootschap (BV), a privately traded entity akin to the US LLC and English Limited (Ltd.) company.

Dutch corporate law follows the incorporation theory: a legal person has the nationality of the state where it is incorporated and/or has its statutory seat (art. 10:118 BW). To be incorporated under Dutch law, a corporation is obliged to have its statutory seat in the Netherlands, as established in art. 2:66(3) for NVs and art. 2:177(3) BW for BVs.[74] The nationality of a corporation's board members or directors, or the location of its shareholders, is in principle of no consequence, nor is the place where the company does the majority of its business or the location of its central administration.

In the past, there has been some discussion about amending Dutch law to incorporate elements of the 'real seat' theory: determining a corporation's nationality based on where it does the majority of its business, or where its directors or central administration are located. Proponents of this approach argue that this does not only better match economic realities, but also potentially prevents abuse of legal personality. However, such proposals have been categorically rejected by the legislature.[75] Note that this ubiquity notion has been included in Art. 63 of Regulation No. 1215/2012 (*Brussels I bis*) on

72 Directive (EU) 2024/1760 of the European Parliament and of the Council of 13 June 2024 on corporate sustainability due diligence and amending Directive (EU) 2019/1937 and Regulation (EU) 2023/2859.

73 Ibid., art. 2(1).

74 See also P. Vlas, Rechtspersonen, Deventer: Kluwer 2017, p. 41, Asser/Kramer & Verhagen 10-III 2015/1.

75 As discussed in the explanatory memorandum to the Wet conflictenrecht corporaties, Kamerstukken II, 1994–1995 24 141, nr 3; the WCC has now been incorporated in Book 10 of the Dutch Civil Code.

jurisdiction and recognition and enforcement of judgments in civil and commercial matters, which is directly applicable in Dutch law. This Regulation however only determines jurisdiction for civil liability purposes, not application of (Dutch) substantive law.

If a corporation has its statutory seat in the Netherlands and thus has Dutch nationality, the corporation and its activities are governed by Dutch law: Dutch corporate law, but also administrative law, tax law, private law,[76] and relevant provisions of labour law and environmental law. Pursuant to art. 51(1) Sr, Dutch corporations are subject to appropriate provisions of criminal law and can be prosecuted just like natural persons. This also means that Dutch corporations can be prosecuted for conduct abroad pursuant to the same jurisdictional principles as apply to natural persons, and are also subject to the same (territorial) enforcement limitations. That said, actual prosecution of corporate entities for crimes committed abroad is relatively rare; in some cases, lack of cooperation by foreign authorities has made evidence gathering difficult,[77] whereas in other cases the choice was made to prosecute the natural persons responsible.[78]

As for foreign-domiciled subsidiaries of Dutch corporations, Dutch law recognizes the separation of legal entities within a corporate structure, and the limited liability of shareholders.[79] Consequently, subsidiaries of Dutch companies with their statutory seat in another state, or incorporated in another state, have the nationality of that state. Consequently, foreign-incorporated subsidiaries are not subject to Dutch law (unless they engage in activities within the Netherlands or employ persons aboard Dutch vessels or airplanes, as noted above).

---

76 Art. 2:5 explicitly equates legal persons with natural persons for the purposes of applying property law.

77 see e.g. Gerechtshof 's-Gravenhage, 12 April 2011 ECLI:NL:GHSGR:2011:BQ1012, and A. Smeulers, Tien jaar Wet Internationale Misdrijven – Een evaluatie, *Delikt & Delinkwent* 2014/25, afl. 4, p. 287, discussed in E.M. van Gelder & C.M.J. Ryngaert, Vervolging van ondernemingen voor schendingen van de mensenrechten: mogelijkheden naar Nederlands strafrecht, *Tijdschrift voor Bijzonder Strafrecht & Handhaving* 2017/3, p. 122.

78 Rechtbank Amsterdam, 23 July 2010, ECLI:NL:RBAMS:2010:BN2193; the case was settled before a decision on appeal was made), especially when the company involved may have been a shell company (Gerechtshof 's-Hertogenbosch, 21 April 2017, ECLI:NL:GHSHE:2017:1760 (*Kouwenhoven*).

79 Art. 2:64 cq art. 2:175 BW; see also A. G. Castermans & J. A. van der Weide, De juridische verantwoordelijkheid van Nederlandse moederbedrijven voor de betrokkenheid van dochters bij schendingen van fundamentele, internationaal erkende mensenrechten, Leiden, September 2009.

Dutch law does contain several possibilities to 'pierce the corporate veil' (a concept generally not used in Dutch law, but used here given the international audience of this book and the expected familiarity with the concept), i.e., to disregard the separation of legal personalities between a company and its shareholder(s), including the separation between a (foreign) subsidiary and its (Dutch) parent company. One can distinguish direct and indirect forms of veil-piercing: direct veil-piercing means directly attributing a subsidiary's conduct to its parent company and holding that parent company responsible for the subsidiary's debts and obligations, whereas indirect veil-piercing means holding a parent company responsible for its own conduct which affects the subsidiary's creditors.[80]

Direct veil-piercing doctrines have generally been developed in case law.[81] In private law, this has been applied quite restrictively, mostly in cases where there is clear and intentional abuse of the corporate form; for instance, where the subsidiary functions as a mere front for its parent company, to shield the parent from debts and claims. In administrative law and tax law, the tests tend to be more lenient and intentional abuse is not required.[82]

Indirect veil-piercing occurs when a parent company is held accountable for its own conduct, insofar as it relates to the subsidiary's conduct and third parties affected by that conduct. This can occur when the parent controls or manages aspects of the subsidiary's operations, which cause harm to others; the parent company can then be held accountable for its own actions, operating through its subsidiary, under normal wrongful act law.[83] Alternatively, a corporation can be held accountable for violating a duty of care under wrongful act law, by failing to exercise oversight or intervene in dangerous activities of its subsidiary when it was in a position to do so.[84]

As mentioned in Section 5, some recent legislative proposals focus specifically on the oversight role of the parent to change business practices of foreign subsidiaries and in transnational supply chains: both the WZK and the parliamentary initiative for a due diligence law require Dutch parent companies and companies selling goods on the Dutch market to conduct human rights

---

80 S. Bartman, A. Dorresteijn & M. Olaerts, Van het Concern, Deventer: Kluwer 2020 (10th ed.), p. 265.

81 HR 9 June 1995, NJ 1996/213 (Krijger/Citco), HR 13 October 2000, NJ 2000/698, m.nt. J.M.M. Maeijer (*Rainbow*).

82 Hof Arnhem 4 September 2012, ECLI:NL:GHARN:2012:BX65, discussed in L.F.H. Enneking et al, Zorgplichten van Nederlandse Ondernemingen Inzake Maatschappelijk Verantwoord Ondernemen, WODC 2015, p. 64.

83 HR 11 September 2009, ECLI:NL:HR:2009:BH4033 (Comsys).

84 Rechtbank Den Haag, 26 May 2021, ECLI:NL:RBDHA:2021:5337 (Milieudefensie/Shell).

due diligence vis-à-vis their subsidiaries and in their supply chains, and take measures to address potential human rights impacts of those subsidiaries and suppliers if they identify risks of such impacts occurring. While this does not involve the direct application of Dutch law to foreign companies, incorporation of these provisions in company-wide policies set by (Dutch) parent companies, and in contractual arrangements by end-tier companies in a supply chain, does give Dutch law effect abroad.

It should be noted that even in cases where the veil is directly or indirectly pierced between a Dutch parent company and a foreign subsidiary, that does not automatically lead to the application of substantive provisions of Dutch law. This depends on how conflict of laws rules are interpreted; in cases of non-contractual disputes, generally the law of the state where the harm materialized (*lex loci damni*) will be applied (Art. 4(1) Rome II Regulation).[85] Some have suggested that the law governing the corporation as a group (*lex societatis*) should be followed,[86] given the control of the parent company over the corporate group, but this approach tends not to be followed in practice. However, Dutch law may in some circumstances be applied if it can be argued that the parent's conduct was the conduct that gave rise to the harmful event, and most relevant conduct took place on Dutch territory (*lex locus delicti commissi*).

7 Interpreting the Geographic Scope of Statutes and Regulations

In the **criminal law**, there is no presumption against extraterritoriality under Dutch law. There is no priority among the jurisdictional provisions of the Dutch Criminal Code, even though the first jurisdictional provision listed is the territoriality principle. The Commentary to the Criminal Code states that the territoriality principle is not necessarily the strongest jurisdictional principle, as exemplified by the limited Dutch interest in prosecution and punishment of a U.S. businessman bribing a Japanese government official in an Amsterdam hotel room.[87]

Given the many jurisdictional grounds listed in the Dutch Criminal Code, there is obviously a clear risk that other States may also have jurisdiction over the same offense. To settle conflicts between the Netherlands and another EU Member State, pursuant to the *Guidance Jurisdictional Conflicts Criminal*

85 see also Enneking et al (2010), p. 65.

86 M.L. Lennarts, Concernaansprakelijkheid, 1999 Deventer: Kluwer pp. 329–333, 362–364.

87 T&C Strafrecht, commentaar op art. 2 Sr.

Procedures (*Aanwijzing rechtsmachtgeschillen bij strafprocedures*),[88] the prosecutor needs to consult his counterpart in the other Member State to find an appropriate solution for potential parallel proceedings. This Guidance implements the EU Council Framework Decision 2009/948/JHA of 30 November 2009 on prevention and settlement of conflicts of exercise of jurisdiction in criminal proceedings. When identifying the appropriate state to exercise jurisdiction over an offense, the *locus delicti* (territoriality) need not play the most important role. Rather, what is important is the 'good administration of justice', which requires an assessment on a case-by-case basis.[89]

There are some indications in **other fields of law** that Dutch courts consider laws to be intended to apply only territorially unless otherwise indicated. The Trade and Industry Appeals Tribunal, one of the appeals bodies for administrative law, has noted that it is presumed that Dutch administrative law applies territorially – and that it may also be limited to that territorial application even absent explicit limitations.[90] This judgment concerned a fine issued by the Dutch Authority for Consumers and Markets on the basis of a violation of Article 4.1 of the *Besluit universele dienstverlening en eindgebruikersbelangen*,[91] which is aimed at protecting the data rights of users of telecommunications products. One element of the dispute between the Authority and the appellant turned on the scope of that provision. The parties disagreed on the question whether the user referred to in the provision is only the Dutch user or whether this includes all users worldwide. The Tribunal argued that the fact that the text and the explanation of the provision did not indicate any limitation to Dutch users does not mean that there is no such limitation. According to the Tribunal, "in connection with the territoriality principle, such a restriction does not have to be explicitly included in Dutch legislation."[92]

8 Countering Extraterritorial Practices of Other States

The Netherlands has not enacted its own blocking statutes, i.e., statutes aimed at countering the effects of extraterritorial jurisdiction by other states, such as extraterritorial economic sanctions promulgated by the United States. It has

88 Stcrt. 2012, 11716.

89 T&C Strafrecht, commentaar op art. 2 Sr, referring to the criteria laid down in Art. 8(1) of the European Convention on the Transfer of Proceedings in Criminal Matters, adopted in the context of the Council of Europe in 1972.

90 CBb 20 June 2013, ECLI:NL:CBB:2013:CA371.

91 Stb. 2004, 203.

92 CBb 20 June 2013, ECLI:NL:CBB:2013:CA371, point 3.4.

limited itself to implementing EU Regulation 2271/96, i.e., the 'EU Blocking Statute'. The relevant implementing legislation (*Wet uitvoering antiboycotverordening*) has amended the Act on Economic Delicts (WED, *Wet Economische Delicten*), which makes failure to comply with the Blocking Statute an offense under Dutch law. There are no cases of Dutch enforcement agencies bringing proceedings against Dutch persons for violating the EU Blocking Statute. In private litigation over whether compliance with US sanctions amounts to *force majeure*, some Dutch courts have referred to the Blocking Statute, but only in passing, without any noticeable impact on the decision.[93]

93 E.g., District Court The Hague, judgment of 25 June 2019, ECLI:NL:RBDHA:2019:6301; District Court Rotterdam, decision of 1 April 2020, ECLI:NL:RBROT:2020:2860. See for a discussion: C. Ryngaert, 'Tussen hamer en aambeeld: de impact van Amerikaanse economische sancties op het Nederlandse contractenrecht', in E.R. de Jong *et al.* (eds.), *Opvattingen Onderzoeken* (Boom 2021) 87–114.

The Extraterritorial Application of Statutes and Regulations

Romania

*Sergiu Popovici**

1 Context and Overview

1.1 *Generalities*

The extraterritoriality of Romanian law is an issue which may arise in several different areas of law, all with specific and often very different rules. In order to sort these out, some distinctions are necessary.

First, Romania is a country with a uniform legislative system, any territorial overlaps between local units being treated as a matter of domestic administrative law.

Second, the most important division of Romanian internal law, a heritage of Romance legal doctrines, is between public and private law. To simplify, every area of law considered to be relevant to Romanian society in general is part of public law; where the interests of individuals are predominant, the respective legal branch is a matter of private law. Constitutional, criminal and administrative law are considered areas of public law. Procedural law, including civil procedure, is also considered public law, and the same is the case with certain areas of civil substantive law, such as most of family law and the procedural aspects of wills and successions. The main areas of private law are contractual and delictual substantive law. The core distinction is that in matters of public law, the will of the parties is secondary to public interest, and relevant only where expressly allowed, while in areas of private law the predominant principle is that of free will, which may still be expressly restricted, if the case.

Another division of Romanian law relevant for extraterritoriality is that between public international law and private international law. The most important point of the division is that the main subjects of public international law are the states themselves.[1] The subjects of every branch of private law (including private international law) and most other areas of public law are private individuals or entities. The Romanian State itself or through its

* Asst. Prof., West University of Timisoara, Faculty of Law.

1 R. Miga-Beşteliu, *Drept internaţional public*, vol. 1, All Beck, Bucharest, 2005, p. 1.

 | DOI:10.1163/9789004720183_013

public institutions or other entities may be party to legal relationships of private law, but only in their capacity as a legal person, not as an entity of public interest.

Private international law itself is a hybrid discipline consisting of international jurisdiction, applicable law (conflicts of laws), and enforcement and recognition of foreign judgments. The extraterritoriality of Romanian law operates differently in every one of these three subdivisions, to which international arbitration may also be added.

Another important distinction, relevant in most areas of law, is between procedural and substantive law. Rules on how litigation should be conducted (competence of courts, subpoena, service of documents, drafting of judgments, etc.) are deemed to be procedural rules, while the norms according to which the solution should be given are considered substantive rules. In private international law, traditionally the regulations on international jurisdiction, enforcement and recognition are part of the international civil trial (procedural rules), while conflict-of-laws norms are considered part of substantive law. As a result, the former category is regulated in the Romanian Civil Procedure Code (hereinafter referred to as RCPC), while conflicts of laws are governed by the Romanian Civil Code (hereinafter referred to as RCC).

Other main areas of Romanian law where extraterritoriality plays an important part are branches of public law, and involve diplomatic immunity, criminal law in cases involving a foreign element, and international aspects of fiscal law.

Finally, before attempting to provide an overview concerning extraterritoriality of Romanian law, all of the above-mentioned divisions of substantive law should be viewed from the perspective of the principle of territoriality of Romanian statutes and jurisdiction, expressly present in most of the major domestic legislative documents.

1.2 *Romania as a Unitary Legal System*

Administrative territorial divisions operate according to the principles of local autonomy and decentralization, according to art. 120 of the Constitution and art. 84 and following of the Romanian Administrative Code. The local normative system leaves close to no room for conflict: the power of every administrative division is limited either to facts and actions occurring within their territory, regardless of the parties involved, or to persons residing within their territory, regardless of the place where the events occur. The subject matter makes it so that these two hypotheses do not overlap. For example, every administrative territorial unit is empowered to impose certain rules of conduct within their area, in the subject matter allowed by the limits of local autonomy, that are compulsory regardless of the parties' origin or residence. Enforcement of the sanctions for breaching these rules, however, is left to the local authorities from the place of domicile or head office of the offender.

The differences between local autonomy and decentralization, on the one hand, and federalism, on the other, have been classified by Romanian doctrine in two categories:[2] institutional and jurisdictional. In essence, institutionally, the transfer of authority in decentralization is only administrative, the local divisions having no legislative, constitutional, judicial or further administrative prerogatives, they may only apply the same legislation in an autonomous manner. The leadership of administrative divisions has no other separation of powers, their representation in state administration is very weak, and there is no political autonomy. From a jurisdictional point of view, any powers that administrative authorities have derive exclusively from the state, through its central legislative process. Moreover, there is no judicial independence for the administrative divisions.

To conclude, because Romania is a state with a uniform legal system, the issue of extraterritoriality arises only in relationship with other countries. Any overlap between the jurisdiction of different territorial units is solved internally as an element of administrative law.

1.3 *Public vs. Private International Law*

The rights and obligations of states as subjects of law are the main object of public international law. In the Romanian legislative system, once a treaty is ratified it becomes part of domestic legislation, according to art. 11 par. 2 of the Romanian Constitution. Moreover, when it comes to the protection of human rights, international treaties that Romania is part of take precedence over less protective domestic legislation, a rule of constitutional value (art. 20 par. 2 of the Constitution). Extraterritoriality of Romanian law as a result of participating in international treaties or conventions[3] will therefore be dealt with only as part of the substantive legal framework relevant for the subject matter under analysis (for example, as elements of international criminal law or international fiscal aspects).

International comity, as an institution originating in public international law, finds itself in private international law under the shape of reciprocity,[4]

2 G. Gîrleşteanu, L. Smarandache, 'Descentralizarea şi autonomia locală în sistemul de drept român' (2009) 2 *Revista de ştiinţe juridice* 38, 45–46.

3 For an overview of the most important international conventions that Romania is part of, see F.G. Păncescu, *Drept procesual civil internaţional*, Hamangiu, Bucharest, 2014, pp. 27–39.

4 F.G. Păncescu, *Drept ...*, p. 6.

especially in matters related to the legal condition of foreigners, international judicial assistance, and enforcement and recognition of foreign judgments.[5] Paradoxically, comity is hardly ever mentioned in the Romanian literature on public international law,[6] probably as a result of the express principle of territoriality, as will be mentioned below.

One particular aspect of the relationship between international law and domestic law, especially relevant for private international law, is the correlation between EU law and Romanian internal law. The principles of direct application and prevalence of EU law[7] in every Member State are now a long-standing constant. However, the concrete effect of European regulations on the international jurisdiction of Romanian courts in private matters, on conflicts of laws, and on enforcement and recognition of foreign judgments has so far proven to be very confusing to the Romanian legislator.

The focus hereinafter will therefore be on Romanian domestic legislation applying to legal relationships with a foreign element based on national statutes and regulations rather than on EU legislation directly applicable in Romania or other international treaties.

1.4 *Extraterritoriality in Private International Law*

The core of Romanian private international law is considered to be the legal relationship with a foreign element.[8] Not autonomous, it is a relationship regulated by private law (contract law, tort, family law, wills and successions, etc.) in cases involving connections with more than one state. Private international law does not deal with the substance of that respective legal relationship, but rather with determining which state's substantive law shall govern it.

5 Ibidem, p. 19.

6 I have selected a few of the most important monographs and treaties in Romanian public international law, both older and more recent, none of which deal with comity as a source of international law: V.Constantin, *Drept internațional public*, UVT, Timisoara, 2004; A. Năstase, C. Jura, B. Aurescu, *Drept internațional public. Sinteze pentru examen*, All Beck, Bucharest, 1999; D. Florea, *Drept internațional public*, Lumen, Iasi, 2017; G. Fabian, *Drept internațional public. Note de curs*, Hamangiu, Bucharest, 2019; C. Moldovan, *Drept internațional public. Principii și instituții fundamentale*, Hamangiu, Bucharest, 2017. It is mentioned in one relevant publication, but not as a source of international law important for Romania, rather as a mention of an institution recognized by the practice of other states: R. Miga-Beșteliu, *Drept internațional public*, vol. I, C.H. Beck, Bucharest, 2014, p. 11.

7 R. Bercea, *Drept comunitar. Principii*, C.H. Beck, Bucharest, 2007, pp. 210–217.

8 I.P. Filipescu, A.I. Filipescu, *Tratat de drept internațional privat*, Universul Juridic, Bucharest, 2008, pp. 19–23; I. Macovei, *Tratat de drept internațional privat*, Universul Juridic, Bucharest, 2017, p. 12.

Should the conflict-of-laws norm lead to Romanian substantive law, we have a case of extraterritoriality: the legal relationship, despite being connected with at least another foreign state, is governed by Romanian law.

There is a very large potential variety of situations where the conflicts-of-laws rules might lead to the application of Romanian domestic law to a legal relationship with a foreign element. Most of these, however, are covered by European regulations, directly applicable in Romania in contractual and delictual or quasi-delictual matters, in maintenance obligations or cross-border successions, as well as in cross-border insolvency. Despite certain exclusions within the declared scope of these regulations, there is only one field generally left to the member states, and that is the civil status of persons and some areas of family law. In the latter, there is a regulation covering divorce and separation, which Romania is part of, however not compulsory in every Member State. There are two regulations in matrimonial property that the Romanian legislator decided not to take part of. In these areas, the nationality of the actor is the most important connecting factor justifying the application of Romanian law.

Apart from conflicts of laws, there is another component mentioned in most of the important private international works in Romania, namely substantive international norms.[9] These are not conflictual rules, since their purpose is not to establish the law of which state, of those connected to the legal relationship, is applicable, but rather to directly establish rights and obligations for the parties involved in the respective legal relationship with a foreign element. Despite, in principle, being applicable only if a conflictual norm leads to Romanian law as applicable law, most are powerful enough to remove the application of foreign law as overriding mandatory provisions or as rules of public policy, thus governing foreign conduct of the parties involved even if the most important connecting factor *ratione materiae* is situated outside of Romania.

1.5 *An Overview of the Operation of Extraterritoriality in Romania*

In the Romanian legal system there is no general doctrine on extraterritoriality. The only rules of Constitutional value consecrate a general principle that foreigners, in principle, benefit from the same rights as Romanian nationals in front of Romanian authorities (art. 18 of the Constitution).

Extraterritoriality thus operates differently according to the relevant legal branch. Private international law covers most situations in which Romanian

9 I. Macovei, *Tratat* ..., p. 33.

private law applies to legal relationships with a foreign element. Diplomatic immunity is a case of extraterritoriality originating from public international law,[10] and is not state specific in the case of Romania. The other major areas of law dealing with international aspects are criminal and fiscal law. Many cross-border aspects of criminal law, such as extradition, are also of international source. Other fields susceptible to extraterritorial effects, such as competition law or other economic measures, are almost completely tributary to EU law, even before accession, as the communist time knew no legal or economical equivalents to them. Of these, competition law has extraterritorial effects specific enough to outline below.

The following discussion provides a general overview of the most important hypotheses where Romanian law may have extraterritorial effects.

1.5.1 The Principle of Territoriality

State sovereignty is an attribute creating the presumption of an absolute international competence of each state as a subject of international law, in a manner which is full, absolute and autonomous,[11] but also implying equality between states. As a corollary of state sovereignty, almost all the major Romanian normative acts expressly consecrate the principle of territoriality of statutes and of jurisdiction.

According to art. 28 RCPC, titled *Territoriality of Procedural Law,* "Provisions of procedural law apply to all litigations taking place in front of Romanian courts, with the reserve of express contrary provisions".[12] Art. 7 RCC, titled *Territoriality of Civil Law,* states in paragraph 1 that "Normative acts adopted by central public authorities and institutions apply on the entire territory of the country, except where expressly mentioned."[13] Art. 8 RCC, titled *Extraterritoriality of Civil Law,* acts as an introduction to the chapter later dedicated to conflicts of laws.

Art. 8 par. 1 of the Romanian Criminal Code, titled *Territoriality of Criminal Law,* stipulates that "Romanian criminal law applies to crimes committed within the territory of Romania". Art. 7 pt. 38 of the Romanian Fiscal Code

10 In general public international law, the extraterritorial effects of legislation are hardly ever mentioned in Romanian doctrine, and where they are, they represent either a side mention within the principle of sovereignty, with references to foreign practices (C. Moldovan, *Drept ...* , pp. 166–167), or as criticism to extrateritorrial practices of the United States (V. Constantin, *Drept* ... (2004), pp. 242–243).

11 R. Miga-Beşteliu (2005), p. 1.

12 All quotes of Romanian legal texts are unofficial translations of the author.

13 Despite not excluding extraterritoriality, the text needs to be read in context. Par. 2 states that local authorities only have limited territorial jurisdiction.

introduces the concept of *residency*, and links taxation, as a principle, to residency within the territory of Romania.

Judicial doctrine in Romania, thus, never mentions a presumption against extraterritoriality. That there is such is deduced from the express mention of the principle of territoriality of statutes and the universally accepted[14] rule that extraterritoriality is possible only where expressly mentioned. It is also possible for Romanian law to have extraterritorial effects where a foreign state allows it. This latter hypothesis is not part of the focus in the present paper.

As mentioned before when outlining public international law, once the Romanian Parliament ratifies an international treaty it becomes part of domestic law. There are several cases of extraterritoriality of Romanian law – as it may be deemed through ratification of international instruments. Of these, one might mention, among others: The Convention on the Law of the Non-navigational Uses of International Watercourses from 1997, the four Geneva Conventions of 1958 concerning the law of the seas, as well as the UN Convention of 1982, The Vienna Conventions on the Law of Treaties (1969 and 1986), the GATT agreement of 1947, the UN Convention on the Reduction of Statelessness from 1961. One of the most infamous (in Romania) of these is the NATO Status of Forces Agreement.[15]

These, however, are not state specific, and are therefore not the main focus of the analyses below.

1.5.2 Extraterritoriality of Romanian Public Law: Diplomatic Immunity, International Criminal Law, International Fiscal Aspects

Romania is party to the Vienna Conventions on Diplomatic Relations (1961) and on Consular Relations (1963). The Romanian legislator has not adopted any domestic legislation in the field,[16] so at the moment, jurisdictional immunity is exclusively subject to international law. Given the widespread application of these two conventions, as well as other more specific conventions, Romanian law covers its diplomatic and consular missions regardless of where

---

14 There is no doctrine or jurisprudence in Romania even suggesting the contrary.

15 There was upheaval in the media concerning the death of a Romanian pop musician in a car accident driven by a US marine allegedly under the influence of alcohol, later cleared by the US jurisdiction (https://www.bbc.co.uk/romanian/news/story/2006/02/060202_teo_peter_sentinta.shtml, accessed 11 February 2022). While this is the reverse of extrateritorriality concerning Romanian law, based on the same international instrument deeds commited by Romanian military abroad are subject to Romanian law.

16 It has been opined that Romania should follow the common-law models on adopting national legislation concerning the immunity of states, at the time not covered by international law: F.G. Păncescu, *Drept …* , p. 45.

they are situated. Since these aspects are not state specific, they will not form the object of further analysis.

There are general regulations of cross-border aspects in both criminal law[17] and fiscal law. They are very much restricted by EU law (in matters of VAT and excise) or treaties of public international law. The state-specific provisions are described further below.

1.6 *Historical Outlook*

The development of extraterritoriality of Romanian law is directly connected with the changes in its international status: from the inter-war period to communism to democratic republic to Member State of the EU.

Aware of the importance of international relations, especially following the fall of the communist regime in December 1989,[18] the Romanian legislator enacted laws on all three aspects of private international law (international jurisdiction, applicable law, enforcement and recognition of judgments) as well as the legal condition of foreigners: Law no. 105/1992, and later on international judicial assistance.

Before that moment, however, there was only one text dealing with the extraterritoriality of Romanian private law,[19] namely art. 2 par. 2 of the previous Civil Code, enacted in 1864. According to that text, the laws on civil status and capacity follow Romanians even when they reside abroad. In the absence of symmetrical provisions for foreigners residing in Romania or addressing Romanian authorities, an entire doctrine and jurisprudence was developed on extraterritoriality, based on French law and jurisprudence. Even in the inter-war period, Romanian private international law was mostly the result of researching French doctrine and jurisprudence in private international law.[20] Extraterritoriality has never been routine in Romanian private law. There is little to no published jurisdiction of Romanian courts on the above-mentioned text; the entire discipline of Romanian private international law in the inter-war period was based on the similarly phrased French normative texts and the way that French courts interpreted them.

This historical background: incipient development of legal sciences in general, international law especially (the inter-war period), closed borders

17 For a comparative look on extraterritoriality of US vs EU criminal law, see F. Ciopec, 'Far and Beyond Territory. Lessons for the EU from the US Legal Practice', *Journal of Eastern European Criminal Law* (2020) 1, 147.

18 F.G. Păncescu, *Drept …*, p. 3.

19 M.V. Jakotă, *Drept internațional privat* vol II, Chemarea, Iași, 1997, pp. 8–9.

20 The most important works surviving from that period are Iorgu Radu's Știința și tehnica dreptului internațional privat, vol. I, Tipografia Națională, Cluj, 1933, and vol. II, 1934.

(communist regime) and Member State of the EU (from 2007 onward), has left little room for extraterritorial practices of the Romanian legislator. Most neighboring states have a similar background, so there has also been little chance for response to extraterritorial practices of other states.[21]

2 Extraterritoriality of Romanian Law as a Legislative Error

Going over several normative texts in different domains of private law may lead to an appearance of prescriptive extraterritoriality, where Romanian normative texts expressly provide for effects over foreign conduct, such as, for instance, the powers and attributes of the liquidator appointed in Romanian insolvency proceedings in front of the courts of other states.

It is my view, however, that most instances of prescriptive extraterritoriality are not the result of an active intention by the Romanian legislator to pursue state interest abroad, but rather of superficial drafting when using international instruments (EU or general international treaties). There is ample evidence that phrasings in Romanian legislation suggesting extraterritorial effects are the result of ignoring the relationship between prescriptive and enforcement jurisdiction[22] or the relationship between EU and domestic law.

These errors are particularly clear in the matter of cross-border insolvency.[23] For instance, art. 316 par. 1 and 2 of the Insolvency Code of Romania,[24] identical to prior legislation on the matter, states that the liquidator named within a procedure opened according to Romanian legislation is entitled to exercise, within the territory of all the Member States, all the powers which they are entitled to exercise in Romania. This provision, mentioned in the case of credit institutions, is reiterated in the matter of insurance, by article par. 1 and 2. Moreover, art. 324 par. 2 stipulates that decisions of Romanian courts

21 Response to extraterritorial practices of major actors in the international community such as the EU (prior to accession), the United States, or the Russian Federation hasn't generally been seen as a viable option.

22 This might be a side-effect of the underdevelopment of the issue in public international law. Differences between the three aspects of jurisdiction are only generally mentioned and given a concise definition, in the context of as a side-note or a subchapter of state sovereignty, in all of the public international law papers quoted within this report.

23 For details, see S. Popovici, 'Cross-Border Insolvency in the New Insolvency Code of Romania', in *The Second World Congress on Resilience: From Person to Society*, Medimond International Proceedings, Bologna, 2014, pp. 907–910.

24 Law no. 85/2014 on Insolvency and Insolvency Prevention Proceedings, published in OMR no. 466 of 25 June 2014.

concerning the opening of winding-up proceedings of a Romanian insurance undertaking, including its branches in other Member States, shall be recognized without further formality within the territory of all other Member States and shall be effective there as soon as the decision is effective in Romania.

Relevant in the matter are Directives No. 2001/24/EC and 2001/17/EC of the European Parliament and Council, on the reorganization and winding up of credit institutions and of insurance undertakings, respectively (despite only the first being expressly mentioned in the Insolvency Code). Both directives uphold the same principles as stated above. In implementing these rules, however, the Romanian legislator may only stipulate that liquidators named in procedures opened in other Member States may exercise all of their rights in Romania without further formalities, and to acknowledge recognition of decisions taken by courts of other Member States in Romania without any formalities. By stating that Romanian liquidators may act in other Member States without restrictions, and that decisions taken by Romanian courts are recognized in other Member States without formalities, the legislator of the new Insolvency Code oversteps the boundaries of its influence. Such rules are only applicable by effect of the instruments which implement the directives in the other Member States, or by effect of the directives themselves, certainly not by effect of Romanian legislation.[25]

The fact that the error is one of substance and understanding, rather than one of form, is confirmed by the final part of art. 331 of the Insolvency Code, which expressly states that the law of the Member State of origin is applicable on grounds of certain Romanian statutory provisions, obviously not the case.

The problem is persistent not only in insolvency matters, but in many situations where domestic legislation is based on international treaties, conventions or other such instruments. To name only a few hypotheses in substantive law where the Romanian legislator seems to forget that a necessary condition for application of domestic texts is the examination of the legal relationship

25 The error of the Romanian legislator is not random or isolated. The conceptual problem is confirmed not only by similar texts such as art. 320 and 321, as well as article 331 of the Insolvency Code which stipulate that authorities in the Member States of origin are the only ones entitled to decide when it comes to Romanian branches of an undertaking or institution situated in that Member State. While the principle is in accordance with the directives, the Romanian legislator, implementing them, may at most stipulate that Romanian courts are not competent when it comes to Romanian branches of undertakings or institutions situated in another Member State. Competence of the foreign courts will be attributed to them by their own *lex fori*, as well as the applicable law in those proceedings.

by a Romanian administrative or judicial authority,[26] art. 2583 par. 1 RCC states that *"a foreign legal person which has been recognized benefits from all of the rights arising out of the law of its organic statute, except those which the recognizing state refuses through its legal provisions."* Unless the recognizing state is Romania, the text is pointless, therefore the final part of the text should read as: *"except those which Romanian law excludes"*, a phrasing actually used in the immediately following paragraph. According to art. 2639 par. 2 let. c NCC, *"the act is still to be deemed as formally valid if it meets the conditions stipulated in one of the following laws ... c) the law applicable according to the private international law rules of the authority examining the validity of the legal act"*. In addition to the only hypothetical applicability of this text because of the Rome I Regulation, it is clear that it makes any sense only if the authority analyzing its validity is a Romanian one.

Civil procedure is also dotted with similar misdrafting, such as art. 1074 RCPC, and art. 1077 RCPC which, despite relating to judicial jurisdiction, strengthen the view that prescriptive extraterritoriality, where present in examples such as the ones above, is not generated by Romania's pursuit of state interest abroad, but rather by incorrect understanding of the relationship between prescriptive and judicial jurisdiction.

3 Extraterritoriality of Romanian Law in Some Matters of Public Law

As mentioned in the introductory part, most cross-border aspects of public law are of international inspiration, and therefore not state specific. Most domestic provisions are only applicable in the absence of an inter-state bilateral or multilateral instrument, and therefore their practical incidence is very restricted. Below is a brief outlook on extraterritoriality of Romanian criminal and fiscal law. Corruption, despite being a part of criminal law in the Romanian legal system, has a separate subchapter dedicated to it. Competition law is also worth mentioning, despite being almost entirely tributary to EU law.

3.1 *Criminal International Law*

Romanian doctrine, in line with western European legal literature of public international law, distinguishes between *international criminal law* and

---

26 S. Popovici, 'Reguli generale ale dreptului internaţional privat consacrate în Noul Cod Civil şi Noul Cod de Procedură civilă, cu o sferă de aplicare mai restrânsă decât ar indica formularea lor', *Revista de Ştiinţe Juridice* (2014) 1, 54.

criminal international law.[27] In essence, the former deals with supranational provisions through which the states, as subjects of international law, aim to suppress illicit conduct which might threaten fundamental rights of the international community. The latter, relevant further on, is the criminal equivalent of private international law, regulating the jurisdiction of Romanian courts and the applicability of Romanian law in criminal cases with a foreign element.

Since application of a foreign law in the criminal trial is only exceptionally and indirectly possible (for instance, if there is a case of bigamy, the foreign law might be relevant to assess whether there are multiple valid marriages), regulation of cross-border cases is much simplified in criminal law.

According to art. 41 of the Romanian Criminal Procedure Code, Romanian courts have jurisdiction if the criminal offence was committed in Romania. That place is, according to par. 2, where the criminal action took place, wholly or partially, or where its effects occurred. Art. 42 governs jurisdiction for crimes committed outside of Romania.

Since jurisdiction of Romanian criminal courts is implicitly connected to application of Romanian criminal law, these texts must be read together with articles 8–14 of the Romanian Criminal Code governing the application of Romanian criminal law in cross-border cases.

Art. 8 of the Criminal Code establishes the principle of territoriality in a similar manner, the main point of focus being the place where a criminal offence was committed.[28] There are, however, several in-depth explanations of what that place is. First, in the meaning of criminal law (criminal procedure included), the Romanian territory is comprised of the land mass, the territorial sea and waters with their ground, underground and airspace within the state borders. For ships and aircraft flying the Romanian flag specific provisions are in force. A criminal offence is deemed to have been committed in Romania if any criminal activity, including as instigator or accomplice, or if the effects of that activity, even in part, are on Romanian territory.

The personality principle, according to art. 9, comes to extend the scope of Romanian law, which applies to criminal offences committed outside the territory of Romania by a Romanian citizen or legal person, if the maximum punishment exceeds 10 years imprisonment. In other situations, Romanian law shall apply only if the action is deemed to be a criminal offence by the

27 For details, see I.C. Paşca, *Drept penal internaţional. Curs universitar*, Universul Juridic, Bucharest, 2020, pp. 7–10.

28 For a more detailed overview on extraterritoriality of Romanian criminal law, as well as its recent implications on cyberspace criminality, see L.M. Stănilă, 'Cyberspaţiul şi teritorialitatea legii penale', *Analele Universiăţii de Vest din Timişoara* – Seria Drept (2020) 2, 21.

law of the state where it was committed or in a territory not covered by other national jurisdiction. Application *in rem* (art. 10) is in fact the passive personality principle, according to which Romanian criminal law shall apply to criminal offences committed outside of Romania by a foreign or stateless citizen against the Romanian state or a Romanian natural or legal person. Finally, based on the principle of universal jurisdiction (art. 11), the same is the case for any other criminal offence if the offender is willingly in Romania and: (a) an offence was committed which the Romanian State engaged to repress based on an international treaty, regardless of incrimination in the state where it was committed, or (b) extradition was declined.

There are no domestic rules on conflicts of jurisdiction, such as *lis pendens* or connected actions in civil procedure. Such conflicts are usually settled by diplomatic means, on ground of international judicial assistance treaties. This is a possible reason for the relatively low doctrinal interest in criminal international law. Even though all general publications on criminal law treat international aspects, there are few works dedicated to them,[29] and not a lot of jurisprudence.

Most controversies observed by Romanian doctrine concerning criminal international law, especially ubiquity, are not whether a state has jurisdiction or not over a crime committed in part within its territory, but whether that jurisdiction extends to the entire activity or just to part of it.[30] Depending on the specific distinctions made by domestic criminal law, the solutions may differ.

In case of continuous or continuated[31] crimes, due to their indivisible nature, Romanian law covers every aspect of the crime, including the foreign ones, regardless of foreign legal provisions. In case of connected crimes, the solution differs. Since these are not indivisible, for example forgery of a document abroad and use of that document in Romania, or theft abroad and concealment of theft in Romania, the different crimes are considered to be fully committed and finalized separately in every state, therefore extraterritoriality is not an issue. In case of crimes by omission, the relevant place is where the

29 See I. Pocean, 'Principiul teritorialității în dreptul penal român, (2020) 10 *Ars Aequi*, 79–104, the source for most of the ideas summarized in this subchapter.

30 For instance, the Romanian Supreme Court (currently HCCJ) decided that the counterfeiting of banknotes in Turkey by a Turkish citizen with the purpose of distributing them in Germany is considered to have been fully committed in Romania, due to the fact that the banknotes were discovered in Romania and the entire criminal conduct was continuous, therefore indivisible.

31 A continuated crime is, in Romanian law, a crime made of separate and individual criminal acts, every one of which might be considered alone a crime (the same crime), connected by the same intent and a uniform result.

omitted action was to take place or its results were to occur. Attempted crimes follow the same regime as full crimes. All forms of participation, regardless of combination (main crime in Romania and participation abroad or main crime abroad and participation from Romania) incur the full application of Romanian law to all aspects investigated.

From a jurisprudence point of view, most examples given in doctrine involve aspects concerning either definitions of territory (for example territorial sea or crimes committed aboard a ship), or diplomatic immunity, none of which are state specific. Of the decisions published on the website of the HCCJ, the tendency is not to establish or pursue extraterritoriality of Romanian law, but rather to confirm the extraterritorial practices of other nations, especially the United States.[32]

3.2 *International Corruption from a Romanian Perspective*

Romania has separately ratified both the Criminal Law Convention on Corruption and the Civil Law Convention on Corruption[33] issued under the guidance of the Council of Europe (CoE). The way that the CoE monitors compliance with the Convention is through The Group of States against Corruption, or GRECO,[34] established in 1999 by the Council of Europe to monitor States' compliance with the organization's anti-corruption standards. Membership in GRECO, as an enlarged agreement, is not limited to Council of Europe member States. Currently, GRECO comprises 49 member States (48 European States and the United States).

The interaction between the mechanisms of the CoE and those of the EU represent a significant part of the European legal landscape, especially, but not only, concerning the jurisdictional power of the European Court of Human Rights versus that of the Court of Justice of the European Union.[35] As regards

32 For example, Decision no. 198/9 March 2021, Decision no. 860/22 December 2020, Decision 3/3 January 2019, etc. Most other published (http://www.scj.ro/736/Cautare-jurisprudenta) are in application of the European warrant of arrest.

33 For full text, (Oct. 9 2018, 9.55 a.m.) https://www.coe.int/fr/web/conventions/full-list/-/conventions/rms/090000168007f3f6 . Romania has ratified this Convention by Law no. 147/2002, published in the Official Monitor of Romania no. 260 of Apr. 18 2002. For details, see S. Popovici, 'The Civil Law Convention on Corruption: Directions from the Council of Europe and how Romanian Legislation Aims to Meet Them', *5th Sino-European International Forum of Criminal Law – New Challenges of Crime Control and Criminal Policy of Countries in Transition in the 21st Century*, Shanghai, 2018, pp. 1–10.

34 (Oct. 9 2018, 10.40 a.m.) https://www.coe.int/en/web/greco .

35 For a brief presentation of some interactions between the two European Institutions (EU and CoE) as seen from the perspective of the latter, see (https://www.coe.int/en/web/portal/european-union accessed October 2018).

the criminal aspects of corruption, two conventions have been established within the system of the EU: the Convention on the fight against corruption involving officials of the European Communities or officials of Member States of the European Union and the Convention on the protection of the European Communities' financial interests.

Another very important forum for international protection against corruption is the United Nations. The United Nations Convention against Corruption (UNCAC),[36] adopted by the UN General Assembly on 31 October 2003, opened for signature in 2003. On the civil side, the UNCAC has a distinct chapter dedicated to asset recovery. The UNCAC was ratified by Romania through Law no. 365/2004, and separately by the European Union itself, by Council Decision 2008/801/EC.

Romania's response to these international instruments was to enact Law 78/2000 on the Prevention, Discovery and Sanctioning of Corruption Deeds,[37] and to establish the National Anticorruption Directorate (Romanian *Direcția Națională Anticorupție*) initially in 2002, later in 2005 under the current denomination. However, there are few substantive differences from common crimes or criminal proceedings. More importantly, from an international perspective, cross-border aspects are not specific in case of corruption, so the rules mentioned in the previous subchapter are indistinctly applicable.

3.3 *International Fiscal Aspects*

When it comes to VAT or excise tax, most domestic legislation is an implementation of European Directives. Most of Romanian customs legislation is also covered by EU Law. Just like other internal rules, provisions in the Romanian Fiscal Code (hereinafter referred to as RFC) dealing with international aspects are subsidiary, and are excluded by international instruments such as conventions for the avoidance of double taxation.

Procedural aspects concerning the extraterritorial application of Romanian fiscal law are regulated in arts. 284–335 of the Romanian Fiscal Procedure Code. They establish the technicalities of international judicial assistance, including cross-border enforcement of fiscal foreign documents and requests for enforcement of Romanian fiscal documents abroad. Since they are mostly of international inspiration and not part of prescriptive jurisdiction, their details are not presented below.

As part of public law, there is no general application of foreign law in fiscal proceedings. Some aspects of foreign law may be relevant in the avoidance of

36 https://www.unodc.org/unodc/en/corruption/uncac.html accessed October 2018.

37 Published in OMR no. 219 of 18 May 2000, with many later amendments.

double taxation, but that is almost always the result of multilateral or bilateral international treaties. The following paragraphs aim to present a general outline of international fiscal aspects[38] contained in the RFC especially on income tax (for natural persons) and profit tax (for legal entities).

International fiscal aspects in Romania are grouped around the specific notion of *residency*, as defined by art. 7 pts. 22 and 27, 28 and 37. Someone being considered foreign or not is generally relevant only as an element of establishing residency. In essence, a company is not a Romanian resident if its office is not registered in Romania; if its central leadership is situated in Romania (art. 8^1), though, even a foreign company may be considered resident. For natural persons, residents are considered those who have their domicile in Romania, whose center of vital interests is in Romania or who are present in Romania for more than 182 days in a consecutive period of 12 months ending in the relevant fiscal year. For economic activities performed either by foreign legal persons or freelancers, an important role is given to their *permanent establishment* in Romania (art. 8 RFC).

For both income and profit tax, the extraterritoriality of Romanian fiscal law may cover either taxation of income gained by Romanian residents abroad, or of income gained by non-residents in Romania. Art. 12 RFC defines twenty different situations, depending on the tax and other circumstances, such as source or destination, of income gained in Romania. For every category of tax these general categories are further detailed and regulated in a different manner.

In principle, both categories mentioned above – income gained in Romania by non-residents and income gained abroad by Romanian residents – are subject to taxation in Romania. There are some subsidiary rules for the avoidance of double taxation found in the RFC, but they are almost never applicable due to the many conventions for the avoidance of double taxation that Romania is part of.

3.4 *Competition Law*

Competition Law no. 21/1996 was first published in Official Journal no. 88/30 April 1996. Exclusively based on EU legislation, it set up the first basic framework of sanctionable anti-competition practices, even before accession. The Competition Council, the administrative authority empowered with the

38 Fiscal law in general, its international aspects, in particular, are governed by a multitude of normative texts, on a very specific and technical level. Anything more complex than a gross oversimplification would take up a comparatively immense amount of room, disproportionate to the rest of the present paper. For some details, see Section 5 of R. Bufan, *Tratat de drept fiscal – Vol. I. Teoria generală a dreptului fiscal*, Hamangiu, Bucharest, 2016.

oversight of competition legislation, was established for the first time following the enactment of Law no. 21/1996. As the market economy gradually grew in Romania after the fall of the communist regime, the activity of the Competition Council also slowly began to increase.

Until now, the law has undergone several substantive revisions, and at present it constitutes the main body of Romanian legislation aimed at transposing EU directives in competition matters. Extraterritorial reach is expressly mentioned within art. 2(3) of Law no. 21/1996, according to which measures provided for by competition legislation shall apply to actions taking place outside of Romania whenever they have effects on the territory of Romania. There is, however, very little practice in application of this text[39] outside the international framework on competition law, predominantly EU law. Internationally, the Competition Council is also part of the International Competition Network (ICN), the United Nations Conference on Trade and Development (UNCTAD), the Organisation for Economic Co-operation and Development (OECD) and the Global Competition Review (GCR).[40]

There are concrete cases where the Competition Council investigates anti-competition practices taking place outside of Romania, however these are entirely tributary to EU legislation and are possible based on the cross-border competences given by the EU to the national authorities investigating practices which affect their domestic market.

In the exercise of its powers, the Competition Council may impose fines as administrative sanctions. According to 5(7) of Law no. 21/1996, in case the party fined is non-resident, regardless of where the sanctioned practice took place, the fines are calculated exclusively based on the income and/or turnover obtained in Romania by the non-resident entity.

39 The extraterritorial reach of the Competition Council regarding conduct taking place outside of Romania is almost exclusively restricted to agreements between foreign parties and Romanian nationals. In such cases, whether the agreement was made in Romania or not became irrelevant, since the main conduct sanctioned was that of the Romanian national which affected the domestic market. Such was the case in Decision no. 127/1998 of the Competition Council, published in the Official Journal no. 68/18 February 1998, and of Decision no. 99/27 December 2011 (available online at the webpage https://www.consiliulconcurentei.ro/wp-content/uploads/2012/01/decizie_parfumuri_pentru_site.pdf.

40 This may explain why, in most of the relevant monographs on competition law, there is no specific mention of cross-border activity, let alone extraterritorial practices. See, for example, A. Almășan, *Dreptul concurenței*, Hamangiu, Bucharest, 2021; G. Gheorghiu, M. Niță, *Dreptul concurenței*, Universul Juridic, Bucharest, 2022.

Law no. 21/1996 establishes that some of its breaches result in criminal liability of the parties involved, in which case the general provisions of Romanian criminal procedure shall apply, including extraterritorial provisions.

4 Conclusions

As there is no general doctrine of extraterritoriality of Romanian law, one must search the different areas of law where international aspects are dealt with. A common feature of all domestic texts is the principle of territoriality: Romanian legislation only applies within the administrative territory of Romania. Despite some legislative errors, extraterritoriality of Romanian law in the geographical/administrative sense is only possible based on international legislation or on domestic legislation of foreign states allowing such a territorial extension.

An established normative system of extraterritoriality is present in criminal law. However, most conflicts concerning criminal jurisdiction are settled diplomatically, which is probably why little focus is given in Romanian law doctrine to international aspects. The trend notifiable in the published jurisprudence of the HCCJ is to confirm extraterritorial practices of other states rather than pursue the application of domestic law to foreign conduct.

While the present study doesn't claim to be an exhaustive presentation of every aspect involving extraterritoriality of Romanian law, it does aim to cover most of the main issues and to leave aside only very specific and technical legislative aspects, as well as non-state specific situations.

The Legislative Practice of Extraterritoriality in Statutes and Regulations of Taiwan

*Rong-Chwan Chen**

1 Introduction

1.1 *Factual Background*

Taiwan bears the 'Republic of China' (the ROC) as its official name.[1] The ROC was established by the Constitution of the ROC and its Amendments. The Chinese Communist Party abolished all the laws promulgated by the Nationalist government after it established the People's Republic of China (the PRC) on 1 October 1949.[2] From then on, the ROC has coexisted with the PRC. The territory that the ROC effectively controls has been limited to the 'Taiwan region' and the application of the ROC's laws is restricted to this jurisdiction.

The original ROC state formed by the Constitution is now composed of four different legal territories. The 'original' ROC legal system was inherited and revised by its government on Taiwan. Mainland China, Hong Kong and Macau have, respectively, developed different legal systems for themselves.

According to the ROC Constitution, the Legislative Yuan (parliament) is its highest legislative organ and shall exercise legislative power on behalf of the people.[3] Basically, it passes laws to be enforced within the territory of the ROC and upon the citizens of the ROC who possess its nationality.[4] Although highest in the legislative system of the ROC, the Legislative Yuan's legislative power

* University Distinguished Professor of Law, National Taipei University, Taiwan.

1 'Taiwan', 'Mainland China', 'Hong Kong' and 'Macau' refer to the separate geographical regions that have been defined in the related statutes of the ROC. The ROC refers to the government that was established in 1912 by Dr. Sun Yat-Sen and has been governing Taiwan effectively since 1949. Taiwan or the ROC currently has jurisdiction over the main island of Taiwan, Penghu, Kinmen and Matsu and the related island groups.

2 Art. 17 of the Common Programme of the People's Political Consultative Conference of China, adopted on 29 Sep. 1949 at the First People's Political Consultative Conference of China, calls for abolishing all laws and regulations and the whole judicial system established by the ROC (Nationalist) government. See Henry R. Zheng, China's Civil and Commercial Law, p. 1, n. 1 (Lexis Pub, 1988).

3 Article 62 of the Constitution of the ROC.

4 Article 3 of the Constitution of the ROC states: "Persons possessing the nationality of the Republic of China shall be citizens of the Republic of China." Article 4 states: "The territory of the Republic of China according to its existing national boundaries shall not be altered except by resolution of the National Assembly."

 | DOI:10.1163/9789004720183_014

is not without limit. The constitutionality of national legislation is subject to judicial review by the Grand Justices. The inherent principles and spirit underlying the articles of the Constitution set out the basic guidelines and boundary for the Legislative Yuan. According to its Article 23, a law is unconstitutional "except by such as may be necessary to prevent infringement upon the freedoms of other persons, to avert an imminent crisis, to maintain social order or to advance public welfare". The legislative power to prescribe conduct committed abroad is thus restrained by these fundamental principles.

1.2 *Definition of Prescriptive Jurisdiction*

It is generally accepted that jurisdiction refers to the ability of a sovereign state to make and enforce its laws. The power of lawmakers relates to the sovereignty of the state to which they belong and links intrinsically to its territory. The lawmakers have the power and responsibility to say how the enactments they make shall be enforced, although some enactments are silent on such issue because it is too basic to be particularly specified in every enactment.

The prescriptive jurisdiction discussed here is different from the jurisdiction of courts over a particular case. It has nothing to do with the particular factor or connection between the court and the legal relationship at issue. However, the problem of prescriptive jurisdiction of a particular enactment might also be disputed in proceedings before a court.

The spatial reach of domestic statutes is of domestic and international significance. When states are willing to extend the reach of their own regulations to conduct occurring abroad, they may unilaterally prescribe to apply their own laws to that conduct. The rules of international jurisdiction are not necessarily explicitly mentioned or referenced in the relevant provisions or legislative documents. Public laws, including criminal law and administrative law, are therefore effectuated once the criteria of applicability set out in the statute are met. The conflicts rules embodied in the Act Governing the Choice of Law in Civil Matters Involving Foreign Elements[5] apply only to private or civil matters involving foreign elements. In that context, multilateral connecting factors are deployed to ascertain the law applicable to the matter in question.[6] This is the reason why private law codes or statutes are silent on their geographic or personal scope.

---

5 This Act was passed in 1953 and comprehensively revised in 2010. Its English version translated by this author, is available at https://law.moj.gov.tw/ENG/LawClass/LawAll.aspx?pcode=B0000007 [last accessed November 30, 2022].

6 For a comprehensive discussion on the objective connecting factors adopted in the Conflict-of-law Act, see Rong-Chwan Chen, Taiwan, pp. 37–42 (paras. 55–72), in Bea Verschraegen *ed., International Encyclopaedia of Laws: Private International Law* (Alphen aan den Rijn, NL: Kluwer Law International, 2021).

Prescriptive jurisdiction of an enactment can be based on territory, nationality or residence of a person, the interests to be protected, or the nature of the conduct at issue. It relates to the applicability of law within a specific territory, to a specific person, or to specific conduct. The principle of territoriality confines the application of a state's statutes to conduct occurring within its territory. Extraterritorial legislative jurisdiction enables legislation to apply to conduct occurring abroad. The issue of territorial or extraterritorial application of statutes or regulations thus concerns only public law, including criminal and administrative law.

From the beginning of establishing its jurisdictional system, the ROC sought to address international issues under its own statutes and to prescribe the relevant rules in accordance with the norms of international law. The general principles of territoriality and extraterritoriality were therefore both adopted and stipulated in statutes since early on. The rules on extraterritoriality flowed from the history of unequal treaties that unfairly restrained the ROC's legislative and judicial jurisdiction. Apparently, the initial adoption of extraterritoriality or jurisdictional expansion reflected the desire to rebuild the national esteem. However, the modern version of extraterritoriality of regulations is a part of participation in building the legal environment and protecting the legal order that is fundamental to enhance international commerce in the context of globalization. Through the coordination and cooperation of states in prescribing the extraterritorial regulations, a global net of national regulations that leaves no hole or gap for certain conduct serves well to combat illegal practices.

1.3 *Constitutional Consideration of Prescriptive Jurisdiction*

The ROC Constitution does not generally address prescriptive jurisdiction over foreign conduct. It is clear in designating the subject matter to be legislated at the national level,[7] but the spatial or geographic scope of a specific legislation or regulation is not totally without question. International law is relevant in this respect to govern the issue of the geographic effect of a national law.

7 Article 107 of the ROC Constitution states: In the following matters, the Central Government shall have the power of legislation and administration: 1. Foreign affairs; 2. National defense and military affairs concerning national defense; 3. Nationality law and criminal, civil and commercial law; 4. Judicial system; 5. Aviation, national highways, state-owned railways, navigation, postal and telegraph service; 6. Central Government finance and national revenues; 7. Demarcation of national, provincial and county (Xian) revenues; 8. State-operated economic enterprises; 9. Currency system and state banks; 10. Weights and measures; 11. Foreign trade policies; 12. Financial and economic matters affecting foreigners or foreign countries; and 13. Other matters relating to the Central Government as provided by this Constitution.

The ROC Constitution is silent on the effect of international law and its relationship with domestic legislation. Article 141 declares that "the foreign policy of the Republic of China shall, in a spirit of independence and initiative and on the basis of the principles of equality and reciprocity, cultivate good neighborliness with other nations, and respect treaties and the Charter of the United Nations, in order to protect the rights and interests of Chinese citizens residing abroad, promote international cooperation, advance international justice and ensure world peace." This Article leads to the opinion that the ROC, including its Legislative Yuan, is constitutionally bound to obey and respect the principles of international law. It also forms the foundation for the Legislative Yuan (the Parliament) to exercise its legislative power to prescribe provisions that are consistent with the principles of international law.

Therefore, while the concept of territoriality is kept in mind as the natural essence of all national legislation, extraterritoriality is also adopted to protect public interests and to cope with legislation of foreign countries and international law. The constitutional declaration of principles of equality and reciprocity of states, and preservation of good neighborliness with other nations, denotes that discord with other states is not encouraged or even allowed in deciding jurisdictional problems. Yet, it has no direct role in defining or limiting the geographic scope of statutes and regulations passed by the Legislative Yuan since it has been considered in the process of legislation and prescribed in them.

It is noteworthy that international comity has been considered by the Supreme Court in its judgment to refrain from over-exercising jurisdiction. The relevant case will be discussed later.

1.4 *Influence of Multilateral or Regional Instruments*

Given the uniqueness of the ROC (Taiwan) and the political reality in the international arena, the ROC is hardly able to sign or accede to multilateral or regional instruments under which the contracting parties are sovereign states. However, the ROC follows the legal development and trends of international law and adopts the spirit of such instruments in its domestic statutes. An illustrative example is the International Convention for the Suppression of the Financing of Terrorism.[8] The spirit of the provisions passed by the UN General

8 UN General Assembly, International Convention for the Suppression of the Financing of Terrorism, 9 December 1999, No. 38349, available at: https://www.refworld.org/docid/3dda0b867.html [[last accessed November 9, 2021].

Assembly is embodied in the Money Laundering Control Act, although the ROC is not a member of the UN.

Article 4 of the Counter-Terrorism Financing Act[9] is also directly influenced by UN instruments. Paragraph 1 provides: "If the competent authority believes that any of the following situations exist with respect to any individual, legal person, or entity, the competent authority may, subject to the approval of the TF review committee and based on the reports from the Investigation Bureau or under the competent authority's own authority, include such individual, legal person and entity on the sanction List and publish such list: 1. (an individual, legal person or entity) suspected of committing an offense specified in Article 8 Paragraph 1 hereof with unspecified persons for the purpose of intimidating the public or pressure the government, a foreign government or institution, or an international organization; or 2. an international treaty or convention in connection with TF prevention so requires or such is necessary to implement international cooperation or United Nations resolutions." Paragraph 2 provides: "Any individual, legal person, or entity who meets the criteria of designation, whether within or outside the territory of the ROC, may be listed in accordance with the foregoing paragraph."

2 The Principle of Territoriality

2.1 *Presumption against Extraterritoriality*

Territoriality relates to the basic nature of national enactments and the fact that they were effectuated because of the state's sovereignty. Such enactments are therefore effective to confer rights and power to individuals or state agencies only within the scope of the state's sovereign power. Their effects cannot reach beyond the state's territorial or geographic boundary unless so prescribed.[10]

Legislation on intellectual property rights, criminal punishment, and administrative penalty are illustrative in this regard. All intellectual property rights are created by legislation of sovereign states. An intellectual property right cannot be created without a relevant enactment to support it. The enactments on intellectual property law are hence territorial in nature. Likewise, a person is not punishable unless the criminal or administrative statute of the

9 The Counter-Terrorism Financing Act was passed in 2016 and last revised in 2018.

10 For general discussion on territoriality, *see* Hannah L. Buxbaum, "Territory, Territoriality, and the Resolution of Jurisdictional Conflict," 57 American Journal of Comparative Law 631 (2009); Toshiyuki Kono, "Territoriality," in Jüngen Basedow et al. ed., Encyclopedia of Private International Law, volume 2, pp. 1702–1709 (Cheltenham, UK: Edward Elgar Publishing Ltd, 2017).

place where his/her conduct was committed imposes punishments or sanctions on such conduct. The criminal statutes or administrative enactments of a state are therefore applicable to impose criminal punishments or administrative sanctions for conduct committed within its territory.

The principles of territoriality and extraterritoriality are both adopted in the basic enactments of criminal law and administrative law. Territoriality is no doubt a principle that can generally apply, yet extraterritoriality is also widely accepted as an exception. The point is whether the offense in question is within the scope of territorial or extraterritorial jurisdiction. The rules on extraterritoriality in the ROC's Criminal Code and the Administrative Penalty Act provide legitimate ground and scope to apply to extraterritorial conduct.

The principle of territoriality is consistent with the constitutional declaration on equality and reciprocity of states. Extraterritoriality is accepted only exceptionally in domestic statutes and regulations. A statute or regulation is thus presumed to lack extraterritorial reach when the legislators are silent on its geographic scope.[11]

2.2 *The ROC Criminal Code*

In 1935, the ROC promulgated its Criminal Code[12] to implement the principle "*nulla poena sine legea*" and establish crimes and their punishments. It addresses the principle of territoriality of criminal law in Article 3: "This Code shall apply to an offense committed within the territory of the ROC. An offense committed on board a vessel or aircraft of the ROC outside the territory of the ROC shall be considered an offense committed within the territory of the ROC."

2.2.1 The Territory of the ROC

The first sentence above prescribes the basic rule that the ROC Criminal Code applies only to offenses committed within the territory of the ROC. An offense committed outside the territory of the ROC, unless otherwise provided, is beyond the reach of the Code's prescriptive jurisdiction. Taiwan's Supreme Court ruled in its precedent that the first sentence of Article 3 of the Criminal Code embodies the principle of territoriality in criminal law.[13] Under this provision, the Criminal Code applies to all offenses committed within the territory of the ROC, regardless of the nationality of the offender or the victim. The exceptions to this basic principle of territoriality will be discussed in the next part on extraterritoriality.

11 Comments to Questionnaire 9.

12 The Criminal Code of the ROC was promulgated in 1935 and last revised in 2022.

13 Supreme Court's Criminal Judgment, Tai-Shang 2902 of 2011.

As a divided state, the boundary of the ROC's territory is problematic. The prescriptive jurisdiction and enforcement jurisdiction of its legislation are likewise not without doubt. The Supreme Court has ruled that the Criminal Code applies to all conduct committed within ROC territory.[14] It also stated that the scope of the ROC's territory remains unchanged since it has never been constitutionally changed according to Article 4 of the ROC Constitution or Article 1 Paragraph 1 of the Additional Articles to the ROC Constitution. Mainland China is, for the purpose of prescriptive jurisdiction, treated as a part of the ROC territory. The ROC Criminal Code therefore applies to any offense committed by anyone in mainland China.[15]

Although the interpretation above apparently ignores the fact that the legislations and statutes passed under the ROC Constitution are not recognized and enforceable in mainland China, it is relied on in practice as an established rule.[16] The unilateral declaration of territorial scope still has the effect to extend the prescriptive jurisdiction of the ROC laws to mainland China.

Article 43 of the Hong Kong and Macau Relations Act[17] adopts a relatively pragmatic view. It stipulates in Paragraph 1 that "provisions of the Criminal Code shall apply to the following offenses committed in Hong Kong, Macau, or on the vessels or aircraft of Hong Kong or Macau: (1) offenses provided in each item of Article 5 of the Criminal Code; (2) offenses provided in each item of Article 6 of the Criminal Code committed by civil servants of the Taiwan Area; and (3) offenses not provided in items (1) and (2) above, which are committed by persons from the Taiwan Area, or against persons from the Taiwan Area, for which the minimum penalty is imprisonment of three years or longer, unless said offenses are not punishable under Hong Kong or Macau laws." In other words, Hong Kong and Macau are treated as territories beyond the reach of ROC criminal law. Offenses committed in Hong Kong or Macau are treated as if they were extraterritorial offenses committed in foreign countries.

14 Supreme Court's Criminal Judgments, Tai-Shang 2271 of 2011, Tai-Shang 3021 of 2015, Tai-Shang 2497 of 2018, Tai-Shang 334 of 2019, and Tai-Fei 94 of 2000.

15 Ibid. In their Interpretation Shi-Zi 328 of 1993, the Grand Justices looked into the problem of national territory of the ROC. Instead of enumerating the components, Article 4 of the Constitution provides that the national territory of the Republic of China is determined "according to its existing national boundaries." It was ruled that the delimitation of national territory is a significant political question and thus it is beyond the reach of judicial review.

16 Supreme Court's Criminal Judgment, Tai-Shang 2686 of 2022.

17 The Hong Kong and Macau Relations Act was promulgated in 1997 and last revised in 2022.

2.2.2 Interpretation of the Territory

The second sentence in Article 3 of the Criminal Code provides a legislative interpretation of the term "an offense committed within the territory of the ROC" that expands its scope. It apparently treats the vessels and aircrafts of a state as floating islands which are assimilated with its territory. An offense committed on such a vessel or aircraft is deemed to be an offense committed within the territory of the ROC, and thus subject to its prescriptive jurisdiction.

Taiwan's Supreme Court interpreted the term "an offense committed on board a vessel or aircraft of the ROC outside the territory of the ROC" in a precedent. It states that under Article 3, the scope of geographic effects of the Criminal Code is basically determined by the principle of territoriality. The provisions "an offense committed on board a vessel or aircraft of the ROC outside the territory of the ROC" cover an offense committed on board either a state-owned or a private vessel or aircraft of the ROC. Whether that vessel or aircraft is located within a foreign state or beyond the territory of any state, an offense committed on it is treated as an offense committed within the territory of the ROC. It is therefore subject to the effects of the Criminal Code. It refers to the so-called "floating territory" theory and says that it is an expansion of the principle of territoriality with the purpose of filling the gap between the territorial effects of criminal laws of different states.[18] For instance, an offender may be punished for illegal fishing on a fishing boat on the high seas under the Criminal Code if the boat is registered in the ROC.[19]

Literally speaking, the principle of territoriality is adopted in the above-mentioned provisions of the ROC Criminal Code. The Code applies to punish the criminalized offense because it was committed within the ROC's territory. The applicability of the Code is based on the connecting factor between the ROC and the criminal offense, ie the place where it was committed. In the event that ROC criminal law is applied on this basis while the vessel or aircraft in question is within the territory of another state or otherwise subject to the jurisdiction of another state, it might create international discord.

Such a conflict of prescriptive jurisdiction is an issue of public international law and must be resolved through international negotiation and diplomatic practice. The incident of the Philippine Coast Guard personnel's opening fire on a fishing boat (Guang Da Xing No. 28) from Taiwan on May 9, 2013 illustrates this conflict of jurisdictions. It happened outside of Taiwan's territorial waters and resulted in the damage of the boat and the death of Mr. Hung Shih Cheng. The ROC asserted its jurisdiction and stated that the Philippine commander

18 Supreme Court's Criminal Judgment, Tai-Shang 1066 of 2005.

19 Supreme Court's Criminal Judgment, Tai-Shang 3363 of 1997.

and shooters were liable for homicide as defined in Article 271 of the ROC Criminal Code. It further demanded that the Philippines cooperate with Taiwan on the investigation, based on a mutual legal assistance agreement, in order that the truth of the incident be revealed and that the perpetrators be punished.[20] The Philippines agreed to these principles and cooperated with Taiwan's investigation team. It started with international sanctions and negotiation and ended up with criminal punishment, civil compensation and diplomatic apology under Philippine law. The requirement and standards of the ROC law were thus also met.[21]

2.2.3 International Comity

Besides the legislative expansion of the "territory of the ROC", the Supreme Court confirmed in its precedent that such term specified in Article 3 of the ROC Criminal Code covers both real and conceptual territory.[22] The floating territory of vessels or aircraft is just one part of this conceptual territory. The Court cautiously refrained from directly extending it by analogy to the ROC embassies and offices located in foreign states. It emphasized that it was not explicitly stipulated whether offenses committed in a ROC embassy or office are offenses committed within the territory of the ROC. As there is no express limitation on a state's exercise of jurisdiction under statutory international law, customary international law shall be observed. The exercise of jurisdiction over criminal offenses by the sending state shall be conditioned on the waiver of the resident state. In case it has been proved that the resident state agreed not to exercise its jurisdiction, the offenses may thus be deemed as ones committed within the territory of the ROC. It is this author's opinion that international comity is considered by the Supreme Court in defining the scope of prescriptive jurisdiction.[23]

2.3 *The Administrative Penalty Act*

The above-mentioned provisions of the ROC Criminal Code are general provisions which can be applied to all criminal statutes. Likewise, the principle

---

20 "ROC and Philippines hold working-level consultations on mutual legal assistance over fatal shooting attack on Taiwan fishing boat Guang Da Xing No. 28 by Philippine government vessel," available at https://en.mofa.gov.tw/News_Content.aspx?n=1331&sms=275&s=34159 [last accessed December 10, 2022].

21 "Philippines and Taiwan Resume Normal Relations with Closure in Guang Da Xing Incident," available at https://www.taiwan-panorama.com/Articles/Details?Guid=7a3d420f-99b3-4fa5-ad59-4771d8064919&langId=3&CatId=10 [last accessed December 10, 2022].

22 Supreme Court's Criminal Judgment, Tai-Fei 129 of 1969.

23 Comments to Questionnaire 4.

of territoriality is also adopted in Article 6 of the Administrative Penalty Act[24] to prescribe the geographic scope of ROC administrative statutes. In its Paragraph 1, it states: "This Act shall be applicable to any act in breach of duty under administrative law that is committed within the territory of the ROC and is punishable." This echoes the territoriality rule in the Criminal Code, taking the same approach for acts committed in breach of duty under administrative law. Such an act is only punishable under the ROC administrative statutes if it was committed within its territory. It means that the ROC administrative statutes are principally territorial and are not effective beyond the reach of the ROC's sovereignty.

Paragraph 2 of the same Article provides: "An act in breach of duty under administrative law committed on board a vessel or aircraft of the ROC outside the territory of the ROC or within an area subject to jurisdiction of the ROC by law shall be punished in the same manner as if it were an act committed within the territory of the ROC." The first part denotes the "floating territory" theory mentioned previously; the second part adds other areas such as the ROC embassies in foreign states to the ROC's conceptual or virtual territory where its administrative statutes are applicable.

2.4 *The Geographic Location of Conduct*

Under the principle of territoriality, domestic criminal statutes and administrative enactments apply only to geographically domestic conduct. Conduct occurring abroad is beyond the ROC's prescriptive jurisdiction. The geographic location of conduct must therefore be determined before applying a particular domestic criminal or administrative statute.

The concept of extraterritoriality refers to the application of domestic law to an activity committed outside the territory of the forum state. This concept is based on the preliminary assumption that such an activity is an extraterritorial or foreign one.

It is noteworthy that the standard for characterizing a conduct as domestic or extraterritorial may differ from state to state. As each state may stipulate in its statutes whether an activity committed partly within its territory or resulting in effects partly within its territory is domestic or exterritorial, specific conduct can be characterized as conduct within the territory of state X and simultaneously as conduct within the territory of state Y. In such circumstances, the prescriptive jurisdictions of the law of state X and of state Y over the specific conduct may overlap.

24 The Administrative Penalty Act was passed in 2005 and last revised in 2011.

3 Legislative Practice of Extraterritoriality

3.1 *Conduct Committed Partly Abroad*

With some exceptional rules on extraterritoriality, the basic rules in the ROC Criminal Code are construed to accord with relevant international instruments such as the United Nations Convention against Transnational Organized Crime.[25] It emphasizes "the principles of sovereign equality and territorial integrity of States and that of non-intervention in the domestic affairs of other States" in Article 4 (1) and stipulates in Article 15 the basic rule and exceptions to establish jurisdiction over an offense.[26]

In Taiwan, a criminal offense is composed of conduct and its effects or result. The places of the conduct may spread over different states, and so may the places of its result. An act committed partly within domestic territory is partly domestic and partly foreign. An act committed wholly outside domestic territory is hardly domestic even if part of its consequence occurred within the domestic territory. In such a case, it will be problematic in ascertaining the place where the offense was committed.

---

25 Comments to Questionnaire 2. United Nations Convention against Transnational Organized Crime was adopted by the UN General Assembly on November 15, 2000, by resolution 55/25 and entered into force on September 29, 2003. Available at https://www.unodc.org/unodc/en/organized-crime/intro/UNTOC.html (last visited: November 5, 2023)

26 Article 15 Jurisdiction

1. Each State Party shall adopt such measures as may be necessary to establish its jurisdiction over the offences established in accordance with articles 5, 6, 8 and 23 of this Convention when:
    (a) The offence is committed in the territory of that State Party; or
    (b) The offence is committed on board a vessel that is flying the flag of that State Party or an aircraft that is registered under the laws of that State Party at the time that the offence is committed.
2. Subject to article 4 of this Convention, a State Party may also establish its jurisdiction over any such offence when:
    (a) The offence is committed against a national of that State Party;
    (b) The offence is committed by a national of that State Party or a stateless person who has his or her habitual residence in its territory; or
    (c) The offence is:
        (i) One of those established in accordance with article 5, paragraph 1, of this Convention and is committed outside its territory with a view to the commission of a serious crime within its territory;
        (ii) One of those established in accordance with article 6, paragraph 1 (b) (ii), of this Convention and is committed outside its territory with a view to the commission of an offence established in accordance with article 6, paragraph 1 (a) (i) or (ii) or (b) (i), of this Convention within its territory.

However, the prescriptive jurisdictional policy adopted in the Criminal Code and the Administrative Penalty Act is highly doctrinal. Article 4 of the ROC Criminal Code states: "Where either the conduct or the result of an offense takes place within the territory of the ROC, the offense shall be considered as committed within the territory of the ROC." This provision focuses on the prescriptive jurisdiction of the Criminal Code and establishes the rule that for the purpose of determining the prescriptive jurisdiction of domestic statutes, any part of the offense can be a valid connecting factor. It is thus clear that if the criminal act (*actus reus*) was committed partly within the territory of the ROC and partly in one or more foreign countries, the Criminal Code applies without considering whether the criminal law of any foreign state applies. The element relating to the result of an offense will be discussed later.

Paragraph 3 of Article 6 of the Administrative Penalty Act states: "Where either the commission of an act in breach of duty under administrative law or the consequence resulting therefrom takes place within the territory of the ROC, it shall constitute a breach of duty under administrative law committed within the territory of the ROC." This is apparently an embodiment of a similar rule adopted in Article 4 of the Criminal Code. It acknowledges the principle of territoriality and states that for the purpose of prescriptive jurisdiction, any part of the commission of the relevant act is sufficient to justify territorial jurisdiction.[27] The significance of the place where the consequence of the act occurred will be discussed later.

The provisions mentioned above in the ROC Criminal Code and the Administrative Penalty Act unilaterally characterize the partly domestic conduct as domestic to support domestic prescriptive jurisdiction on the basis that the conduct at issue is partly territorially linked with the domestic state. The quality, significance and relativity of the territorial links is not explicitly prescribed and hence not considered in the court's judgments or decisions. Although this may create some problems of jurisdictional conflict with foreign countries, it is consistent with the principle of territoriality in international law. There is therefore no concern about jurisdictional overreach because it is also other states' legislative policy to expand their prescriptive jurisdiction over conduct in this way.

27 In the Supreme Administrative Court's Decision Shang 167 of 2021, the server and website in question were established outside of the ROC territory, the advertisements on them violated the provisions of the Pharmaceutical Affairs Act. The Supreme Administrative Court ruled that since they can be reached via internet by the people within the ROC territory, the effects of violation occurred within the ROC territory. The conducts are thus culpable under the the Pharmaceutical Affairs Act.

3.2 *Extraterritoriality and the Effects Theory*

A bigger concern is the provisions on effects, results or consequences of conduct mentioned in Article 4 of the ROC Criminal Code and Article 6 Paragraph 3 of the Administrative Penalty Act. As noted above, such provisions are applicable to wholly extraterritorial conduct whose result or consequence occurs within the territory of the ROC. However, they follow the logic of treating such conduct as committed partly domestically and characterizing it as domestic conduct. The domestic statutes apply to punish or sanction the conduct without a second thought. Because the effect or consequence resulting from the conduct is considered an integral part of the whole conduct, it is reasonable to characterize the whole conduct as a domestic one since it is partly domestic in this sense.

It is noteworthy that the effect or consequence resulting from conduct may also be characterized as a fact separate from the conduct itself. On this logic, extraterritorial conduct with domestic effect or consequence is still extraterritorial in its nature. If so, the application of a domestic statute to such extraterritorial conduct needs to stand on some other jurisdictional ground. Extraterritoriality is not necessarily the outcome of sovereignty. The aforementioned provisions may, by adopting a different view on characterization, extend the arm of territoriality to embrace extraterritorial conduct and lead to the applicability of domestic criminal law and administrative law. Although the terminology of extraterritoriality was avoided delicately and successfully in such provisions, this author is of the opinion that the wine of extraterritoriality is contained in a bottle labelled "territoriality". It is therefore honest to conclude that extraterritoriality is adopted also as a basic principle in the ROC criminal law and administrative law. The effects theory is legislatively adopted to apply domestic statutes and regulations to extraterritorial conduct.

Article 339-4, Paragraph 1 of the ROC Criminal Code may provide an illustration. It stipulates: "A person who commits the offense of fraud under Article 339 and who has any of the following events shall be sentenced to imprisonment for no less than one year and no more than seven years; in addition thereto, a fine of no more than one million yuan may be imposed: … 2. offense by three or more persons … " In its Criminal Judgment, Tai-Shang 3920 of 2020, the Supreme Court stated that offense includes the actors' "conduct" to commit fraud, another person's delivering property, and the "effects" that the property is acquired by the actor or third party. If no place of conduct, delivery or acquirement is located within the ROC territory, it cannot be deemed an offense within the ROC territory.[28]

28 Supreme Court's Criminal Judgment, Tai-Shang 3920 of 2020.

In judicial practice, the prescriptive jurisdiction of a domestic statute is determined according to the jurisdictional provisions prescribed in it. Once the provisions are cited to support extraterritorial application, the theory underlying the jurisdictional provisions is seldom challenged. The Supreme Court's Criminal Judgment Tai-Shang 6001 of 1997 may illustrate its reasoning. The fact found by the lower court is that the owner of a domestic travel agency assigned an unlicensed Taiwanese tour guide to lead a tourist group to Palau. It ended with the result of a tourist's drowning death in Palau. The Supreme Court ruled that the owner is punishable for the alleged crime committed abroad according to Articles 3 and 4 of the Criminal Code.[29] The statutory word "consequence" or "effect" is interpreted broadly to include the tourist's death in Palau. The causation between the tourist's death and the owner's wrongful assignment of tour guide for the group was not challenged. The requirement of directness, reasonableness or fairness in causation is not yet explicitly prescribed in statutes and is therefore not discussed by the Supreme Court.[30]

3.3 *Universal Jurisdiction and Protective Jurisdiction*

Article 5 of the ROC Criminal Code provides that the Code shall apply to several offenses that have no link of conduct or effects to ROC territory. They are characterized as foreign offenses or offenses outside the ROC territory. Prescriptive jurisdiction over such offenses is based either on the principle of international law embodied in universal jurisdiction or on the security of the state or the integrity of governmental functions that justifies protective jurisdiction over offenses committed abroad.

The prescribed offenses are the following: 1. the offense of sedition specified in Article 100; 2. The offense of treason specified in Article 103; 3. the offense of obstructing governmental operation specified in Articles 135, 136 and 138; 4. the offenses against public safety specified in Articles 185-1 and 185-2; 5. the offenses of counterfeiting state's currency specified in Articles 195 to 199; 6. the offenses of counterfeiting securities specified in Articles 201 to 202; 7. the offenses of forgery specified in Articles 211, 214 and 218, and the offenses of using the forged official documents as specified in Articles 211, 213 and 214 (Article 216); 8. the offenses relating to opium and other drugs, while the offenses of drug abuse, possession of drugs, seeds, and application tools or drug are excluded; 9. the offenses against personal freedom specified in Articles 296

29 Supreme Court's Criminal Judgment, Tai-Shang 6001 of 1997.

30 Comments to Questionnaire 5.

and 296–1; 10. the offenses of piracy specified in Articles 333 and 334; and 11. the offenses of aggravated fraud specified in Articles 339-4.

The nature of Article 5 is relevant to the scope of its application. In their Interpretation 176 of 1982, the Grand Justices ruled that it is an exception to the principle of territoriality and shall be interpreted strictly.[31] The Hong Kong and Macau Relations Act stipulates similarly in Article 43, Paragraph 2: "The Criminal Code shall also apply to offenses provided in each item of Article 5 of the Criminal Code, which are committed by Hong Kong or Macau Residents in foreign areas..." The time factor of the listed item has been disputed in practice. In its Criminal Judgment, Tai-Shang 3920 of 2020, the Supreme Court ruled that because Article 339-4, Paragraph 1 was not listed in Article 5 of the ROC Criminal Code as Item 11 of it until December 2, 2016, it does not apply to an offense committed in Hong Kong or Macau before that date.[32]

Those offenses listed in Article 5 of the ROC Criminal Code are subject to the ROC's prescriptive jurisdiction partly due to their nature as offenses against the public interests of the ROC. It is noteworthy that all states similarly assert universal jurisdiction over such offenses irrespective of national links. The overreach or conflict of states' jurisdictions is therefore inevitable.

3.4 *Nationality of the Actor (Active Personality)*

In the ROC Criminal Code, the status of the actor with respect to the ROC nationality is stipulated as a basis for prescriptive jurisdiction over some violations. Article 7 provides that the Code shall apply where any ROC national commits outside the territory of the ROC an offense which is not specified in Articles 5 and 6 but is punishable by not less than 3 years of imprisonment. However, if the offense is not punishable by the law of the place where the offense is committed, the Code shall not apply to it.

Such provision does not concern any specific sort of crimes. It focuses on the punishment that is imposed on the crime at issue. The Supreme Court has relied on it in practice. It ruled in its judgments that Article 7 supported the prosecution of a foreign act of robbery prescribed in Article 328, Paragraph 1,[33]

31 Interpretation of Grand Justices of Judicial Yuan, No. 176, announced on August 13, 1982.

32 Supreme Court's Criminal Judgment, Tai-Shang 3920 of 2020.

33 Supreme Court's Criminal Judgment, Tai-Shang 3508 of 2008. Article 328, Paragraph 1 of the ROC Criminal Code provides: "A person who uses violence, threats, drugs, hypnosis, or other means to render resistance impossible and to take away property of another or cause him to deliver it over for purpose to exercise unlawful control over other's property for himself or for a third person commits robbery and shall be sentenced to imprisonment for not less than five years."

but not the prosecution of foreign fraud prescribed in Article 339, Paragraph 1.[34]

3.5 *The "Passive Personality" Principle*

Article 7 of the ROC Criminal Code allows courts to exercise active personality jurisdiction over offenses committed by its nationals abroad. Article 8 stipulates that the provisions of Article 7 shall apply *mutatis mutandis* to an alien who commits an offense outside the territory of the ROC against a national of the ROC. Accordingly, the ROC Criminal Code applies to such offenses to protect the ROC nationals even though the relevant conduct was committed abroad by an alien. The prescriptive jurisdiction resulting from Article 8 focuses on the nationality of the victims and meets the definition of passive personality jurisdiction.

The mixed bases of prescriptive jurisdiction included in the Personal Data Protection Act[35] attract the interest of this author. Article 43 of that Act states that the provisions of Articles 41[36] and 42[37] on criminal punishment also apply to any offense specified therein if it is committed outside of the ROC's territory by nationals of the ROC against any other national of the ROC. It emphasizes the extraterritorial application of such criminal provisions. However, both the actor and the victim are required to be ROC nationals to apply these provisions.

34 Supreme Court's Criminal Judgment, Tai-Fei 121 of 2008. Article 339, Paragraph 1 of the ROC Criminal Code provides: "A person who by fraud causes another to deliver to him property belonging to such other or to a third person for purpose to exercise unlawful control over other's property for himself or for a fourth person shall be sentenced to imprisonment for not more than five years or short-term imprisonment; in lieu thereof, or in addition thereto, a fine of not more than five hundred thousand yuan may be imposed."

35 The Personal Data Protection Act was passed in 1995 and last revised in 2015.

36 Article 41 of the Personal Data Protection Act states: "If a person, with the intention of obtaining unlawful gains for himself/herself or a third party, or with the intention of impairing another person's interests, is in violation of Paragraph 1, Article 6, Articles 15, 16, 19, and Paragraph 1, Article 20, or an order or decision relating to the restrictions on cross-border transfers made by the central government authority in charge of the industry concerned in accordance with Article 21 of the PDPA, thereby causing damage to others, the person shall be sentenced to imprisonment for no more than five years; in addition thereto, a fine of no more than NT$ 1 million may be imposed."

37 Article 42 of the Personal Data Protection Act states: "If a person, with the intention of obtaining unlawful gains for himself/herself or for a third party, or infringing upon the interests of others, illegally changes or erases personal data files, or otherwise compromises the accuracy of another's personal data files, thereby causing damages to others, the person shall be sentenced to imprisonment for no more than five years or detention, and/or a fine of no more than NT$ 1 million."

This reflects a new combination of the principles of active personality and passive personality.

In addition, the Personal Data Protection Act extends the traditional principle of jurisdiction to the protection of personal data in cyberspace. It stipulates in Paragraph 2 of Article 51 that the Act applies extraterritorially to protect the personal data of the ROC nationals even if the conduct of collecting, processing, or using that data are committed abroad.[38] Without mentioning the nationality of the actors in question, it applies exceptionally to conduct committed abroad if the person to whom the personal data belong is an ROC national. This Paragraph reflects the passive personality principle as well as the effects principle since the effects of the breach of protection will be felt by an ROC national in the ROC.

The approach adopted in the ROC Personal Data Protection Act is different from the EU General Data Protection Regulation (GDPR).[39] Without mentioning the prescriptive label of "extraterritoriality" in Article 3,[40] the GDPR emphasizes that it applies when the "establishment of a controller or a processor" or the data subject is "in the Union". Its successful extension to the activities or data processing outside EU territory by a foreign controller or processor illustrates a new trend of relevant legislation. It is hoped that the Taiwanese provisions will be seriously assessed in light of the nature of the cyberworld in which extraterritoriality is of less meaning, and the legislative trend in this regard.

---

38 It states: "This Act also applies to the conducts of the governmental and the non-governmental agencies of collecting, processing or using the personal data of the ROC nationals outside the territory of the ROC."

39 REGULATION (EU) 2016/679 OF THE EUROPEAN PARLIAMENT AND OF THE COUNCIL of 27 April 2016 on the protection of natural persons with regard to the processing of personal data and on the free movement of such data, and repealing Directive 95/46/EC (General Data Protection Regulation).

40 Article 3 of the GDPR provides:

1. This Regulation applies to the processing of personal data in the context of the activities of an establishment of a controller or a processor in the Union, regardless of whether the processing takes place in the Union or not.
2. This Regulation applies to the processing of personal data of data subjects who are in the Union by a controller or processor not established in the Union, where the processing activities are related to: (a) the offering of goods or services, irrespective of whether a payment of the data subject is required, to such data subjects in the Union; or (b) the monitoring of their behaviour as far as their behaviour takes place within the Union.
3. This Regulation applies to the processing of personal data by a controller not established in the Union, but in a place where Member State law applies by virtue of public international law.

3.6 *Corporate Nationality*

Corporate criminal liability and corporate nationality are not specifically addressed in the ROC Criminal Code. In theory, to the extent that corporate criminality is recognized, the provisions shall apply to corporations as well as individuals.

Article 2 of the Money Laundering Control Act[41] defines the offense of money laundering as conduct committed by any person whose indirect activity is specified in it. Article 15 further stipulates further the punishments imposed on anyone who accepts, possesses, or uses the property or the benefits of the property without a reasonable account of the origin of such assets, or whose income is obviously disproportionate to the size of such assets in the prescribed circumstances.

The Money Laundering Control Act provides for corporate criminal liability. Article 11 Paragraph 1 of it provides: "A legal person shall be held severally liable for any offense set out in Article 8 or Article 9 committed by its representative, agent, employee or staff during the performance of duty and charged with corresponding penalty." In Article 16 Paragraph 1, it states that when a representative, an agent, an employee or employed personnel of a legal person commits such an offense during his/her performance of duties of business, the offender shall be punished, and the legal person shall also be charged with a fine in accordance with the provisions of the respective applicable provision.[42]

Article 16 Paragraph 3 of the Money Laundering Control Act provides for active personality jurisdiction over prescribed offenses committed by citizens of the ROC outside the territory of the ROC. The Supreme Court further ruled in a recent judgment that the Money Laundering Control Act applies even to acts of money laundering utilizing accounts of foreign financial institutions.[43]

Article 16 Paragraph 4 of the Money Laundering Control Act further provides such offenses apply extraterritorially. It states that unless the specified unlawful activity is not punishable by the law of the place of the act, the Act applies regardless of whether or not the unlawful activity was undertaken in or its result was felt within the territory of the ROC.

The active personality jurisdiction mentioned above applies to both individuals and corporations. The nationality of a legal person is basically decided

41 The Money Laundering Control Act was promulgated in 1996 and last amended in 2018.

42 Article 11 Paragraph 1 of the Counter-Terrorism Financing Act provides similarly: "A legal person shall be held severally liable for any offense set out in Article 8 or Article 9 committed by its representative, agent, employee or staff during the performance of duty and charged with corresponding penalty."

43 Supreme Court's Criminal Judgment, Tai-Shang 5864 of 2020.

by the law of the state concerned. A legal person has the nationality of the ROC if it was incorporated under its law. Article 4 of the Company Act[44] therefore defines a foreign company as a company, for the purpose of profit making, organized and incorporated in accordance with the laws of a foreign country. Foreign companies that are owned or controlled by domestic corporations are not ROC companies. A foreign company, within the limits prescribed by laws and regulations, is entitled to the same legal capacity as a ROC company. However, it is not subject to provisions applicable only to offenders who are ROC nationals.[45]

3.7 *Counter-Reaction to Extraterritorial Application of Foreign Laws: Blocking Statutes*

Theoretically, unless otherwise permitted by international law or jurisdictional provisions in domestic statutes, every state shall restrain from applying its domestic laws outside its territory to avoid international discord. If a foreign statute or regulation simply stipulates its extraterritorial prescriptive jurisdiction, it may unfairly reach into the territory of other states and infringe interests that are protected under their domestic laws. To counter such unfair overreach of foreign statutes, some states deploy blocking statutes.[46]

Blocking statutes are so far not an option in Taiwan's legislative practices.[47] One of the reasons is that the adoption of a blocking statute by a state is a form of political countermeasure to react to a foreign state's unlawful, offensive legal measures that infringe its national interests. It is made to increase political leverage on the government of the foreign state and to display the adopting state's plan to use its own domestic statutes as a weapon in international conflicts of interests. It is doubtful whether such statutes have legal legitimacy and constitutional basis.

The general consideration is that the battle of legitimacy or constitutionality of a state's extraterritorial statute or regulation should be fought in that state. Given the fact that an individual or corporation of another state is hardly capable of fighting against it in an unfriendly venue, however, it is suggested that legislation for blocking a particular foreign state shall be seriously considered as a necessary choice. The ROC constitutional declaration of international

---

44 The Company Act was passed in 1929 and last revised in 2018.

45 Comments to Questionnaire 8.

46 For general discussion on blocking statutes, see Jürgen Basedow, "Blocking Statutes," in Jürgen Basedow et al. ed., Encyclopedia of Private International Law, volume 1, pp. 209–214 (Cheltenham, UK: Edward Elgar Publishing Ltd, 2017).

47 Comments to Questionnaire 10.

reciprocity and comity can also be interpreted to call for reasonable and equitable solutions to the unfair overreach of foreign extraterritorial statutes.

4 Conclusion

Territoriality and extraterritoriality are adopted as principle and exception in Taiwan's enactments on criminal law and administrative law. Territoriality signals the messages of sovereign power and self-restraint of a state. Extraterritoriality follows the principle of international law and copes with the trend of foreign legislation. The effects theory is integrated to extend the scope of territoriality rather than extraterritoriality. The distinction between them is thus covered by an illusional veil.

Active personality jurisdiction, passive personality jurisdiction, protective jurisdiction and universal jurisdiction are all adopted in Taiwan's legislative practice. No blocking statute has been enacted to protect the national interests infringed by unfair overreach of foreign extraterritorial legislations. The geographic scope of the Personal Data Protection Act follows the traditional principle to protect digital data that has no concrete physical location. It is suggested to reconsider the option of adopting blocking statutes to protect national interests, and to make some proper revisions to Taiwan's data protection law in light of the scope of the EU GDPR.

The Extraterritoriality of Statutes and Regulations

United Kingdom

*Matteo Angelini**

1 Trends and Practices in the Extraterritorial Application of Statutes and Regulations

The UK has traditionally adopted a restrictive attitude towards the extraterritorial application of its statutes. Historically, this primarily territorial approach to jurisdiction was reflected in (i) a presumption by English courts against the extraterritorial application of legislation and (ii) the UK Parliament enacting expressly extraterritorial legislation only in very limited circumstances.

While the presumption against the extraterritorial application of statutes remains an important principle of statutory interpretation today, the past three decades have seen an increased willingness by the UK Parliament to enact legislation with express extraterritorial application, particularly in response to international crime and commerce. The English courts have also, on occasion, shown themselves to be willing to apply a purposive approach to statutory interpretation in order to find an intent that certain modern statutes should have extraterritorial effect.

1.1 *Traditional Approach*

The primacy of a territorial approach to jurisdiction under English law is founded upon the principle that every State is entitled to regulate the conduct of persons within its territory and is not concerned with the behaviour of those within the territory of other States.[1] It also reflects the reality that the authorities of the State in whose territory an offence is committed are generally best placed to prosecute that offence because of advantages in securing the evidence and witnesses necessary for a successful prosecution.[2] For example, the English courts have traditionally had no power to compel someone out of the jurisdiction to come to the UK to give oral evidence or to present documents to

* Counsel, WilmerHale, London, England

1 The Law Commission Published Working Paper No. 29 (12 May 1970) at para. 4.

2 United Kingdom Mission to the United Nations, Letter to the Office of Legal Affairs of the United Nations (23 March 2020) available at: https://www.un.org/en/ga/sixth/75/universal_jurisdiction/unitedkingdom_e.pdf.

 | DOI:10.1163/9789004720183_015

the court.[3] Letters of request can be issued through diplomatic channels seeking the voluntary assistance of foreign authorities. However, this is not always an effective procedure, as it relies on a foreign State's willingness to provide legal assistance.[4]

Underpinning this territorial approach to jurisdiction is a well-established and long-standing presumption under English law against the extraterritorial effect of legislation. This presumption manifests itself in two general, and widely applied, principles of statutory construction. First, unless a contrary intention appears, the UK Parliament is taken to intend a statute to extend to each territory of the UK but not to any territory outside the UK. Second, unless a contrary intention appears, the UK Parliament is also taken to intend a statute to apply to persons and matters within each territory of the UK, but not to foreigners regarding their conduct abroad.[5]

These two principles of statutory construction underpin a traditionally restrictive approach of English law to the extraterritorial application of its statutes and regulations.[6] Traditionally, the UK Parliament has enacted legislation which expressly applies to conduct outside the territory of the UK only in limited circumstances. Generally, these statutes can be divided into three categories, which are examined in more detail below[7]:

1. Statutes which make persons liable for certain specific offences when they are committed abroad based on a particular connection with the UK.
2. Statutes which extend all or large parts of English law to persons outside the UK who constitute a particular class, usually based on their relationship with the UK government.
3. Statutes which extend all of English law to all persons within certain specific geographic territories or physical structures outside the UK.

1.1.1 Particular connection with the UK

Although international law permits a State to exercise jurisdiction over its nationals travelling or residing abroad,[8] the UK has traditionally taken the view

3 The 'Roskill Report' (Fraud Trials Committee Report), 1987 at para. 5.20m available at: https://www.sfo.gov.uk/download/the-roskill-report-fraud-trials-committee-report/.

4 The 'Roskill Report' (Fraud Trials Committee Report), 1987 at para. 5.20m available at: https://www.sfo.gov.uk/download/the-roskill-report-fraud-trials-committee-report/.

5 *R (Al-Skeini) v. Secretary of State for Defence* [2007] UKHL 26 at para. 11.

6 *See* Bennion, *Statutory Interpretation,* 4th ed. (2002), p. 282, section 106, approved by the House of Lords in *R (Al-Skeini) v. Secretary of State for Defence* [2007] UKHL 26 at para. 11 and *Lawson v. Serco Ltd* [2004] 2 All ER 200 at para. 16.

7 The Law Commission Published Working Paper No. 29 (12 May 1970) at paras. 41, 75 and 84.

8 *See, e.g., R (Al-Skeini) v. Secretary of State for Defence* [2007] UKHL 26 at para. 46.

that the general body of English law does not apply to UK persons acting abroad. Instead, only certain specific statutory offences apply to foreign conduct, on the basis of a particular connection with the UK.

The particular connection which makes individuals liable under English law for such offences committed abroad is, in most cases, possession of British subject status.[9] For example, the Slave Trade Act 1824 made it an offence for "any Subject or Subjects of His Majesty" to knowingly and willfully assist in the dealing of any persons as slaves "upon the High-Seas." Similarly, the Official Secrets Act 1911 extends a number of offences to "British Officers or subjects" wherever they may be.

On some occasions, something less than residence or nationality is sufficient to trigger the extraterritorial application of a statutory provision. For example, under the long-standing Treason Act 1351 any person owing allegiance to the Crown, who engages in or supports treasonable activities, whether within the realm or elsewhere, is guilty of treason.[10] That Act recognises that the duty of allegiance to the Crown is not only based on residence or nationality but may also be owed by a foreigner not within the realm.[11]

1.1.2 Constituting a Particular Class

Some statutes extend English law, entirely or in part, to certain classes of persons when they are abroad. Generally, these are government employees, representatives, and other persons connected with government service. The rationale behind the broad application of English law to these classes is that they represent the UK and may escape prosecution in the host State if they have diplomatic protection.[12]

The earliest statute of this type is the Act 11 Will. 3 c. 12 (1698–9), which contained a provision for trial in England of any offence contrary to "the laws of this realm" or contrary to laws in force in a colony, committed by governors and commanders-in-chief in colonial territories under their jurisdiction. A more recent example is the Armed Forces Act 2006, which makes a "person subject to service law, or a civilian subject to service discipline" liable for any act that "is punishable by the law of England and Wales" or that "if done in England or Wales, would be so punishable."[13]

---

9 The Law Commission Report No. 91 (13 December 1978) at para. 85.

10 *See Joyce v. D.P.P.* [1946] A.C. 347.

11 *Ibid.* at p. 349.

12 The Law Commission Report No. 91 (13 December 1978) at para. 78.

13 Armed Forces Act 2006 sec. 42.

1.1.3 Geographic Areas and Physical Structures

Occasionally, the UK Parliament has extended the reach of English law based on a person's presence in a designated geographic area or physical structure outside the territory of the UK, thereby holding even foreign persons situated outside the UK liable for their actions under English law.

Given the UK's historically restrictive attitude towards extraterritoriality, such provisions were generally enacted with the specific objective of implementing a relevant multilateral agreement. Examples include certain provisions of the Health and Safety at Work Act 1974, which apply in designated areas outside the UK, and section 1(1) of the Tokyo Convention Act 1967, which extends English criminal law to persons on board British-controlled aircraft in flights outside the UK. For more information on these two statutes and the treaties they implement, see Section 2.

Apart from the legislation discussed above, the UK's restrictive stance on extraterritoriality can also be seen in market regulation, where a longstanding view was that jurisdiction should be based on territoriality.[14] In competition law, the UK government submitted an Aide-Mémoire to the Commission in the case of *Dyestuffs,* insisting that a state should not exercise jurisdiction against "a foreigner who or a foreign company which has committed no act within its territory."[15] This attitude was also reflected in the Protection of Trading Interests Act 1980, which aimed to thwart any extraterritorial application of US antitrust law which was considered excessive. The 1980 Act was invoked once in relation to a competition matter, though not specifically objecting to extraterritoriality.[16]

1.2 *Current Approach to Extraterritoriality*

As crime and commerce became more international, the UK's restrictive position became increasingly difficult to justify. The UK Parliament eventually intervened by enacting legislation to extend the jurisdiction of UK authorities for certain crimes when part or all the relevant criminal conduct occurred overseas.[17] In the 1960s, the Law Commission was tasked with considering how closely connected to the territory of the UK a conduct must be to constitute an

---

14 *See* R. Y. Jennings, Extraterritorial Jurisdiction and the United States Antitrust Laws (1957) 33 British Yearbook of International Law 146.

15 United Kingdom Aide-Mémoire of 20 October 1969 to Commission of the European Communities, reprinted in I. Brownlie, *Principles of Public International Law* 310, 313 (1979), at p. 313.

16 Protection of Trading Interests (US Antitrust Measures) Order 1983, SI 1983/900.

17 Dixon, *Textbook on International Law*, 7th ed. (2013) at sec. 6.2.1(b).

offence under English law.[18] Its proposals resulted in the enactment of sections 1 to 3 of the Criminal Justice Act 1993. Those provisions authorise the English courts to exercise jurisdiction over certain crimes where a constituent element of the crime occurred within UK territory.

Since then, UK statutes and regulations have been more mindful of the international elements of crime and the past three decades have seen an increasing number of statutes which are expressly stated to have extraterritorial application.[19] For example, section 63C of the Terrorism Act 2000 extends jurisdiction extraterritorially over acts of terrorism targeting the UK, regardless of the actor's location or nationality. Other UK statutes have broadened the "particular connection" with the UK that is required for a statute to have extraterritorial effect. For example, under the Bribery Act 2010, a company conducting business or part of a business in the UK can be liable for the foreign actions of a foreign subsidiary, because the two are "affiliated."[20]

Recently, the English courts have shown a willingness to find that the UK Parliament intended a statute to have extraterritorial effect even when the statute does not expressly provide for extraterritorial application. For example, in *R v. Rogers,* which concerned the conversion of criminal property contrary to section 327 of the Proceeds of Crime Act 2002, the Court of Appeal indicated that the modern approach to jurisdiction required an adjustment to the circumstances of international criminality and noted: "[t]he offence of money laundering is par excellence an offence which is no respecter of national boundaries. It would be surprising indeed if Parliament had not intended the Act to have extra-territorial effect (as we have found it did)."[21] This decision shows that the English courts may hold that a statute has extraterritorial effect when it is silent on the issue but is clearly enacted to address an international matter, and therefore requires extraterritorial application in order to be effective.

An important example of this approach is the landmark decision of *R (Al-Skeini) v. Secretary of State for Defence.*[22] In that case, the families of Iraqi citizens killed by British armed forces in Iraq began judicial review proceedings in England. The families claimed that the Secretary of State for Defence had violated Article 2 (right to life) and Article 3 (freedom from torture) of the European Convention on Human Rights (ECHR), which have force in the UK

---

18 *Ibid.*

19 *See, e.g.*, in the context of economic crime, Global Investigative Report, *Extraterritoriality: The* UK *Perspective*, 3 January 2020, accessed 20 December 2020, available at: https://globalinvestigationsreview.com/guide/the-practitioners-guide-global-investigations/2020/article/extraterritoriality-the-uk-perspective.

20 *See R v. Sweett Group* PLC discussed in Section 6.

21 *R v. Rogers* [2014] EWCA Crim 1680 at para. 52.

22 *R (Al-Skeini) v. Secretary of State for Defence* [2007] UKHL 26.

by virtue of the Human Rights Act 1998. The core issue in the case was whether the Act had extraterritorial application. The House of Lords held that it did: the Act necessarily applied to acts of UK public authorities abroad which were within the "jurisdiction" of the UK for the purposes of Article 1 ECHR. The court arrived at that conclusion by emphasising that the fundamental purpose of the Human Rights Act (i.e., the protection of fundamental human rights) would be undermined if it is not given extraterritorial effect.[23]

The globalised nature of economic activity has also prompted the UK to reconsider its position on extraterritoriality in competition law. EU competition law has adopted the "qualified effects" doctrine as a basis for jurisdiction, catching conduct outside the EU as long as it has foreseeable, immediate and substantial anti-competitive effect within the EU.[24] In 2018, the English High Court applied the qualified effects doctrine in a claim against Google for breach of EU competition regulation along with the Competition Act 1998.[25] More recently, the Court of Appeal interpreted the Competition Act 1998 as having extraterritorial effect, in both its prohibitions and its investigation and enforcement regimes.[26] The court considered the presumption against the extraterritorial application of statutes but held that Parliament intended the relevant sections of the Competition Act to have extraterritorial effect, as admissible pre-legislative material made clear that the Act was intended to be consistent with EU law.[27] Consequently, the Competition and Markets Authority (CMA) has the power to issue information requests even to foreign-domiciled companies with no UK presence.

The expanding extraterritorial reach of the CMA was recently codified in law by the Digital Markets, Competition and Consumers Act, which received royal assent in May 2024. Prohibitions on anticompetitive agreements and cartels now explicitly apply to activities implemented outside the UK.[28] The CMA's power to give notice to a person outside the UK even where that person has no UK connection is also codified.[29]

---

23 *R (Al-Skeini) v. Secretary of State for Defence* [2007] UKHL 26, at para. 54 ("the purpose of the 1998 Act is to provide remedies in our domestic law to those whose human rights are violated by a United Kingdom public authority. Making such remedies available for acts of a United Kingdom authority on the territory of another state would not be offensive to the sovereignty of the other state.")

24 Case C-413/14 P *Intel v Commission* EU:C:2017:632.

25 *Unlockd Ltd v. Google Ireland Ltd* [2018] EWHC 1363 (Ch).

26 *Competition and Markets Authority v Volkswagen* AG [2023] EWCA Civ 1506

27 *Ibid.* at para. 50.

28 Competition Act 2018 sec. 2(1), as substituted by the Digital Markets, Competition and Consumers Act 2024 sec. 119(2).

29 Digital Markets, Competition and Consumers Act 2024 sec. 111.

Last but not least, the UK's General Data Protection Regulation (GDPR) regime also expressly incorporates far-reaching extraterritorial elements. For example, it applies to the processing of personal data in the context of an establishment of a controller or a processor in the UK, regardless of whether the processing takes place in the UK.[30] Equally, data controllers or processors entirely outside the UK may be subject to GDPR where a data subject is in the UK.[31]

1.3 *Conclusion*

In conclusion, the UK largely retains its restrictive approach to extraterritoriality. In particular, the presumption against the extraterritorial application of legislation continues to play an important role in statutory interpretation, and the UK Parliament maintains its position against the unilateral imposition of UK laws abroad. The general rule also continues to be that UK nationals are not subject to English law when acting outside the UK.

In recent years, however, the UK Parliament has been increasingly willing to enact legislation with express extraterritorial application. Courts have taken note and are willing to adopt a purposive approach to find that the UK Parliament had an extraterritorial intent when a multi-jurisdictional issue is at stake and the purpose of the statute would be undermined if it were not given extraterritorial effect.

2 The Influence of Multilateral or Regional Instruments

The UK has implemented several multilateral agreements pursuant to which English prescriptive jurisdiction is applied extraterritorially. The extraterritorial application of these statutes is generally based on UK nationality or residence; a UK nexus; or universal jurisdiction.

2.1 *Treaties: Extraterritorial Jurisdiction based on UK Nationality or Residence*

The UK is a party to certain multilateral treaties which encourage it to prosecute its nationals and residents for specific crimes they may have committed abroad. These include:

- The Bribery Act 2010, section 12 of which implements an extended nationality principle that covers all persons who have "a close connection with

---

30 Data Protection Act 2018 sec. 207(2).

31 Data Protection Act 2018 sec. 207(3).

the UK", including not only UK citizens, but also individuals ordinarily resident in the UK and bodies incorporated under English law (including UK subsidiaries of foreign companies). This provision goes to the UK's compliance with Article 42 of the United Nations Convention Against Corruption, which encourages states to establish extraterritorial jurisdiction in appropriate circumstances.
- The International Criminal Court Act 2001, which gives effect to the Statute of the International Criminal Court and applies to acts committed outside the UK by a UK national, a UK resident or a person subject to UK service jurisdiction;[32] and
- The Domestic Abuse Act 2021, which was enacted as part of the UK's efforts to comply with Article 44 of the Istanbul Convention, and applies to conduct committed outside the UK by any UK national or person who is habitually resident in the UK.[33]

2.2 *Treaties: Extraterritorial Jurisdiction based on a UK Nexus*

The UK has also implemented certain international treaties under which English domestic legislation applies extraterritorially regardless of nationality, provided there is some connection with the UK. Examples include:
- The Health and Safety at Work Act 1974 (Application outside Great Britain) Order 2013, which applies to specified offshore areas and work activities occurring in designated areas within the Exclusive Economic Zone adjacent to British territorial waters. The UK designated its extraterritorial Exclusive Economic Zone per the United Nations Convention of the Law of the Sea, and jurisdiction is based on proximity to the British Coast.[34]
- The Tokyo Convention Act 1967, section 1 of which extends English law to all persons on board British-controlled aircraft, regardless of their nationality, even when they are flying outside the UK. This provision was enacted in furtherance of the Tokyo Convention on Offences and certain other Acts Committed on board Aircraft.
- The Antarctic Act 1994, which implements, *inter alia*, the 1959 Antarctic Treaty and its 1994 Protocol. Sections 8 through 12 of the Act hold any "non-national on a British expedition" to Antarctica liable for certain

32 *See, e.g.*, International Criminal Court Act 2001 at secs. 51, 52, 54.

33 Domestic Abuse Act 2021 sec. 72.

34 The United Nations Convention on the Law of the Sea defines an Exclusive Economic Zone as an area not extending beyond 200 nautical miles from shore, within which the coastal state has the right to explore and exploit, and the responsibility to conserve and manage, both living and non-living resources.

offences under the Act. Under section 3, a British expedition is one which was organised in or which departed from the UK but was not authorised or organised by another Contracting Party to the Protocol.

2.3 *Treaties: Universal Extraterritorial Jurisdiction*

Lastly, there are some international treaties pursuant to which the UK exercises universal extraterritorial jurisdiction. These include:

- The Geneva Conventions Act 1957, which implements Geneva Conventions I, II, III and IV. sSection 1 of the Act provides that "[a]ny person, whatever his nationality, who, whether in or outside the United Kingdom, commits, or aids, abets or procures the commission by any other person of a grave breach of any of the scheduled conventions" shall be guilty of an offence.
- The Criminal Justice Act 1988, section 134 of which is related to the Convention against Torture and Other Cruel, Inhuman or Degrading Treatment or Punishment. It provides that "a public official or person acting in an official capacity, whatever his nationality, commits the offence of torture if in the United Kingdom or elsewhere he intentionally inflicts severe pain or suffering on another in the performance or purported performance of his official duties".
- The United Nations Personnel Act 1997, which implements the Convention on the Safety of UN and Associated Personnel 1994. Section 1(1) provides that "[i]f a person does outside the United Kingdom any act to or in relation to a UN worker which, if he had done it in any part of the United Kingdom, would have made him guilty of any of the offences mentioned in subsection (2), he shall in that part of the United Kingdom be guilty of that offence".

For more information about universal jurisdiction under English law, see Section 6.

2.4 *Brexit*

The UK withdrew from the European Union on 31 January 2020 and the withdrawal transition period ended on 31 December 2020.

The multilateral agreements entered into by the UK in its own capacity (and not as a member of the EU) automatically continued to apply to the UK after its withdrawal from the EU, and after the end of the transition period. However, treaties signed and concluded by the EU which fall exclusively within the EU's competence no longer apply to the UK after the end of the transition period. Where an agreement was unlikely to apply after the end of the transition period, the UK government has in some cases negotiated the UK's accession to or entry into a new arrangement. For example, in the run-up to

Brexit, the UK Parliament enacted the European Union (Withdrawal) Act 2018 to retain EU-derived domestic law after the UK's exit from the EU and the end of the transition period.

3 The Role of International Law

International law plays an important role in defining and limiting the territorial scope of the UK's statutes and regulations. International law principles of state sovereignty, in particular, impact the English courts' interpretation of the territorial application of statutes and account in part for English law's primarily territorial approach towards the application of legislation.

Under English law, every statute is interpreted, "so far as its language permits, so as not to be inconsistent with the comity of nations or the established rules of international law."[35] One such established rule of international law is the requirement that one State should not by the claim or exercise of jurisdiction infringe the sovereignty of another State in breach of rules of international law. Hence, the presumption that statutes do not apply extraterritorially unless the UK Parliament indicates otherwise is, at least in part, founded on international law. This was directly stated by Lord Lloyd-Jones in *R (On the Application of* KBR*) v. Director of the Serious Fraud Office*, in which he held that:

> The presumption reflects, in part, the requirements of international law that one State should not by the claim or exercise of jurisdiction infringe the sovereignty of another State in breach of rules of international law. Thus, for example, legislation requiring conduct in a foreign State which would be in breach of the laws of that State or otherwise inconsistent with the sovereign right of that State to regulate activities within its territory may well be a breach of international law.[36]

In that case, the Supreme Court found that section 2(3) of the Criminal Justice Act 1987, which empowers the Serious Fraud Office (SFO) to require a person to collate material held abroad and produce it to the SFO on pain of criminal penalty, does not extend to foreign companies with no fixed UK place of business and/or those which are not carrying on business in the UK. Similarly, in

35 Lord Reid in *R (Al-Skeini) v. Secretary of State for Defence* [2007] UKHL 26 at para. 45, citing Maxwell, *The Interpretation of Statutes* (12th edition, 1969), p. 183.

36 *R (On the Application of* KBR*) v. Director of the Serious Fraud Office* [2021] UKSC 2 at para. 24.

R v. Jameson, the court noted that the presumption that a statute will not be construed as applying to foreigners in respect of acts done by them abroad "is a rule based on international law by which one sovereign power is bound to respect the subjects and the rights of all other sovereign powers outside its own territory."[37] An issue in that case was whether section 11 of the Foreign Enlistment Act 1870 applied to non-UK subjects acting outside "the Queen's dominions." The Court held that it did not.

The UK has also enacted "blocking statutes" in order to restrain the application of extraterritorial laws within its borders or with respect to British legal persons. Part of the reasoning behind these blocking statutes is the international law principle that the unilateral imposition of laws on another sovereign State is illegal under international law. For more information about the UK's blocking legislation, see Section 10.

Conversely, international law also recognises that States have a legitimate interest in legislating regarding the conduct of their nationals abroad. As a result, the strength of the presumption against the extraterritorial application of legislation is weaker with regard to UK nationals abroad.[38] Indeed, in *R v. Jameson* the court held that, unlike non-UK subjects, "subjects of the Queen" were subject to section 11 of the Foreign Enlistment Act 1870 "wherever they might be."[39] More recently, Lord Rodger stated the matter in *Al-Skeini* in the following terms:

> Subjects of the Crown, British citizens, are in a different boat. International law does not prevent a state from exercising jurisdiction over its nationals travelling or residing abroad, since they remain under its personal authority: *Oppenheim's International Law*, 9th ed (1992), vol 1, Pt 1, para 138. So there can be no objection in principle to Parliament legislating for British citizens outside the United Kingdom, provided that the particular legislation does not offend against the sovereignty of other states.[40]

Thus, international law principles of state sovereignty play an important role in both limiting and defining the territorial scope of UK legislation. On the one hand, the principle that a State shall not infringe on the sovereignty of another State curtails the extraterritorial application of laws to foreigners outside the

37 *R v. Jameson* [1896] 2 QB 425 at p. 430.
38 *Masri v. Consolidated Contractors International* (UK) *Ltd* (*No 4*) [2009] UKHL 43 at para. 10.
39 *R v. Jameson* [1896] 2 QB 425 at p. 431.
40 *R* (*Al-Skeini*) *v. Secretary of State for Defence* [2007] UKHL 26 at para. 46.

UK. On the other hand, the principle that a State may exercise sovereignty over its nationals wherever they may be allows the application of certain UK statutes to UK nationals based abroad.

4 The Role of International Comity

It is important to note that English law does not recognise international comity as a binding international legal obligation. International comity has instead been described in case law as "something less than a rule of international law"[41] and in legal writing as "a species of accommodation"[42] that is "far from a binding norm, but [...] more than mere courtesy exercised between state courts."[43] However, the English courts have recognised, on more than one occasion, international comity as one of the reasons behind the UK's primarily territorial approach to jurisdiction. For example, in *Lawson v. Serco*, Lord Hoffmann held that:

> The general principle of construction is, of course, that legislation is *prima facie* territorial. The United Kingdom rarely purports to legislate for the whole world. Some international crimes, like torture, are an exception. But usually such an exorbitant exercise of legislative power would be both ineffectual and contrary to the comity of nations.[44]

More recently, in *Al-Skeini*, Lord Rodger stated that:

> It would usually be both objectionable in terms of international comity and futile in practice for Parliament to assert its authority over the subjects of another sovereign who are not within the United Kingdom. So, in the absence of any indication to the contrary, a court will interpret legislation as not being intended to affect such people.[45]

41 *R (On the Application of* KBR) *v. Director of the Serious Fraud Office* [2021] UKSC 2 at para. 24

42 Crawford, Brownlie's *Principles of Public International Law*, 9th ed (2019), p. 21; cited by *R (On the Application of* KBR) *v. Director of the Serious Fraud Office* [2021] UKSC 2 at para. 24

43 Crawford, Brownlie's *Principles of Public International Law*, 9th ed (2019), p. 468 cited by *R (On the Application of* KBR) *v. Director of the Serious Fraud Office* [2021] UKSC 2 at para. 24

44 *Lawson v. Serco* [2006] ICR 250 at para. 6.

45 *R (Al-Skeini) v. Secretary of State for Defence* [2007] UKHL 26 at para. 45.

Thus, it is clear that international comity, despite not being a binding legal obligation, does have a role in defining and limiting the territorial scope of English law. This is because international comity provides a rationale behind the presumption against the extraterritorial application of UK legislation.

This is confirmed by the recent Supreme Court decision in KBR, where the Court drew an express link between international comity and the presumption against the extraterritorial application of UK legislation. As discussed in Section 3 above, KBR concerned the question whether section 2(3) of the Criminal Justice Act 1987 extends to foreign companies with no fixed place of business and not carrying on business in the UK. The Supreme Court held that it did not. In coming to this conclusion, the Court was required to address the tension between the domestic law presumption that "legislation is generally not intended to have extra-territorial effect" and international law's recognition of "a legitimate interest of States in legislating in respect of the conduct of their nationals abroad."[46] The Supreme Court held that:

> The [domestic law] presumption reflects, in part, the requirements of international law that one State should not by the claim or exercise of jurisdiction infringe the sovereignty of another State in breach of rules of international law. […] However, the rationale and resulting scope of the presumption are wider than this. They are also rooted in the concept of comity. The term "comity" is used here to describe something less than a rule of international law. […]
>
> The lack of precisely defined rules in international law as to the limits of legislative jurisdiction makes resort to the principle of comity as a basis of the presumption applied by courts in this jurisdiction all the more important. As a result, the presumption in domestic law is more extensive and reflects the usages of States acting out of mutual respect and, no doubt, the expectation of reciprocal advantage. *Accordingly, it is not necessary, in invoking the presumption, to demonstrate that the extra-territorial application of the legislation in issue would infringe the sovereignty of another State in violation of international law.*[47]

In other words, the Supreme Court took the view that, since the domestic law presumption against the extraterritorial application of legislation is founded in part on the principle of the comity of nations, contravention of this principle

46 *R (On the Application of* KBR) *v. Director of the Serious Fraud Office* [2021] UKSC 2 at paras. 21.
47 *Ibid.* at paras. 24–25 (emphasis added).

alone can be sufficient to deny the extraterritorial application of a statute or regulation.

In conclusion, international comity has long been one of the reasons behind the UK's primarily territorial approach to jurisdiction. Recently, the Supreme Court in KBR has strengthened the link between comity and the domestic presumption against extraterritorially. In doing so, it may have opened the door for international comity to play a greater role in limiting the extraterritorial reach of legislation.

5 Reasonableness in the Extraterritorial Application of Statutes and Regulations

When interpreting a statute, the English courts will always presume that Parliament intended to act reasonably rather than unreasonably. Accordingly, while there is no express requirement of "reasonableness" in the extraterritorial application of statutes unless the UK Parliament has so provided, a standard of "reasonableness" nevertheless exists and will be implemented as a result of the way the courts interpret legislation.

Where a statute is silent or ambiguous, the application of principles of statutory construction will determine the scope of its extraterritorial effect. In this regard, the UK's Supreme Court has stated that "[t]he answer will depend on the wording, purpose and context of the legislation considered in light of relevant principles of interpretation and principles of international law and comity."[48] In addition to a purposive approach to interpretation, the courts will consider the legislative history and intention of Parliament when determining whether a statute has extraterritorial application. The Supreme Court has confirmed that "[t]he more exorbitant the jurisdiction, the more is likely to be required of the statutory provisions in order to rebut the presumption against extraterritorial effect."[49]

Accordingly, even though there is no express requirement of reasonableness, the English courts through their approach to statutory interpretation will ensure that a standard of reasonableness governs the extraterritorial application of statutes. For example, in KBR, discussed in Section 3 above, the statute in question (the Criminal Justice Act 1987) was silent as to its extraterritorial

48 *R (On the Application of* KBR) *v. Director of the Serious Fraud Office* [2021] UKSC 2 at para. 27.

49 *Ibid.* at para. 28.

effect.[50] The Supreme Court held that the Director of the SFO's power to compel disclosure of materials under the Act does not extend to foreign companies with no fixed UK place of business and/or those which are not carrying on business in the UK, as such an extension "would be inconsistent with the Parliamentary intention as evidenced by the scheme and history of the legislation" and "any attempt to [hold otherwise] would exceed the appropriate bounds of interpretation and usurp the function of Parliament."[51] The Court ultimately found that the legislative history and purpose of the statute supported a reasonable finding that the power to compel disclosure did not extend to foreign companies beyond what was provided in the statute.

Another illustration of the application of a reasonableness standard when considering the extraterritorial effect of statutes is found in the approach of the UK to jurisdiction in criminal cases. In cases involving multiple jurisdictions, Crown Prosecutors, pursuant to Director's Guidance, will consider whether the UK would be the most appropriate to prosecute the offender(s), taking into consideration, *inter alia*, whether the prosecution could be divided into separate cases in two or more jurisdictions; the location and interests of the victim(s) and witness(es) and the accused; and delay.[52] While there is no explicit reasonableness requirement in these guidelines, these considerations come close to applying a reasonableness standard to determine the most appropriate forum.

6 Application of UK Law to Wholly Foreign Conduct

6.1 *UK Nationality or Residence*

The UK has statutes and regulations that apply to wholly foreign conduct on the basis of the nationality of the actor. Although international law permits a State to exercise jurisdiction over its nationals travelling or residing abroad,[53] British persons acting outside the UK are only liable for specific statutory offences under English law. These offences operate extraterritorially based on one or more types of UK nationality or residence.

The connection with the UK that makes legal persons liable under English law for such offences committed abroad is, in most cases, possession of British

50 *See* Tim Cochrane, *The Presumption Against Extraterritoriality, Mutual Legal Assistance, and the Future of Law Enforcement Cross-Border Evidence Collection*, Modern Law Review (Aug. 2021).

51 *R* (KBR, *Inc*) *v. Director of the Serious Fraud Office* [2021] UKSC 2 at para. 65.

52 *Jurisdiction*, Crown Prosecution Service (2 Sept. 2020), https://www.cps.gov.uk/legal-guidance/jurisdiction.

53 *See, e.g.*, *R* (*Al-Skeini*) *v. Secretary of State for Defence* [2007] UKHL 26 at para. 46.

subject status. For example, section 72 of the Sexual Offences Act 2003 applies to certain acts done outside the UK, where the person who does the act is a UK national or resident at the time the act in question is done or when the proceedings are brought.

In other cases, something less than nationality or residence may suffice to justify the extraterritorial application of a statute. Certain provisions of the *Bribery Act 2010* are of particularly broad application. Under section 7 of that Act, for example, a "commercial organisation" can be guilty of an offence if it fails to take reasonable steps to prevent a person "associated with" it from bribing another to obtain or retain business or an advantage in the conduct of business for that organisation. A "relevant commercial organisation" is defined broadly to include any body corporate or partnership "(wherever incorporated) which carries on a business, or part of a business, in any part of the United Kingdom." Moreover, the act of bribery may take place anywhere in the world. This provision was applied recently in *R v. Sweett Group Plc* to find a UK parent company liable for a bribe paid by its Cypriot subsidiary to a non-British national in the United Arab Emirates.[54]

Other specific extraterritorial offences applicable based on one or more types of UK nationality or residence include: murder or manslaughter;[55] corruption;[56] offences under official secrets legislation;[57] and certain offences related to explosive substances.[58]

6.2 *Passive Personality*

The UK historically did not claim, or recognise claims to, criminal jurisdiction based on "passive personality" (i.e., the nationality of the person harmed by the conduct in question).[59] However, it has recently adopted the "passive personality" principle regarding some terrorist offences. For example, section 63C

54 *R v Sweett Group plc* (2016, unreported). *See also* DPP *v. Joyce*, in which the House of Lords held that the Treason Act 1351 applied to any person owing allegiance to the Crown, wherever located ("if an alien is under British protection he occupies the same position when abroad as he would occupy if he were a British subject. Each of them owes allegiance, and in so doing each is subject to the jurisdiction of the British Crown." per Lord Porter at pp. 375–76).

55 Offences Against the Person Act 1861 sec. 9 (as amended by the Criminal Law Act 1967 sec. 10(2)).

56 The Bribery Act 2010 sec. 12.

57 The Official Secrets Act 1911 sec. 10; Official Secrets Act 1989 sec. 15.

58 The Explosive Substances Act 1883 secs. 2, 3.

59 Michael Hirst, Murder As An Offence Under English Law, 68 JoCL 315 (2004) (noting that prior to the Terrorism Act 2000, "English law ha[d] never before embraced this "passive personality principle" of jurisdiction").

of the Terrorism Act 2000 extends jurisdiction extraterritorially over acts of terrorism if they are "done to, or in relation to, a United Kingdom national, a United Kingdom resident or a protected person."

6.3 *Protective Principle*

The English courts have recognised the existence of the protective principle (i.e., a State asserting jurisdiction over those who are not nationals but whose actions have an adverse effect on the State irrespective of where those actions have been committed). However, as far as the author is aware, they have not relied on the protective principle alone as a basis to assert extraterritorial jurisdiction.[60]

In DPP *v. Joyce*, a British passport holder was convicted of treason under the Treason Act 1351 for broadcasting pro-German propaganda from Germany during the Second World War. He appealed his conviction on, *inter alia*, the ground that "no English court has jurisdiction to try an alien for a crime committed abroad." The House of Lords disagreed, with Lord Jowitt L.C. stating that:

> No principle of comity demands that a state should ignore the crime of treason committed against it outside its territory. On the contrary a proper regard for its own security requires that all those who commit that crime, whether they commit it within or without the realm should be amenable to its laws.[61]

Thus, the House of Lords recognised that a State may pursue extraterritorial jurisdiction based on the protective principle. This was stated in *obiter dicta*, however, as the House of Lords ultimately determined that "since [the Treason Act 1351] is declaratory of the crime of treason, it can apply only to those who are capable of committing that crime", namely those who owe allegiance to the UK. Since Joyce was a British passport holder, the UK had a duty to protect him and he in turn owed a duty of allegiance to the King. In other words, extraterritorial jurisdiction was based on Joyce's status as a British subject rather than the protective principle alone.

More recently, the Privy Council in *Somchai Liangsiriprasert v. Government of the United States of America* recognised the protective principle.[62]

---

60 *Halsbury's Laws of England*, International Law and Foreign Relations (Volume 61 (2018)), 10. Jurisdiction, 216. Protective principle, footnote 2.

61 *DPP v. Joyce* [1946] AC 347.

62 *Somchai Liangsiriprasert v. Government of the United States of America* [1991] 1 A.C. 225.

Liangsiriprasert concerned a conspiracy to import heroin to the United States from Thailand, the proceeds of which were to be collected in Hong Kong. In the context of considering the Hong Kong courts' jurisdiction under the common law, Lord Griffiths held:

> Unfortunately in this century crime has ceased to be largely local in origin and effect. Crime is now established on an international scale and the common law must face this new reality. Their Lordships can find nothing in precedent, comity or good sense that should inhibit the common law from regarding as justiciable in England inchoate crimes committed abroad which are intended to result in the commission of criminal offences in England. Accordingly a conspiracy entered into in Thailand with the intention of committing the criminal offence of trafficking in drugs in Hong Kong is justiciable in Hong Kong even if no overt act pursuant to the conspiracy has yet occurred in Hong Kong.[63]

The Privy Council, therefore, recognised extraterritorial jurisdiction based on the protective principle. However, in establishing jurisdiction, the Council then went on to rely on the fact that at least one act in furtherance of the conspiracy had been committed in Hong Kong,[64] making this another case in which jurisdiction was not based solely on the protective principle.

The decision in *Liangsiriprasert* was subsequently relied upon by the Court of Appeal in *R v. Sansom*, in which four defendants were charged with conspiring to evade the prohibition on the importation of a controlled drug by entering into an agreement to smuggle cannabis resin in bulk from Morocco to England. Unlike *Liangsiriprasert,* in which the conspiracy charge was based on the common law, the conspiracy in *Sansom* was based in statute, namely the Criminal Law Act 1977.[65]

At trial, jurisdiction was asserted based on an extraterritorial conspiracy that, if carried out, would produce effects within the UK. When the case came before the Court of Appeal, the bench expressly adopted the Privy Council's reasoning in *Liangsiriprasert* in the context of statutory conspiracy offences. However, as with jurisdiction in *Liangsiriprasert,* the Court of Appeal ultimately found that it had jurisdiction because one of the defendants had taken steps to advance the conspiracy (arranging for a vessel) in the UK.[66]

---

63 *Ibid.* at p. 251.
64 *Ibid.* at p. 251.
65 *R v. Sansom* [1991] 2 All ER 145.
66 *Ibid.* at p. 150.

Thus, while the English courts have recognised the existence of the protective principle, the author is not aware of a decision in which an English court has found extraterritorial jurisdiction based solely on the protective principle.

6.4 *Universal Jurisdiction*

The UK considers the term "universal jurisdiction" to refer to national jurisdiction established over a crime, irrespective of the location of the alleged crime, the nationality of the alleged perpetrator, the nationality of the victim, or other links to the prosecuting State.[67] The UK has statutes and regulations that apply to wholly foreign conduct on the basis of the principle of universal jurisdiction. These include provisions regarding genocide, crimes against humanity and war crimes,[68] torture,[69] piracy,[70] hostage-taking,[71] and hijacking.[72]

The fact that the UK has decided to provide for such jurisdiction as a matter of domestic law does not mean that such jurisdiction should always be exercised. The UK has previously highlighted the importance of using procedural requirements to ensure that universal jurisdiction is exercised responsibly, believing such requirements to be an important safeguard.[73] Domestic prosecuting authorities in the UK would not usually seek to institute proceedings against a suspect who was not present in the jurisdiction, and may need prior permission to proceed.[74] For example, national proceedings for an offence under section 1A of the Geneva Conventions Act 1957 (i.e., for grave breaches of the Geneva Conventions) can only be instituted in the UK with the consent of the Attorney General – who would ensure that public interest considerations, including considerations of international law and comity when appropriate, are taken into account before a decision to prosecute is made.

---

67 United Kingdom Mission to the United Nations, Letter to the Office of Legal Affairs of the United Nations (23 March 2020) available at: https://www.un.org/en/ga/sixth/75/universal_jurisdiction/unitedkingdom_e.pdf.

68 International Criminal Court Act 2001 secs. 51, 52, 54.

69 The Criminal Justice Act 1988 sec. 134.

70 The Tokyo Convention Act 1967 sec. 4.

71 The Taking of Hostages Act 1982 sec. 1.

72 The Aviation Security Act 1982 secs. 1, 2, 6.

73 United Kingdom Mission to the United Nations, Letter to the Office of Legal Affairs of the United Nations (23 March 2020) available at: https://www.un.org/en/ga/sixth/75/universal_jurisdiction/unitedkingdom_e.pdf.

74 *See* above.

6.5 *Conclusion*

In summary, under English law, the main bases for extraterritorial jurisdiction are the nationality of the actor and the principle of universal jurisdiction. Extraterritorial jurisdiction based on the passive personality and protective principles is more limited and controversial. The Terrorism Act 2000 is the first time the UK has passed legislation based on passive personality jurisdiction. English case law has considered the protective principle as a basis for extraterritorial jurisdiction but has yet to find extraterritorial jurisdiction of a statute exclusively on this basis.

7 Local Conduct as the Basis for Extraterritorial Application of Statutes and Regulations

The UK has several statutes that apply to conduct occurring in a foreign jurisdiction on the basis of territorial links. However, these territorial links vary depending on what the UK Parliament has prescribed in the statute.

Historically, the jurisdiction of the English courts has been linked to territory – namely, where the crime or act has been committed. As crime increased in organisation, sophistication and globalisation, it became difficult to justify the inability to prosecute wrongdoers who committed all of the preliminary steps in the UK but completed the crime abroad. Consequently, the Law Commission was tasked with reconsidering the difficult question of how closely connected with UK territory a conduct must be before it constitutes an offence under English law.

The review of the Law Commission ultimately resulted in the enactment of the Criminal Justice Act 1993. It is important to note that the 1993 Act preserves the principle of territoriality in criminal matters: the starting point under the Act is that the UK does not have jurisdiction over acts occurring outside the territory. In this way, the Criminal Justice Act 1993 continues to reflect the UK's traditional approach which is that it would be inappropriate and contrary to international law to impose the UK's prescriptive criminal laws extraterritorially.[75]

Instead of extending the scope of its jurisdiction extraterritorially, the Criminal Justice Act 1993 broadens the definition of what constitutes sufficient conduct within its territory to justify the UK exercising jurisdiction. In this way, the 1993 Act extends the jurisdiction of the UK by authorising the English courts

75 The Bribery Act, on the other hand, extends jurisdictional reach to acts occurring outside the UK but involving actors connected to the UK, as discussed in Section 6.

to exercise jurisdiction over certain crimes where a constituent element of the crime occurred within UK territory, whether or not the final element was completed therein.

The Terrorism Act 2000 adopts a similar approach. It allows the English courts to claim jurisdiction over offences and breaches which are commenced within the UK, even if the rest of the offence or breach is committed in a foreign country. For example, Section 59 establishes that it is an offence for a person "to incite[] another person to commit an act of terrorism wholly or partly outside the United Kingdom."[76] The Terrorism Act 2000 expressly states that for the purpose of this offence "it is immaterial whether or not the person incited is in the United Kingdom at the time of the incitement."[77]

The principal money laundering offences created by the Proceeds of Crime Act 2002 (POCA) are also of broad extraterritorial application. The purpose of POCA is to criminalise all forms of money laundering.[78] Under POCA, the location of the underlying criminal conduct is immaterial. The relevant question for the purpose of establishing jurisdiction is whether the conduct in question would constitute a criminal offence had it occurred in the UK. This was confirmed in *R v. Rogers*. In that case, a UK citizen resident in Spain allowed the proceeds of a fraudulent scheme to be paid into a Spanish bank account he controlled and to be withdrawn by another individual. The defence argued that the English courts did not have jurisdiction under POCA against a non-UK resident in circumstances where the conduct occurred entirely outside the United Kingdom. The Court dismissed this defence, noting that Parliament had intended the primary criminal offences under POCA to be extraterritorial in effect. The Court concluded that there was jurisdiction on the basis that the acts that "a significant part of the criminality underlying the case took place in England, including the continued deprivation of the victims of their monies."[79] The decision confirmed that a person may be guilty of an offence under POCA where both the criminal conduct that gives rise to money laundering, and the act of money laundering, take place outside the UK.

---

76 Terrorism Act 2000 sec. 59(1).

77 Terrorism Act 2000 sec. 59(4).

78 POCA establishes three key criminal offenses: (I) concealing, disguising, converting, transferring or removing from the UK, any criminal property (sec. 327); (II) entering or becoming concerned in arrangements that one knows or suspects facilitate the acquisition, use, etc., of criminal property (sec. 328); and (III) acquiring, using or possessing criminal property (sec. 329).

79 *R v. Rogers (Bradley) and others* [2014] EWCA Crim 1680 at para. 55.

The Fraud Act 2006 also has broad extraterritorial application. The Fraud Act 2006 establishes three classes of statutory fraud: (I) fraud by false representation, (II) fraud by failing to disclose information and (III) fraud by abuse of position. Where any element of these offenses occurs within the UK, the English courts will have jurisdiction regardless of whether the person charged is a UK citizen or was in the jurisdiction at the time of the offence.

As a final example, the Extradition Act 2003 sets out the relevant UK legal framework for extradition between EU Member States. Notably, extradition between EU Member States is governed by the European arrest warrant, which is based on principles of mutual trust and was created to ensure speedy extradition proceedings. After Brexit, however, the UK will need new arrangements with EU Member States to maintain appropriate degrees of co-operation regarding extradition.

In summary, the UK has several statutes relating to criminal offences that apply to activity occurring partly in foreign countries. Particularly in the context of economic crimes, the UK is willing to extend its jurisdiction and prosecute in the UK even where the criminal conduct in question occurred in foreign countries. In such cases, a key consideration for the UK courts when deciding if there is a sufficient jurisdictional nexus is whether the criminal conduct in question had an impact on victims in the UK.

8 Corporate Nationality in the Extraterritorial Application of Statutes and Regulations

As discussed in Sections 1 and 6 above, certain UK statutes and regulations are applied to foreign conduct based on the nationality of the actor. In such cases, corporate nationality is determined by the seat of the corporation, meaning UK-seated corporations are subject to UK laws, and corporations seated outside the UK generally are not. Since corporations have a separate legal personality under English law, the nationalities of their shareholders and subsidiaries do not matter. A rare exception to this principle is when a court decides to pierce the corporate veil.

8.1 *Corporate Nationality under English Law*

The domicile of a corporation, under English law, is in the country under whose law it is incorporated. Therefore, under English law, a company formed under the Companies Act 2006 will have an English domicile if it is registered in England. Companies that are incorporated outside the UK but which establish a branch within the UK are nevertheless subject to certain obligations under the Companies Act 2006.[80]

In the case of a company registered in England under the Companies Act 2006 or any other Act (notwithstanding that the company's business is entirely abroad), the company is deemed to be present in England by virtue of its incorporation in England. Consistently with this principle, a corporation's nationality under the Civil Jurisdiction and Judgments Act (CJJA) of 1982 is determined by its seat of corporation or association, which is treated as its domicile. A corporation has its seat in the UK if (I) it was incorporated under a law of a part of the UK and has either a registered office or some other official address in the UK; or (II) its central management and control is exercised in the UK.[81] The nationality of the shareholders and the principal place of business or headquarters are not determinative of corporate nationality under the CJJA.

Statutes and regulations that are applied to foreign conduct based on the actor's nationality will generally only apply to domestic corporations which are domiciled in the UK. There is a limited exception to this principle, known as "piercing the corporate veil", which could involve holding a parent company directly liable for the subsidiary's obligations. The English courts have repeatedly emphasised that this is a very narrow doctrine, which applies only in cases of impropriety where a company is set up for fraudulent purposes or to evade an existing legal obligation.[82]

8.2 *Jurisdiction over the Conduct of a Foreign Corporation*

The foreign conduct of a foreign-domiciled corporation or subsidiary could still be subject to English law on some other basis which does not arise from its corporate nationality.[83]

Certain statutes and regulations are specifically stated to apply to foreign companies. The Bribery Act of 2010, for example, contains a corporate offence under section 7 which applies to foreign businesses having a trading presence,

80 *See* Companies Act Pt 34 and Overseas Companies Regulations 2009 (SI 2009/1801).

81 Civil Jurisdiction and Judgments Act (1982) sec. 42(3)(a)–(b).

82 *Prest v. Petrodel Resources Ltd* [2013] UKSC 34; *Hurstwood Properties (A) Ltd v. Rossendale* [2021] UKSC 16.

83 Separately, the English courts may establish jurisdiction over a foreign corporation or subsidiary where the relevant cause of action arises within the UK. For example, in *Newby v. von Oppen (1871–72) L.R. 7 Q.B. 293*, the court ruled that a foreign corporation not incorporated in England but carrying on business in England may be sued in the English courts in respect of a cause of action – in this case contract law – which arose within the jurisdiction.

however small, in the UK and to UK businesses trading abroad. Under the Act, commercial organisations are implicated where they fail to prevent bribery. Pursuant to section 7(1), a commercial organisation is guilty of an offence if a person associated with it bribes another person, intending to obtain or retain business or a business advantage for the organisation. The Act defines a "relevant commercial organisation" broadly as a body which is incorporated, or a partnership which is formed, under the law of any part of the UK and which carries on a business whether in the UK or elsewhere, or any other corporate body or partnership wherever incorporated or formed which carries on business in any part of the UK. Section 8 of the Act also includes agents, employees, or subsidiaries of the corporations. Thus, in the context of the Bribery Act, the law covers not only domestic corporations abroad and foreign businesses with a UK trading presence, but also their subsidiaries.

8.3 *Jurisdictional Reach over the Conduct of Subsidiaries of Domestic Corporations*

In addition, parent companies domiciled in the UK can be liable for the conduct of their foreign subsidiaries. An English court could establish jurisdiction over a claim against a parent company of a subsidiary under Article 4 of the Recast Brussels Regulation (1215/2012/EU), which allows claimants to bring a claim against a company based in an EU Member State before that Member State's courts. This prevents the English courts from refusing to hear a claim where a parent company is domiciled in England. As a consequence of Brexit, the Recast Brussels Regulation does not apply to claims initiated after 31 December 2020. Therefore, UK-domiciled defendants can challenge the jurisdiction of the English courts on the basis that England is not the appropriate forum.

In two important decisions, the UK Supreme Court has recently clarified that a parent company may owe a duty of care to those affected by the acts or omissions of its foreign subsidiary. In *Lungowe and others v. Vedanta Resources plc* the Supreme Court confirmed that UK parent companies can have liability for the overseas operations of their non-UK subsidiaries.[84] The Supreme Court considered that "if claims are brought in relation to matters arising outside the jurisdiction against multiple defendants, and one of the defendants is properly an anchor defendant, then the English courts have jurisdiction over all of the claims against all of the defendants, including those not domiciled

84 *Lungowe and others v. Vedanta Resources Plc* [2019] UKSC 20.

in the jurisdiction, even in relation to matters that have occurred outside the jurisdiction."[85]

More recently, in *Okpabi v. Royal Dutch Shell Plc*, approximately 40,000 Nigerians alleged they had suffered damage as a result of oil spills from infrastructure operated by the foreign subsidiary of Royal Dutch Shell, an English-domiciled company. The Supreme Court reiterated that an English court has jurisdiction to hear claims against a parent company for the actions of a foreign subsidiary, where the parent company has superior knowledge and expertise regarding, and control over, the subsidiary's operations. The Court applied a broad test to hold that "control is just a starting point. The issue is the extent to which the parent did take over or share with the subsidiary the management of the relevant activity. [...] That may or may not be demonstrated by the parent controlling the subsidiary. In a sense, all parents control their subsidiaries. That control gives the parent the opportunity to get involved in management. But control of a company and de facto management of part of its activities are two different things. A subsidiary may maintain de jure control of its activities, but nonetheless delegate de facto management of part of them to emissaries of its parent."[86]

Such jurisdiction of the English courts can be challenged on the ground that England is not the appropriate forum for the case. A stay of English proceedings will be granted if there is another available forum, having competent jurisdiction, in which the case may be tried more suitably for the interests of all the parties and the ends of justice.[87]

8.4 *The English Courts' Interpretation of Statutory Jurisdictional Reach over Foreign Corporations*

The English courts also determine the scope of statutes' applicability to corporations. For example, the UK Supreme Court's decision in KBR ruled that the SFO's power to compel disclosure of materials under section 2(3) of the Criminal Justice Act 1987 does not extend to foreign companies with no fixed UK place of business and/or those which are not carrying on business in the UK.[88]

The Supreme Court highlighted that if KBR had been a UK company or had a registered office or fixed place of business in the UK, and held documents abroad, then the 1987 Act would have been effective to require production of those documents. The decision, therefore, does not apply to foreign companies

85 *Ibid.* at para. 3.

86 *Okpabi v. Royal Dutch Shell Plc* [2021] UKSC 3 at para. 147.

87 *Spiliada Maritime Corp v Cansulex Ltd* [1986] UKHL 10.

88 *R* (KBR, *Inc*) *v. Director of the Serious Fraud Office* [2021] UKSC 2.

with businesses in the UK, which would fall squarely within the Act's contemplation of "corporate nationality."

In *Gaudiya Mission v. Brahmachary* the Court of Appeal considered the extraterritorial application of the *Charities Act 1993* to a foreign corporation incorporated and registered in India.[89] Under section 96(1) of the Act, a "charity" is any institution, corporate or not, which is established for charitable purposes and is subject to the control of the High Court in the exercise of the court's jurisdiction with respect to charities. The issue was whether the foreign corporation was an institution established for charitable purposes and subject to the control of the High Court with respect to charities within the meaning of the Act. The Court of Appeal held that the Charities Act 1993 neither expressly nor impliedly applied to corporations established for charitable purposes outside England and Wales in accordance with the law of a foreign state. It reasoned that to hold otherwise would be incompatible with established principles of territoriality and inconsistent with authority. The statute's lack of express or implied extraterritoriality prevented the court from holding foreign-established corporations accountable under the Act.

One notable exception to the extraterritorial application of UK statutes on foreign companies is in the realm of competition law, where the Competition and Markets Authority has the power to issue information requests even to foreign-domiciled companies with no UK presence. This was discussed in Section 1 above.

9 Interpreting the Territorial Reach of Ambiguous Statutes

The English courts apply two presumptions against extraterritoriality when a statute is silent as to its territorial scope. These are discussed in turn below.

9.1 *Presumption against Extraterritorial Application of Legislation*

The first is a presumption that UK legislation is generally not intended by Parliament to cover conduct outside the territorial jurisdiction of the UK. In *Clark v. Oceanic Contractors*,[90] Lord Scarman identified the general principle as follows:

> Unless the contrary is expressly enacted or so plainly implied that the courts must give effect to it, United Kingdom legislation is applicable

89 Gaudiya Mission v. Brahmachary [1998] Ch 341.

90 *Clark v. Oceanic Contractors* [1983] 2 A.C. 130 at p. 145.

> only to British subjects or to foreigners who by coming to the United Kingdom, whether for a short or a long time, have made themselves subject to British jurisdiction.[91]

More recently, in *Al-Skeini*,[92] Lord Bingham reviewed the authorities and endorsed the following statements from *Bennion, Statutory Interpretation*:

> Unless the contrary intention appears, Parliament is taken to intend an Act to extend to each territory of the United Kingdom but not to any territory outside the United Kingdom.[93]

> Unless the contrary intention appears … an enactment applies to all persons and matters within the territory to which it extends, but not to any other persons and matters.[94]

As discussed above, there are two rationales behind this presumption. First, the presumption against extraterritoriality reflects the international law requirement to respect State sovereignty. Second, the presumption arises from the concept of international comity.[95] The *Clark* case established that the presumption against extraterritoriality is not an irrebuttable presumption but a rule of construction only.[96] The UK Parliament may override this presumption by expressly providing for the extraterritorial application of a statute.

Even absent express language from the UK Parliament, the extraterritorial application of a statute may be implied by the context and scheme of the statute. For example, the English courts may be willing to imply an intent by the UK Parliament that a statute should apply extraterritorially where the purpose of a statute would otherwise be thwarted.[97]

The Supreme Court recently confirmed that extraterritoriality may be implied "from the scheme, context and subject matter of the legislation."[98] However, the "more exorbitant the jurisdiction, the more is likely to be required" to rebut the presumption of territoriality.[99] Particular factors supporting extraterritoriality may include "the breadth of [the statutory] provisions", and

91 *Ibid.* at p. 145.
92 *Al-Skeini* [2008] 1 AC 153.
93 *Bennion, Statutory Interpretation*, 4th ed (2002) at p. 282, sec. 106.
94 *Ibid.* at p. 306, sec. 128.
95 *See* Section 4 above.
96 *Clark v. Oceanic Contractors* [1983] 2 A.C. 130 at p. 145.
97 *R (KBR, Inc) v. Director of the Serious Fraud Office* [2021] UKSC 2 at paras. 27, 32.
98 *Ibid.* at para. 29.
99 *Ibid.* at para. 28.

where "the purpose of the legislation could not effectually be achieved" otherwise. Factors against extraterritoriality may include the "impracticability of enforcement" which will suggest that the UK Parliament intended a statute to be territorially limited.[100]

9.2 *Presumption against Application to Non-nationals Outside the UK*

The second presumption is a presumption that a statute will not be construed as applying to foreigners regarding acts done by them abroad. Lord Russell CJ explained the presumption in *R v. Jameson*:

> One other general canon of construction is this – that if any construction otherwise be possible, an Act will not be construed as applying to foreigners in respect to acts done by them outside the dominions of the sovereign power enacting.[101]

This presumption is rebuttable. The strength of the presumption will depend on the subject matter of the statute under consideration.[102] Important factors to be considered include the mischief that the statute was intended to remedy, the purpose of the statute, and public interest.

10 Blocking Statutes under UK Law

In the UK, a blocking statute is understood as legislation which prohibits UK persons and businesses from complying with the extraterritorial laws of a foreign State. The UK has enacted blocking statutes in the context of protecting trade interests.

The Protection of Trading Interests Act 1980 is an important example of a blocking statute. The Act permits the Secretary of State to prohibit compliance with any foreign law being applied in a way that could harm the commercial interests of the UK. Three orders have been made under the provisions of the Act: the Protection of Trading Interests (US Re-export Control) Order 1982; the Protection of Trading Interests (US Antitrust Measures) Order 1983; and the Protection of Trading Interests (US Cuban Assets Control Regulations) Order 1992.[103]

---

100 *Ibid.* at para. 29.
101 *R v. Jameson* [1896] 2 QB 425 at p. 430.
102 *Air India v. Wiggins* [1980] 2 All ER 593 at p. 597.
103 Protection of Trading Interests (retained blocking regulation) – GOV.UK available at https://www.gov.uk/guidance/protection-of-trading-interests-retained-blocking-regulation.

The Blocking Regulation (Council Regulation (EC) 2271/96) and Implementing Regulation (Commission Implementing Regulation (EU) 2018/1101) also form part of the retained EU law applying in the UK under the European Union (Withdrawal) Act 2018. The UK has also implemented the Protecting against the Effects of the Extraterritorial Application of Third Country Legislation (Amendment) (EU Exit) Regulations 2020.

Together, these regulations protect UK persons trading with countries affected by the extraterritorial application of certain laws by making it illegal for the protected persons to:

- comply with the legislation imposing the proscribed sanctions (Article 5 of Council Regulation (EC) No 2271/96); and
- fail to inform the Secretary of State for International Trade within 30 days of obtaining information that their economic interests have been affected by the legislation imposing the proscribed sanctions (Article 2 of Council Regulation (EC) No 2271/96).

Breaches of Articles 2 and 5 of Council Regulation (EC) No 2271/96 are criminal offences in the UK, punishable by a fine. However, these provisions are intended to protect UK persons from the extraterritorial effect of legislation imposing the proscribed sanctions. In exceptional circumstances, protected persons may be authorised by the Secretary of State for International Trade to comply with legislation imposing the proscribed sanctions.

Thus, the UK has a legal framework in place to block the application of foreign statutes to UK companies and persons. Currently, the United States sanctions against Iran and Cuba, which seek to regulate the activities of non-United States persons in any jurisdiction, are subject to the UK's blocking statutes.

The Extraterritorial Application of Statutes and Regulations

United States

Franklin A. Gevurtz *

1 Introduction

This report, prepared for the 2022 General Congress of the International Academy of Comparative Law, examines United States law regarding the extraterritorial application of statutes and regulations. This is a particularly worthwhile topic for comparative law study.[1] After all, we would not compare laws if all nations' were always the same. This divergence, in turn, inevitably leads to questions regarding what nation's law will apply to a given situation, which, itself, may elicit different answers from different nations.

Commonly, we think of this sort of problem in terms of courts choosing which nation's law to apply in litigation when there are two or more differing laws potentially applicable – the topic variously referred to as conflicts-of-laws or private international law. Yet often the question is whether a given statute or regulation applies to the situation regardless of whether another nation's conflicting law is also potentially applicable. This, in turn, invokes a frequently different line of analysis – most especially asking whether the legislature intended its statute to apply. It is this inquiry we address.

One constant, embedded in the framing of this topic as the "extraterritorial" application of statutes and regulations, is that nations (including the United States) normally apply their statutes and regulations to what goes on inside their borders. Hence, the interesting question is when nations apply their statutes and regulations to what happens outside their borders.

The approach of this report is to examine the overall approaches used by the United States in applying its statutes and regulations to events occurring outside the country. While it aids understanding of the overall approaches to give specific examples, it is beyond the scope of this report to provide an examination of this question for each individual statute that might be of interest. The reader should consult works addressing specific fields of substantive U.S. law for such an examination.

* Distinguished Professor of Law, University of the Pacific, McGeorge School of Law.

1 Which is why I proposed it to the International Academy.

 | DOI:10.1163/9789004720183_016

2 Historical Evolution

The extraterritorial application of U.S. statutes and regulations has, not surprisingly, grown as a legal issue since the beginning of the nation and, perhaps less inevitably, gone through a cycle in terms of judicial attitudes toward such application. This began with the rare instances in which the issue arose that one would expect with a relatively weak nation – both in terms of power on the world stage and in terms of the role of its federal government.

In this early stage, the issue of applying U.S. law beyond the young nation's borders largely involved happenings on ships, such as piracy,[2] murder at sea,[3] and customs duties.[4] While willing to apply U.S. laws to such events, the United States Supreme Court expressed circumspection. Specifically, the Supreme Court explained that even though a statute used broad, general language regarding its reach, the Court presumed in the absence of explicit language that Congress only intended to legislate within Congress's "authority and jurisdiction."[5] This probably referred to events within the territory of the United States and certain other situations (actions of U.S. nationals and pirates) consistent with the Court's understanding of what was permissible under international law at the time.[6]

Toward the close of the Nineteenth and beginning of the Twentieth Century, a larger industrialized United States had greater power, both internationally and in the role of its federal government. Laws regulating economic dealings, when such dealings extended beyond the nation's borders, increasingly raised the issue of the laws' extraterritorial application. In its 1909 decision in *American Banana Co. v. United Fruit Co.*,[7] the Supreme Court expressed strong hostility toward such application. In rejecting a claim that the defendant violated the Sherman Antitrust Act by blocking the plaintiff's efforts in Central America to establish a competing business growing bananas for import into the United States, Justice Holmes' opinion for the Court asserted that the legality of an act nearly universally depends upon the

2 *E.g.*, United States v. Klintock, 18 U.S. 144 (1820).

3 *E.g.*, United States v. Furlong, 18 U.S. 184 (1820). The tenth clause of Article I, Section 8, of the U.S. Constitution gives Congress authority to punish piracies and felonies committed on the high seas.

4 The Apollon, 22 U.S. 362, 368–69 (1824).

5 22 U.S. at 370.

6 *See, e.g.*, J. Knox, 'A Presumption Against Extrajurisdictionality' (2010) 104 *American Journal of International Law* 351, 363–66.

7 213 U.S. 347 (1909).

law of the nation in which the act takes place. Hence, the U.S. antitrust law did not cover the defendant's conduct in Central America.

Justice Holmes's strict notions of territoriality subsequently fell out of favor, including with respect to the very law involved in *American Banana*.[8] In its 1945 decision in *United States v. Aluminum Company of America* (*Alcoa*),[9] the United States Court of Appeals for the Second Circuit[10] applied the Sherman Act against a cartel of foreign companies producing aluminum outside the United States. The cartel members had agreed to limit their production, including that intended for export to the United States. *Alcoa* is emblematic of an era in which the U.S. courts readily,[11] but not always,[12] applied various U.S. laws despite extraterritorial aspects of the case.

The cycle reversed with the Supreme Court's 1991 decision in EEOC *v. Arabian American Oil Co.* (*Aramco*).[13] Invoking a presumption against extraterritoriality, the Supreme Court held that Title VII of the 1964 Civil Rights Act did not apply to the discriminatory firing of an American citizen by an American company when the firing took place in Saudi Arabia. While Congress reacted by amending Title VII to generally cover such cases,[14] Supreme Court decisions after *Aramco* have increasingly invoked this presumption to reject the application of other U.S. laws to situations in which critical (in the Court's view) aspects of the case occurred outside the United States.[15]

At the same time, some legislation and executive branch actions provide a counterpoint to the judicial retrenchment on the extraterritorial application of U.S. statutes and regulations. This especially involves statutes and regulations designed to achieve foreign policy objectives.

8 *E.g.*, United States v. Sisal Sales Corp., 274 U.S. 268 (1927).

9 148 F.2d 416 (2d Cir. 1945).

10 Recusal by most of the Supreme Court justices led Congress to enact special legislation allowing this case to be heard by an appellate court the level below the Supreme Court. The primary claim in this action was against Alcoa for monopolization.

11 *E.g.*, W. Dodge, 'The New Presumption Against Extraterritoriality' (2020) 133 *Harvard Law Review* 1582, 1591–95.

12 *E.g.*, Foley Bros. v. Filardo, 336 U.S. 281 (1949).

13 499 U.S. 244 (1991).

14 42 U.S.C. §§ 2000e(f), 2000e-1(b)–(c) (2012).

15 *E.g.*, RJR Nabisco, Inc. v. European Community, 136 S. Ct. 2090 (2016); Kiobel v. Royal Dutch Petroleum Co., 569 U.S. 108 (2013); Morrison v. Nat'l Austl. Bank, 561 U.S. 247 (2010).

3 Sources

U.S. courts start with the language of the relevant statute when deciding whether U.S. statutes and regulations apply extraterritorially.[16] This works well enough when the statute clearly specifies whether and when it applies to events outside the United States. Unfortunately, U.S. statutes usually do not contain language explicitly addressing the statute's geographic reach.[17] While U.S. courts could approach such situations the same way they would for any other question of statutory interpretation, they often look to sources more specific to this context in making their decision. As suggested above and discussed in detail later, the primary source is a judicially created presumption that Congress does not intend extraterritorial application of its statutes. Before getting to this, however, it is useful to examine several other sources to which U.S. courts might look in resolving issues of extraterritorial application of U.S. statutes.

3.1 *Customary International Law*

U.S. courts follow two basic propositions regarding customary international law and the extraterritorial application of U.S. statutes. First, if a U.S. statute clearly indicates that it applies in the situation, the fact that such an application violates customary international law does not stop U.S. courts from applying the statute.[18] On the other hand, U.S. courts presume that Congress does not intend U.S. statutes to violate international law.[19] Hence, courts will interpret the reach of the statute to avoid such a violation in situations in which the statute's language is not entirely clear.[20] This, not surprisingly, may lead to disagreements among U.S. judges regarding what limits customary international law imposes on the extraterritorial application of statutes.

3.2 *Treaties and International Instruments*

The United States is party to various treaties under which nations can, or even must, apply their statutes extraterritorially to address topics such as

16 *E.g.*, *Aramco*, 499 U.S. at 248.

17 *E.g.*, J. Meyer, 'Dual Illegality and Geoambiguous Law: A New Rule for Extraterritorial Application of U.S. Law' (2010) 95 *Minnesota Law Review* 110, 128.

18 *E.g.*, United States v. Yousef, 327 F.3d 56 (2d Cir. 2003). This is because U.S. courts must follow U.S. statutes unless the statute is unconstitutional and nothing in the U.S. Constitution requires statutes to comply with international law.

19 This is known as the Charming Betsy doctrine after the name of the leading case, *Murray v. Schooner Charming Betsy*, 2 Cranch 64 (1804).

20 *E.g.*, McCulloch v. Sociedad Nacional de Marineros de Honduras, 372 U.S. 10 (1963).

international human rights violations,[21] aviation and maritime safety,[22] and other matters of special international concern.[23]

One area in which treaties dominate the extraterritorial reach of U.S. (and other nations') laws is taxation. This is because nationality provides a tempting additional basis to territoriality for applying tax laws. If nations impose tax on income made within their territory, as well as upon their nationals for income wherever made, then persons will be subject to double taxation on the same income. Avoiding such double taxation has led the United States, like other nations, to enter numerous treaties.[24]

Sometimes, however, U.S. courts might miss the significance of treaties on the reach of U.S. statutes. For instance, in *Sale v. Haitian Centers Council, Inc.*,[25] the Supreme Court refused to apply a U.S. statute, which prohibited the return of aliens to a country where they faced persecution, to the Coast Guard's interception of Haitian vessels in international waters. Yet, limiting the reach of the statute in this manner may have put the United States in violation of its treaty obligations.[26]

3.3 *Comity*

U.S. courts have a complicated history in applying the notion, commonly referred to as comity, that nations will seek to avoid conflict by declining to apply their laws to the extent they otherwise might. This became a major consideration during the era in which U.S. courts took a generally expansive approach to the extraterritorial application of law.

Decisions such as *Alcoa* engendered significant pushback from other nations.[27] Lower U.S. federal courts responded by invoking this notion of comity when deciding whether to apply U.S. antitrust or other laws to situations

---

21 *See, e.g.*,18 U.S.C. §§ 1583–1584 (implementing Convention to Suppress the Slave Trade and Slavery); 18 U.S.C. § 2340A (implementing Convention Against Torture).

22 *See, e.g.*, 18 U.S.C. § 32 (implementing Convention for the Suppression of Unlawful Acts Against the Safety of Civil Aviation); 18 U.S.C. § 2280 (implementing Convention for the Suppression of Unlawful Acts Against the Safety of Maritime Navigation).

23 *See, e.g.*, 18 U.S.C. §§ 112, 878, 1116 (implementing Convention on the Prevention and Punishment of Crimes Against Internationally Protected Persons, Including Diplomatic Agents); 18 U.S.C. § 831 (implementing Convention on the Physical Protection of Nuclear Material).

24 *E.g.*, Internal Revenue Service, *U.S. Tax Treaties*, Publication 901 (09/2016), available at https://www.irs.gov/publications/p901.

25 509 U.S. 155 (1993).

26 509 U.S. at 190 (Blackmun, J. dissenting)

27 *E.g.*, G. Born, 'A Reappraisal of the Extraterritorial Reach of U.S. Law' (1993) 24 *Law and Policy in International Business* 1, 32–33.

having a significant foreign dimension. This took off with the Ninth Circuit's 1976 decision in *Timberlane Lumber Co. v. Bank of America*,[28] followed by similar decisions in other circuits.[29]

The mechanism for applying this notion of comity in these cases was to use a multifactor balancing test. Among the factors were: (1) the degree of conflict between U.S. and foreign law or policy; (2) the nationality of the parties; (3) the relative significance of effects in the United States as opposed to elsewhere; (4) whether the defendant intended to affect U.S. commerce or, if not, whether the effect was foreseeable; (5) the extent of any activity within the United States; (6) the enforceability of any remedy ordered; (7) the availability of a remedy abroad; (8) the effect of exercising jurisdiction on foreign relations; (9) the U.S. reaction if the roles were reversed; (10) whether the relief demanded would subject the defendant to conflicting requirements under U.S. and foreign law; and (11) the impact of any relevant treaties.[30]

This sort of multifactor balancing drew heavily on the interest-balancing approach to conflicts of law that had emerged in the context of civil litigation in the United States a decade or so earlier.[31] The American Law Institute's Third Restatement of Foreign Relations Law,[32] in turn, adopted this approach. In a nutshell, the Third Restatement started with a broad view of permissible bases for applying national law to events having a foreign dimension.[33] It then, in its noted Section 403, called upon nations to avoid resulting conflicts between their laws by refusing to apply them when, under a multifactor test, it would be unreasonable to do so.[34]

The Supreme Court's treatment of comity has been indirect and inconsistent. In *Hartford Insurance Inc. v. California*,[35] Justice Scalia argued that

---

28 549 F.2d 597 (9th Cir. 1976).

29 *E.g.*, Montreal Trading Ltd. v. Amax Inc., 661 F.2d 864, 869–70 (10th Cir. 1981); In re Uranium Antitrust Litig., 617 F.2d 1248, 1255–56 (7th Cir. 1980).

30 *E.g.*, Mannington Mills, Inc. v. Congoleum Corp., 595 F.2d 1287, 1297–98 (3d Cir. 1979).

31 *E.g.*, H. Buxbaum, 'Territory, Territoriality, and the Resolution of Jurisdictional Conflict' (2009) 57 *American Journal of Comparative Law* 631, 647–48, 650.

32 The American Law Institute is a non-governmental organization that promulgates works attempting to summarize (or restate) the rules emerging from judicial decisions. Among the topics covered in the Restatement of Foreign Relations Law is prescriptive jurisdiction – in other words, the reach of U.S. statutes to events having a foreign dimension. The ALI promulgated the Third Restatement of Foreign Relations Law in 1986. A Fourth Restatement has recently supplanted the Third.

33 *Restatement (Third) of the Foreign Relations Law of the United States* § 402.

34 The Restatement, without citing authority, treated this as a matter of customary international law rather than comity.

35 509 U.S. 764, 814–818 (1993).

international law required the application of comity and a multifactor balancing approach in cases of conflict between otherwise applicable U.S. and foreign laws. The majority in *Hartford Insurance*, however, dismissed this as irrelevant to the case since there was no "true" conflict: While English law did not bar the English re-insurance companies from engaging in the boycott that violated the Sherman Act, it also did not require them to do so.

This cramped view of a conflict that would trigger comity did not survive a second Supreme Court decision addressing the reach of the Sherman Act. In *F. Hoffmann-LaRoche Ltd. v. Empagran S.A.*,[36] the Court faced the question of whether a statute,[37] which clarified that the Sherman Act reached conduct causing anticompetitive effects in the United States but not conduct causing anticompetitive effects solely in foreign markets, precluded claims by purchasers injured in foreign markets by a worldwide conspiracy of vitamin producers who also raised prices in the United States. As one of two reasons for reading the statute to exclude these claims, the Court pointed to considerations of comity. This, the Court asserted, followed from the need to construe statutes to avoid unreasonable interference with the sovereign authority of other nations, which the Court, citing Justice Scalia's dissent in *Hartford*, treated as part of construing statutes to avoid violation of international law. Nevertheless, while pointing to comity in its arguments about statutory interpretation, the Court specifically rejected the case-by-case balancing approach as unworkable.

The Supreme Court has also made indirect and inconsistent use of comity in justifying the presumption against applying statutes extraterritorially. In *Aramco*, the court pointed to avoiding "unintended clashes between our laws and those of other nations which could result in international discord"[38] as one reason for the presumption. The Court repeated this in *Kiobel v. Royal Dutch Petroleum Co.*[39] In between, Justice Scalia's opinion for the Court in *Morrison v. National Australian Bank Ltd.*[40] states that the presumption against extraterritoriality is not about avoiding conflicts with other nations' laws. Ironically, while disclaiming that avoiding conflicts had anything to do with the Court's decision, one of the arguments made by Justice Scalia in *Morrison* was a backdoor attempt to apply this notion to the issue the Court faced. Specifically, as one of the arguments for holding that U.S. law did not prohibit domestic acts of fraud impacting overseas sales of securities, Justice Scalia asserted

36 542 U.S. 155 (2004).
37 Foreign Trade Antitrust Improvements Act, 15 U.S.C. § 6a (2012).
38 499 U.S. at 248.
39 569 U.S. 108, 115 (2013).
40 561 U.S. 247, 255 (2010).

that Congress would have done more to address possible conflicts with foreign securities laws had it intended U.S. law to reach foreign sales.

Despite the occasional invocation of comity by the Supreme Court to support its statutory interpretations, case-by-case fact-specific conflict avoidance has waned in the United States.[41] This remains so even in the face of foreign laws[42] seeking to block extraterritorial application of U.S. economic sanctions.[43] (Interestingly, the United States has not found it necessary to enact statutes seeking to block extraterritorial application of other nations' laws).

3.4 *Reasonableness*

Section 403 of the Third Restatement of Foreign Relations had called upon courts to consider the reasonableness of applying laws extraterritorially by engaging in a case-by-case balancing of multiple factors. While this approach often overlaps with seeking comity, the overlap is not complete. To begin with, lower federal courts, in applying the so-called "conduct" and "effects" test (or tests) discussed later in this report, had engaged in case-by-case multifactor evaluation not only in the interest of avoiding conflict with other nations' laws but also to determine whether the extraterritorial application of a U.S. statute in a particular instance facilitated Congressional policy or was just wasting resources on matters of little U.S. concern.[44]At the other end of the spectrum, Supreme Court decisions such as *Empagran* invoked comity as part of their grounds for decision but rejected any sort of case-by-case multifactor evaluation of reasonableness.

It is unclear to what extent a case-by-case reasonableness evaluation survives *Empagran* as well as *Morrison* (in which the court rejected the case-by-case multifactor approach in addressing the reach of the U.S. prohibition of securities fraud). Despite the Supreme Court's hostility, this sort of approach retains it attraction to some lower federal courts in cases in which the claim

41 *But see* In re Vitamin C Antitrust Litigation, 8 F.4th 136, 159–63 (2d Cir. 2021) (continuing to follow *Timberlane* approach in antitrust).

42 *E.g.*, Council Regulation (EC) No 2271/96

43 *E.g.*, S. Lohmann, 'Extraterritorial U.S. sanctions: only domestic courts could effectively curb the enforcement of U.S. law abroad' (5.2019) 7 SWP *Comment*. Berlin: Stiftung Wissenschaft und Politik -SWP- Deutsches Institut für Internationale Politik und Sicherheit available at https://doi.org/10.18449/2019C05 (The U.S. district courts hearing challenges to prosecutions for violating U.S. economic sanctions did not engage in weighing the respective interests of the United States and those of the other nations involved).

44 *E.g.*, Eur. & Overseas Commodity Traders, S.A. v. Banque Paribas London, 147 F.3d 118, 129–31 (2d Cir. 1998).

makes it through the bright line review called for under *Empagran* and *Morrison*.[45]

In *Parkcentral Global Hub Ltd. v. Porsche Auto. Holdings* SE,[46] the Second Circuit held that meeting *Morrison*'s test for the geographic reach of the U.S. prohibition of securities fraud was a necessary but not a sufficient condition for applying the prohibition to situations involving a non-U.S. dimension. The Second Circuit then held that the purchase of swap contracts in the United States, while meeting *Morrison*'s test for U.S. law to apply, was nevertheless insufficient to trigger application of U.S. law when the value of the contracts depended upon the price of stock in a German company which was listed only on the German stock exchange and the German company's fraudulent misrepresentations occurred and had been prosecuted in Germany – meaning that foreign elements dominated the case. Courts in some other circuits have rejected this approach.[47]

Even if cases such as *Parkcentral* open the door to the return of reasonableness and multifactor case-by-case review, it will be different from before *Empagran* and *Morrison*. Previously, such review was a way to mitigate the inherent overreach resulting from an expansive approach to extraterritorial application. Now, it becomes a vehicle to give defendants a second bite at the apple if they are unable to prevent application of U.S. law under bright line tests designed to limit the reach of U.S. laws. The result is to create an asymmetry in which the disadvantages of both bright line tests and multifactor case-by-case review fall on plaintiffs and not defendants.[48]

4 Application

4.1 *Non-territorial Bases for Applying Statutes and Regulations*

Nations typically apply their laws to what goes on inside their borders and not to what goes on outside – in other words, they usually base the application of their law upon a territorial connection.[49] In some circumstances, however,

45 *E.g.* Hannah L. Bauxbaum & Ralf Michaels, *Reasonableness as a Limitation on the Extraterritorial Application of U.S. Law*, in The Restatement and Beyond: The Past, Present, and Future of U.S. Foreign Relations Law (Paul B. Stephan & Sarah H. Cleveland, eds. 2020).

46 763 F.3d 198 (2d Cir. 2014).

47 *E.g.*, SEC v. Morrone, 997 F.3d 52, 60 (1st Cir. 2021).

48 *E.g.*, F. Gevurtz, 'Extraterritoriality and the Fourth Restatement of Foreign Relations Law: Opportunities Lost' (2020) 55 Willamette Law Review 446, 467–70.

49 *E.g.*, *Restatement (Fourth) of Foreign Relations Law* § 408 Reporter's Note 1 (2018) ("Territorial jurisdiction is the oldest, most common, and least controversial basis for exercising jurisdiction to prescribe.").

nations will apply their laws upon a different basis. This is true for the United States as well.

4.1.1 Nationality

The most obvious non-territorial connections that might lead a nation to apply its laws are ties either to the party whom the law seeks to control or to the party whom the law seeks to protect.

4.1.1.1 *Nationality of the Party the Law Seeks to Control (Active Personality)*

Jurists in the United States have long recognized that the nation may legitimately apply its laws to control its nationals even for their activities outside the nation.[50] A variety of U.S. statutes take this approach.

Nations have the most obvious incentive to apply their laws to their nationals even for activities outside the nation when it comes to taxation. Hence, the United States, subject to treaties and statutory exceptions, taxes its nationals on income made abroad.[51] In addition, U.S. statutes sometimes criminalize the actions of U.S. nationals even when those actions occurred outside the United States.[52] The common denominator in many of these statutes appears to be the foreign policy impact of the condemned actions. Specifically, these are often instances in which the overseas behavior of U.S. nationals might create negative blowback upon U.S. foreign policy (as with the bribery of foreign officials by U.S. firms prohibited by the Foreign Corrupt Practices Act (FCPA)[53]), or U.S. law is conscripting U.S. firms into efforts to carry out U.S. foreign policy (as with economic sanctions).

4.1.1.2 *Nationality of the Party the Law Seeks to Protect (Passive Personality)*

Applying a nation's law to protect its nationals in other countries is often referred to as passive personality – to contrast it with the term "active personality" sometimes used for applying a nation's law to control the actions of its nationals in other countries.[54] At one time, the United States took the position

---

50 *E.g.*, *The Apollon*, 22 U.S. at 370.

51 *E.g.*, J. Harvey, Jr, 'Worldwide Taxation of U. S. Citizens Living Abroad: Impact of FATCA and Two Proposals' (1.3.2013) Villanova University School of Law Public Law and Legal Theory Working Paper No. 2013–3057, available at http://ssrn.com/abstract=2318463.

52 *E.g.*, 18 U.S.C. § 229(c)(2) (use of chemical weapons that "takes place outside of the United States and is committed by a national of the United States"). 18 U.S.C. § 1956(f)(1) (money laundering "by a United States citizen"); 18 U.S.C. § 2332f(b)(2)(A) (bombing public places if "a perpetrator is a national of the United States").

53 15 U.S.C. §§ 78dd-1, -2.

54 *E.g.*, *Restatement (Fourth) of Foreign Relations Law* at § 411.

that international law barred nations from applying their laws based upon passive personality.[55] The U.S. attitude has changed[56] and some U.S. statutes apply on this basis.

As with applying U.S. laws to control the overseas conduct of U.S. nationals, the U.S. statutes seeking to protect U.S. nationals abroad often involve some foreign policy or other added dimension that makes the United States unwilling to leave matters to the domestic laws of wherever the misconduct occurred – as the United States would, for instance, if an American tourist was robbed on an overseas vacation. Examples include war crimes or terrorism,[57] or occur in locations with considerable transit to and from the United States, such as international airports,[58] or result in more extreme harm.[59] Some statutes protecting U.S. nationals outside the United States go beyond criminal prohibitions and establish private claims for injured parties.[60]

4.1.1.3 *Determining Nationality*

U.S. statutes addressing overseas conduct by, or harm to, U.S. nationals often refer to the definition in Section 101 of the Immigration and Nationality Act:[61] "The term 'national of the United States' means (A) a citizen of the United States, or (B) a person who, though not a citizen of the United States, owes permanent allegiance to the United States."[62] U.S. statutes sometimes also attempt to control the overseas actions of residents of the United States.[63]

---

55 *E.g.*, Dept. of State, 'Report on Extraterritorial Crime and the Cutting Case' (1887) *Foreign Relations Law of the United States* 751–867.

56 *E.g.*, *Yousef*, 327 F.3d at 96.

57 *E.g.*, 18 U.S.C. § 229(c)(3) (use of chemical weapons "against a national of the United States while the national is outside the United States"); 18 U.S.C. § 2339C(b)(2)(C)(iii) (financing terrorism directed at "any national of the United States or the property of such national"); 18 U.S.C. § 2441(b) (war crimes if the victim is "a national of the United States").

58 18 U.S.C. § 37(b)(2) (violence at international airports if "a victim is a national of the United States").

59 *E.g.*, 18 U.S.C. § 2332 (homicide, attempt or conspiracy with respect to homicide, and serious bodily injury of a national of the United States outside the United States).

60 *E.g.*, 18 U.S.C. § 2333 (providing treble damages for "[a]ny national of the United States injured in his or her person, property, or business by reason of an act of international terrorism").

61 8 U.S.C. § 1101(a)(22).

62 Examples of statutes applying outside the United States based upon nationality as so defined include: 18 U.S.C. § 7(9); 18 U.S.C. § 37(b)(2); 18 U.S.C. § 1203(c).

63 *E.g.*, 22 U.S.C. § 2780(l)(3)(A) ("United States person" for purposes of prohibiting transactions with countries supporting terrorism includes "any citizen or permanent resident alien of the United States").

Other statutes may have a specialized reach, for example by applying based upon the individual's relationship to the U.S. Armed Forces.[64]

Determining the nationality of a business or non-profit corporation or similar entity for purposes of applying U.S. law obviously involves different criteria. Normally, this is incorporation under the law of a state or other jurisdiction within the United States[65] – which invites regulatory arbitrage.[66] A less manipulable criterion sometimes used is the corporation's principal place of business.[67]

Some U.S. statutes and regulations take even more expansive approaches to making companies and those associated with them subject to U.S. law. For example, the FCPA's prohibition on overseas bribery applies not only to domestic firms but also to foreign firms issuing securities subject to registration under the U.S. securities law by virtue of the securities' trading in U.S. markets.[68] Moreover, the prohibition also applies to agents, employees, officers, directors and shareholders of companies subject to the FCPA even if such individuals are not U.S. nationals.[69] Some U.S. statutes and regulations go even further by treating firms incorporated in foreign jurisdictions as U.S. firms when controlled by U.S. persons.[70] This has been particularly controversial when used in connection with economic sanctions.[71]

---

64 Military Extraterritorial Jurisdiction Act, 18 U.S.C. § 3261(a) (applying to persons who are members of, employed by, or accompanying U.S. Armed Forces).

65 *E.g.*, 26 U.S.C. § 7701(a)(4) & (30)(B)–(C) (defining "United States person" under the Internal Revenue Code to include domestic corporations and providing that "[t]he term 'domestic' when applied to a corporation ...means created or organized in the United States or under the law of the United States or of any State"). Except for certain specialized businesses (banks), incorporation in the United States occurs under the laws of individual states (such as Delaware) rather than under federal law.

66 While many nations require incorporation under the laws of the jurisdiction within which the corporation has its headquarters (the real seat doctrine), many others, including the United States, allow incorporation under the laws of any jurisdiction that the founders of the corporation choose without regard to the corporation's lack of other connection to the state (the incorporation doctrine).

67 *E.g.*, 15 U.S.C. § 78dd-2(h)(1)(B) ("domestic concerns" subject to the Foreign Corrupt Practices Act includes not only corporations formed under domestic laws, but also those having their principal place of business in the United States).

68 15 U.S.C. § 78dd-1(a).

69 Ibid. *See also* U.S. v. Hoskins, 902 F.3d 69 (2d Cir. 2018) (pointing to the FCPA's reach of those working for U.S. corporations as precluding the statute also reaching others conspiring with such corporations).

70 *See, e.g.*, 42 U.S.C. § 2000e-1(c)(1) ("If an employer controls a corporation whose place of incorporation is a foreign country, any practice prohibited by section 2000e-2 or 2000e-3 of this title engaged in by such corporation shall be presumed to be engaged in by such employer.").

71 *E.g.*, S. Lohmann, 'Extraterritorial U.S. sanctions: only domestic courts could effectively curb the enforcement of U.S. law abroad' (5.2019) 7 SWP *Comment*. Berlin: Stiftung

4.1.2 Application based upon State Interest (Protective Principle)

Nations sometimes apply laws extraterritorially to protect critical state interests. This is commonly referred to as the protective principle.[72] A few U.S. statutes follow this approach. Most address obvious subjects such as counterfeiting[73] and other attacks on core government functions.[74] Some U.S. efforts to invoke this principle, such as for laws addressing narcotics trafficking by sea,[75] are more controversial.[76]

4.1.3 Universal Jurisdiction

Nations have traditionally considered certain crimes, such as piracy and more recently genocide, to be subject to universal jurisdiction under which any nation may apply its law to prosecute the conduct no matter where committed, by whom, and against whom.[77] Various U.S. statutes apply this approach.[78] This includes U.S. laws against piracy,[79] the slave trade,[80] and similar offenses.[81] The United States also has statutes following universal jurisdiction to attack terrorism related offenses.[82] In a particularly expansive and hence controversial

---

Wissenschaft und Politik -SWP- Deutsches Institut für Internationale Politik und Sicherheit available at https://doi.org/10.18449/2019C05 pp. 6–7.

72 *E.g.*, *Restatement (Fourth) of Foreign Relations Law* § 412.

73 *E.g.*, 18 U.S.C. § 470 (counterfeiting outside the United States).

74 *E.g.*, 18 U.S.C. §§ 792–799 (espionage); 18 U.S.C. § 1114 (murder of government officials); 18 U.S.C. § 1546 (fraud and misuse of visas, permits, and other documents).

75 Maritime Drug Law Enforcement Act, 46 U.S.C. § 70501 (congressional finding that "trafficking in controlled substances aboard vessels is a serious international problem, is universally condemned, and presents a specific threat to the security and societal well-being of the United States").

76 *Compare* United States v. Cardales, 168 F.3d 548, 553 (1st Cir. 1999) ("Therefore, application of the MDLEA to the defendants is consistent with the protective principle of international law because Congress has determined that all drug trafficking aboard vessels threatens our nation's security."), *with* United States v. Wright-Barker, 784 F.2d 161, 168 n.5 (3d Cir. 1986) ("international agreements have yet to recognize drug smuggling as a threat to a nation's security as a state or the operation of its governmental functions warranting protective jurisdiction").

77 *E.g.*, *Restatement (Fourth) of Foreign Relations Law* § 412.

78 The only "jurisdictional" limit is to require that the defendant be present in the United States because the United States does not conduct criminal trials in absentia.

79 18 U.S.C. § 1651.

80 18 U.S.C. §§ 1583–1584, 1596.

81 *E.g.*, 18 U.S.C. §§ 1589, 1596 (forced labor); 18 U.S.C. §§ 1590–1591, 1596 (trafficking persons); 18 U.S.C. § 2442(c)(3) (recruitment of child soldiers).

82 *E.g.*, 18 U.S.C. § 2332f(b)(2)(C) (bombings of places of public use); 18 U.S.C. § 2339B(d)(1)(C) (providing material support or resources to designated foreign terrorist organizations); 18 U.S.C. § 2339C(b)(2)(B) (financing terrorism).

view of crimes subject to universal jurisdiction, the United States has asserted that this applies to narcotics trafficking on the high seas.[83]

4.2 *Territoriality*

4.2.1 The Presumption against Extraterritoriality

The normal basis for application of a U.S. statute or regulation is the occurrence of some relevant event within the United States – in other words, a territorial connection. Typically, however, U.S. statutes do not come out and say this. Rather, this is the way U.S. courts interpret the reach of U.S. statutes that are, as is normally the case, silent or ambiguous on the question.

As stated earlier, the Supreme Court increasingly speaks of this interpretation as applying a presumption against extraterritoriality. This presumption has several rationales. Perhaps the simplest and least articulated is that lawmakers, like human beings generally (and like many other species), think in terms of geographic territory and controlling what goes on in that territory. Hence, it is sensible to assume that a statute, which is silent as to its reach, intends to govern what goes on inside the nation's territory and not what goes on outside the nation's borders, regardless of the nationality of the parties involved or other factors. The Supreme Court has also articulated a couple of policy grounds for the presumption. As mentioned earlier, it avoids multiple nations applying conflicting laws to the same events. It also reflects a "someone else's problem" philosophy to what goes on outside a nation's territory.

4.2.2 Rebutting the Presumption

4.2.2.1 *In General*

The presumption against extraterritoriality does not mean that U.S. statutes cannot apply extraterritorially. Rather, it means that U.S. courts start with the assumption that Congress does not intend such an application and, therefore, U.S. courts require some showing that Congress had a different intent for the statute involved in the case.[84]

Unfortunately, Supreme Court opinions are not entirely clear or consistent on how strong such a showing must be.[85] Recent opinions talk of the need for

---

83 U.S. court decisions disagree on this assertion. *Compare* United States v. Perlaza, 439 F.3d 1149, 1163 (9th Cir. 2006), *with* United States v. Estupinan, 453 F.3d 1336, 1338 (11th Cir. 2006).

84 *E.g.*, *Aramco*, 499 U.S. at 248.

85 *E.g.*, W. Dodge, 'Understanding the Presumption Against Extraterritoriality' (1998) 16 *Berkeley Journal of International Law* 85, 96–7 (discussing statements by the Supreme Court with different formulations regarding the evidence necessary to overcome the presumption against extraterritoriality).

"clear" evidence.[86] These opinions, however, explain that the requirement for clear evidence does not impose a so-called "clear statement rule" under which the statute would need language explicitly stating that it applies outside the United States to overcome the presumption. Instead, as the Supreme Court stated in RJR *Nabisco v. European Community*,[87] the context of less explicit statutory language might establish Congress' intent to have extraterritorial reach.

4.2.2.2 *Specific Evidence of Intent to Apply Extraterritorially*

The most persuasive evidence showing Congress intended a statute to apply extraterritorially is language in the statute explicitly calling for its application to events outside the United States. The U.S. statute that criminalizes terrorist acts against U.S. nationals outside the United States[88] provides a simple example.

Sometimes, however, language that might seem to explicitly indicate extraterritorial application does not really do so. This has been the Supreme Court's longstanding view of statutory language prohibiting various actions when the actions involve commerce with foreign countries.

Beyond the language of the statute, there is legislative history and purpose. While one can read the Supreme Court's opinion in *Aramco* to rule out going beyond the statutory language to rebut the presumption against extraterritoriality,[89] other decisions seem more open-minded. For example, the Supreme Court's *Kiobel* opinion pointed to events preceding Congress' enactment of the Alien Tort Statute to show that Congress viewed the statute as addressing claims by foreign ambassadors accosted in the United States rather than addressing tort claims for violations of international law occurring abroad.

4.2.3 What is Territorial versus Extraterritorial

The failure to rebut the presumption against extraterritoriality does not mean that a U.S. statute cannot apply to any case involving events outside the United States. Instead, in cases in which events occurred both outside and inside the United States, the court must decide whether the application of the statute would be extraterritorial. A classic example is when the defendant, who is standing in one nation, shoots a rifle and kills the intended victim, who is

86 *Morrison*, 561 U.S. at 255.

87 136 S. Ct. 2090 (2016).

88 18 U.S.C. § 2332.

89 *See, e.g.*, *Aramco*, 499 U.S. at 263 (Marshall, J., dissenting) ("The majority converts the presumption against extraterritoriality into a clear-statement rule").

standing near the border in another nation. While such shootings are infrequent,[90] in a world of growing economic interaction, the overall problem is pervasive.

4.2.3.1 *The Rise and Fall of Looking to Conduct or Effects*

As expressed in *American Banana*, the most traditional approach to determining territoriality looks to the location of the conduct that the law seeks to govern[91] In the cross-border shooting example this means that the nation in which the victim stood would be applying its law extraterritorially while the nation in which the shooter stood would not.[92] By contrast, *Alcoa,* as well as the Court of International Justice's opinion in *Lotus*,[93] uphold application of a law based not just upon conduct but also upon effects within a nation. This allows either nation in the cross-border shooting example to apply its law.

For a time, courts in the United States followed this broad view by applying U.S. securities[94] and some other statutes[95] based upon either conduct or effects in the United States – albeit mitigated by applying a case-by-case balancing of factors. This approach was referred to as the conduct and effects test or tests. The Supreme Court rejected this approach in 2010.

4.2.3.2 *The Focus Test*

In 2010, the United States embarked upon a new path for determining whether the application of a U.S. statute in a particular case is extraterritorial. This approach, referred to as the focus test, comes from the Supreme Court's 2010 decision in *Morrison*.

---

90 But they happen. *E.g.*, Hernandez v. Mesa, 140 S.Ct. 735 (2020) (refusing to allow a judicially created "*Bivens* action" for violation of U.S. Constitutional protections when a U.S. official standing in the United States shot and killed a Mexican national on the Mexican side of the border).

91 *E.g.*, W. Dodge, 'The New Presumption Against Extraterritoriality' (2020) 133 *Harvard Law Review* 1582, 1605–06.

92 Seeking to avoid such a result, some state court decisions in the United States have asserted that the shooter's conduct also occurs where the victim is hit. *E.g.*, Simpson v. State, 17 S.E. 984, 985 (Ga. 1893) ("[I]f a man in the State of South Carolina criminally fires a ball into the State of Georgia, the law regards him as accompanying the ball, and as being represented by it, up to the point where it strikes.").

93 S.S. "Lotus" (Fr. v. Turk.), 1927 P.C.I.J. (ser. A) No. 10, (Sept. 7).

94 *E.g.*, SEC v. Berger, 322 F.3d 187, 192–93 (2d Cir. 2003).

95 *E.g.*, Poulos v. Caesars World, Inc., 379 F.3d 654, 663 (9th Cir. 2004) (applying the test to RICO).

In *Morrison*, the Court confronted a situation in which the plaintiffs argued that the case did not involve extraterritoriality because the misrepresentations inflating the price of the stock that they purchased originated in Florida.

In response, the Court held that extraterritoriality depends upon where the event constituting the focus of the statute occurred. The Court then held that the focus of the Securities Exchange Act's prohibition of fraud in connection with the purchase or sale of a security is the purchase or sale rather than the fraud, and so the location of the sale, rather than of the fraud, dictates extraterritoriality. Since the plaintiffs purchased their stock in Australia, the case involved extraterritoriality and U.S. securities law did not cover the claim. What is most interesting is that the Court did not look to where the proscribed conduct occurred, which, as stated earlier, is the most traditional test for extraterritoriality. Indeed, the sales of stock upon which the Court in *Morrison* focused (pun intended) were neither the defendant's conduct (since the plaintiffs purchased their stock from other innocent shareholders) nor prohibited.

4.2.3.3 *Determining the Focus*

If the location of the event constituting the statute's focus provides the test for determining whether the situation involves extraterritoriality, what is the test for determining the statute's focus? Unfortunately, Supreme Court opinions applying the focus test provide no useful guidance – a reflection of the inherent indeterminacy of the test.

In *Morrison*, the Court concluded that the focus of the prohibition on fraud in connection with the purchase or sale of a security is the sale, not the fraud, based upon conventional statutory interpretation arguments purporting to show that Congress did not intend to regulate overseas sales of securities – an approach which renders the presumption against extraterritoriality superfluous.

In *RJR Nabisco*, the Supreme Court concluded that the section of the Racketeer Influenced and Corrupt Organizations Act (RICO) creating a private cause of action for persons injured by a violation of the statute[96] only applies if the injury occurs in the United States. This reflects an implicit conclusion[97] that the focus of RICO's private cause of action section is the injury rather than the violation. Yet, the Court never bothers to explain why this should be so.

By contrast, the Supreme Court's subsequent application of the focus test in *WesternGeco LLC* v. *ION Geophysical Corp*[98] reached the opposite result from

96 18 U.S.C. § 1964(c).

97 The Court never comes out and says this.

98 138 S. Ct. 2129 (2018).

RJR *Nabisco* and decided that when it comes to patent cases the focus of the section of the U.S. patent statute allowing parties to recover damages from patent infringement is the infringement rather than the damages – thereby allowing the plaintiff to recover overseas damages resulting from a patent infringement in the United States.

The bottom line from this set of decisions is that the Supreme Court's application of its focus test either requires a determination that Congress does not wish the statute to apply unless a particular event occurs inside the United States – in which case the presumption against extraterritoriality is redundant – or else simply becomes an ipsa dixit that decrees one way for one statute and the opposite way for another. Indeed, one gets the feeling that the focus test is simply a vehicle for the Court to look at whatever it wants about the statute, no matter how inconsistent with the approach in other decisions, to get the result that the Court sought before it looked at the statute.

4.2.3.4 *Specialized Alternatives to the Focus Test*

Applying the focus test is unnecessary for some U.S. statutes whose language specifies the sufficient territorial connection. For example, Congress responded to *Morrison* by enacting a provision reestablishing the conduct and effects tests as the basis for government prosecutions of those violating the U.S. prohibition on securities fraud.[99] Congress responded to the OECD Convention on Combating Bribery of Foreign Public Officials in International Business Transactions by amending the FCPA to prohibit non-U.S. persons from engaging in any act in furtherance of overseas bribery while in the territory of the United States[100] – the "any act in furtherance" language suggesting a fairly expansive view of what domestic conduct is sufficient.

4.2.3.5 *Locating Relevant Events*

Not only might there be uncertainty about what event dictates extraterritoriality under a particular statute, there also might be uncertainty regarding where the relevant event occurred.[101]

For example, in arguing that aiding and abetting violations of international law occurred in the United States, the plaintiffs in *Nestlé* USA, *Inc. v. Doe*,[102]

99 Dodd-Frank Wall Street Reform and Consumer Protection Act of 2010, Pub. L. No. 111–203, §§ 929P(b), 929Y(a)(2), 124 Stat. 1376 (2010).

100 15 U.S.C. § 78dd-3.

101 We earlier encountered an example of this issue when noting how some state courts had concluded that the wrongful conduct in the cross-border shooting situation also occurred where the victim is struck.

102 141 S.Ct. 1931 (2021).

pointed to their allegation that major corporate "operational decisions" by the defendant company occurred in this country. The Court rejected this as a "generic" allegation of corporate decision-making akin to a domestic corporate presence. Left unanswered is whether a specific decision and order by corporate higher-ups in the United States to have the corporation engage overseas in conduct that is the statute's focus is enough to render the case not extraterritorial.

A similar problem occurs under *Morrison*'s holding that the focus of the U.S. prohibition on securities fraud is the sale of securities. Determining where the sale occurred is simple enough when the plaintiffs purchased stock through an exchange. World financial markets, however, often involve transactions that occur off the exchange. In *Absolute Activist Value Master Fund Ltd v. Ficeto*,[103] the Second Circuit held that in such cases the sale occurs both where the parties become irrevocably bound to the contract and where title to the purchased security was transferred. The first alternative makes the application of U.S. securities law to a transborder deal made over the phone or the Internet turn on the happenstance of which statement in a back-and-forth conversation irrevocably committed the parties to the transaction.

The location of the relevant event can be particularly controversial in applying tax laws. Specifically, determining how much income a taxpayer made from activities within the United States is subject to a host of accounting decisions by the taxpayer – for example, what price the taxpayer "paid" for goods or services supplied by a related firm operating in another country. This creates an obvious temptation for parties subject to tax on income made in the United States (or other high tax rate countries) to manipulate such decisions to decrease the amount of income "made in" the United States and increase the amount of income "made in" countries with lower tax rates.[104] The approaches taken by U.S. tax law to deal with this problem are complex and beyond the scope of this report.

4.2.4 Overarching Puzzles

4.2.4.1 *Slicing and Dicing*

One issue potentially impacting both whether the presumption against extraterritoriality is rebutted and the focus of the statute is whether to take the statute as a whole or instead to look at individual provisions, and, if looking at

103 677 F.3d 60 (2012).

104 E.g., C. Fuest, et al., 'Profit Shifting and "Aggressive" Tax Planning by Multinational Firms: Issues and Options for Reform' (10.2013) Discussion Paper No. 13–078, available at https://ftp.zew.de/pub/zew-docs/dp/dp13078.pdf.

individual provisions, how narrowly to do so. In RJR *Nabisco*, the Court sometimes subdivided the statute and sometimes grouped provisions together both in deciding whether the presumption against extraterritoriality was rebutted and in determining the focus of a statutory provision. The result is to leave it unclear when the Court will treat statutory provisions separately and when it will lump them together in applying the presumption.

4.2.4.2 *Nature of the Plaintiff*

A results-oriented explanation for many of the Supreme Court's decisions in this area is that they reflect hostility toward claims by foreign plaintiffs who the Court suspects are forum shopping for laws more conducive to private actions than available in their home countries – or, as the Court put it in *Morrison*, lawyers seeing the United States as "the Shangri – La of class-action litigation."[105]

This is perhaps most explicit in *Empagran*. As part of its rationale for rejecting claims by parties injured because of price fixing in foreign markets, the Court noted the opposition of many other countries to allowing private claims, as opposed to government prosecutions, for violation of antitrust laws.

RJR Nabisco reflects a similar viewpoint and outcome. By holding that RICO's private cause of action provision only reaches injuries occurring in the United States, while at the same time holding that RICO criminalizes some conduct occurring outside the United States, the Court allows U.S. government prosecutions, but not private lawsuits, for some racketeering taking place and injuring parties outside the United States. In reaching this result, the Court not only repeats *Empagran*'s concerns about other nations' opposition to allowing private claims for violations of criminal and other public laws, but also notes that private suits lack the check provided by prosecutorial discretion against litigation creating international friction.

Some Congressional action also supports this distinction. In a provision of the Dodd-Frank Act,[106] Congress sought to reverse *Morrison* when it came to government actions for securities fraud but directed the SEC to further study what the rule should be for private actions.

While policy might support a distinction between private plaintiffs and government enforcement, the results in the cases suggest a different judicial motive. Specifically, the cases betray a hostility toward foreign plaintiffs seeking the advantage of U.S. laws. So, the fact that the European Commission, rather than some entirely private party, was the plaintiff is RJR *Nabisco*

105 561 U.S. at 270.

106 Dodd-Frank Wall Street Reform and Consumer Protection Act of 2010, Pub. L. No. 111–203, §§ 929P(b), 929Y(a)(2), 124 Stat. 1376 (2010).

produced scorn and charges of hypocrisy by the majority of the Supreme Court. By contrast, in *WesternGeco*, the Court flipped its view of the focus of private remedy provisions to allow a U.S. company holding a U.S. patent to recover lost overseas profits.

4.3 *Mixing and Matching Territorial and Non-territorial Application*

Some U.S. statutes can apply based both upon events occurring in the United States or upon nationality or other non-territorial grounds. For example, as mentioned earlier the FCPA applies based upon either nationality (U.S. issuers and firms) or territoriality (acts in furtherance of bribes by non-U.S. parties occurring in the United States).

An especially controversial example of a "whatever works" approach to applying U.S. law has occurred with the imposition of economic sanctions by the United States. The primary statutory authority for U.S. economic sanctions is the International Emergencies Economic Powers Act (IEEPA).

The IEEPA empowers the President to prohibit currency or other banking transactions involving foreign countries or nationals, as well as any other transaction involving any property in which any foreign country or a national has an interest "by any person, or with respect to any property, subject to the jurisdiction of the United States."[107] Extending the statute's reach to any person or property subject to U.S. jurisdiction without defining what makes persons or property subject to jurisdiction leaves things rather open-ended. This has led the executive branch to fill the gap through administrative regulations or prosecutorial decisions imposing and enforcing various sanctions.

Insofar as regulations bar U.S. nationals from doing business with sanctioned parties, or the export of goods or services from the United States to sanctioned parties, then nationality and territoriality provide recognized bases for applying U.S. law and such bans are obviously contemplated by the statute whether extraterritorial or not. Hence, legal challenges to sanctions in U.S. courts have fared poorly.[108]

Things become dicier when the sanctions regime, to avoid circumvention or otherwise increase its impact, seeks to control persons from other nations acting outside of the United States. One mechanism is to expand the list of sanctioned parties to include not only the nation or other foreign parties who are the principal targets of the sanctions, but also to bar dealings with foreign firms that do business with the principal targets (so-called

107 15 U.S.C. § 1702(a)(1)

108 See, e.g., M. Malloy, United States Economic Sanctions: Theory and Practice, Kluwer Law International 2001, p. 337.

secondary sanctions) and thereby coerce cooperation by parties not otherwise subject to U.S. law.[109] While the effect of such coercion is extraterritorial and controversial (as illustrated by foreign blocking statutes), it is difficult to say that this is beyond the reach of the IEEPA so long as the mechanism remains the same control over U.S. persons and exports as used for the primary sanctions.

Not satisfied with such economic coercion, the U.S. has also criminally prosecuted foreign parties who enticed or fooled U.S. nationals into selling to sanctioned parties. Lower federal courts have upheld such prosecutions based upon an elastic view of territoriality – the role of the foreign defendant, even if acting outside the United States, in triggering banking or other transactions in the United States.[110] Occasionally, a court may throw in for good measure the argument that the Congress intended the IEEPA to apply extraterritorially following the protective principle.[111] Such decisions seem rather casual in explaining whether each U.S. statute allegedly violated by the foreign party[112] applies extraterritorially or else how the domestic events involved in the case constitute each statute's focus.

Yet another approach to extend the reach of economic sanctions (as well as to control the distribution of items with military use[113]) is to limit re-exports – in other words, the export of items originating in the United States (or items that contain such items) from a non-sanctioned to a sanctioned nation.[114] The notion that the United States retains jurisdiction over property that goes from one country to another because of the property's U.S. origin seems expansive – although international conventions and common practice make this widely accepted when dealing with items having military use.[115]

109 E.g., M. Rathbone, et al., 'Sanctions, Sanctions Everywhere: Forging a Path through Complex Transnational Sanctions Laws' (2013) 44 Georgetown Journal of International Law 1055, 1112–13.

110 E.g., United States v. Halkbank, 2020 WL 5849512, at *6 (S.D.N.Y. 2020); United States v. Zarrab, 2016 WL 6820737, at *8 (S.D.N.Y. 2016).

111 Ibid.

112 In addition to violation of the IEEPA, the defendants in these cases have been charged with conspiracy to defraud the United States, bank fraud and money laundering.

113 Arms Export Control Act of 1976, 22 U.S.C. Ch 39; Export Controls Act of 2018, 50 U.S.C. Ch 58.

114 E.g., H. Clark, 'Dealing with U.S. Extraterritorial Sanctions and Foreign Countermeasures' (2004) 25 University of Pennsylvania Journal of International Economic Law 455, 462–64.

115 H. Clark, 'Dealing with U.S. Extraterritorial Sanctions and Foreign Countermeasures' (2004) 25 University of Pennsylvania Journal of International Economic Law 455, 465.

5 Beyond U.S. Statutes

5.1 *Regulations*

While the topic of this report is the extraterritorial application of statutes and regulations, the discussion so far has largely focused on statutes. This is because, as a general matter, a court's interpretation of the reach of a U.S. statute dictates the reach of regulations promulgated pursuant to the statute.

For example, the plaintiffs in *Morrison* alleged a violation of Rule 10b-5 – a regulation promulgated by the Securities and Exchange Commission pursuant to Section 10(b) of the Securities Exchange Act. The Supreme Court focused on the reach of the statute rather than the regulation. The Court explained that a regulation cannot have a broader reach than Congress intended for the statute pursuant to which the agency issued the regulation.

Addressing the potential extraterritorial reach of a regulation raises, however, one additional issue: Should the court give any deference to the views of the agency promulgating the regulation regarding either rebutting the presumption against extraterritoriality or the focus of the statute? The Fourth Restatement of Foreign Relations Law takes the position that courts should give the same deference to agency interpretations of the geographic reach of statutes administered by the agency that courts give to agency interpretations of statutes generally.[116] The continued significance of this may wane, however, due to decreased judicial deference to administrative interpretations in general. Still, when dealing with regulations adopted to implement foreign policy in areas such as economic sanctions, even a court determined to decrease the influence of the "administrative state" might be inclined to defer to agencies in the executive branch.

5.2 *State Statutes*

While this report has focused on U.S. (or federal) statutes, statutes enacted by the fifty individual states in the United States can also raise issues of extraterritorial application. Indeed, not only can events outside the United States trigger such issues under state statutes, but events occurring in other states within the United States do so as well.[117]

---

116 E.g., Restatement (Fourth) of Foreign Relations Law § 404 Reporter's Note 12.

117 See, e.g., W. Dodge, 'Presumptions against Extraterritoriality in State Law' [hereinafter "Dodge, 'Extraterritoriality in State Law'"] (2020) 53 U.C. Davis Law Review 1389, 1421–22 (state courts generally do not distinguish between application of state statutes to events in other states or to events outside the United States when considering the extraterritorial application of statutes).

Many state courts invoke a presumption against extraterritoriality; many others do not; the law in some is unclear.[118] Not surprisingly, the state court decisions applying the presumption show variation in the amount of evidence necessary to rebut it. One state court follows a clear statement rule under which statutory language must explicitly call for extraterritorial application,[119] another goes even further by holding that the legislature lacks the power to apply its statutes extraterritorially,[120] and most state courts adopt the fuzziness exhibited by federal decisions.[121] State courts also vary in how they determine whether a particular application of a statute would be extraterritorial. Some follow the traditional location of the conduct approach[122] – albeit sometimes with an expansive view of where the relevant conduct occurred.[123] Others reach eclectic results that often look to the determinative event for similar federal statutes – albeit without necessarily using the focus test.[124]

State courts not employing a presumption against extraterritoriality either treat the matter as one of ordinary statutory interpretation without prejudging the outcome one way or the other[125] or look solely to conflicts-of-law doctrines to decide whether state statutes will apply to events with a significant foreign dimension.[126]

5.3 *Common Law*

Our topic is the extraterritorial application of statutes and regulations, which, at first glance, might seem to create an important omission in reports from common law countries like the United States. After all, courts in the United States often face the issue of when to apply various common law doctrines to litigation involving events that occurred outside the United States. When

118 Dodge, 'Extraterritoriality in State Law' pp. 1403–04 (table listing what approach each state follows).

119 Nevares v. M.L.S., 345 P.3d 719, 727 (Utah 2015).

120 Doctors Hosp. of Augusta, LLC v. CompTrust AGC Workers' Comp. Tr. Fund, 636 S.E.2d 862, 863 (S.C. 2006).

121 E.g., Dodge, 'Extraterritoriality in State Law' pp. 1407–08.

122 E.g., Diamond Multimedia Sys., Inc. v. Superior Court, 968 P.2d 539, 554 n.20 (Cal. 1999).

123 E.g., Kearney v. Salomon Smith Barney, Inc., 137 P.3d 914, 931 (Cal. 2006) (asserting that a Georgia company's recording in Georgia of its phone calls with California customers effectively took place in California; analogizing to the view that someone in Nevada shooting a person standing in California has acted in California).

124 E.g., Dodge, 'Extraterritoriality in State Law' pp. 1408–09.

125 E.g., Dodge, 'Extraterritoriality in State Law' pp. 1415–17.

126 E.g., Taylor v. Eastern Connection Operating, Inc., 988 N.E.2d 408 (Mass. 2013) (albeit leaving open the possibility of a different approach to cases involving events outside the United States rather than just in another state).

dealing with common law, however, such issues are generally addressed through the doctrines of conflicts-of-laws rather than through the question of whether a common law rule would not apply even in the absence of another jurisdiction's conflicting law.[127]

Perhaps this is simply because, without the prompt of a statute triggering the question of what reach the legislature intended, courts have overlooked the issue in the absence of a conflict between potentially applicable laws. There is, however, a more fundamental explanation. Courts, unlike legislatures, are not empowered to enact laws for the governance of society. Rather, courts exist to resolve specific disputes between parties. Common law finds its justification in the need to resolve such disputes in the absence of statutory guidance and to follow the principle that like cases should produce like results. This justification means that, unlike legislation, common law applies unless supplanted by some other law.[128]

6 Conclusion

This report has provided an overview of the extraterritorial application of U.S. statutes and regulations. I hope that the report will enable both domestic and foreign readers to understand the U.S. approach and that the occasionally critical analysis of U.S. law in this report might warn foreign jurists of some foibles found in the U.S. approach.

127 E.g., Dodge, 'Extraterritoriality in State Law' p. 1412 (finding no cases in which state courts applied the presumption against extraterritoriality to common law); J. Meyer, 'Extraterritorial Common Law: Does the Common Law Apply Abroad?' (2014) 102 Georgetown Law Journal 301, 304.

128 Indeed, if a common law court reaches a different result for cases arising from events outside the court's state than it would by applying the common law covering domestic cases and does not base this on application of another jurisdiction's law, then the court is making up a substantive rule for cases involving events outside the court's state. This means that the court is still applying its common law (a rule created by courts in the state) to extraterritorial events.

L'Application Extraterritoriale des Lois et Règlements

Vietnam

Quoc Chien Ngo et Duc Vinh Nguyen***

Avant de fournir des réponses aux questions selon l'ordre établi par le Rapporteur général, il nous semble opportun de donner des précisions terminologiques. Deux notions doivent être précisées, à savoir la juridiction et l'extraterritorialité.

La notion de juridiction. Bien qu'étant un pays « socialiste » influencé par l'idéologie soviétique pendant la guerre froide, le Vietnam peut être classé dans la catégorie des pays de tradition civiliste, vu sa tradition de codification ancienne et l'influence exercée par la France pendant près de cent ans de colonisation. Et bien que connaissant des influences américaines pendant la guerre de 1956–1975, le système vietnamien reste étranger à la notion de juridiction de la Common Law. Ainsi, les termes « jurisdiction »[1] et « competence » ne sont pas compris de la même manière entre les pays de la Common Law et le Vietnam. En droit vietnamien, le terme de « jurisdiction » ou de « competence » (*thẩm quyền*) désignent le pouvoir du juge d'examiner, d'interroger (*thẩm*) pour se prononcer (*phán*) sur un problème juridique conformément à la loi. La *jurisdiction* relève donc du seul pouvoir judiciaire. Édicter les règles de droit pour régir les rapports sociaux est dans la main du pouvoir législatif et le terme consacré est *quyền lập pháp*, tandis que faire exercer les règles est dans la main du pouvoir exécutif – *quyền hành pháp*. Au Vietnam les trois pouvoirs sont désignés communément par un terme « puissance de l'Etat » (art. 2, Constitution de 2013). La *jurisdiction* a donc un sens très limité.

Aux fins du présent rapport, le terme « jurisdiction » doit avoir une acception plus large que son sens en droit national ou en droit international privé. La compétence en droit public international concerne non seulement le pouvoir des tribunaux de statuer, le pouvoir de l'État de prescrire, mais implique également le droit de l'État d'appliquer les lois.

* Professeur, Ecole supérieure de commerce extérieur de Hanoi, Vietnam.

** Professeur, Ecole supérieure de commerce extérieur, campus de Ho Chi Minh-ville, Vietnam.

1 Aux Etats-Unis, par exemple, selon le *The Third Restatement of Foreign relation law of the United States*, la jurisdiction se compose d'une juridiction pour prescrire, une juridiction pour statuer et une juridiction pour faire appliquer.

 | DOI:10.1163/9789004720183_017

La notion d'extraterritorialité. En droit vietnamien, la territorialité des lois se comprend comme leur application à l'intérieur du territoire d'un Etat. Le terme consacré par la doctrine est *trị nội lãnh thổ* (ou « autorité à l'intérieur du territoire »). Le territoire vietnamien comprend les « continents, îles, mers et espace aérien ». Le droit vietnamien ne définit pas l'extraterritorialité, mais par un raisonnement *a contrario*, on peut dire qu'est extraterritoriale une norme dont l'application dépasse les frontières de l'Etat qui l'a émise. Lorsqu'une loi est extraterritoriale, la doctrine vietnamienne s'accorde à lui donner le nom « autorité au-delà du territoire »[2] (*trị ngoại lãnh thổ*).

Aux fins du présent rapport, l'extraterritorialité ne doit pas être limitée uniquement à l'application spatiale (à l'extérieur du territoire), mais implique également des situations où une loi, appliquée par l'Etat à l'intérieur de son territoire, produit des effets à l'étranger.

1 Veuillez identifier les tendances au fil du temps dans l'attitude de votre pays à l'égard de l'application extraterritoriale des lois et règlements. Existe-t-il des cas ou des lois particuliers – ou des différends impliquant d'autres pays – qui marquent des changements importants dans l'approche de votre pays en matière d'extraterritorialité ? Existe-t-il actuellement une pratique d'application extraterritoriale des lois et règlements dans votre pays ?

Jusqu'à nos jours, parler de l'extraterritorialité des lois et règlements pourrait choquer les juristes vietnamiens dont beaucoup d'entre eux ont été enseignés que les lois édictées par un Etat ne pouvaient produire effets que sur le territoire de celui-ci. Dans un pays où les manuels de droit enseignent toujours la territorialité absolue des lois et plaident contre toute ingérence étrangère aux affaires intérieures, on n'est pas surpris de l'absence totale de recherche sur l'extraterritorialité des lois pendant plus de trente ans depuis l'ouverture du pays à l'international[3]. Il faut attendre jusqu'à 2011 pour qu'un premier article sur « l'application extraterritoriale des règles de concurrence aux États-Unis et en Europe et renseignements pour le Vietnam » ait été publié[4]. Toujours en se

2 Thu Phuong TRAN, 'Extraterritorial Jurisdiction: From Theory to International Practices and the Case of Vietnam Law', *Journal of Politics and Law* (2020); Vol. 13, n° 1; 2020;

3 Marquée par la polilitique de renouveau ou Đổi *mới* mise en place en 1986.

4 Dương Văn Học, « Từ kinh nghiệm của Hoa Kỳ và châu Âu, bàn về nguyên tắc áp dụng ngoài lãnh thổ của Luật cạnh tranh Việt Nam » (l'application extraterritoriale des règles de

basant sur l'analyse comparative des droits américain et européen, le même auteur a ensuite proposé, dans un article publié en 2014[5], des solutions pour élargir le champ d'application spatiale de la loi vietnamienne de concurrence qui fait l'objet d'une réforme importante en 2018.

Cette pauvreté doctrinale pourrait faire croire que le droit vietnamien ignore les règles dont l'application peut dépasser le territoire vietnamien. Bien au contraire, le législateur vietnamien a introduit, depuis quelques années, des dispositions extraterritoriales dans nombre de codes et lois lors des réformes entamées à la suite de l'adoption d'une nouvelle Constitution en 2013. Mais, à dire vrai, l'introduction de nouvelles solutions sur l'application extraterritoriale des règles n'est qu'opportuniste, faute de recherche approfondie. Jusqu'à nos jour, il n'y a pas de politique, ni de pratique d'extraterritorialité au Vietnam. Comme l'a remarqué Duong Van Hoc, les lois d'application extraterritoriale sont souvent considérées comme une arme impérialiste utilisée par les pays développés à la merci des pays sous-développés ou en voie de développement[6]. À l'occasion des réformes de la Loi sur la concurrence et du Code de procédure civile[7], la question de l'extraterritorialité des règles a été considérée non seulement comme un problème purement juridique, mais avant tout et surtout comme un problème politico-économique.

Du point de vue textuel, de *prime abord* le droit vietnamien n'est pas favorable à l'application extraterritoriale des lois. Ainsi, l'article 3 de la Loi sur l'élaboration et la promulagation des lois et règlements de 2015, révisée en 2020, définit les normes juridiques comme « les règles générales de conduite, obligatoires et applicables [...] sur l'ensemble du territoire ou dans une unité administrative déterminée ». L'art. 155 de ladite loi prévoit, quant à lui, que les règles édictées par les organes du pouvoir central sont d'application sur l'ensemble du pays ». Il en résulte que les lois et règlements vietnamiens ne s'appliquent que sur le territoire vietnamien, sauf les règles de droit international privé qui permettent d'élargir la compétence des tribunaux vietnamiens pour connaître

---

concurrence aux États-Unis et en Europe et renseignements pour le Vietnam), *Tạp chí Khoa học Pháp lý Việt Nam* (*Revue Science juridique vietnamienne*), n° 5(66)/2011, pp. 29–35.

5 Dương Văn Học, « Nguyên tắc ngoài lãnh thổ trong pháp luật cạnh tranh Hoa Kỳ và việc xem xét lại đối tượng điều chỉnh của pháp luật cạnh tranh Việt Nam » (L'extraterritorialité en droit de la concurrence américain et l'extension du champ d'application de la loi vietnamienne sur la concurrence), *Tạp chí Nghiên cứu lập pháp* (*Revue Études législatives*), n° 22(278), nov. 2014.

6 Certes émergeant, le Vietnam reste néanmoins un pays moins développé.

7 À l'occasion desquels l'auteur de ces lignes a assisté aux séances de consultations expertes en vue de finalisation des projets de loi.

des litiges civils internationaux et d'appliquer la loi vietnamienne aux rapports comportant élément d'extranéité.

Et pourtant, on constate la montée en nombre des règles d'application extraterritoriale à partir de 2015, suite à l'adoption de la Résolution n° 22 du Comité central du Parti communiste sur l'intégration internationale[8] et de la nouvelle Constitution en 2013. En effet, la Résolution 22 ordonne aux autorités vietnamiennes de participer activement à l'intégration internationale et de prendre l'initiative dans la construction des normes et institutions internationales en vue de tirer profit de l'intégration, de mieux protéger la sécurité nationale[9]. Il en résulte que des lois et règlements doivent être modifiés ou nouvellement élaborés. C'est ainsi que l'on voit la naissance de nombre de règles d'application extraterritoriale.

Ainsi, en matière pénale, le champ d'application spatiale des dispositions du nouveau Code pénal de 2015 s'élargit aux actes criminels commis à l'extérieur du territoire vietnamien lorsqu'ils affectent les intérêts des citoyens vietnamiens ou de l'Etat vietnamien (art. 6). On voit ici la consécration de la théorie des effets. Les règles pénales vietnamiennes sont également applicables aux actes criminels ou les conséquences d'actes criminels survenant à bord d'aéronefs, de navires ayant la nationalité vietnamienne, et à d'aéronefs, de navires n'ayant pas la nationalité vietnamienne mais se trouvant dans les eaux maritimes du Vietnam (art. 5). Dans toutes ces hypothèses, la nationalité des auteurs des actes n'est pas considérée. Ces dispositions faisaient défaut dans les législations pénales antérieures.

En matière de concurrence, la Loi sur la concurrence de 2018 a élargi le champ d'application des règles de concurrence vietnamiennes à « toutes entités, organisations et personnes vietnamiennes ou étrangères concernées » (art. 2). La nouvelle loi a également rajouté le vocable « susceptible d'affecter » dans la précision des pratiques tombées sous le coup des règles de concurrence. Ainsi, en vertu de l'art. 1 de ladite loi, les règles de concurrence vietnamiennes sont applicables à toutes pratiques restrictives de concurrences et aux concentrations économiques qui affectent ou qui sont susceptibles d'affecter la concurrence sur le marché vietnamien. Ces règles sont donc dotées d'une application extraterritoriale à la condition que l'on prouve l'affectation

8 Il est à noter que cette résolution ne traite pas directement la question d'extraterritorialité des lois. À noter également qu'au Vietnam, les résolutions du Parti Communiste jouent un rôle de première importance. Les lois et règlements se résument en l'institutionnalisation de ce qui est dit par les Résolutions.

9 Point II-2.

ou la possibilité d'affectation des pratiques anticoncurrentielles, qu'elles soient réalisées par les nationaux ou par les étrangers, au Vietnam ou à l'étranger. Aucun degré d'affectation et de possibilité d'affectation n'est exigée par le droit vietnamien.

S'agissant des entreprises réalisant des investissements à l'étranger, la Loi sur les entreprises de 2020 leur impose de « rapatrier les bénéfices pendant le délai de six mois courant de la remise des bilans fiscaux ».

En examinant le contenu des règles d'application extraterritoriale, on peut dire que le législateur vietnamien a inspiré de toutes les théories relatives à l'extraterritorialité, telles que la théorie de la nationalité, la théorie de protection, la théorie des effets … Mais le manque d'explications[10] quant au choix de chaque théorie dans la consécration des solutions nous rend difficile à dire qu'il existe au Vietnam une politique systématique dans l'édiction des règles d'application extraterritoriale.

2 Les instruments multilatéraux ou régionaux ont-ils eu une influence sur l'application extraterritoriale des lois ou règlements dans votre pays ? Par exemple, votre pays a – t – il adhéré à des traités contre la corruption ou à d'autres instruments qui encouragent l'application extraterritoriale du droit interne dans des circonstances particulières ?

Du point de vue géopolitique, le Vietnam est le terrain d'élection des idées concurrentes de toutes les grandes puissances mondiales. Depuis l'ouverture à l'économie internationale, le Vietnam s'intègre très activement à l'internationale. L'économie vietnamienne est parmi des plus ouvertes de la région. En effet, les échanges commerciaux représentent aux alentours de 200% de son PIB depuis quelques années[11]. Étant une économie ouverte dont la croissance est de plus en plus dépendante des échanges commerciaux et des investissements étrangers, le Vietnam a besoin des accords commerciaux avec les pays de par le monde. Force est de constater que suite à l'échec du multilatéralisme marqué par la crise de gouvernance qui affecte l'OMC, ainsi qu'en témoigne l'enlisement du Cycle de Doha, le Vietnam se prête au bilatéralisme tout en signant des accords de libre-échange avec ses grands partenaires commerciaux,

10 Vainement cherchera-t-on des explications dans les rapports sur les projets de lois soumis au Comité permanent de l'Assemblée Nationale.

11 Tổng Cục thống kê Việt Nam (Direction Nationale des statistiques) (2021), *Import et export*. URL : https://www.gso.gov.vn/xuat-nhap-khau/ (consulté le 14 sept. 2021).

tels que le Japon[12] et la Corée du Sud[13], l'Union européenne (EVFFTA).... D'autres accords sont en cours de négociation. Ces accords de « nouvelle génération » couvrent non seulement les aspects commerciaux, mais également les droits humains, ce qui exige le Vietnam à adhérer à nombre de conventions dans le cadre de l'OIT, de conventions en matière environnementale. Hormis les traités commerciaux, le Vietnam a également adhéré à des conventions et des instruments des Nations-Unis contre le blanchiment d'argent[14] et financement du terrorisme[15], contre la corruption[16]. Le Vietnam est devenu membre du Groupe Asie-Pacifique sur le blanchiment d'argent (APG) depuis 2007.

L'adhésion à des conventions internationales influence grandement à l'extraterritorialité des lois et règlements au Vietnam. Étant donné que le Vietnam est un système mixte, certaines stipulations internationales s'appliquent directement sur le sol vietnamien dès leur ratification, d'autres doivent faire l'objet de transposition[17]. La place du droit international dans l'ordre juridique vietnamien n'est pas prévue clairement par la loi, de telle sorte qu'il est permis de dire que le Vietnam n'est fidèle ni à la théorie moniste, ni à la théorie dualiste. Il applique les deux, de façon opportune. L'option pour l'une ou pour l'autre dépend du contexte socio-politique[18]. En réalité, très peu de règles internationales sont d'application directes sur le territoire vietnamien. La plupart d'entre

12 Signé le 25 décembre 2008 et entre en vigueur depuis le 1er octobre 2009.

13 Signé le 5 mai 2015 et entre en vigueur depuis le 20 décembre 2015.

14 Il s'agit de Convention des Nations Unies contre le trafic illicite de stupéfiants et de substances psychotropes (1988) ; Convention des Nations Unies contre la criminalité transnationale organisée (2000) ; Déclaration politique et Plan d'action contre le blanchiment d'argent (1998) ; Déclaration politique de Naples et Plan mondial d'action contre la criminalité transnationale organisée.

15 Convention internationale pour la répression du financement du terrorisme (1999) ; Résolution 1373 (2001), adoptée par le Conseil de sécurité à sa 4385e séance, le 28 septembre 2001 ; Résolution 1377 (2001), adoptée par le Conseil de sécurité à sa 4413e séance, le 12 novembre 2001

16 Il s'agit de Convention des Nations Unies contre la corruption de 2005.

17 En effet, L'art. 6–2 de la Loi sur le droit des traités de 2016 prévoit qu'« En fonction des exigences, du contenu et de la nature du traité en question [soumis à l'adhésion], l'Assemblée Nationale, le Président de la République, le Gouvernement, ordonnent, dans l'acte acceptant d'être lié par ce traité, ou bien l'application directe totalement ou partiellement de ce traité pour les organes, les organisations et les individus lorsque les stipulation de ce traité sont suffisamment claires et complètes ; ou bien décident ou proposent, dans le même acte, de modifier, d'amender ou d'abroger les textes juridiques en vue d'appliquer ce traité ».

18 Sur ce sujet, v. Duc Vinh NGUYEN et Quoc Chien NGO, "Les enjeux de la transposition des règles sociales des accords de libre-échange en droit vietnamien", *La Revue de Droit des Affaires Internationales*, n° 5-6/2020, pp. 689–699.

elles doivent faire l'objet de transposition, de telle sorte que la doctrine parle de l'internationalisation du droit vietnamien[19]. Prenons le cas de la Loi sur la lutte contre le blanchiment d'argent de 2012. Cette loi s'applique à toutes organisations et tous individus, vietnamiens ou étrangers, effectuant ou participant aux opérations de blanchiment d'argent (art. 2-4). Le législateur vietnamien de 2012 s'est inspiré largement des solutions conventionnelles internationales dans la définition des termes « blanchiment d'argent » (art. 4-1), « opérations douteuses » (art. 4-6), « identification des clients » (art. 8)… Cette loi est en cours de révision pour tenir compte du cyber-délit et de monnaie numérique.

De même, en matière de corruption internationale, la Loi sur la lutte contre la corruption de 2018 s'est inspirée des solutions de la Convention des Nations Unies contre la corruption de 2005. Ainsi, l'art. 1 de ladite loi énonce de manière très générale que « La présente Loi prévoit la prévention, la détection et la sanction de la corruption ». On voit ici le rapprochement avec l'art. 1 de la Convention de 2005. À la différence d'autres textes dans lesquels le législateur précise, très souvent dans l'article premier, que « la présente loi s'applique… au Vietnam », la Loi sur la lutte contre la corruption de 2018 ne délimite pas son champ d'application spatiale au Vietnam. Il en résulte que ses dispositions sont susceptibles d'être appliquées à tout acte de corruption concernant le Vietnam, peu importe le lieu de réalisation de l'acte et la nationalité de son auteur. La Loi de 2018 consacre ensuite tout un chapitre[20] sur la coopération internationale en matière de prévention et de lutte contre la corruption qui permet aux autorités vietnamiennes de procéder au rapatriement des biens.

3 En général, quel rôle le droit international joue-t-il dans la définition ou la limitation de la portée géographique des lois et règlements dans votre pays ?

Le droit international joue un rôle important dans la limitation de la portée géographique des lois et règlements au Vietnam. En effet, l'article 12 de la Constitution de 2013 énonce que la République socialiste du Vietnam « respecte la Charte des Nations Unies et d'autres traités internationaux auxquels elle est partie ». De même, l'article 3 de la Loi sur le droit des traités de 2016

19 NGO Quoc Chien (s.dir.de), *Manuel de droit international privé*, éd. Lao Dong, 2019. Dans le même sens : DAO Le Thu, « Xu hướng quốc tế hóa của luật hình sự Việt Nam và vấn đề đặt ra cho lập pháp hình sự » (Les enjeux de l'internationalisation du droit pénal vietnamien), *Tạp chí Nghiên cứu Lập pháp*, n°12 (412), juin, 2020.

20 Chapitre VII.

prévoit la priorité d'application des normes internationales[21], à l'exclusion de la Constitution. Si les conventions internationales auxquelles le Vietnam a adhéré prévoient des solutions extraterritoriales, le législateur n'hésite pas à prévoir des solutions semblables lors de la transposition au droit interne. Les exemples cités à la Question 2 ont montré que le droit vietnamien est internationalisé. Au Vietnam, les coutumes internationales sont acceptées comme source du droit international.

4 En général, quel rôle joue la courtoisie internationale dans la définition ou la limitation de la portée géographique des lois et règlements dans votre pays ?

Aucun texte vietnamien ne prévoit la courtoisie internationale dans la définition ou la limitation de la portée géographique des lois et règlements. L'art. 4 de la Loi sur l'élaboration des lois énonce 6 principes généraux dans l'élaboration et la promulgation des lois et règlements, mais aucune mention n'est faite à la courtoisie internationale. Le même constat s'impose à la lecture d'autres textes. On ne trouve aucune trace de la coutoisie internationale dans les règles extraterritoriales vietnamiennes. Par contre, il existe des dispositions relatives à la réciprocité internationale. Ainsi, sur la base de réciprocité le juge vietnamien peut donner effet à des décisions étrangères alors même qu'il existe aucune convention de reconnaissance mutuelle entre le Vietnam et l'Etat d'origine desdites décisions.

5 Existe-t-il une exigence de caractère raisonnable dans l'application extraterritoriale des lois et règlements de votre pays ? Si oui, comment est-il défini et mis en œuvre ?

Non, aucun texte n'exige le juge à mesurer le degré raisonnable dans l'application extraterritoriale des lois et règlements, que ce soit dans les domaines de lutte contre la corruption, de sécurité ou dans le domaine de concurrence et de droit international privé. Ainsi, en matière de concurrence, la Loi sur la concurrence a retenu la théorie des effets pour ses règles d'application extraterritoriale et accorde au juge le pouvoir souverain dans la détermination du degré d'affectation. En matière de mariage et de famille, le mariage des couples

21 Cette priorité est encore rappelée par différents textes spéciaux dans des matières spéciales, telle que la Loi sur les investissements de 2014 (art. 4), la Loi sur le commerce de 2005 (art. 5), etc…

vietnamo-étrangers est soumis à la loi vietnamienne[22]. Le droit vietnamien se trouve applicable à leur divorce[23], même si le couple a la résidence commune à l'étranger. Dans toutes ces hypothèses, la nationalité vietnamienne d'une partie suffit pour fonder la compétence juridictionnelle et législative, sans qu'aucun autre lien de proximité ne soit nécessaire.

6 Existe-t-il des lois ou des règlements qui s'appliquent à une conduite entièrement étrangère sur la base de l'un des éléments suivants ?

Il existe en droit vietnamien des règles qui s'appliquent à une conduite entièrement étrangère sur la base de nationalité de l'acteur, de la nationalité d'une personne lésée par le comportement, des effets internes du comportement en question. Ainsi, la nationalité est prise en compte pour déterminer l'application extraterritoriale des lois et règlements vietnamiens au statut personnel des vietnamiens, qu'ils résident au Vietnam ou à l'étranger[24]. La loi vietnamienne se trouve également appliquée sur la base de la nationalité de l'auteur d'une violation aux règles administratives vietnamiennes. Ainsi, l'article 20 de la Loi sur les sanctions administratives de 2012, révisée en 2020, prescrit que « sont soumis à la présente loi tous citoyens et organisations vietnamiens qui violent les règles administratives vietnamiennes même à l'étranger ». L'application extraterritoriale est déterminée sur le seul critère de la nationalité des auteurs de l'acte. Le même constat s'impose en matière pénale.

La nationalité de la personne lésée par un comportement nuisible est également prise en considération. En effet, en matière de compétence internationale, le juge vietnamien a la compétence générale pour connaître des affaires mettant en cause les relations civiles qui sont établies, modifiées, interrompues sur le territoire d'un pays étranger mais dont l'objet porte sur les droits et obligations des personnes physiques et des organisations vietnamiennes ou des personnes physiques et des organisations étrangères ayant leur domicile ou leur siège au Vietnam[25].

Le droit interne vietnamien ne prévoit pas la compétence universelle. Le Code pénal et le Code de procédure pénale exigent l'existence d'un lien de rattachement entre l'acte commis et le Vietnam pour que les règles pénales

---

22 Art. 126 de la Loi sur le mariage et la famille.

23 Art. 127 de la Loi sur le mariage et la famille.

24 Les art.s 673–675 du Code civil de 2015.

25 Art. 469-1-f du Code de procédure civile de 2015.

s'appliquent. Par contre, la compétence universelle du Vietnam peut s'établir sur la base des conventions internationales et des accords de coopération.

7 Existe-t-il des lois ou règlements qui s'appliquent à une activité se déroulant en partie dans un autre pays sur la base d'un comportement local (liens territoriaux) ? Dans l'affirmative, y a – t – il des limites fondées sur l'importance relative des liens territoriaux ou sur un autre facteur ?

Oui, en matière de responsabilité extracontractuelle, le droit vietnamien se trouve appliqué lorsque le préjudice est subi au Vietnam, peu importe le lieu du fait générateur qui s'est produit au Vietnam ou à l'étranger. C'est ce qui résulte de l'article 687 du Code civil de 2015. Il s'agit d'une disposition générale applicable à toutes les responsabilités extracontractuelles, que le fait générateur se soit déroulé dans le monde réel ou dans monde virtuel. Aucun centre de gravité n'est exigé.

8 Dans la mesure où les lois ou règlements s'appliquent au comportement étranger sur la base de la nationalité de l'acteur, comment la question de la nationalité de l'entreprise est-elle abordée ? Les lois s'appliquent – elles uniquement aux sociétés nationales, par exemple, ou également aux sociétés détenues ou contrôlées par des sociétés nationales ?

De manière générale, la nationalité des personnes morales est déterminée conformément à la loi de l'État où elles ont été enregistrées. C'est la loi du lieu de l'enregistrement de la personne morale qui régit la capacité juridique en matière civile, la raison sociale, la représentation légale, l'organisation, la réorganisation, la dissolution de la personne morale, la relation entre la personne morale et ses membres, la responsabilité de la personne morale et de ses membres envers les obligations de la personne morale sont déterminées selon la loi de l'État dont la personne morale porte la nationalité. La personnalité juridique des personnes morales étrangères qui concluent ou exécutent des actes de la vie civile au Vietnam est soumise à la loi vietnamienne[26].

26 Art. 676 du Code civil de 2015.

Il n'existe aucune disposition dans le droit interne vietnamien qui exige le juge à lever la voile des sociétés. Le juge doit procéder au dévoilement seulement lorsqu'une convention internationale l'exige[27].

9 Si une loi ou un règlement est muet quant à sa portée géographique, existe-t-il des règles d'interprétation législatives pertinentes, telles qu'une « présomption contre l'extraterritorialité » ?

Au Vietnam, la mission de l'interprétation des règles législatives obscures est confiée au Comité permanent de l'Assemblée Nationale[28]. Cet organe, depuis sa création, n'a jamais interprété une loi. Le conseil des juges suprêmes, quant à lui, peut rendre des jurisprudences[29]. En regardant les 72 jurisprudences qui ont été publiées sous l'empire de la loi de 2014[30], nous ne trouvons aucun élément de réponse à la question posée. Aucune jurisprudence ne traite la question de l'extraterritolité des lois. Étant donné que les juges de fond au Vietnam sont « la bouche de la loi », il nous parait peu probable qu'ils accordent le caractère extraterritorial à des règles nationales en cas d'absence de précision légale.

10 Votre pays a – t – il adopté des « lois de blocage » ou d'autres lois destinées à limiter les effets des pratiques extraterritoriales d'autres États ?

Non, le Vietnam n'a adopté aucune loi de blocage, ni de loi destinée à limiter les effets des pratiques extraterritoriales d'autres États. Victime des lois extraterritoriales étrangères, le Vietnam cherche à résoudre le problème via les échanges diplomatiques.

---

27 Il s'agit par exemple de l'Accord de Partenariat trans-pacifique global et progressiste qui exige le dévoilement des sociétés pour prévenir du chalandage des traités. V. Quoc Chien Ngo, Van Anh Ly, « Le chalandage de traités à l'épreuve des accords d'investissement de nouvelle génération », *Revue internationale de droit* économique, 2017/3 (t. XXXI), pp. 85–108.

28 Art. 49 de la Loi sur l'organisation de l'Assemblée Nationale de 2014, révisée en 2020.

29 Art. 22 de la Loi sur l'organisation judiciaire de 2014.

30 Il est à noter que le terme de jurisprudence au Vietnam ne s'entend pas de la même manière qu'en France. Ainsi, au Vietnam, tous les arrêts de la cour ne sont pas jurisprudences. Seulement les décisions contenant dans des jugements des tribunaux qui sont sélectionnées par le Conseil des juges suprêmes deviennent Jurisprudences. Les jurisprudences, pour avoir force de lois, doivent être publiées. On peut les retrouver en ligne: https://anle.toaan.gov.vn/webcenter/portal/anle/home.

PART 3

Special Report

The Extraterritorial Application of Statutes and Regulations

European Union

*Lena Hornkohl**

1 Introduction[1]

European Union (EU) law deploys increasingly extraterritorial effects. The EU has always seen itself as an important worldwide economic player that seeks to extend its influence in a variety of ways. The many free trade and association agreements already indicate a desire for great influence beyond its own territory. However, digitalisation and globalisation, in particular, have led to the introduction of more and more regulations in the EU that result in extraterritorial application and entail a global range of influence. Recently, the discussion has picked up speed again due to legislative initiatives on the introduction of rules on supply chain liability or the new Foreign Subsidies Regulation. However, while the EU is trying to extend its sphere of influence further and further, it takes a rather critical view of the extraterritoriality of the laws of third countries, as the *Bank Melli* judgment of the Court of Justice of the European Union (CJEU) illustrates.

This chapter deals with this phenomenon of extraterritorial application of statutes and regulations in European Union law (prescriptive jurisdiction). In that sense, it answers the question if and to what extent EU law applies beyond the EU's territory. It assesses the legal instruments themselves and throws light on the CJEU interpretation. It maps out the understanding of extraterritoriality in EU law and explains the logic and rationale behind applying the concept for EU law. Furthermore, the chapter illustrates the general principles, trends, and evolution of EU extraterritoriality, focusing on the concept of universal

* Tenure Track Assistant Professor for European Law, University of Vienna; postdoctoral researcher (Habilitandin), Heidelberg University.

1 The author would like to thank Prof. Dr. Dres. h.c. Burkhard Hess for his extremely valuable comments and Anne-Catherine Kern, Lena Scheiwen, Paula Luz Y Graf, and Jasmin Wittmann for their research and editorial assistance. The chapter was written in November 2023; subsequent legal developments had to be disregarded. This chapter is a revised and slightly shortened version of Hornkohl, The Extraterritorial Application of Statutes and Regulations in EU Law, (2022) 1 MPIL *Research Paper Series*, https://ssrn.com/abstract=4036688.

 | DOI:10.1163/9789004720183_018

jurisdiction. It describes the triggers for the extraterritorial application of EU law: nationality, presence, conduct, effects, anti-evasion, counterparty, and property. The chapter demonstrates the limits to extraterritoriality, such as comity and reasonableness. Lastly, it discusses blocking statutes of the EU against extraterritorial laws of third states.

2 Scope and Definition

This chapter deals with the extraterritoriality of statutes and regulations in EU law. In this sense, it covers the question of legislative prescriptive jurisdiction *per se* and does not concern issues related to the enforcement of these statutes and regulations.[2] Moreover, it covers EU law *strictu sensu*. This limitation includes the EU treaties as well as regulations and directives. It excludes the laws of the Member States in principle, even when they transpose EU law directives or supplement EU regulations, unless their discussion is directly relevant to the extraterritoriality of EU law itself. Moreover, it excludes specific European Economic Area (EEA) law discussions, even if some EU regulations and directives apply *mutatis mutandis* in the EEA.[3] Lastly, it generally excludes the European Convention on Human Rights (ECHR) law unless directly relevant via Article 6(3) TEU to EU law.

In the EU context, the term 'extraterritoriality' does not have an agreed or common definition. Rather, extraterritoriality is an ambiguous term.[4] The EU law literature often uses the term inconsistently for various divergent concepts. This chapter focuses on examining the extraterritorial reach of EU legislation (prescriptive jurisdiction), *i.e.*, when EU law applies irrespective of a territorial connection to the EU or beyond the territorial scope as defined by the EU Treaties to conduct outside of the EU. At the same time, the chapter excludes the concepts of transterritoriality and the so-called 'Brussels Effect' from its scope.

2 See Cremona and Scott, Introduction: EU Law Beyond EU Borders, in Cremona and Scott (eds), EU *Law Beyond* EU *Borders – The Extraterritorial Reach of* EU *Law*, Oxford University Press 2019, pp. 13–14.

3 See, on the question of extraterritoriality and EEA law, Müller, EWR-Recht und Extraterritorialität, (2020) 41(1) *Liechtensteinischen Juristenzeitung* 91.

4 The general terminology regarding 'jurisdiction' in public international law appears equally largely unsettled Ryngaert, *Jurisdiction in International Law*, 2nd ed, Oxford University Press 2015.

The concept of transterritoriality[5] inherently connects to the general territorial scope of EU law. Articles 52 TEU and 355 TFEU regulate the territorial scope of the EU primary law, the EU Treaties, and, consequently, of the legal acts adopted based on them, the EU secondary law.[6] According to these provisions, the territorial scope of EU law, in principle, covers the cumulated territories of the EU Member States. The 'territories of the EU Member States' relates to the entire territory according to Article 29 of the 1969 Vienna Convention on the Law of Treaties, subject to the special rules laid down in Articles 355, 349 TFEU, *inter alia,* for overseas territories. Otherwise, the 'entire territory' includes the complete geographical area over which the EU Member States exercise territorial sovereignty. This includes the land areas, the coastal sea that is also part of the national territory and the airspace above the land and coastal sea.[7] Furthermore, the territorial scope of Union law also extends to vessels[8] and aircraft[9] registered in one of the Member States.[10]

At the same time, due to the lack of territorial sovereignty, the exclusive economic zone and the continental shelf are not part of the territory of the Member States.[11] The concept of transterritoriality refers to just these zones. In that regard, the CJEU has adopted a functional understanding and applies EU law to the exclusive economic zone and the continental shelf.[12] Even though

5 Terminology used in this context by Müller, EWR-Recht und Extraterritorialität, (2020) 41(1) *Liechtensteinischen Juristenzeitung* 91, 92.

6 Case 61/77, *Commission of the European Communities v. Ireland,* ECLI:EU:C:1978:29, 46; Case 214/94, *Ingrid Boukhalfa v. Bundesrepublik Deutschland,* ECLI:EU:C:1996:174, 13.

7 Von der Decken, Article 29, in Dörr and Schmalenbach (eds), *Vienna Convention on the Law of Treaties,* vol. 2, Springer 2018, p. 23.

8 Article 91(1) United Nations Convention on the Law of the Sea [1982] OJ L 179/3.

9 Article 17 Convention on International Civil Aviation [1944] OJ L 187/7.

10 See, for secondary-law examples, Article 20(b) Council Regulation (EU) 2017/2063 of 13 November 2017 concerning restrictive measures in view of the situation in Venezuela (2017 Venezuela Sanctions Regulation) [2017] OJ L295/21; Article 17(b) Council Regulation (EU) No 269/2014 of 17 March 2014 concerning restrictive measures in respect of actions undermining or threatening the territorial integrity, sovereignty and independence of Ukraine (2014 Russia Sanctions Regulation) [2014] OJ L78/6; Article 15(b) Council Regulation (EU) No 359/2011 of 12 April 2011 concerning restrictive measures directed against certain persons, entities and bodies in view of the situation in Iran (2011 Iran Sanctions Regulation) [2011] OJ L100/1.

11 Dörr, Artikel 52 EUV, in Grabitz and others (eds), *Das Recht der Europäischen Union,* 4th ed, Beck 2021, p. 15.

12 Case C-6/04, *Commission of the European Communities v. United Kingdom of Great Britain and Northern Ireland*, ECLI:EU:C:2005:626, 117; Case 347/10, *A. Salemink v. Raad van bestuur van het Uitvoeringsinstituut werknemersverzekeringen*, ECLI:EU:C:2012:17, 35 et.seq.; see also Article 3 (1) c) Directive 2005/35/EC of the European Parliament and of

the EU Member States cannot exercise territorial sovereignty over these areas, they can exercise sovereign rights there, particularly the right to extensive use of resources.[13] While transterritoriality technically includes an EU law application beyond the territorial sovereignty of Member States and, thus, a form of extraterritoriality of EU law, it is not further analysed in the chapter as the legal issues largely relate to the use of resources or the question of pollution in these areas.[14]

In contrast, the so-called 'Brussels Effect'[15] entirely falls out of the understanding of extraterritoriality of this chapter, although it is often mentioned in this context because it likewise serves to extend the reach of EU law. With the 'Brussels Effect', *Bradford* describes the 'global power that the European Union is exercising through its legal institutions and standards, and how it successfully exports that influence to the rest of the world'.[16] It concerns a form of unilateral regulatory globalisation, either in the form of a *de facto* or *de jure* 'Brussels Effect'.[17] A '*de facto* Brussels Effect' occurs when third-country companies must comply with EU standards when they produce goods for the EU market and decide to comply with these standards even when they produce goods for markets outside of the EU. A '*de jure* Brussels Effect' occurs when a third country incorporates EU legal standards into its domestic law by choice. However, both do not concern extraterritoriality in the defined sense but rather deal with EU rules' influence on regulation outside of the EU. A good example is the EU Product Liability Directive[18] that influenced product liability standards worldwide.

Instead, this chapter provides a targeted discussion of extraterritoriality and, like *Scott*, focuses on (1) genuine extraterritoriality and (2) territorial

---

the Council of 7 September 2005 on ship-source pollution and on the introduction of penalties for infringements (Ship-Source Pollution Directive) [2005] OJ L 255/11.

13 Case C-6/04, *Commission of the European Communities v. United Kingdom of Great Britain and Northern Ireland*, ECLI:EU:C:2005:626, 117; Case 347/10, *A. Salemink v. Raad van bestuur van het Uitvoeringsinstituut werknemersverzekeringen*, ECLI:EU:C:2012:17, 35 et.seq.

14 Krämer, Extraterritoriale Wirkungen des Unionsrechts – eine normanalytische Skizze, (2021) 2 *Europarecht* 137, 143.

15 Bradford, The Brussels Effect, (2015) 107(1) *Northwestern University Law Review* 1; Bradford, *The Brussels Effect – How the European Union rules the world*, Oxford University Press 2020.

16 Bradford, The Brussels Effect, (2015) 107(1) *Northwestern University Law Review* 1, 3.

17 Bradford, The Brussels Effect, (2015) 107(1) *Northwestern University Law Review* 1, 6.

18 Council Directive 85/374/EEC of 25 July 1985 on the approximation of the laws, regulations and administrative provisions of the Member States concerning liability for defective products (Product Liability Directive) [1985] OJ L178/27.

extension.[19] In the case of genuine extraterritoriality, EU law applies irrespective of a territorial connection of the relevant conduct to the territory of an EU Member State – for example, when EU law applies to the conduct of EU nationals beyond EU borders. On the other hand, territorial extension 'is triggered by the existence of a territorial connection with the EU' but 'requires an evaluation of foreign conduct' – for example, when EU applies to the conduct of a foreign national operating in the EU. Sometimes, genuine extraterritoriality and territorial extension are hard to differentiate and are in whole or in part covered by the general term 'extraterritoriality' used in this chapter. However, the concepts are not identical and require a certain categorisation.

3 Objectives and Justification

It is undeniable that the EU is a global player. Developments like the 'Brussels Effect' alone demonstrate the substantial external influence of the EU. However, the motives behind the extraterritoriality of statutes and regulations in EU law are not of an external but mostly of an internal nature;[20] that is, EU law mainly pursues internal rather than external objectives, even when measures give rise to genuine extraterritoriality or territorial extension. In that sense, the extraterritoriality of EU law does not stem from an effort to expand the reach of EU law *per se*. Extraterritoriality of EU law is often necessary to achieve essentially internal goals.[21]

Despite the overarching principle of primacy of EU law, the internal reach of EU law alone is limited, and the EU's regulatory powers follow a carefully balanced approach in relation to Member States' powers. (Legislative) action by the EU, therefore, requires justification and needs to follow a clear-cut objective that the EU is allowed to regulate.[22] EU laws giving rise to genuine extraterritoriality or territorial extension follow such objectives in the areas of competence of the EU. Examples stretch from consumer protection, to the

19 Scott, The Global Reach of EU Law, in Cremona and Scott (eds), EU *Law Beyond EU Borders – The Extraterritorial Reach of EU Law*, Oxford University Press 2019, pp. 21–22; Scott, Extraterritoriality and Territorial Extension in EU Law, (2014) 62 (1) *American Journal of Comparative Law* 87; Scott, The new EU "Extraterritoriality", (2014) 51(5) *Common Market Law Review* 1343.

20 Equally, Scott, The Global Reach of EU Law, in Cremona and Scott (eds), *EU Law Beyond* EU *Borders – The Extraterritorial Reach of* EU *Law*, Oxford University Press 2019, p. 29.

21 See, for example, Case 507/17, *Google* LLC *v. Commission nationale de l'informatique et des libertés* (CNIL), ECLI:EU:C:2019:772, 54 et.seq.

22 See Article 5 TEU.

protection of competition in the EU markets, privacy of EU citizens, their safety or their other fundamental rights and interests, discussed in this chapter.

EU law, thus, essentially aims to protect EU internal interests and the interests of EU citizens.[23] Solely as a consequence attached to this pursuit of the objective, EU law may require extraterritorial applicability to achieve the respective goal. Extraterritoriality in itself is not the prime objective. Yet, in some instances, particularly when it comes to digital activities, the necessity for an extraterritorial reach of EU law and the intent to apply EU law externally is more obvious. In EU data protection and privacy law, for example, EU law broadly applies to foreign conduct and is specifically intended to also cover foreign conduct, for example, data transfers to third countries.[24] Nevertheless, the motivation behind the extraterritorial reach is also policy-oriented towards internal EU goals: the EU wants to defend its own substantive legal data protection and privacy standards and, finally, to protect its own citizens and enterprises.[25] This demonstrates that there is usually a direct link between the scope of application of EU law and the internal policy objectives it wants to pursue.[26] This makes it necessary to establish the policy objectives of a specific EU law to determine its territorial scope.[27]

Nevertheless, exceptions exist where EU law aims to achieve an objective entirely outside of the EU, without a connection to an internal goal or the protection of EU citizens. Some of those objectives relate to universal principles that the EU wants to promote, such as universal fundamental rights protection. For example, the Anti-Torture Regulation[28] covers the monitoring of trade in goods which could be used in committing acts of capital punishment

---

23 See, similarly, Kuner, The Internet and the Global Reach of EU Law, in Cremona and Scott (eds), EU *Law Beyond* EU *Borders – The Extraterritorial Reach of* EU *Law*, Oxford University Press 2019, p. 139.

24 See, for example, Articles 3, 44 et seq. Regulation (EU) 2016/679 of the European Parliament and of the Council of 27 April 2016 on the protection of natural persons with regard to the processing of personal data and on the free movement of such data, and repealing Directive 95/46/EC (GDPR) [2016] OJ L 119/1; see in detail, Kuner, Protecting EU Data Outside EU Borders under the GDPR, (2023) 60 *Common Market Law Review* 77.

25 See, similarly, Kuner, The Internet and the Global Reach of EU Law, in Cremona and Scott (eds), EU *Law Beyond* EU *Borders – The Extraterritorial Reach of* EU *Law*, Oxford University Press 2019, p. 139.

26 Cremona and Micklitz, Introduction, in Cremona and Micklitz (eds), *Private Law in the External Relations of the* EU, Oxford University Press 2016, pp. 1 et seq.

27 Jääskinen and Ward, The External Reach of EU Private Law in the Light of L'Oréal versus eBay and Google and Google Spain, in Cremona and Micklitz (eds), *Private Law in the External Relations of the* EU, Oxford University Press 2016, p. 145.

28 Regulation (EU) No 2019/125 of the European Parliament and of the Council of 16 January 2019 concerning trade in certain goods which could be used for capital punishment,

or torture orbidden in the EU,[29] outside of the EU. Here, non-EU citizens that are not residents or present in the EU should be protected from capital punishment or torture. Furthermore, the proposed Corporate Sustainability Due Diligence Directive (Draft CSDDD)[30] wants to promote, *inter alia*, universal human rights and environmental protection in the supply chain, also in third countries.[31] EU companies relying on global supply chains should be subject to legal obligations in terms of human rights and environmental due diligence obligations in the supply chain, including the part of the supply chain located outside of the EU.[32]

External objectives also predominate in problems the EU wants to address which extend beyond the bloc's territory. In light of the transboundary and worldwide nature of many environmental problems, in addition to the environmental aspects covered by the proposed Corporate Sustainability Due Diligence Directive, other EU environmental law also includes measures to protect the environment beyond the EU's territory.[33] For example, the Draft Regulation on waste shipments[34] aims at ensuring that the EU does not export its waste challenges and pollution to third countries. Moreover, the Ship-Source Pollution Directive applies also in the high seas in order to guarantee a high level of safety and environmental protection.[35] Action beyond the EU's borders is often necessary to achieve global environmental protection and tackle climate change.

---

torture or other cruel, inhuman or degrading treatment or punishment (Anti-Torture Regulation) [2019] OJ L 30/1.

29 Articles 2(2), 4 EU Charter of Fundamental Rights.

30 Proposal for a Directive of the European Parliament and of the Council on Corporate Sustainability Due Diligence and amending Directive (EU) 2019/1937 (Draft CSDDD) [2022] COM/2022/71 final.

31 Hereto also European Parliament resolution of 10 March 2021 with recommendations to the Commission on corporate due diligence and corporate accountability (2020/2129(INL)) [2021] OJ C 474/11; see, for example, Patz, The EU's Draft Corporate Sustainability Due Diligence Directive: A First Assessment, (2022) 7(2) *Business and Human Rights Journal* 291.

32 Article 1 Draft CSDDD.

33 See wording of Article 191 TFEU.

34 Proposal for a Regulation of the European Parliament and of the Council on shipments of waste and amending Regulations (EU) No 1257/2013 and (EU) No 2020/1056 (2021/0367 (COD)) [2021] COM(2021) 709 final.

35 Article 3(1)(e) Ship-Source Pollution Directive; see Case C-308/06, *The Queen, on the application of International Association of Independent Tanker Owners (Intertanko) and Others v. Secretary of State for Transport*, ECLI:EU:C:2008:312.

4 General Principles, Trends, and Evolution

Like EU law in general, the extraterritorial application of EU statutes and regulations is an ever changing and growing field. As the extraterritoriality of EU law is primarily linked to the internal EU competencies and objectives of the EU, respective internal developments influence the extraterritorial application of EU law. Accordingly, there are no specific judgments or legislative measures that generally bar extraterritoriality in EU law. Extraterritoriality in an EU law context depends on the subject matter. In some cases, even EU primary law itself demands its extraterritorial application. The EU competition law rules, for example, are directly located in Articles 101, 102 TFEU, EU primary law. In such circumstances, extraterritoriality is in principle as old as the EU law itself.[36]

4.1 *No Uniform Principle of Extraterritoriality*

In general, there is no universal practice of extraterritorial application of EU law. Extraterritoriality in an EU law context varies according to the respective sub-field of EU law and subject matter.

Several sub-fields of EU law are especially susceptible to extraterritoriality. They either want to guarantee a high level of protection for EU citizens and EU values or are more prone to extraterritoriality due to influences of globalisation and digitisation that transcend EU borders. Notable examples where extraterritoriality plays a more prominent role include EU competition, data protection and data governance, financial regulation, consumer protection, IP, trade, and environmental law. In these fields, cases of genuine extraterritoriality as the further-reaching concept without territorial links to the EU are rarer than cases of territorial extension.[37]

4.2 *The Role of Public International Law*

International law plays some role in defining or limiting the geographic scope of statutes and regulations in EU law. The case law mentioned above on the applicability of EU law on the exclusive economic zone and the continental shelf, for example, refers to the United Nations Convention on the Law of the Sea.[38] Yet, the existence of international standards or international agreements

---

36 Already Case 22/71, *Béguelin Import v. S.A.G.L. Import Export*, ECLI:EU:C:1971:113, 11.

37 See Scott, The Global Reach of EU Law, in Cremona and Scott (eds), EU *Law Beyond* EU *Borders – The Extraterritorial Reach of* EU *Law*, Oxford University Press 2019, p. 24.

38 Case C-6/04, *Commission of the European Communities v. United Kingdom of Great Britain and Northern Ireland*, ECLI:EU:C:2005:626, 117; Case 347/10, *A. Salemink v. Raad van*

is generally not a precondition for the extraterritoriality of EU law.[39] The CJEU rarely refers to international law obligations[40] to justify or limit the extraterritorial reach of EU law. However, examples exist in the field of environmental protection, fisheries and transportation law, for example, in the *Poulsen* or *Air Transport Association of America* case discussed in more detail below.[41] On the contrary, as also discussed in more detail below, the EU has initiated a blocking statute against extraterritorial embargo rules of the United States, based on its understanding that the embargos are contrary to international law.[42]

4.3 *General Principles of Comity*

Even though there is no universal across-the-board practice of EU law extraterritorial application, some general principles are identifiable.

First of all, the territorial scope of EU law generally does not limit EU extraterritoriality.[43] As mentioned above, EU law generally limits its territorial scope in Articles 52 TEU and 355 TFEU to the Member 'States' territories. Critics of EU extraterritoriality who question the normative extraterritoriality with reference to the territorial scope of the EU,[44] however, misunderstand the meaning of Articles 52 TEU and 355 TFEU. These rules are relevant in establishing the territorial scope of the rights and obligations of the Member States and Union institutions, but not for the admissibility of extraterritoriality orders in primary or secondary law.[45] As mentioned above, the extraterritoriality of EU law depends on its respective objective.

---

bestuur van het Uitvoeringsinstituut werknemersverzekeringen, ECLI:EU:C:2012:17, 35 et. seq.

39 Scott, The Global Reach of EU Law, in Cremona and Scott (eds), EU *Law Beyond EU Borders – The Extraterritorial Reach of EU Law*, Oxford University Press 2019, p. 36.

40 See, hereto, Ryngaert, *Jurisdiction in International Law*, 2nd ed, Oxford University Press 2015, pp. 47 et seq.

41 See, for example, Case 286/90, *Anklagemyndigheden v. Peter Michael Poulsen and Diva Navigation Corp*, ECLI:EU:C:1992:453, 9; Case 366/10, *Air Transport Association of America and Others v. Secretary of State for Energy and Climate Change*, ECLI:EU:C:2011:864, 123; see Hadjiyianni, *The EU as a Global Regulator for Environmental Protection*, Bloomsbury 2019; see below V. 3.

42 See below VII.

43 Krämer, Extraterritoriale Wirkungen des Unionsrechts – eine normanalytische Skizze, [2021] *Europarecht* 137, 140.

44 See, for example, Brauneck, Marktortprinzip der DSGVO: Weltgeltung für EU-Datenschutz?, [2019] *Europäische Zeitschrift für Wirtschaftsrecht* 494, 499; with regard to the so called *lex loci solutionis* according to Article 3(2) GDPR.

45 Equally Krämer, Extraterritoriale Wirkungen des Unionsrechts – eine normanalytische Skizze, [2021] *Europarecht* 137, 140.

Second, only a few EU instruments explicitly state their applicability in an extraterritorial context, even though there is a growing number of instruments that include at least textual hints at extraterritorial application. For example, Article 3(2) GDPR[46] regulates the *lex loci solutionis,* according to which the concerned data processor does not need to have a physical establishment within the EU for the GDRP to apply.[47] Another prominent example is the EU sanctions regime (also called restrictive measures), which is applicable to, *inter alia,* nationals of a Member State that carry out business with sanctioned entities inside or outside the territory of the Union.[48]

Otherwise, EU law observes neither a presumption of extraterritoriality nor a presumption excluding extraterritoriality. As indicated above, the extraterritoriality of EU law must be identified on a case-by-case basis with regard to the objective of the EU instrument. The CJEU has explicitly set out such an approach in *Google v* CNIL by underlining the connection between the objective of 'high level of protection of personal data throughout the European Union' and the measure in question, the 'scope of a dereferencing outside the Union'.[49] Nevertheless, the lack of guidance by the EU legislator regarding the extraterritoriality of a respective law means uncertainty for practice and entails an increased workload for courts.[50] Moreover, it could lead to an incoherent and inconsistent application of EU law with political interests unduly influencing the legal discourse.[51]

Lastly, there are instances where EU statutes or regulations apply to wholly foreign conduct, for example, when EU law applies because of an anti-evasion trigger.[52] It is worth reiterating that the application of EU law to wholly foreign conduct is closely linked to the objective of the EU measure in question.

46 See below V. 3. on the text of Article 3(2) GDPR; and other data and digital related rules containing rules on *lex loci solutionis.*

47 See Case 131/12, *Google Spain* SL *and Google Inc. v. Agencia Española de Protección de Datos* (AEPD) *and Mario Costeja González,* ECLI:EU:C:2014:317.

48 See, for example, Article 20(c) 2017 Venezuela Sanctions Regulation; Article 17(c) 2014 Russia Sanctions Regulation; Article 15(c) 2011 Iran Sanctions Regulation.

49 Case 507/17, *Google* LLC *v. Commission nationale de l'informatique et des libertés* (CNIL), ECLI:EU:C:2019:772, 54 et. seq.

50 Jääskinen and Ward, The External Reach of EU Private Law in the Light of L'Oréal versus eBay and Google and Google Spain, in Cremona and Micklitz (eds), *Private Law in the External Relations of the* EU, Oxford University Press 2016, p. 145.

51 Kuner, The Internet and the Global Reach of EU Law, in Cremona and Scott (eds), EU *Law Beyond* EU *Borders – The Extraterritorial Reach of* EU *Law*, Oxford University Press 2019, p. 140.

52 See below at V.5.

4.4 *Universal Jurisdiction and EU Law*

Connected to the previous point, the principle of universal jurisdiction in EU law is developing in different stages.

Generally, universal jurisdiction is an acknowledged principle of international criminal law. The concept of universal jurisdiction allows claiming criminal jurisdiction regardless of where the alleged crime was committed, the accused's nationality, country of residence, or any other relation with the prosecuting entity.[53] Since the EU has only very limited competencies concerning criminal law,[54] universal criminal jurisdiction plays a minor role in EU law. An exception seems to be, for example, the mentioned Ship-Source Pollution Directive, which also applies in the high seas outside of Union territory to guarantee a high level of safety and environmental protection and foresees criminal offences for pollution infringements.[55]

Several EU Member States know and apply the concept of universal criminal jurisdiction. Here, the EU largely limits its activities to the promotion and support of the Member States with regard to international criminal justice, including universal criminal jurisdiction.[56]

Universal civil jurisdiction refers to jurisdiction exercised by a State over a civil case when there are no significant connections between that case and the forum state. Universal civil jurisdiction is also not a general principle underpinning European Union legislation, although there are some gradual developments as well as discussions in academia.[57]

The principle of universal civil jurisdiction may gain some general significance on the EU level in the future. The overall debate on universal civil

---

53 See, for example, O'Sullivan, *Universal jurisdiction in international criminal law: the debate and the battle for hegemony*, Routledge 2017.

54 Articles 67, 82 – 86 TFEU; see also Herlin-Karnell, EU Competence in Criminal Law after Lisbon, in Biondi and others (eds), *EU Law after Lisbon*, Oxford University Press 2012, p. 331.

55 Articles 3(1)(e), 4 Ship-Source Pollution Directive.

56 Krebs, Ryngaert and Jeßberger, Universal jurisdiction and international crimes: Constraints and best practices, [2018] *Report requested by the European Parliament's Subcommittee on Human Rights*, https://www.europarl.europa.eu/RegData/etudes/STUD/2018/603878/EXPO_STU(2018)603878_EN.pdf

57 See, for example, Forlati and Franzina (eds), *Universal Civil Jurisdiction – Which Way Forward?*, Brill 2021; Bonfanti (ed), *Business and Human Rights in Europe: International Law Challenges*, Routledge 2019; Hess and Mantovani, Current developments in forum access: Comments on jurisdiction and forum non conveniens – European perspectives on human rights litigation, (2019) 1 MPIL *Research Paper Series*, https://ssrn.com/abstract=3325711. For an overview of the full discussion, see Hornkohl, The Extraterritorial Application of Statutes and Regulations in EU Law, (2022) 1 MPIL *Research Paper Series*, 9 – 13, https://ssrn.com/abstract=4036688

jurisdiction has flared up again in two contexts. In the context of the possible forthcoming revision of the Brussels I^{bis} Regulation,[58] jurisdiction over third state matters and the relationship of the Regulation with third states are again being discussed.[59] Moreover, broader principles of universal civil jurisdiction might be addressed in the context of the already mentioned planned Corporate Sustainability Due Diligence Directive on supply chain liability, especially in connection with civil liability for human rights violations abroad.[60] It remains to be seen how and to what extent the EU legal framework will change when it comes to the principle of universal civil jurisdiction. Nevertheless, the discussions show a general trend towards a principle of universal civil jurisdiction, the parameters and limits are still unclear and need to be defined by future legislation and case law.

5 Triggers for the Extraterritorial Application of EU Law

Based on the above-mentioned categories of genuine extraterritoriality and territorial extension, certain triggers for the extraterritorial application of EU law can be established. It is worth mentioning that these factors *can* trigger the extraterritorial application of EU law but do not *have* to be applicable across

58 Regulation (EU) No 1215/2012 of the European Parliament and of the Council of 12 December 2012 on jurisdiction and the recognition and enforcement of judgments in civil and commercial matters (Brussels I^{bis} Regulation) [2012] OJ L351/1.

59 See Rass-Masson, Rouas, Trivellato and Vona (Mileu SRL), Study to support the preparation of a report on the application of Regulation (EU) No 1215/2012 on jurisdiction and the recognition and enforcement of judgments in civil and commercial matters (Brussels Ia Regulation), [2023] *Final report*, Publications Office of the European Union, 91 et seq., https://op.europa.eu/en/publication-detail/-/publication/4e4370d0-cead-11ed-a05c-01aa75ed71a1/language-en; Hess, Althoff, Bens, Elsner and Järvekülg, The Reform of the Brussels I^{bis} Regulation, (2022) 6 MPIL *Research Paper Series*, 15 et seq., https://ssrn.com/abstract=4278741; Hess, Reforming the Brussels I^{bis} Regulation: Perspectives and Prospects, (2021) 4 MPIL *Research Paper Series* 5 et seq., https://ssrn.com/abstract=3895006

60 Article 19(2) Annex to the European Parliament resolution of 10 March 2021 with recommendations to the Commission on corporate due diligence and corporate accountability (2020/2129(INL)) [2021] OJ C 474/11; for example, foresaw that EU undertakings should 'be held liable and provide remediation for any harm arising out of potential or actual adverse impacts on human rights, the environment or good governance that they, or undertakings under their control, have caused or contributed to by acts or omissions', which includes a quite far-reaching concept of liability for the wrongful acts of third parties abroad. Contrary, Article 22 Draft CSDDD relies more on the EU company's own failure to comply with certain obligations; see, on civil liability in supply chains comprehensively, Hübner, *Unternehmenshaftung für Menschenrechtsverletzungen*, Mohr Siebeck 2022, *passim*.

the board for all spheres of EU law. They are each only applicable in specific contexts for specific subject matters defined by the EU law itself or interpretation following the rationale and aim of the respective EU legal instrument.

Furthermore, with the emerging principle of universal jurisdiction in EU law, wholly foreign conduct will fall more and more in the extraterritorial realm of EU law. In the future, for example, under a broad supply chain liability regime, none of these triggers might be needed to apply the envisaged EU rules. Depending on the final configuration of the Corporate Sustainability Due Diligence Directive, civil liability might be solely reliant on the objective to promote universal human rights protection abroad.[61] Today, an example of an extended form of genuine extraterritoriality where the extraterritorial application of EU law is already no longer dependent on these triggers is the mentioned Ship-Source Pollution Directive. The anti-pollution rules of the Ship-Source Pollution Directive also apply in the high seas to third-country vessels to guarantee a high level of safety and environmental protection.[62]

5.1 *Nationality*

As a non-territorial connecting factor that triggers the application of EU law, EU nationality of the actor or the person affected can be relevant. The nationality principle is primarily relied on in cases of genuine extraterritoriality when EU law applies irrespective of a territorial connection of the relevant conduct to an EU Member State. The nationality trigger can be relevant for natural and legal persons but also for ships, vessels or aircraft operating under an EU flag or operating license.

Applying the active or passive personality principle to the conduct of natural persons is quite rare and generally limited either to (quasi-) criminal law or closely connected to universal fundamental rights protection or external policy reasons. The active personality principle, the EU nationality of the actor, for example, applies in the EU sanctions regime. The EU sanctions regime prohibits, *inter alia*, nationals of Member States from carrying out business with sanctioned entities inside or outside the territory of the Union.[63] The active personality principle also plays a role in the jurisdiction of Member States over EU nationals for offenses under the Human Trafficking Directive.[64]

---

61 Contrary, as Article 22 Draft CSDDD stands now, it relies on the EU company's own failure to comply with certain obligations, such as monitoring obligations in the supply chain.

62 Articles 3(1)(e), (2), 4 Ship-Source Pollution Directive.

63 See, for example, Article 20(c) 2017 Venezuela Sanctions Regulation; Article 17(c) 2014 Russia Sanctions Regulation; Article 15(c) 2011 Iran Sanctions Regulation.

64 Article 10 Directive 2011/36/EU of the European Parliament and of the Council of 5 April 2011 on preventing and combating trafficking in human beings and protecting its victims, and replacing Council Framework Decision 2002/629/JHA [2011] OJ L101/1.

Examples of the passive personality principle, acts committed against EU nationals, are likewise scarce.[65] Some directives on consumer protection contain provisions based on this passive personality principle.[66] While several EU laws and measures aim to protect EU citizens, they primarily apply only when there is a connection to EU territory, and therefore fall under the category of territorial extension. Article 6(2) of the Unfair Contract Terms Directive,[67] for example, states that 'Member States shall take the necessary measures to ensure that the consumer does not lose the protection granted by this Directive by virtue of the choice of the law of a non-Member country as the law applicable to the contract if the latter has a close connection with the territory of the Member States.'

Concerning legal persons, the distinction between the nationality-trigger and the presence-trigger discussed below is sometimes not easy to establish, especially when subsidiaries are involved.[68] Essentially, the extraterritorial application of EU law and whether the trigger is nationality-based or presence-based depend on the subject matter of the EU law. For a nationality-based trigger, in the case of legal persons, the respective EU law usually requires a registered office, central administration or principal place of business in the EU, a more permanent and centred connection to the EU.[69] Sometimes, the mere act of establishing or creating a legal entity within a particular member state's legal framework can be enough for the nationality-based trigger. As discussed further below, for the presence-trigger, on the other hand, the simple establishment of a branch of the company is relevant.[70]

In EU sanctions law, the incorporation or constitution under the laws of a Member State is sufficient to establish a nationality trigger for legal persons. Similar to natural persons, the EU sanctions regime relies on the active personality principle: EU sanctions apply to legal persons incorporated or

65 See on the overlap with the counterparty principle below at v.6.

66 See Szpunar, The Territorial Scope of Application of EU Private Law Directives, in Burkhard Hess and others (eds), *Europa als Rechts- und Lebensraum – Liber amicorum für Christian Kohler zum 75. Geburtstag*, Gieseking Verlag 2018, p. 504.

67 Council Directive 93/13/EEC of 5 April 1993 on unfair terms in consumer contracts [1993] OJ L 95/29.

68 See Scott, The Global Reach of EU Law, in Cremona and Scott (eds), EU *Law Beyond* EU *Borders – The Extraterritorial Reach of* EU *Law*, Oxford University Press 2019, p. 23.

69 Hess, *The Private Public Divide in International Dispute Resolution, Collected Courses of the Hague Academy of International Law*, vol. 388, Brill 2018; p. 49, 66.

70 See below at v.2.

constituted under the law of a Member State, both inside and outside the territory of the Union.[71] Furthermore, the Dual-Use Export Control Regulation[72] requires authorization, *inter alia*, for legal persons to provide technical assistance on dual-use items – items useable for both civil and military purposes –, in line with the EU Strategy against Proliferation of Weapons of Mass Destruction.[73] The Dual-Use Export Control Regulation applies also to providers of technical assistance in form of legal persons 'established' in a Member State that provide technical assistance within the territory of a third country.[74]

Internal market law, on the contrary, establishes a nationality trigger for legal persons based on the registered office, central administration, or principal place of business in the EU, for example in Article 54(1) TFEU. Other examples of such nationality-based triggers can be found in financial law.[75] For example, the Directive on Alternative Investment Fund Managers[76] states that an Alternative Investment Fund is considered to be an EU investment fund, even if it is not authorised or registered in a Member State, but has its registered office and/or head office in a Member State.[77] In the context of such nationality-based triggers, provisions that apply to the entirely foreign conduct of third-country subsidiaries or branches of EU companies can lead to a quite far-reaching extraterritoriality of EU law. For example, several provisions of the

71 See, for example, Article 20(d) 2017 Venezuela Sanctions Regulation; Article 17(d) 2014 Russia Sanctions Regulation; Article 15(d) 2011 Iran Sanctions Regulation.

72 Regulation (EU) 2021/821 of the European Parliament and of the Council of 20 May 2021 setting up a Union regime for the control of exports, brokering, technical assistance, transit and transfer of dual-use items (recast) (Dual-Use Export Control Regulation) [2021] OJ L 206/1.

73 Council of the European Union, EU Strategy against Proliferation of Weapons of Mass Destruction [2003], <https://data.consilium.europa.eu/doc/document/ST%2015708%20 2003%20INIT/EN/pdf>.

74 Article 2(10)(b) Dual-Use Export Control Regulation.

75 See also Schweigl, Extraterritorial Effects of EU Financial Markets Laws, in Cunha Rodrigues (ed), *Extraterritoriality of* EU *Economic Law*, Springer 2021, 251.

76 Directive 2011/61/EU of the European Parliament and of the Council of 8 June 2011 on Alternative Investment Fund Managers and amending Directives 2003/41/EC and 2009/65/EC and Regulations (EC) No 1060/2009 and (EU) No 1095/2010 (Directive on Alternative Investment Fund Managers) [2011] OJ L174/1.

77 Article 2 (1)(k) Directive on Alternative Investment Fund Managers.

Capital Requirements Directives[78] apply to third country and offshore subsidiaries or branches of EU firms.[79]

Similarly, the single economic entity doctrine for the concept of undertakings in EU competition law makes third-country subsidiaries, sister, and parent companies liable for competition law infringements of EU companies.[80] According to the single economic entity doctrine, initially, a third-country parent company exercising decisive influence over its EU subsidiary is liable for breaches of competition law of its subsidiary because the parent company and its subsidiaries form a single economic entity.[81] The CJEU has also expanded the single economic entity doctrine to (foreign) sister companies and subsidiaries of EU companies[82] and expanded the concept to private enforcement of competition law.[83]

5.2 *Presence*

The stable[84] presence of non-EU entities may also trigger the extraterritoriality of EU law.[85] Since presence is a trigger connected to the EU's territory, it

78 Directive 2013/36/EU of the European Parliament and of the Council of 26 June 2013 on access to the activity of credit institutions and the prudential supervision of credit institutions, amending Directive 2002/87/EC and repealing Directives 2006/48/EC and 2006/49/EC (Capital Requirements Directive) [2013] OJ L 176/338; in its current amended form by Directive (EU) 2021/338 of the European Parliament and of the Council of 16 February 2021 amending Directive 2014/65/EU as regards information requirements, product governance and position limits, and Directives 2013/36/EU and (EU) 2019/878 as regards their application to investment firms, to help the recovery from the COVID-19 crisis [2021] OJ L 68/14.

79 Article 92(1) Capital Requirements Directive; see also: Article 104c Directive (EU) 2019/878 of the European Parliament and of the Council of 20 May 2019 amending Directive 2013/36/EU as regards exempted entities, financial holding companies, mixed financial holding companies, remuneration, supervisory measures and powers and capital conservation measures [2019] OJ L 150/253.

80 Generally, Bailey and Odudu, The single economic entity doctrine in EU competition law, (2014) 51(6) *Common Market Law Review* 1721.

81 See Case 48–69, *Imperial Chemical Industries Ltd. v. Commission of the European Communities*, ECLI:EU:C:1972:70, 64; Case 6–72, *Europemballage Corporation and Continental Can Company Inc. v. Commission of the European Communities*, ECLI:EU:C:1973:22, 15.

82 See the latest judgment by the CJEU on the single economic entity doctrine, Case C-882/19, *Sumal, S.L. v. Mercedes Benz Trucks España, S.L.*, ECLI:EU:C:2021:800; see Kersting, Liability of Sister Companies and Subsidiaries in European Competition Law, (2020) 41 *European Competition Law Review* 125.

83 Case C-724/17, *Vantaan kaupunki v Skanska Industrial Solutions Oy and Others*, ECLI:EU:C:2019:204; see, for example, Hornkohl, The economic continuity test in private enforcement of competition law – The ECJ's judgment in Skanska Industrial Solutions (C-724/17), (2019) 29 *European Competition Law Review* 339.

84 We cover transient presence together with the conduct trigger, see below at V.3.

85 Scott, The new EU "Extraterritoriality", (2014) 51(5) *Common Market Law Review* 1343, 1353.

applies in cases of territorial extension, making an evaluation of foreign conduct necessary.

For natural foreign nationals, many EU laws apply particularly if they have a stable presence in the EU – generally, in the form of residence or domicile in an EU Member State. For example, irrespective of the EU nationality of the defendant, persons domiciled in an EU Member State can be sued in the courts of that Member State, applying the procedural rules of that Member State to the dispute according to Article 4(1) Brussels I^{bis} Regulation.[86] Similarly, the Dual-Use Export Control Regulation applies also to providers of technical assistance resident in a Member State, irrespective of their nationality, that provide technical assistance within the territory of a third country.[87]

As indicated above, for legal persons, the distinction between the nationality-trigger and the stable presence-trigger can be hard to identify and relies on the interpretation of the concepts of nationality and establishment for legal persons.[88] Contrary to the incorporation or constitution of a company under the laws of a Member State or a registered office, central administration or principal place of business in the EU, which is connected to the nationality-based trigger, establishment pertains to the stable presence of a legal person in the EU. The presence trigger becomes relevant for EU branches and subsidiaries of non-EU national companies, *i.e.* incorporated or constituted under third-country laws and with a registered office, central administration or principal place of business outside of the EU.[89] For example, in data protection law, according to Article 3(1) GDPR, the GDPR 'applies to the processing of personal data in the context of the activities of an establishment of a controller or a processor in the Union, regardless of whether the processing takes place in the Union or not.' The GDPR followed the CJEU decision in *Google Spain*, according to which the data processing activity itself does not need to occur within the EU, as long as the third country processor has an establishment in the EU.[90] In *Google Spain*, the actual operator and data controller of the respective search engine at hand was located outside of the EU but the actual operator and data controller also had an establishment in the

86 Hess, *Europäisches Zivilprozessrecht*, 2nd ed., De Gruyter 2021, pp. 5.10 et.seq.

87 Article 2(10)(b) Dual-Use Export Control Regulation.

88 See above at V.1.

89 Equally Scott, The new EU "Extraterritoriality", (2014) 51(5) *Common Market Law Review* 1343, 1353.

90 Case C131/12, *Google Spain* SL *and Google Inc. v. Agencia Española de Protección de Datos* (AEPD) *and Mario Costeja González*, ECLI:EU:C:2014:317, 43, 60; similar: Kuner, Protecting EU Data Outside EU Borders under the GDPR, (2023) 60 *Common Market Law Review* 77, 82.

EU.[91] EU financial law also largely applies to branches of credit institutions having their head office in a third state or holding special obligations to these branches.[92] Sometimes, EU law even makes market access for third nationals conditional on having a stable EU subsidiary.[93]

5.3 *Conduct*

The most prevalent trigger for the extraterritorial application of EU law relates to an activity that occurs at least partly in EU territory, the so-called conduct trigger.[94] Similarly to stable presence, the conduct trigger becomes relevant in cases of territorial extension. For the conduct trigger, some activity of a foreign entity needs to connect to the EU's territory.

Examples of the conduct trigger are numerous. EU law relates to many different types of conduct for its applicability. Transient, temporary presence, for example, plays a large role in EU environmental, transportation, or fisheries law.[95] Third-country aircraft, ships, or fishing vessels flying to or out of the EU, operating an intra-EU flight or entering an EU port must often comply with specific EU standards. In EU fisheries law, in *Poulsen*, for example, the CJEU decided that the predecessor of the Technical Measures Regulation[96] applies to third-country vessels operating in inland waters or ports of a Member State by referring to the relevant rules of the international law of the sea.[97] Similarly, EU animal welfare rules apply to animal transport from or to the territory of the Union, including the part of the journey taking place in third countries,

91 See Gömann, The new territorial scope of EU data protection law: Deconstructing a revolutionary achievement, (2017) 54 *Common Market Law Review* 567, 571.

92 See, for example, Article 47 Capital Requirements Directive.

93 See, for example, Article 41 Directive 2014/65/EU of the European Parliament and of the Council of 15 May 2014 on markets in financial instruments and amending Directive 2002/92/EC and Directive 2011/61/EU [2014] OJ L 173/349.

94 Krämer, Extraterritoriale Wirkungen des Unionsrechts – eine normanalytische Skizze, [2021] *Europarecht* 137, 142.

95 See Puetz, 'Extraterritoriality' in European Law: Airfreight and Beyond, (2021) 46(6) *Air and Space Law* 763.

96 Regulation (EU) 2019/1241 of the European Parliament and of the Council of 20 June 2019 on the conservation of fisheries resources and the protection of marine ecosystems through technical measures, amending Council Regulations (EC) No 1967/2006, (EC) No 1224/2009 and Regulations (EU) No 1380/2013, (EU) 2016/1139, (EU) 2018/973, (EU) 2019/472 and (EU) 2019/1022 of the European Parliament and of the Council, and repealing Council Regulations (EC) No 894/97, (EC) No 850/98, (EC) No 2549/2000, (EC) No 254/2002, (EC) No 812/2004 and (EC) No 2187/2005 [2019] OJ L 198/105.

97 Case 286/90, *Anklagemyndigheden v. Peter Michael Poulsen und Diva Navigation Corp*, ECLI:EU:C:1992:453, 9.

since the arrival or departure from the Union constitute conduct in the EU, and thus create a sufficiently strong EU nexus.[98]

Moreover, non-European airlines operating flights from and to the EEA, for example, are required to monitor, report and verify their emissions and to surrender allowances against those emissions under the EU emissions trading system.[99] The initial system was extended to also apply to emissions from flights from and to the EEA, including the portion of an international flight which takes place outside the airspace of Member States.[100] This amendment sparked the judgment in the prominent *Air Transport Association of America* case.[101] In this judgment, the CJEU upheld the extension of the EU emissions trading system to aviation, including flights from and to the EEA of non-EEA airlines. By relying on *Poulsen*, the CJEU explicitly delved into the compatibility of such a scheme with the customary international law principles for extraterritoriality.[102] The CJEU established that 'European Union legislation may be applied to an aircraft operator when its aircraft is in the territory of one of the Member States'. Such legislation 'does not infringe the principle of territoriality or the sovereignty which the third States from or to which such flights are performed have over the airspace above their territory, since those aircraft are physically in the territory of one of the Member States of the European Union and are thus subject on that basis to the unlimited jurisdiction of the European Union.' For

---

98 Article 14 Council Regulation (EC) No 1/2005 of 22 December 2004 on the protection of animals during transport and related operations and amending Directives 64/432/EEC and 93/119/EC and Regulation (EC) No 1255/97 [2005] OJ L 3/1; see: Case C-424/13, *Zuchtvieh-Export GmbH v. Stadt Kempten*, ECLI:EU:C:2015:259, 47.

99 Articles 12(2a), 14(3), Annex I(6) Directive 2003/87/EC of the European Parliament and of the Council of 13 October 2003 establishing a system for greenhouse gas emission allowance trading within the Union and amending Council Directive 96/61/EC [2003] OJ L 275/32.

100 Annex I(6) Directive 2003/87/EC as amended by Directive 2008/101/EC of the European Parliament and of the Council of 19 November 2008 amending Directive 2003/87/EC so as to include aviation activities in the scheme for greenhouse gas emission allowance trading within the Community [2009] OJ L 8/3; see also: recital 16 Directive 2008/101/EC of the European Parliament and of the Council of 19 November 2008 amending Directive 2003/87/EC so as to include aviation activities in the scheme for greenhouse gas emission allowance trading within the Community [2009] OJ L 8/3.

101 Case C-366/10, *Air Transport Association of America and Others v. Secretary of State for Energy and Climate Change*, ECLI:EU:C:2011:864; see, generally on the extraterritoriality of EU emission trading, Mullen, The European Union Overstepping Its Bounds and Borders: The Extraterritorial Effect of the Emissions Trading System and Its Call for Multilateral Action, (2013) 74 *University of Pittsburgh Law Review* 783.

102 Case C-366/10, *Air Transport Association of America and Others v Secretary of State for Energy and Climate Change*, ECLI:EU:C:2011:864, 121–130.

the CJEU, the physical connection to the territory of a Member State is sufficient to satisfy customary international law, irrespective that 'certain matters contributing to the pollution of the air, sea or land territory of the Member States originate in an event which occurs partly outside that territory.' Consequently, the CJEU underlined that the EU emissions trading system does not 'apply as such to international flights flying over the territory of the Member States of the European Union or of third States when such flights do not arrive at or depart from an aerodrome situated in the territory of a Member State' due to the lack of conduct in the EU territory. Despite the case law of the CJEU, the EU subsequently temporarily limited the scope to flights within the EEA[103] after third countries continued to widely condemn the system (even introducing blocking statutes)[104] and to facilitate progress at the International Civil Aviation Organisation to reach an international agreement to reduce greenhouse gas impacts from aviation.[105]

Furthermore, the Passenger Rights Regulation applies to all flights departing from the EU, even if operated by non-EU carriers.[106] This Regulation does not apply to flights departing from an airport located in a third country to an airport situated in the EU if a non-EU carrier operates the flight.[107] However,

103 Article 1 Decision No 377/2013/EU of the European Parliament and of the Council of 24 April 2013 derogating temporarily from Directive 2003/87/EC establishing a scheme for greenhouse gas emission allowance trading within the Community [2013] OJ L 113/1; Article 1 Regulation (EU) No 421/2014 of the European Parliament and of the Council of 16 April 2014 amending Directive 2003/87/EC establishing a scheme for greenhouse gas emission allowance trading within the Community, in view of the implementation by 2020 of an international agreement applying a single global market-based measure to international aviation emissions [2014] OJ L 129/1; Article 1 Regulation (EU) 2017/2392 of the European Parliament and of the Council of 13 December 2017 amending Directive 2003/87/EC to continue current limitations of scope for aviation activities and to prepare to implement a global market-based measure from 2021 [2017] OJ L 350/7.

104 US European Union Emissions Trading Scheme Prohibition Act of 2011, Publ. L. 112–200, 126 STAT. 1477 (2011).

105 See recital 5 Regulation (EU) 2017/2392 of the European Parliament and of the Council of 13 December 2017 amending Directive 2003/87/EC to continue current limitations of scope for aviation activities and to prepare to implement a global market-based measure from 2021 [2017] OJ L 350/7.

106 Article 3(1)(a) Regulation (EC) No 261/2004 of the European Parliament and of the Council of 11 February 2004 establishing common rules on compensation and assistance to passengers in the event of denied boarding and of cancellation or long delay of flights, and repealing Regulation (EEC) No 295/91 (Passenger Rights Regulation) [2004] OJ L 046; Article 7(1) Brussels I^bis^ Regulation is largely interpreted in that sense, see Case 204/08, *Peter Rehder v. Air Baltic Corporation*, ECLI:EU:C:2009:439; Burkhard Hess, *Europäisches Zivilprozessrecht*, 2nd ed., De Gruyter 2021, p. 6.61.

107 Article 3(1)(b) Passenger Rights Regulation.

the general Civil Aviation Regulation applies to aircraft operation by a third country operator into, within, or out of the EU's territory.[108]

An area in which the conduct trigger frequently leads to extraterritoriality is market access and imports to the EU. Many EU laws impose EU standards on goods imported into the EU or services provided partly in the EU. The requirements laid down in the Animal Slaughter Regulation, for example, equally apply to imports from third countries.[109]

Furthermore, EU trade defence law aims at shielding the EU industry with anti-dumping, anti-subsidy, or safeguard measures against international trade distortions through imports in the EU.[110] In EU anti-dumping law, the Commission can impose import duties when manufacturers from a non-EU country sell goods in the EU below the sales price in their domestic market or below the cost of production, causing Union injury.[111] Similarly, in EU anti-subsidy law, the Commission can impose import duties on products when a non-EU government provides financial assistance to importing companies, which are unfairly injuring EU competitors.[112] EU safeguard law covers unforeseen, sharp and sudden increases of imports causing (or threatening) serious injury to EU domestic industry. As a reaction, the Commission can impose quantitative restrictions on imports from any non-EU country and/or surveillance, including a system of automatic import licensing.[113] Moreover, the EU Regulation on the International Procurement Instrument entails a trade policy tool that

---

108 Article 2(1)(c) Regulation (EU) 2018/1139 of the European Parliament and of the Council of 4 July 2018 on common rules in the field of civil aviation and establishing a European Union Aviation Safety Agency, and amending Regulations (EC) No 2111/2005, (EC) No 1008/2008, (EU) No 996/2010, (EU) No 376/2014 and Directives 2014/30/EU and 2014/53/EU of the European Parliament and of the Council, and repealing Regulations (EC) No 552/2004 and (EC) No 216/2008 of the European Parliament and of the Council and Council Regulation (EEC) No 3922/91 (Civil Aviation Regulation) [2018] OJ L 212/1.

109 Article 12 Council Regulation (EC) No 1099/2009 of 24 September 2009 on the protection of animals at the time of killing (Animal Slaughter Regulation) [2009] OJ L 303/1.

110 See, comprehensively, Van Bael and Bellis, EU *Anti-Dumping and Other Trade Defence Instruments*, 6th ed., Kluwer Law International 2019, *passim*.

111 Article 1 Regulation (EU) 2016/1036 of the European Parliament and of the Council of 8 June 2016 on protection against dumped imports from countries not members of the European Union [2016] OJ L 176/21.

112 Article 1 Regulation (EU) 2016/1037 of the European Parliament and of the Council of 8 June 2016 on protection against subsidised imports from countries not members of the European Union [2016] OJ L 176/55.

113 Articles 10 – 21 Regulation (EU) 2015/478 of the European Parliament and of the Council of 11 March 2015 on common rules for imports; Articles 7 – 16 Regulation (EU) 2015/755 of the European Parliament and of the Council of 29 April 2015 on common rules for imports from certain third countries (recast) [2015] OJ L 83/16.

aims at facilitating EU companies access to third country public procurement markets on equal terms in reciprocity to access to the EU procurement markets. Under the Instrument, the Commission can investigate if EU companies are repeatedly and significantly denied access to the public procurement markets of a third country and, after consultations with the concerned country, the Commission can limit access of companies from that country to Union procurement markets, including total exclusion from procurement procedures.[114]

Market access is also relevant in EU sanctions law. EU sanctions law applies, *inter alia*, to 'any legal person, entity or body in respect of any business done in whole or in part within the Union'.[115] A foreign company, for example, must abide by the EU sanctions regime if it conducts some of its business within the EU, *i.e.*, wants access to the EU internal market. Consequently, foreign companies (partly) active in the EU are, for example, prohibited to contract with other companies in the sanctioned country.[116]

Market access also plays a large role in EU data protection law. With Article 3(2) GDPR, as mentioned above, the EU introduced the *lex loci solutionis* into its data protection regime.[117] For the offering of goods and services to data subjects in the Union pursuant to Article 3(2)(a) GDPR, for example, it is sufficient to provide addresses or phone numbers reachable from the EU or using a language or currency of a Member State.[118] Accordingly, the concerned data processor does not need to have a physical establishment within the European Union, as long as there is some territorial nexus concerning market access or targeting data subjects in the Union. *De Hert/Czerniawski* rightly point out the vast extraterritorial reach of Article 3(2)(a) GDPR particularly for cases where the service, payment, or location of the provider is located outside of the EU but the data subject in the EU – not necessarily an EU citizen – booked the

114 Article 6 Regulation (EU) 2022/1031 of the European Parliament and of the Council of 23 June 2022 on the access of third-country economic operators, goods and services to the Union's public procurement and concession markets and procedures supporting negotiations on access of Union economic operators, goods and services to the public procurement and concession markets of third countries (International Procurement Instrument) [2022] OJ L 173/1.

115 See, for example, Article 20(e) 2017 Venezuela Sanctions Regulation; Article 17(e) 2014 Russia Sanctions Regulation; Article 15(e) 2011 Iran Sanctions Regulation.

116 See, for example, Article 3 2017 Venezuela Sanctions Regulation.

117 See hereto, for example, Kuner, Extraterritoriality and Regulation of International Data Transfers in EU Data Protection Law, (2015) 5 *International Data Privacy Law* 242; critically: Brauneck, Marktortprinzip der DSGVO: Weltgeltung für EU-Datenschutz?, [2019] *Europäische Zeitschrift für Wirtschafsrecht* 494.

118 Kuner, Protecting EU Data Outside EU Borders under the GDPR, (2023) 60 *Common Market Law Review* 77, 83.

service.[119] The level of protection of the personal data does not play any role for the application of EU data protection law under Article 3(2) GDPR.[120] At the same time, the GDPR understands that enforcement against non-EU data controllers or processors under Article 3(2) GDPR might be difficult and therefore requires data controllers and processors to appoint a representative in the Union.[121]

Other new EU data laws follow the GDPR model. The Data Governance Act[122] does not contain an explicit provision like Article 3(2) GDPR but implies its principles by stating in Article 11(3) that 'a data intermediation services provider that is not established in the Union, but which offers the data intermediation services referred to in Article 10 within the Union, shall designate a legal representative in one of the Member States in which those services are offered.'[123] Article 1(3) of the new Data Act,[124] on the other hand, seems to fully follow the Article 3(2) GDPR approach of *lex loci solutionis*.[125]

The new Digital Markets Act[126] also follows the market access concept of *lex loci solutionis* of the EU data laws. According to Article 1(2) Digital Markets Act the Regulation applies 'to core platform services provided or offered by gatekeepers to business users established in the Union or end users established or located in the Union, irrespective of the place of establishment or

119 De Hert and Czerniawski, Expanding the European data protection scope beyond territory: Article 3 of the General Data Protection Regulation in its wider context, (2016) 6 *International Data Privacy Law* 230, 239.

120 Kuner, Protecting EU Data Outside EU Borders under the GDPR, (2023) 60 *Common Market Law Review* 77, 85.

121 Article 27(1) GDPR; see Millard and Kamarinou, Article 27, in Kuner, Bygrave and Docksey (eds.), *The EU General Data Protection Regulation: A Commentary, Oxford University Press* 2020, pp. 589, 590.

122 Regulation (EU) 2022/868 of the European Parliament and of the Council of 30 May 2022 on European data governance and amending Regulation (EU) 2018/1724 (Data Governance Act) [2022] OJ L 152/1.

123 Hennemann and Von Ditfurth: Datenintermediäre und Data Governance Act, [2022] *Neue Juristische Wochenschrift* 1905, 1907; generally: Von Ditfurth, and Lienemann, The Data Governance Act: – Promoting or Restricting Data Intermediaries?, (2022) 23(4) *Competition and regulation in network industries* 270.

124 Regulation of the European Parliament and of the Council on harmonised rules on fair access to and use of data and amending Regulation (EU) 2017/2394 and Directive (EU) 2020/1828 (Data Act) [2023] OJ L 409/1.

125 Specht-Riemenschneider, Der Entwurf des Data Act, [2022] *Multimedia und Recht* 809, 812.

126 Regulation (EU) 2022/1925 of the European Parliament and of the Council of 14 September 2022 on contestable and fair markets in the digital sector and amending Directives (EU) 2019/1937 and (EU) 2020/1828 (Digital Markets Act) [2022] OJ L 265/1.

residence of the gatekeepers and irrespective of the law otherwise applicable to the provision of service.' Importantly, similar to the GDPR, under the Digital Markets Act, the users only have to be located in the EU, not nationals of a EU Member State. The subsequently adopted Digital Services Act[127] almost copies the wording of the Digital Markets Act in Article 2(1) Digital Services Act.

Another sub-form of the conduct trigger are EU rules on activities conducted from the territory of the EU for the benefit of the territory of a third country, such as export, transfer, or transmission from the EU to third countries. Export, for example, consists of sending goods or other items from the EU out of the territory of the Union[128] and, thus, relates to an activity that occurs at least partly in EU territory. From time to time, exports from the EU can be exempt from EU obligations, for example, in product safety law.[129] Yet, when the EU has a special public interest in the exported goods, exports from the EU also need to meet EU obligations or exports from the EU are controlled. This can lead to total export bans, for example, for goods that have no practical use other than in connection with capital punishment or for torture and other cruel, inhuman, or degrading treatment or punishment.[130] Another example is the mentioned Draft Regulation on waste shipments, which aims at ensuring that the EU does not export its waste challenges to third countries. Furthermore, the Dual-Use Export Control Regulation requires an authorization for the export of dual-use items, which can lead to the prohibition of such exports.[131] Any outbound strategic investment control, which the EU Commission is contemplating at the moment,[132] unless entirely connected to nationality, might

127 Regulation (EU) 2022/2065 of the European Parliament and of the Council of 19 October 2022 on a Single Market For Digital Services and amending Directive 2000/31/EC (Digital Services Act) [2022] OJ L 277/1.

128 See, for example, Article 269(1) Regulation (EU) No 952/2013 of the European Parliament and of the Council of 9 October 2013 laying down the Union Customs Code (recast) (Union Customs Code) [2013] OJ L 269/1; Article 2 Dual-Use Export Control Regulation.

129 Many of the New Approach Directives do not apply to EU goods that are manufactured for export, see, for example, the obligations on manufacturers of toys laid down in Article 4 Directive 2009/48/EC of the European Parliament and of the Council of 18 June 2009 on the safety of toys [2009] OJ L 170/1, which only apply when placing their toys on the EU market.

130 Article 3(1) Anti-Torture Regulation.

131 For example, Art. 3 Dual-Use Export Control Regulation.

132 Joint Communication to the European Parliament, the European Council, and the Council – on "European Economic Security Strategy" [2023] JOIN(2023) 20 final.

also fall under this sub-category of the conduct trigger, depending on the exact set-up of such outbound strategic investment control.[133]

Comparable to the export of goods, the GDPR also includes rules to ensure that the transfer of personal data by the controller and processor from the EU to third countries does not undermine the level of protection of natural persons ensured in the Union by the GDPR.[134] The conduct is connected to EU territory, since the processor or controller transfers personal data from the EU to a third country. Under the strict framework provided by the GDPR, data transfers to third states are only possible in specific, pre-defined situations, to essentially allow for data processing equivalent to EU standards.[135] The Data Governance Act now contains similar rules for data held by public sector bodies[136] and re-used by natural or legal persons for commercial or non-commercial purposes.[137,138] Any intended third-country transfer by a re-user must first be notified to the public sector body.[139] The public sector body may only transfer the requested data to the re-user intending to transfer the data to a third country if the Commission has deemed the recipient country's rules on the protection of intellectual property and trade secrets to be equivalent by legal act,[140] or if the re-user contractually guarantees to comply with the conditions of the Data Governance Act.[141] A comparable approach to the data related laws when it comes to authorisation for transmission of software or technology to a territory outside of the customs territory of the Union is followed by Article 2(2)(d) Dual-Use Export Control Regulation.

133 See, Herrmann, Das Ende der Kapitalausfuhrfreiheit? – Die EU-Kommission deutet Überlegungen zu einer Investitionsexportkontrolle an, [2022] *Europäische Zeitschrift für Wirtschafsrecht* 1081.

134 Recital 101 GDPR; see Articles 44 et seq. GDPR; see also Case C-311/19, *Data Protection Commissioner* v. *Facebook Ireland Limited and Maximilian Schrems*, ECLI:EU:C:2020:559, 88.

135 See Articles 44 et seq. GDPR; see also, Case C-362/14, *Maximillian Schrems v. Data Protection Commissioner*, ECLI:EU:C:2015:650, 90; Opinion of Advocate General Mengozzi, Case 1/15, EU-*Canada* PNR *Agreement*, ECLI:EU:C:2016:656, 212–215; Case C-311/18, *Data Protection Commissioner v. Facebook Ireland Limited and Maximillian Schrems*, ECLI:EU:C:2020:559, 184; see, in detail, for example, Zalnieriute, Data Transfers after Schrems II: The EU-US Disagreements Over Data Privacy and National Security, (2022) 55(1) *Vanderbilt Journal of Transnational Law* 1.

136 Article 3(1) Data Governance Act.

137 Article 1(2) Data Governance Act.

138 See Tolks, Die finale Fassung des Data Governance Act, (2022) 6 *Multimedia und Recht* 444, 445.

139 Article 5(9) Data Governance Act.

140 Article 12 Data Governance Act.

141 Article 5(10) Data Governance Act.

The Dual-Use Export Control Regulation also provides an example of another sub-form of the conduct trigger, where an activity is conducted from the territory of the EU but otherwise entirely relates to the territory of a third country. The Regulation covers brokering services, which includes '(a) the negotiation or arrangement of transactions for the purchase, sale or supply of dual-use items from a third country to any other third country; or (b) the selling or buying of dual-use items that are located in third countries for their transfer to another third country.'[142] The broker can be 'any natural or legal person or any partnership that provides brokering services from the customs territory of the Union into the territory of a third country.'[143]

EU competition law gives us another example of a sub-form of the conduct trigger. The CJEU held already half a century ago that the fact that an undertaking participating in an anticompetitive agreement is situated in a third country does not prevent the application of EU competition law if that agreement is operative in the territory of the internal market.[144] Consequently, in EU competition law, the CJEU also applies the doctrine of implementation as a sub-form of the conduct trigger.[145] According to the implementation doctrine established in *Woodpulp I*, recently upheld in the *Airfreight Cartel*[146] case, agreements, decisions or concerted practices formed outside of the EU by EU or non-EU companies are subject to EU jurisdiction if the anticompetitive activity is implemented in the EU and it affects trade between the Member States.[147] The problematic conduct falling under EU competition law jurisdiction, the restrictive business practice, can occur entirely outside the Union's territory. Yet, the implementation doctrine is part of the conduct trigger, since other conduct implementing the restrictive business practice within the EU territory is necessary. For this, mere sales within the internal market are sufficient.[148]

---

142 Article 2(7) Dual-Use Export Control Regulation.

143 Article 2(8) Dual-Use Export Control Regulation.

144 Case 22/71, *Béguelin Import v. S.A.G.L. Import Export*, ECLI:EU:C:1971:113, 11.

145 See, on the various tests in competition law, Behrens, The extraterritorial reach of EU competition law revisited: The "effects doctrine" before the ECJ, [2016] Discussion Paper No. 3/16, *Europa-Kolleg Hamburg*, 1, 8 – 14.

146 The Airfreight Cartel case concerns many different proceedings, see, inter alia, Case T-323/17, *Martinair Holland* NV *v. European Commission*, ECLI:EU:T:2022:174, 102 et seq.

147 Joined cases 89, 104, 114, 116, 117 and 125 to 129/85, *A. Ahlström Osakeyhtiö and others v. Commission of the European Communities* (*Woodpulp I,*) ECLI:EU:C:1988:447,16.

148 See: Case 102/96, *Gencor Ltd v. Commission of the European Communities*, ECLI:EU:T:1999 :65, 85.

Similarly, the competition-akin new Foreign Subsidies Regulation[149] is applicable to undertakings receiving foreign subsidies and 'engaging in an economic activity in the internal market'.[150] While the Regulation does not demand that the undertakings themselves be foreign, third countries will likely only grant subsidies to their own undertakings.[151] The Regulation mainly aims at specific conduct on the internal market, *i.e.,* an undertaking acquiring control or merging with an undertaking established in the Union or an undertaking participating in a public procurement procedure in the EU.[152] These procedures even demand a prior notification with the Commission, similar to EU merger control.[153] On the other hand, the *ex officio* tool of the Foreign Subsidies Regulation covers all other economic activities in the internal market. Undertakings receiving foreign subsidies and engaging in any economic activity, i.e., conduct, in the EU, therefore fall under the scrutiny of the European Commission. The opening of procedures in case of *ex officio* investigations largely lies in the discretion of the Commission.[154]

Lastly, the EU FDI Screening Regulation[155] falls within the long range of the conduct trigger. Foreign direct investments naturally require conduct, an investment, in an EU Member State. While it ultimately lies with the Member States to introduce a foreign direct screening mechanism, the FDI Screening Regulation increases harmonisation within the EU by creating a framework for national FDI screening mechanisms.[156] This includes minimum requirements for Member States' screening mechanisms of foreign investments.[157]

---

149 Regulation (EU) 2022/2560 of the European Parliament and of the Council of 14 December 2022 on foreign subsidies distorting the internal market (Foreign Subsidies Regulation) [2022] OJ L 330/1; see Hornkohl, The EU Foreign Subsidy Regulation – Why, what and how?, in Pohl, Warchol, Papadopoulos and Wiesenthal (eds), *Weaponising Invesments,* vol. 2, *forthcoming*, online first, https://link.springer.com/chapter/10.1007/17280_2023_15.

150 Article 1(2) Foreign Subsidies Regulation.

151 Hornkohl, Protecting the Internal Market from Subsidisation with the EU State Aid Regime and the Foreign Subsidies Regulation: Two Sides of the Same Coin?, 2023(3) *Journal of European Competition Law & Practice*, 137, 146.

152 Article 1(2) Foreign Subsidies Regulation .

153 Chapter 3, 4 Foreign Subsidies Regulation.

154 Chapter 2 Foreign Subsidies Regulation.

155 Regulation (EU) 2019/452 of the European Parliament and of the Council of 19 March 2019 establishing a framework for the screening of foreign direct investments into the Union (FDI Screening Regulation) [2019] OJ LI 79/1; see, for example, Verellen, When Integration by Stealth Meets Public Security: The EU Foreign Direct Investment Screening Regulation, (2021) 48 (1) *Legal issues of economic integration* 19.

156 See hereto recently, Opinion of Advocate General Capeta, Case C-106/22, *Xella Magyarország Építőanyagipari Kft v. Innovációs és Technológiai Miniszter,* ECLI:EU:C:2023:267.

157 Article 3 FDI Screening Regulation.

5.4 (*Qualified*) *Effects*

Sometimes, the EU exercises prescriptive jurisdiction over wholly foreign conduct on the basis of its domestic effects in the EU. This trigger is territorially ambiguous as the conduct of the relevant (foreign) entities may lack any connection to the EU's territory. Nevertheless, the effects of their conduct directly impact the territory of the Union.

The effects doctrine is particularly known in EU competition law, where the above-mentioned implementation[158] and single economic entity-doctrines continue to play a central role.[159] In EU merger control law, the *Gencor* decision of the General Court clarified early on that the Merger Control Regulation[160] applies to mergers between wholly foreign companies when immediate and substantial effects of the merger within the EU are foreseeable.[161] Nevertheless, even for mergers between wholly foreign companies, the merger would also need to exceed the EU turnover thresholds,[162] which are calculated on the basis of products sold and services provided in the Union.[163]

Concerning competition law *strictu sensu*, with *Intel*, the CJEU has explicitly backed[164] the qualified effects approach, which the Commission had already applied for some time.[165] Simple domestic effects of the conduct are not sufficient. The conduct must have qualified effects: the restrictive third country

158 In the *Airfreight Cartel case*, the General Court has recognised implicitly that the Commission can rely on both the implementation and the effects doctrine, see, for example, Case T-323/17, *Martinair Holland* NV *v. European Commission*, ECLI:EU:T:2022:174, 104.

159 See Case 413/14 P, *Intel Corp. v. European Commission*, ECLI:EU:C:2017:632, 42, 43, which specifically backs the other tests next to the qualified effects test; see, generally on extraterritoriality of EU competition law, for example, Martyniszyn, Intel, iiyama and Air Cargo: Far-Reaching Extraterritorial Application of EU Competition Law, (2022) *43(11) European Competition Law Review* 505.

160 Council Regulation (EC) No 139/2004 of 20 January 2004 on the control of concentrations between undertakings (Merger Control Regulation) [2004] OJ L 024.

161 Case 102/96, *Gencor Ltd v. Commission of the European Communities*, ECLI:EU:T:1999:65, 79.

162 See, for the different worldwide and EU turnovers Articles 1(2), (3) Merger Control Regulation; see Case 102/96, *Gencor Ltd v. Commission of the European Communities*, ECLI:EU:T:1999:65, 78, 87.

163 Article 5(1) Merger Control Regulation.

164 Case 413/14 P, *Intel Corp. v. European Commission*, ECLI:EU:C:2017:632, 49; see Fox, Extraterritorial Jurisdiction, Antitrust, and the EU Intel Case: Implementation, Qualified Effects, and the Third Kind, (2019) 42 *Fordham International Law Journal* 981.

165 See already Commission Decision 69/243/EEC of 24 July 1969 relating to a proceeding under Article 85 of the EEC Treaty (IV/26 267 – Colouring matters) [1996] OJ L195; on the discussion, Geradin, Reysen and Henry, Extraterritoriality, Comity, and Cooperation in EU Competition Law, in Guzman (ed), *Cooperation, Comity, and Competition Policy*, Oxford University Press 2010, p. 21.

business practice must have foreseeable, immediate, and substantial effects in the EU.[166] The *Intel* case law was recently backed in the *Airfreight Cartel*[167] case.[168] The General Court underlined again that qualified effects in the EU must be foreseeable, immediate, and substantial but also held that probable effects are sufficient.[169]

Although the discussion is most prominent in competition law, other areas of EU law also rely on the effects doctrine. Some EU financial law regulations, for example, apply effects tests of varying intensity to promote financial stability in the EU.[170] The clearing obligations of the Market Instrument Regulation,[171] for example, apply to OTC derivative contracts between third-country entities that would be subject to those obligations if they were established in the Union when the contract has 'a direct, substantial and foreseeable effect within the Union'.[172] Similarly, the obligation of the Markets in Financial Instruments Regulation[173] to trade certain derivates in an organised manner also applies 'to third-country entities that would be subject to the clearing obligation if they were established in the Union, which enter into derivatives transactions pertaining to a class of derivatives that has been declared subject to the trading obligation, provided that the contract has a direct, substantial and foreseeable effect within the Union […].'[174] The Market Abuse Regulation[175]

166 Case C-413/14 P, *Intel Corp. v. European Commission*, ECLI:EU:C:2017:632, 49.

167 The Airfreight Cartel case concerns many different proceedings, see, inter alia, Case T-323/17, *Martinair Holland* NV *v. European Commission*, ECLI:EU:T:2022:174.

168 See, in detail, Martyniszyn, Intel, iiyama and Air Cargo: Far-Reaching Extraterritorial Application of EU Competition Law, (2022) *43(11) European Competition Law Review* 505.

169 See, inter alia, Case T-323/17, *Martinair Holland* NV *v. European Commission*, ECLI:EU:T:2022:174, 108.

170 See Schweigl, Extraterritorial Effects of EU Financial Markets Laws, in Cunha Rodrigues (ed), *Extraterritoriality of* EU *Economic Law*, Springer 2021, p. 251.

171 Regulation (EU) No 648/2012 of the European Parliament and of the Council of 4 July 2012 on OTC derivatives, central counterparties and trade repositories (Market Instrument Regulation) [2012] OJ L 201/1.

172 Article 11(12) Market Instrument Regulation; see Commission Delegated Regulation (EU) No 285/2014 of 13 February 2014 supplementing Regulation (EU) No 648/2012 of the European Parliament and of the Council with regard to regulatory technical standards on direct, substantial and foreseeable effect of contracts within the Union and to prevent the evasion of rules and obligations [2014] OJ L 85.

173 Regulation (EU) No 600/2014 of the European Parliament and of the Council of 15 May 2014 on markets in financial instruments and amending Regulation (EU) No 648/2012 (Markets in Financial Instruments Regulation) [2014] OJ L 173/84.

174 Article 28(2) Markets in Financial Instruments Regulation.

175 Regulation (EU) No 596/2014 of the European Parliament and of the Council of 16 April 2014 on market abuse and repealing Directive 2003/6/EC of the European Parliament and

goes even further by not even requiring qualified effects, applying on the basis of any effects in EU territory.[176] It is sufficient that financial instruments are traded the 'price or value of which depends on or has an effect on the price or value of a financial instrument' traded on an EU market.[177]

5.5 *Anti-evasion*

A quite rare non-territorial connecting factor in EU law that triggers extraterritorial application concerns the evasion of EU law. Anti-evasion clauses in EU laws serve to extend the geographical scope of EU law to include extraterritorial conduct to the extent it is necessary or appropriate to prevent the evasion of EU law.[178] In any case, due to the novelty of the concept in EU law, the anti-evasion trigger still appears to be quite vague, making clarifying case law necessary.

With the introduction of the (qualified) effects doctrine in several EU financial market regulations, the EU has included anti-evasion triggers in some of the financial law instruments.[179] The above-mentioned clearing obligations of the Market Instrument Regulation, for example, apply to OTC derivative contracts between third-country entities that would be subject to those obligations if they were established within the Union, 'where such obligation is necessary or appropriate to prevent the evasion of any provision of this Regulation'.[180] Similarly, the above-mentioned obligation of the Markets in Financial Instruments Regulation to trade certain derivatives in an organised manner also applies extraterritorial for anti-evasion reasons.[181]

The anti-evasion trigger is sometimes applicable only together with other triggers of EU extraterritoriality. In EUIP law, for example, the CJEU decision in *L'Oréal v. eBay*[182] demonstrates a mixture of the effects, conduct and anti-evasion doctrines.[183] In this case, the CJEU had to decide whether EU

of the Council and Commission Directives 2003/124/EC, 2003/125/EC and 2004/72/EC (Market Abuse Regulation) [2014] OJ L 173/1.

176 Similar conclusion Scott, The new EU "Extraterritoriality", (2014) 51 *Common Market Law Review* 1343, 1358.

177 Articles 2(1)(d), (2)(a), (2)(b) Market Abuse Regulation.

178 See Scott, The new EU "Extraterritoriality", (2014) 51 *Common Market Law Review* 1343, 1359.

179 See Schweigl, Extraterritorial Effects of EU Financial Markets Laws, in Cunha Rodrigues (ed), *Extraterritoriality of* EU *Economic Law*, Springer 2021, p. 251.

180 Article 11(12) Market Instrument Regulation.

181 Article 28(2) Markets in Financial Instruments Regulation.

182 Case 324/09, *L'Oréal* SA *and Others v. eBay International* AG *and Others*, ECLI:EU:C:2011:474.

183 Similarly, Jääskinen and Ward, The External Reach of EU Private Law in the Light of L'Oréal versus eBay and Google and Google Spain, in Cremona and Micklitz (eds), *Private*

trademark law is relevant to offers for the sale of goods from outside the EU by means of eBay's websites accessible in the EU. The CJEU held that EU trademark law applies if it is clear from the website, which has to be assessed on a case-by-case basis, that the offer for sale of a trademarked product located outside of the EU targeted consumers in the EU; otherwise, one could escape EU trademark law simply by using e-commerce to the detriment of the effectiveness of those rules.[184] Targeting EU consumers points to the effects and conduct trigger, while the referencing to escaping EU trademark law hints at an application of the anti-evasion trigger.

Similarly, the EU Anti Money Laundering Directive[185] contains a combination of the anti-evasion and nationality triggers for its extraterritorial application. According to Article 45(3) Anti Money Laundering Directive, the minimum EU anti-money laundering and countering the financing of terrorism obligations apply to branches or majority-owned subsidiaries of EU companies located in third countries where the minimum requirements are less strict. The branch and subsidiary requirement connect to the nationality trigger, while the minimum obligations relate to the anti-evasion of EU law.

EU sanctions law also includes anti-evasion triggers in combination with other triggers. The EU sanctions against Russia in the context of Russia's aggression against Ukraine, for example, contain rules on the circumvention of the sanctions.[186] Since the 8th package of sanctions against Russia in the context of Russia's aggression against Ukraine, the EU approach goes even further and applies sanctions to persons facilitating infringements of the prohibition against circumvention of EU sanctions.[187] As discussed in this chapter,

Law in the External Relations of the EU, Oxford University Press 2016, pp. 125, 128; referring a necessary final element, Krämer, Extraterritoriale Wirkungen des Unionsrechts – eine normanalytische Skizze, [2021] *Europarecht* 137, 142.

184 Case 324/09, *L'Oréal* SA *and Others v. eBay International* AG *and Others*, ECLI:EU:C:2011:474, 62.

185 Directive (EU) 2015/849 of the European Parliament and of the Council of 20 May 2015 on the prevention of the use of the financial system for the purposes of money laundering or terrorist financing, amending Regulation (EU) No 648/2012 of the European Parliament and of the Council, and repealing Directive 2005/60/EC of the European Parliament and of the Council and Commission Directive 2006/70/EC (Anti Money Laundering Directive) [2015] OJ L 141/73.

186 Article 9 2014 Russia Sanctions Regulation.

187 Council Regulation (EU) 2022/1905 of 6 October 2022 amending Regulation (EU) No 269/2014 concerning restrictive measures in respect of actions undermining or threatening the territorial integrity, sovereignty and independence of Ukraine [2022] OJ LI 259/76; see Zimmermann, Umgehungsverbote und Sekundärsanktionen: Sanktionspolitische Wende der EU?, [2022] *Ukraine Krieg und Recht* 716.

sanctions law generally falls under the nationality and conduct trigger.[188] If EU nationals outside of the EU violate the circumvention provision or facilitate an infringement of the prohibition against circumvention, for example, the triggers of both nationality and anti-evasion apply.

5.6 *Counterparty*

Some EU laws rely on the counterparty principle. According to this principle, third-country nationals need to follow certain obligations of EU law because they contract or otherwise engage in or outside of the EU with an EU national or resident counterparty.[189] For the foreign national, this is largely a non-territorial connecting factor that triggers the application of EU law because only the counterparty has a connection to the territory of the EU. The overlaps with the passive personality principle are fluid.

Many examples can be found in financial law. For example, the Market Instrument Regulation obliges third parties entering into an OTC derivate contract with an EU counterparty to follow the clearing obligations.[190] According to Article Art 4(1)(a)(IV) Market Instrument Regulation, OTC derivative contracts pertaining to a class of OTC derivatives that has been declared subject to the clearing obligation in accordance with the Market Instrument Regulation, fall under the clearing obligations when conducted, *inter alia*, 'between a financial counterparty or a non-financial counterparty meeting the conditions referred to in Article 10(1)(b) and an entity established in a third country that would be subject to the clearing obligation if it were established in the Union'.

5.7 *Property*

Lastly, EU law may sometimes apply when only the property of a third-country national is located in the EU.[191] Here, the territoriality connecting factor is just the object. The presence of the parties or the location of the contract or other conduct is irrelevant.

According to Article 24(1) Brussels I^{bis} Regulation, for example, in proceedings which have as their object rights *in rem* in immovable property, the courts of the Member State in which the property is situated have jurisdiction regardless of the domicile of the parties.[192] Moreover, in financial law, the Short Selling

188 See above V.1. and 3.

189 Scott, The new EU "Extraterritoriality", (2014) 51 *Common Market Law Review* 1343, 1360.

190 Art 4(1)(a)(IV) Market Instrument Regulation.

191 Scott, The new EU "Extraterritoriality", (2014) 51 *Common Market Law Review* 1343, 1361.

192 Similarly, Article 10 Regulation (EU) No 650/2012 of the European Parliament and of the Council of 4 July 2012 on jurisdiction, applicable law, recognition and enforcement of decisions and acceptance and enforcement of authentic instruments in matters of

Regulation,[193] for example, applies to shares traded outside the EU when they are admitted to trading on an EU trading venue.[194] The trading venue in the EU is a sufficient connection to the location of the shares in the EU.

6 Limits and Exceptions

Irrespective of the above-mentioned triggers for the extraterritorial application of EU law, EU law acknowledges limits to extraterritoriality. Most notably, the principles of comity, reasonableness, proportionality, balancing of interests and equivalence can become relevant. EU law itself is largely silent concerning these principles. Yet, the CJEU has applied some of the principles in the context of extraterritoriality of EU law.

6.1 *Comity*

Comity is generally understood as an underlying principle of international relations, according to which states voluntarily take other states' interests into account, even when exercising extraterritorial jurisdiction.[195] Unfortunately, EU legislation is silent on the principle of comity. While it has not been accepted as a general principle of EU law and EU external relations, however, it can be found in some EU bilateral agreements.

Particularly in EU competition law, comity has played a role when it comes to extraterritoriality.[196] Competition law is particularly hospitable to comity principles. This is due to the fact, as *Geradin/Reysen/Henry* observe, that 'a system of overlapping review by different antitrust authorities, however, without taking into account the other parties' interests, leads to undesired consequences such as forum shopping, divergent results, duplicate sanctions, and a misallocation of administrative resources and can have detrimental effects

succession and on the creation of a European Certificate of Succession (EU Succession Regulation) [2012] OJ L 201/107 provides for jurisdiction in case of property located in a Member State of the deceased not located within the Union.

193 Regulation (EU) No 236/2012 of the European Parliament and of the Council of 14 March 2012 on short selling and certain aspects of credit default swaps (Short Selling Regulation) [2012] OJ L 86/1.

194 Articles 5, 6, 12 Short Selling Regulation.

195 See, in the context of competition law OECD, Committee on Competition Law and Policy Report on Positive Comity (1999), 5.

196 See, for example, Sousa, The Three Body Problem: Extraterritoriality, Comity and Cooperation in Competition Law, in Cunha Rodrigues (ed), *Extraterritoriality of* EU *Economic Law*, Springer 2021, p. 119.

on other legal systems.'[197] Moreover, comity could become relevant in EU data and digital law, where the extent of EU extraterritoriality due to the abovementioned *lex loci solutionis* is quite far-reaching.[198]

In the absence of a general principle of comity in EU law, in order to temper the effects of the unilateral assertion of extraterritorial jurisdiction, the EU has included comity principles in several bilateral competition comity and cooperation agreements. For example, early competition cooperation agreements with the United States include comity provisions. Each party should take into account the important interests of the other party and notify the other party if anticompetitive activities occur on the territory of the other party.[199] The provisions are non-binding. Nevertheless, both parties have invoked them, for example, unsuccessfully by the Commission regarding the *Boeing/McDonnell Douglas*[200] merger, which almost led to a trade war between the United States and EU.[201]

This case demonstrates the limits of comity. Even if a territorial entity abides by comity principles and turns to cooperation attempts as a recourse, in cases of real conflict, each party, in the end, can claim its overriding interest in enforcement and disregard the non-binding principle of comity.[202] The CJEU has itself criticised the lack of comity and cooperation provisions.[203] With such mechanisms, states could weigh their interests against one another and coordinate enforcement.

197 Geradin, Reysen and Henry, Extraterritoriality, Comity, and Cooperation in EU Competition Law, in Guzman (ed), *Cooperation, Comity, and Competition Policy*, Oxford University Press 2010, pp. 21, 29, 30.

198 See Taylor, Reasonableness in its reasoning: How the European Union can mitigate problematic extraterritoriality on a de-territorialised internet, (2019) 62 *Questions in Law* 35, 39.

199 Agreement between the Government of the United States of America and the Commission of the European Communities regarding the application of their competition laws (1991); Agreement between the European Communities and the Government of the United States of America on the application of positive comity principles in the enforcement of their competition laws (1998).

200 Commission Decision 97/816/EC of 30 July 1997 declaring a concentration compatible with the common market and the functioning of the EEA Agreement (Case No IV/M.877 – Boeing/McDonnell Douglas) [1997] OJ L 336, 11.

201 See Boeder and Dorman, The Boeing/McDonnell Douglas Merger: The Economics, Antitrust Law and Politics of the Aerospace Industry, (2000) 45(1) *Antitrust Bull* 119.

202 Geradin, Reysen and Henry, Extraterritoriality, Comity, and Cooperation in EU Competition Law, in Guzman (ed), *Cooperation, Comity, and Competition Policy*, Oxford University Press 2010, pp. 21, 22.

203 With regard to data protection law, specifically: Case 507/17, *Google* LLC *v. Commission nationale de l'informatique et des libertés* (CNIL), ECLI:EU:C:2019:772, 63.

6.2 *Reasonableness, Proportionality, and Balancing*

The vague doctrine of reasonableness could limit the exercise of prescriptive jurisdiction. Reasonableness relates to the close connection of a given conduct or situation with the laws of a territorial entity. Extraterritorial application is unreasonable when a state with weaker interests exercises prescriptive extraterritorial jurisdiction and does not defer to the state with stronger interests.[204] Furthermore, proportionality and interest-balancing play a role, as 'one State's jurisdictional assertion does not encroach upon the interests of another State to an extent that is disproportionate to the object or aim of that assertion'.[205] Reasonableness as a limitation on extraterritorial regulation is very prominent with regard to the extraterritoriality of US law.[206]

An explicit reference to the concept of reasonableness is largely missing in EU law. Yet, particular reflections can be seen in several CJEU judgments on the extraterritoriality of EU law or occasionally in EU regulatory instruments. However, the concept is not as established as in US law. Predominantly, the CJEU has had recourse to reasonableness in its case law on the extraterritoriality of data protection and privacy law, as demonstrated by the *Google Spain*[207] and *Google v* CNIL[208] cases. The CJEU applied the reasonableness approach by adopting a proportionality and balancing-of-interests test.[209] The extraterritorial application of EU data protection law needs to be proportionate, *i.e.*, adequately related in size or degree to that objective, and needs to be balanced against other interests, particularly of third states.[210]

In *Google Spain,* the CJEU balanced an individual's data protection and privacy rights concerning an extraterritorial right to erasure against other

204 Ryngaert, *Jurisdiction in International Law*, 2nd ed., Oxford University Press 2015, pp. 145 – 188.

205 Ryngaert, *Jurisdiction in International Law*, 2nd ed., Oxford University Press 2015, pp. 158, 159.

206 See Buxbaum and Michaels, Reasonableness as a Limitation on the Extraterritorial Application of U.S. Law, in Stephan and Cleveland (eds), *The Restatement and Beyond: The Past, Present, and Future of U.S. Foreign Relations Law*, Oxford University Press 2020, p. 283.

207 Case 131/12, *Google Spain* SL *and Google Inc. v. Agencia Española de Protección de Datos* (AEPD) *and Mario Costeja González,* ECLI:EU:C:2014:317.

208 Case 507/17, *Google* LLC *v. Commission nationale de l'informatique et des libertés* (CNIL), ECLI:EU:C:2019:772.

209 Similar Taylor, Reasonableness in its reasoning: How the European Union can mitigate problematic extraterritoriality on a de-territorialised internet, (2019) 62 *Question of International Law* 35, 46.

210 See, in connection to the reasonableness-approach, Ryngaert, *Jurisdiction in International Law*, 2nd ed., Oxford University Press 2015, pp. 158, 159.

competing interests, *i.e.*, of the operator of the search engine and the general interest in freedom of information.[211] With that judgment, the CJEU showed its openness to a balancing and proportionality test regarding the extraterritoriality of EU law. In *Google v* CNIL, the Court was even more explicit. It directly mentioned other rights and the principle of proportionality that need to be considered.[212] In its interest-balancing- and proportionality-exercise with regard to the territorial scope of the obligation to dereference, the CJEU took into account the connection of the conduct to the territory of the EU but also the rationale of the law to protect personal data throughout the European Union and data protection as a fundamental right. Furthermore, in an apparent reference to the reasonableness of the extraterritorial EU measure, it mentioned the interests of other states by stating that 'numerous third States do not recognise the right to de-referencing or have a different approach to that right'.

Generally, the principles of proportionality and interest-balancing are deeply rooted in EU primary law.[213] The European legislator cannot take disproportionate measures, which also limits the EU concerning prescriptive extraterritoriality.[214] Accordingly, some extraterritorial EU legal instruments refer to the principle of proportionality and interest-balancing or aspects of it. In financial law, for example, recourse to the anti-evasion trigger is essentially only possible where the extraterritorial application of the financial law obligations is 'necessary or appropriate to prevent the evasion of the provisions of the respective law'.[215]

7 Blocking Extraterritoriality

Blocking statutes aim at limiting the effects of extraterritorial practices by other states.[216] A limited number of Union rules exist to defend against third-country

211 Case 131/12, *Google Spain* SL *and Google Inc. v. Agencia Española de Protección de Datos* (AEPD) *and Mario Costeja González*, ECLI:EU:C:2014:317, 93 et. seq.

212 Case 507/17, *Google* LLC *v. Commission nationale de l'informatique et des libertés* (CNIL), ECLI:EU:C:2019:772, 52 et. seq.

213 See Article 5(4) TEU.

214 See Layton and Parry, Extraterritorial jurisdiction – European Responses, (2004) 26 *Houston Journal of International Law* 309, 322–323.

215 See, for example, Article 11(12) Market Instrument Regulation .

216 See, on the general historical development, Basedow, *The Law of Open Societies: Private Ordering and Public Regulation in the Conflict of Laws*, Brill 2015, pp. 388 et seq.

extraterritoriality orders by prohibiting private parties from complying with the prohibitions or restrictions contained therein or based thereon.[217]

The so-called EU Blocking Regulation[218] was a response to the extraterritorial application of US embargos and secondary sanctions against Cuba, Iran and Libya, which the EU considered contrary to international law.[219] Specifically, the Blocking Regulation was designed to protect EU individuals and companies engaged in lawful international trade, as well as related commercial activities, against the effects of extraterritorial legislation adopted by third countries.[220] For example, according to the Blocking Regulation, no judgment or decision from outside the Union's territory giving direct or indirect effect to the US laws specified in the Annex of the Blocking Regulation could be recognised or enforced by the Member States of the EU.[221] Moreover, EU operators are prohibited from complying with any requirement or prohibition resulting from the annexed laws, unless they are authorised by the European Commission.[222]

While the United States and the European Union were able to reach an agreement concerning the laws initially included in the Annex of the Blocking Regulation, the so-called US Helms-Burton[223] and D'Amato[224] Acts,[225] the Blocking Regulation reached new prominence with regard to the so-called Iran Nuclear Deal.[226] The Trump administration unilaterally decided to withdraw from the Iran Nuclear Deal and reintroduced sanctions against Iran as well as secondary sanctions with extraterritorial effects on, among other things, EU

---

217 In detail Hornkohl, (Miss-)Achtung des Fremden? – Extraterritoriale Drittstaatenregelungen, EU-Blocking-Statuten und deren Auswirkungen im Privatrecht, in Heindler, Melcher (eds), *Achtung des Fremden,* Mohr Siebeck 2024, 169.

218 Council Regulation (EC) 2271/96 of 22 November 1996 protecting against the effects of the extra-territorial application of legislation adopted by a third country, and actions based thereon or resulting therefrom (Blocking Regulation) [1996] OJ L 309.

219 Article 1 and Annex Blocking Regulation; on the legality of secondary sanctions in international law see, Sandrock, Völkerrechtliche Grenzen staatlicher Gesetzgebung, (2016) 115 *Zeitschrift für Vergleichende Rechtswissenschaft* 1, 79.

220 Recital 6 Blocking Regulation; Case 124/20, *Bank Melli Iran v. Telekom Deutschland GmbH,* ECLI:EU:C:2021:1035, 35; see also: Huber, The Helms-Burton Blocking Statute of the European Union, (1996) 20 *Fordham International Law Journal* 699.

221 Article 3 Blocking Regulation.

222 Article 5 Blocking Regulation.

223 Cuban Liberty and Democratic Solidarity (Libertad) Act. 22 U.S.C. §§ 6021 ff. (1996) (Helms – Burton Act).

224 Iran and Libya Sanctions Act. 50 U.S.C. § 1701 ff. (1996) (D'Amato Act).

225 See Smis and Borght, The EU-U.S. Compromise on the Helms-Burton and D'Amato Acts, (1999) 93(1) *American Journal of International Law* 227.

226 Joint Comprehensive Plan of Action (2015).

individuals and companies.[227] As a reaction, the EU updated the Annex of the old Blocking Regulation.[228] In the meantime, the revived Blocking Regulation was applied in several civil cases throughout the EU involving, for example, contract terminations with blocked persons based on extraterritorial US laws aimed against Iran.[229] As Advocate General *Hogan* recently pointed out, the Blocking Statute could create problems for EU companies with large activities in the United States.[230] They are at the moment torn between risking US secondary sanctions or violating the EU prohibition to comply with such US sanctions based on the Blocking Statute.

The recent *Bank Melli Iran* judgment perfectly demonstrates such a conundrum.[231] It relates to a dispute between the *Bank Melli Iran* and *Deutsche Telekom*. *Deutsche Telekom*, acting without authorisation of the Commission according to Article 5 Blocking Regulation, had terminated contracts for telecommunication services to Bank Melli Iran after the latter was added to a list of blocked entities by extraterritorial US laws. In this case, the CJEU, for the first time, had the opportunity to rule on the validity and interpretation of the Blocking Statute.

The CJEU held that the prohibition on complying with the extraterritorial laws adopted by the United States[232] can be relied on in civil disputes and applies even in the absence of an order or instruction directing compliance issued by a US administrative or judicial authority – if the respective

227 See Mulligan, Withdrawal from International Agreements: Legal Framework, the Paris Agreement, and the Iran Nuclear Agreement, [2018] *Congressional Research Service*, https://sgp.fas.org/crs/row/R44761.pdf.

228 Commission Delegated Regulation (EU) 2018/1100 of June 6, 2018 amending the Annex to Council Regulation (EC) No 2271/96 protecting against the effects of extra-territorial application of legislation adopted by a third country, and actions based thereon or resulting therefrom [2018] OJ L 199 I/1; Commission Implementing Regulation (EU) 2018/1101 of August 3, 2018, laying down the criteria for the application of the second paragraph of Article 5 of Council Regulation (EC) No 2271/96 protecting against the effects of the extra-territorial application of legislation adopted by a third country, and actions based thereon or resulting therefrom [2018] OJ LI 199/7.

229 See Report from the Commission to the European Parliament and the Council relating to Article 7(a) of Council Regulation (EC) No 2271/96 (Blocking Statute) [2021] COM(2021) 535 final; see, for example, Haellmigk, Das aktuelle US-Iran-Embargo und seine Bedeutung für die deutsche Exportwirtschaft: Das US-Sanktionsregime der Primary und Secondary Sanctions, (2018) 1 *Corporate Compliance Zeitschrift* 33.

230 Opinion of Advocate General Hogan, Case 124/20, *Bank Melli Iran v. Telekom Deutschland GmbH*, ECLI:EU:C:2021:1035, 136.

231 See, for example, Ryngaert, Interpreting an unsatisfactory EU Blocking Statute: Bank Melli Iran, (2023) 60 *Common Market Law Review* 517.

232 Article 5 Blocking Regulation.

company decides on its own to comply with the American laws – to reach the above-mentioned objectives of the Regulation.[233] The CJEU further clarified that termination in breach of a statutory prohibition, such as the one stemming from the Blocking Regulation, would be null and void under German law.[234] This, according to the CJEU, creates a high evidentiary burden for the party relying on the breach of Article 5(1) Blocking Regulation.[235] The CJEU considered that it would be too difficult to prove such a violation due to the lack of accessible evidence by the concerned party, which undermines the prohibition laid down in the Blocking Regulation.[236] Therefore, it held that in the context of civil proceedings, when 'all the evidence available to a national court tends to indicate *prima facie* that, by terminating the contracts in question', an EU company acting without authorisation of the Commission has complied with the extraterritorial US laws, it has to prove that its termination did indeed not seek to comply with those extraterritorial laws.[237]

The CJEU concluded by stating that while the rules of the Blocking Regulation limit the freedom to conduct business resulting from Article 16 EU Charter of Fundamental Rights, such limitations are necessary to counteract the extraterritorial effects of the foreign laws, thereby protecting the established legal order and the interests of the European Union and its citizens in general.[238] As a result, the Court interpreted the blocking statute broadly in order to facilitate countermeasures against the extraterritorial application of foreign law. However, the Grand Chamber also held that these measures are subject to limitations of proportionality to be strictly applied by the courts of EU Member States.[239]

Apart from these embargo issues, there is currently no across-the-board regulation generally blocking the extraterritorial application of third-country legal measures. Nevertheless, some EU laws block exorbitant assertions of jurisdiction by third countries for specific subject matters when the measure conflicts with its own values.[240] Data protection law, for example, contains

233 Case 124/20, *Bank Melli Iran v. Telekom Deutschland GmbH*, ECLI:EU:C:2021:1035, 39, 49, 50, 59.
234 Section 134 BGB, which states that any legal act contrary to a statutory prohibition shall be void except as otherwise provided by law.
235 Case 124/20, *Bank Melli Iran v. Telekom Deutschland GmbH*, ECLI:EU:C:2021:1035, 64.
236 Case 124/20, *Bank Melli Iran v. Telekom Deutschland GmbH*, ECLI:EU:C:2021:1035, 65.
237 Case 124/20, *Bank Melli Iran v. Telekom Deutschland GmbH*, ECLI:EU:C:2021:1035, 67.
238 Case 124/20, *Bank Melli Iran v. Telekom Deutschland GmbH*, ECLI:EU:C:2021:1035, 91.
239 Case 124/20, *Bank Melli Iran v. Telekom Deutschland GmbH*, ECLI:EU:C:2021:1035, 95.
240 See Kuner, The Internet and the Global Reach of EU Law, in Cremona and Scott (eds), EU *Law Beyond* EU *Borders – The Extraterritorial Reach of* EU *Law*, Oxford University Press 2019, p. 134.

a blocking statute in Chapter 5 GDPR.[241] According to Article 48 GDPR, 'any judgment of a court or tribunal and any decision of an administrative authority of a third country requiring a controller or processor to transfer or disclose personal data may only be recognised or enforceable in any manner if based on an international agreement, such as a mutual legal assistance treaty, in force between the requesting third country and the Union or a Member State, without prejudice to other grounds for transfer pursuant to this Chapter.'

This provision was first tested in the *Schrems* II case law,[242] where the Court of Justice, *inter alia*, invalidated the so-called EU-US Privacy Shield.[243] The EU-US Privacy Shield regulated transatlantic exchanges of personal data for commercial purposes between the EU and the United States, allowing EU companies to legally transfer personal data to US-based companies listed in the Privacy Shield list.[244] The CJEU held that the United States has invasive surveillance programmes that are considered to create disproportionate interference with the rights to protection of data and privacy of Article 45(1) GDPR and Articles 7, 8 and 52(1) EU Charter of Fundamental Rights and does not provide for an essentially equivalent, and therefore sufficient, level of protection as guaranteed by the GDPR and the EU Charter of Fundamental Rights.[245] Recently, the EU issued a new adequacy decision for the transfer of personal data to the United States on the basis of the new 'EU-US data protection framework' as

241 See Kessler, Nowak and Khan, The Potential Impact of Article 48 of the General Data Protection Regulation on Cross Border Discovery From the United States, (2016) 17 *The Sedona Conference journal* 575; Swire, When Does GDPR Act as a Blocking Statute: The Relevance of a Lawful Basis for Transfer, [2019] *Georgia Tech Scheller College of Business Research Paper* No. 3473187.

242 Case 311/18, *Data Protection Commissioner v. Facebook Ireland Limited and Maximillian Schrems* (Schrems II), ECLI:EU:C:2020:559; D'Ath, Arrêt « Schrems II » : sur la légalité des transferts de données personnelles fondés sur une décision d'adéquation ou moyennant des garanties appropriées, [2020] *Journal de droit européen* 442; Sandfuchs, The Future of Data Transfers to Third Countries in Light of the CJEU's Judgment C-311/18 – Schrems II, [2021] GRUR *International* 245.

243 See Commission Implementing Decision (EU) 2016/1250 of 12 July 2016 pursuant to Directive 95/46/EC of the European Parliament and of the Council on the adequacy of the protection provided by the EU-U.S. Privacy Shield [2016] OJ L 207/1.

244 See, generally, Spies, EU-US-Privacy-Shield – eine schwierige Reparatur, (2021) *Zeitschrift für Datenschutz* 478.

245 Case 311/18, *Data Protection Commissioner v. Facebook Ireland Limited and Maximillian Schrems* (Schrems II), ECLI:EU:C:2020:559, 185.

defined in Art. 45 GDPR.[246] Today, Article 48 GDPR is primarily aimed against the so-called US CLOUD Act,[247] which allows US criminal investigation authorities to access all data stored on servers regardless of whether the data are stored in the United States or on foreign soil, provided that the company is based in the United States or is subject to US law, which also applies to companies doing business in the United States.[248]

8 Conclusion and Outlook

The chapter has shown that the extraterritorial effect of EU law has already taken a comprehensive shape. However, a general doctrine of extraterritoriality does not yet apply. Extraterritoriality depends on the respective EU law subject matter. Nevertheless, the phenomenon of extraterritoriality is already widespread in many such subject areas. Foremost among these are competition law, data protection law, financial law, and environmental law due to the increasing digitalisation, globalisation and global effects of certain phenomena, such as climate change. In EU law, cases of territorial extensions are currently even more frequent than cases of genuine extraterritoriality. With increasing discussion of the possibility of universal civil jurisdiction, for example, in the area of civil liability for human rights violations abroad, this tide may soon turn.

In the future, I envisage further applications of extraterritoriality, especially in the context of ongoing digitalisation. The GDPR and other data and digital law, in particular, provides for far-reaching extraterritorial rules that have yet to be fully explored in the CJEU's case law. Furthermore, globalisation will also remain a relevant factor for extraterritoriality. This is demonstrated by developments such as the Foreign Subsidies Regulation or the FDI Screening

---

246 Commission Implementing Decision of 10.07.2023 pursuant to Regulation (EU) 2016/679 of the European Parliament and of the Council on the adequate level of protection of personal data under the EU-US Data Privacy Framework, [2022], C(2023) 4745 final.

247 Clarifying Lawful Overseas Use of Data Act of 2018 (CLOUD Act), Publ. L. 115–141, 132 STAT. 1213 (2018).

248 Critically EDPB-EDPS Joint Response on the US Cloud Act, https://edps.europa.eu/data-protection/our-work/publications/opinions/edpb-edps-joint-response-us-cloud-act_en; Gausling, Offenlegung von Daten auf Basis des CLOUD Act, [2018] *Multimedia und Recht* 578; Brauneck, Europa-Cloud: Zwingt der US CLOUD Act EU-Unternehmen zur EU-rechtswidrigen Datenherausgabe?, [2019] *Europäisches Wirtschafts- und Steuerrecht* 307.

Regulation. It remains to be seen to what extent the EU Green Deal will impact further extraterritorial EU environmental law. Moreover, the global application of EU universal principles will also remain a topic of conversation. The discussions on supply chain liability show this. On the other hand, *Bank Melli* demonstrated the general value of blocking statutes in the EU, especially in relation to US extraterritorial regulations. Concerning the blocking statute rules of the GDPR, the United States and its CLOUD Act will likely also become the subject of future proceedings at the highest court of the EU.

PART 4

Appendix

Questionnaire

General Notes

The goal of the report is to provide a comprehensive description of the law and practice in your country regarding the extraterritorial reach of legislation. In addition to addressing the questions below, *please add any other information* that you find necessary or interesting.

Scope and Terminology

The topic is limited to the extraterritoriality of *statutes and regulations*. As a result, the report will not address extraterritoriality involving other sources of law, such as the extraterritorial reach of constitutional law or the extraterritorial obligations of states under international human rights law.

The report will address only *legislative (prescriptive) jurisdiction*. Issues related to the enforcement of statutes and regulations will be excluded.

The terms "extraterritorial," "extraterritorial jurisdiction," and "extraterritoriality" do not have consensus definitions. Please use them as they are used in practice in your country.

The aim of the questions that follow is to elicit an overview of state practice in interpreting the geographic scope of legislation; applying domestic legislation in situations presenting foreign elements; and, if relevant, responding to extraterritorial practices of other states. The practice of extraterritoriality in individual substantive areas (e.g., competition law, securities regulation, economic sanctions, data protection, criminal law, intellectual property law, etc.) should be discussed by way of example or illustration, or in connection with the historical development of extraterritorial practices in your jurisdiction. However, due to page limits, it will probably be impossible to delve too far into the technicalities of each individual area.

 | DOI:10.1163/9789004720183_019

Questionnaire

1. Please identify any trends over time in your country's attitude toward the extraterritorial application of statutes and regulations. Are there particular cases or laws – or disputes involving other countries – that mark significant shifts in your country's approach to extraterritoriality? Is there currently a practice of extraterritorial application of statutes and regulations in your country?
2. Have multilateral or regional instruments had any influence on the extraterritorial application of statutes or regulations in your country? For instance, has your country joined anti-corruption treaties or other instruments that encourage the extraterritorial application of domestic law in particular circumstances?
3. In general, what role does international law play in defining or limiting the geographic scope of statutes and regulations in your country?
4. In general, what role does international comity play in defining or limiting the geographic scope of statutes and regulations in your country?
5. Is there a requirement of reasonableness in the extraterritorial application of statutes and regulations in your country? If so, how is it defined and implemented?
6. Are there statutes or regulations that apply to *wholly* foreign conduct on the basis of any of the following?
   - Nationality of the actor
   - Nationality of a person harmed by the conduct (the "passive personality" principle)
   - Domestic effects of the conduct in question
   - The principle of universal jurisdiction
7. Are there statutes or regulations that apply to activity occurring *partly* in another country on the basis of local conduct (territorial links)? If so, are there limits based on the relative significance of the territorial links or some other factor?
8. To the extent that statutes or regulations are applied to foreign conduct on the basis of the actor's nationality, how is the question of corporate nationality addressed? Do the laws apply only to domestic corporations, for instance, or also to companies that are owned or controlled by domestic corporations?

9. If a statute or regulation is silent as to its geographic scope, are there any relevant rules of statutory interpretation, such as a "presumption against extraterritoriality"?
10. Has your country enacted any "blocking statutes" or other legislation intended to limit the effects of extraterritorial practices by other states?

Index

www.ingramcontent.com/pod-product-compliance
Lightning Source LLC
Chambersburg PA
CBHW051356240926
51852CB00001B/45
9789004720176